Communications
in Computer and Information Science 905

Commenced Publication in 2007
Founding and Former Series Editors:
Phoebe Chen, Alfredo Cuzzocrea, Xiaoyong Du, Orhun Kara, Ting Liu,
Dominik Ślęzak, and Xiaokang Yang

More information about this series at http://www.springer.com/series/7899

Mayank Singh · P. K. Gupta
Vipin Tyagi · Jan Flusser
Tuncer Ören (Eds.)

Advances in Computing and Data Sciences

Second International Conference, ICACDS 2018
Dehradun, India, April 20–21, 2018
Revised Selected Papers, Part I

Springer

Editors
Mayank Singh
University of KwaZulu-Natal
Durban, South Africa

P. K. Gupta
Jaypee University of Information
Technology
Solan, India

Vipin Tyagi
Jaypee University of Engineering
and Technology
Guna, Madhya Pradesh, India

Jan Flusser
Institute of Information Theory
and Automation
Prague 8, Czech Republic

Tuncer Ören
University of Ottawa
Ottawa, Canada

ISSN 1865-0929   ISSN 1865-0937 (electronic)
Communications in Computer and Information Science
ISBN 978-981-13-1809-2   ISBN 978-981-13-1810-8 (eBook)
https://doi.org/10.1007/978-981-13-1810-8

Library of Congress Control Number: 2018909291

This Springer imprint is published by the registered company Springer Nature Singapore Pte Ltd.
The registered company address is: 152 Beach Road, #21-01/04 Gateway East, Singapore 189721, Singapore

Preface

Computing techniques like big data, cloud computing, machine learning, Internet of Things etc. are playing a key role in processing of data and retrieving of advanced information. Several state-of-art techniques and computing paradigms have been proposed based on these techniques. This volume contains the papers presented at the Second International Conference on Advances in Computing and Data Sciences (ICACDS 2018) held during April 20–21, 2018, at the Uttaranchal Institute of Technology, Uttaranchal University, Dehradun, Uttarakhand, India. The conference was organized specifically to help bring together researchers, academics, scientists, and industry and to derive benefits from the advances of the next generation of computing technologies in the areas of advanced computing and data sciences (ACDS).

The Program Committee of ICACDS 2018 is extremely grateful to the authors who showed an overwhelming response to the call for papers, with over 598 papers being submitted in two tracks in "Advanced Computing" and "Data Sciences." All submitted papers went through a peer review process and, finally, 110 papers were accepted for publication in two volumes of Springer's CCIS series. The first volume is devoted to advanced computing and the second deals with data sciences. We are very grateful to our reviewers for their efforts in finalizing the high-quality papers.

The conference featured many distinguished personalities like Prof. Ling Tok Wang, National University of Singapore, Singapore; Prof. Viranjay M. Srivastava, University of KwaZulu-Natal, Durban, South Africa; Prof. Parteek Bhatia, Thapar Institute of Engineering and Technology, Patiala, India; Prof. S. K. Mishra, Majmaah University, Saudi Arabia; Prof. Arun Sharma, Indira Gandhi Delhi Technical University for Women, India; Dr. Anup Girdhar, CEO and Founder, Sedulity Solutions and Technology, India, among many others. We are very grateful for the participation of these speakers in making this conference a memorable event.

The Organizing Committee of ICACDS 2018 is indebted to Sh. Jitendra Joshi, Chancellor Uttaranchal University, and Dr. N. K. Joshi, Vice Chancellor, Uttaranchal University for the confidence that they have invested in us for organizing this international conference, and all faculty members and staff of UIT, Uttaranchal University, Dehradun, for their support in organizing the conference and making it a grand success.

We would also like to thank the authors of all submitted papers for their hard work, adherence to the deadlines, and patience with the review process. Our sincere thanks to CSI, CSI SIG on Cyber Forensics, Consilio Intelligence Research Lab, and LWT India for sponsoring the event.

September 2018

Mayank Singh
P. K. Gupta
Vipin Tyagi
Jan Flusser
Tuncer Ören

Organization

Steering Committee

Chief Patron
Jitender Joshi
  (Chancellor)

Uttaranchal University, Dehradun, India

Patron
N. K. Joshi (Vice
  Chancellor)

Uttaranchal University, Dehradun, India

Honorary Chair
Arun Sharma

Indira Gandhi Delhi Technical University for Women,
  Delhi, India

General Chair
Mayank Singh

University of KwaZulu-Natal, Durban, South Africa

Program Chairs
Shailendra Mishra
Viranjay M. Srivastava

Majmaah University, Kingdom of Saudi Arabia
University of KwaZulu-Natal, Durban, South Africa

Convener
Pradeep Kumar Gupta

Jaypee University of Information Technology, Solan, India

Co-convener
Vipin Tyagi

Jaypee University of Engineering and Technology, Guna,
  India

Advisory Board Chair
Tuncer Ören

University of Ottawa, Canada

Technical Program Committee Chairs
Jan Flusser

Institute of Information Theory and Automation,
  Czech Republic

Dirk Draheim

Tallinn University of Technology, Estonia

Conference Chairs

Manoj Diwakar	Uttaranchal University, Dehradun, India
Sandhaya Tarar	Gautham Buddha University, Greater Noida, India

Conference Co-chairs

Anand Sharma	Mody University of Science and Technology, Sikar, India
Vibhash Yadav	Rajkiya Engeering College, Banda, India
Purnendu S. Pandey	THDC Institute of Hydropower Engineering and Technology, Tehri, India
D. K. Chauhan	Noida International University, Greater Noida, India

Organizing Chairs

Devendra Singh	Uttaranchal University, Dehradun, India
Amit Kumar Sharma	Uttaranchal University, Dehradun, India
Sumita Lamba	Uttaranchal University, Dehradun, India
Niranjan Lal Verma	Mody University of Science and Technology, Sikar, India

Organizing Secretariat

Kapil Joshi	Uttaranchal University, Dehradun, India
Punit Sharma	Uttaranchal University, Dehradun, India
Vipin Dewal	Krishna Engineering College, Ghaziabad, India
Krista Chaudhary	Krishna Engineering College, Ghaziabad, India
Umang Kant	Krishna Engineering College, Ghaziabad, India

Finance Chair

Tarun Kumar	Uttaranchal University, Dehradun, India

Creative Head

Deepak Singh	MadeEasy Education, Delhi, India

Organizing Committee

Registration

Ugra Mohan	Uttaranchal University, Dehradun, India
Vivek John	Uttaranchal University, Dehradun, India
Meenakshi	Uttaranchal University, Dehradun, India
Vinay Negi	Uttaranchal University, Dehradun, India

Publication

Sumita Lamba	Uttaranchal University, Dehradun, India
Prashant Chaudhary	Uttaranchal University, Dehradun, India

Cultural

Shivani Pandey   Uttaranchal University, Dehradun, India
Rubi Pant   Uttaranchal University, Dehradun, India

Transportation

Pankaj Punia   Uttaranchal University, Dehradun, India
Arvind Singh Rawat   Uttaranchal University, Dehradun, India
Avneesh Kumar   Uttaranchal University, Dehradun, India

Hospitality

Sonam Rai   Uttaranchal University, Dehradun, India
Shruti Sharma   Uttaranchal University, Dehradun, India
Nitin Duklan   Uttaranchal University, Dehradun, India

Stage Management

Punit Sharma   Uttaranchal University, Dehradun, India
Arti Rana   Uttaranchal University, Dehradun, India
Musheer Vaqar   Uttaranchal University, Dehradun, India

Technical Session

Mudit Baurai   Uttaranchal University, Dehradun, India
Manish Singh Bisht   Uttaranchal University, Dehradun, India
Sunil Ghildiyal   Uttaranchal University, Dehradun, India
Ravi Batra   Uttaranchal University, Dehradun, India

Finance

Sanjeev Sharma   Uttaranchal University, Dehradun, India
Amit Kumar Pal   Uttaranchal University, Dehradun, India
Sudhir Jugran   Uttaranchal University, Dehradun, India

Food

Sourabh Agarwal   Uttaranchal University, Dehradun, India
Arpit Verma   Uttaranchal University, Dehradun, India
Ankur Jaiswal   Uttaranchal University, Dehradun, India
Gaurav Singh Negi   Uttaranchal University, Dehradun, India

Advertising

Kapil Joshi   Uttaranchal University, Dehradun, India
Himanshu Gupta   Uttaranchal University, Dehradun, India
Ravi Dhaundiyal   Uttaranchal University, Dehradun, India

Press and Media

Shreya Goyal   Uttaranchal University, Dehradun, India
Rachna Juyal   Uttaranchal University, Dehradun, India

Editorial

Parichay Durga   Uttaranchal University, Dehradun, India
Nishi Chachra   Uttaranchal University, Dehradun, India

Technical Sponsorship

Computer Society of India, Dehradun Chapter
Special Interest Group – Cyber Forensics, Computer Society of India

Financial Sponsorship

Consilio Intelligence Research Lab
LWT India Private Limited

Contents – Part I

Contents – Part II

Two Stage Histogram Enhancement Schemes to Improve Visual Quality of Fundus Images

Farha Fatina Wahid[✉], K. Sugandhi, and G. Raju

Department of Information Technology, Kannur University, Kannur, Kerala, India
farhawahid@gmail.com, sugandhikgs@gmail.com,
kurupgraju@gmail.com

Abstract. A fundus image plays a significant role to analyze a wide variety of ophthalmic conditions. One of the major challenges faced by ophthalmologist in the analysis of fundus images is its low contrast nature. In this paper, two stage histogram enhancement schemes to improve the visual quality of fundus images are proposed. Fuzzy logic and Histogram Based Enhancement algorithm (FHBE) and Contrast Limited Adaptive Histogram Equalization (CLAHE) algorithm are cascaded one after the other to accomplish the two stage enhancement task. This results in two new enhancement schemes, namely FHBE-CLAHE and CLAHE-FHBE. The analysis of the results based on its visual quality shows that two stage enhancement schemes outperforms individual enhancement schemes.

Keywords: Image enhancement · Fundus images · CLAHE · FHBE

1 Introduction

Image enhancement is one of the prominent pre-processing steps in image processing applications. In image enhancement, importance is given more to subjective quality of the image rather than objective quality. There are mainly two types of image enhancement- edge enhancement and contrast enhancement. In edge enhancement, image edges are enhanced in order to improve the sharpness of edges whereas contrast enhancement enhances image contrast thereby increases the visual quality of images [1]. Image enhancement is equally significant in both gray and color images. But, color image enhancement is complex than gray images because color images can be represented by different color models and each color model has its own component structure. In order to enhance a color image, one has to fix the color model and the component which is to be enhanced [2]. Several approaches for enhancing color images for different applications are available to choose from [3–5]. An efficient color image enhancement scheme for enhancing low contrast and low bright natural images using Fuzzy logic and Histogram Based Equalization, FHBE, was proposed in [6].

Medical image processing is a key research area in medical imaging; especially with the wide spread use of digital images. Even though image enhancement is a pre-processing step, it plays a major role in medical image processing facilitating accurate diagnostics. Specialized medical imaging techniques such as X-ray, CT, MRI, PET, Ultrasound, etc. are broadly used to capture various parts of human body for diagnostics.

© Springer Nature Singapore Pte Ltd. 2018
M. Singh et al. (Eds.): ICACDS 2018, CCIS 905, pp. 1–11, 2018.
https://doi.org/10.1007/978-981-13-1810-8_1

Generally, captured medical images are low-contrast and noisy in nature. Thus, contrast enhancement is an inevitable step in certain medical image modality. Many algorithms are developed to enhance low-contrast medical images from different modality [7–10]. Among them, Contrast Limited Adaptive Histogram Equalization (CLAHE) has a noticeable role [11].

A fundus image is a photograph of the interior surface of the eye captured using a fundus camera with specialized low power microscope. The fundus image covers the retina, optic disc, retinal vasculature, macula and posterior pole [12]. The specialty of eye fundus is that one can observe microcirculation directly. Fundus images of the diabetic retinopathy patients may contain haemorrhages, exudates, cotton wool spots, blood vessel abnormalities (tortuosity, pulsation and new vessels) and pigmentation [13]. But, the major barrier of ophthalmoscopy is the low contrast of fundus images which decreases the visibility of medical signs of retinopathy. Hence, enhancement of low contrast fundus image has a key role in ophthalmoscopy.

Now a day, many researchers are working on the enhancement of low contrast fundus images. As fundus images are color images, enhancement can be performed on any color model. Generally, enhancements are done on value (V) component of HSV color model and green channel of RGB color model [6, 14]. In [14], the authors have proposed an enhancement scheme for fundus images using CLAHE algorithm. They suggested that CLAHE algorithm on green channel of RGB color model outperforms the enhancement results obtained by performing CLAHE on V component of HSV color model.

In this paper, two stage fundus image enhancement schemes are proposed. FHBE and CLAHE algorithms are selected for the two stages of enhancement. The enhanced results using the two stage enhancement schemes give better performance than individual enhancement results based on visual quality.

The paper is organized as follows. Section 2 gives a description of FHBE followed by CLAHE in Sect. 3. The proposed two stage enhancement schemes are discussed in Sect. 4. Experimental results and discussions are given in Sect. 5.

2   Fuzzy Logic and Histogram Based Enhancement (FHBE)

A Fuzzy logic and Histogram Based Enhancement (FHBE) scheme was developed in [6] to enhance low contrast and low bright natural color images. In this scheme, the original low contrast image is initially converted from RGB color space to HSV color space and computations are performed only on the V component of image thereby maintaining the chromatic information (hue and saturation) in the image [6].

The basic methodology of FHBE scheme is to stretch the V component of an image based on its average intensity, M, and stretching parameter, K. M is computed from the histogram of image using Eq. 1.

$$M = \frac{\sum_x x * H(x)}{\sum_x H(x)} \tag{1}$$

where x is the intensity value, $0 \leq x \leq 255$ and H(x) is the number of pixels in the V component of image with intensity value x.

Intensity stretching is the key operation of FHBE. Stretching is performed independently on two classes, C1 and C2 where C1 and C2 contains intensity values in the range $[0 - (M - 1)]$ and $[M - 255]$ respectively. The stretching is controlled by the stretching parameter, K, using the membership given to each intensity value of an image. For intensity values in class C1, a fuzzy membership function is defined such that if the current intensity value, x, is close to M, then membership is high and vice-versa. For class C2, the degree of membership depends on how far x is from the extreme value of intensity, E, in which the membership value for x is directly proportional to its distance from E.

Let μ_1 and μ_2 denote memberships of intensity values in class C1 and C2 respectively.

$$\mu_1(x) = 1 - \frac{M - x}{M} \tag{2}$$

$$\mu_2(x) = \frac{E - x}{E - M} \tag{3}$$

where $x \in$ C1 in Eq. 2 and $x \in$ C2 in Eq. 3 respectively.

The stretching parameter, K, is a constant which behaves differently for classes C1 and C2 when combined with respective membership values. For class C1, the stretching limit for intensity value x is $[0 - K]$ based on $\mu_1(x)$ and for class C2, the stretching limit is $[(E-K) - E]$ based on $\mu_2(x)$.

Once membership values are obtained, the enhancement operation is carried out independently on classes C1 and C2. For class C1, the enhanced intensity, x' is obtained as

$$x' = x + \mu_1(x) * K \tag{4}$$

And for class C2,

$$x' = x * \mu_2(x) + \left(E - \mu_2(x) * K\right) \tag{5}$$

The final enhanced image using FHBE is obtained by converting the image from HSV to RGB color model.

3 Contrast Limited Adaptive Histogram Equalization (CLAHE)

Contrast Limited Adaptive Histogram Equalization (CLAHE) is a well-known indirect contrast enhancement technique [11, 15–17]. It is an improved version of Adaptive Histogram Equalization (AHE) technique [15]. The major limitation of AHE is the presence of noise in the enhanced image. These noisy areas are characterized by high peak in the histogram. To overcome this problem with AHE, CLAHE was introduced. CLAHE works similar to AHE as the original image is divided into contextual regions (tiles) and local histograms are computed individually on each contextual region. As high peak in histogram indicates the presence of noise, a clipping is performed in CLAHE on individual histograms where clipped intensity values are redistributed equally among all the bins. The cumulative histograms from each contextual region give the final enhanced image [11].

The importance of dividing an image into contextual region lays in the fact that local contrast enhancement is more effective than global contrast enhancement especially for medical images. The number of contextual regions depends on the type of image and is generally fixed as 8×8 windows with 64 contextual regions [11]. The major distinguishing feature of CLAHE over AHE is the application of clip limit to high peak histogram bins of contextual regions. The clip limit for a contextual region's histogram is based on its average height and a user defined contrast factor, γ. It is defined as

$$\text{cliplimit} = \gamma * \text{avg}_{\text{height}} \tag{6}$$

where

$$\text{avg}_{\text{height}} = \frac{R \times C}{L} \tag{7}$$

In Eq. 7, R x C indicates the size of contextual region and L indicates the maximum possible gray level of the image. The user defined contrast factor, γ, controls the degree of cliplimit. It is in the range $0 < \gamma < 1$ [11].

Once clipping is performed on each contextual region's histogram, histogram specification is carried out to transform each clipped histogram to a specified distribution. The distributions can be either uniform, Rayleigh or exponential. It can be fixed based on the type of input image. Finally, the enhanced histograms of contextual regions are combined using bilinear interpolation to obtain histogram of CLAHE enhanced image.

4   Two Stage Histogram Enhancement Scheme

Even though majority of medical images are in gray scale, fundus images obtained using fundus camera are in color format where each color component might represent distinguishing features in the interior surface of eye. It is difficult for the physicians to analyze hemorrhages, exudates, cotton wool spots, blood vessel abnormalities, etc. from the captured fundus images due to its low contrast nature. Hence, enhancing low contrast fundus images is an efficient way to help the physicians for ophthalmoscopy.

FHBE and CLAHE are two contrast enhancement schemes which work in different manner. In the former scheme, stretching is carried out on the entire image's histogram [6] whereas in the latter one, histogram specification is performed on tiles rather than the entire image [11]. FHBE is well suited for enhancing low contrast and low bright natural color images. CLAHE, on the other hand is used to enhance low contrast medical images. In this work, FHBE and CLAHE are selected for the design of a cascaded system for enhancing low contrast fundus images. The input image is first subjected to enhancement using Method I and the enhanced image is given as input to Method II. If FHBE is chosen as Method I, then CLAHE becomes Method II and vice-versa. The output of Method II is taken as the final enhanced image.

4.1 Two Stage Framework

In the first stage, the low contrast fundus image is given as input to FHBE and CLAHE enhancement schemes. These results in two individual enhanced fundus images, namely FHBE enhanced and CLAHE enhanced fundus images. If FHBE algorithm is selected for the first stage, the FHBE enhanced image is given as input to CLAHE algorithm in the second stage to attain the final FHBE-CLAHE enhanced image. Similarly, FHBE algorithm on CLAHE enhanced image results in CLAHE-FHBE enhanced fundus image. The block diagram of two stage enhancement scheme is depicted in Fig. 1.

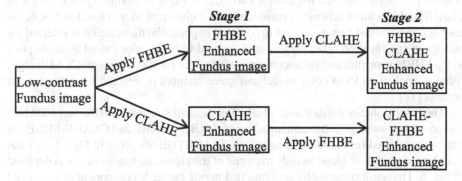

Fig. 1. Block diagram of two stage histogram enhancement schemes

4.2 Fusion on Independently Enhanced Images

Initially, each fundus image is enhanced using CLAHE (I_C) and FHBE (I_B) independently. Then the two enhanced images are converted to HSV color model and the V component of both images are fused using the following rule.

Consider a pixel, x, in I_C. Let μ_x be the average of 3×3 neighborhood of x and $dx = |x - \mu_x|$ be the variation of x from the average intensity of its pixel neighborhood. Similarly, let 'y' be a pixel in I_B which has the same position as x in the fundus image. Assume μ_y as the average of 3×3 neighborhood of y. Then, $dy = |y - \mu_y|$ is the variation of y from μ_y. Now, the fusion rule is that new pixel value, z, of the fused image (I_F) is obtained using Eq. 8.

$$z = \begin{cases} \dfrac{2x+y}{3} & ifdx \geq dy \\ \dfrac{x+2y}{3} & ifdy > dx \end{cases} \tag{8}$$

5 Experimental Results and Discussions

Experiments are carried out with fundus images obtained from Standard Diabetic Retinopathy database (DIARETDB) [18, 19]. It consists of two public databases namely DIARETDB0 [18] and DIARETDB1 [19] for diabetic retinopathy detection from fundus images. DIARETDB0 fundus images are captured with 50° field of view digital fundus camera and it consists of 130 color fundus images which include 20 normal images and 110 with signs of retinopathy. This data set is also known as calibration level 0 fundus images [18]. On the other hand, DIARETDB1 consists of 89 color fundus images of which 84 contains signs of retinopathy and is also known as calibration level 1 fundus images [19].

For the implementation of FHBE enhancement scheme, the stretching parameter K is fixed to 128 for class C1 [6] and for class C2, K value is modified to 64. As far as CLAHE enhancement scheme is considered, the number of tiles is fixed to 8×8, the user defined contrast factor, γ, is set to 0.03 and exponential distribution is selected for histogram specification. The images are converted to HSV color model as in [6] prior to the FHBE algorithm and enhancement is carried out on V component. CLAHE algorithm is applied on RGB color model and green channel is selected for enhancement process [11].

The results obtained using individual enhancement schemes (FHBE and CLAHE) and proposed two stage enhancement schemes (FHBE-CLAHE and CLAHE-FHBE) on randomly selected set of fundus images from DIARETDB are given in Figs. 2, 3, 4 and 5. Enlarged portion of blood vessels from one of the enhanced fundus image is depicted in Fig. 6. The result obtained by applying fusion rule on the V component of individual enhanced images is given in Fig. 7.

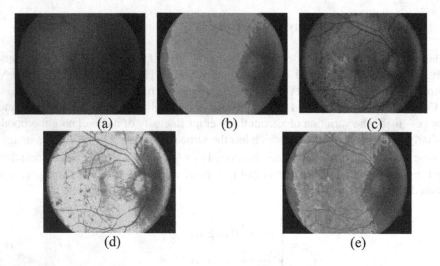

(a) (b) (c)

(d) (e)

Fig. 2. Enhancement results of image019 from DIARETDB0: (a) Original Image (b) FHBE (c) CLAHE (d) CLAHE-FHBE (e) FHBE-CLAHE

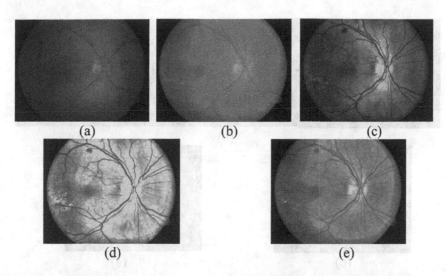

Fig. 3. Enhancement results of image029 from DIARETDB0: (a) Original Image (b) FHBE
(c) CLAHE (d) CLAHE-FHBE (e) FHBE-CLAHE

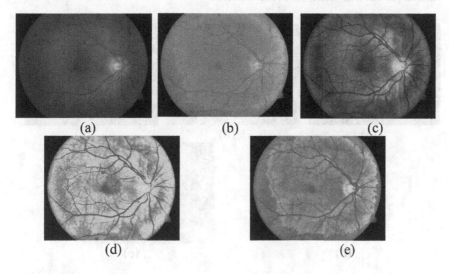

Fig. 4. Enhancement results of image077 from DIARETDB0: (a) Original Image (b) FHBE
(c) CLAHE (d) CLAHE-FHBE (e) FHBE-CLAHE

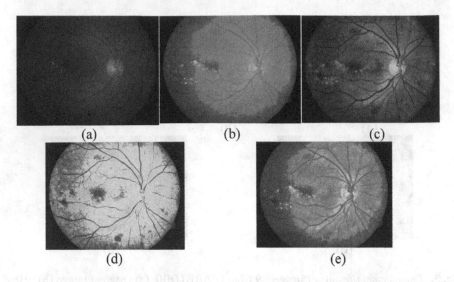

Fig. 5. Enhancement results of image007 from DIARETDB1: (a) Original Image (b) FHBE (c) CLAHE (d) CLAHE-FHBE (e) FHBE-CLAHE

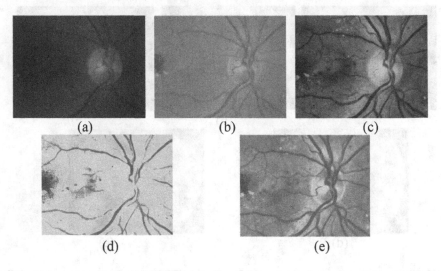

Fig. 6. Enlarged portion of blood vessels from the enhanced results of image007 from DIARETDB1: (a) Original Image (b) FHBE (c) CLAHE (d) CLAHE-FHBE (e) FHBE-CLAHE

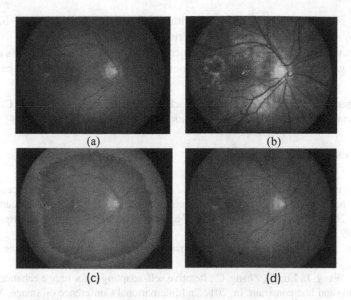

(a)   (b)

(c)   (d)

Fig. 7. Enhancement results of image007 from DIARETDB0: (a) Original Image (b) CLAHE (c) FHBE (d) Fusion of CLAHE and FHBE

From the experiments carried out, it is evident that enhancement of low-contrast fundus images gives better visibility of features in the interior surface of eye. As mentioned earlier, FHBE and CLAHE work differently. Hence, the visual perception of the results obtained using these algorithms are different. The cascading of these two algorithms improves the visual quality of features compared to individual results. It is clearly visible from Figs. 2, 3, 4 and 5. From Fig. 6, it is clear that the blood vessels of the original image are enhanced using all the algorithms while best results are obtained using FHBE-CLAHE two stage enhancement scheme. Figure 7 shows that the enhanced results obtained independently using FHBE and CLAHE has its own merits and demerits based on visual quality and the fusion of these individual enhanced images using specific fusion rule on the V component of the images in HSV color model is an alternate and efficient method to enhance low contrast fundus images.

6   Conclusion

CLAHE and FHBE are two independent enhancement algorithms, the former widely used in medical image enhancement and the latter in enhancing low contrast and low bright natural color images. In this work, CLAHE and FHBE are cascaded to enhance fundus images. Also, a fusion rule is applied on the V component of enhanced fundus images obtained by applying CLAHE and FHBE algorithms independently in HSV color model. The results of the experiments carried out with a set of images shows that the proposed cascaded schemes gives better results compared to individual algorithms and FHBE-CLAHE outperforms CLAHE in terms of visual quality. Also, fusion of both the algorithms outperforms individual algorithms. The enhancement can be further improved by making changes in the fusion rule.

Analysis with objective metrics and subjective metrics by domain experts as well as comparison with other prominent enhancement algorithms is required to be carried out.

Acknowledgement. The authors would like to acknowledge the University Grants Commission for the financial support extended under the Major Project Scheme.

References

1. Shanmugavadivu, P., Balasubramanian, K.: Image edge and contrast enhancement using unsharp masking and constrained histogram equalization. In: Balasubramaniam, P. (ed.) ICLICC 2011. CCIS, vol. 140, pp. 129–136. Springer, Heidelberg (2011). https://doi.org/10.1007/978-3-642-19263-0_16
2. Koschan, A., Abidi, M.: Digital Color Image Processing. Wiley-Interscience, Hoboken (2008)
3. Dou, Y., Wang, J., Lu, G., Zhang, C.: Iterative self-adapting color image enhancement base on chroma and hue constrain. In: 2017 2nd International Conference on Image, Vision and Computing (ICIVC) (2017)
4. Chi, J., Eramian, M.: Wavelet-based texture-characteristic morphological component analysis for color image enhancement. In: 2016 IEEE International Conference on Image Processing (ICIP) (2016)
5. Purushothaman, J., Kamiyama, M., Taguchi, A.: Color image enhancement based on Hue differential histogram equalization. In: 2016 International Symposium on Intelligent Signal Processing and Communication Systems (ISPACS) (2016)
6. Raju, G., Nair, M.: A fast and efficient color image enhancement method based on fuzzy-logic and histogram. AEU Int. J. Electron. Commun. **68**, 237–243 (2014)
7. Tebini, S., Seddik, H., Ben Braiek, E.: Medical image enhancement based on New anisotropic diffusion function. In: 2017 14th International Multi-Conference on Systems, Signals & Devices (SSD) (2017)
8. Hsu, W., Chou, C.: Medical image enhancement using modified color histogram equalization. J. Med. Biol. Eng. **35**, 580–584 (2015)
9. Gu, J., Hua, L., Wu, X., Yang, H., Zhou, Z.: Color medical image enhancement based on adaptive equalization of intensity numbers matrix histogram. Int. J. Autom. Comput. **12**, 551–558 (2015)
10. Yelmanova, E., Romanyshyn, Y.: Medical image contrast enhancement based on histogram. In: 2017 IEEE 37th International Conference on Electronics and Nanotechnology (ELNANO) (2017)
11. Zuiderveld, K.: Contrast limited adaptive histogram equalization. In: Heckbert, P.S. (eds.) Graphics Gems IV, Chap. VIII.5, pp. 474–485. Academic Press, Cambridge (1994)
12. Color Fundus Photography, Department of Ophthalmology. http://ophthalmology.med.ubc.ca/patient-care/ophthalmic-photography/color-fundus-photography/. Accessed 20 Nov 2017
13. Fundus (eye). https://en.wikipedia.org/wiki/Fundus_(eye). Accessed 20 Nov 2017
14. Shamsudeen, F., Raju, G.: Enhancement of fundus imagery. In: 2016 International Conference on Next Generation Intelligent Systems (ICNGIS) (2016)
15. Pizer, S.M., et al.: Adaptive histogram equalization and its variations. Comput. Vis. Graph. Image Process. **38**(3), 355–368 (1987)

16. Sherouse, G., Rosenman, J., McMurry, H., Pizer, S., Chaney, E.: Automatic digital contrast enhancement of radiotherapy films. Int. J. Radiat. Oncology*Biology*Physics **13**, 801–806 (1987)
17. Rosenman, J., Roe, C., Cromartie, R., Muller, K., Pizer, S.: Portal film enhancement: technique and clinical utility. Int. J. Radiat. Oncology*Biology*Physics **25**, 333–338 (1993)
18. DIARETDB0 - Standard Diabetic Retinopathy Database. http://www.it.lut.fi/project/imageret/diaretdb0/. Accessed 20 Nov 2017
19. DIARETDB1 - Standard Diabetic Retinopathy Database. http://www.it.lut.fi/project/imageret/diaretdb1/. Accessed 20 Nov 2017

A Secure and Efficient Computation Outsourcing Scheme for Multi-users

V. Sudarsan Rao[1](✉) and N. Satyanarayana[2]

[1] Department of CSE, Khammam Institute of Technology
and Sciences (KITS), Khammam, (T.S), India
sudharshan.cse2008@gmail.com
[2] Department of CSE, Nagole Institute of Technology
and Sciences (NITS), Hyderabad, (T.S), India
nsn2008@gmail.com

Abstract. The outsourcing process is computationally secure if it is performed without unveiling to the other external agent or cloud, either the original data or the actual solution to the computations. Secure multiparty computation computes a certain function without revealing their private secret information.

In this paper, we presented a new secure and computationally efficient protocol utilizing multi cloud servers view. In our proposed protocol, encrypted data by different users is transformed to cloud. The protocol being non-interactive between users, gives the comparatively lesser computational and communication complexity. The analysis of our proposed protocol is also presented at the end of the paper.

Keywords: Access control · Lattice Based Encryption
Secure outsourcing · Cloud computing · Key issuing · Privacy

1 Introduction

Beside the tremendous advantages of outsourcing, client faces some challenges by outsourcing the computational task to cloud [8,9]. These are security, input-output privacy and verification of result. Consider a scenario where some mutually distrusted members are present, and they want to compute a complex function, which involves their own private inputs [10]. This scenario may be termed as secure multi-party computation. Suppose, $U_1, U_2, \cdots, U_m$ are m users, and each posses a private number $n_1, n_2, \cdots, n_m$. Consider function is,

$$\text{FUNC} = f(n_1, n_2, \cdots, n_m), \tag{1}$$

which they want to co-operatively compute, but they don't want to expose n_i of corresponding U_i to other users U_j, $i \neq j$ & $i, j \in (1, 2, \cdots, m)$. Also they should guarantee that FUNC should not be known by any of the unauthorized user. Its observable that the computation and communication complexities are

© Springer Nature Singapore Pte Ltd. 2018
M. Singh et al. (Eds.): ICACDS 2018, CCIS 905, pp. 12–24, 2018.
https://doi.org/10.1007/978-981-13-1810-8_2

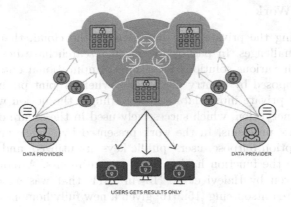

Fig. 1. General computational outsourcing scenario

mostly dependant on the complex nature of computation function. The scenario is shown as Fig. 1.

Recently, as the development of cloud computing [25], users' concerns about data security are the main obstacles that impedes cloud computing from wide adoption. These concerns are originated from the fact that sensitive data resides in public cloud [18], which is maintained and operated by untrusted cloud service provider (CSP) [20,22]. The expectation of users is that the cloud should compute the function having the inputs as private parameters of users in the encrypted/transformed form.

2   Secure Outsourcing Algorithms Classification

Increasing no. of smart equipments and their growing need to execute computationally large task resulting the outsourcing of any scientific computation to the cloud server an encouraging solution. The general nomenclature is represented as Fig. 2 below:-

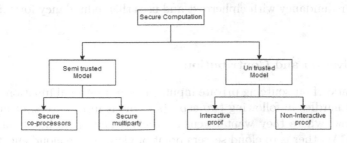

Nomenclature of secure outsourcing algorithms

Fig. 2. Secure outsourcing algorithms nomenclature

2.1 Related Work

While outsourcing the private data functions to the cloud, there exist many problems and challenges. In past years, much research have been carried out to come up with various solutions for secure computational outsourcing. One solution was proposed by Gentry [2], in 2009 where a joint public key is used to encrypt their private input data and accordingly the notion was termed as Homomorphic encryption, which successively used in the secure outsourcing of practical complex problems. In the work presented by [7] has given a scheme where for encryption purpose, users' public keys are utilized, and cloud will be able to compute the function having their private inputs. A more secure outsourcing was given by Halevi et al. [13] in 2011, that was a non-interactive method for secure outsourcing [15]. [16] given a new fully homomorphic scheme, multikey FHE, which applied bootstrapping concept for secure outsourcing of computations. ABE, introduced as fuzzy identity-based encryption in [24], was firstly dealt with by Goyal et al. [1]. Two distinct and interrelated notions of ABE were determined in [1]. Accordingly, several constructions supporting for any kinds of access structures were provided [3,4] for practical applications [5,6]. Atallah et al. [8] offered an structure for secure outsourcing of scientific computations e.g. multiplication of matrices. Although, the solution used the disguise technique and thus leaded to leakage of private information. Atallah and Li [9] given an efficient protocol to outsource sequence comparison with two servers in secure manner. Furthermore, Benjamin and Atallah [10] addressed the problem of secure outsourcing for widely applicable linear algebraic computations. Atallah and Frikken [11] further studied this problem and gave improved protocols based on the so-called weak secret hiding assumption. Recently, Wang et al. [12] presented efficient mechanisms for secure outsourcing of linear programming computation.

In [14], a novel paradigm for outsourcing the decryption of ABE is given. Compared with our work, the two lack of the consideration on the eliminating the overhead computation at attribute authority. In 2014, Sudarshan et al. [27] proposed an Attribute-Based Encryption mechanism, applied for cloud security. Recently Lai et al. [17] given a construction with verifiable decryption, which achieves both security and verifiability without random oracles. Their task supplements a redundancy with ciphertext and uses this redundancy for correctness checking.

2.2 Motivation and Contribution

In the scenario of outsourcing private inputs or computational function to cloud, There exist hurdles in following two aspects - One is in the users' or customers point of view, where they want to ensure the privacy of its input parameters and results. Another is to cloud servers point of view, where cloud entity is worried about feasibleness of encrypted/transformed inputs and operating on them. In computational outsourcing, users are not participating in the computational function, rather than they outsource the private problem along with parameters to the cloud, but users and cloud servers are not mutually trusted entities. Thus, users would not like to submit their private problem data inputs to the cloud. Thus, encrypting/transforming the private data prior to submission to cloud is a usual solution. Our contribution in this paper is as -

- We have proposed protocol for secure and an efficient computational outsourcing to cloud. The protocol is completely non-interactive between users.
- We have performed the computational security analysis for our proposed system.

2.3   Organization of the Paper

Remaining paper organized as - Preliminaries are given in Sect. 3. Secure outsourcing using FHE scheme is given in Sect. 4. Experimental results are presented in Sect. 5. Section 6 presents our proposed scheme along with correctness, security analysis and our experimental simulation results. Section 7 concludes the paper.

3   Preliminaries

This section discusses some of the significant preliminaries required for secure computational outsourcing.

3.1   Computational Verifiability

Various different solutions exist for secure computational outsourcing. Homomorphic encryption(HE) can be assumed as a better solution to secure outsourcing of scientific computations, but it is useful when the returned result can be trusted.

Lemma 1. *It is infeasible to factorizing the N in polynomial time if integer factorization in large scale in infeasible.*

Proof. Assume x is an adversary who is able to factorize a number N into primes p and q of probable same bit length in polynomial time. Suppose this operations probability as p'. Each factor $fact_i$ of a number N will at least posses two prime factors. So the probability p''_r that the attacker can factorize it is - almost lesser than p'. Thus the resultant probability that attacker can factorize N is $\prod_{i=1}^{m} p''_r \leq (p')^m$. Now if p' is negligible, the resultant probability is also negligible.

3.2   Lattice-Based Encryption

As we know that the computational complexity as well as the input parameters' privacy is mostly dependant on the encryption procedure adopted by user. Lattice-Based Encryption [16,28] is considered as secure against quantum computer attacks and much efficient as well as potent than RSA and Elliptic curve cryptosystems.

Lattice based cryptosystem, whose security is based on core lattice theory problems, was introduced by Mikls Ajtai, in 1996. In the same year, first lattice based public key encryption scheme (NTRU) was proposed. Later, much work and improvement [2] was carried out towards this direction involving some additional cryptographic primitives LWE(learning with errors).

4 Secure Outsourcing Using FHE

This section summarizes the scheme [26] for secure outsourcing of large matrix multiplication computations on cloud. The complete description and steps involved in this scheme are summarized as below:-

---

Algorithm 1

1: Generate secret key pair: $\{H, Y\}$
   where, H: is a Hadamard matrix [23] and
   Y: is a diagonal matrix selected randomly.
2: Consider, M_1 and M_2 are two large matrices, for which the multiplication needs to be computed, thus client will outsource this computation problem to cloud side.
3: Client computes,
$$M_1' = H \times M_1 \times Y$$
$$M_2' = Y^{-1} \times M_2$$
4: Client sends M_1' and M_2' to cloud server.
5: $Result' \leftarrow M_1' \times M_2'$
6: The cloud server sends back the computed result to client side.
7: After getting the computed result, client will retransform it and get the original result for MM problem. The procedure is given as below Algorithm -
8: $Result \leftarrow H^{-1} \times Result'$

---

5 Experiment Results

This section presents our experimental analysis.

5.1 System Specifications

Our system specifications are as below:-

– *Software Specifications* -
  OS - Ubuntu 16.04 LTS, 64 bit
  Python version - 'Python 3.6.0'

– *Hardware Specifications* -
  RAM size - 4 GB
  Processor - Intel core i3 4030U CPU @$1.90 GHz \times 4$

5.2 Our Results

The graph for overall algorithm execution for various sized input parameters is given below:-

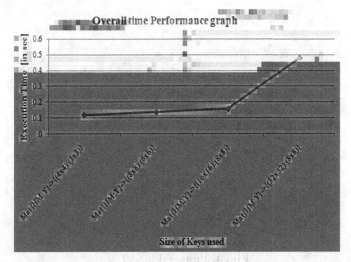

The end results of execution performance for varying key sizes is presented as Table 1 below:-

Table 1. Execution performance

S.No	Dimensions				Exec Performance		
	HM	M1	M2	Y	T[encry](in sec)	T[dec](in sec)	T[Overall](in sec)
1	4×4	4×3	3×4	3×3	0.0994174	0.115151	0.1187498
2	8×8	8×6	6×4	6×6	0.1260472	0.1349868	0.1377818
3	16×16	16×8	8×8	8×8	0.1321644	0.1473488	0.1589264
4	32×32	32×8	8×8	8×8	0.165747	0.146771	0.4791004
Tabular form							

6 Proposed Scheme

In this section, we have proposed an efficient secure computational outsourcing mechanism applicable for multi-users. The system model and proposed mechanism steps are given in subsections below:-

6.1 System Model

The proposed system model is represented as diagram below (Fig. 3):-
Notations used are given in Table 2.

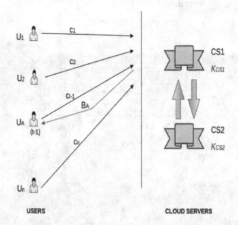

Fig. 3. Proposed model

Table 2. Notations used in proposed system

$CS1$:	First cloud server
$CS2$:	Second cloud server
c_i:	Ciphertexts (encrypted data of each customer/user U_i)
n:	No. of users
α_i:	Private input corresponding to U_i
ψ:	Probability density function
q:	Prime order
$RAND_i$:	Random number for i^{th} user
$\mathscr{C}_{FUN}$:	Function circuit
R:	Ring structure space
β:	Final computed result

6.2   Protocol Steps

The proposed secure computational outsourcing protocol executes in the below phases -

---

Key Gen() and Set up -

- Perform sampling for ring element space vector $a_i \leftarrow R_q^N$, $\forall$ $i = (1, 2, \cdots, n)$; Ring element $SK_i \leftarrow \psi$; $\alpha_i \leftarrow \psi^N$ (ψ represents: probability density function), where -

$$\psi = \int_{-\infty}^{x} P(\xi)d\xi$$

- Key pairs of U_i: Public key - $(a_i.SK_i + 2\alpha_i) \in R_q^N$; Private key - SK_i.
- $CS1$ has its private no. as K_{CS1} & $CS2$ has its private no. as K_{CS2}.
- U_i shares a random no. $RAND_i$ with $CS1$.
- Each user U_i initiates protocol and sends $RAND_i.SK_i$ to $CS2$.
- $CS2$ reckons $K_{CS2}.RAND_i.SK_i$ and sends back to $CS1$.
- $CS1$ can get $K_{CS2}.SK_i$ by extracting $RAND_i$.

$\forall i \in (1, 2, \cdots, n)$,
U_i uses Lattice based encryption method to encrypt its own problem input α_i. The sub-steps involved in this are as below:-

---

Lattice based Encryption -

- First U_i perform sampling as: $e_i \leftarrow \psi^N$. where,
  ψ is: probability density function(PDF), defined as -

$$\psi = \int_{-\infty}^{x} P(\xi)d\xi$$

- Next, each user U_i computes -

$$c_0^i \leftarrow \; < u_i, e_i > + \; \alpha_i \in R_q$$
$$c_1^i \leftarrow \; < a_i, e_i > \; \in R_q$$

- Further, it gives output as ciphertext,

$$c_i = (c_0^i, c_1^i) \in R_q^N; \; (N = 2)$$

$CS1$ stores all ciphertexts coming from user $U_i (1 \leq i \leq n)$, then further steps are as below:-

Circuit Computation on Outsourcing -

- First, $CS1$ transforms the ciphertexts as $c_i \rightarrow c_i^{TR_1}$
  where, $c_i^{TR_1} = (c_0^{i^{TR_1}}, c_1^{i^{TR_1}}) = (K_{CS1}.c_0^i, K_{CS1}.(K_{CS2}.SK_i).c_1^i)$.
- $CS1$ sends above $c_i^{TR_1}$ to $CS2$.
- After receiving $c_i^{TR_1}$, $CS2$ again transforms $c_i^{TR_1}$ into

$$c_i^{TR_2} = (K_{CS2}.K_{CS1}.c_0^i, K_{CS1}.(K_{CS2}.SK_i).c_1^i)$$

take, $K = K_{CS1}.K_{CS2}$
then, $c_i^{TR_2} = (c_0^{i^{TR_2}}, c_1^{i^{TR_2}}) = (K.c_0^i, K.SK_i.c_1^i)$
- $CS2$ then reckons the ciphertext of result by transformed ciphertext of every user's private i/p.
  - Additive oprn. for each add. gate -
    $\Rightarrow c_i^{TR_2} \oplus c_j^{TR_2}$
    $\Rightarrow (c_1^{i^{TR_2}} - c_0^{i^{TR_2}}) \oplus (c_1^{j^{TR_2}} - c_0^{j^{TR_2}})$
    $\Rightarrow (K.SK_i.c_1^i - K.c_0^i) \oplus (K.SK_j.c_1^j - K.c_0^j)$
    $\Rightarrow (K.(SK_i.c_1^i - c_0^i) \oplus K.(SK_j.c_1^j - c_0^j))$
    $\Rightarrow K.[(SK_i.c_1^i - c_0^i) \oplus (SK_j.c_1^j - c_0^j)]$
    $\Rightarrow K.[\alpha_i + \alpha_j]$
  - Multiplicative oprn. for every mul. gate -
    $\Rightarrow c_i^{TR_2} \otimes c_j^{TR_2}$
    $\Rightarrow (c_1^{i^{TR_2}} - c_0^{i^{TR_2}}) \otimes (c_1^{j^{TR_2}} - c_0^{j^{TR_2}})$
    $\Rightarrow (K.SK_i.c_1^i - K.c_0^i) \otimes (K.SK_j.c_1^j - K.c_0^j)$
    $\Rightarrow (K.(SK_i.c_1^i - c_0^i) \otimes K.(SK_j.c_1^j - c_0^j))$
    $\Rightarrow K^2.[(SK_i.c_1^i - c_0^i) \otimes (SK_j.c_1^j - c_0^j)]$
    $\Rightarrow K^2.[\alpha_i \times \alpha_j]$

Production of the result by cloud servers will follow as steps below:-

Production of Result -

- When $CS2$ performed gate by gate computation on circuit $\mathscr{C}_{FUN}$, it gets some intermediate meta result, which is encrypted by K_{CS1} and K_{CS2} of the cloud servers $CS1$ and $CS2$.
  If $\beta = FUN(\alpha_1, \alpha_2, \cdots, \alpha_n)$ and let's θ is the no. of multiplicative gates of $\mathscr{C}_{FUN}$.
  then, $\beta' = K^{\theta+1}.\beta = (K_{CS1}^{\theta+1}.K_{CS2}^{\theta+1}).\beta$
- To provide results for each user, and ensure that only authorized user set must get final result [*Assume*, $U_{\mathbb{A}}$, $\mathbb{A} \in (1,2,3,\cdots,n)$ *is authorized user set to access result*], $CS2$ first sends β' to $CS1$.
- $CS1$ removes $K_{CS1}^{\theta+1}$ and ties $RAND_{\mathbb{A}}$ to compute $\beta'_{\mathbb{A}} = RAND_{\mathbb{A}}.K_{CS2}^{\theta+1}.\beta$
- Then $CS1$ sends $\beta'_{\mathbb{A}}$ to $CS2$.
- $CS2$ finally removes $K_{CS2}^{\theta+1}$ and gets $\beta_{\mathbb{A}} = RAND_{\mathbb{A}}.\beta$
- Further $CS2$ sends it to authorized users set $U_{\mathbb{A}}$, $\mathbb{A} \in (1,2,3,\cdots,n)$.

> Secure Results Reconstruction at Users' side -
>
> – For each $U_\mathbb{A}$, $\mathbb{A} \in (1, 2, 3, \cdots, n)$, it successfully gets the final result β by deposing $RAND_\mathbb{A}$.

6.3 Analysis of Proposed Scheme

Here, we have presented the correctness and security analysis of our proposed scheme.

– Correctness analysis -

The correctness analysis of given scheme is as follows:-

Theorem 1. *Due to Homomorphic properties of the transformed ciphertexts, the given scheme is correct.*

Let, P and Q are rings a function $f : P \rightarrow Q$ will be ring homomorphism if $\forall x_1, x_2 \in P$.

- $f(x_1 + x_2) = f(x_1) + f(x_2)$
- $f(x_1 * x_2) = f(x_1) * f(x_2)$

– Security analysis -

The security analysis of proposed scheme can be analysed as below:-

Theorem 2. *As long as Lattice based encryption is secure and cloud servers CS1 and CS2 are noncolluding, the given protocol is secure enough.*

In proposed protocol, each user U_i encrypts its private input α_i with the help of its own public key, which is being produced by triggering lattice based encryption scheme. Further, U_i sends $RAND_i.SK_i$ to $CS2$. Then, $CS2$ reckons $K_{CS2}.RAND_i.SK_i$ and sends back to $CS1$. Here, $U_i's$ private key is SK_i, which is protected by $RAND_i$. In the entire process, the user's private keys are not being revealed.

After transferring computed results, cloud ensures in the protocol that only authorized user set must get final result; (Assume, $U_\mathbb{A}$, $\mathbb{A} \in (1, 2, 3, \cdots, n)$ is authorized user set to access result.)

6.4 Comparative Analysis

This section presents the comparison of our scheme with existing schemes on several factors/parameters. The representation is given in Table 3.

Table 3. Comparison with related work

Schemes	Feasible data size	Encry() technique adopted	Download result and decry()	Users	Speed-up	Cloud-Efficiency
Wang et al. (2015)	Low and medium sized	Parameters transformation	Slow on large size data	Single user	Good for medium sized problem	Moderate
Li et al. (2015)	Medium sized	Identity based encryption	Slow on large size data	Single user	Good upto medium sized problem	Moderate
Our construction	Medium to large sized	Lattice based encryption	Comparatively faster	Multi user supported	Better for large sized problem	Good

7   Conclusion and Future Work

When users have to compute some complex function, which involves their private inputs then to perform outsourcing is the possible scenario from user side. There exist hurdles in following two aspects - One is in the users' or customers point of view, where they want to ensure the privacy of its input parameters and results. Another is to cloud servers point of view, where cloud entity is worried about feasibleness of encrypted/transformed inputs and operating on them.

In this paper, we have constructed a scheme for secure outsourcing based on multi cloud servers. The computational complexity and security analysis is also given for our proposed system. Finding an efficient, practical and computationally secure outsourcing solution for various specific scientific problems will be our further research work.

References

1. Goyal, V., Pandey, O., Sahai, A., Waters, B.: Attribute-based encryption for fine-grained access control of encrypted data. In: Proceedings of 13th ACM Conference on Computer and Communications Security, pp. 89–98 (2006)
2. Gentry, C.: A fully homomorphic encryption scheme [Doctoral dissertation], Stanford University (2009)
3. Cheung, L., Newport, C.: Provably secure ciphertext policy ABE. In: Proceedings of 14th ACM Conference on CCS, pp. 456–465 (2007)
4. Nishide, T., Yoneyama, K., Ohta, K.: Attribute-based encryption with partially hidden encryptor-specified access structures. In: Bellovin, S.M., Gennaro, R., Keromytis, A., Yung, M. (eds.) ACNS 2008. LNCS, vol. 5037, pp. 111–129. Springer, Heidelberg (2008). https://doi.org/10.1007/978-3-540-68914-0_7
5. Han, F., Qin, J., Zhao, H., Hu, J.: A general transformation from KP-ABE to searchable encryption. Future Gen. Comput. Syst. **30**, 107–115 (2014)
6. Zhao, H., Qin, J., Hu, J.: Energy efficient key management scheme for body sensor networks. IEEE Trans. Parallel Distrib. Syst. **24**(11), 2202–2210 (2013)

7. Asharov, G., Jain, A., López-Alt, A., Tromer, E., Vaikuntanathan, V., Wichs, D.: Multiparty computation with low communication, computation and interaction via threshold FHE. In: Pointcheval, D., Johansson, T. (eds.) EUROCRYPT 2012. LNCS, vol. 7237, pp. 483–501. Springer, Heidelberg (2012). https://doi.org/10.1007/978-3-642-29011-4_29

8. Atallah, M.J., Pantazopoulos, K., Rice, J.R., Spafford, E.E.: Secure outsourcing of scientific computations. In: Zelkowitz, M.V. (ed.) Trends in Software Engineering, vol. 54, pp. 215–272. Elsevier, Amsterdam (2002)

9. Atallah, M.J., Li, J.: Secure outsourcing of sequence comparisons. Intl. J. Inf. Secur. 4(4), 277–287 (2005)

10. Benjamin, D., Atallah, M.J.: Private and cheating-free outsourcing of algebraic computations. In: Proceedings of 6th Annual Conference on PST, pp. 240–245 (2008)

11. Atallah, M.J., Frikken, K.B.: Securely outsourcing linear algebra computations. In: Proceedings of 5th ACM Symposium on ASIACCS, pp. 48–59 (2010)

12. Wang, C., Ren, K., Wang, J.: Secure and practical outsourcing of linear programming in Cloud Computing. In: Proceedings of IEEE INFOCOM, pp. 820–828 (2011)

13. Halevi, S., Lindell, Y., Pinkas, B.: Secure computation on the web: computing without simultaneous interaction. In: Rogaway, P. (ed.) CRYPTO 2011. LNCS, vol. 6841, pp. 132–150. Springer, Heidelberg (2011). https://doi.org/10.1007/978-3-642-22792-9_8

14. Green, M., Hohenberger, S., Waters, B.: Outsourcing the decryption of ABE ciphertexts. In: Proceedings of 20th USENIX Conference on SEC, p. 34 (2011)

15. Brakerski, Z., Vaikuntanathan, V.: Efficient fully homomorphic encryption from (standard) LWE. In: Proceedings of the IEEE 52nd Annual Symposium on Foundations of Computer Science (FOCS 2011), pp. 97–106 (2011)

16. López-Alt, A., Tromer, E., Vaikuntanathan, V.: Cloud-assisted multiparty computation from fully homomorphic encryption. IACR Cryptology ePrint Archive, vol. 2011, Article 663 (2011)

17. Lai, J., Deng, R., Guan, C., Weng, J.: Attribute-based encryption with verifiable outsourced decryption. IEEE Trans. Inf. Forensics Secur. 8(8), 1343–1354 (2013)

18. Zhang, Y., Blanton, M.: Efficient secure and verifiable outsourcing of matrix multiplications. In: Chow, S.S.M., Camenisch, J., Hui, L.C.K., Yiu, S.M. (eds.) ISC 2014. LNCS, vol. 8783, pp. 158–178. Springer, Cham (2014). https://doi.org/10.1007/978-3-319-13257-0_10

19. Atallah, M.J., Frikken, K.B.: Securely outsourcing linear algebra computations. In: ASLACCS, 13–16 April 2010, Beijing, China (2010)

20. Lei, X., Liao, X., Huang, T., Li, H., Hu, C.: Outsourcing large matrix inversion computation to a public cloud. IEEE Trans. Cloud Comput. 1(1), 1 (2013)

21. Benjamin, D., Atallah, M.J.: Private and cheating-free outsourcing of algebraic computations. In: Sixth Annual Conference on Privacy, Security and Trust, PST 2008. IEEE (2008)

22. Xiang, C., Tang, C.: Securely verifiable outsourcing schemes of matrix calculation. Int. J. High Perform. Comput. Netw. 8(2), 93–101 (2015)

23. http://homepages.math.uic.edu/leon/mcs425-s08/handouts/Hadamard_codes.pdf

24. Sahai, A., Waters, B.: Fuzzy identity-based encryption. In: Cramer, R. (ed.) EUROCRYPT 2005. LNCS, vol. 3494, pp. 457–473. Springer, Heidelberg (2005). https://doi.org/10.1007/11426639_27

25. Zeng, D., Guo, S., Hu, J.: Reliable bulk-data dissemination in delay tolerant networks. IEEE Trans. Parallel Distrib. Syst. doi.ieeecomputersociety.org/10.1109-TPDS.2013.221
26. Sudarshan, V., Satyanarayana, N.: An efficient protocol for secure outsourcing of scientific computations to an untrusted cloud. In: International Conference on Intelligent Computing and Control (I2C2), Karpagam College of Engineering, Tamilnadu (2017)
27. Sudarshan, V., Satyanarayana, N., Dileep Kumar, A.: Lock-in to the meta cloud with attribute based encryption without outsourced decryption. IJCST **5**(4) (2014)
28. Brakerski, Z., Vaikuntanathan, V.: Fully homomorphic encryption from ring-LWE and security for key dependent messages. In: Rogaway, P. (ed.) CRYPTO 2011. LNCS, vol. 6841, pp. 505–524. Springer, Heidelberg (2011). https://doi.org/10.1007/978-3-642-22792-9_29

Detecting the Common Biomarkers for Early Stage Parkinson's Disease and Early Stage Alzheimer's Disease Associated with Intrinsically Disordered Protein

Sagnik Sen[✉] and Ujjwal Maulik

Department of Computer Science, Jadavpur University,
Kolkata 32, West Bengal, India
sagnik.sen2008@gmail.com

Abstract. Mild cognitive Impairment is in charge of slight but effective changes in cognitive activities e.g., thinking capability, memory etc. Cases of mild cognitive impairment can be upgraded to neuro-degenarative diseases which are also associated with intrinsically disordered proteins. A bunch of proteins without unique and ordered protein structures are known as Intrinsically Disordered Proteins. In this article, we screened out 164 differentially expressed protein biomarkers at mild cognitive impairment stage which are common in alzheimer's disease and parkinson's disease and also associated with structural disordered. Among them top ten disordered protein biomarkers are taken for further evaluation under KEGG and GO analysis. Fetched pathway and GO information are related to cognitive changes which lead to early stages of alzheimer and parkinson. Hence, it can be concluded that the differentially expressed protein biomarkers with structural disorder can be associated with both of alzheimer and parkinson.

Keywords: Intrinsically disordered proteins · Mild cognitive impairment Parkinson's disease · Alzheimer's disease

1 Introduction

Mild Cognitive Impairment (MCI) [1–3] is responsible for slight but effective changes in cognitive activities e.g., thinking capability, memory etc. The chances of few neuro-degenerative diseases increase after MCI stage. More than half who suffered from MCI is upgraded to dementia e.g., amnestic MCI enhances the chances of the Alzheimer's disease. There are few cases of Parkinson's also where MCI is working as an intermediate stage.

Intrinsically Disordered Proteins (*IDPs*) are common type of proteins without proper or no three dimensional structures [6]. *IDPs* work as indicator of evolutionary rate [7]. Mostly for their unusual structural orchestration the structure- function paradigm is affected [11]. Around 30% of the human proteins have partial or complete disorder [4, 10]. Mostly proteins having disorder at binding site are highly performing

© Springer Nature Singapore Pte Ltd. 2018
M. Singh et al. (Eds.): ICACDS 2018, CCIS 905, pp. 25–34, 2018.
https://doi.org/10.1007/978-981-13-1810-8_3

unusual functionalities. Usually IDPs are associated with three different kind of diseases such as Heart Diseases, Malignancies and Neurodegenerative Diseases [5, 6].

It is observed that Parkinson and Alzheimer are sharing same biomarkers at early stages. However, *IDP*s are directly associated with both of the diseases e.g., amyloid β, α-synuclein which are responsible for AD, PD respectively are known examples of *IDP*s [8, 12]. Protein biomarkers which are related to AD and PD might have disordered regions or have complete structural disorder. Unfortunately, very few works have been done with structural disorder of protein biomarkers. In this article, we propose one framework which can help to fetch common differentially expressed protein biomarkers in terms of autoantibodies which are highly associated with protein disorders.

This article is divided in four sections. In Sect. 1, a background study of the field is given. Subsequently, Sects. 2 and 3 are given to describe proposed framework and corresponding results and discussion on it. Finally, Sect. 4 concludes the article.

2   Methods

In this section, the proposed a framework for the objective of selecting common *IDP* biomarkers of AD and PD have been described. We start with a group of autoantibodies for AD and PD separately which are stored in Ab_{AD} and Ab_{PD} respectively. The samples stored in aforementioned matrices are used for data pre-processing. Subsequently, the differentially behaved in terms of auto antibodies activities. The main objective of the work is find common biomarkers at early stages of two diseases. The flow of the proposed framework is given in Fig. 1 the steps of the experiment are more elaborately discussed below:

2.1   Experimental Dataset

In this article, we use list of autoantibodies (NCBI Ref. id: GSE74763) [13] which consists of 9480 proteins having either Alzheimer and/or Parkinson. It has 25 diseased (parkinson and alzheimer individually) samples and 25 control (MCI stage) samples.

2.2   Data Pre-processing

Under Ab_{AD} and Ab_{PD}, all the autoantibodies are divided in two groups i.e., proteins at MCI stages are considered as controlled and similarly proteins at AD and PD stages are considered as diseased. 'Two sample T-test' is performed on both of the data set to find differentially expressed autoantibodies. In case of 'two sample T-test', the means of two data samples are considered and the variations in terms of differences between samples are calculated. Hence, hypothesis type is being chosen by the variation scoring in terms of p-value. The p-value is calculated from cumulative distribution function. Let, for each transcripts i, group 1 consists of k_1 diseased samples, with mean l_1 and standard deviation s_{n1}, and group 2 contains k_2 control samples, with mean l_2 and standard deviation s_{n2}. Therefore, t-test is defined as follows.

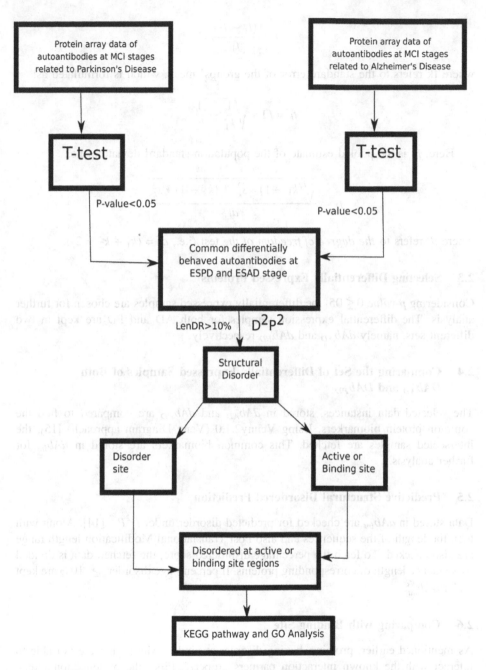

Fig. 1. A schematic for brief description of the proposed framework

$$t = \frac{(l_1 - l_2)}{f_1}$$

where fk refers to the standard error of the groups' mean, which is formulated as:

$$f_l = f1 * \sqrt{\frac{1}{k_1} + \frac{1}{k_2}}$$

Here, $f1$ is the pooled estimate of the population standard deviation; i.e.,

$$f_1 = \frac{\sqrt{(k_1 - 1) * s_{k_1}^2 + (k_2 - 1) * s_{k_2}^2}}{df}$$

where df refers to *the degree of freedom of the* test (i.e., $df = (k_1 + k_2 - 2)$).

2.3   Selecting Differentially Expressed Proteins

Considering *p-value* $0 \leq 05$, the differentially expressed samples are chosen for further analysis. The differential expression samples for both AD and PD are kept in two different sets, namely dAb_{AD} and dAb_{PD} respectively.

2.4   Comparing the Set of Differentially Expressed Samples of Both DAb_{AD} and DAb_{PD}

The selected data instances, stored in dAb_{AD} and dAb_{PD} are compared to find the common protein biomarkers. Using Venny2.1.0 (Venn Diagram approach) [15], the intersected samples are fetched. This common biomarkers are stored in dAb_{int} for further analysis.

2.5   Predictive Structural Disordered Prediction

Data stored in dAb_{int} are checked for predicted disorder under D^2P [14]. Along with that, the length of the sequences and also Post Translational Modification length range are also checked. To fetch the percentage disordered score, the fetched data is divided by sequence length of corresponding proteins. If percent- age disorder $\geq$ 10% are kept under dAb_{int}^{dis}.

2.6   Comparing with Binding Site

As mentioned earlier, proteins, having disorder at binding site region are not able to interact with the known interaction partners properly. First, the protein biomarkers, kept in dAb_{int}^{dis}, are checked with Uniport database for known binding site information. Subsequently, the predicted binding site are also examined from an online tool, RAPTORX [16]. Resultant binding site information are compared with disordered residues from the protein structural facet.

2.7   KEGG Pathway Analysis and Gene Ontology

The functionality of protein biomarkers can be analyzed using pathway analysis and gene ontological observation. It helps to evaluate our findings. *IDP*s which are kept in dAb_{int}^{dis}, are revised under KEGG pathway analysis and Gene Ontology Analysis.

3   Result and Discussion

Following the aforementioned framework, step wise screening of protein biomark- ers are mentioned in this section. In Ab_{AD} and Ab_{PD}, individually 9480 proteins are kept initially. After preforming two sample T-test, there are 789 unique differentially expressed protein biomarkers under dAb_{AD}. Similarly, there are 2372 unique differentially expressed samples under dAb_{PD}. Subsequently, the 508 common differentially expressed biomarkers are kept in dAb_{int}. In Fig. 2, common biomarkers from two different sets are shown. Following that, the chosen samples are sent for disordered predictions. As mentioned in the Sect. 2, the rate of percentage disordered $\geq 10\%$ are considered as disordered protein biomarkers. Among 508 common protein biomarkers from 264 common biomarkers, 152 proteins are predicted with 10% rate of structural disorder. In Table 1, top ten protein biomarkers from dAb_{int}^{dis} are described with corresponding rate of percentage disorder and rate of post translational modifications. Finally, disordered site and corresponding binding site informations are shown in Table 2. In Table 1, top ten disordered protein biomarkers are shown. Among the first ten proteins, uniprot id P63313 and O14604 have 100% structural disorder. The range of structural disorder is from 100% to 67.04%. Other information is related to type of Post Translational Modifications at some region of a protein sequence. For first two proteins, any binding site should fall under disordered regions. Under structure-function paradigm, unusual functional activity can be expected.

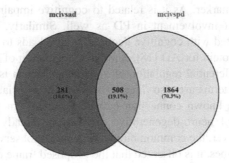

Fig. 2. Venn diagram to show number of common differentially expressed protein biomarkers for both AD and PD cases

Table 1. Top ten disordered protein biomarkers (in terms of percentage disorder) and corresponding percentage disordered and PTM scores associated with both AD and PD

Uniprotid	LenDR	PTM
P63313	100%	0.431818182
O14604	100%	0.068181818
O76087	98.2905983%	0.05982906
Q96B54	92.5531915%	0.015957447
Q13065	84.8920863%	0.043165468
P20396	82.6446281%	0
Q6ICT4	79.5275591%	0
Q8NEY8	76.8558952%	0.104803493
Q9NYV4	69.7315436%	0.079865772
P09017	67.0454545%	0.011363636

Table 2 is showing the relationship between binding site and disordered regions. All of the top ten samples have at least one binding site which is a part of disordered region of the similar proteins.

Table 3 has all pathway and GO information for top ten disordered protein biomarkers. Among the top ten results, no information regarding KEGG and GO for five proteins viz., P63313, O76087, Q96B54, Q8NEY8 and P09017 have been found. From rest of the protein biomarkers two proteins such that O14604 and P20396 are associated with two different pathways i.e., Regulation of actin cytoskeleton Homo sapiens hsa04810 (pvalue 0.017) and Thyroxine (Thyroid Hormone) Production Homo sapiens WP1981 (pvalue 0.0003).

Proteins in MCI are carrying more propensities to initiate NDs. However it is not necessary whereas thyroid function is one of the issues implicating cognitive impairment and associated with AD [17]. It is validating the involvement of P20396 as disordered protein biomarker. As it is related to cognitive impairment, it can be said that there is chance of involvement in PD as well. Similarly, Regulation of actin cytoskeleton is associated with cognitive declined which leads to unusual behavior of *amyloid-β*, the main protein for AD [18]. Similarly, regulation of actin cytoskeleton is also responsible for differential regulation of *α-synuclein* which is responsible for PD. Listed Gene Ontology terms are also directly or partially associated with both or any one of the diseases. A known connection between protein structural disordered and individual categories of neuro-degenerative diseases is already shown in different research articles. However, the common biomarkers are not observed previously. From the evaluation of outcomes, it is observed that the proposed frame can detect disordered common protein biomarkers for multiple diseases associated with MCI.

Table 2. Comparative study to find disordered at active site or binding site for top ten protein biomarkers

Uniprot Id	Dis_Strt	Dis_End	Binding site
O14604	1	44	13,14,17
P63313	1	44	34,35,38,39,42
O76087	1	6	61,63,64,68
Q96B54	9	117	149,161,173
	1	164	
	179	188	
Q13065	1	6	116,120,123,124,60,63
	9	115	
	135	139	
P20396	20	40	8-13,53,54,61,64,65,73
	60	208	
	213	242	
Q6ICT4	2	2	12,15
	6	10	
	12	28	
	37	39	
	41	41	
	43	61	
	68	68	
	74	127	
Q8NEY8	1	1	227,231,330,433,434
	3	3	
	9	49	
	52	55	
	60	60	
	63	119	
	122	297	
	347	406	
	448	458	
Q9NYV4	1	72	8-17,733-736,741,754,756,813-817,819
	74	79	
	81	707	
	709	711	
P09017	21	21	198,199,203,206,210
	23	26	
	28	133	
	150	162	
	211	211	
	213	264	

Table 3. List of KEGG pathway and Gene Ontology terms along with corresponding $p - value$ for top ten selected protein biomarkers

Uniprot	KEGG pathway and corresponding p-value	Gene Ontology and corresponding p-value	GO-type
P63313	-	-	
O14604	Regulation of actin cytoskeleton Homo sapiens hsa04810(p-value-0.017)[18]	regulation of actin filament polymerization(p-value-0.0085)	Go:BP
	-	regulation of actin filament depolymerization(p-value-0.00045)	Go:BP
	-	regulation of actin polymerization or depolymerization(p-value-0.0005)	Go:BP
	-	sequestering of actin monomers(0.00075)	Go:BP
O76087	-	-	
Q96B54	-		
Q13065	-	intracellular defense response(p-value-0.0029)	Go:BP
	-	cellular defense response(p-value-0.00285)	Go:BP
P20396	Thyroxine (Thyroid Hormone) Production Homo sapiens WP1981(p-value-0.0003) [17]	negative regulation of glutamate secretion, neurotransmission(p-value-0.0007)	Go:BP
	-	positive regulation of insulin secretion(p-value-0.0055)	Go:BP
	-	positive regulation of insulin secretion involved in cellular response to glucose stimulus(p-value-0.00195)	Go:BP
	-	thyrotropin-releasing hormone activity(0.00255)	Go:MF
Q6ICT4	-	nuclear speck(p-value-0.02625)	Go:CC
	-	omega speckle(p-value-0.0139)	Go:CC
	-	negative regulation of protein dephosphorylation(p-value-0.0004)	Go:BP
	-	mRNA catabolic process(p-value-0.0066)	Go:BP
	-	negative regulation of phosphoprotein phosphatase activity(p-value-0.00375)	Go:BP
	-	RNA catabolic process(p-value-0.003)	Go:BP
	-	DNA replication, removal of RNA primer(p-value-0.00205)	Go:BP
	-	mRNA binding involved in posttranscriptional gene silencing(p-value-0.00485)	Go:MF
	-	sequence-specific mRNA binding(p-value-0.005)	Go:MF
	-	mRNA CDS binding(p-value-0.0049)	Go:MF
	-	mRNA cap binding(p-value-0.00535)	Go:MF
	-	protein serine/threonine phosphatase inhibitor activity(p-value-0.0009)	Go:MF
Q8NEY8	-	-	-
Q9NYV4	-	autosome(p-value-0.00225)	Go:CC
	-	cyclin/CDK positive transcription elongation factor complex(p-value-0.00045)	Go:CC
	-	phosphorylation of RNA polymerase II C-terminal domain serine 2 residues(p-value-0.0003)	Go:BP
	-	inactivation of MAPKKK activity(p-value-0.00115)	Go:BP
	-	pyruvate dehydrogenase (acetyl-transferring) kinase activity(p-value-0.00845)	Go:MF
	-	protein serine/threonine/tyrosine kinase activity(p-value-0.00885)	Go:MF
P09017	-	-	-

4 Conclusion

In this article, we try to establish a frame to find common protein biomarkers for AD and PD which have structural disordered specially at binding sites. For this purpose, a statistical methodology has been developed where initially screening of protein is started with t-test for AD and PD. Subsequently, the common protein biomarkers are chosen for percentage disordered search. Finally, 164 proteins are selected in a stringent way. The top ten protein biomarkers are analyzed for binding site. From the result, it is observed that almost all the top ten disordered proteins with 100% to 67.08% percentage disordered are actually having disordered at binding site. As discussed, the relation between binding site and disordered region justifying its unusual functionalities during both of the diseases. From the evaluation of the outcomes of the proposed frame, it is established that statistically common disordered protein biomarkers for multiple diseases related to MCI can be detected.

Acknowledgement. The work of Sagnik Sen is supported by DST-INSPIRE. The work of Ujjwal Maulik is supported by UGC-UPE Phase-II project

References

1. Gauthier, S., et al.: Mild cognitive impairment. Lancet **367**(9518), 1262–1270 (2006)
2. Petersen, R.C.: Mild cognitive impairment. Continuum: Lifelong Learning in Neurology, vol. 22, no. 2 Dementia, p. 404 (2016)
3. Petersen, R.C., et al.: Mild cognitive impairment: a concept in evolution. J. Int. Med. **275**(3), 214–228 (2014)
4. Van Der Lee, R., et al.: Classification of intrinsically disordered regions and proteins. Chem. Rev. **114**(13), 6589–6631 (2014)
5. Uversky, V.N., Oldfield, C.J., Dunker, A.K.: Intrinsically disordered proteins in human diseases: introducing the D2 concept. Annu. Rev. Biophys. **37**, 215–246 (2008)
6. Babu, M., van der Lee, R., de Groot, N.S., Gsponer, J.: Intrinsically disordered proteins: regulation and disease. Curr. Opin. Struct. Biol. **21**(3), 432–440 (2011)
7. Brown, C.J., Takayama, S., Campen, A.M., et al.: Evolutionary rate heterogeneity in proteins with long disordered regions. J. Mol. Evol. **55**(1), 104–110 (2002)
8. Breydo, L., Wu, J.W., Uversky, V.N.: Synuclein misfolding and Parkinson's disease. Biochimica et Biophysica Acta (BBA) Mol. Basis Dis. **1822**(2), 261–285 (2012)
9. Uversky, V.N.: Unusual biophysics of intrinsically disordered proteins. Biochimica et Biophysica Acta (BBA) Proteins Proteomics, **1834**(5), 932–951 (2013)
10. Cheng, J., Sweredoski, M., Baldi, P.: Accurate prediction of protein disordered regions by mining protein structure data. Data Min. Knowl. Disc. **11**(3), 213–222 (2005)
11. Dunker, A.K., et al.: Function and structure of inherently disordered proteins. Curr. Opin. Struct. Biol. **18**(6), 756–764 (2008)
12. Linding, R., et al.: A comparative study of the relationship between protein structure and aggregation in globular and intrinsically disordered proteins. J. Mol. Biol. **342**(1), 345–353 (2004)
13. DeMarshall, C.A., Nagele, E.P., Sarkar, A., Acharya, N.K., et al.: Detection of Alzheimer's disease at mild cognitive impairment and disease progression using au- toantibodies as blood-based biomarkers. Alzheimers Dement (Amst) **3**, 51–62 (2016). PMID: 27239548

14. Oates, M.E., et al.: D2P2: database of disordered protein predictions. Nucleic Acids Res. **41** (D1), D508–D516 (2012)
15. Venny, J.C.O.: An interactive tool for comparing lists with Venn's diagrams (2007–2015). http://bioinfogp.cnb.csic.es/tools/venny/index.html
16. Kllberg, M., et al. RaptorX server: a resource for template-based protein structure modeling. Protein Structure Prediction, pp. 17–27 (2014)
17. Tan, Z.S., Vasan, R.S.: Thyroid function and Alzheimers disease. J. Alzheimers Dis. **16**(3), 503–507 (2009). https://doi.org/10.3233/JAD-2009-0991
18. Penzes, P., Vanleeuwen, J.E.: Impaired regulation of synaptic actin cytoskeleton in Alzheimer's disease. Brain Res Rev. **67**(1–2), 184–192 (2011). https://doi.org/10.1016/j.brainresrev.2011.01.003
19. Uversky, V.N.: Intrinsically disordered proteins and their (disordered) proteomes in neurodegenerative disorders. Front. Aging Neurosci. **7**, 18 (2015)

Assamese Named Entity Recognition System Using Naive Bayes Classifier

Gitimoni Talukdar[1]([✉]), Pranjal Protim Borah[2], and Arup Baruah[3]

[1] Department of Computer Science and Engineering, Royal Group of
Institutions, Guwahati, India
talukdargitimoni@gmail.com
[2] Department of Design, Indian Institute of Technology Guwahati,
Guwahati, India
pranjalborah777@gmail.com
[3] Department of Computer Science and Engineering,
Assam Don Bosco University, Guwahati, India
arup.baruah@gmail.com

Abstract. Named Entity Recognition (NER) is crucial when it comes to taking care of information extraction, question-answering, document summarization and machine translation which are undoubtly the important Natural Language Processing (NLP) tasks. This work is a detailed analysis of our previously developed NER system with more emphasis on how individual features will contribute towards the recognition of person, location and organization named entities and how these features in different combinations affect the performance measure of the system. In addition to these, we have also evaluated the behaviour of the features with the increase in training and test corpus. Since this system is based on supervised learning, we need to have a large parts of speech tagged and named entity tagged Training Corpus as well as a parts of speech tagged Test Corpus. The maximum value of performance measure of the overall system is obtained when the training corpus is of size with 5000 words and the amount of named entities present in the test corpus is 50 and the values obtained are 95% in terms of precision, 84% in terms of recall and 89% in terms of F1-measure. This work will add a new dimension in the usage of features for recognition of ENAMEX tags in Assamese corpus.

Keywords: Named entity · Corpus · Naive Bayes classifier · Machine learning

1 Introduction

Names of person, time and money, location, date, organization and percentage expressions often called information units are necessary to be detected in many NLP tasks as well as information extraction tasks. Two stages clearly plays an important role in Named Entity Recognition comprising of detection of proper nouns in the first phase and then assignment of these proper nouns into a set of categories namely person name, organization names (e.g., private organizations, school names etc.), location names (e.g., roads and cities etc.) and miscellaneous names (e.g., monetary expressions, time, number, date, percentage). For example in Assamese – ডাঃ (Dr.) বোলেন(Bolen)

M. Singh et al. (Eds.): ICACDS 2018, CCIS 905, pp. 35–43, 2018.
https://doi.org/10.1007/978-981-13-1810-8_4

পাঠক(Pathak) শিশু (hikhu) চিকিৎসক (sikitshok) হিচাপে (hisape) কাম (kam) কৰে (kore) |Here in this sentence since ডাঃ(Dr.) বলেন(Bolen) পাঠক(Pathak) is a person, the Assamese NER system should be able to classify it as person NE.

This paper is arranged in the following sequence. Section 2 of this paper discusses some related work. In Sect. 3 various features used in our NER system are illustrated. Section 4 elaborates in detail about the methodology and implementation used in this Naive Bayes Assamese NER system. Section 5 highlights the overall experimental results and Sect. 6 finally concludes our work.

2 Related Work

In Assamese language the first system that was reported to perform named entity recognition was a rule based system. This was the first step towards Assamese named entity recognition. The system initially worked on a manually tagged corpus. It enumerated a set of rules in Assamese by analyzing the corpus which helped in finding person, location and organization names [1]. Another system that was reported to perform named entity recognition was a suffix stripping based system for finding locations. The system took advantage of the fact that in Assamese some location named entities often combines with common suffixes [2].

NER in Assamese was done using rule based approach and conditional random fields in [3] which was able to achieve an F-measure of 90–95%. The system while using only CRF gave an 83% accuracy and using both CRF and rule based approach gave an F-measure of 93.22%. Another work in [4] stated that hybrid approach is much more powerful than rule based approach and machine learning approaches. This system recognized four types of named entities- person, location, organization and miscellaneous. Hybrid approach obtained an accuracy of 85%–90%. It is found that in NER community, the most studied types are three specializations of proper names such as names of persons, locations and organizations.

These types are collectively known as ENAMEX since the MUC-6 competition. The type location can in turn be divided into multiple subtypes of fine grained locations as city, state, country etc. [5, 6]. Similarly, fine-grained person sub-categories like politician and entertainer appear in the work of [7]. The type person is quite common and used at least once in an original way by [8] who combines it with other cues for extracting medication and disease names. The type miscellaneous is used in the CONLL conferences and includes proper names falling outside the classic ENAMEX. The class is also sometimes augmented with the type product [9].

A recent interest in bioinformatics and the availability of the GENIA corpus [10] led to many studies dedicated to types such as protein, DNA, RNA, cell line and cell type as well as studies targeted to protein recognition. For 200 entity types an NER system was developed with handcrafted rules when sufficient amount of training examples were not available [11].

The current dominant technique for addressing the NER problem is supervised learning. Supervised learning techniques include Hidden Markov Models (HMM) [12], Decision Trees [13], Maximum Entropy Models (ME) [14], Support Vector Machines (SVM) [15], and Conditional Random Fields (CRF) [16].

3   Features Used in Assamese NER System

Features play an important role in any machine learning technique for giving good performance. In supervised approach the system must be able to find some distinctive features by analyzing the training data so that the classifier can eventually utilize this knowledge to assign the appropriate class in the testing phase. In this Assamese NER system, we have used four features to train the classifier which has given reasonable performance for the system. The detailed explanation of the features that we have used is given below:

3.1   First Word of the Compound Proper Noun

Compound proper noun's first word can be used for identification of named entities. If W_1...........W_k represent a word sequence in a particular text sentence and W_i.....W_j refer to a sequence of words forming the open compound proper noun and that exist within W_1...........W_k where the value of i >= 1 and the value of j is j > i and j <= k then the word W_i which is the first word of the compound proper noun indicate the presence of a particular named entity. A detailed understanding regarding this feature can be obtained from the explanation of the examples given below:

Example 1. স্বৰ্গীয় - Word স্বৰ্গীয় refers to a person who is dead. The name of a person who is dead can be an open compound proper noun as স্বৰ্গীয়(SwargiyA) ইন্দিৰা (Indira) গান্ধী(Gandhi) where the compound proper noun w_i....w_j in this case has three constituents namely স্বৰ্গীয় (SwargiyA), ইন্দিৰা (Indira) and গান্ধী (Gandhi) where the first word w_i is স্বৰ্গীয় (SwargiyA) and last word w_j is গান্ধী (Gandhi). Therefore, first word w_i স্বৰ্গীয় (SwargiyA) indicates that there is the possibility of the presence of a person named entity.

Example 2. ড° as first word – ড° is often found before the name of a person in Assamese indicating the name of a person named entity. The word ড° refers to a person who holds Ph.D. degree or the equivalent from an academic institution. Similarly, শ্ৰীযুত (Srijut), শ্ৰীমান (Sriman), শ্ৰীমতী (Srimati) are some examples of first word feature.

Example 3. মেচাৰ্চ as first word – The word মেচাৰ্চ is often used as first word of some organization named entities. For example – মেচাৰ্চ (Mesars) লক্ষ্মী (Lakshmi) বুক (Book) ষ্টল (Stall) নামৰ (namor) প্ৰতিষ্ঠানটোৱে (protisthantuwe) এখন (ekhon) কৰ্মশালা (karmahala) আয়োজন (aayujon) কৰে (kore) | Here the word মেচাৰ্চ (Mesars) indicates that there is the possibility of the presence of an organization named entity.

3.2   Last Word of the Compound Proper Noun

In Assamese, compound proper noun's last word can be used for identification of named entities. If W_1.....W_k represent a sequence of words in a particular sentence of text and W_i.....W_j refer to a sequence of words forming the open compound proper noun and if that exist within W_1...........W_k where the value of i >= 1 and the value of j is j > i and j <= k then the word W_j which is the last word of the compound proper noun can be used to find the presence of a distinct entity in Assamese.

A detailed understanding regarding this feature can be obtained from the explanation of the examples given below:

Example 1. নগৰ as last word – When নগৰ (Nagar) is found to be happening as this feature then it signifies a location named entity. For example – তেওঁ (Teu) গান্ধী (Gandhi) নগৰত (NagarAt) থাকে (thake) | Here নগৰ refers to the presence of a location named entity.

Similarly চহৰ (Sahar), গাওঁ (Gaon) and জিলা (Jila) are some examples of last words of compound proper nouns indicating the presence of location named entities.

Example 2. কলেজ as last word – কলেজ when present as last word indicates the presence of an named entity in terms of organization. Example – আজি (aaji) ৰয়েল (Royal) ক্লাব (Club) আৰু (aru) দৰং (Darang) কলেজৰ (Collegor) মাজত (majot) খেল (khel) হব (hobo) |Here the last word কলেজ indicates the presence of a named entity in terms of organization.

Similarly ক্লাব (Club), এছচিয়েচন (Association) বিদ্যালয় (Bidyalay), সংস্থা (Hongstha), স্কুল (School), প্রতিষ্ঠান (Protisthan) etc. are some examples of last words of compound proper nouns indicating the presence of organization named entities.

3.3   Previous Word

Previous word is another feature that is used for training our classifier. These words are some of the words that occur frequently at previous positions of a word thereby indicating the presence of a particular named entity in the next position. Previous word feature is actually a part of surrounding word feature. If $W_1....W_k$ refers to a sequence of words in a sentence and if $W_i......W_j$ of $W_1........W_k$ constitute a simple proper noun or open compound proper noun then the previous word feature is the word W_{i-1} that occurs before W_i and its part of speech information (POS). This feature gives information regarding the presence of particular named entities. A detailed understanding regarding this feature can be received from the elaboration of the examples given below:

Example 1. অধিনায়ক as previous word – অধিনায়ক (Adhinayak) may occur as the previous word indicating the presence of an entity which may be a person. Let us consider the example – ভাৰতৰ (Bharator) অধিনায়ক (adhinayak) শ্রী (Sri) মহেন্দ্র (Mahendra) সিং (Singh) ধোনীয়ে (Dhonie) আজি (aaji) ষ্টেডিয়ামত (stadiumot) কঠোৰ (kothor) পৰিশ্রম (porishrom) কৰা (kora) দেখা (dekha) গৈছে (goise) | In the above example the previous word w_{i-1} is অধিনায়ক (Adhinayak) which indicates the presence of a named entity which may be a person in the immediate next position.

Similarly প্রধানশিক্ষক can be used as previous word indicating the occurrence of named entity which may be a person.

3.4   Next Word

Next word is another feature that is used for training our classifier. These words occur often at target word's next position thereby indicating the occurrence of a particular named entity in the previous position. Next word feature is actually a part of the surrounding word feature. If $W_1....W_k$ refers to a sequence of words in a sentence and if $W_i......W_j$ of $W_1........W_k$ constitute a simple proper noun or open compound proper noun then the next word feature is the word W_{j+1} that occurs after W_j and its part of speech information (POS). This feature gives information regarding the presence of particular named entities for our task. A detailed understanding regarding this feature can be received from the elaboration of the examples given below:

Example 1. দা as next word – When দা (Da) is used then it implies the existence of a named entity which is a person named entity. Word দা is used to address a person who is elder brother in relation in Assamese. For example – আজিৰ (aajir) তাৰিখত (tarikhot) ভূপেন (Bhupen) দাই (dAi) সংগীত (hongeet) জগতক (jogotok) বহু (bohu) ধুনীয়া (dhuniya) গীত (geet) দি (di) থৈ (thoi) গৈছে (goise) | Here the next word w_{j+1} দাই indicates the existence of a person named entity.

Similarly বাইদেউ (Baidew), কক়া (Koka) can be seen to be used as next words implying the existence of named entities in terms of person.

Example 2. অনুষ্ঠিত as next word – The word অনুষ্ঠিত may indicate the existence of a location. Considering the example – আজি (aaji) নেহেৰু (Nehru) স্টেডিয়ামত(Stadiumot) অনুষ্ঠিত (onusthitA) হব (hobo) লগা (loga) খেলখন (khelkhon) ভাৰত (Bharot) আৰু (aaru) অষ্ট্ৰেলিয়াৰ (Australiar) মাজত (majot) হব (hobo) | In the above example the word অনুষ্ঠিত indicates the presence of a location named entity.

Some other common next words are দল (Dol), খেলপথাৰত (Khelpotharot) etc.

4   Methodology

In this project the proposed system is to identify and recognize person, location and organization names from Assamese text. The development of the system starts with creating the corpus a part of which is used for training and another part is used for testing. The text in the corpus is first annotated with POS information. A separate NE tag list is maintained to keep track of the named entities present in each sentence. The implementation of the NER system is done by using supervised approach that uses Naive Bayes classification model.

To implement the Assamese NER system in the training phase first every sentence in the corpus has to be tokenized followed by tokenization of the words for each sentence. When the words are tokenized then for each sentence it is checked whether there are any words whose POS tag is NNP (proper noun) since location name, person name and organization name is grammatically a proper noun. The next step in the training phase is to collect the relevant features which will be used for training the classifier for recognizing person, location and organization names. Features such as previous and next words of a word, compound proper noun's last word and compound proper noun's first word are implemented as has been discussed earlier. The input to the system is Assamese text and output is a word classified as person, location or organization by the Naive Bayes classifier in the text. The system's performance is evaluated by the performance metrics such as recall, F1-Measure and precision as given by [17]:

Precision (P) = Number of correct tags assigned/Total number of tags.

Recall (R) = Number of correct tags assigned/Total number of tags in the annotated test corpus.

F1-measure = (2 × Precision × Recall)/(Precision + Recall)

The Assamese NER system has been tested for Training Corpus of different sizes. The overall performance measure of our previous system [18] containing 50 NEs and current system containing 200 NEs are given in Table 1.

Table 1. Performance measure of the NER System for different size of training corpus and when different number of named entities are present in test corpus.

Size of training corpus	No. of NEs	Precision	Recall	F1 measure
2500 Words	50	77%	70%	73.33%
5000 Words	50	95%	84%	89%
5000 Words	200	82.08%	71%	76.14%

Training Phase. A separate Named Entity Tag list is maintained to keep track of the named entities present in each sentence during the training phase. To provide the named entity information for training the system, a named entity (NE) tag list is separately maintained where the named entities present in each sentence of the corpus is represented as –

$$< NE\,Tag >$$
$$< NE > Sentence\,id, Word\,id, NE\,type < /NE >$$
$$< /NE\,Tag >$$

The way of storing the named entity information in the NE tag list present in the training corpus can be seen from Fig. 1 as shown below.

5   Results and Discussion

The results that we have obtained when the size of the training corpus is 5000 words and number of named entities in test corpus is 200 are as follows (Table 2):

Table 3 shows how the F1-measure changes with the use of different features when the size of the training corpus is with 5000 words and number of named entities present in the test corpus were 50. It is seen that first word of compound NNP feature works good for person and location but gives unsatisfactory performance for organization and for overall system gives 76% F1-measure. Last word of compound NNP feature works

```
<NETag>
<NE>0,0-2,org</NE>
<NE>0,4,loc</NE>
<NE>0,5-7,org</NE>
<NE>0,9-12,per</NE>
<NE>0,21-23,org</NE>
<NE>0,25,loc</NE>
<NE>0,26-28,org</NE>
<NE>2,0,loc</NE>
<NE>2,4,loc</NE>
<NE>2,10,loc</NE>
<NE>3,8-10,per</NE>
```

Fig. 1. Named entity tag list for training corpus

Table 2. Performance measure of the NER System for 200 entities in test corpus.

Type of NE	No of NE	Correctly classified	Wrongly classified	Precision (%)	Recall (%)	F1-measure (%)
Person	90	65	12	84.41	72.22	77.84
Location	70	53	8	86.88	75.71	80.91
Organization	40	24	11	68.57	60	63.99
Person, Location & Organization	200	142	31	82.08	71.0	76.14

Table 3. F1 Measures of person, location, organization and overall system for different features

S. N.	Features	F1 measure for person	F1 measure for location	F1 measure for organization	F1 measure for overall
1	First Word of Compound NNP	72	86	57	76
2	Last Word of Compound NNP	25	82	100	59
3	Both First & Last Word of Compound NNP	72	86	100	80
4	Previous Word	41	79	28	55
5	Next Word	61	86	25	67
6	Both Previous & Next Word	69	83	25	70
7	All four features	88	87	100	89

well for location and organization giving F1-measure values 82 and 100 but gives poor performance for person with F1-measure value 25. When both first and last word of compound NNP features are used then 80% F1-measure is obtained for the overall system.

Previous word feature works reasonably well for location as compared to person and organization and gives 55% F1-measure for overall system. On the other hand next word feature works well for location with F1-measure value of 86% and gives poor performance for organization with F1-mesure value of 25%. When both previous word and next word features are used then for location a good F1-measure value of 83% is obtained and 70% F1-measure value is obtained for the entire system but for person 69% F1-measure value is obtained. For all combination of features 88% F1-measure is obtained for person, 87% F1-measure is obtained for location and 89% for the overall system.

6   Conclusion and Future Work

In our project we have used a supervised approach of Naïve Bayes classification model to recognize the names of person, location and organization from Assamese text. We have achieved a reasonable performance of F1-measure 89% for our system using the Naive Bayes approach when the size of the training corpus is 5000 words and numbers of named entities in the test corpus were 50. In this paper we have explained our work in detail with more emphasis on features. Further work includes to increase the size of our training corpus for better results and to include the identification of the TIMEX and NUMEX named entity tags as well and also to use a large set of features at the constituent level as it is seen that keeping the size of the training corpus constant if the number of named entities in test corpus is increased then the accuracy of the system is decreased. Since research of named entity recognition task has just started only recently in Assamese language we can perform the named entity recognition task with some other machine learning techniques which has already been applied to other Indian languages.

References

1. Sharma, P., Sharma, U., Kalita, J.: The first Steps towards Assamese named entity recognition. Brisbane Convention Center, Brisbane, Australia (2010)
2. Sharma, P., Sharma, U., Kalita, J.: Suffix stripping based NER in Assamese for location names. In: Computational Intelligence and Signal Processing (CISP) (2012)
3. Sharma, P., Sharma, U., Kalita, J.: Named entity recognition in Assamese using CRFS and rules. In: 2014 International Conference on Asian Language Processing (IALP), pp. 15–18. IEEE, October 2014
4. Sharma, P., Sharma, U., Kalita, J.: Named entity recognition in Assamese: a hybrid approach. In: 2016 International Conference on Advances in Computing, Communications and Informatics (ICACCI), pp. 2114–2120. IEEE, September 2016
5. Fleischman, M.: Automated subcategorization of named entities. In: ACL (Companion Volume) (2001)

6. Lee, S., Lee, G.G.: Heuristic methods for reducing errors of geographic named entities learned by bootstrapping. In: Dale, R., Wong, K.-F., Su, J., Kwong, O.Y. (eds.) IJCNLP 2005. LNCS (LNAI), vol. 3651, pp. 658–669. Springer, Heidelberg (2005). https://doi.org/10.1007/11562214_58

7. Fleischman, M., Hovy, E.: Fine grained classification of named entities. In: Proceedings of the 19th International Conference on Computational Linguistics-Volume 1. Association for Computational Linguistics (2002)

8. Bodenreider, O., Zweigenbaum, P.: Identifying proper names in parallel medical terminologies. Stud. Health Technol. Inform. **77**, 443 (2000)

9. Bick, E.: A named entity recognizer for Danish. In: LREC (2004)

10. Ohta, T., Tateisi, Y., Kim, J.-D.: The GENIA corpus: an annotated research abstract corpus in molecular biology domain. In: Proceedings of the Second International Conference on Human Language Technology Research. Morgan Kaufmann Publishers Inc. (2002)

11. Sekine, S., Nobata, C.: Definition, dictionaries and tagger for extended named entity hierarchy. In: LREC (2004)

12. Bikel, D.M., et al.: Nymble: a high-performance learning name-finder. In: Proceedings of the Fifth Conference on Applied Natural Language Processing. Association for Computational Linguistics (1997)

13. Sekine, S.: NYU: description of the Japanese NE system used for MET-2. In: Proceedings of the Seventh Message Understanding Conference MUC-7 (1998)

14. Borthwick, A., et al.: NYU: description of the MENE named entity system as used in MUC-7. In: Seventh Message Understanding Conference (MUC-7): Proceedings of a Conference Held in Fairfax, Virginia, 29 April–1 May 1998

15. Asahara, M., Matsumoto, Y.: Japanese named entity extraction with redundant morphological analysis. In: Proceedings of the 2003 Conference of the North American Chapter of the Association for Computational Linguistics on Human Language Technology-Volume 1. Association for Computational Linguistics (2003)

16. McCallum, A., Li, W.: Early results for named entity recognition with conditional random fields, feature induction and web-enhanced lexicons. In: Proceedings of the Seventh Conference on Natural Language Learning at HLT-NAACL 2003-Volume 4. Association for Computational Linguistics (2003)

17. Nadeau, D., Sekine, S.: A survey of named entity recognition and classification. Lingvisticae Investigationes **30**, 3–26 (2007)

18. Talukdar, G., Borah, P.P., Baruah, A.: Supervised named entity recognition in Assamese language. In: International Conference on Contemporary Computing and Informatics, India (2014)

Medical Image Multiple Watermarking Scheme Based on Integer Wavelet Transform and Extraction Using ICA

R. Nanmaran, G. Thirugnanam[✉], and P. Mangaiyarkarasi

Department of Electronics and Instrumentation Engineering, Annamalai University, Chidambaram, India
ggtt_me@yahoo.com

Abstract. In this paper, a medical image multiple watermarking technique rely on integer wavelet transform is proposed. Medical image watermarking is a unique division of image watermarking in the intellect that images have particular necessities. Watermarked medical images should not diverge relating to their creative complement because clinical interpretation of images should not be pretentious. Watermarking methods rely on discrete wavelet transform (DWT) are described in numerous writings excluding forcefulness and defense by means of integer wavelet transform is enhanced while equate to DWT. The important confront in traverse angles in images arrives from the discrete environment of the information. In this paper, input image is scaled to two level by means of integer wavelet transform and the two watermarks are embedded in the ensuing coefficients. To extract the watermark, Pearson ICA is applied and it has a novel feature, it does not necessitate the alteration procedure to extract the watermark. Simulation results illustrate that proposed method is robust against attacks such as Gaussian noise, Salt and Pepper noise, rotation and translation. PSNR, Similarity measure and Normalized correlation are the performance measures applied to evaluate and it is compared with Wavelet Packet Transform (WPT). Simulations are conceded in using Matlab.

Keywords: Image watermarking · Independent component analysis
Telemedicine · Integer wavelet transform

1 Introduction

Digital watermarking is the process by which watermark a discrete data stream is hidden inside the input image by impressive invisible changes on the image. To embed and extract the watermark, a secret key is used in many proposed techniques. Copyright protection is one of the main sources of power for research in this area for digital medium. Copy protection code is the main application to protect and to allocate possession. By altering the watermarked image, attacker tries to extract the watermark. Thus, it is struggled to embed the watermark and it is hard to extract without key except the watermarked image is drastically imprecise. A trendy similarity for watermarking is the system of data connections in which the ambition is to efficiently converse the watermark

© Springer Nature Singapore Pte Ltd. 2018
M. Singh et al. (Eds.): ICACDS 2018, CCIS 905, pp. 44–53, 2018.
https://doi.org/10.1007/978-981-13-1810-8_5

information using embedding algorithms. Consequently, it is vital for the outlook progress of associated hypermedia structure that strong procedure are urbanized to look after the logical belongings precise of data in chargers alongside unofficial repetition and redeployment of the substance made obtainable on the system. In addition to the above it is a significant concern to widen a strong watermarking proposal by means of an enhanced swapping between sturdiness and indistinct [1]. From copyright infringement watermarking transpire as an instrument for defensive the multimedia statistics. To identify the ownership watermark is embedded into the input image. After embedding the watermark, perceptual deprivation should not be there. Unauthorized person should not be able to remove the watermark and it is necessary to develop the robust watermarking against intended and unintended attacks [2]. Various watermarking systems are published in the literature. This work contemplates the scrupulous crate of medicinal image watermarking. Watermarking has grown to be a vital matter in medical image safety measures, privacy and veracity. In order to validate and inspect the reliability of medical images, the medical image watermarks are used. Medical image watermarking special requirements is the key problem in watermarking [5]. A stiff obligation is that the image might not endure any deprivation which affects the interpretation of images. Normally, images are necessary to stay behind integral to attain this with no visible modification to their original shape. The three obligatory defense distinctiveness are:

- Privacy is the allowed users have admission to the in sequence.
- Accessibility is the capability of the information arrangement to be used in the typical planned environment of admittance.
- Consistency is based on the aftermath of reliability and validity.

Integer Wavelet Transform is applied to offer a lossless compression. Sub-bands of IWT are identified by restricted exactness information and this used for lossless coding. IWT stress for less data length than the floating point DWT and hence DWT is extra time overwhelming. The image is reconstructed of no loss as the coefficients of IWT are integers and placed devoid of rounding off errors [6]. Here IWT applies lifting scheme. Lifting Scheme is an effectual technique of implementing the wavelet filtering procedure by Sweldens. Lifting scheme is categorized into three stages:

Split: Here the initial signal is separated into two samples of even and odd.

Predict: In this, the odd samples are anticipate from the even samples.

Update: At this stage, the original even samples are added to the predicted odd samples to generate the new even samples. Inverse lifting transform is conceded with the dissimilarity that its signs are upturned. Moreover, the intelligent detection technique, Pearson ICA is applied for extraction devoid of the utilize of preceding information of the watermark and still the conversion procedure. Sturdiness and lucidity of the exceeding technique is established with outcome. This work is prepared like this: 2nd section scrutinizes the IWT; Sect. 3 investigates the watermark implant technique. In 4th section, watermark taking out technique ICA is expressed. The output results are accessible in 5th section and termination are pinched in Sect. 6.

Telemedicine removes inconvenience arising from different geographic locations and provides health services at far-away places. In the recent years, use of digital equipment's in health care sector has increased considerably. Modern technology allows doctors to diagnose their patients using digital parameters. In numerous medical applications, distinct protection and secrecy is needed for patient records, reason being thorough analysis on health pictures is needed for proper diagnosis. Tampering images will lead to surface unwanted consequences as an aftermath of defeat of crucial information.

2   Integer Wavelet Transform

Wavelet construction is a novel technique. Lifting schemes are almost applied in all traditional wavelets. IWT stress for less data length than the floating point DWT and hence DWT is extra time overwhelming. The image is reconstructed of no loss as the coefficients of IWT are integers and placed devoid of rounding off errors. Yet, the lifting strategy in IWT maps integer to integer devoid of rounding misconception (ii) IWT is effortless to comprehend, execute and overturn [4]. During mathematical calculations IWT are performed fast in position, and supplementary reminiscence is not requisite as shown in Fig. 1. The above stuffs of IWT are applied to conserve imperceptibility and increase the robustness. The IWT has three widespread lifting steps:

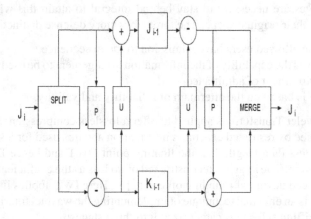

Fig. 1. Integer wavelet transforms decomposition and reconstruction

- Split — It is called as lazy wavelet as the input image is shared into even and odd polyphase mechanism.
- Predict — by finding out the linear combination of trial of even polyphase module, the new odd polyphase modules are calculated. The samples of the odd polyphase constituent are restored by the variation between the odd polyphase component and the anticipate assessment. The envisage procedure is furthermore mentioned as dual lifting step.
- Update — the novel even polyphase modules are shaped rely on a linear combination of various samples prevailed from the predict procedure. This step is also mentioned as the primal lifting step.

Discrete Wavelet Transform (DWT) is appropriate for distinguish the places of the input image and the watermark be able to be invisibly entrenched since of its exceptional time frequency localization belongings. The Integer Wavelet Transform (IWT) is a focused adaptation of universal DWT which maps integers to integers. The benefit of applying IWT is that it can be executed with merely basic arithmetic process. Devoid of deformation is the competent technique to conceal furtive messages [7]. In DWT, the resultant is not consisting of integers when the input consists of integers. So it produces complexity in reinstatement of the input image. But in IWT, integers are present in the output. In IWT, LL coefficients become visible to be secure reproduction of the input image with lesser range while in DWT the resultant LL is indistinct faintly.

3   Watermark Embedding

The input colour medical image is analysis to 2 levels using IWT is revealed. LL2 coefficients which are a low frequency are not selected to embed watermark as it will critically disgrace image eminence [8]. Likewise, the diagonal high frequency sub-bands HH2 are too not measured since safety is underprivileged when watermark is entrenched as shown in Fig. 2.

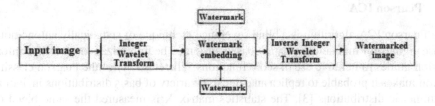

Fig. 2. Proposed block diagram of watermark embedding using IWT

Therefore, the center subband HL2 and LH2 are selected in this paper to entrench multiple watermarks based on the exchange between imperceptibility and robustness. A random replica of the input image is practical to an ability to change watermark by calculating Noise Visibility Function (NVF) with variable variance Gaussian replica. Here, NVF can be uttered by

$$NVF(i,j) = \frac{1}{1 + \sigma_x^2(i,j)} \tag{1}$$

where $\sigma_x^2(i,j)$ indicate inconsistency of the input image in a transom middled on the pixel with interrelate (i, j). By implementing NVF, the surface and corners get powerful than in smooth regions in the watermark. Embedding the watermark in HL2 by means of the subsequent equation:

$$I'HL_2(i, j) = HL_2(i, j) + E(HL_2)\alpha_1(1 - NVF(i, j))W(i, j)+$$
$$\frac{E(HL_2)}{10}.\alpha_1.NVF(i, j).W(i, j) \tag{2}$$

Where $I'HL_2(i,j)$ is watermarked renovate sub-bands, $E(HL_2)\alpha_1$ signify the watermark power of surface and $\frac{E(HL_2)}{10}.\alpha_1$ designate the watermark potency of corner area for HL coefficients. α_1 is the embedding strength issue on the grain areas and plane areas and E represents the mean and watermark $W(i,j)$. Watermarked image is obtained by inversing IWT.

4   Independent Component Analysis

It is an arithmetical method that procures autonomous sources S from even combination X. The input sources and the real addition A are recognized. It is attained by capitalizing superior regulate sign information and optimization methods. Pearson ICA technique applied here for extraction of watermark is explained underneath:

4.1   Pearson ICA

The Pearson ICA algorithm is a blind severance technique of statistically autonomous cause signals for mutual information based system. The minimization of mutual information guides to iterative use of score functions. The elasticity of the Pearson classification makes it probable to replica an extensive variety of basis distributions including asymmetric distributions [3]. The statistics matrix X is measured the same blend of demographically autonomous apparatus as

$$X = AS \tag{3}$$

where mixing matrix is A and the values of S enclose the independent constituents has Gaussian allotment. The ambition of ICA is to locate a matrix W that the yield,

$$\hat{S} = WX \tag{4}$$

is an approximation of perhaps covered and sequence basis matrix S. In order to take out the autonomous component sources for a demixing matrix W, this reduces the shared in sequence of the origin

$$W_{k+1} = W_k + D\left(E\{\phi(y)y^T\} - diag(E\{\phi(y_i)y_i\})\right) \tag{5}$$

5   Simulation Results

The future watermarking technique is applied on input Medical image (Patient) of size 256 × 256. Integer wavelet transform for two levels is accomplished on the input image. The two middle coefficients HL2 and LH2 are chosen to embed watermarks. Watermark1 (EEG) of size 64 × 64 and watermark2 (Prescription) are used and α is set to 0.3 by frequent replication to make sure the imperceptibility of the watermark. Figure 3 shows the colour Input image (Patient), and it is converted into YUV components. Y component is shown in Fig. 4. Patient Input image is decomposed to one level using IWT to obtain 4 sub-bands LL1, HL1, LH1 and HH1 as shown in Fig. 5 and LL1 is further decomposed to second level to obtain another 4 sub-bands LL2, HL2, LH2 and HH2 as shown in Fig. 6. Watermark 1(EEG) colour image of size 64 × 64 as shown in Fig. 7 is taken and it is converted to Y, U, V components and Y component is shown in Fig. 8. Arnold Transform is applied for Y component of watermark 1 as shown in Fig. 9. Watermark 2 (Prescription) colour image of size 64 × 64 as shown in Fig. 10 is taken and it is converted to Y, U, V components and Y component is shown in Fig. 11. Fibonacci Transform is applied for Y component of watermark 2 as shown in Fig. 12. Two watermarks are embedded in two sub-bands HL2 and LH2. Inverse IWT is done to obtain the Y component of watermarked image as shown in Fig. 13. U and V components are concatenated to obtain colour watermarked image as shown in Fig. 14. The toughness of the over watermarking method is authorized beside various assault similar to Gaussian noise addition, Salt and Pepper noise, Rotation and Translation done on watermarked image. Figures 15 and 16 show Gaussian noise added and Salt & Pepper noise, respectively. Similarly, Figs. 17 and 18 show Rotation and Translation attacks performed on watermarked image respectively. Besides executing a variety of ambush, integer wavelet transform acquire an elevated PSNR rate while contrast to wavelet packet transform. Watermarks 1 and 2 are extracted from Translation attack is shown in Figs. 19 and 20 using Pearson ICA. Comparing the values of PSNR, Similarity Measure and Normalized Correlation intended for integer wavelet and wavelet packet transform is tabulated in Table 1.

Fig. 3. Input image (Patient)

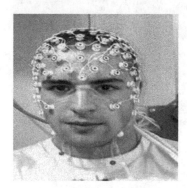

Fig. 4. Y component of input image

Fig. 5. One level IWT decomposition

Fig. 6. Two level IWT decomposition

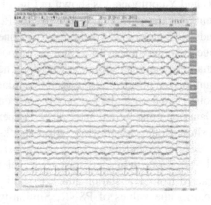

Fig. 7. Watermark1 (EEG)

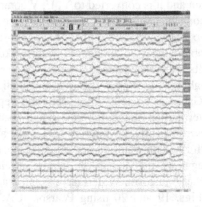

Fig. 8. Y component of watermark1

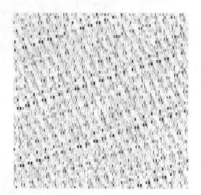

Fig. 9. Arnold transform of watermark1

Fig. 10. Watermark2 (Prescription)

Fig. 11. Y component of watermark2

Fig. 12. Fibonacci transform

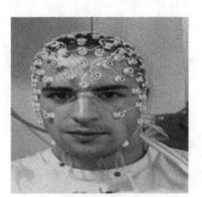

Fig. 13. Y component of watermarked image

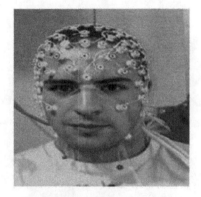

Fig. 14. Watermarked image

Fig. 15. Gaussian Noise attack

Fig. 16. Salt & Pepper noise

Fig. 17. Rotation attack

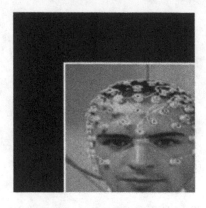

Fig. 18. Translation attack

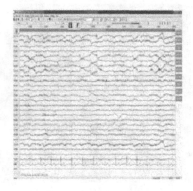

Fig. 19. Extracted watermark1 from translation   Fig. 20. Extracted watermark2 from translation

Table 1. Evaluation indices of WPT and IWT for various attacks

Input images	PSNR (dB)		Similarity measure		Normalized correlation	
	WPT	IWT	WPT	IWT	WPT	IWT
Watermarked image	45.1768	47.1286	0.9416	0.9617	0.9312	0.9621
Gaussian noise	43.8094	45.8432	0.9267	0.9535	0.9298	0.9592
Salt & pepper noise	43.7863	45.3098	0.9381	0.9582	0.9223	0.9597
Rotation	42.9279	44.9965	0.9316	0.9407	0.9210	0.9492
Translation	42.9987	44.8359	0.9356	0.9485	0.9386	0.9474

6 Conclusion

Healthcare diligence currently requires additional complicated services like transmitting medical images. Improvement in statistics technology made it feasible to clutch such requirements crossways wireless communication. Excluding protection is imperative issue. In this paper, proposed an impressively robust multiple image Watermarking with higher defense with accurate recovery of watermark for image, providing PSNR equal to 47 and correlation factor equals to 0.96.

References

1. Bender, W., Gruhl, D., Morimoto, N., Lu, A.: Techniques for data hidhing. IBM Syst. J. **35**(3), 313–336 (1996)
2. Mallat, G.: A theory for multiresolution signal decomposition: the wavelet representation. IEEE Trans. Pattern Anal. Mach. Intel. **11**(7), 674–693 (1989)
3. Bounkong, S., Toch, B., Saad, D., Lowe, D.: ICA for watermarking digital images. J. Mach. Learn. Res. **4**, 1471–1498 (2003)
4. Calderbank, A.R., Daubechies, I., Sweldens, W.: Wavelet transform that maps integers to integers. Appl. Comput. Harmonic Anal. **5**(3), 332–369 (1998)
5. Wong, P.H.W., Au, O.C., Yeung, G.Y.M.: A novel blind multiple watermarking technique for images. IEEE Trans. Circuits Syst. Video Tech. **9**, 813–830 (2003)
6. Giakoumaki, A., Pavlopoulos, S., Koutsouris, D.: Multiple image watermarking applied to health information management. IEEE Trans. Inf Technol. Biomed. **10**(4), 267–274 (2006)
7. Lu, L., Sun, X., Cai, L.: A robust image watermarking based on DCT by Arnold transform and spread spectrum. Adv. Comput. Theory Eng. **1**, 254–259 (2010)
8. Swanson, M.D., Kobayashi, M., Tewfik, A.H.: Multimedia data embedding and watermarking technologies. IEEE Trans. Biomed. Inf. **86**, 814–821 (2006)

Recognizing Real Time ECG Anomalies Using Arduino, AD8232 and Java

Pratik Kanani[✉] and Mamta Padole

Department of Computer Science and Engineering,
The M.S. University of Baroda, Vadodara, India
pratikkanani123@gmail.com, mamta.padole@gmail.com

Abstract. Living being remains alive, only, as long as its heart is functional. Hence, proper functioning of Heart is essential. The functioning of Heart can be checked by continuous monitoring of heartbeats through Electrocardiogram (ECG). Irregularity in the rhythm of the heartbeat results in arrhythmia. Arrhythmia can be classified based on the origins that cause it. ECG signal comprises of PQRST wave. Analysis of PQRST wave helps identifying the type of arrhythmia. Thus, real-time analysis of ECG is of utmost priority, to acquire immediate medical aid and to avoid fatality. The paper discusses the use of the AD8232 sensor to capture ECG signals and its interfacing with Arduino Nano. Arduino is used as a Sampler and Analog to Digital Converter (ADC). The intervals of PQRST wave is analyzed using Java APIs and windowing algorithm. The results are compared with standard ECG signals to detect abnormalities and further analysis. The paper aids the reader to understand and develop a handy and low cost ECG analysis system, thus, reducing the treatment costs.

Keywords: IoT · Arduino · AD82332 · ADC · ECG · Arrhythmias
ECG filtering techniques · ECG intervals · PQRST wave · Filters · Sampling
Interfacing

1 Introduction

Proper functioning of Heart is essential for life of a being. Thus, one needs to perform regular checkup to ensure that the heart is functioning normally. The proper functioning of Heart can be checked by regular tracking of the heartbeats and through continuous monitoring of Electrocardiogram (ECG). Heart is a mechanical device that pumps blood to and from itself. The human heart is divided into Atria and Ventricles. The pumping action of heart occurs through an electrical conduction system which generates an electrical signal known as Electrocardiogram (ECG). The ECG wave is the representation of heart beat. On the basis of the ECG signal the human heart health can be predicted and cured. The ECG signal comprises of PQRST wave, which is represented as a collection of key points known as PQRST. These PQRST points are used to mark certain intervals which are compared with the standard results to identify the ECG abnormality or arrhythmia. So the procedure starts with getting an ECG signal from heart and

© Springer Nature Singapore Pte Ltd. 2018
M. Singh et al. (Eds.): ICACDS 2018, CCIS 905, pp. 54–64, 2018.
https://doi.org/10.1007/978-981-13-1810-8_6

processing it till the results are acquired. The block diagram of the proposed system is as shown below (Fig. 1).

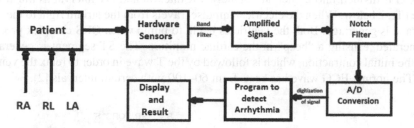

Fig. 1. Proposed system block diagram

Different electrical lead, commonly known as ECG electrodes are used to get the electrical activity of the heart. After the electrodes are placed on the body, at Right Arm (RA), Right Lower (RL) and Left Arm (LA), some sensors are needed to convert these electrical signals to waveform. In this paper the AD8232 IC is used. But ECG signal also comes with some sort of noise in it. This noise is introduced because of low frequency due to movements of muscles, improper placement of electrodes on the body, or baseline wonder and power line interferences. The different techniques to effectively handle and remove such noises are also discussed in this paper. After the removal of noise, one needs to make use of analog to digital converter to get the ECG signal on a computer system. But before this, the sampling frequency and different quantization levels need to be defined. In this paper, sampling and ADC is achieved with the help of Arduino. The code in Arduino's firmware needs to be tailored according to the goals and objectives. Now, on the hardware part outside the computer system, the signal is ready in time domain in the form of discrete signal, sampled at 500 Hz. This signal has to get inside the system for further processing. In this project, Java programming is used to analyze the static and real time ECG signals. There are many Java libraries and APIs to make that allow us to serial communication of Arduino and system, and this paper intends to explore them in detail. For visual appearance of ECG signal, a Java library JFreeChart is being used. The Time domain ECG signal is stored in the data structure called ArrayList and analyzed to detect PQRST points and their time intervals. To get the actual intervals on real time basis for each and every ECG cycle, the novel windowing algorithm is used which gives 99% accuracy. At last, the obtained intervals are compared with standard intervals already defined to get the ECG signal is normal or abnormal. The final obtained results are acknowledged to the user.

2   Electrocardiogram (ECG)

ECG is a Graph test that helps to analyze and determine whether or not the heart is working normally. It records the heart rhythm and electrical activity. Some of the things an ECG reading can detect include cholesterol clogging up your heart's blood supply, a heart attack in the past, enlargement of one side of the heart and abnormal heart rhythms [1].

ECG is divided into 2 intervals, namely, PR interval and QT interval as illustrated in the Fig. 2 below. When the electrical impulse travels from the atrium right to the left, PR wave is generated. Both the ventricles begin to pump when QRS complex process is generated, causing a "beep" in the cardiac monitors. The ST segment is generated after the initial contraction, which is followed by the T wave in order to relax the ventricles. The normal ECG wave has beats from 60–100 with certain intervals [2].

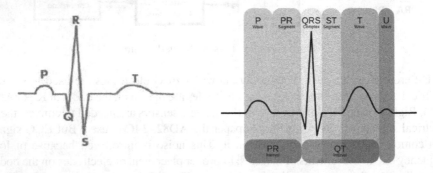

Fig. 2. ECG waveform reference points and its intervals [3]

2.1 Heart Arrhythmia

The rate of heartbeat may vary significantly. Sometimes it can be too fast or too slow. This variation in the rate of heartbeat is called Arrhythmias. Arrhythmia is a generalized term used to denote disturbances in heart's rhythm and can be recognized by evaluating the ECG in systematic manner. [4]

Arrhythmia is also known as cardiac dysrhythmia. There are 4 steps which helps us recognize the types of arrhythmias:

1. Take the patient's medical history into consideration. It begins by labelling P wave, PR interval, QRS complex, OT interval and T wave.
2. Calculate heart rates of Atrial and Ventricle. A rate lesser than 60 bpm indicates slow heartbeat rate, a value between 60 bpm and 100 bpm is considered normal and a rate higher than 100 bpm suggests fast heart rate.
3. Check if the rhythm is regular or irregular. This can be determined by analysing if RR intervals and PP intervals are regularly spaced. Once the irregularity is identified, the next step is to determine if the irregularity is occasional, regularly irregular or irregularly irregular.
4. Carefully and meticulously evaluate the waveform of the ECG.

Arrhythmias can be broadly divided into 3 types [5]:

1. Arrhythmia origination from Atria.
2. Arrhythmia origination from Ventricle.
3. Sinus irregularity.

2.2 Obtaining ECG Strip

ECG waveforms represent the heart's depolarization and repolarization. Different numbers of bipolar and unipolar leads are used to measure ECG. The numbers can vary as 3 lead, 4 lead, 5 lead, 6 lead and 12 lead [6]. The advantage of the three lead approach, however, is that it is more convenient, pervasive and IoT friendly (Fig. 3).

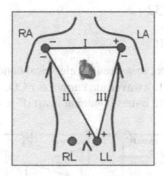

Fig. 3. Einthoven's Triangle [7]

Three sensors are used to record voltage coming from 3 limb electrodes. These electrodes are placed on right arm, left arm and left leg forming a triangle. This triangle is known as Einthoven's Triangle. Einthoven's law states that sum of LEAD I and III are equal to that of lead II. Also, the polarity of lead II is anticlockwise whereas that of lead I and III is clockwise [8].

2.3 ECG Filtering Techniques

The ECG signal comes along with the noise. To deal with this, different types of filtering techniques can be used [9, 10]:

(1) **Adaptive notch filtering:** This type of filtering is used to remove the power line interference of 50–60 Hz noise when superimposed on the signals.
(2) **High pass IIR Filtering**: This filtering process is applicable when low frequency noise is present in the signal. Such types of noise can get added because of loose contact with skin, or due to the patient's body movement (muscle noise) while recording the signal.
(3) **Zero Phase Filtering:** In this technique, a short window is applied backward and forward in time domain to achieve characteristics like zero phase distortion.
 4) **Moving Average Approach:** Here the moving averaging window is applied on the signal to remove the low frequency noises present in time domain which smoothens the signal.
(5) **Savitzky-Golay Filtering:** It is also commonly referred to as least squares smoothing filter. It derives the polynomial coefficients and then applies them to the signal with two parameters; one as window size and the other as the degree of

polynomial. This filter is known to smooth the ECG signal while keeping their original features intact.

(6) **Polynomial Fitting:** This method removes baseline by fitting polynomials into the curve while keeping original features of the signal and removes the low frequency noises.

3 Arduino and AD8232

3.1 AD8232 ECG Sensor IC

AD8232 [11] is a tiny chip that measures the electrical conduction of human heart and then converts this conduction to a waveform known as ECG. This ECG signal is analyzed further to determine any health issues in human heart (Fig. 4).

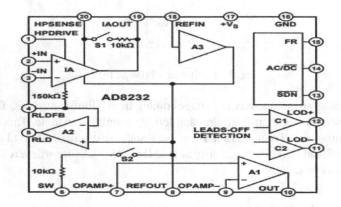

Fig. 4. AD8232 Functional Block diagram [11]

The IC mainly consists of the following

1. A specialized Instrumentation amplifier
2. An operational amplifier
3. A right leg drive amplifier
4. A mid supply reference buffer
5. High pass and low pass filters

Application: AD8232 is also known as an ECG module. ECG is a time VS voltage graph. Heart activities are measured with ECG. This is done by placing electrodes on left chest, right chest and right leg. This module can also be used for Electromyography (Study of activity in the skeletal muscles).

3.2 Arduino

Arduino is an Open-source hardware and software programmable board, which can read and process electrical inputs. It is designed to work on platforms like Windows, Linux and Mac. Its key features are [12]:

- It is inexpensive
- It has a simple and clear programming environment
- It is open-source and have extensible hardware and software.

Presently, Arduino is available in many sizes and shapes and used in many applications like controlling systems using sensors, Internet of Things (IoT), home automation systems, intrusion alarms, LCD displays, email-notifier, Maze solver, UPS systems, plot sensor values and decision making, robots and solar panels [13, 14].

3.3 Interfacing of Arduino Nano and AD8232

The hardware interfacing of AD8232 ECG sensor and Arduino board [15] is, the input to the sensor can be applied either by the input jack or by using the three pins: RA, LA and RL. The output pin of the sensor is given to the any one of the analog pin of Arduino. Inside the Arduino, these sensor output is processed by the firmware code, burned to it.

4 Arduino as ADC and Sampling Device

4.1 Arduino as Analog to Digital Converter

Arduino has multiple analog pins. The analog input is given at any of these pins and Arduino can be programmed to make these values as digital. The function used to convert analog values to digital is AnalogRead(). It has 10-bit resolution that is the given analog is converted into 10 bit binary number which varies from 0–1023. An input between 0 to 3.3 V or 5 V will be shown as a digital output in the range of 0 to 1023 $((2^{10}) - 1)$. One can achieve the maximum reading of 10000 samples per second [16, 17]. The obtained digital value x can also be converted back to its equivalent analog value y by using the following mathematical formula:

$$Y = (x * \text{analog range}/1023) \tag{1}$$

4.2 ADC Program Code

```
void setup() {Serial.begin(9600);}
  void loop() {Serial.println(analogRead(A0)); }
```

4.3 Arduino as a Sampling Device

Sampling is the process of converting a continuous analog signal to a discrete one, Arduino can serve this purpose [18–21]. And if these discrete sampling values are quantized, then it becomes digital time domain signal. The time interval between the two samples should always remain the same. Arduino gives many functions, like delay(), to halt the program state for a while. But the problem with such functions is that they do not always delay for exactly the specified amount of time for each execution of the function. As a result, one may find that the time gap varies. Hence one cannot use delay functions for sampling. The other way of achieving the constant interval is with the help of timers. They have three timers: two 8-bit timer(Counter 0 and Counter 2) and one 16-bit timer(Counter 1).

An 8-bit timer uses a 8-bit register and counts from 0 to 255 while a 16-bit timer uses a 16-bit register and ranges from 0 to 65535. Once the timer has reached the highest count (255 or 65535, depending on the timer used), the register resets to zero and starts again.

4.4 Arduino Program Code to Achieve Sampling Rate of 500 Hz

To achieve the sampling of 500 Hz, System should have the interval as 2000 ms. The mentioned sampling is implemented with the help of the following code.

```
long i = 0;        String s;    unsigned long times;
void setup() {
Serial.begin(115200);  cli(); //stop interrupts
//set timer1 interrupt at 500Hz
TCCR1A = 0; // set entire TCCR1A register to 0
TCCR1B = 0; // same for TCCR1B
TCNT1  = 0; //initialize counter value to 0
// set timer count for 500hz increments
OCR1A = 3999; // = (16*10^6) / (500*8) - 1
//had to use 16 bit timer1 for this bc 3999>255,
TCCR1B |= (1 << WGM12); // turn on CTC mode
TCCR1B |= (1 << CS11);  // Set CS11 bit for 8 prescaler
TIMSK1 |= (1 << OCIE1A);
sei();//allow interrupts      }
void loop() {}
ISR(TIMER1_COMPA_vect)       {
s=String("");
 s+=String(micros());
 s+=String(",");
 s+=String(analogRead(A0));
Serial.println(s)            }
```

  Ouput:
  2056 337
  4056 337
  6056 338

In the above output one can observe the difference between first two consecutive fields are 2000 ms which is the current time of Arduino board while the second column shows the respective analog reading after conversion to digital.

5 ECG Analyzing Algorithm and Java

5.1 Novel Windowing ECG Algorithm

There exist several algorithms for ECG signal analysis. The prominent algorithm approaches are: by using wavelet analysis and wavelet transforms, pen and tompkins algorithm, QRS peak detection, template based matching, using Neural Networks, windowing algorithm and combined methods. These approaches work on the principles of time and frequency domain. The novel windowing algorithm suggested by Muhammad Umer et al. in [9] gives 99% accuracy and is best suitable for time domain discrete signals which are implemented in the proposed system by considering Q point at 30 ms, x as 8 and BPM as the ratio of t_{rr} to f_s multiplied by 60.

5.2 Implementation Using Java

The first guiding path is to get the real time ECG signals inside the programming space, so that working logic can be applied on it. The jSerialComm [22] is the Java communication library jar file which helps to get any outside signal in the computing system, using their serial ports without requiring any external libraries. It can also configure multiple ports simultaneously. This library provides different methods and classes which can read and write byte streams of data to any port. In any system the visual appeal matters a lot. There is an API, which plots and displays real time data or any static data stored in a file on the professional looking charts called as JFreeChart [23]. This jar library has inbuilt paint() and repaint() methods.

The reading values of ports and sensors are stored in the data structure called as ArrayList. Then different methods of such data structures are used to detect the minimum and maximum values from the list in the intervals specified by windowing size. After different key points are identified the time interval between two consecutive points are found out. The sampling size used in this system is 500 Hz for reading an ECG signal. This concludes the time gap between two points in the array list is 2 ms. This principle is used to find time interval between any two key points which is 2 ms multiplied by number of existing points between two key points.

5.3 Standard ECG Intervals

The ECG health can be determined by different intervals mainly PR, QRS and QT when heart is beating at normal BPM i.e., between 60 and 100. The normal ECG intervals are given in the Table 1 below [24–26], one can identify the ECG abnormality by comparing the intervals with the standard ones.

Table 1. Standard ECG Intervals.

Parameters	Intervals
PR Interval	120–200 ms
QRS Interval	80–120 ms
QT Intervals	Less than 400–440 ms
BPM	*60–100* bpm

6 Implementation Results

1. The patient name and age are entered and the static and real time mode at which user wants to operate the system is selected.
2. The real time user mode where user has to enter the sampling frequency and the port at which the Arduino is being connected.
3. If it is static mode, user enters the sampling frequency, name and type of the file.
4. Final window in Fig. 5, animates the given ECG signal and shows different intervals and its nature.

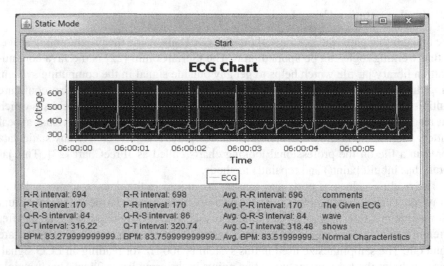

Fig. 5. Final Output window showing ECG interval and its normality

The above window shows, the real time ECG signal and their corresponding PQRST point interval values. The voltage levels shown on the Y axis is the quantized levels given by Arduino in the range of 0–1023. The parameter listed in third column illustrates the average of the previous intervals. And the forth column concludes that whether the input ECG signal is normal or abnormal.

7   Conclusion

In conclusion, the human heart is one of the most important organs of the human body. It supplies blood and oxygen to different parts of our body using ECG signals. A properly functioning human heart is an indication of good health, wellness and longevity of human life. On the other hand, any anomaly in ECG, called arrhythmia, can indicate anything from subtle to serious health issues. Early stage detection of these anomalies can be instrumental in averting and treating fatal heart-related disease and irregularities. For this, one should first identify the different types of arrhythmia and their causes and then subsequently try to pinpoint their presence. In this paper, authors have successfully proposed and implemented a system in Java that detects real-time anomalies in heartbeat. This system can be used by medical practitioners in both real-time and as well as in static modes. While both the modes require sampling frequencies, the real-time mode also makes use of a port connected to Arduino, a highly effective IoT unit. The AD8232 senor is then interfaced with Arduino. The final result displays the ECG signal on a Voltage-Time graph and also gives the R-R, P-R, Q-R-S and Q-T intervals. The practitioners can easily and very accurately detect anomalies from the output.

References

1. ECG. http://www.bloodpressureuk.org/BloodPressureandyou/Medicaltests/ECG
2. Standard range of intervals, E MEDICINE. http://emedicine.medscape.com/article/2172196-overview
3. PQRST INTERVAL and AD8232 guide, SPARK FUN. https://learn.sparkfun.com/tutorials/ad8232-heart-rate-monitor-hookup-guide
4. Conduction System, QCG. http://www.qcg.com.au/conduction_system.html
5. Types of heart arrhythmia, MEMORIAL HERMANN. http://heart.memorialhermann.org/types-of-heart-arrhythmia/
6. American Heart Association, Lead Placement and Acquisition of the 12-Lead Electrocardiogram. https://www.heart.org/idc/groups/heart-public/@wcm/@mwa/documents/downloadable/ucm_464992.pdf
7. Einthoven's Triangle, CV PHYSIOLOGY. http://www.cvphysiology.com/Arrhythmias/A013a
8. Einthoven's triangle, Wickipedia. https://en.wikipedia.org/wiki/Einthoven%27s_triangle
9. Bilal, M.U., Ahmed, B., et al.: Electrogram feature extraction and pattern recognition using a novel windowing algorithm. Adv. Biosci. Biotechnol. 5, 886–894 (2014)
10. Kaur, M., Singh, B.: Comparison of different approaches for removal of baseline wander from ECG Signal. In: 2nd International conference and workshop on Emerging Trends in Technology (ICWET) (2011)
11. Analog Devices AD8232. http://www.analog.com/en/products/application-specific/medical/ecg/ad8232.html
12. Arduino. https://www.arduino.cc/en/Guide/HomePage
13. Project Ideas. https://playground.arduino.cc/Projects/Ideas
14. Sparkfun, what is an Arduino? https://learn.sparkfun.com/tutorials/what-is-an-arduino
15. Arduino Based ECG & Heartbeat Monitoring Healthcare System. http://www.instructables.com/id/ECG-Monitoring-System-by-Using-Arduino-or-AD8232/
16. Arduino. https://www.arduino.cc/reference/en/language/functions/analog-io/analogread/

17. Sparkfun, Analog to Digital conversion. https://learn.sparkfun.com/tutorials/analog-to-digital-conversion
18. Introduction to AVR Timers. https://maxembedded.wordpress.com/2011/06/22/introduction-to-avr-timers/
19. Arduino Timer and Interrupt Tutorial. https://oscarliang.com/arduino-timer-and-interrupt-tutorial/
20. Embedded Systems - Timer/Counter. https://www.tutorialspoint.com/embedded_systems/es_timer_counter.htm
21. Read Analog Voltage. https://www.arduino.cc/en/Tutorial/ReadAnalogVoltage
22. What is jSerialComm? http://fazecast.github.io/jSerialComm/
23. Welcome To JFreeChart! http://www.jfree.org/jfreechart/
24. Standard range of intervals, June 2017. E MEDICINE. http://emedicine.medscape.com/article/2172196-overview
25. Cardiology Teaching Package. http://www.nottingham.ac.uk/nursing/practice/resources/cardiology/function/normal_duration.php
26. Normal ECG. https://meds.queensu.ca/central/assets/modules/ECG/normal_ecg.html

Interpretation of Indian Sign Language Using Optimal HOG Feature Vector

Garima Joshi[1(✉)], Anu Gaur[2], and Sheenu[1]

[1] UIET, Panjab University, Chandigarh, India
joshi_garima5@yahoo.com
[2] UIET, Himachal Pradesh University, Shimla, India
anugaur1508@gmail.com

Abstract. This paper presents a Histograms of Orientation Gradient (HOG) based feature vector for design of Sign Language Recognition System (SLRS). HOG is known to be independent of segmentation task. In this work an attempt has been made to explore the need and motivation to recognize ISL, which can provide opportunities for hearing impaired person in working environment to become more self reliant. For experimentation, Indian Sign Language (ISL) uniform background alphabet dataset and the Triesch's database has been taken. Triesch's database comprises of hand gesture recognition images in uniform as well as complex background condition. The optimal feature vector is computed by identifying the HOG parameters which vary the feature vector size. By repeated experimentation, the feature vector size has been reduced by increasing the number of pixels per cell without compromising accuracy. Performance evaluation has been done on the basis of accuracy for different classifiers such as Support Vector Machine (SVM), Naïve Bayes (NB) and Simple Logistic. For ISL dataset, SVM exhibits the best performance with highest accuracy of 94.5%.

Keywords: Indian Sign Language · Sign Language Recognition System
Complex background · Histograms of Orientation Gradient

1 Introduction

Since Stone Age drawn gestures had been the source of communication. With development in science and technology, society is surrounded by machines to interact and communicate, hence again the age old tradition of communicating using gestures is used and this technique is called gesturing. Gesturing can be used for Human Computer Interface (HCI) to eliminate the use of peripheral devices such as mouse, keyboards and keypads [1]. Gesturing also plays an important role in human to human interaction especially for hearing impaired, deaf and mute people [2]. Hence, HCI has been proved to be the useful technique by the researchers in the field of Sign Language (SL) interpretation also [3]. SL interpretation can help hearing impaired people to interact with others via computer. The basic idea of SL interpretation systems is to convert SL into text. In order to have a natural interface, an automatic system which can process the input SL gesture and convert it into meaningful text. The input gesture can be of any

© Springer Nature Singapore Pte Ltd. 2018
M. Singh et al. (Eds.): ICACDS 2018, CCIS 905, pp. 65–73, 2018.
https://doi.org/10.1007/978-981-13-1810-8_7

form like hand gestures, arm gestures or facial expressions [2]. It has been found that very little attention has been paid by researchers [4]. ISL is quite complex in contrast to the ASL because most of the gestures in ISL are performed with both the hands [5]. Moreover, complexity due occlusion relative to position of hand on hand or on face exists [6]. Thus, it is a very challenging task to prepare a robust ISL recognition system which can recognize double hands signs. This paper focuses recognition of static alphabet signs of ISL.

2   Literature Survey

Viswanathan and Idicula analyzed recent developments in ISL recognition. The paper reported that voluminous work has been carried out in ASL and other SLs. It was also seen that the system which has high recognition rate for ASL may not give the same results when employed in ISL [7]. The overview of literature is presented in Table 1. Rekha *et al.* proposed an automatic gesture recognition system for ISL. The shape, texture and finger features of each hand are extracted using Principle Curvature Based Region (PCBR) detector, Wavelet Packet Decomposition (WPD-2) and complexity defects algorithms for hand posture, respectively. This system applied skin color segmentation and was able to achieve 91.3% overall accuracy for static gestures [8]. Adithiya *et al.* proposed a method for recognition of 36 signs of ISL. In this Fourier descriptors are used for feature extraction and classification was done using Artificial Neural Network (ANN). The overall system was tested for 180 images and resulted in 91% recognition rate. YCbCr color model was used to segment the hand region from the background [9]. Collumeau *et al.* presented the comparative study of global, semi-local and local approaches for hand gesture recognition. It was concluded that semi-local approach such as HOG proved more efficient as compared to other methods [10]. Gupta *et al.* proposed a work on ISL static images of alphabets both with single and double hand. HOG and Scale Invariant Feature Transform (SIFT) features were extracted. Combining HOG with other descriptors gave an accuracy of 90% [11]. Kaur

Table 1. Literature survey

Ref.	Dataset	Segmentation	Feature extraction	RR%
2013 [8]	ISL	YCbCr	Fourier descriptor	91%
2015 [9]	ISL	Skin color	PCBR and WPD-2	91.3% for static
2016 [11]	26 ISL UB	Not required	HOG	78.80%
2016 [12]	10 ISL numbers	Skin color	KM till 3rd order for 5 ROI	90%
2017 [21]	26 ISL UB	Skin color	ZM + HM + Geometric features	92.70%
Proposed work	26 ISL UB	Not required	HOG	94.50%

HM: Hu Moments; KM: Krawtchouk Moments; PCBR: Principle Curvature Based Region, UB: Uniform Background; WPD-2: Wavelet Packet Decomposition; ZM: Zernike Moments.

and Joshi considered hand gesture of 10 distinct looking ISL alphabets and used Krawtchouk polynomials at lower orders by varying Region of Interest (ROI). Comparison of reduced and original feature set was done. The reduced feature dimensionality gave competent accuracy as compared to the original feature-set for all the proposed classifiers. 84.9% accuracy was achieved. Skin color segmentation was done during preprocessing [12].

2.1 Overview of HOG

Histogram of Orientation Gradients (HOG) features were proposed by Dalal and Triggs for robust object recognition in complex background. They used HOG features and Support Vector Machine (SVM) for pedestrian human detection. HOG gave very promising results. It completely outperformed existing feature sets for human detection [13].

HOG are local image descriptors. Local image descriptors are regarded as more robust in terms of image description capability [14]. Later, HOG was also used for face detection [15, 16], in challenging viticulture applications also [17] and in hand gesture recognition [18–20]. Feng and Yuan extracted the gradient direction histogram features for uniform background hand gesture dataset by adjusting the contrast of gray scale images. The system gave recognition rate of 92.5% in brighter and 91.3% in darker images [18]. Therefore, contrast variation affects the HOG response. Lin and Ding combined HOG features with motion trajectory for temporal classification of six gestures resulting in high overall accuracy [19]. Pang et al. presented two ways of increasing the efficiency of HOG features for human detection. One way was to reuse the features in the blocks to construct the HOG features for a detection window. Another way was to utilize sub-cell based interpolation to efficiently compute the HOG features for each block. The first way significantly reduced the computational cost without sacrificing any detection accuracy [20].

2.2 Findings of Literature Review

Following interpretations are drawn from the literature survey

1. The adoption of methods which shows high accuracy for ASL does not give the same result for ISL [4].
2. Most of ISL datasets are user dependent and are acquired in limited background settings. SLRS should be able to understand sign made by every user. ISL dataset reported in [3] is a signer independent dataset
3. Most of the algorithms are based on skin-color segmentation. The performance of system is adversely affected when any other skin color object is present. There is need to design a system where segmentation is not required and HOG feature extractions do not require segmentation [12].
4. It is found that performance of system drops for complex background images. There is need to design such a system which gives promising results for uniform as well as complex background images.

5. HOG can be computed efficiently in the case of grayscale images also [11].
6. HOG feature characteristics depend on several parameters. There is a need to determine optimal value of these parameters [14].

Therefore, HOG based features are suitable for hand gesture recognition because they do not require segmentation during preprocessing. However, there is a need to determine an optimal set of features for sign language recognition by varying HOG parameters.

3 Methodology

3.1 Image Database

In this work, testing is done on hand gesture datasets. These include the ISL database, Jochen-Triesch's standard database also known as Treisch's dataset. ISL uniform background database consist of images with different skin tones from 90 users under varying light intensity condition with constant black background. The first step for the hand gesture recognition is the image acquisition of the hand gestures. The hand gestures have been performed in front of 2 MP camera placed at a constant distance from the subject. The images being acquired have varying skin tones under varying light intensity condition with constant black background [6].

The process flow of Sign Language Recognition System (SLRS) is shown in Fig. 1.

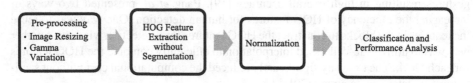

Fig. 1. Process flow of sign language recognition system

3.2 Pre-processing

Images are resized to [50 × 50] and converted to gray scale. The contrast of the images is adjusted using gamma normalization (gamma = 0.5, 1, 1.5). This also helps in reducing the impact of local image shadows and illumination changes, at the same time suppressing the noise interference. Gamma > 1 ($\gamma = 1.5$) expands the intensity range by decreasing the intensity values, which results to the darker image as compare to original image, whereas gamma < 1 ($\gamma = 0.5$) compresses the intensity range by increasing the intensity values, which makes the image brighter.

3.3 Feature Extraction

The computation steps of HOG features are shown in Fig. 2. HOG is used for feature extraction without any segmentation task. The basic idea of using HOG is that local hand appearance and shape can often be characterized by the distribution of local intensity gradients or edge directions, even without precise knowledge of the corresponding gradient or edge positions. During preprocessing, the images are resized followed by contrast enhancement. For calculating HOG features, the image is divided into Cells. Gradient magnitudes and orientations are computed. Range of gradient orientation is decided by selecting an appropriate bin. For each cell, the weighted vote of each gradient falls in the respective bin to which it belongs. Orientation histogram are computed for each cell. Histograms are combined and normalized for each block. In experimental results the objective is to check the best suitable parameters for ISL database. The block normalization is carried out as follows: let V be a non-normalized vector, $\|V\|$ k be its k-norm for k = 1, 2 and ε is a small constant. The normalization methods are:

$$L1 - \text{norm}, \quad V = V/(\|V\|1 + \varepsilon) \tag{1}$$

$$L2 - \text{norm}, \quad V = \frac{V}{\sqrt{\|V\|2^2 + \varepsilon^2}} \tag{2}$$

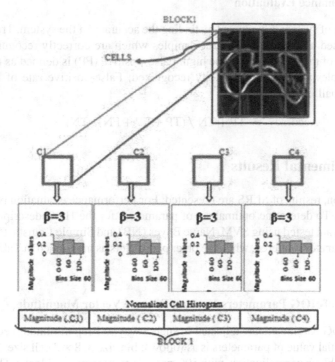

Fig. 2. Computational of HOG features

L2-hys is L2-norm followed by clipping (limiting the max. value of V to 0.2). Table 2 shows HOG parameters that vary feature vector dimension and the parameters that vary HOG feature value. The descriptor must be capable of representing the contents of information from image. Also, the dimension of feature vector must not be too long otherwise it takes long execution time during classification.

Table 2. HOG parameters variation

HOG parameters that vary feature vector dimension		HOG parameters varying feature values (Magnitude)	
Parameter	Variation	Parameter	Variation
Bins = β	3, 4, 5, 6, 9, 12	Gamma normalization	γ = 0, 0.5, 1.5
Block size	2 × 2, 3 × 3, 4 × 4	Gradient Mask	Un-centered [− 1, 1], Centered [− 1, 0, 1], Sobel [− 1 0, 0 1]
Cell size	8 × 8, 10 × 10, 12 × 12	Normalization methods	L1-norm, L2-norm, L2-hys
Block overlap	No overlapping, ½ overlapping ¾ overlapping		

3.4 Performance Evaluation

Performance of system is evaluated by finding the accuracy of the system. True-positive (TP) is defined as the number of true samples which are correctly recognized. True-positive rate of the system should be high. False-positive (FP) is defined as the number of true samples which are incorrectly recognized. False-positive rate of the system should be small.

$$\text{Accuracy} = \text{TP} + \text{TN} / (\text{TP} + \text{FP} + \text{FN} + \text{TN}) \tag{3}$$

4 Experimental Results

In this section, results of SLRS are presented. For performance evaluation two datasets are selected. To determine optimal set of parameters for the HOG descriptors several learning sets are tested using SVM, Naïve Bayes (NB) and Simple Logistic (SL). Firstly a single parameter is altered, while the other parameters as mentioned in Table 2 remain fixed.

4.1 Study of HOG Parameters Varying Feature Vector Magnitude

Initially, HOG parameters are adjusted in such a way to keep minimum vector dimension. The initial value of parameters is as follows: bin size 3, 8 × 8 cell size, 2 × 2 block size, L2-hys block normalization, with 50% or (1/2) overlapping of blocks. The resulting feature vector size is 300. Firstly, the parameters which affect the magnitude of feature values is varied one at a time. The first parameter that is varied is gamma normalization value (γ). Then best resulted value of gamma is selected and set fixed for other parameters. It is observed that γ = 0.5 gives the best accuracy because at this value of gamma image appears neither too dark nor too bright. Similarly, for different gradient masks centered (C) [−1,0,1], un-centered (UC) [−1,1] and Sobel mask[− 1 0; 0 1], then block normalization schemes such as L1-norm, L2-norm, L2-hys the experiments are repeated. It is observed that $\gamma = 0.5$, centered mask and L2-hys normalization turns out to be the best for all the classifiers.

4.2 Study of HOG Parameters Varying Feature Vector Dimension

In the next step, effort is made to tune those parameters which change the dimension of feature vector. As shown in Table 3, these parameters are: bin size, block size, cell size and block overlap. It is seen that keeping cell division 2×2, blocks 5×5 fixed and varying Block overlapping, the dimension of feature vector varies from 108 for no overlapping to 300 with 50% overlapping.

Table 3. Accuracy (%) based on parameters which vary HOG magnitude values.

Gamma Normalization				Gradient Mask				Normalization			
γ	SVM	NB	SL	Mask	SVM	NB	SL	Type	SVM	NB	SL
0	88.3	81.3	88.2	C	**90**	83.3	88.2	L1-norm	87.8	79	86
0.5	90	83.3	89	UC	86.1	79	86.1	L2-norm	90.1	80	89.2
1.5	88.1	78	87	Sobel	84	76.1	84	L2-hys	**90.2**	84	89.3

Result listed in Table 4 show that the higher value of accuracy is obtained with 50% overlapping. Therefore, selecting the value of 50% overlapping, next the bin size is varied from as 3, 5, 6 and 9. It gives high recognition results for bin = 5 and 6. For higher value of bin size, there is no significant increase in the performance. Hence, bin = 5 with overlapping of block is chosen.

Table 4. Accuracy (%) for parameters which vary HOG Feature Vector (FV) dimension.

Overlapping	Overlapping					Bin Variation			
	SVM	NB	SL	FV	Bins	SVM	NB	SL	FV
No	86.3	75.6	84.8	108	3	90.2	84	89	300
					5	**92.8**	83.5	88.4	500
50%	**90.2**	**84**	89	300	6	**92.8**	83.8	89	600
					9	92.2	84.9	90	900
					12	92.3	86	90.3	1200

On the basis of results obtained the HOG various parameters are: $\gamma = 0.45$; $[-1\ 0\ 1]$ centered mask; bins = 5; 2×2 cells per block; block overlapping and L2-hys normalization. Table 5 shows the results based on variations in pixels per cell. It is observed that 18×18 pixels per cell (Cell Size) give the best result, while the accuracy drops below and above these values. The dimension of feature vector is 80. Hence, with feature reduction good accuracy is obtained.

Table 5. Recognition results for variations in pixels per cell

ISL Dataset					Treisch's Database					
Cells	FV	SVM	NB	SL	Dataset	Pixels/Cell	FV	SVM	NB	SL
8 × 8	500	92.8	86.8	88	LB	18 × 18	144	**95.55**	86	90
10 × 10	180	92.8	86	88.1	DB	18 × 18	144	**94.20**	84.10	89
12 × 12	180	92.5	86	88	CB	8 × 8	1296	92.30	82.70	89.30
14 × 14	80	94	87	89.2		10 × 10	729	**93.10**	82.50	89
18 × 18	80	**94.5**	87	90.2		12 × 12	324	88.90	81	88
20 × 20	80	94	86.8	89.5		18 × 18	144	85.60	80	88.60

CB: Complex Background; DB: Dark Background; LB: Light Background.

The parameters value found for HOG are applied on the Triesch's Database. For feature vector of size 144 the accuracy is good in case of light and dark background. For complex background, smaller cell size of 10 × 10, resulting in the larger feature vector of size 729 gives highest accuracy of 93.1% for Treisch's complex background dataset.

5 Conclusion and Future Work

This paper proposes a novel approach for recognizing hand gestures in uniform as well as complex backgrounds on the basis of HOG descriptor and SVM classifier. The HOG descriptor computation does not require any segmentation during preprocessing. In this work, bin size, block size, cell size and block overlap are determined as the parameters on which the feature vector dimensions depend, while, gamma variation, normalization method and type of gradient mask are the parameters on which the magnitude of the feature vector depends. Using repeated experimentation method, the variation of these parameters is done to find an optimal feature vector. Results show that SVM exhibits the best performance with highest accuracy of 94.5% for ISL dataset. Though HOG based method holds good for both uniform and complex background in terms of accuracy but dimension of feature vector is large in case of complex background.

The drawback of that proposed method is that proper design of experiments approach has not been applied which results in large number of experimental run. Also, only feature vector dimension and accuracy are considered. However, computational time is also a very important parameter. In near future, we would further optimize the accuracy, computation time and feature vector dimension using some standard optimizing technique.

References

1. Mitra, S., Acharya, T.: Gesture recognition: a review. IEEE Trans. Syst. Man Cybern. Part C Appl. Rev. **37**, 311–324 (2007)
2. Melnyk, M., Shadrova, V., Karwatsky, B.: Towards computer assisted international sign language recognition system: a systematic survey. Int. J. Comput. Appl. **89**(17), 44–51 (2014)

3. Ong, S.C.W., Ranganath, S.: Automatic sign language analysis: a survey and the further beyond lexical meaning. IEEE Trans. Pattern Anal. Mach. Intell. **27**(6), 837–891 (2007)

4. Badhe, P., Kulkarni, V.: Indian sign language translator using gesture recognition algorithm. In: IEEE International Conference on Computer Graphics, Vision and Information Security, pp. 195–200 (2015)

5. Mullur, K.M.: Indian sign language recognition system. Int. J. Eng. Trends Technol. **21**(9), 450–454 (2015)

6. Joshi, G., Vig, R., Singh, S.: CFS-Infogain based combined shape based feature vector for signer independent ISL database. In: Proceedings of 6th International Conference on Pattern Recognition Applications and Methods, pp. 541–548 (2017)

7. Viswanathan, D.M., Idicula, S.M.: Recent developments in Indian sign language recognition: analysis. IEEE Int. J. Comput. Sci. Inf. Technol. **6**, 289–293 (2015)

8. Rekha, J., Bhattacharya, J., Majumder, S.: Shape, texture and local movement hand gesture features for indian sign language. In: 3rd International Conference on Trendz in Information Sciences and Computing (TISC), pp. 30–35 (2011)

9. Adithya, V., Vinod, P.R., Gopalakrishnan, U.: Artificial neural network based method for indian sign language recognition. In: IEEE Conference on Information and Communication Technologies, pp. 1080–1086 (2013)

10. Collumeau, J.F., Leconge, R., Emile, B., Laurent, H.: Hand-gesture recognition: comparative study of global, semi-local and local approaches. In: 7th International Symposium on Image and Signal Processing and Analysis, pp. 247–253 (2011)

11. Gupta, S., Shukla, P., Mittal, A.: K-nearest correlated neighbor classification for Indian sign language gesture recognition using feature fusion. In: International Conference on Computer Communication and Informatics, pp. 1–5 (2016)

12. Kaur, B., Joshi, G.: Lower order Krawtchouk moment-based feature-set for hand gesture recognition. Adv. Hum. Comput. Interact. **2016**, 1–10 (2016)

13. Dalal, N., Triggs, B.: Histograms of oriented gradients for human detection. In: IEEE International Conference on Computer Vision and Pattern Recognition (CVPR) 2005, San Diego, USA, pp. 886–893 (2005)

14. Chen, J., et al.: WLD: a robust local image descriptor. IEEE Trans. Pattern Anal. Mach. Intell. **32**(9), 1705–1720 (2010)

15. Déniz, O., Bueno, G., De la Torre, F.: Face recognition using histograms of oriented gradients. Pattern Recogn. Lett. **32**(12), 1598–1603 (2011)

16. Albiol, A., Monzo, D., Martin, A., Sastre, J., Albiol, A.: Face recognition using HOG–EBGM. Pattern Recogn. Lett. **29**(10), 1537–1543 (2008)

17. Škrabánek, P., Dolezel, P.: Robust grape detector based on SVMs and HOG features. Comput. Intell. Neurosci. **2017**, 1–18 (2017)

18. Feng, K., Yuan, F.: Static hand gesture recognition based on HOG characters and support VectorMachines. In: 2nd International Symposium on Instrumentation and Measurement, Sensor Network and Automation, pp. 936–938 (2013)

19. Lin, J., Ding, Y.: A temporal hand gesture recognition system based on HOG and motion trajectory. Optik **124**, 6795–6798 (2010)

20. Pang, Y., Yuan, Y., Li, X., Pan, J.: Efficient HOG human detection. Sig. Process. **91**, 773–781 (2011)

21. Kaur, B., Joshi, G., Vig, R.: Indian sign language recognition using Krawtchouk moment-based local features. Imaging Sci. J. **65**(3), 171–179 (2017)

Stable Reduced Link Break Routing Technique in Mobile Ad Hoc Network

Bhagyashri R. Hanji[1(✉)] and Rajashree Shettar[2]

[1] Department of CSE, Global Academy of Technology, Bengaluru 98, India
bhagyashri@gat.ac.in
[2] Department of CSE, R V College of Engineering, Bengaluru 59, India
rajashreeshettar@rvce.edu.in

Abstract. A Mobile Ad hoc Network is a wireless network with the aim of coming collectively when need arises. In modern days improving the Quality of Service in MANETs is considered as the major research area in wireless communication systems. Each node in the network functions as both a host and a router. Each intermediate node forwards data packets to the next node in the path independently. The greatest visible challenge in the design of wireless ad hoc network is the limited availability of energy resources and mobility of nodes. Mobility is measured as the major cause of damage and disruption leading to path breakage, topology change, traffic overhead, long lasting disconnection, network partitions. In the proposed method the node mobility, direction of motion and energy are the major parameters considered to establish a stable path. The proposed method is evaluated with AODV and MTPR routing protocol and confirm better in terms of end-to-end delay, number of packets sent in a session, energy consumed, control and routing overhead.

Keywords: Link stability · Energy · Overhead · End to end delay
Quality of service · Throughput

1 Introduction

MANETs have received great attention and raises several research challenges as they operate without any central administration and fixed infrastructure. Nodes move in diverse directions resulting in self-motivated topology. The challenge in finding stable route and reduce control overhead and extending the route lifetime are the critical issues. Any route is said to be stable if it offers connectivity for longer time between source and destination during data transmission. The link breakage leads to generation of huge control packets in the network reducing throughput, raising overhead and energy consumption. This paper devises a new method to reduce the link break and maintain the balance between mobility and energy of node. The purpose of the proposed method is to find the path which remains alive for maximum possible amount of time. The amount of power consumed along different paths differs as it depends on interference levels of noise and how far communicating nodes are located.

© Springer Nature Singapore Pte Ltd. 2018
M. Singh et al. (Eds.): ICACDS 2018, CCIS 905, pp. 74–83, 2018.
https://doi.org/10.1007/978-981-13-1810-8_8

Ad hoc On-Demand Distance Vector (AODV) Routing algorithm allows dynamic self starting multihop routing between mobile nodes in ad hoc network [1]. Minimum Total Transmission Power Routing (MTPR) is one of the primary energy efficient routing which concentrates on end-to-end energy efficiency selecting the minimum hop path. The energy consumed to forward data along the route is considered as a major parameter to select nodes, but does not consider the available energy of node. A node before making any routing decision must know networks energy state. Hence this node must interact with other nodes to obtain information [2, 3].

2 Related Work

More amount of work has been done earlier towards improving the routing, retaining energy, ensuring security in MANET. However the problem of routing still remains unsettled. Some of the works used to address this issue are as under.

In [4] the authors propose a scheme to decrease the link break by finding an optimal path by calculating the signal power and link expiration time in the system. In [5] the authors concurrently consider two parameters mobility and residual energy in formation of path. Considering both the parameters helps to reduce the link break due to displacement of node or energy exhaustion of a node. In [6] the authors compare four different types of node movement namely horizontal, vertical, square path and specified area among which horizontal motion origins majority of node dislocation relative to corresponding nodes. The nodes will not be able to forward any data once they are out of range and continue to be out of range further affecting the performance of MANET. In [7] the authors conclude that packet drop rate is directly proportional to node mobility. On demand protocols are more advantageous as they do maintain route only when source destination pair have data to send. At the same time generate huge amount of overhead while constructing path. In [8] the authors think of a new idea in handling routing decision. Source node chooses shortest path with better link lifetime if available else will go on with hop-count as the major routing metric. In [9] the authors propose a simple and powerful networking protocol based on tree routing to support the creation of wired and wireless connections over different media. Network layer administers the node addressing and MAC address is used only during initial network configuration. The method provides effective low overhead, supporting a variety of transmission media through custom tree based routing scheme. In [10] the authors present less complex, strongly asymmetrical, extremely lightweight ToLHnet protocol with reduced latency, increasing the overall network efficiency, with insignificant raise in network complexity. The protocol resides at network layer able to span different transmission media independent of lower layers. Experimental results show improvement in communication at baud rates compared with total cable length. In [11] the authors present service oriented architecture allowing heterogeneous wireless sensor networks to communicate in a distributed way with higher ability to recover errors. In [12] the authors propose a simple and robust hybrid communication solution for wired/wireless multi master architecture. Considering only node remaining energy, node location stable link can be found which remains active only for short time. In this work we want the stable link to persist for longer time keeping in mind of certain parameters like if two neighbor nodes are within each other range and are moving along almost same direction with negligible angular displacement then the two nodes remain connected for a longer time. If two neighbors are moving away from each other with huge angular displacement they will soon be disconnected leading to new path discovery.

3   Proposed Work

The proposed work aims to achieve more stable links, which remain alive and support communication between two nodes for a longer time. As the links persist for longer time the possibility of route breaks during a communication session is reduced. The choice of AODV protocol is because it performs better in terms on energy efficiency and mobility when compared to other reactive protocols. [13, 14] the vital reason for link break are due to node moving out of range of its neighboring node, node failing of energy exhaustion, software or hardware failures in node [15]. Each node follows linear node movement without sudden drastic changes with respect to direction of motion, speed and velocity [6].

Our previous study [16, 17] mentions about the work being carried out using nodes location and energy as a major criteria for a node to participate in route discovery phase. A simple technique using these parameters to obtain a better path is presented. The outcome is proficient with respect to existing AODV protocol. The proposed method proves to be efficient routing capable of minimizing routing overhead and thereby enhancing network lifetime. The prime features of the proposed study are:

- Develop routing protocol in MANET for reducing Routing overhead.
- Reduce the number of route breaks and maintaining better data delivery ratio and energy efficiency.

When we say nodes are mobile this mobility comes with a particular direction which also needs to be given prime importance. For example at time T if the two nodes are within range of each other and the node is selected as the next intermediate node in the path. After time $T + \Delta t$ (small time interval), if the two nodes move in exactly opposite direction to each other then very soon they will exceed a certain extent where signals cannot be received correctly leading to link breakage. But if the two nodes are moving almost in a similar direction they remain connected for a longer time. Along with this factor, the node must also have enough energy required to transmit and receive data, so that node will not die because of energy depletion which also leads to path break. Here we consider the first two major important reasons stated for link break to make sure that link must be active for the session.

Consider two nodes A and B as shown in Fig. 1, at a distance D apart. $A(X_{a1}, Y_{a1})$, $B(X_{b1}, Y_{b1})$ be the initial coordinates of nodes A and B and are moving in the direction at angle Θ_a and Θ_b with respect to Y-axis. V_a and V_b represent the velocity of the node. The distance D and the angular displacement between two nodes play an important role in deciding the stability of the link. The Link Stability [18, 19] can be calculated using the following formula (1).

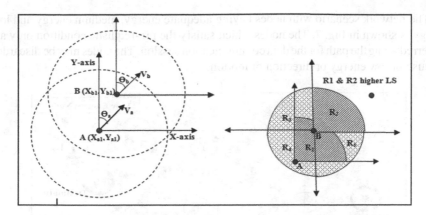

Fig. 1. Important parameters & example of preferable node selection region

$$Link\ Stability = \frac{term_1 + \sqrt{term_2 * r^2 - term_3^2}}{term_2} \qquad (1)$$

Where

$term_1 = \left(\left(-(V_a Cos(\Theta_a) - V_b Cos(\Theta_b) * (X_{a1} - X_{b1}) + ((V_a Sin(\Theta_a) - V_b Sin(\Theta_b)) * (Y_{a1} - Y_{b1})\right)\right)$

$term_2 = \left((V_a Cos(\Theta_a) - V_b Cos(\Theta_b))^2 + ((V_a Sin(\Theta_a) - V_b Sin(\Theta_b))^2\right)$

$term_3 = \left((V_a Cos(\Theta_a) - V_b Cos(\Theta_b)) * (Y_{a1} - Y_{b1}) - (X_{a1} - X_{b1}) * (V_a Sin(\Theta_a) - V_b Sin(\Theta_b))\right)^2$

Steps followed to select a node in a path:

```
If the node is an intermediate node then
    The node checks for duplicate RREQ received.
If Duplicate RREQ
    RREQ is discarded.
Else
    Compute Link Stability & Residual Energy of neighbors.
    Select higher Link Stability & Residual Energy node.
    Update the RREQ Packet.
    Forward the RREQ packet to its neighbors.
Else if node is destination then
    If RREQ Sequence number>Routing Table sequence number
then
    Compute the best available route.
    Update the RREP packet and send.
Else
    Drop the RREQ packet.
```

The network scenario with nodes having adequate energy, medium energy and low energy is shown in Fig. 2. The nodes which satisfy the pre-requisite condition only are preferred along the path for the data communication session. The nodes may be discarded because of low energy or direction of motion.

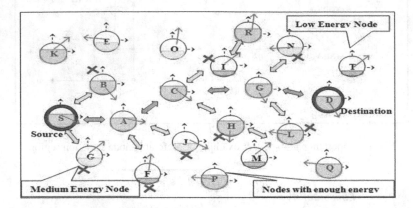

Fig. 2. Stable Path formed between Source and Destination

Table 1 illustrates few values of Link Stability calculated for various parameters. The Link Stability value highly depends on node position, angular displacement and Velocity. Each node chooses its subsequent neighbor node along the path with high stability value.

Table 1. Calculation of Link Stability for different values

(X_{a1}, Y_{a1})	(X_{b1}, Y_{b1})	(V_a, V_b)	(Θ_a, Θ_b)	Link stability
(100,100)	(150,150)	(2,2)	(0,45)	113.54
(100,100)	(150,150)	(2,2)	(46,45)	152.1
(100,100)	(150,150)	(2,2)	(98,86)	97.71
(100,100)	(150,150)	(2,2)	(130,75)	65.46
(100,100)	(150,150)	(3,3)	(0,45)	77.89
(100,100)	(150,150)	(2,3)	(0,45)	78.12
(100,100)	(150,150)	(4,4)	(0,45)	56.77
(100,100)	(150,150)	(8,8)	(0,45)	28.38
(100,100)	(150,150)	(8,4)	(0,45)	14.21
(100,100)	(150,150)	(15,10)	(0,45)	18.91
(100,100)	(250,250)	(2,2)	(46,45)	27.17
(100,100)	(250,250)	(2,2)	(130,75)	14.44
(100,100)	(250,250)	(3,3)	(46,45)	10.78
(100,100)	(250,250)	(8,8)	(0,45)	11.09

4 Simulation Results and Discussion

To evaluate the performance simulation is carried out with NS2.35 [20]. The mobile nodes are randomly placed with Random Waypoint mobility model using IEEE 802.111 MAC Protocol as link layer protocol. The transmission and carrier sensing range is taken as 250 m. The sender receiver pair is selected at random over the defined network. The energy model in NS2.35 is used that lets know any node about its instant energy level. Three important parameters Initial Energy, transmission power and reception power are used in calculation of energy usage for transmission and reception of packets.

The following graphs in Figs. 3 and 4 shows the amount of time the link remains stable plotted against the angular displacement. Figure 3 shows, the Link Stability increases as the Angular Displacement and Distance decreases and Link Stability decreases as the Angular Displacement and Distance increases.

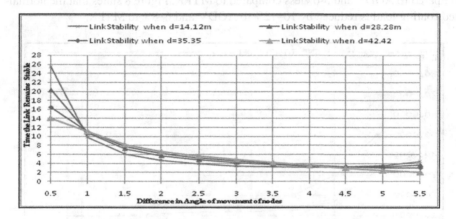

Fig. 3. Link Stability Vs Difference in Angle of movement of nodes

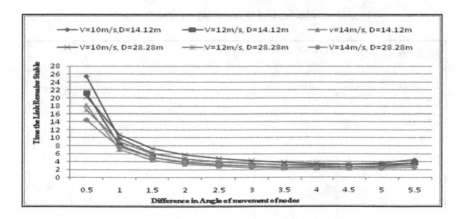

Fig. 4. Link Stability Vs Difference in Angle of movement of nodes (varying velocity).

Figure 4 shows, the relation between Link Stability and Velocity. Link stability decreases as the velocity between nodes increases for the same distance between nodes. The analysis states that if the nodes move with greater speed with any angular difference between them, the link lifetime decreases.

To begin with nodes are set to battery full capacity of 100 J. Figures 5, 6, 7 and 8 shows the result by varying simulation time from 25 s to 500 s, for 50 nodes. Figure 5 shows that the proposed method (S-AODV) has less end to end delay than MTPR and AODV once the path is setup. The results show that S-AODV has 12–15% lesser time than AODV and 8–10% lesser time than MTPR. Figure 6 depicts the number of packets transmitted successfully to the target to those produced at the source is higher in S-AODV than the other two protocols. When the simulation model is run for 25 s then S-AODV, MTPR, AODV have transmitted 4520, 3240 and 2240 packets respectively. Figure 7 results prove that the proposed method consumes less energy by 8–10% compared to AODV and 5-6%less compared to MTPR. Figure 8 states that the normalized routing load is reduced by 10–12% to AODV and 6–8% to MTPR.

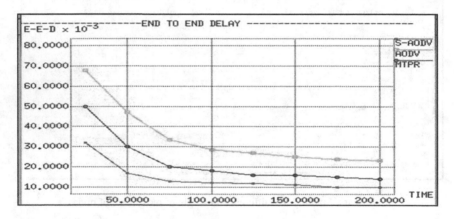

Fig. 5. End to end delay vs time

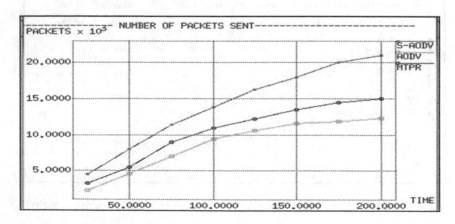

Fig. 6. Number of packets sent vs time

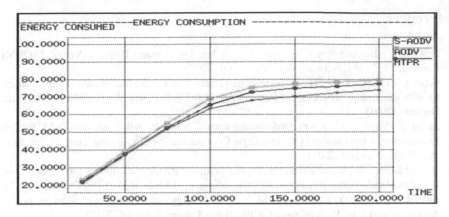

Fig. 7. Protocol energy consumption vs time.

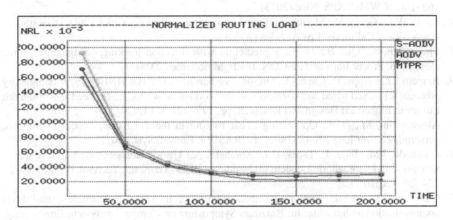

Fig. 8. Normalized routing load vs time.

5 Conclusion

S-AODV proposed method is a proficient method for finding stable path in MANETs which has increased the number of data packets that can be sent over a session before link break. The method reduces the number of link breaks, hence on an average around 8–10% improvement is found with delay, 7–8% reduced power consumption and 8–10% reduced normalized routing overhead. The AODV routing protocol does not consider the transmission power, energy of node but only considers the shortest path. MTPR considers the transmission energy required and based on this value decides the routing path. But the transmission power required changes as nodes move closer to each other and apart from each other. The proposed method takes care of these factors and behaves efficiently. The fundamental method in this work is greatly extensible supporting Quality of Service for end users.

References

1. Perkins, C., Belding-Royer, E., Das, S.: Ad hoc On-Demand Distance Vector (AODV) Routing, RFC 3561, Network Working Group (2003)
2. Scott, D., Toh, C., Cobb, H.: Performance evaluation of battery life aware routing schemes for wireless Adhoc networks. In: Proceedings of IEEE ICC, vol. 9, pp. 2824–2829. IEEE, Helsinki (2001)
3. Zhonj, Z., Yuming, M.: A new QoS routing scheme in mobile Adhoc network-Q-MTPR. In: Proceedings of International Conference on Communication Circuits and Systems, pp. 389–393. IEEE, Chengdu (2004)
4. Senthil Kumar, R., Kamalakkannan, P.: Personalized RAODV algorithm for Reduce Link Break in Mobile Adhoc Networks. In: Proceedings of IEEE ICoAC. IEEE, Chennai (2012)
5. Rashid, U., Waqar, O., Kiani, A.K..: Mobility and energy aware routing algorithm for mobile Adhoc networks. In: Proceedings of ICEE, IEEE, Lahore, Pakistan (2017)
6. Alzaylaee, M., DeDourek, J., Pochec, P..: Linear Node Movement Patterns in MANETs, pp. 162–166. ICWMC, XPS, Nice (2013)
7. Su, W.W.L., Gerla, M.: Motion prediction in mobile/wireless networks. Ph.D. Dissertation, University of California, Los Angeles (2000)
8. Sithitavorn, K., Qiu, B.: Mobility prediction with direction tracking on dynamic source routing. In: Proceedings of TENCON. IEEE, Melbourne (2005)
9. Biagetti, G., Crippa, P., Curzi, A., Orcioni, S., Turchetti, C.: TOLHNET: a low-complexity protocol for mixed wired and wireless low-rate control networks. In: Proceedings of the 6th European Embedded Design and Research, pp. 177–181. IEEE (2014)
10. Alessandrini, M., et al.: Optimizing linear routing in the ToLHnet protocol to improve performance over long RS-485 buses. EURASIP J. Embed. Syst. (2017)
11. Corchado, J.M., Bajo, J., Tapia, D.I., Abraham, A.: Using heterogeneous wireless sensor networks in a telemonitoring system for healthcare. IEEE Trans. Inf. Technol. Biomed. **14**(2), 234–240 (2010)
12. Guarese, G.B., et al.: Exploiting modbus protocol in wired and wireless multilevel communication architecture. In: Brazilian Symposium on Computing System Engineering, pp. 13–18 (2012)
13. Amjad, K., Stocker, A.J.: Impact of node density and mobility on the performance of the AODV and DSR in MANETS. In: Proceedings of Communication Systems Networks and Digital Signal Processing, CSNDSP, pp. 61–65. IEEE, Newcastle upon Tyne (2010)
14. Lei, Q., Xiaoqing, W.: Improved energy aware AODV routing protocol. In: Proceedings of International Conference on Information Engineering (ICIE), pp. 18–21. IEEE, Taiyuan (2009)
15. Sofian, Hamad., Noureddine., Hamed, Al-Raweshidy.: Link Stability and energy aware for reactive routing protocol in mobile Adhoc network. In. Proceedings of 9th ACM International symposium on Mobility Management and Wireless Access, pp. 195–198, Miami Florida,USA (2011)
16. Hanji, B.R., Shettar, R.: Enhanced AODV multipath routing based on node location. In: Proceedings of International Conference on Computational Systems and Information Systems for Sustainable Solution, CSITSS, pp. 158–162. IEEE, Bengaluru (2016)
17. Hanji, B.R., Shettar, R.: Improved AODV with restricted route discovery area. In: Proceedings of International Conference on Computer Communication and Informatics, ICCCI. IEEE, Coimbatore (2015)

18. Sun, J., Liu, Y.A., Hu, H., Yuan, D.: Link stability based routing in mobile Adhoc networks. In: 5th IEEE Conference on Industrial Electronics and Applications, pp. 1821–1825. IEEE, Taichung (2010)
19. Su, W., Lee, S.J., Gerla, M.: Mobility prediction and routing in Adhoc wireless networks. Int. J. Netw. Manage. **11**(1), 3–30 (2001)
20. Fall, K., Varadhan, K.: The NS Manual. The VINT Project (2011)

Disguised Public Key for Anonymity and Enforced Confidentiality in Summative E-Examinations

Kissan G. Gauns Dessai[1(✉)] and Venkatesh V. Kamat[2]

[1] Government College of Arts Science and Commerce, Quepem, Goa, India
kissangd@gmail.com
[2] Goa University, Taleigao Plateau, Goa, India
vvkamat@gmail.com

Abstract. The two crucial assets of summative examination are question paper and the answers-scripts. Maintenance of secrecy of question paper/answers-scripts within its defined perimeters is extremely important to protect the sanctity and fairness of the summative examination. In addition to the secrecy of question paper/answers-scripts, anonymity between students and examiners is also equally important for ensuring an unbiased evaluation. Anonymity and secrecy is required in an examination environment to prevent the student and any other entity from coercing with each other and indulging in unfair means. It appears that, establishing secrecy of answers-scripts from examination authority is a bit tricky task as examination authority itself needs to receive the answers-scripts submitted by students for forwarding it to the examiners for evaluation. In this paper, we propose a dual purpose cryptographic scheme for achieving anonymity of students and examiners from each other besides the secrecy of answers-scripts from recipient examination authority, which we refer to as enforced confidentiality. We intend to achieve anonymity and enforced confidentiality by disguising the public key (public key cryptosystem) of the final recipient entity from the sender of the information based on the concept of blind signature scheme. The proposed mechanism is suitable for achieving anonymity and enforced confidentiality in applications where communication between the sender and the recipient needs to be carried through the intermediate entity.

Keywords: Anonymity · Enforced confidentiality · Blind signature
Disguised public key · Public key cryptosystem · Summative E-Examination

1 Introduction

Summative examination comprises of two key ingredients, namely question paper and the answers-scripts. As summative examinations are high stake examinations, it is often targeted by malicious entities infringing the secrecy of the question paper/answers-scripts. The secrecy of the question paper needs to be protected before the conduct of the examination to safeguard the fairness and reliability of the examination system. Similarly, the identity of the examiner and students' needs to be kept secret from each other to prevent malicious acts such as unfair evaluation, illicit demands, bribes/threats, etc. In addition to the secrecy of question paper and anonymity requirement, it is also

© Springer Nature Singapore Pte Ltd. 2018
M. Singh et al. (Eds.): ICACDS 2018, CCIS 905, pp. 84–94, 2018.
https://doi.org/10.1007/978-981-13-1810-8_9

essential to ensure the secrecy of answers-script from the examination authority and all others except the examiners concerned. It is desirable to maintain secrecy of answers-scripts from examination authority to prevent any violation of answers-scripts integrity without getting detected.

In the current examination system (conventional/electronic) the anonymity of the student is achieved by mapping student identity to a unique and random pseudonym. Some of the security paradigms used in achieving the anonymity in electronic examinations are based on blind signature [1], group digital signatures [2], mix-network approach [3], etc. The current approaches address anonymity requirement comprehensively, but lacks in maintaining secrecy of answers-scripts from examination authority.

1.1 Motivations

The current process of summative examination suffers from a variety of security vulnerabilities as apparent from frequent cases of malpractices. One such vulnerability is a violation of confidentiality/integrity of answers-scripts during delivery of answers-scripts. It is essential to deliver answers-scripts from students to examination authority and examination authority to examiners to prevent any act of coercion between student and examiners. Although, this approach ensures anonymity of student and examiners, but it leads to exposure of answers-scripts to many entities before evaluation and thus challenging the integrity of answers-scripts. Thus, we require a comprehensive solution that can safeguard anonymity as well as protects confidentiality of the exchanged data.

1.2 Scope and Outline of the Paper

We need a mechanism for delivering the answers-scripts produced by the students to the examiner, in such a way that, it satisfies the following security goals

1. Do not reveal the identity of the examiner to the student
2. Do not reveal the identity of the student to the examiner and
3. Do not reveal the answers-scripts to the examination authority.

The first two goals listed above, refer to the anonymity property of hiding the identity of sender/receiver from each other as defined in [4]. Coupled with the anonymity (first two goals above), we also need to keep the transmitted information secret from the intermediate receiver (third goal above). We use the term "**Enforced confidentiality**" to refer to the process of hiding the part of information from the intermediate receiver of the information. In a nutshell, we need a dual purpose approach, satisfying both anonymity and enforced confidentiality.

Contribution: This paper proposes a cryptographic scheme to achieve the following goals

1. De-link the receiver of the message from the sender of the message (to achieve anonymity) and
2. Keep the message secret from the intermediary receiver (to achieve enforced confidentiality)

We present a mathematical proof of the proposed cryptographic scheme to validate and support our claim. The methodology proposed to achieve anonymity and enforced confidentiality in this paper is a novel and to the best of our knowledge, no such/similar work has formed the basis of any research.

Outline: The remainder of this paper is structured as follows: Sect. 2 describes the summative examinations and related work on security in e-examinations. Section 3 describes the proposed disguised public key scheme in detail. Section 4 provides the working of answers-script exchange with disguised public key. Section 5 validates disguised public key scheme using mathematical proofs. Section 6 draws the conclusion and outlines the future work.

2 Background and Related Work

This paper discusses University based summative examination along with the related work addressing security requirements of those examinations

2.1 Summative Examination

The main communicating entities of the summative examination are: question paper setters, students, supervisors, examiners, and examination authority. Paper setter is an entity who sets the questions based on predefined syllabus. A subset of such questions is randomly selected for examination based on the requirement of question paper. Eligible students answer the examination electronically and produce answers-scripts corresponding to the given question paper. The supervisor is an entity who is responsible for controlling and monitoring the conduct of the examination. Examination authority is an entity responsible for conducting the examination in a fair manner. Examination authority collects the answers-scripts and assigns those answers-scripts to examiners for evaluation. The examiner is an entity who evaluates the answers-scripts at the end of the examination and allots the marks/grades for each answer based on the marking scheme.

The main purpose of summative examination is grading, certification and placement [5]. Summative examinations are high stake examinations and need to be conducted in a manner that increases its robustness and reliability. Due to the high-stake nature of the summative examinations, these examinations remain a target for user security challenges [6].

The confidentiality of question paper needs to be protected before the conduct of the examination. Similarly, the confidentiality of answers-scripts needs to be protected from all entities except the examiner concerned. If the secrecy of the question paper/answers-scripts is violated (out of the defined perimeters), it can make entire examination process null and void. In addition to the confidentiality, anonymity needs to be satisfied between the following entities:

1. Student and paper setter (Student is not required to know who is the paper setter)
2. Examiner and student (Examiner is not required to know whose answer-scripts he is evaluating and vice versa) and

Normally, each student is assigned a pseudonym to hide the identity of student from others for establishing the anonymity. However, the problem of achieving the secrecy of answers-scripts from examination authority becomes a challenging task as the answers-scripts produced by students are routed through examination authority to the respective examiners.

2.2 Related Work

Any secure computer system is built on 3 main pillars of security, namely: confidentiality (C), integrity (I) and availability (A) [7]. In particular, confidentiality protects the data item from interception, integrity protects the data from modification and availability protects it from interruption [8].

Cryptography has many uses in electronic communications, including providing the basic security principles of confidentiality and integrity, among many other vital information security functions. The notions of symmetric key cryptography [9] and public key cryptography [10] play a major role in information security.

In cryptography, a blind signature as introduced by [1] is a form of digital signature in which the sender disguises (blinds) the message before it is sent to signer for obtaining the his/her signature. The blind signature scheme is used effectively in achieving anonymity in applications such as e-voting [11], e-auction [12] and e-cash [13] protocols.

Now, we discuss some of the existing research work, towards the deployment of the security goals as a solution for most data security issues in e-examination. There are exam protocols for obtaining confidentiality of information exchanged [14, 15]. These protocols use public key infrastructure (PKI) as an adequate technology to provide confidentiality, authenticity, integrity and non-repudiation security goals. There is a formal framework using applied π calculus to define and analyse authentication and privacy requirements for examinations through formalization of several individual and universal verifiability properties [16]. There exists an exam protocol without the need of a trusted third party that guarantees several security properties including anonymity for anonymising the student's test [17]. The said protocol allows the student and the examiner to jointly generate a pseudonym that anonymises the student's test. The pseudonym is revealed only to the student when the exam starts. The e-examination setup proposed in [18] achieves the security goals of confidentiality and anonymity using ElGamal encryption [19] and reusable anonymous return channel [20].

There is a considerable work in the area of e-examinations, handling the issue of security. However, there is difficulty in adopting existing solutions per se, as they do not fully model security requirements of the typical examination under our consideration.

We need a comprehensive solution to transfer the answers-scripts produced by the students to examination authority/examiner without revealing the identity of student and examiners to each other. We also need to protect the confidentiality of answers-scripts from the examination authority. In this paper, we define a cryptographic scheme built on top of public key cryptosystem to fulfill the security goals specific to summative subjective e-examinations. The proposed mechanism is inspired from blind signature scheme. As per our best knowledge, no such research work has been done in general and specific to e-examinations.

3 Disguised Public Key

In a public key cryptosystem, each communicating entity is in possession of two keys: a public key and a private key. The public key is known to the public in general. Any user A wishing to communicate with user B, uses the public key of B to encrypt the message intended for B. Only user B can decrypt the said message, using his/her own private key (i.e., private key of B).

3.1 Basic Notations

The elementary notations used to describe the proposed security scheme to achieve anonymity and enforced confidentiality is listed in Table 1

Table 1. Glossary of notations.

Notation	Description
K_{Ai}; K_{Ai}^{-1}	Public key and private key of an entity A_i
K_{Ai} (m)	Message m is encrypted using public key of entity A_i
K_{Ai}^{-1} (c)	Ciphertext c is decrypted using the private key of entity A_i

3.2 Equational Theory

The proposed mechanism is based on the RSA public key cryptosystem [21] and blind signature scheme [1]. We use the following predicates to construct our disguised public key cryptosystem:

1. An encryption function *aenc* and the corresponding inverse *adec*, such that

$$adec(aenc(m, K_x), K_x^{-1}) = m \tag{1}$$

and given *aenc* it is infeasible to derive *adec*.

2. The message blinding function, blind and the corresponding inverse *unblind,* s.t.

$$unblind(blind(m, r), r^{-1}) = m \tag{2}$$

and given *blind* it is infeasible to derive r.

3. The message blinding and unblinding function as defined in item 2 above and the message signing function *sign* (i.e., message signed with the private key), s.t.

$$\$\, unblind(sign(blind(m, r), K_x^{-1}), r^{-1}) = sign(m, K_x^{-1}) \tag{3}$$

and given blind, it is infeasible to derive r.

4. A randomization imposing function r, having corresponding inverse r^{-1} to make the search for valid public key impractical.

Along with the above predicates, we propose following predicate in the equational theory

- A disguising function *hide* and the corresponding inverse unhide, such that:

$$unhide\big(aenc\big(m, hide\big(K_E, r\big)\big), r^{-1}\big) = aenc\big(m, K_E\big). \qquad (4)$$

It is not possible to derive public key K_E or randomization factor r, *given hide (K_E, r)* and aenc

Definition 1 (Disguised Public Key). Let there be three entities: producer (A) - the creator of a message, intermediary (B) - the intermediate recipient of a message and consumer (E) - the final recipient of a message. Given a public key, (K_A, n_A) of the producer of the message m, a public key (K_E, n_E) and a private key (K_E^{-1}, n) of the consumer of the message (m). Let (r, n_r) be the random blind factor and (r^{-1}, n_r) be the inverse of r, selected by an intermediary, then the disguised public key produced by the intermediary is defined as $K_{E'}$, such that

$$K_E' = \big(K_E * r\big)^{K_A} \big(mod\, n_A\big) \qquad (5)$$

having a corresponding recovery function:

$$c = c'^{r^{-1}} \big(mod\, n_r\big) \qquad (6)$$

Here c' represents the message encrypted by the producer of the message with the disguised public key $\big(K_E'\big)$ of the consumer.

4 Protocol for Anonymity and Enforced Confidentiality Using Disguised Public Key

In this section we illustrate the use of disguised public key in delivering examination content anonymously

Let A (student) be the producer of a message m, C (examiner) be the final consumer of a message m and B (examination authority) be the intermediary, whose task is to collect the message from A and deliver it to C. A wants to exchange answers-script (AS) with B without revealing the answers-scripts to B and B wants to deliver answers-scripts to C without revealing identity of C to A. All partners rely on existing public-key infrastructure, such as X.509. The exchange of cryptographic keys is not covered by our protocol.)

The detailed protocol steps are illustrated below:

1. Initially, B takes the public key K_C of C and chooses a random number (r). It disguises the selected public key K_C of the consumer, using the random number (r). B, encrypts the disguised public key K_C using the public key, K_A of A to produce m'. m' is sent to entity A.

2. B sends the encrypted disguised public key, m' to A for encrypting the answers-script (AS) produced by it.

3. Entity A decrypts m' using its private key, K_{A_i} to get the disguised public key s'. Answers-scripts AS produced by A is encrypted using s' to create c'. A sends c' to B.

4. Entity B on receipt of c', applies r^{-1} to it, the inverse of r, chosen in step 1 to unhide the public key of C. This produces c, i.e. an encrypted answers-script produced through the use of public key of C.

5. Entity B, subsequently sends encrypted answers-scripts(c), to the examiner.

6. Entity C can decrypt the answer-scripts c using its private key, K_C^{-1} as c is encrypted using its public key K_C.

In this way, although student (A) gets the public key of the examiner, he/she is not in a position to get the identity of the examiner (C). Similarly, although examination authority (B) gets the answers-script from the student, it cannot view the actual answers-scripts as it is encrypted using the public key of the examiner (C). In the next section, we prove that, the proposed disguised public key scheme successfully achieves the stated security goals of anonymity and enforced confidentiality.

The proposed protocol is useful in achieving anonymity and enforced confidentiality in situations where information is exchanged between two parties through an intermediary.

5 Evaluation of Disguised Public Key Scheme

We analyze our disguised public key scheme described in Sect. 4 based on the cryptographic principles and equational theory defined in Sect. 3.2. We provide a mathematical proof to validate the working of the proposed scheme.

Theorem 1. In a Public Key Cryptosystem

1. Message encrypted with the disguised public key of the recipient achieves recipient anonymity.
2. $unhide\ (aenc(m, hide(K_C, r)), r^{-1}) = aenc(m, K_C)$
3. Message encrypted with the disguised public key, achieves enforced confidentiality of a message.

Proof. Let there be 3 entities, viz., producer (A), intermediary (B) and consumer (C)

Let the public/private key pair of entity A, B and C derived from public key cryptosystem be represented K_A / K_A^{-1}, K_B / K_B^{-1}, K_C / K_C^{-1} respectively. Here, each public key is known to the public in general and corresponding private key is known only to the owner of the private key. Each public/private key pair satisfies the equations as defined in equational theory (refer Sect. 3.2). Let r represent a random number, having corresponding inverse r^{-1} known to entity B only. According to te RSA blind signature scheme, any message (m) is blinded with the random factor (r) to obtain the signature of signer as follows:

$$m' = m * r^{K_x}(mod\, n) \tag{7}$$

We adopt a similar approach as used in Eq. 7 to disguise the public key of entity C to hide it from the entity A. B encrypts disguised public key of C, using the public key of A as follows (refer Sect. 3.2):

$$m' = (K_c * r)^{K_A}(mod\, n) \tag{8}$$

Encrypted disguised public key (m') is sent to A. On receipt of m', A decrypts m' as follows (refer Sect. 3.2)

$$s' = \left(m'\right)^{K_A^{-1}}(mod\, n) \tag{9}$$

Using Eq. 8 it is evident that

$$s' = (K_c * r)^{K_A K_A^{-1}}(mod\, n) \tag{10}$$

i.e., entity A get

$$s' = (K_c * \mathrm{r})(mod\, n) \tag{11}$$

Now in order to prove our theorem statement (1): **Message encrypted with the disguised public key of the recipient, achieves recipient anonymity**

We need to prove that: "Given s' and list of t unique public keys K_1, K_2,..., K_t, where $s' = K_C * \mathrm{r}$ and one of the $K_i \equiv K_C$, K_C cannot be predicted with certainty." Based on the knowledge of A, it can try to infer the value of K_C as follows,

$$r_1 = \frac{s'}{K1}, r_2 = \frac{s'}{K2}, \dots, r_t = \frac{s'}{Kt}$$

It is evident from the above equations that, if we divide the given disguised public key by each of the known public key K_i, we get quotient r_i. Let us assume that each r $_i$ = r. However, it is not possible to get identical quotient when a division is carried between common numerator and different denominator (public keys are unique). Such division will produce different quotient each time. In other words, our assumption that r_i = r is false. Since A is in possession of t public keys and unaware of random factor r used to disguise the public key K_C, we can say that, A can only find the public key K_C hidden in s' with probability $\frac{1}{t}$. Hence, we can state that: **Message encrypted with the disguised public key of recipient achieves recipient anonymity.** Thus, it is not possible for A to obtain the identity of C if disguised public keys are used for encryption.

A uses s' as a key to encrypt the message (m) as follows

$$c' = (m)^{s'}(mod\, n) \tag{12}$$

Using Eq. 11, we can simplify Eq. 12 as

$$c' = (m)^{K_c * r} (mod \, n) \tag{13}$$

A sends c' to B. B applies r^{-1} the inverse of r to c' using the same principle as defined in Eq. 3 (refer Sect. 3.2). Therefore,

$$c = \left(c'\right)^{r^{-1}} (mod \, n) \tag{14}$$

From Eqs. 12 and 14, we get

$$c = (m)^{K_c * r * r^{-1}} (mod \, n) \tag{15}$$

i.e. the undisguised encrypted message(c) produced by B is

$$c = (m)^{K_c} (mod \, n) \tag{16}$$

based on Eqs. 3, 14 and 16, we have

$$unhide \left(aenc \left(m, hide(K_C, r)\right), r^{-1}\right) = aenc \left(m, K_C\right) \tag{17}$$

Thus, we prove statement 2 of Theorem 1. As per the Eq. 17, on application of inverse function on a message encrypted with disguised public key produces a message encrypted with the public key (K_C).

Now since, the recovered message in Eq. 16 is encrypted with the public key of C, B cannot decrypt it with his/her private key. This proves statement 3 of Theorem 1, i.e.: **Message encrypted with the disguised public key, achieves enforced confidentiality of a message**.

6   Conclusion

In summative examinations, the two crucial security requirements are the anonymity and the enforced confidentiality. Anonymity is required to hide the identity of the student and the examiner from each other and the enforced confidentiality is necessary to maintain the secrecy of answers-scripts from the examination authority. In this paper, we propose a dual purpose cryptographic scheme, namely "disguised public key" to achieve anonymity and enforced confidentiality in summative e-examinations. In our approach, examination authority provides students with the disguised public key of the examiner to de-link the identity of the examiner from the student. The proposed mechanism is suitable in general, for achieving anonymity and enforced confidentiality in applications where communication between the sender and recipient is achieved through the intermediate third party.

References

1. Chaum, D.: Blind signatures for untraceable payments. In: Chaum, D., Rivest, R.L., Sherman, A.T. (eds.) Advances in Cryptology, pp. 199–203. Springer, Boston (1983). https://doi.org/10.1007/978-1-4757-0602-4_18
2. Lysyanskaya, A., Ramzan, Z.: Group blind digital signatures: a scalable solution to electronic cash. In: Hirchfeld, R. (ed.) FC 1998. LNCS, vol. 1465, pp. 184–197. Springer, Heidelberg (1998). https://doi.org/10.1007/BFb0055483
3. Danezis, G.: Mix-networks with restricted routes. In: Dingledine, R. (ed.) PET 2003. LNCS, vol. 2760, pp. 1–17. Springer, Heidelberg (2003). https://doi.org/10.1007/978-3-540-40956-4_1
4. Pfitzmann, A., Kohntopp, M.: Anonymity, unobservability, and pseudonymity - a proposal for terminology. In: Federrath, H. (eds.) Designing Privacy Enhancing Technologies. LNCS, vol. 2009, pp. 1–9. Springer, Heidelberg (2001). https://doi.org/10.1007/3-540-44702-4_1
5. Harlen, W.: Teachers' summative practices and assessment for learning-tensions and synergies. Curric. J. **16**(2), 207–223 (2005)
6. Apampa, K.M., Wills, G., Argles, D.: An approach to presence verification in summative e-assessment security. In: 2010 International Conference on Information Society (i-Society), pp. 647–651. IEEE (2010)
7. Gollman, D.: Computer Security. Wiley, London (1999)
8. Pfleeger, C.P., Pfleeger, S.L.: Security in Computing. Prentice Hall Professional Technical Reference (2002)
9. Daemen, J., Rijmen, V.: The Design of Rijndael: AES - The Advanced Encryption Standard. Springer, Heidelberg (2013)
10. Diffie, W., Hellman, M.E.: New directions in cryptography. IEEE Trans. Inf. Theory **22**(6), 644–654 (1976)
11. Kaliyamurthie, K.P., Udayakumar, R., Parameswari, D., Mugunthan, S.N.: Highly secured online voting system over network. Indian J. Sci. Technol. **6**(6), 4831–4836 (2013)
12. Cao, G.: Secure and efficient electronic auction scheme with strong anonymity. JNW **9**(8), 2189–2194 (2014)
13. Miers, I., Garman, C., Green, M., Rubin, A.D.: Zerocoin: anonymous distributed e-cash from bitcoin. In: 2013 IEEE Symposium on Security and Privacy (SP), pp. 397–411. IEEE (2013)
14. Weippl, E.R.: Security in e-Learning, vol. 16. Springer, Heidelberg (2005)
15. Castella-Roca, J., Herrera-Joancomarti, J., Dorca-Josa, A.: A secure e-exam management system. In: The First International Conference on Availability, Reliability and Security, ARES 2006. IEEE (2006)
16. Dreier, J., Giustolisi, R., Kassem, A., Lafourcade, P., Lenzini, G.: A framework for analyzing verifiability in traditional and electronic exams. In: Lopez, J., Wu, Y. (eds.) ISPEC 2015. LNCS, vol. 9065, pp. 514–529. Springer, Cham (2015). https://doi.org/10.1007/978-3-319-17533-1_35
17. Bella, G., Giustolisi, R., Lenzini, G., Ryan, P.Y.A.: A secure exam protocol without trusted parties. In: Federrath, H., Gollmann, D. (eds.) SEC 2015. IAICT, vol. 455, pp. 495–509. Springer, Cham (2015). https://doi.org/10.1007/978-3-319-18467-8_33
18. Huszti, A., Petho, A.: A secure electronic exam system. Publicationes Mathematicae Debrecen **77**(3–4), 299–312 (2010)

19. ElGamal, T.: A public key cryptosystem and a signature scheme based on discrete logarithms. In: Blakley, G.R., Chaum, D. (eds.) CRYPTO 1984. LNCS, vol. 196, pp. 10–18. Springer, Heidelberg (1985). https://doi.org/10.1007/3-540-39568-7_2
20. Golle, P., Jakobsson, M.: Reusable anonymous return channels. In: Proceedings of the 2003 ACM Workshop on Privacy in the Electronic Society, pp. 94–100. ACM (2003)
21. Rivest, R.L., Shamir, A., Adleman, L.: A method for obtaining digital signatures and public-key cryptosystems. Commun. ACM, **21**(2), 120–126 (1978)

Early Diabetes Prediction Using Voting Based Ensemble Learning

Adil Husain[⊠] and Muneeb H. Khan

Department of Computer Engineering, Zakir Husain College of Engineering and Technology,
Aligarh Muslim University, Aligarh, U.P, India
{adilhusain,muneebhkhan}@zhcet.ac.in

Abstract. Machine Learning Techniques are gaining a lot of momentum in constant improvement of disease diagnosis. In this study, we have investigated the discriminative performance of ensemble learning model for diabetes prediction at an early stage. We have used different machine learning models and then ensemble it to improve the overall prediction accuracy. The dataset used is NHANES 2013-14 comprising of 10,172 samples and 54 feature variables for diabetes section. The feature variables used are in the form of questionnaire, a set of questions suggested by NHANES (National Health and Nutrition Examination Survey). An Ensemble model using majority voting technique was developed by combining the unweighted prediction probabilities of different machine learning models. Also, the model is evaluated and validated for real user input data for user friendliness. The overall performance was improved by Ensemble Model and had an AUC (Area under Curve) of 0.75 indicating high performance.

Keywords: Machine learning · Ensemble model · Voting · AUC

1 Introduction

Today, around 415 million people have diabetes around the world [1]. In 2015, about 4.5 million people died due to diabetes around the world. In medical sciences, diabetes diagnosis is responsible for other diseases such as heart failure, coronary angioplasty etc. due to chronic vascular complications [1]. It is difficult to understand the exact diagnosis at an early stage by clinical examination and patient records [2].

Predicting the onset of diabetes at early stage is a complex problem as it is a lifestyle disease and requires intervention of self-assessment prevention at every step. There is a need of machine learning based decision making tool that focuses on learning the trained samples of various age groups and validate it on the real input data to assess the diabetes risk. The potential gains of early diabetes prediction include prolonged quality life, reduced health cost [3]. There is a limited knowledge of building relationship between different features that initiates the diabetes risk. The machine learning predictive model aims to predict the various correlated features and learning is done based on the labels fed by experts. The data collected in hospitals is large and instead of analyzing, this machine learning based health tool identifies the patterns, learn it and predicts the onset in an efficient and cost-effective manner.

© Springer Nature Singapore Pte Ltd. 2018
M. Singh et al. (Eds.): ICACDS 2018, CCIS 905, pp. 95–103, 2018.
https://doi.org/10.1007/978-981-13-1810-8_10

The aim of the paper is to predict diabetes at an early stage using voting based ensemble learning. This is a binary classification problem which predicts the class labels like Diabetic or Non-Diabetic and outputs a risk probability of any unseen sample over a trained ensemble learning model. The class label diabetic includes both diagnosed and undiagnosed. The risk probability greater than or equal to 0.5 comes in diabetic class and less than 0.5 comes in non-diabetic class.

The paper is organized as follows- Sect. 2 will be a description of related work. Then, Sect. 3 will describe the proposed work and methodology. In addition, there will be a description of dataset and the learning steps along with evaluation and validation. In Sect. 4, results will be presented that describe the comparative analysis of the models.

2   Related Work

Alghamdi et al. [1] have developed an Ensembling-based predictive model for Henry Ford Exercise Testing Project. The study used data of 32,555 patients and 62 attributes. The combined decision tree methods (Random Forest, Naïve Bayes Tree, LMT) improve the prediction accuracy considering a cardio respiratory fitness data and a follow-up of 5 years. *Semerdjian et al.* [4] have presented an ensemble model to predict the onset of type II diabetes. They have used NHANES 1999-2004 dataset. An ensemble model using five classification algorithms was developed using 16 features indicating overall high performance. *Yu et al.* [5] have presented a useful approach based on Support Vector Machine (SVM) techniques to classify persons with and without diabetes. They have also used NHANES 1999-2004 dataset.

Vijayan et al. [6] proposed a decision support system for predicting diabetes that uses AdaBoost algorithm along with Decision Stump as base classifier for classification. *Sanakal, et al.* [7] presented a diagnostic FCM (Fuzzy c-means algorithm) and SVM using SMO(Sequential Minimal Optimization) and investigated that the technique is useful in diagnosis of diabetes disease. *Anand, et al.* [8] presented a novel approach to Pima Indian diabetes data diagnosis using PCA (principle component analysis) and HONN (Higher Order Neural Network). *Meng et al.* [9] uses three machine learning models(decision tree, artificial neural network and logistic regression)for diabetes and pre-diabetes prediction. *Radha, et al.* [10] have developed an application using five classification techniques (SVM, C4.5, K-NN, PLR(Penalized Logistic Regression), and BLR(Binary Logistic Regression)) to predict the diabetes. They showed that using, these five techniques BLR has the lowest computing time with 75% accuracy and error rate of 0.27.

3   Proposed Work and Methodology

The previous work, although gave predictions but is not user friendly and this was done on the NHANES 1999-2004, PIMA and other datasets. The proposed work focuses on learning in NHANES 2013-14 dataset, offering good predictions, validating in real-time user data, and thus provides a good user friendly environment to self-assess the diabetes risk at an early stage.

Ensemble Learning Model
In this paper, the four machine learning models that are used in diabetes prediction are Logistic Regression, K-Nearest Neighbor, Random Forests, and Gradient Boosting. Other Models are excluded due to training time overhead and over fitting/under fitting. Each trained model outputs a probability p. The ensemble model is fed by probabilities of each models, calculates the un-weighted average probability p [4], and thus outputs a class label based on average probability (risk probability) as shown in Fig. 1.

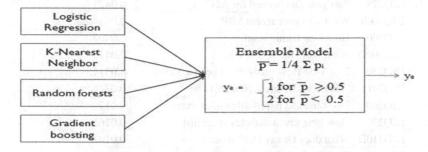

Fig. 1. Schematic diagram of ensemble learning model

There is also a need of voting technique for calibration of Ensemble Model. **Voting** is an aggregating technique that combines the results of the multiple machine learning models. There are two types of voting- Majority Voting and Weighted Voting. Majority Voting is independent of parameter tuning until the models have been trained while Weighted voting require weights of votes for different models [11]. In this paper, the voting technique used is Majority Voting.

From Fig. 1, y_e is the class label classifying Diabetic vs. Non-Diabetic and p is the risk probability which describe the overall risk of diabetes in future. The decision boundary is 0.5. The class labels are 1 for Diabetic and 2 for Non-Diabetic.

Data Preprocessing
National Health and Nutrition Examination Survey (NHANES) is an on-going cross-sectional sample survey of U.S population where information is collected by a set of questions suggested by doctors or nutritionals. The target age group is 1–150 years old. This dataset is a questionnaire where each questions have certain labels of a particular range. NHANES 2013-14 diabetes dataset consists of 10,172 samples and 54 feature variables [15]. NHANES dataset have some missing values that are imputed with most common labels of each column. The categorical values if any must be transformed into numeric values.

Feature Selection
The feature variables are too large for this high dimensional dataset. With presence of large features, learning model over fits and thus overall performance is degraded. For reducing dimensionality, feature selection is the most important step as selecting subset of features not only improves performance but also reduces cost of computation [12].

Table 1 below lists all the 24 feature variables selected on the basis of feature importance scores in descending order.

Table 1. Feature importance score based on random forest classifier

Codes	Feature name	Feature score
DID260	How often check blood for glucose/sugar	0.4671
DID330	What does Dr say LDL should be	0.1221
DIQ275	Past year Dr checked for A1C	0.0823
DIQ300S	What was your recent SBP	0.0637
DID060	How long taking insulin	0.0497
DIQ300D	What was your recent DBP	0.0479
DID250	Past Year How many times seen a doctor	0.0314
DIQ291	What does Dr say A1C should be	0.0226
DIQ360	Last time had pupils dilated for exam	0.0179
DIQ230	How long saw a diabetes specialist	0.0166
DID310D	What does Dr say DBP should be	0.0147
DIQ070	Take Diabetic Pills to lower blood sugar	0.0139
DID310S	What does Dr say SBP should be	0.0139
DIQ260U	Unit of measure (day/week/month/year)	0.0142
DIQ280	What was your last A1C level	0.0104
DID320	What was most recent LDL number	0.0078
DIQ240	Is there one Dr you see for diabetes	0.0025
DIQ060U	Unit of Measure	0.0024
DIQ050	Taking Insulin Now	0.0018
DIQ080	Diabetes affected eyes/had retinopathy	0.0016
DIQ341	Past year times Dr check feet for sores	0.0015
DID350	How often do you check your feet	0.0013
DIQ350U	Unit of measure (day/week/month/year)	0.0011

Model Generation

In order to prevent over fitting, we train the machine learning algorithm on a set consisting of 80% of the data, and test it on another set consisting of 20% of the data. Hyper-parameter tuning is also done to optimize the best candidate sets for learning. It defines a **grid of parameters** that will be **searched** using K-fold cross-validation. First, the dataset is separated into K parts called folds, and all the folds have instances of equal size. Except one fold for testing, the training process is applied on K - 1 folds [13]. In this paper, 10-fold cross-validation is used, with 2 candidates requiring total 20 fits for Logistic Regression, Random Forest, KNN models and 4 candidates requiring total 40 fits for Gradient Boosting model.

Model Evaluation

The model evaluation is done on the test dataset that are unseen samples and are not learned by the model. First, of all, we find the class label and risk probability of all unseen samples in test set and then compute the mean error rate between the predicted and actual values. Then, we compute the True Positive, False Positive, True Negative, and False Negative. Using these, we calculate the precision, recall, F1-score, and accuracy. Finally, we plot the ROC (Receiver Operating Characteristics Curve), which is a plot against true positive and false positive while separating the default decision boundary, 0.5. Finally, we have computed the AUC (Area under curve) score, which indicates the overall performance of model.

Model Validation

Until now, the ensemble model gave the reasonable predictions and computes the class labels and risk probability of all the un-trained samples of test dataset. These samples belong to the original NHANES dataset and there is a need of user to use the model and predict their class label and risk probability. For this, user input data labels into the comma separated file based on certain ranges and values in the feature space. Then, the comma separated file is read and then the trained ensemble model predicts the class label and risk probability. This is a validation approach to check how the trained ensemble model actually find out correct class label with relevant and relatable risk probability. All modeling was done in scikit-learn, a python-based machine learning toolkit for efficient and effective data analysis [14].

4 Results and Discussion

Table 2 below lists all the True Positives, False Positives, True Negatives, False Negatives and Mean error (error between predicted and actual samples) in which the main goal is minimize the false positive rate in order to get good evaluation.

Table 2. TP/FP/TN/FN/ME model metrics

Model	True positives	False positives	True negatives	False negatives	Mean error
Logistic regression	34	10	1910	81	0.044
K-Nearest neighbor	44	8	1912	71	0.039
Gradient boosting	43	9	1911	72	0.039
Random forests	41	7	1913	74	0.038
Ensemble	42	9	1911	73	0.040

Table 3 below lists all the performance metrics such as Precision, Recall, Accuracy, F1-Score and AUC (Area under ROC curve). Except accuracy, which don't have significant effect of class imbalance; Precision, Recall, and F1-score has been calculated based on weighted averaging by support (the no. of true instances of each label).

Table 3. Model Metrics using Weighted Averaging

Model	AUC	Precision	Recall	Accuracy	F1-Score
Logistic regression	0.71	0.949	0.955	0.955	0.945
K-Nearest neighbor	0.74	0.958	0.961	0.961	0.954
Gradient boosting	0.74	0.956	0.960	0.960	0.953
Random forests	0.73	0.957	0.960	0.960	0.952
Ensemble	0.75	0.955	0.960	0.960	0.952

ROC Curve Snapshots

ROC (Receiver Operating Characteristics) curve can be used to select a threshold for a classifier which maximizes the true positives, while minimizing the false positives. The most widely-used measure is the area under the curve (AUC).

From Fig. 2, ROC curve for Logistic Regression, the curve follows towards the y-axis and at end deviates towards the decision boundary and ROC curve for KNearest-Neighbor, the curve follows towards the y-axis and at end follows towards decision boundary.

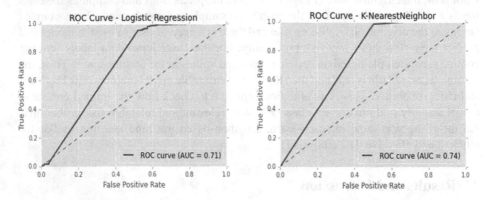

Fig. 2. ROC curve for logistic regression and KNearestNeighbor

From Fig. 3, ROC curve for Random Forest, the curve follows towards the y-axis and at end deviates more abruptly towards the decision boundary and ROC curve for Gradient Boosting, the curve follows towards the y-axis and at end deviate but not abruptly towards the decision boundary.

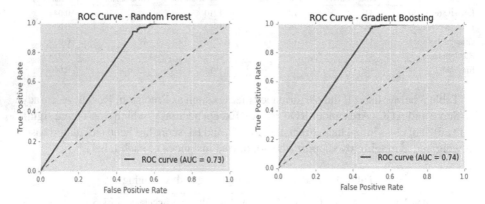

Fig. 3. ROC curve for random forest and gradient boosting

From Fig. 4, ROC curve for Ensemble Model, the curve follows towards the y-axis and at end deviates slightly and then follow towards decision boundary and the comparative ROC curve of all 4 models and ensemble and it shows that AUC of Ensemble

Classifier is best among all other four models. So the overall discriminative performance of Ensemble Model is very good in comparison to other four models.

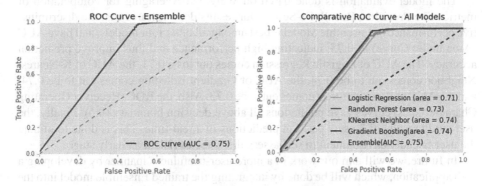

Fig. 4. ROC curve for ensemble and all models

User Study Results (Validation)
A user study is conducted in which user input the 24 feature labels of various questions related to diabetes prediction. All the feature labels are stored in comma separated file, and then proposed system predicts the class label and risk probability of user in real time. A total of 7 users input the feature variables and check their class label and risk probability, which they are quite satisfied about it as shown in Table 4.

Table 4. User-Input Validation of 7 users

S.No	Class	Probability
1	Diabetic	0.548
2	Non-Diabetic	0.122
3	Non-Diabetic	0.389
4	Non-Diabetic	0.064
5	Non-Diabetic	0.204
6	Non-Diabetic	0.125
7	Non-Diabetic	0.349

5   Conclusion and Future Work

In this paper, we have designed and implemented a Early diabetes Prediction System using voting based Ensemble learning. We have trained the 4 machine learning models (logistic Regression, KNearest Neighbor, Random Forest, and Gradient Boosting) on 80% data, optimize the candidate sets using 10-fold cross validation, test them on 20% remaining data, and finally perform Ensemble Learning upon them using soft voting technique. Once trained, we have performed model evaluation on the test set of NHANES dataset and finally we have performed a user study, a validation step to input real time data labels of user and check whether it classifies a target person into Diabetic or Non-Diabetic Class and what will be the associated risk probability of diabetes in future.

The model evaluation is done based on Weighted Averaging for computation of metrics like Precision, Recall, F1-Score. Our results demonstrated that the discriminative performance of Ensemble Model is best among all other four models, and have AUC (Area under Curve) of 0.75, indicating high performance and thus improve prediction accuracy. The AUC of Logistic Regression comes out to be 0.71, the AUC of K-Nearest Neighbor comes out to be 0.74, the AUC of Gradient Boosting comes out to be 0.74, and the AUC of Random forest comes out to be 0.73. Also, the ROC (Receiver Operating Characteristics) curves gave predictions all above decision boundary (0.5). Finally, the user study results of 7 users perform predictions in a real-time. This is done to initiate the user friendly environment to self-assess the diabetes risk at an early stage.

In future, we will aim our work in a more user-usefulness manner by developing a web application, which will be done by integrating the trained Ensemble model into the python flask framework. Also, we will do model evaluation on another diabetes dataset to check the model performance. Finally, machine learning model that undergo high training time overhead, under fitting/over fitting will need sampling to account a class balance giving reasonable predictions.

References

1. Alghamdi, M., Al-mallah, M., Keteyian, S., Brawner, C., Ehrman, J., Sakr, S.: Predicting diabetes mellitus using SMOTE and ensemble machine learning approach: The Henry Ford Exercise Testing (FIT) project. PLoS ONE **12**(7), e0179805 (2017). https://doi.org/10.1371/journal.pone.0179805
2. Fatima, M., Pasha, M.: Survey of machine learning algorithms for disease diagnostic. J. Intell. Learn. Syst. Appl. **9**, 1–16 (2017). https://doi.org/10.4236/jilsa.2017.91001
3. Kavakiotis, L., Tsave, O., Salifoglou, A., Maglaveras, N., Vlahavas, L., Chouvarda, L.: Machine learning and data mining methods in diabetes research. Comput. Struct. Biotechnol. J. **15**, 104–116 (2017)
4. Semerdjian, J., Frank, S.: An Ensemble Classifier for predicting the onset of Type-II Diabetes. Cornell University Library. arXiv:1708.07480v1*[stat.ML]* 24 August 2017 (2017)
5. Yu, W., Liu, T., Valdez, R., Gwinn, M., Khoury, M.J.: Application of support vector machine modelling for prediction of common diseases: the case of diabetes and prediabetes. BMC Med. Inform. Decis. Mak. **10**, 16 (2010)
6. Vijayan, V., Ravikumar, A.: Study of data mining algorithms for prediction and diagnosis of diabetes mellitus. Int. J. Comput. Appl. (0975 – 8887) **95**(17), 12–16 (2014)
7. Sanakal, R., Jayakumari, T.: Prognosis of diabetes using data mining approach-fuzzy C means clustering and support vector machine. Int. J. Comput. Trends Technol. (IJCTT) **11**(2), 94–98 (2014)
8. Anand, R., Singh Kirar, V.P., Burse, K.: K-fold cross validation and classification accuracy of PIMA Indian diabetes data set using higher order neural network and PCA. Int. J. Soft Comput. Eng. (IJSCE) **2**(6) (2013). ISSN: 2231-2307
9. Meng, X.H., Huang, Y.X., Rao, D.P., Zhang, Q., Liu, Q.: Comparison of three data mining models for predicting diabetes or prediabetes by risk factors. Kaohsiung J. Med. Sci. **29**(2), 93–99 (2013). https://doi.org/10.1016/j.kjms.2012.08.016

10. Radha, P.: Srinivasan Dr., B.: Predicting diabetes by co sequencing the various data mining classification techniques. IJISET Int. J. Innov. Sci. Eng. Technol. **1**(6), 334–339 (2014)
11. Zhang, Y., Zhang, H., Cai, J., Yang, B.: A weighted voting classifier based on differential evolution. In: Abstract and Applied Analysis, vol. 2014. Hindawi Publishing Corporation (2014)
12. Blum, A.L., Langley, P.: Selection of relevant features and examples in machine learning. Artif. Intell. **97**(1), 245–271 (1997). https://doi.org/10.1016/S0004-3702(97)00063-5
13. Bengio, Y., Grandvalet, Y.: No unbiased estimator of the variance of k-fold cross-validation. J. Mach. Learn. Res. **5**(Sep), 1089–1105 (2004)
14. Sci-Kit Learn. Machine learning in python. http://scikit-learn.org/. Accessed 02 Dec 2017
15. NHANES Dataset. https://www.cdc.gov/nchs/nhanes/nhanes_questionnaires.htm. Accessed 02 Dec 2017

A System that Performs Data Distribution and Manages Frequent Itemsets Generation of Incremental Data in a Distributed Environment

Vinaya Sawant[1(✉)] and Ketan Shah[2]

[1] Dwarkadas J. Sanghvi College of Engineering, Mumbai, India
vinaya.sawant@djsce.ac.in
[2] MPSTME, Mumbai, India
KetanShah@nmims.edu

Abstract. Association rule mining (ARM) algorithms are typically developed to work on the data that is centralized and non-dynamic. When data is dynamic, the usage of input/output (I/O) resources in a centralized approach waste computational costs and they impose excessive communication overhead when data is distributed. When large amount of data is available, there is a need to perform data distribution using fragmentation techniques in a faster and inevitable manner so that overhead of manually performing fragmentation can be reduced. Also, there is a need of effective implementation of incremental data mining methods for ensuring system scalability and facilitating knowledge discovery when data is dynamic and distributed. In this paper, two issues are addressed; one is automatic generation of horizontal fragments and thus making data distribution as a part of Distributed ARM and another in the perspective of frequent itemsets generation on incremental data. The significance of distributed approach is that it generates local models of frequent itemsets from each node connected in a distributed environment and also generates global model aggregating all the local models.

Keywords: Distributed Data Mining · Incremental mining
Distributed databases · Horizontal fragmentation

1 Introduction

Association Rules are used to describe the set of strong rules using the measure of interestingness from the set of transactions data or retail basket. One of the key practices of ARM is Market Basket Analysis which is used by retailers to find associations between products that are bought together in a given set of transactions. It allows retailers to identify relations between the products that people buy. The very popular algorithm used for generating association rules is Apriori Algorithm which makes use of two measures. One measure is support threshold for finding the frequent itemsets and another measure is confidence threshold for finding the strong association rules between the set of items.

The process of data mining can be categorized as centralized and distributed based on the location of data. The data in a centralized data mining process is located on a

M. Singh et al. (Eds.): ICACDS 2018, CCIS 905, pp. 104–113, 2018.
https://doi.org/10.1007/978-981-13-1810-8_11

single node whereas data in a distributed process is located into multiple nodes. The distributed process makes use of shared-nothing architecture, where the data is owned by each node separately or an enormous amount of data may be distributed into multiple data nodes. The paper proposes a system that efficiently performs data distribution using horizontal fragmentation technique using web based framework and also generate frequent itemsets from the transactional data located in a distributed environment with the objective of minimizing execution time and communication overhead and to handle incremental data effectively [3, 4].

As new set of transactions are inserted or deleted from dataset, the older association rules may no longer be useful and new interesting rules could appear in the newly added dataset. The process of generating new association rules by combining old association rules and generating new rules based on the updated part of the dataset is called incremental association rules. In fact, some lager itemsets in the old database could remain large in the new database, for these large itemsets, it is unnecessary to recompute their support count from the scratch, since we already have their support in the old database. In this case, much computation time can be saved [5, 7].

2   Related Work

The literature survey involves study of different algorithms that are used for Distributed Association Rule Mining (DARM). The main working of DARM algorithms is to perform local analysis at local nodes and then perform global analysis using knowledge integration techniques. Various algorithms such as Count Distribution Algorithm (CDA) [10], Fast Data Mining Algorithm (FDM) [9] and Optimized Distributed Association Mining (ODAM) [8] related to DARM are proposed in the literature where the major focus is on generation of frequent itemsets with minimum execution time and reduced communication cost. Performance evaluation of mentioned algorithms is tested in the distributed environment on the datasets described in Sect. 5 and the work is published in paper [2]. The implementation details and experimental results of above mentioned algorithms are presented and described in [2]. The impact of message exchange size in a distributed environment of current DARM algorithms that can affect the communication costs in a distributed environment is also highlighted in [2]. The results show that the ODAM performs better than CDA and FDM and hence considered as the base algorithm for the proposed work mentioned here.

The research work can be further improved by combining the concept of distributed association rule mining with incremental mining. The work of ODAM can be extended to efficiently execute the incremental data in a distributed environment [1]. The proposed approach not only involves improvement of DARM architecture to handle local data, global data and incremental data but also generates horizontal fragments using web based framework. The incremental algorithm Fast Update Algorithm (FUP) [9] was reviewed to handle the incremental data. By combining above mentioned concepts, the algorithm Incremental Optimized Distributed Association Mining (IODAM) is proposed that effectively handles incremental data in a distributed environment and presented in paper [1].

3 Proposed Architecture

The below Fig. 1 represents the proposed architecture with different modules. The architecture combines the concept of distributed association rule mining with incremental mining. The dataset is horizontally fragmented and distributed among the nodes in a distributed environment. The data is local data and incremental data. The incremental data are the records that are added in the existing local dataset.

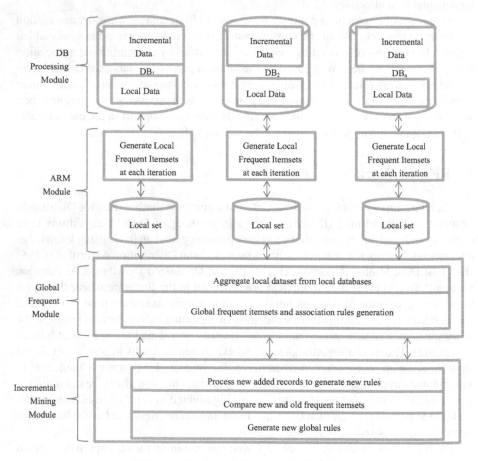

Fig. 1. Proposed architecture for DARM

As many organizations are moving towards distributed databases, so any change in one of the dataset may change local and global rules. An incremental approach for maintaining association rules in a distributed environment is proposed. The Apriori algorithm is used to generate the frequent itemsets and association rules. The proposed approach is based on Apriori due to its parallel nature.

The main aim of the proposed system is to work on own local data and at the same time, benefit from the data that is available at other data sites without transferring or directly accessing that data. Also, if the data is growing at constant rate, then there is a need to generate the solution that will handle the incremental data and local data to generate association rules. As new data is being added to existing ones, there is a need to accurately reflect the varying consequences in the association rules.

To address the above challenges, an architecture and functional modules of the system are proposed over which ODAM can be implemented using the concept of incremental mining. This new approach will work on base dataset as well as on incremental dataset.

4   Functional Modules of Proposed System

The following Fig. 2 represents the functional modules used for the proposed system. The system involves many steps to be performed for complete execution of the process form data preprocessing that involves representing transactions using sparse matrix, and then performing data distribution to generate horizontal fragments and allocate to the nodes in the distributed environment. Further, frequent itemsets and association rules generation on base data and incremental data is done to obtain the desired result.

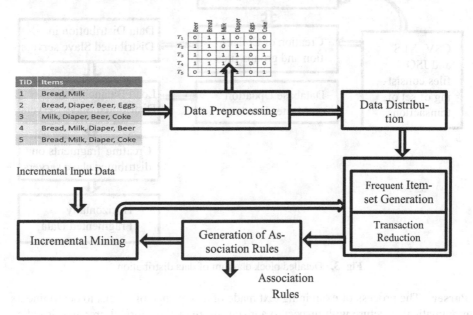

Fig. 2. Functional modules of proposed system

4.1   Data Preprocessing

In data preprocessing module, the dataset containing the transactions done at the shopping market or groceries shops are converted into sparse binary matrix. For market-basket analysis, the transactions are collection of items that are bought together by the customers from the grocery shop. The data preprocessing involves reading text/csv files consisting of the collection of transactions maintaining the list of items purchased by the customers, determining the total number of items across all the transactions given in a file, converting the set of transactions read from a file to a sparse matrix representation, filling the missing or null values in the transaction set with zeros in sparse matrix and finally exporting the sparse matrix to text/csv file to be used for further processing.

4.2   Data Distribution

The processed data retrieved from the previous steps is now ready for fragmentation. The input database is distributed among nodes to create a distributed environment. This block implements the concept of horizontal fragmentation where database is divided into subset of rows. A distributed database is a collection of multiple interconnected databases, which are spread physically across various locations that communicate via a computer network. The following figure Fig. 3 represents the detailed blocks involved in data distribution.

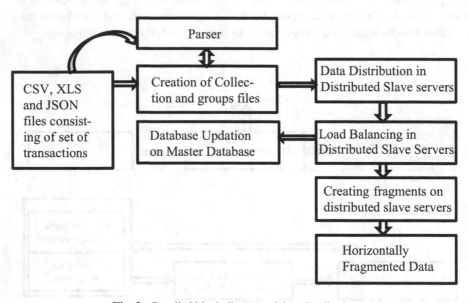

Fig. 3.   Detailed block diagram of data distribution

Parser.   The process of examining text made of a sequence of tokens to determine its grammatical structure with respect to a given (more or less) formal grammar is called parsing. The parser then builds a data structure based on the tokens. Here, the input file given for data distribution to create horizontal fragments can be in the form of XLS, CSV, XML and JSON (JavaScript Object Notation) formats. CSV stands for "comma-separated values," and CSV files are simplified spreadsheets stored as plaintext files. JSON is a lightweight data-interchange format. It is easy for humans to read and JSON files are easy for machines to parse and generate. The file formats with xls, csv and xml are parsed into JSON format for further processing in the next modules.

Creation of Collections and User Groups. A **collection** is analogous to a table of an RDBMS. A collection may store documents those who are not same in structure. The user can see the collections created and those that are shared with him. The user can create a new collection and add new users to it. It can also assign read write permissions to the other users and can retrieve the created collections. The user can also modify his creations. All the created collections and the users' information is stored in the database.

Data Distribution in Distributed Slave Servers. The data uploaded by the collection and group files are then distributed among the distributed slave servers depending upon the size of data fragments.

Load Balancer in Distributed Slave Servers. The functionality of load balancing to distribute work load across multiple servers. The load balancing in distributed slave servers is achieved by balancing the fragments in all the nodes depending upon the number of fragments created from the input collection size.

Creation of Horizontal Fragments. The entire data is divided into equal size horizontal fragments at different servers. The entire data can then be retrieved via the retrieval page on entering the collection details.

4.3 Frequent Itemsets Generation

This module is implemented using the Apriori Algorithm in the distributed environment. Initially, frequent itemsets are generated at each pass and at each node based on the minimum support threshold. This is called local pruning. The local frequent itemsets at each node is uploaded to global server for calculating global frequent itemsets. These global frequent itemsets are then used by all the nodes for generating candidate itemsets for next pass [6].

Transaction Reduction. The main aim of this module is to reduce the number of transaction scans at each local node that will significantly reduce the execution time in a distributed environment. This module deletes those transactions from the transaction file which contains infrequent itemsets for all passes thus reducing the transaction size and making the algorithm memory efficient.

4.4 Incremental Mining

This module processes the incremental data that are arriving after the association rules on base dataset are generated. This module follows the incremental mining algorithm in a distributed environment. The new set of transactions is given as an input at each client node. The output of previous transactions is combined with the new set of transactions to generate the revised set of association rules [9, 10]. This module is the one of the contribution to the existing DARM algorithms and the related work and few experiments using new algorithm IODAM is available in [1].

5 Experiments

This section describes the experimental setup, datasets and experiments used for the complete system to execute in a distributed environment. The major focus of the experiments is on data distribution and incremental mining in distributed environment.

5.1 Experiment Setup

The system is implemented on one to three nodes and a server. The configuration of each workstation on the network was an Intel Core i3 CPU @2.90 GHz, 4 GB RAM, 64-bit OS and Windows 8.1 Pro One 400 model. Remote Method Invocation Mechanism (RMI) is used for communications between the nodes in the network for incremental mining algorithm and for data distribution, web based framework was designed and developed to generate horizontal fragments.

5.2 Datasets Used

The datasets from UCI Machine Learning Repository [4] was used for testing the performance of ODAM and Proposed Algorithm in a distributed environment. The following are the different datasets used for testing the results.

Tic-Tac-Toe Dataset	DS (8*10000)	Grocery
– 9 items	– 8 items	– 60 items
– 958 transactions	– 10000 transactions	– 300000 transactions

5.3 Experiment 1: Correctness Measure of Data Distribution

The data distribution modules read the dataset and perform horizontal fragmentation by partitioning the dataset according to rows and then assigning the partitions to active nodes in the distributed environment. The correctness measure such as completeness, reconstruction and disjointness of data fragmentation and allocation in distributed environment were accurately satisfied. The following figures Figs. 4, 5 and 6 represents the steps that are required to generate horizontal fragments using proposed web based framework.

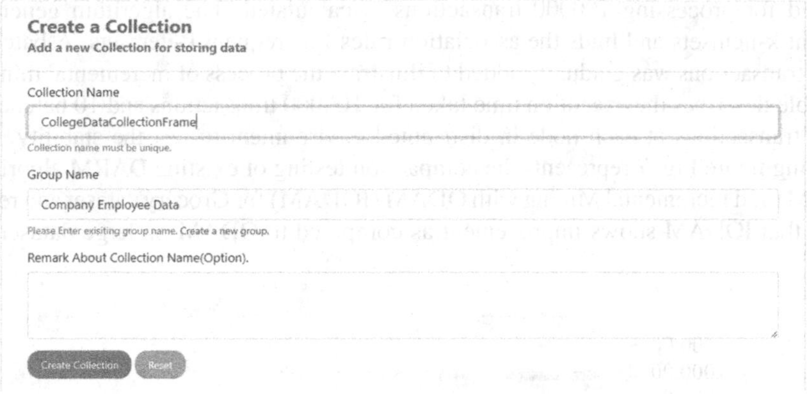

Create a Collection
Add a new Collection for storing data

Collection Name

CollegeDataCollectionFrame

Collection name must be unique.

Group Name

Company Employee Data

Please Enter exisiting group name. Create a new group.

Remark About Collection Name(Option).

Create Collection   Reset

Fig. 4. Step 1 to create a Collection

Insert Data.
Insert a data into a new Collection.
Collection Name

CollegeDataCollection_3

Create a new collections.

Choose File EmployeeData.xlsx

Submit

Fig. 5. Step 2 to insert the Data

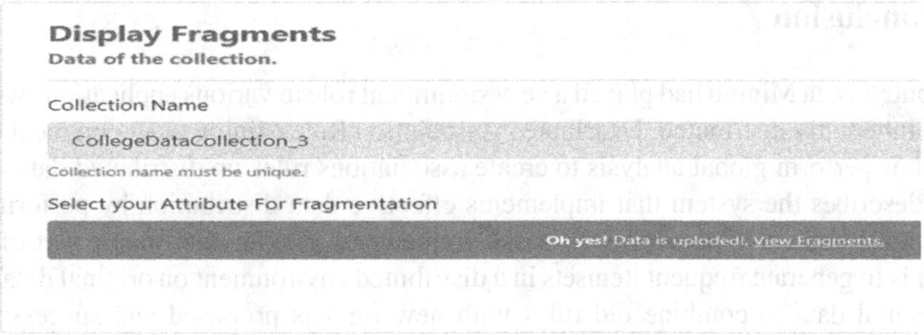

Display Fragments
Data of the collection.

Collection Name

CollegeDataCollection_3

Collection name must be unique.

Select your Attribute For Fragmentation

Oh yes! Data is uploded!, View Fragments.

Fig. 6. Step 3 to display the fragments

5.4 Experiment 2: Performance of Incremental Mining in Distributed Environment

For the given experiment, a grocery dataset consisting of 300000 transactions made by customers at various places were considered. This dataset was horizontally fragmented into equal fragments and distributed on 3 different nodes. Initially, execution time required for processing 100000 transactions is calculated. The algorithm generates frequent k-itemsets and finds the association rules for frequent k-itemsets. A batch of 10000 transactions was gradually added to illustrate the process of incremental mining. The table describes the execution time taken for 100000 transactions and 10 batches of 10000 transactions at each node in distributed environment to test the stability. The following figure Fig. 7 represents the comparison testing of existing DARM algorithm (ODAM) and Incremental Mining with ODAM (IODAM) for Grocery dataset and result shows that IODAM shows improvement as compared to ODAM on large datasets as well.

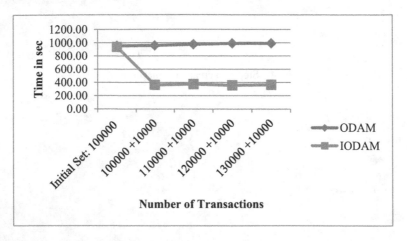

Fig. 7. Comparison of ODAM and IODAM algorithms for Grocery Dataset

6   Conclusion

Distributed Data Mining had played a very significant role in various applications where data is inherently distributed. Distributed Association Rule Mining works on local data as well as perform global analysis to create associations rules on distributed data. The paper describes the system that implements effective data distribution by performing horizontal fragmentation using web based framework. The another major part of the system is to generate frequent itemsets in a distributed environment on original data and incremental data to combine old rules with new ones is proposed and successfully implemented and compared with the existing algorithm with respect to execution time.

References

1. Sawant, V., Shah, K.: An incremental mining with ODAM (IODAM). Presented at 2017 International Conference on Intelligent Computing, Instrumentation and Control Technologies (ICICICT). IEEE Explore (2017)
2. Sawant, V., Shah, K.: Performance evaluation of distributed association rule mining algorithms. Procedia Comput. Sci. **79**, 127–134 (2016)

3. Xu, L., Zhang, Y.: A novel parallel algorithm for frequent itemset mining of incremental dataset. In: International Conference on Information Science and Control Engineering. IEEE (2015)
4. Bache, K., Lichman, M.: UCI Machine Learning Repository. University of California, School of Information and Computer Science, Irvine, CA (2013). http://archive.ics.uci.edu/ml
5. Sreedevil, M., Vijay Kumar, G., Reddy, L.S.S.: Parallel and distributed approach for incremental closed regular pattern mining. IEEE (2014)
6. Darwish, M., Elgohery, R., Badr, N., Faheem, H.: Association rules mining based on distributed databases. In: International Conference on Computer Science and Network Technology (2013)
7. Chandraker, T., Sao, N.: Incremental mining on association rules. Res. Inven. Int. J. Eng. Sci. 1(11), 31–33 (2012). ISBN 2319-6483. ISSN 2278-4721
8. Ashrafi, M., Taniar, D., Smith, K.: ODAM: an optimized distributed association rule mining. IEEE Distrib. Syst. Online 5(3) (2004). https://doi.org/10.1109/MDSO.2004.1285877
9. Cheung, D., Han, J., Ng, V., Fu, A., Fu, Y.: A fast-distributed algorithm for mining association rules. In: Fourth International Conference on Parallel and Distributed Information Systems (1996)
10. Agrawal, R., Shafer, J.: Parallel mining of association rules. IEEE Trans. Knowl. Data Eng. 8(6), 962–969 (1996)

Assessing Autonomic Level for Self-managed Systems – FAHP Based Approach

Arun Sharma[1(✉)], Deepika Sharma[1], and Mayank Singh[2]

[1] Department of Information Technology, Indira Gandhi Delhi Technical University for Women, Delhi, India
arunsharma@igdtuw.ac.in, sharmadeepika817@gmail.com
[2] University of KwaZulu-Natal, Durban 4041, South Africa
dr.mayank.singh@ieee.org

Abstract. Autonomic computing when first introduced, there was apprehension whether it would become a reality. It is a concept that merges many fields of computing area to give a system which is easily manageable and thus reduce the complexities faced by IT industry today. The term Autonomic Level gives the quantification measurement about the autonomic features, a system has. This paper starts by brief introduction to autonomic systems. It proposes a framework for assessing the Level of Autonomic features of the system and also presents some of the quality metrics that may be used in future to evaluate the proposed framework. The evaluation section contains the mathematical model of the framework and case study shows the implementation of the model using fuzzy-AHP soft computing technique.

Keywords: Autonomic level · Quality · Self-management · Framework Fuzzy-AHP

1 Introduction

The world of computers has come a long way from first computer ENIAC in 1946 to PC and laptops. But the real challenges were introduced in IT field when Internet came. The growing challenges of IT industry in coming days can be identified as follows: First, complexity that comes with business processes, organizations and resources. It is measured in terms of cost, time, size and probability of fault-occurrence. Second, complexity faced in process of evolving a system which includes design, implementation, testing, evolving, and restructuring. Third, systems management, security management and all others issues related to efficiency and service providing complexities.

All these complexities are adding up to the existing complex architecture of Internet. To handle this ever growing network, we need some new computing strategies. In the past decade, the cost of acquiring systems has fallen drastically. Now days the cost maintaining the human force is approx. equal to the cost of producing and managing that network. As seen in the report published [1], almost 50% of the budget is spent in preventing and recovering the systems from crashes.

© Springer Nature Singapore Pte Ltd. 2018
M. Singh et al. (Eds.): ICACDS 2018, CCIS 905, pp. 114–123, 2018.
https://doi.org/10.1007/978-981-13-1810-8_12

One possible area that has risen to all the above challenges is Autonomic Computing Systems (ACS). Autonomic computing is a concept that merges many fields of computing area to give a system which is easily manageable and thus reduce the complexities faced by IT industry today.

Introduced in 2001 by IBM [2], autonomic computing is a concept that visions the shift of responsibilities from administrators to the systems which are guided by high level policies [3]. These high level policies are defined by administrators. Thus these systems have self-managing properties. There are main four properties that define Autonomic Systems (AS). They are referred to as self - * properties or self – CHOP properties. These are further defined in Sect. 3.

2 Literature Review

We have come a long way from the first mention of this term by Horn [2] in 2001. Since then, industry has integrated some of the autonomous features with the existing software. Kephart et al. [4] have first discussed all the characteristics in detail and given an architecture of AS. Later they had presented the engineering challenges as well as scientific challenges that IT industry will face when developing AS. Salehie et al. [5] has presented a comprehensive study of projects that are developed in academics and industry and the various features they incorporate. It is evident that there is no single such software that is fully autonomic and not all the features are implemented in the existing projects of the industry.

Many survey papers are published which tell us various developments in the field and also the problems that are not been addressed till now. One such survey paper done by Nami et al. [6] presented an overview of autonomic elements architecture and presented the importance of studying the field. Paper provides a through survey on topic and gives a relationship between AC properties and the quality factors that are affected.

Sharma et al. [7] have discussed the generic architecture and have proposed a software life-cycle for developing autonomous systems software. Taking a step further Sahdev et al. [8] proposed an autonomic SDLC model which maps security and privacy in the early requirement and designing phases of the model. According to Chauhan et al. [9] the autonomic systems can be developed efficiently using agile modelling concept. Authors have proposed a generic architecture consisting of life cycle model and Agile Modeling Approach (AMA) because it is flexible.

There have been numerous discussions about the architecture of the autonomic systems. The building blocks for any system are the autonomic elements (AE) [10]. Each AE has two parts: the managed element and the autonomic manager (AM). Another type of architecture defined for AE is "Intelligent Machine Design". [11] Discusses the shortcoming of the IBM proposed architecture and has introduced this new design. It is made of 3 layers: Reaction layer, Routine layer and Reflection layer.

Singh et al. [12] proposed some factors that should be taken care of while judging any autonomic system. Ferreira et al. [15] used the concept of autonomic systems to configure and execute the applications across various clouds. For this purpose, authors proposed and evaluated an autonomic and goal-oriented system with the implementation of self-configuration, self-healing, and context-awareness properties [16].

Dehraj et al. [14] proposed a new software quality model by incorporating autonomicity and trustworthiness factors into the existing ISO 25010 software quality model.

3 Proposed Framework

As the systems become more interconnected and diverse, communication between components become more complex; the administrators find it a difficult task to design and maintain such infrastructure. The AS reduces this hassle by reducing the human part in its own maintenance and routine working. But such AS must also conform to any standards. Based on the ISO 9126 model which is of hierarchical nature, we propose a similar hierarchy for attributes that affect the Autonomic Level of the system. In this framework, first some base attributes are identified that give us 2nd level sub-attributes.

These sub-attributes then are combined to give main four attributes of autonomic system i.e. CHOP properties. Some of the sub-attributes contribute to all the main first level attributes while some sub-attributes under one criterion are independent of other three main attributes. For evaluation purposes only those attributes are considered which affect all the main attributes. These base sub-attributes are defined as follows:

Complexity: Includes the complexity of the autonomic agent, the managed element and the interface. It will also include the size of the autonomic agent software itself. Hence the base values that may be used are:

(a) LOC
(b) Component coupling (tight/loose).

LOC directly affects the complexity while more coupling means greater communication which increases complexity.

Response time: Time taken in start responding to changing conditions. It will also include after the change is identified the time taken to start the adaptation.

Activation time for agent: Time taken by autonomic agent to start the healing process.

Reduction in Failure: It may also be viewed as no. of problems solved. The two base values for this sub-attribute are:

• Pre-errors: Errors those are present before the system is autonomic.
• Post-errors: Errors those are present after the autonomic agent is introduced.

Based on these two parameters, Reduction Failure may be defined as:

Reduction in Failure = Pre Errors − Post Errors

Throughput: It depends on impact of introducing agent in the non- autonomic system. The base values that may be used in evaluation are (a) change in cost (b) change in performance. Further change in cost includes cost of new dedicated resources and change in cost of human labor.

Fault Tolerance: It is related to reliability factor of the system. What is the level of errors that system can handle and still continue to perform close or its ideal or expected behavior will define the fault tolerance factor.

4   Proposed Methodology for Evaluation

Determining autonomic level can be viewed as a multi-criteria decision making problem with much complexity, vagueness and uncertainty (Fig. 1).

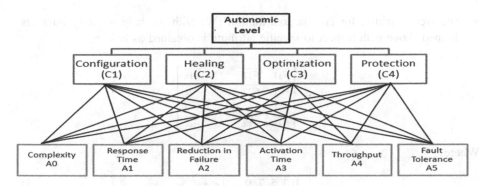

Fig. 1. Hierarchical structure for the problem

4.1   Fuzzy Analytical Hierarchy Process (FAHP)

Analytical Hierarchy Process (AHP) is a well organized decision making process for multiple criteria problems. FAHP can be considered as an advancement on AHP technique. FAHP uses fuzzy triangular membership function to accommodate for uncertainty of decision-maker. To get ranking of choices it uses many methods like geometric mean, least square, fuzzy preference programming etc. Sagar et al. [13] used FAHP approach for ranking of the components to be used in component based software development and found to be an effective approach for ranking problem.

In this paper, we have used fuzzy extent analysis to solve the matrices. For removal of unreliable comparisons, alpha-cut analysis is done on fuzzy performance matrix. The fuzzy triangular numbers are defined in triplet i.e. M (lower, middle, upper) values which are interpreted as per Table 1 below:

- The membership function for obtaining triplet is defined in Eq. (1):

$$
\mu_A(X) = \begin{cases} \frac{(x-a_1)}{(a_2-a_1)}, & a_1 \leq x \leq a_2 \\ \frac{(a_2-x)}{(a_3-a_2)}, & a_2 \leq x \leq a_3 \\ 0, & otherwise \end{cases} \tag{1}
$$

Table 1. Interpretation for Fuzzy Triangular Numbers

Fuzzy number	Triangular fuzzy values (L,M,U)	Interpretation
1	(1,1,1) and (1,1,3)	Equal contribution of i and j attribute
3	(1,3,5)	i contributes slightly more than j
5	(3,5,7)	i contributes strongly more than j
7	(5,7,9)	i contributes very strongly more than j
9	(7,9,9)	i contributes fully more than j
Reciprocals	(1/U, 1/M, 1/L)	If i has less contribution than j

- The weight matrix for criteria contribution (W) with the help of fuzzy numbers defined above with respect to specific attribute is obtained as below:

$$W = \begin{bmatrix} \overline{a_{11}} & \overline{a_{12}} & \cdots & \overline{a_{1k}} \\ \overline{a_{21}} & \overline{a_{22}} & \cdots & \overline{a_{2k}} \\ \cdots & \cdots & \cdots & \cdots \\ \overline{a_{k1}} & \overline{a_{k2}} & \cdots & \overline{a_{kk}} \end{bmatrix} \tag{2}$$

Where,

$$\overline{1}, \overline{3}, \overline{5}, \overline{7}, \overline{9}, \quad l < s, \tag{3}$$

$1, l = s, l, s = 1, 2\ldots k, k = m$ or $n, 1/a_{sl}, l > s.$

- Using Eqs. (1) and (4), fuzzy extent analysis is carried out on (wj) or (xij) as:

$$\left(x_{ij} \right) \text{ or } \left(w_j \right) = \frac{\sum_{s=1}^{k} \overline{a_{ls}}}{\sum_{i=1}^{k} \sum_{s=1}^{k} \overline{a_{ls}}} \tag{4}$$

- The resultant decision matrix (X) and weight matrix (W) are given as below:

$$X = \begin{bmatrix} \overline{x_{11}} & \overline{x_{12}} & \cdots & \overline{x_{1m}} \\ \overline{x_{21}} & \overline{x_{22}} & \cdots & \overline{x_{2m}} \\ \cdots & \cdots & \cdots & \cdots \\ \overline{x_{n1}} & \overline{x_{n2}} & \cdots & \overline{x_{nm}} \end{bmatrix} \tag{5}$$

$$W = \left(w_1, \quad w_2, \quad \ldots, \quad \ldots, \quad w_m \right) \tag{6}$$

- Fuzzy Performance Matrix (Z) is calculated as a product of X and W:

$$Z = (X) \times (W) \tag{7}$$

- Applying alpha-cut analysis we obtain interval performance matrix ($Z\alpha$):

$$Z_\alpha = \begin{bmatrix} ([z_{11l}^{\propto}, \ z_{11r}^{\propto}]) & \cdots & \cdots & ([z_{1ml}^{\propto} & z_{1mr}^{\propto}]) \\ \cdots & \cdots & \cdots & & \cdots \\ \cdots & \cdots & \cdots & & \cdots \\ [z_{n1l}^{\propto} & z_{n1r}^{\propto}] & \cdots & \cdots & [z_{nml}^{\propto} & z_{nmr}^{\propto}] \end{bmatrix}$$

- Hwang and Yoon [17] proposed algorithm for avoiding worst decision outcome by selecting maximum value and minimum value across all the alternatives with respect to each criterion. Hence we get the positive ideal solution $A_\alpha^{\lambda+}$ and the negative ideal solution $A_\alpha^{\lambda-}$ as follows:

$$\begin{cases} A_\alpha^{\lambda+} = \left(Z_{1\alpha}^{\lambda+}, Z_{2\alpha,\cdots,\dots}^{\lambda+}, Z_{m\alpha}^{\lambda+} \right) \\ A_\alpha^{\lambda-} = \left(Z_{1\alpha}^{\lambda-}, Z_{2\alpha,\cdots,\dots}^{\lambda-}, Z_{m\alpha}^{\lambda-} \right) \end{cases} \tag{8}$$

- To calculate degree of similarity between each alternative, the positive ideal solution and the negative ideal solution, vector matching function is applied in Eq. (9) and (10):

$$S_\alpha^{\lambda+} = \frac{A_{i\alpha}^{\lambda} \ A_\alpha^{\lambda+}}{\max \left(A_{i\alpha}^{\lambda}, A_{i\alpha}^{\lambda}, A_\alpha^{\lambda+}, A_\alpha^{\lambda+} \right)} \tag{9}$$

and

$$S_\alpha^{\lambda-} = \frac{A_{i\alpha}^{\lambda} \ A_\alpha^{\lambda-}}{\max \left(A_{i\alpha}^{\lambda}, A_{i\alpha}^{\lambda}, A_\alpha^{\lambda-}, A_\alpha^{\lambda-} \right)} \tag{10}$$

- Finally each alternative is ranked according to its overall performance index calculated by Eq. (11). Higher index value indicates more contribution of the alternative.

$$S_{i\alpha}^{\lambda} = \frac{S_{i\alpha}^{\lambda+}}{S_{i\alpha}^{\lambda+} + S_{i\alpha}^{\lambda-}}, i = 1, 2, \dots, n. \tag{11}$$

4.2 Implementation of Framework

The input matrices are the fuzzy reciprocal judgement matrices for each main attribute as shown below:

$$
C1 = \begin{array}{c|cccccc}
 & A1 & A2 & A3 & A4 & A5 & A6 \\
\hline
A1 & 1 & 1 & 3 & 1/3 & 1 & 1/5 \\
A2 & 1 & 1 & 1/3 & 1 & 1 & 1/3 \\
A3 & 1/3 & 3 & 1 & 1/3 & 1/3 & 1 \\
A4 & 3 & 1 & 3 & 1 & 1 & 3 \\
A5 & 1 & 1 & 3 & 1 & 1 & 1/5 \\
A6 & 5 & 3 & 1 & 1/3 & 5 & 1
\end{array}
$$

$$
C2 = \begin{array}{c|cccccc}
 & A1 & A2 & A3 & A4 & A5 & A6 \\
\hline
A1 & 1 & 1/7 & 1/7 & 1/7 & 1 & 5 \\
A2 & 7 & 1 & 5 & 1 & 5 & 3 \\
A3 & 7 & 1/5 & 1 & 7 & 5 & 3 \\
A4 & 5 & 1 & 1/7 & 1 & 1 & 5 \\
A5 & 1 & 5 & 1/5 & 1 & 1 & 1/5 \\
A6 & 1/5 & 3 & 1/3 & 1/5 & 5 & 1
\end{array}
$$

$$
C3 = \begin{array}{c|cccccc}
 & A1 & A2 & A3 & A4 & A5 & A6 \\
\hline
A1 & 1 & 1/5 & 1/3 & 1/3 & 1/5 & 1/3 \\
A2 & 5 & 1 & 1 & 1/3 & 1/5 & 3 \\
A3 & 3 & 1 & 1 & 1 & 1/5 & 1/5 \\
A4 & 3 & 3 & 1 & 1 & 3 & 5 \\
A5 & 5 & 5 & 5 & 1/3 & 1 & 3 \\
A6 & 3 & 1/3 & 5 & 1/5 & 1/3 & 1
\end{array}
$$

$$
C4 = \begin{array}{c|cccccc}
 & A1 & A2 & A3 & A4 & A5 & A6 \\
\hline
A1 & 1 & 1/7 & 1/3 & 1 & 1/3 & 3 \\
A2 & 7 & 1 & 7 & 1 & 5 & 5 \\
A3 & 3 & 1/7 & 1 & 1/3 & 3 & 5 \\
A4 & 1 & 1 & 3 & 1 & 7 & 5 \\
A5 & 3 & 1/5 & 1/3 & 1/7 & 1 & 1/3 \\
A6 & 1/3 & 1/5 & 1/5 & 1/5 & 3 & 1
\end{array}
$$

The input weight matrix for the main four attributes is:

$$
W = \begin{array}{c|cccc}
 & C1 & C2 & C3 & C4 \\
\hline
C1 & 1 & 5 & 3 & 3 \\
C2 & 1/5 & 1 & 1 & 1/7 \\
C3 & 1/3 & 1 & 1 & 1/3 \\
C4 & 1/3 & 7 & 1/3 & 1
\end{array}
$$

The resultant decision matrix (X) and weight matrix (W) is:

$$X = \begin{bmatrix} (0.039,0.157,0.639) & (0.048,0.116,0.301) & (0.026,0.052,0.104) & (0.032,0.098,0.279) \\ (0.027,0.088,0.392) & (0.086,0.235,0.611) & (0.037,0.121,0.382) & (0.141,0.323,0.772) \\ (0.035,0.136,0.493) & (0.104,0.254,0.592) & (0.027,0.074,0.303) & (0.061,0.161,0.387) \\ (0.048,0.217,0.863) & (0.049,0.127,0.376) & (0.089,0.285,0.824) & (0.117,0.289,0.715) \\ (0.036,0.149,0.627) & (0.047,0.116,0.311) & (0.115,0.314,0.798) & (0.021,0.047,0.14) \\ (0.072,0.249,0.829) & (0.055,0.149,0.363) & (0.064,0.151,0.356) & (0.027,0.078,0.202) \end{bmatrix}$$

$$W = \begin{bmatrix} (0.141,0.423,1.089) \\ (0.037,0.082,0.27) \\ (0.059,0.188,0.564) \\ (0.151,0.305,0.645) \end{bmatrix}$$

The fuzzy performance matrix (Z) is:

$$Z = \begin{bmatrix} (0.005,0.066,0.696) & (0.002,0.009,0.081) & (0.001,0.009,0.058) & (0.005,0.0306,0.181) \\ (0.003,0.037,0.427) & (0.003,0.019,0.165) & (0.002,0.022,0.215) & (0.021,0.100,0.501) \\ (0.005,0.057,0.537) & (0.003,0.021,0.161) & (0.001,0.014,0.171) & (0.009,0.050,0.251) \\ (0.006,0.092,0.940) & (0.001,0.011,0.101) & (0.005,0.053,0.466) & (0.0183,0.089,0.464) \\ (0.005,0.063,0.684) & (0.001,0.009,0.084) & (0.006,0.059,0.451) & (0.002,0.0106,0.041) \\ (0.01,0.105,0.904) & (0.002,0.012,0.098) & (0.003,0.028,0.201) & (0.004,0.024,0.131) \end{bmatrix}$$

The degree of similarity between each alternative and the positive ideal solution and the negative ideal solution are:

$$S_{1\alpha}^{\lambda+} = 0.397 \; S_{1\alpha}^{\lambda-} = 0.660, \; S_{2\alpha}^{\lambda+} = 0.741 \; S_{2\alpha}^{\lambda-} = 0.309$$

$$S_{3\alpha}^{\lambda+} = 0.581 \; S_{3\alpha}^{\lambda-} = 0.473, \; S_{4\alpha}^{\lambda+} = 0.886 \; S_{4\alpha}^{\lambda-} = 0.267$$

$$S_{5\alpha}^{\lambda+} = 0.555 \; S_{5\alpha}^{\lambda-} = 0.365, \; S_{6\alpha}^{\lambda+} = 0.530 \; S_{6\alpha}^{\lambda-} = 0.505$$

The final result and ranking shows the top alternative contributes the most to the framework. The ranking is as follows (Table 2):

Table 2. Ranking of sub-attributes based on fuzzy-AHP

Ranking	Performance index
A3	0.768
A1	0.705
A4	0.603
A2	0.551
A5	0.511
A0	0.375

5   Future Work

Autonomic Level of a system may be an excellent indicator to know about the autonomic features provided by that system. A number of research work has been done in this direction. However, majority of the work done so far in evaluating the Autonomic systems has been found theoretical. This paper is an attempt to propose a framework to assess the autonomic level in AS.

However, in implementation of the above framework we have considered only those factors that have effect on all four main factors and fuzzy – AHP has been used for these factors evaluation. As a future work, researchers may include all the factors that are left out by calculating their effect individually and try to aggregate them with this implementation using neuro-fuzzy, neural networks, fuzzy logic, AHP etc. Researchers may also try using different methods to evaluate different sub-attributes and then applying any of the above said techniques to assess the final autonomic level.

References

1. Patterson, D., et al.: Recovery-oriented computing (ROC): Motivation, definition, techniques, and case studies. UC Berkeley Computer Science (2002)
2. Horn, P.: Autonomic Computing: IBM's Perspective on the State of Information. IBM (2001)
3. Parashar, M., Hariri, S.: Autonomic computing: an overview. In: Banâtre, J.-P., Fradet, P., Giavitto, J.-L., Michel, O. (eds.) UPP 2004. LNCS, vol. 3566, pp. 257–269. Springer, Heidelberg (2005). https://doi.org/10.1007/11527800_20
4. Kephart, J.O., Chess, D.M.: The vision of autonomic computing. IEEE Comput. 36(1), 41–50 (2003)
5. Salehie, M., Tahvildari, L.: Autonomic computing: emerging trends and open problems. ACM SIGSOFT Softw. Eng. Notes 30(4), 1–7 (2005)
6. Nami, M.R., Sharifi, M.: A survey of autonomic computing systems. In: Shi, Z., Shimohara, K., Feng, D. (eds.) IIP 2006. IIFIP, vol. 228, pp. 101–110. Springer, Boston, MA (2006). https://doi.org/10.1007/978-0-387-44641-7_11
7. Sharma, A., Chauhan, S., Grover, P.: Autonomic computing: paradigm shift for software development. CSI Commun. 35 (2011)
8. Sahadev, K., Yadav, S.K., Sharm, A.: A new SDLC framework with autonomic computing elements. Int. J. Comput. Appl. 54(3), 17–23 (2012)
9. Chauhan, S., Sharma, A., Grover, P.: Developing self managing software systems using agile modeling. ACM SIGSOFT Softw. Eng. Notes 38(6), 1–3 (2013)
10. McCann, Julie A., Huebscher, Markus C.: Evaluation Issues in Autonomic Computing. In: Jin, H., Pan, Y., Xiao, N., Sun, J. (eds.) GCC 2004. LNCS, vol. 3252, pp. 597–608. Springer, Heidelberg (2004). https://doi.org/10.1007/978-3-540-30207-0_74
11. Shuaib, H., Anthony, R., Pelc, M.: A framework for certifying autonomic computing systems. In: The Seventh International Conference on Autonomic and Autonomous Systems (2011)
12. Singh, P.K., Sharma, A., Amit, K., Saxena, A.: Autonomic computing: a revolutionary paradigm for implementing self-managing systems. In: International Conference on Recent Trends in Information Systems(ReTIS) (2011)

13. Sagar, S., Mathur, P., Sharma, A.: Multi-criteria selection of software components using fuzzy-AHP approach. Int. J. Innov. Comput. Inf. Control **11**(3), 1045–1058 (2015)
14. Singh, M., Srivastava, V.M., Gaurav, K., Gupta, P.K.: Automatic test data generation based on multi-objective ant lion optimization algorithm. In: 2017 Pattern Recognition Association of South Africa and Robotics and Mechatronics (PRASA-RobMech), Bloemfontein, pp. 168–174 (2017)
15. Dehraj, P., Sharma, A., Grover, P.S.: Incorporating autonomicity and trustworthiness aspects for assessing software quality. Int. J. Eng. Technol. **7**(1.1), 421–425 (2018)
16. Leite, A.F., Alves, V., Rodrigues, G.N., Tadonki, C., Eisenbeis, C., De Melo, A.C.: Autonomic provisioning, configuration, and management of inter-cloud environments based on a software product line engineering method. In: 2016 International Conference on Cloud and Autonomic Computing (ICCAC), pp. 72–83 (2016)
17. Hwang, C.L., Yoon, K.: Methods for multiple attribute decision making. In: Multiple Attribute Decision Making. Lecture Notes in Economics and Mathematical Systems, vol 186, pp 58–191. Springer, Heidelberg (1981)

Bounded Paths for LCR Queries in Labeled Weighted Directed Graphs

B. Bhargavi[✉] and K. Swarupa Rani

School of Computer and Information Sciences,
University of Hyderabad, Hyderabad, Telangana, India
bhargavibbv@uohyd.ac.in, swarupacs.uoh@nic.in

Abstract. Most of the data in the Big Data era is semi-structured or unstructured that can be modeled as graphs where nodes could be objects and edges represent the relations among the objects. Given a source and destination vertex along with label-constraint set, the Label-Constraint Reachability(LCR) query finds the existence of a path between the source vertex and destination vertex within the label-constraint. The objective of the paper is to find the label-constrained paths efficiently bounded by cost. We extend and propose landmark based path indexing to compute bounded paths for LCR queries in graphs. It involves choosing a subset of nodes as landmark nodes, constructing an index that constitutes their reachable nodes and corresponding path information. For each non-landmark node, an additional index is constructed that constitutes the reachability to landmark nodes and their corresponding path information. In query processing, these indices are used to check for the reachability and find the bounded paths efficiently. Experiments were conducted on real graphs and benchmark synthetic datasets.

Keywords: Edge label-constraints · Graph databases
Bounded paths · Reachability

1 Introduction

Graph is a powerful modeling tool used in many modern applications, ranging from chemical, bio-informatics and other scientific disciplines to social networking and social-based applications such as recommender systems. One of the challenges is to develop algorithms that can store, manage and provide analysis over a large number of graphs for the real-world applications. Another challenge might be to develop efficient graph database systems. Neo4j [14] and Infinite-Graph [15] are some of the graph database systems optimized for handling graph data. In addition, big data companies like Twitter and Google designed graph database systems such as Twitter's FlockDB [16] and Google's graph processing framework, Pregel [10] for their purposes.

Graph reachability is one of the basic operations to manage graph data. Many reachability techniques like interval-based cover, 2-hop and 3-hop are proposed [11]. But, in real-time, nodes and edges have attributes and are labeled

© Springer Nature Singapore Pte Ltd. 2018
M. Singh et al. (Eds.): ICACDS 2018, CCIS 905, pp. 124–133, 2018.
https://doi.org/10.1007/978-981-13-1810-8_13

and weighted. For example, the edge weights can be the bandwidth of a link in communication networks, the reliability of an interaction between two proteins in protein-protein interaction (PPI) networks and the distance in road networks [7]. Edges are labelled depending upon the properties and interaction between nodes in a data set. For instance, the edge labels can be *isFriendOf*, *isRelativeOf* in social networks and enzymes in PPI networks [1]. Reachability techniques cannot be directly applied to the constrained reachability queries. Jin et al. [12] were the first to formally define the label-constraint reachability(LCR) problem that finds for the given two vertices s, t and a label-set L, if t is reachable from s with its path-label within the given label-constraint set L.

Landmark index based query processing [1] is one of the efficient techniques to solve LCR queries, in which subset of nodes are selected as landmark nodes and index is constructed for all the nodes based on landmark nodes. We study the LCR problem in the context of labeled weighted directed graphs. We extend the landmark index based query processing technique [1] to find the bounded paths between the two given vertices for the LCR query.

We describe the problem of finding bounded paths for the LCR query as follows: Given two vertices s and t in an edge-labeled weighted directed graph G $(V, E, \Sigma, \lambda, w)$ (where V is the set of vertices, E is the set of edges, Σ is the set of labels in G and for every edge $e \in E$, $w(e) \in \mathbb{R}$ and $\lambda(e) \in \Sigma$), label-set $L \subseteq \Sigma$ and maximum bound for the path-weight $\delta \in \mathbb{R}$, the problem of bounded paths for the LCR query is to find simple L-paths p from s to t whose path-weight $C(p) \leq \delta$. The path-weight C(p) is obtained by the sum of edge weights $w(e_i)$ along the path p.

This problem is challenging as we need to handle exponential number of label combinations while finding the resultant bounded paths. Shortest path finding techniques [5,8] are proposed which can compute only the approximate paths. These observations motivate us towards realistic network scenarios as we handle the real-valued edge weight constraints, categorical edge label constraints and find exact paths bounded by cost.

One of the applications of bounded path based LCR problem is in road networks. We consider for road networks, the different locations as nodes and the link between two adjacent locations with national highways or state highways or local routes as edge labels. The edge weights can be the distance or travel time. For instance, the bounded path based LCR query in road networks can be to find the paths between two locations A and B within a distance δ which are connected via roads labeled as national highways and state highways only.

Figure 1 illustrates the bounded path based LCR query for the given labeled weighted directed graph, G with V = {v1, v2, v3, v4, v5, v6, v7} and E = {(v1, v2), (v1, v4), (v1, v5), (v2, v5), (v3, v2), (v4, v3), (v5, v6), (v6, v3), (v6, v4), (v6, v7)} , Σ = {'a', 'b', 'c'}, for instance, λ(v1, v2) = 'a' and w(v1, v2) = 2. The bounded path-based LCR query is to find the path for s = v4, t = v7, L = 'ac' and δ = 50. The resultant bounded-path p is 'v4-v3-v2-v5-v6-v7'. The path cost C(p) = w(v4, v3) + w(v3, v2) + w(v2, v5) + w(v5, v6) + w(v6, v7) = 31 (Fig. 1(b)).

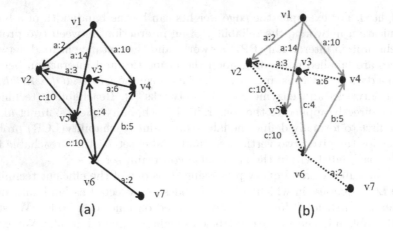

Fig. 1. (a) Labeled weighted directed graph and (b) Resultant path for bounded path based LCR query (*v4, v7, 'ac', 50*)

In this paper, we propose a novel idea to find bounded paths for LCR queries in labeled weighted directed graphs using landmark based path indexing. By adding bounded paths constraint and through incorporating Dijkstra's relaxation property, we extend landmark based indexing technique [1] to find bounded paths for LCR queries. In Sect. 2, we describe the related work and techniques. Section 3 describes our contributions of bounded path indexing and query processing. Section 4 deals with experiments and evaluation of path indexing on real and synthetic graphs. Finally, we conclude with scope for further research in Sect. 5.

2   Related Work

In this section, constrained reachability techniques and path finding techniques are reviewed. Supergraph search, constraint graph reachability and graph pattern mining are some of the current research trends in graph pattern matching [2]. They have broad applications in social networks, biology, chemistry, Resource Description Framework (RDF), image processing and software engineering. Many variants of reachability formed by adding constraints to nodes and edges have been proposed [3,5,7]. The constraints proposed are edge weights, node labels, edge labels and preserving the order of edge labels.

Jin et al. [12] initiated spanning tree based solution to LCR problem. Fan. et al [9] proposed bidirectional BFS technique and used constraint reachability solution as the base technique for finding matching graph patterns. Zou et al. [4] proposed augmented Directed Acyclic Graph(DAG) based transitive closure technique and partition-based technique to solve LCR queries. Valstar et. al. [1] proposed landmark based indexing technique which can handle LCR queries efficiently for large graphs.

Barrett et al. [13] used formal language to define label and weight constraints of graph and computed constrained simple and shortest paths based on dynamic programming. Likhyani et al. [8] computed approximate label-constrained shortest paths for reachability queries based on shortest path distance sketch index constructed for landmark nodes grouped in sets. Bonchi et al. [6] computed approximate shortest paths based on distance to selected subset of landmark nodes in labeled directed graphs. Chen et al. [5] proposed sampling based techniques to find approximate shortest paths constrained by distance in uncertain graphs. Qiao et al. [7] formalized weight constraint reachability query in which every edge weight through the path must satisfy the given range constraint. Erez et al. [3] proposed SAT-based graph aware strategy to find cost-bounded paths in positively weighted undirected graphs.

3   Bounded Paths for LCR Queries

In this section, our contributions are explained. We extended and modified the landmark based indexing [1] to find the bounded paths for LCR queries. We proposed LWPathIndex algorithm to compute path index and QBPath algorithm to find the bounded paths for the LCR query. In the landmark based indexing technique [1], 'k' landmark nodes were selected based on highest total degree. Min-heap based prioirty queue with path-label size as priority was used to add labelsets satisfying minimality. To find bounded paths, we included path labels as well as path weights and path while indexing. We considered path-weight as prioirty in min-heap based priority queue. While adding paths, we incorporated Dijsktra's relaxation property when path labels are same. While processing the bounded path based LCR (s, t, L) query, we find the L-paths using BFS-based query processing along with the path index and return the L-paths whose path-weights are bounded by δ.

3.1   Path Indexing Algorithm

In LWPathIndex algorithm, for each landmark node, all reachable nodes, their labels, the path and path-weight are computed using LWPathIndexPerLM() and stored in Path LandMark index (PLM). In AddPathInfo() method, we add paths to path index by considering minimality of labelsets [1] and cost constraints. While adding paths with same labels, we add only paths that preserve Dijkstra's relaxation property. For any reachable node v from s, let (L', cost') be the labelset and path-weight for path p' that is already inserted and (L, cost) represent the labelset and cost for path p that is to be inserted based on Table 1. For instance, let 'v1' be one of landmark nodes for the graph G in Fig. 1(a), Suppose PLM[v1] for node 'v6' has L' = 'ac', p' = 'v1-v5-v6' and cost' = 24. If a tuple ('v6', L, p, cost) with L = 'ac', p = 'v1-v2-v5-v6' and cost = 22 is encountered, it is inserted into PLM[v1] and the record ('v6', L', p', cost') is deleted.

Table 1 describes how label constraints and weight constraints are considered while indexing. In cases 5–8, minimality of labelsets is preserved as well as Dijkstra's relaxation property for weights is not violated. But, for the cases 1–4, we

---

Algorithm 1. LWPathIndex

---

1 PLM[v_i]←`LWPathIndexPerLM` (v_i)// i ∈ 1:k
2 PNL[v_j]←`LWPathIndexPerNM` (v_j)// j ∈ remaining (n-k) nodes
3 **procedure** `LWPathIndexPerLM` (v) // Let q be priority queue
4 **while** *q is not empty* **do**
5 | Dequeue u and add its path information to PLM[s] through `AddPathInfo` ()
6 | Add u to transL[s][S] if same labeled data exists else add(u, L) to transL[s]
7 | **if** *u is indexed* **then**
8 | | `ExpandOut` (); **continue**
9 | **for** *w* ∈ *adj*(*u*) **do**
10 | | **if** *PathLength(s,w)*≤ ⌈*diameter(g)/2*⌉ **then**
11 | | | Enqueue w

12 **procedure** `LWPathIndexPerNM` (v, b)
13 **while** *q is not empty* **do**
14 | Add u and its path information to PNL[s] through `AddPathInfo` ()
15 | **if** *u is indexed* **then**
16 | | `ExpandOutNM` (s, u, L, iv, cost) upto b landmark nodes
17 | **for** *w* ∈ *adj*(*u*) **do**
18 | | Enqueue w

19 **procedure** `AddPathInfo` (s, v, L, intv, cost)
20 **if** *(v, L′, intv′, cost′)* ∈ *PInd[s]* and *L′* ⊆ *L* **then**
21 | **return false**
22 Remove every (v, L′, intv′, cost′) with L⊂ L′ or (L′ = L and cost′ > cost) from PInd[s].
23 Add (v, L, intv, cost) to PInd[s].// PInd=PLM for LM index, else PInd=PNL
24 **return true**

---

have performed trade-off for faster indexing by adding paths preserving minimality of labelsets. We add only those simple paths to path index whose path length≤ ⌈diameter/2⌉ and we set k = ⌈ $\sqrt{n}$ ⌉ for faster indexing. An additional index transL is created for the landmark nodes for which we either create a new entry (L, v) or add v to an existing entry in transL[l_i][L] used for efficient pruning in query processing. For each non-landmark vertex, LWPathIndexPerNM() computes P̲ath N̲on-L̲andmark index(PNL). ExpandOut() and ExpandOutNM() methods propogate the reachability information of indexed vertices that lead to faster index construction for PLM and PNL respectively.

3.2   Query Algorithm

We modified and extended the BFS-based query processing approach [1] by accessing the path index and returning the label constrained paths whose pathweight is within given maximum bound. The query processing of bounded-path based LCR queries is evaluated based on QBPath Algorithm. If *s* is landmark

Table 1. Cases of label constraints and cost constraints while indexing

Case No.	Label set condition	Cost condition	$(L', cost')$ removed?	$(L, cost)$ added?	Dijkstra's property preserved?	Minimality preserved?
1	$L' \subset L$	cost<cost'	No	No	No	Yes
2	$L \subset L'$	cost>cost'	Yes	Yes	No	Yes
3	$L \not\subset L'$ and $L' \not\subset L$	cost<cost'	No	Yes	No	Yes
4	$L \not\subset L'$ and $L' \not\subset L$	cost>cost'	No	Yes	No	Yes
5	$L \subset L'$	cost $\leq$ cost'	Yes	Yes	Yes	Yes
6	$L = L'$	cost $\leq$ cost'	Yes	Yes	Yes	Yes
7	$L = L'$	cost > cost'	No	No	Yes	Yes
8	$L' \subset L$	cost $\geq$ cost'	No	No	Yes	Yes

vertex, then QPathLM() is invoked that checks if there exists (l, p, $cost$) in PLM[s] for the target node t where l is path-label for path p and $cost$ is path-weight with $l \subseteq L$ and $cost \leq maxcost$, then p is returned. If s is nonlandmark vertex, the vertices are either traversed Breadth-first wise or checked in non-landmark path index (PNL) till t is reached. The nodes from s along the path that cannot reach t are marked as visited using QCheckMark().

Algorithm 2. QBPath

Input : s, t, L, maxcost
Output: Bounded Paths p_i

1   **if** $s \in V_L$ **then**
2   QPathLM (s, t, L, maxcost)

3   **for** $(v, L', intv', cost') \in PNL[s]$ **do**
4   **if** ($L' \subseteq L$ **and** QCheckMark $(v, t, L, marked, maxcost)=true$) **then**
5   Add path s~v~t to p

6   **while** q *is not empty* **do**
7   **if** $v=t$ **then**
8   Add path s~t to p; **break**

9   **if** $v \in V_L$ **and** QCheckMark $(v, t, L, marked, maxcost)=true$ **then**
10   Add path s~v~t to p
11   **for** $w \in adj(v)$ **do**
12   **if** $(marked(w)=false$ **and** $\lambda(v, w) \subseteq L)$ **then**
13   Insert w into q

14   **if** $(p$ *is not empty* **and** $pcost(p_i) \leq maxcost, p_i \in p)$ **then**
15   return p_i

3.3　Space and Time Complexity

Each landmark vertex may store $O(2^{|\Sigma|})$ entries for each of the remaining vertices and each non-landmark vertex may store $O(b)$ entries. The total index size is $O((n(k2^{|\Sigma|} + b)(n + |\Sigma|))$ bits. For each non-landmark, each call to AddPathInfo() requires only $O(b)$ time. Hence, the time complexity for index construction is $O(n(\log n + 2^{|\Sigma|} + m)k2^{|\Sigma|}) + O((n(\log n + b) + m)(n - k)2^{|\Sigma|})$ $= O((n\log n + m + 2^{|\Sigma|} k + b(n - k))n\,2^{|\Sigma|})$. While query processing, in the worst case, we call QCheckMark() for each of k landmarks. QCheckMark() compares L to at most $2^{|\Sigma|}$ label sets and sets at most n vertices in marked. Thus, the query time complexity is $O(m + k(2^{|\Sigma|} + n))$.

4　Experiments and Evaluation

In this section, we evaluate our proposed methods on both real and synthetic datasets. We conducted our experiments on Linux CentOS 64 GB server with 32-core Intel Xeon 2.6 Ghz processors using R programming. We generated the synthetic graphs in SNAP [17] using 'Preferential Attachment' (P-A) and 'Erdos-Renyi' (E-R) models. The direction is chosen based on binomial distribution and the edge labels are exponentially distributed ($\lambda = 1.7$) with $|L| = 8$.

Table 2. Description of real and synthetic data sets

S.No	Dataset	n	m	$|\Sigma|$	Real/synthetic
1	Robots	1724	3596	4	Real
2	AdvogatoS	1800	5969	4	Real
3	E-R Graph	987	2000	8	Synthetic
4	P-A graph	1000	1997	8	Synthetic

We also conducted experiments on real datasets such as Robots[1] and Advogato trust networks [18]. We considered Advogato sample (AdvogatoS) derived from random vertex sampling of Advogato dataset. Table 2 describes the number of vertices (n), number of edges (m) and number of labels ($|\Sigma|$) for the datasets. The edge weights are distributed randomly from set {10, 20, 30, 40, 50, 60, 70, 80, 90, 100, 110, 120} for all the datasets in Table 2.

Figure 2(a) shows the total index size and Fig. 2(b) shows the total index time for the datasets with degree and eigenvector (EV) centrality measures as criteria for landmark selection. LWPathIndex algorithm is implemented with b = 20 [1]. We observe that eigenvector centrality as criteria has lesser total index size than that of degree for all the graphs. We generated query sets for real datasets using number of labels, $nl = 2, 3$ and for synthetic datasets using $nl = 4, 6$. For each query set, 100 queries are generated based on BFS-based query generation process [1] with $\delta = 999$.

---

[1] http://tinyurl.com/gnexfoy.

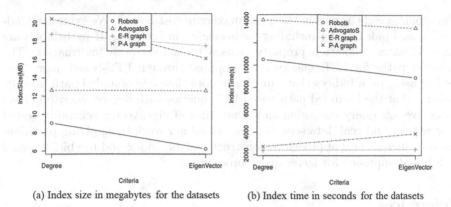

(a) Index size in megabytes for the datasets   (b) Index time in seconds for the datasets

Fig. 2. Total index size and total index time for the datasets using degree and eigen-vector centrality as criteria

Table 3. Average query execution time and the false negative ratio (τ) of true queries (tq) and average query execution time of false queries (fq) in seconds using degree (D) and eigen vector centrality (EV) as criteria with the number of labels, nl

Dataset	nl	tq(D)	tq(EV)	τ (D)	τ (EV)	fq(D)	fq(EV)
Robots	2	.120	.115	.064	.075	.153	.132
	3	.128	.141	.01	.01	.265	.264
AdvogatoS	2	.490	.807	.042	.064	.379	1.049
	3	.773	1.056	.01	.01	.448	1.033
E-R graph	4	.187	.252	.220	.266	.172	.226
	6	.486	.588	.205	.266	.835	1.389
P-A graph	4	.103	.187	.053	.053	.082	.200
	6	.111	.212	.01	.01	.154	.456

Table 3 summarizes the average query execution time of set of 100 true queries and set of 100 false queries with degree (D) and eigenvector centrality (EV) measure as criteria for landmark selection with nl number of labels in each query set. As labelset size increases, there is decrease in the false negative ratio [8] for true queries. The average query execution time for the graphs with degree criteria is faster than that of EV. The resultant τ values in Table 3 indicate that a trade-off is required to be done between index time and path length consideration during landmark based path index construction.

5   Conclusion

In this paper, we addressed a novel problem of bounded path based LCR query where we find simple L-paths from given source vertex to destination vertex whose path-weight is within the given maximum cost bound. We extended landmark based indexing by including path-weights in indexing. If path labels are same, Dijsktra relaxation property is used to include path information. The bounded paths for LCR queries are computed through BFS-based query processing using path indices that can return more than one bounded path. Results indicate that the bounded path based LCR queries with degree as criteria have faster average query execution time than that of eigenvector centrality tested on synthetic and real data sets. We can extend our work by applying partition-based or incremental approach to construct scalable index and use bidirectional BFS based approach for faster query processing.

References

1. Valstar, L.D.J., Fletcher, G.H.L., Yoshida, Y.: Landmark indexing for evaluation of label-constrained reachability queries. In: Proceedings of 2017 ACM International Conference on Management of Data, SIGMOD, Chicago (2017)
2. Singh, K., Singh, V.: Graph pattern matching: a brief survey of challenges and research directions. In: 3rd International Conference on Computing for Sustainable Global Development, pp. 199–204. IEEE(2016)
3. Erez, A., Nadel, A.: Finding bounded path in graph using SMT for automatic clock routing. In: Kroening, D., Păsăreanu, C.S. (eds.) CAV 2015. LNCS, vol. 9207, pp. 20–36. Springer, Cham (2015). https://doi.org/10.1007/978-3-319-21668-3_2
4. Zou, L., Xu, K., Chen, L., Xiao, Y., Zhao, D., Yu, J.X.: Efficient processing of label-constraint reachability queries in large graphs. J. Inf. Syst. **40**, 47–66 (2014)
5. Chen, M., Gu, Y., Bao, Y., Yu, G.: Label and distance-constraint reachability queries in uncertain graphs. In: Bhowmick, S.S., Dyreson, C.E., Jensen, C.S., Lee, M.L., Muliantara, A., Thalheim, B. (eds.) DASFAA 2014. LNCS, vol. 8421, pp. 188–202. Springer, Cham (2014). https://doi.org/10.1007/978-3-319-05810-8_13
6. Bonchi, F., Gionis, A., Gullo, F., Ukkonen, A.: Distance Oracles in edge-labeled graphs. In: Proceedings of the 17th International Conference on Extending Database Technology, pp. 547–558. EDBT (2014)
7. Qiao, M., Cheng, H., Qin, L., Yu, J.X., Yu, P.S., Chang, L.: Computing weight constraint reachability in large networks. VLDB J. **22**(3), 275–294 (2013)
8. Likhyani, A., Bedathur, S.: Label constrained shortest path estimation. In: 22nd International Conference on Information and Knowledge Management, pp. 1177–1180. ACM (2013)
9. Fan, W., Li, J., Ma, S., Tang, N., Wu, Y.: Adding regular expressions to graph reachability and pattern queries. In: 27th IEEE Proceedings of ICDE, pp. 39–50 (2011)
10. Malewicz, G., et al.: Pregel: a system for large-scale graph processing. In: Proceedings of the 2010 ACM SIGMOD International Conference on Management of Data, pp. 135–146 (2010)
11. Aggarwal, C.C., Wang, H.: Managing and Mining Graph Data. Advances in Database Systems Series. Springer, New York (2010). https://doi.org/10.1007/978-1-4419-6045-0
12. Jin, R., Hong, H., Wang, H., Ruan, N., Xiang, Y.: Computing label-constraint reachability in graph databases. In: Proceedings of the ACM International Conference on Management of Data, USA, pp. 123–134 (2010)

13. Barrett, C., Jacob, R., Marathe, M.: Formal-language constrained path problems, SIAM J. Comput. **30**(3), 809–837 (2000)
14. Neo4j. https://neo4j.com/
15. InfiniteGraph.http://www.objectivity.com/infinitegraph
16. Twitter FlockDB. https://github.com/twitter/flockdb
17. SNAP: A general purpose network analysis and graph mining library in C++. http://snap.stanford.edu/snap
18. Konect - the Koblenz Network Collection. http://konect.uni-koblenz.de/

An Efficient Image Fusion Technique Based on DTCWT

Sonam[⊠] and Manoj Kumar

Department of Computer Science, BBA University, Lucknow, India
sonam870115@gmail.com, mkjnuiitr@gmail.com

Abstract. We introduce a novel image fusion technique for multifocus and multimodal image fusion based on dual-tree complex wavelet transform (DTCWT) in this paper. The motive of this work is to reconstruct a new and improved image retaining more significant detail from all the input/source images. The proposed fusion framework has been divided into three parts. In the first part, source images are transformed in frequency domain using DTCWT and high and low frequency sub-bands are obtained. In second part, obtained high-low frequency sub-bands are combined using two fusion methods: maximum rule and gradient based fusion rule. In the end, a single output fused image is reconstructed by merging all new fused frequency subbands using inverse DTCWT. Experimental results indicate that our proposed fusion framework yields more accurate analysis for fusion of multifocus or multimodal images. The obtained results from the proposed fusion framework prove that the proposed framework outperforms than several existing methods in qualitative and quantitative ways.

Keywords: Image fusion · Multifocus image fusion
Multimodal image fusion · Dual-tree complex wavelet transform

1 Introduction

The integration of images has become an important subarea in image processing and computer vision due to the limitation of optical lens, improper capturing conditions, poor visibility and clarity in a single image [1]. The term image fusion refers to as image processing technique with the aim to integrate all the important information from several source images in such a manner that the produced output image contains most of the relevant information as compared to any of the single input image [2]. In application of optical cameras, it is often not possible to capture a well focussed image because of the problem of limited depth of focus (DOF). When images are captured at a particular distance (having large depth of field) are focussed in everywhere while at larger distance (having limited depth of field) images are not well focussed. Thus, an image having better visual information cannot be obtained. To extend the depth of defocused/multifocus images, multifocus image fusion which is the main research

© Springer Nature Singapore Pte Ltd. 2018
M. Singh et al. (Eds.): ICACDS 2018, CCIS 905, pp. 134–143, 2018.
https://doi.org/10.1007/978-981-13-1810-8_14

field of image fusion is employed. It has been developed as a solution which aims to merge the information of different focused source/input images into one image which contain all objects in focus [3,4]. Medical imaging is another application of image fusion for extracting the complementary detail from the medical images. For instance, magnetic resonance imaging (MRI) and computed tomography (CT) medical images are captured by using different cameras and retain different information of the same body part. For instance, CT image provides information of the hard tissues. On the other hand, MRI image provides details of soft tissues. Consequently, CT and MRI are two different images which can not separately yield the complete information of the same organ so that we are unable to obtain both of the information in a single image. Therefore, when these two image are combined into a single image then it suitably can provide the complete description of the same organ. This fusion process is referred to multimodal image fusion [5,6].

Image fusion techniques have been categorized by Stathaki into spatial domain and transform domain [7]. The fusion techniques based on spatial domain works directly over the spatial data (pixel intensities) to generate the resultant fused image in spatial domain. Alternatively, in transform domain many different transforms are used over the input images which decomposes the images into different frequency sub-bands. The obtained frequency sub-bands are processed by using fusion methods to generate the fusion result in transform domain. This result requires an inverse transform to create the final fused image [8]. Agrawal et al. [9] have introduced a fusion method using weighted averaging in spatial domain which is the simplest method. But this method generates unsatisfactory outcomes because of the features present in one source image, which is not present in another source images are provided in the fused image which reduces the contrast of fused image. Metwalli et al. [10] have proposed a pixel level fusion technique to integrate the images using principal component analysis (PCA). This technique is low in complexity and yields fused image having low contrast salient information. To overcome this problem, multi resolution based fusion techniques have been developed. Burt et al. [11] and Toet [12] were presented the multiresolution fusion techniques based on laplacian and ratio of low pass pyramid. Wavelet decomposition based fusion method like discrete wavelet transform (DWT) do not suffer from the problem of introducing any artifacts and therefore it has been broadly used in image fusion to capture the image features at different resolution as well as different orientations. Li et al. [13] have given a fusion technique using DWT to merge the source images using consistency verification and maximum selection method. Later, another image fusion technique based on DTCWT have been developed which provides better directionality and shift invariance as compared to DWT [14]. Singh et al. [15] have developed a method to fuse the medical images using DTCWT in which two fusion rules are employed.

This paper presents a new image fusion framework for multifocus and multimodal images using DTCWT. It is based on the concept of pixel-level image fusion in which pixels of input images are integrated using pixel by pixel approach. The transform domain based fusion method is proposed due to its easy computation and simplicity. Over the source images, DTCWT is performed to obtain high-low frequency sub-bands. To fuse these frequency sub-bands, maximum rule and gradient based fusion rule are employed. The maximum method selects the largest information of high frequency subbands whereas, gradient method is employed to provide sharp details of low frequency subbands. The obtained resultant image retains more sharp details by the combination of these methods and also enhance the visual information. It is structured as follows: the dual tree complex wavelet transform is explained in Sect. 2. Section 3 presents the proposed fusion framework. Experimental results and analysis followed by a brief discussion of evaluation metrics can be found in Sect. 4. Finally, a conclusion of this paper is drawn in Sect. 5.

2 Dual Tree Complex Wavelet Transform

The properties of DTCWT such as, better directionality and shift invariance over the DWT have motivated for image fusion purpose. A small change in source signals can cause the large change in DWT coefficients because of the shift variance in DWT. For DWT, aliasing may be occurs because of large changes in downsampling and wavelet coefficients. Inverse DWT removes this aliasing. It has inability to distinguish between positive and negative frequencies because of poor directionality [16]. These disadvantages of DWT can be solved by employing complex wavelet transform (CWT). Selesnick [17] and Kingsbury [14] have proposed a DTCWT, which yields better shift invariance and directional selectivity. The DTCWT provide better image fusion results than DWT because of the containing above advantages. DTCWT decomposes the input signal into two parts: real and imaginary. The obtained real coefficients are used to compute amplitude whereas the imaginary coefficients are used to compute phase information. In Fig. 1, the structure of DTCWT is illustrated in which two DWT are designed over the same data and filters for DTCWT. The real part is denoted in upper part of DWT whereas, the imaginary part is represented in lower part of DWT. When DTCWT is performed over an image, it divided that image into low-high frequency subbands. At each level of decomposition, two low and six distinct high frequency subbands (at orientations $\pm 15°$, $\pm 45°$ and $\pm 75°$) are obtained. 2D DTCWT [18] decomposes an image I into different scales y^j as:

$$y = \{x^j, y^1, y^2, y^3 ....., y^J\} \tag{1}$$

$$y^j = \begin{cases} y^j_{real,1}(c,s), y^j_{real,2}(c,s), ..., y^j_{real,6}(c,s) \\ y^j_{imag,1}(c,s), y^j_{imag,2}(c,s), ..., y^j_{imag,6}(c,s) \end{cases}$$

Where, x^j and y^j are referred as low and high frequency subbands, by combining six real and imaginary directional subbands y^j is obtained and (c,s) and $d = 1, 2, 3, ...6$ represent spatial position of the coefficients and orientation.

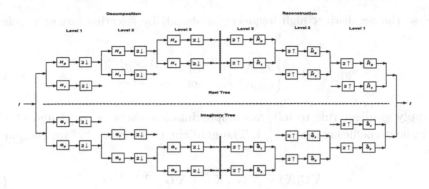

Fig. 1. 3-level DTCWT decomposition and reconstruction of DTCWT coefficients with filters H_0 and H_1 for real part decomposition, G_0 and G_1 for imaginary part decomposition, $\hat{H}_0$ and $\hat{H}_1$ for real part reconstruction, $\hat{G}_0$ and $\hat{G}_1$ for imaginary part reconstruction.

3 Proposed Framework

The brief discussion of the proposed fusion framework is presented in this Section. Here, A and B images of same size are considered as source images which are taken to create one fused image F. The diagram of the proposed framework is depicted in Fig. 2. In the proposed framework, DTCWT is performed over the input images by which high and low frequency subbands are achieved. The high frequency subbands usually include sharp informations such as boundaries, edges and texture of the image. The most popular selection for high frequency subbands is to select largest absolute values, therefore to fuse high frequency subbands maximum method is used. Low frequency sub-bands represent the approximation part and contain average detail of the image. The simplest rule is pixel averaging method to produce composite bands but it may not provide the high quality images because of the contrast reduction. Although, the averaging method is widely used for the fusion of approximation parts but the gradient based method may fuse the directional and smooth change also. Therefore, gradient rule is employed to merge the approximation parts. In the end, the resultant fused image is achieved after performing an inverse DTCWT over the new fused coefficients. The proposed fusion framework can be described as follows:

1. Take images A and B which are considered as input images.
2. Apply DTCWT decomposition at j-level over the input images to achieve low x^j and six high $y^j (j = 1, 2, ..., J)$ frequency subbands at each level.

$$A : (x_A^j, y_{A,d}^j), \quad B : (x_B^j, y_{B,d}^j) \tag{2}$$

where, low and high frequency subbands at j-level are represented as x_*^j and $y_{*,d}^j$ in the d orientation and $*$ represents source images A or B.

3. Fuse the six distinct high frequency subbands by selecting largest absolute value.

$$y_{F,d}^{j}(c,s) = \begin{cases} y_{A,d}^{j}(c,s), & y_{A,d}^{j}(c,s) \geq y_{B,d}^{j}(c,s) \\ y_{B,d}^{j}(c,s), & otherwise \end{cases} \tag{3}$$

4. Apply gradient rule to integrate approximation parts (x_A^j, x_B^j) and obtain gradient coefficients $(x_{A'}^j, x_{B'}^j)$. The gradient coefficients [19] are computed as:

$$\nabla G(X) = [\nabla G_e(X)^2 + \nabla G_f(X)^2]^{1/2} \tag{4}$$

where, $\nabla G_e(X), \nabla G_f(X)$ can be defined as:

$$\nabla G_e(X) = \Big\{ -z(e-1,f-1,g,h) - 2z(e-1,f,g,h) - z(e-1,f+1,g,h)$$

$$+z(e+1,f-1,g,h) + 2z(e+1,f,g,h) + z(e+1,f+1,g,h) \Big\}$$

$$\nabla G_f(X) = \Big\{ z(e-1,f-1,g,h) + 2z(e,f-1,g,h) + z(e+1,f-1,g,h)$$

$$-z(e-1,f+1,g,h) - 2z(e,f+1,g,h) - z(e+1,f+1,g,h) \Big\}$$

Let $X = (e,f,g,h)$ denotes index of particular multi-scale decomposition coefficients. e, f denote spatial position, g represents level of decomposition and h multiscale decomposition frequency band.

5. Compare $x_{A'}^j$ and $x_{B'}^j$ using a step function and achieve the decision map D.

$$D(c,s) = \begin{cases} 1, & if(x_{A'}^j(c,s) > x_{B'}^j(c,s)) \\ 0, & otherwise \end{cases} \tag{5}$$

6. Choose the pixels from (x_A^j, x_B^j) using decision map $D(c,s)$ to achieve new fused low coefficients x_F^j.

$$x_F^j(c,s) = D(c,s)x_A^j + (1 - D(c,s))x_B^j \tag{6}$$

7. Perform j-level inverse DTCWT over the new fused high $(y_{F,d}^j(c,s))$ and low $(x_F^j(c,s))$ frequency subbands to reconstruct the final fused image F.

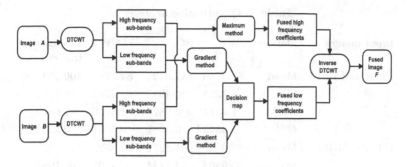

Fig. 2. The diagram of the proposed framework

4   Experimental Results and Analysis

In this Section, the effectiveness of the proposed framework is evaluated through experimental results. Figure 3 (a–b) are FLIR (visible) and LLTV (infrared) images and Fig. 4(a–b) are CT and MRI images. The size of multi-focus images is 512×512 as given in Figs. 5(a–b) and 6(a–b). Figures 3(a–b) and 5(a–b) images are obtained from the help of Dr. V.P.S. Naidu [20]. Figures 4(a–b) and 6(a–b) are obtained by using http://www.metapix.de/download.htmlink. The proposed framework is compared against DWT (avg-max) [13,20], PCA [20] and DTCWT [14,15] based image fusion. The results of proposed framework are illustrated in Figs. 3, 4, 5 and 6(f). The proposed framework is compared in two aspects of subjective and objective image quality measurements.

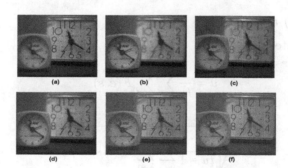

Fig. 3. (a) Right part concentrated; (b) left part concentrated; (c) DWT; (d) PCA; (e) DTCWT; (f) proposed method.

The qualitative analysis is not sufficient way to analyze the quality of image. Therefore, for quantitative analysis we used some metrics such as, mean, SD, SCD, $Q^{AB/F}$. By combination of quantitative and qualitative results, it can be analyzed that the above discussed framework produces better informative

Table 1. Quantitative analysis

Input images	Metrics	DWT	PCA	DTCWT	Proposed framework
FLIR and LLTV	Mean	84.3786	151.312	84.378	100.363
	SD	48.1265	96.4685	63.2763	74.1559
	SCD	1.4611	0.0874	1.6666	1.6810
	$Q^{AB/F}$	0.4365	0.3987	0.5511	0.5238
CT and MRI	Mean	32.0820	51.8274	31.8523	45.5972
	SD	35.9304	54.1734	58.1705	60.1984
	SCD	1.3617	1.3452	1.7570	1.6958
	$Q^{AB/F}$	0.5035	0.6518	0.7255	0.7883
Saras	Mean	227.666	227.666	227.666	227.666
	SD	46.3984	45.9007	49.9141	50.0429
	SCD	0.4286	0.3936	0.7543	0.7754
	$Q^{AB/F}$	0.5941	0.6135	0.7368	0.7371
Clock	Mean	97.0389	97.037	97.038	96.556
	SD	49.4888	49.3160	51.7481	51.9456
	SCD	0.3205	0.5867	0.6240	0.6481
	$Q^{AB/F}$	0.6131	0.3020	0.6688	0.6691

synthesized image. The Table 1 shows the result obtained from the above metrics. The used metrics are described as:

4.1 Mean ($\hat{\mu}$) and SD (σ)

It can be computed as:

$$\hat{\mu} = \frac{1}{tu} \sum_{c=1}^{t} \sum_{s=1}^{u} F(c, s) \tag{7}$$

$$\sigma = \sqrt{\frac{1}{tu-1} \sum_{c=1}^{t} \sum_{s=1}^{u} (F(c, s) - \hat{\mu})^2} \tag{8}$$

where, fused image is denoted as F. The image of high contrast having high SD values.

4.2 Sum of the Correlation of Differences (SCD)

It evaluates the maximum amount of complementary detail transferred from input images.

$$SCD = r(D_1, A) + r(D_2, B) \tag{9}$$

where, D is the difference image and $r(.)$ function computes the correlation between A and D_1, B and D_2 can be defined as:

$$D_1 = F - B, \quad D_2 = F - A \tag{10}$$

and

$$r(D_w, I) = \frac{\sum_c \sum_s (D_w(c,s) - \bar{D}_w) \cdot (I(c,s) - \bar{I})}{\sqrt{\sum_c \sum_s (D_w(c,s) - \bar{D}_w)^2 \cdot \sum_c \sum_s (I(c,s) - \bar{I})^2}} \tag{11}$$

where, $w = 1, 2$ and I represents image A or B, and $\bar{D}_w$ and $\bar{I}$ denote average pixel values of D_w and I, respectively. The good quality resultant image F contains higher values.

4.3 $Q^{AB/F}$

The information of edges transferred from (A, B) to F is measured by using this metric. This metric is computed for images A and B as:

$$Q^{AB/F} = \frac{\sum_{c=1}^{t} \sum_{s=1}^{u} (Q^{AF}(c,s).p^A(c,s) + Q^{BF}(c,s).p^B(c,s))}{\sum_{c=1}^{t} \sum_{s=1}^{u} (p^A(c,s) + p^B(c,s))} \tag{12}$$

where, Q^{AF} and Q^{BF} are the edge information preservation values, $p^A(c,s)$ and $p^B(c,s)$ reflect the importance of Q^{AF} and Q^{BF}. The 0 value represents the loss of input detail and 1 value represents a better fused image.

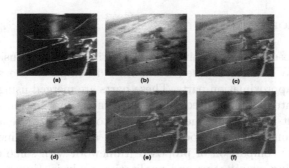

Fig. 4. (a) Visible; (b) infrared; (c) DWT; (d) PCA; (e) DTCWT; (f) proposed method.

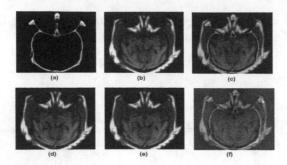

Fig. 5. (a) CT image; (b) MRI image; (c) DWT; (d) PCA; (e) DTCWT; (f) proposed method.

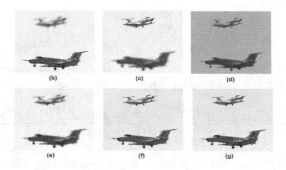

Fig. 6. (a) Lower part concentrated; (b) upper part concentrated; (c) DWT; (d) PCA; (e) DTCWT; (f) proposed framework.

5   Conclusions

Our paper proposes a novel multifocus and multimodal image fusion framework based on DTCWT. The proposed framework decomposed the source images into detail and approximation parts. These parts are merged using two different methods to create one final fused image with more information and improved quality. Gradient based fusion method is used to synthesize the approximation parts whereas, maximum method is employed as the fusion measurement of detail parts. The comparison of proposed framework with some other existing is performed using quantitative and qualitative analysis. Experimental results of different images show that the proposed framework outperforms and also enhance the visual information of final fused image.

Acknowledgment. We would like to thank Dr. V.P.S. Naidu to provide the images.

References

1. Wald, L.: Some terms of reference in data fusion. IEEE Trans. Geosci. Remote Sens. **37**(3), 1190–1193 (1999)
2. Mitchell, H.B.: Image Fusion: Theories, Techniques and Applications. Springer, Heidelberg (2010)
3. Piao, Y., Zhang, M., Wang, X., Li, P.: Extended depth of field integral imaging using multi-focus fusion. Opt. Commun. **411**, 8–14 (2018)
4. Zhang, Q., Liu, Y., Blum, R.S., Han, J., Tao, D.: Sparse representation based multi-sensor image fusion for multi-focus and multi-modality images: a review. Inf. Fusion **40**, 57–75 (2018)
5. Manchanda, M., Sharma, R.: An improved multimodal medical image fusion algorithm based on fuzzy transform. J. Vis. Commun. Image Representation **51**, 76–94 (2018)
6. Qu, G.H., Zhang, D.L., Yan, P.E.: Medical image fusion by wavelet transform modulus maxima. Opt. Express **9**(4), 184–190 (2001)
7. Stathaki, T.: Image Fusion: Algorithms and Applications. Elsevier, Oxford (2008)
8. Aymaz, M., Kose, C.: A novel image decomposition-based hybrid technique with super-resolution method for multi-focus image fusion. Inf. Fusion **45**, 113–127 (2019)
9. Agrawal, D., Singhai, J.: Multifocus image fusion using modified pulse coupled neural network for improved image quality. IET Digit. Libr. **4**(6), 443–451 (2010)
10. Metwalli, M., Nasr, A., Farag, O., El-Rabaie, S.: Image fusion based on principal component analysis and high pass filter. In: Proceedings of IEEE Computer Engineering and Systems (ICCES), pp. 63–70 (2009)
11. Burt, P.J., Adelson, E.H.: The Laplacian pyramid as a compact image code. IEEE Trans. Commun. **31**, 532–540 (1983)
12. Toet, A.: Image fusion by a ratio of low-pass pyramid. Pattern Recog. Lett. **9**(4), 245–253 (1989)
13. Li, H., Manjunath, B., Mitra, S.: Multisensor image fusion using the wavelet transform. Graph. Models Image Process. **57**(3), 235–245 (1995)
14. Kingsbury, N.: Image processing with complex wavelets. In: Silverman, B., Vassilicos, J. (eds.) Wavelets: The Key to Intermittent Information, pp. 165–185. Oxford University Press (1999)
15. Singh, R., Srivastava, R., Prakash, O., Khare, A.: DTCWT based multimodal medical image fusion. In: Proceedings of International Conference on Signal, Image and Video Processing, pp. 403–407 (2012)
16. Diwakar, M., Sonam, Kumar, M.: CT image denoising based on complex wavelet transform using local adaptive thresholding and bilateral filtering. In: Proceedings of International Symposium on Women in Computing and Informatics (WCI), pp. 297–302 (2015)
17. Selesnick, I.W., Baraniuk, R.G., Kingsbury, N.C.: The dual-tree complex wavelet transform. IEEE Sig. Process. Mag. **22**(6), 123–151 (2005)
18. Bal, U.: Dual tree complex wavelet transform based denoising of optical microscopy images. Biomed. Opt. Express **3**(12), 1–9 (2012)
19. Sonam, Kumar, M.: An effective image fusion technique based on multiresolution singular value decomposition. INFOCOMP **14**(2), 31–43 (2015)
20. Naidu, V.P.S., Raol, J.R.: Pixel level image fusion using wavelets and principal component analysis. Defence Sci. J. **58**(3), 338–352 (2008)

Low-Delay Channel Access Technique for Critical Data Transmission in Wireless Body Area Network

M. Ambigavathi[✉] and D. Sridharan

Department of ECE, CEG Campus, Anna University, Chennai, India
ambigaindhu8@gmail.com, sridhar@annauniv.edu

Abstract. The healthcare, e-health, and other entertainment services have attracted researcher's interest in Wireless Body Area Network (WBAN). IEEE 802.15.6 MAC protocol is recently developed to overcome the challenges and issues present in the existing IEEE 802.15.4 MAC Protocol. The decisive role of WBAN is to transmit the critical or emergency data packet with minimum delay over the transmission medium. The delay minimization problem was concentrated by several researchers under IEEE 802.15.4 and IEEE 802.15.6 MAC protocols. However, there are no complete solutions to resolve the channel access problem of the critical data packet. This paper introduces an effective Low-Delay Channel Access Technique (LDCAT) to minimize the transmission delay of the critical data packet. For that purpose, an additional field termed as Severity Indicator (SI) is appended in the MAC header in order to indicate the severity condition of the data packets before the coordinator node starts to allocate the time slots during the data transmission phase. Subsequently, the header information is analyzed, after that the slots are allocated to the nodes based on the importance of data traffic. Finally, the simulation results are evaluated to the proposed technique in terms of energy consumption, average delay and throughput using OMNet++ network simulator tool to show that the achieved results outperforms better with existing MAC protocols.

Keywords: Wireless Body Area Network · Channel access · Delay
Energy consumption

1 Introduction

Wireless Body Area Network is comprised of low-power sensor devices to monitor the vital parameters and forward the sensed data to the coordinator. The gathered information will be transferred to the other medical repositories for further analysis. IEEE 802.15.6 standard was intentionally designed to improve the performance of the WBAN system [1]. The overall structure of WBAN system is illustrated in Fig. 1. WBAN supports real-time applications such as healthcare, military and defense, sports, and entertainment etc. Several researchers in the existing literature address the following challenges such as latency, energy consumption, collisions etc. [2]. To resolve these challenges in WBAN, different MAC protocols have been developed. These MAC protocols work on either TDMA or CSMA based. The sleep mechanism for improvising

© Springer Nature Singapore Pte Ltd. 2018
M. Singh et al. (Eds.): ICACDS 2018, CCIS 905, pp. 144–153, 2018.
https://doi.org/10.1007/978-981-13-1810-8_15

the energy efficiency of the nodes is proposed under IEEE 802.15.6 MAC protocol in [3]. In this mechanism, nodes alter to sleep state when there are no packets to transmit. Otherwise, the node is still maintained at an active state. So, thus reduces the energy consumption but if the node fails to promptly wakeup during the packet arrival, then latency will be increased to the core. Further, the energy consumption issue is solved by authors in [4] using Network Longevity Enhancement by Energy Aware MAC Protocol (NLEEAP) with the considering the relay request, relay response, and super-frame adjustment. However, it is developed only to increase the lifetime of nodes rather than the degree of importance of the data traffic.

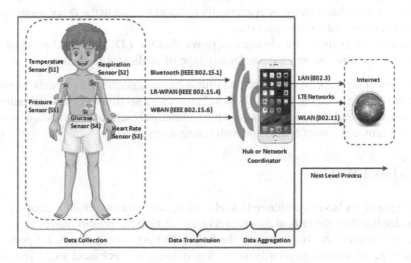

Fig. 1. Layout of wireless body area network

Also, both energy and delay constraints-based MAC protocol is developed using heuristic approach (i.e.) fixed wake-up interval and reference time in [5]. In general, the sensed data from body sensors are not normal at all time, since scheduling is widely used mechanism to send the critical data packets based on the assigned priority values. A robust beacon scheduling technique is introduced with modified beacon frame format in [6]. This method includes the extra elements (i.e. resource request and information element, respectively) in the beacon frame that is comprised of element ID, length, network identifier and requested resources. Based on the Reserved Beacon Period (RBP), a slot is allocated to the nodes only for a specific interval. Since, if any node receives critical data packet after this duration it will be dropped. The overall QoS performance of WBAN is also enhanced by using Ransom Contention- based Resource Allocation (RACOON) MAC protocol [7]. Prioritization of data packet plays a signif- icant role in WBAN. Priority is fixed to the data packet as either using static or dynamic approach. The coordinator node allocates the time slots according to the user priority level of the data traffic. Adaptively Tuned MAC (AT-MAC) protocol is developed based on the IEEE 802.15.4 [8] that supports and enhances the reliability of critical nodes by optimizing MAC-frame payload. The criticality index of each node is estimated and their payloads are adjusted based on the incoming data transmission, thus leads to maximize the packet delivery ratio. For evaluation, different types of data traffic are considered in [9]. As well, this method assigned the fixed delay values for video traffic that has maximum of 250 milliseconds. Accordingly, the time slots are assigned to the sensor nodes. Though, many researchers have concentrated on scheduling the data packet in accordance with urgency and energy-aware schemes. Still, there are a lot of issues to be addressed. The main objectives of this paper are outlined as follows:

- All medicinal data packet is delay sensitive, since an additional field (i.e. severity indicator) is included in the MAC header format to predict the node's criticality before it starts the data transmission process.
- Size of contention window is dynamically handled to sustain the delay-aware transmission of the critical data packets.
- Performance analyses are obtained to prove that the LDCAT MAC protocol is a feasible and effective mechanism for any type of medical applications.

The rest of this paper is organized into following sections: Sect. 2 presents the recent research works carried out in WBAN MAC protocols. Sections 3 and 4 elaborate the proposed model and then Sect. 5 discusses the simulation results of the proposed method. Section 6 provides a brief conclusion with future research work.

2 Related Works

Many researchers have concentrated on scheduling mechanisms, channel access mechanisms for handling the critical data packets by assigning the priority values to the data traffic. The authors in [10] increased the length of EAP access phases for providing exclusive access to the high priority nodes. But, it does not use channel access procedure like CSMA/CA or slotted aloha to transmit the data packet. In the designed superframe, the allocation slots are divided into mini slots with 25% of allocations and normal with 75% of allocation slots. Normal slots are assigned for both critical and normal sensor nodes. Thus, the mini slots reduce the delay but it will maximize the delay of critical data packets when it is not received. Based on this scheme, the data packets are allocated with minimum slots based on their data rates, since critical packets which are not supposed to have higher data rates at all time.

To handle emergency data packet, authors proposed an Inter-WBAN Scheduling and Aggregation (IWSA) mechanism in order to improve the QoS in [11]. The value of delay for critical data frames is computed and the packet form sensor node with minimum delay is transmitted to reduce the transmission delay. TDMA-based MAC protocol is introduced in [12] to maintain QoS by adjusting the transmission duration with the corresponding channel status. To achieve this, synchronization scheme is used to schedule the sleep time and sensing time for the nodes to minimize the energy consumption. Authors also introduced backoff counter reservation scheme to avoid collision problem in [13]. In this, the next backoff value is added to the data frame in order to identify the future backoff duration by the coordinator. If the data frame is not arrived at the predicted transmission slot, a Guaranteed Time Slot (GTS) is allocated to the sensor node in the next superframe duration. Since, the sensor node reserves the slot for next packet transmission but the unused time slot will increase the bandwidth waste when it is not utilized by the sensor nodes. Therefore, most of the research works have been focused on the issues such as energy efficiency, delay and throughput under IEEE 802.15.4 and IEEE 802.15.4 MAC protocols. However, they are failed to achieve higher throughput on prioritizing the data packets by providing prior information to the coordinator node.

If the data frame is not arrived at the predicted transmission slot, a Guaranteed Time Slot (GTS) is allocated to the sensor node in the next superframe duration. Since, the sensor node reserves the slot for next packet transmission but the unused time slot will increase the bandwidth waste when it is not utilized by the sensor node. The comparative analysis of different MAC protocols is presented. Therefore, most of the research works have been focused on the issues like energy efficiency, delay and channel-based concepts using IEEE 802.15.6 standard. But failed to achieve higher throughput on prioritizing the data packets with initial information from sensor nodes and also existed with certain limitations.

3   Modification in MAC Header

IEEE 802.15.6 MAC protocol for WBAN is specially designed to provide short-range communication approximately up to 2 meters and 10 Mbps of data rate speed. Generally, this standard dealt with different user-priorities and the values are ranging from minimum to maximum in accordance with variations in the contention window values. Different access modes are used in IEEE 802.15.6. But, this paper focused only on the beacon-enabled access mode. Accessing the communication channel depends on the user priority levels. In this, MAC header plays a key role to identify a severity condition of the data packet using Severity Indicator (SI). This is the field which additionally included in the MAC header and checked initially in every WBAN communication. This field occupies a size of 1 octet. Also, this field is defined by the nodes based on the importance of sensed values. For this, three different data types are considered such as critical data, normal and periodic.

The coordinator node checks the header information with assigned SI values and then it is assigned minimum and maximum Contention Window (CW) size respectively. According to the assigned CW value, the back- off value is determined. Back-off (B_{off}) is the waiting time for a node to transmit its data packets. Hence the value of back-off is expressed as,

$$B_{off} = \frac{CW_{min} * T_l}{2} \tag{1}$$

All sensor nodes wait for packet transmission until the computed Boff value reaches zero, Table 1 lists the CW bounds for different data traffic. Severity Indicator (SI) is included in each packet for the determination of data's severity. SI is defined as the measure of criticality or seriousness of human health metric which is predicted by means of body sensors placed in the human body. Figure 2 shows the modified MAC header format. The node's state information is obtained by using DTMC model which is discussed in further section.

Table 1. Contention window values

Service Type	CWmin	CWmax
Critical Data (CD)	0	4
Non-Critical Data (NCD)	4	16
Periodic Data (PD)	16	32

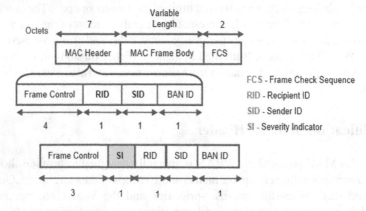

Fig. 2. Modified MAC header of LDCAT

4 Modification in Superframe Structure

IEEE 802.15.6 MAC protocol for WBAN is specially designed to provide short-range communication approximately up to 2 meters and 10 Mbps of data rate speed. Generally, this standard dealt with different user-priorities and the values are ranging from minimum to maximum in accordance with variations in the contention window values. Different access modes are used in IEEE 802.15.6. But, this paper focused only on the beacon-enabled access mode. Accessing the communication channel depends on the user priority levels. In this, MAC header plays a key role to identify a severity condition of the data packet using Severity Indicator (SI). This is the field which additionally included in the MAC header and checked initially in every WBAN communication. This field occupies a size of 1 octet. Also, this field is defined by the nodes based on the importance of sensed values.

For this, three different data types are considered such as critical data, normal and periodic. The coordinator node checks the header information with assigned SI values and then it is assigned minimum and maximum Contention Window (CW) size respectively. All sensor nodes wait for packet transmission until the computed Boff value reaches zero, Table 1 lists the CW bounds for different data traffic. Severity Indicator (SI) is included in each packet for the determination of data's severity. SI is defined as the measure of criticality or seriousness of human health metric which is predicted by means of body sensors placed in the human body. Figure 2 shows the modified MAC header format.

4.1 Contention Window Mechanism

LDCAT design uses beacon-enabled mode with superframe that performs under CSMA/CA procedure. In CSMA/CA, Cwmin and CWmax denote the minimum and maximum CW size of a node with user priority UP = 0, 1, 2. If a node with data packets for transmission, it will sustain a CW value which is given with respect to user priority in this work. The value of CW is represented as CW $\in$ (CWmin, Cwmin), the backoff value is estimated $B_{off} \in [1, CW]$. On determining the backoff value, the node initiates channel sensing in pCSMA slot, this slot length is fixed by pCSMA slot length. Sensor node minimizes the backoff value based on each idle CSMA slot. When the backoff timer value reaches zero, then the sensor node starts its packet transmission.

In CSMA/CA, sensor waits for Short Interframe Space (SIFS) during Random Access Period (RAP) phase and its duration is denoted as pSIFS. CSMA/CA procedure is followed for RAP and Contention Access Phase (CAP) field presented in the superframe. The total transmit time of a data packet is formulated as,

$$T_{SI} = T_{SI-CW} + T_{data} + 2T_{pSIFS} + 2\alpha \qquad (2)$$

Where T_{SI} represents the severity indicator, T_{SI-CW} is the backoff time obtained with respect to SI of body sensor node, Tdata is the time taken for packet transmission, T_{pSIFS} is the interframe spacing time and α denotes the delay time. The value of pSIFS and α is multiplied by 2 that defined as Round Trip Time (RTT). Due to RTT, TpSIFS and α is doubled the time taken to reach the coordinator and return back to the body sensor nodes. The total time taken for data packet transmission is defined as the sum of the time period of a preamble, physical header, MAC header, MAC frame body and Frame check sequence respectively.

5 Performance Evolution

5.1 Simulation Environment

The LDCAT is implemented using OMNeT++ environment and it is a generic, discrete event simulator, enabled to support channel and radio models with several MAC and routing protocol design. This simulation setup consists of four sensor nodes with a single coordinator connected in a star topology. Table 2 represents the significant performance parameters that are specified for this WBAN simulation.

Table 2. Simulation parameters

Parameters	Value
Number of coordinator	1
Number of BANs	10
Slot Duration	1 S
Superframe Slots	16
MAC header length	24 bits
Body Sensor Listening time	61 ms
Bandwidth	1000 MHz
Data rate	0.24 bps
Energy Consumption (Txn)	0.5 mW
Transmission Range	–15 dBm
Packet Size	512 Bytes
Transmission power	100 mW
Simulation Time	150 s

5.2 Comparative Analysis

5.2.1 Energy Consumption

Energy remains a significant constraint in sensor nodes which performs sensing process to gather vital information. In this section, the average energy consumption analysis of LDCAT is compared with other techniques [11–13].

Figure 3 shows the average energy consumption, where BCR, AMAC and MCMAC is consumed a large amount of energy but LDCAT consumes less amount of energy in this work. The value of contention window varies for each node with the corresponding user priority. From this analysis, LDCAT minimizes the energy consumption during the data transmission packet. Hence, this method extends the node's lifetime.

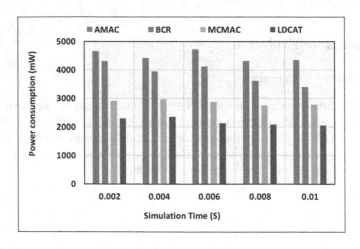

Fig. 3. Energy consumption

5.2.2   Average Delay

Data transmission delay is plotted with respect to packet size in bytes. The number of transmission increases then delay occurrence leads to poor throughput since the data packets are not delivered to coordinator successfully. This LDCAT design minimizes the delay by using the additional field in MAC frame. Figure 4 illustrates the reduction of delay based on the proposed LDCAT. Delay is greatly minimized by using the specified contention window values and these values are responsible for either increase or decrease in backoff time. As long as the packet size increases the value of delay during the data packet transmission process also increases but the proposed technique reduces the average delay as much as possible compared with other techniques.

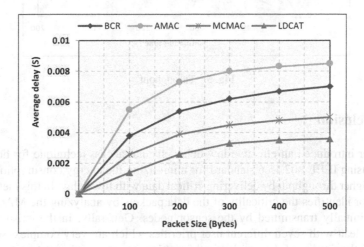

Fig. 4. Delay

5.2.3   Throughput

Throughput plays a major role in evaluating the overall performance of the network. Figure 5 shows the comparison results of throughput with respect to the simulation time in seconds.

The existing techniques show the gradual increase in throughput at an initial stage, when the simulation time increases and then the throughput will get reduced. From this observation, LDCAT increases the throughput based on the selection of contention window mechanism.

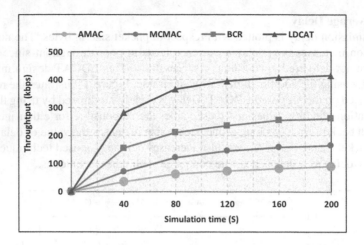

Fig. 5. Throughput

6 Conclusion

This paper introduced an effective low delay channel access technique for body area network using IEEE 802.15.6 standard for minimizing the energy consumption and to achieve higher throughput by delivering critical data with low delay. In this method, the coordinator identifies the criticality of the data packets by analyzing the MAC header which is initially transmitted by the sensor nodes. Generally, in the existing MAC protocols dealt with seven different user priorities which are very complex, so in this work only three types of data packets are considered to reduce the system complexity according to the sensed data. The simulation results describe the results achieved using LDCAT design and compared with other existing techniques. The same technique will be extended in future, using a novel backoff algorithm in order to maximize the throughput and minimize the delay.

References

1. Cavallari, R., Martelli, F., Rosini, R., Buratti, C., Verdona, R.: A survey on wireless body area networks: technologies and design challenges. IEEE Commun. Surv. Tutor. **16**, 1635–1657 (2014)
2. Barakah, D.M., Ammad-uddin, M.: A survey of challenges and applications of wireless body area network (WBAN) and role of a virtual doctor server in existing architecture. In: IEEE International Conference on Intelligent Systems Modelling and Simulation, pp. 214–219 (2012)
3. Jacob, A.K., Kishore, G.M., Jacob, L.K.: Lifetime and latency analysis of IEEE 802.15.6 WBAN with interrupted sleep mechanism. Sādhanā **42**, 865–878 (2017)
4. Cai, X., Li, J., Jingjing Yuan, W., Zhu, Q.W.: Energy-aware adaptive topology adjustment in wireless body area networks. Springer Telecommun. Syst. **58**(2), 139–152 (2015)

5. Alam, M.M., Hamida, E.B., Berder, O., Menard, D., Sentieys, O.: A heuristic self-adaptive medium access control for resource-constrained WBAN systems. IEEE Access **4**, 1287–1300 (2016)
6. Kim, J.-W., Hur, K., Lee, S.-R.: A robust beacon scheduling scheme for coexistence between UWB based WBAN and WiMedia networks. Springer Wirel. Pers. Commun. **80**(1), 303–319 (2015)
7. Cheng, S.H., Huang, C.Y., Tu, C.C.: RACOON: a multiuser QoS design for mobile wireless body area networks. Springer J. Med. Syst. **35**(5), 1277–1287 (2011)
8. Moulik, S., Misra, S., Das, D.: AT-MAC: adaptive MAC-frame payload tuning for reliable communication in wireless body area networks. IEEE Trans. Mob. Comput. **16**(6), 1516–1529 (2017)
9. Bradai, N., Charfi, E., Fourati, L.C., Kamoun, L.: Priority consideration in inter-WBAN data scheduling and aggregation for monitoring systems. Trans. Emerg. Telecommun. Technol. **27**(4), 589–600 (2016)
10. Liu, B., Yan, Z., Chen, C.W.: Medium access control for wireless body area networks with QoS provisioning and energy efficient design. IEEE Trans. Mobile Comput. **16**(2), 1–14 (2016)
11. Li, C., Zhang, B., Yuan, X., Ullah, S., Vasilakos, A.V.: MC-MAC: a multi-channel-based MAC scheme for interference mitigation in WBANs. Wirel. Netw. **18**(5), 1–15 (2016)
12. Shin, H., Kim, Y., Lee, S.: A backoff counter reservation scheme for performance improvement in wireless body area networks. In: IEEE International Conference on Consumer Communications and Networking (2015)
13. Kim, R.H., Kim, J.G.: Adaptive MAC protocol for critical data transmission in wireless body sensor networks. Int. J. Softw. Eng. Its Appl. **9**(9), 205–216 (2015)

Lexicon-Based Approach to Sentiment Analysis of Tweets Using R Language

Nitika Nigam and Divakar Yadav[✉]

Department of CSE, M.M.M. University of Technology,
Gorakhpur 273010, U.P., India
nigamniti8@gmail.com, dsy99@rediffmail.com

Abstract. Sentiment analysis is a method to study the opinions of user on a subject like product reviews, appraisal or expressing any emotion on the entity. There are mainly two approaches used for sentiment analysis: lexicon based and machine learning based approach. We emphasis on lexicon based approach which depends on an external dictionary. Our aim is to classify the given set of tweets into two classes: Positive and Negative. We extract the semantics from the tweets and calculate the score. This score helps in classification of tweets either in positive or negative class. In this experiment of sentiment analysis, we used R language as a tool. R is a freely available software which is used for statistical computation, data manipulation, and graphical display.

Keywords: Sentiment analysis · Twitter · Lexicon based approach

1 Introduction

Recently, many people in the world use social sites like Twitter, Facebook, LinkedIn to share their views with the world. It is one of the best communication tools. Thus, the bulk of data is generated (known as big data) and for analysis the reviews, sentiment analysis was introduced. Sentiment Analysis (SA) is the process of finding whether the given texts have a positive, negative or neutral opinion. It also uses to detect the emotion of people, decision making process, etc. The formal definition of Sentimental Analysis is "extracting the semantics and determining the attitude of a speaker which conclude either positive, negative or neutral reaction." It was first time used in 2003.

It was also for analysis of pre-or-post criminal activities on social media, product reviews, movie reviews, news, and blogs, etc. The advantage of sentiment analysis is to improve the products, leads to innovations, growth in market etc. [1]. This method is also known opinion mining. This analysis totally depends upon the context provided by the speaker. Sentiment analysis is handled at many levels of granularity i.e. at the document level, sentence level, and phrase level. The most well-known use of sentiment analysis is in reviews of items and services given to the users. It is the application of natural language processing (NLP) and it is commonly used in a recommender system. In our paper, we are using

© Springer Nature Singapore Pte Ltd. 2018
M. Singh et al. (Eds.): ICACDS 2018, CCIS 905, pp. 154–164, 2018.
https://doi.org/10.1007/978-981-13-1810-8_16

data from Twitter. Twitter is an online social networking site, which provides a virtual environment for the people who are interested in hanging out together. It helps the people to express the thoughts on a subject. People post their views on numerous topics like a recent issue, party-political issue, Bollywood-Hollywood etc. There are many NLP technique which detects the sentiments of Twitter like Stop word removing, Parts of Speech Tagging, Name Entity Recognition (NER) which is trailed by bags of words etc. These techniques use dictionaries as the references. Since no training is provided, it requires less computational power. We are using lexicon approach which is used to classify the text into two classes: "Positive" and "Negative" with the help of dictionaries. The challenges that arise during extraction of the features and then doing classification of that text are given below but some of the challenges are removed by cleaning the text data set.

- Handling the big data which consist of the opinions given by the people.
- Informal languages, slang word/abbreviation or emoticons usage.
- Spelling mistakes/typo mistakes.
- Detection of sarcasm. [2]. E.g. Don't bother me. I am living happily ever after. Sarcasm: Speaker is taunting as well as hurting the person.
- Ambiguous sentences used by a user. E.g. I have never tasted a pizza quite like that one before! Ambiguity: Was the pizza good or bad
- Hashtag based text detection [3].
- Detecting hidden sentiment of a user.
- Polarity Shifting detection [4].

2 Related Work and Techniques Used on Twitter Dataset

Hearst in 1992 and Kessler et al. in 1997 initiated the research of sentiment analysis. There are two major techniques which are used for classification of sentiments of text Lexical analysis and Machine learning based analysis. In Lexical analysis, a dictionary-based approach is considered which is manually created by an expert. These dictionaries are used to interpret the word's meaning so that classification could be done easily. Dictionary contains adjectives words as pointers equivalent with semantic orientation (SO) (polarity or strength of text) value. The tokens are compared with the given dictionary which has been compiled already. The matched tokens are decorated with corresponding SO values by using a dictionary and, SO values are combined into a single score.

In [5] the author gave the method for opinion mining by using the lexicon based approach. The data set used was the reviews of products. They extracted features of reviews and classify whether opinions were positive or negative. These results were summarized so that shopper could get useful information. In [6] the author emphasized to resolve two major problems that occur in lexicon based method, i.e. (1) the context based dependent words, (2) combination of multiple opinion words in one sentence. A holistic lexicon based approach was proposed in which they compare another customer review if an ambiguous review was present. In [7] author extracted the sentiments from the text by using monolingual dictionary. In this approach, they calculated the semantic orientation (SO) value with help of dictionaries. These dictionaries consist of the collection of words with their strength and polarity which was created manually. The list consists of semantic-bearing words like adjective, noun, and adverb with their SO values. The model given by them is to handle the negation and intensification words (shifter valence). Without using any prior knowledge or training, their approach performs well and result well in the cross domain. In Machine learning based analysis, the opinions are extracted automatically i.e. it allows the computer to learn without explicitly programmed [8]. It gains more popularity due to adaptiveness and extracts many features easily. It is divided into 3 subcategories: Supervised learning, Unsupervised learning, and semi-supervised techniques. These techniques are used to extract the features like terms with their frequency count, Part of Speech, negation and syntactic dependency. In Supervised learning, the technique is applied under the guidance of a supervisor and it is an unlabelled data. Naive Bayes algorithm is a supervised technique and used for classification [9]. It is the best method at document level of classification. Support Vector machine is another algorithm which provides the maximum accuracy in text classification [10].

In [2] author proposed the pattern based approach which spots the cynicism on twitter. To find sarcasm they used a pattern based approach with the help of Parts of Speech (PoS) and for classification, machine learning approach. The feature extracted by them was classified as (i) Sentiment based (ii) punctuation based (iii) syntactic and semantic based (iv) pattern based. This classification helps in removal of noisy or useless data. They detect whether the text was sarcastic or not, in which they successfully achieve the accuracy of 83.1% with precision 91.1%. In [11] author proposed an innovative supervised technique in which the pattern analysis is done on writing skills and unigrams of tweets. SENTA tool (an open source tool) was used for extracting the features from the text which was classified into 7 classes "happy", "sad", "anger", "hate", "love", "fun", "neutral". The accuracy of multi class classification was almost 60.2% and after removal of neutral tweets, it was 70.1%.

In [4] author overcome the problem of polarity shift detection by proposing a model called "Dual Sentiment Analysis (DSA)". The DSA used the pair of reviews, original reviews and reversed reviews. These reversed reviews were created through data expansion technique which was the set of both training and testing reviews. The supervised technique was used for classification with the help of a dictionary, which was domain adaptive as well as language independent. They remove the dependency on external antonym dictionary which improves the performance but due to dual reviews, it consumes space as well as time. In [12] used the supervised learning approach and found unigram feature which results 73% accuracy. In Unsupervised learning, the data provided as input is unlabelled data without any output. No pattern is followed, and it contains discrete values. It is further subdivided into 2 categories: Clustering and Regression. Expectation-maximization is the algorithm of unsupervised learning. In [13] focuses on the sentiment analysis of social media site's data like Twitter, Myspace, and Digg. They projected a lexicon based, less domain specific, spontaneous and unsupervised learning algorithm to get a better result. The solution given by them was pertinent for subjectivity detection and polarity classification. The advantage of given approach was that it providess a robust and reliable solution. In Semi-Supervised learning, the features are extracted by using a combination of supervised and unsupervised learning. In [14] emphases on the extraction of features from phrase level in which they differentiate between the semantic orientation and contextual polarity. Their goal was to extract the important features which identify contextual polarity. Their experiment was 2 step procedures, firstly they identify all instances of a clue with the help of lexicon and after that, they classify each of them into polar or neutral class. In the second step, it disambiguates the contextual polarity of each instance. It improved the accuracy and the main advantage of their approach was that it solved the higher-level NLP tasks.

In [15] proposed the approach for analysis the sentiments of tweets. They focuses on data mining classifiers like k-nearest neighbour, random forest, Naive Bayes and BayesNet classifiers. Basically they are comparing the accuracy of these classifiers by considering stop words and without stop words. In [16] uses the "Naive Bayes classifiers", which is a probability based method. They uses the dataset on movie opinion given on twitter, a social site blog. The sentiments of tweets was calculated by using Hadoop framework. They baiscally, compares the datasets with and without emoticons. In case of emoticons, the emoticons are changed into its equivalent words while in other case, these are neglacted. In their approach the performance is increase in case of emoticons. In [17] author proposed a noval system for Hindi dialects given by user on different movies. This system is known as Hindi Opinion Mining System (HOMS). They uses the Niave Bayes classifier which also includes the combination of Parts of Speech (PoS) tagging and machine learning approaches for classifying the dataset into "positive", "negative" and "neutral" class. In the caseof PoS tagging only words which comes under adjective domain are taken into picture. The drawback of "HOMS" is that it can't handle "Discourse relation" like "but".

In [18] author done the sentiment analysis by using the machine learning approaches in different dialects(English, French and Dutch Languages). Their motive was to classifies the opinions given by the users on the products used by them. Since, they were extracting the feelings of people they train the set of opinions which was already decorated by tagging the words into "positive", "negative" and "neutral" class. This was done manually. They acheived 83% accuracy in case of English language, 70% for Dutch text and 68% in French language. In [20], the authors have concentrated on distributed data over the web which is in terms of reviews. Opinion mining is self-administer content investigation and rundowns of things accessible on networks which control our feeling and recognize positive and negative viewpoint for examining positive and negative feeling of the client.

3   The Proposed Method

The investigation of Twitter information is a rising field that needs more necessities substantially more consideration. There are various methods to classifies tweets into positive or negative class. Some researchers use machine learning approach and some uses lexical based method. The ultimate goal is to extract the sentiments of the given dataset.

In our paper, we use R language for our experiment. R is a freely available software which is used for statistical computation, data manipulation, and graphical display. It is a dialect of S which was designed by John M. Chambers in 1980. It provides many statistical techniques like clustering, classification etc. It can be easily run on any operating system (Windows, Unix, MacOS). It becomes popular because it provides following facilities:

1. Handles Big data.
2. Open source software and free.
3. Provides storage facilities.
4. Good graphical facilities as it produces graphical output in jpg, png, pdf, svg format and table format in latex and html. It can be easily extended via packages.

In our approach we have collected data from twitter and evaluated the result with the help of R language. The proposed methodology is illustrated in the form of flow chart and represented in Fig. 1.

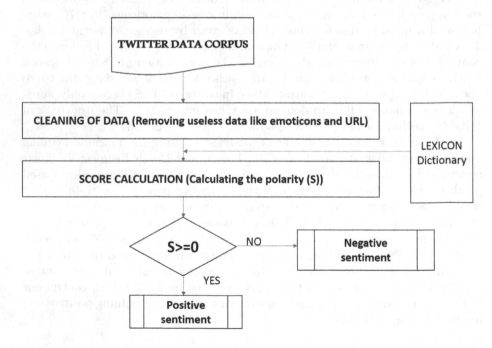

Fig. 1. Flow Chart on proposed methodology.

It consists of four steps which are enlisted below:

1. Collection of dataset.
2. Noise removal from tweets.
3. Lexical Analysis
4. Classification and calculation of score.

A comprehensive explanation of these steps in our approach has been explained in next sub sections.

3.1 Collection of Dataset:

The corpus is the collection of tweets on our Hon'ble Prime Minister Narendra Modi. The dataset is a collected with the help of twitter streaming API. API provides the authentication to access the tweets. In this, we acquire about 150 tweets and for that we used the following command of R for extracting the tweets:

#extract the tweets

modi.tweets <– searchTwitter("Modi", n = 150)

where, modi.tweets is a variable in which data is stored regarding the search on topic "Modi".searchTwitter() is a function which comes under "CRAN" package [19]. We passed two arguments which contain topic name (on which particular topic we need to collect tweets) and numbers of tweets required. In Fig. 2 we have shown extracted tweets.

3.2 Noise Removal from Tweets:

To enhance the performance, the dataset given as shouldn't contain any type of noise i.e. it should be clean dataset. In this section, we are removing noise from

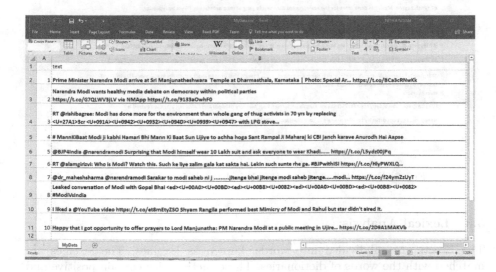

Fig. 2. Extracted tweets (10) about Prime Minister Modi.

tweets after extracting them. These are removed because it doesn't provide any time of knowledge regarding the output we want. While scanning the dataset, the useless data is also scanned which consume lots of time (CPU cycles are wasted). Due these reasons we are eliminating the noise (useless data) from tweets. Using R tool, the tweets are extracted and the next step is to clean the data. In the cleaning of data, the emoticons, URL punctuation marks/Target/ are removed shown in Fig. 3.

The useless data is explained properly below:

- *Emoticons:* These are facial expressions which are pictorially represented by using punctuation and letters. Emoticons prompt the attitude of a user.
- *URL:* User sometime attached the url with their tweet, which shows the address of a page. *Hashtag:*Users usually use to mark subjects.
- *Target :* Users use the @ symbol to refer to other users, which automatically alerts them. This is primarily done to increase the visibility of their tweets.

These are cleaned because we can easily understand the sentiments of the user by removing these useless data. For example, "I like a @YouTube video http://t.co/et8m Shyam Rangilla performed good" after cleaning it will look like "I like a @YouTube video Shyam Rangilla performed good". Likewise, "I love my India ☺" and after cleaning "I love my India" emoticons are removed.

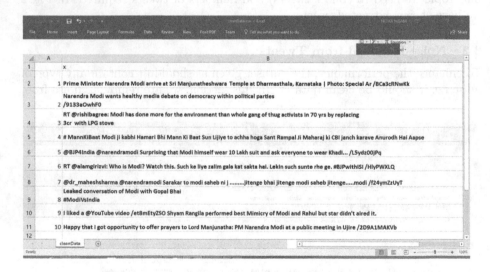

Fig. 3. Extracted clean tweets (10) about Prime Minister Modi.

3.3   Lexical Analysis:

The tweets are subdivided into words, known as lexemes. The lexemes are matched with the words of dictionaries. These dictionaries contain positive and negative words and it is manually created. These dictionaries consist of almost all types of words for example, "most of user uses short forms to express their views: You are looking good can be written as U r looking gud". So, we have consisdered all types of possible words that are used by people to express their opinion.

Some people uses hybrid language i.e. Hinglish "the combination of Hindi and English dialects". For example, "modi saheb jitenge" written by a user which express the feeling of user that he wants Modi ji to win. The hybrid language is not considered by us for sentiment analysis. As it will consume time in preparing a dictionary for hybrid language. The resources for these types of language are less in comparison of other language. Thus, our dictionary doesn't consider hybrid language words.

3.4   Classification and Calculation of Score:

In this section, lexemes are tagged with the help of dictionaries. The process of tagging helps in the classification of tweets, whether these are in positive sense or in a negative sense. The classification is done by calculating the score. The tweets words are matched with the dictionary words and if it is a positive word then score will be +1, negative words then score will be −1, otherwise 0.

The formula for calculating "score" is given below:

$$Score = Pos(x, \text{``}pos\_word\text{''}) - Neg(x, \text{``}neg\_word\text{''}) \qquad (1)$$

where, x is a phrase, pos_word is positive words and neg_word is negative words. The result of some tweets is shown in Fig. 4. In this, each lexeme in a sentence is compared with the dictionary words and assign the score accordingly.

	Text	Score	Positive	Negative
1	Text	Score	Positive	Negative
2	Prime Minister Narendra Modi arrive at Sri Manjunatheshwara Temple at Dharmasthala, Karnataka | Photo: Special Ar /BCa3cRNwKk	0	0	0
3	Narendra Modi wants healthy media debate on democracy within political parties /9135aOwhF0	1	1	0
4	RT @rishibagree: Modi has done more for the environment than whole gang of thug activists in 70 yrs by replacing 3cr with LPG stove	-1	0	1
5	# MannKiBaat Modi ji kabhi Hamari Bhi Mann Ki Baat Sun Lijiye to achha hoga Sant Rampal Ji Maharaj ki CBI janch karave Anurodh Hai Aapse	0	0	0
6	@BJP4India @narendramodi Surprising that Modi himself wear 10 Lakh suit and ask everyone to wear Khadi... /L5ydz00jPq	0	0	0
7	RT @alamgiritzvi: Who is Modi? Watch this. Such ke liye zalim gala kat sakta hai. Lekin such sunte rhe ge. #BJPwithISI /HlyPWXLQ	0	0	0
8	@dr_maheshsharma @narendramodi Sarakar to modi saheb ni j ....jitenge bhai jitenge modi saheb jitenge.....modi /f24ymZzUyT	0	0	0
9	RT @aartic02: Must Hear Leaked conversation of Modi with Gopal Bhai #ModiVsIndia /khV9BUkb0G	0	0	0
10	I liked a @YouTube video /et8mEtyZSO Shyam Rangila performed best Mimicry of Modi and Rahul but star didn't aired it.	2	2	0
11	Happy that I got opportunity to offer prayers to Lord Manjunatha: PM Narendra Modi at a public meeting in Ujire /2D9A1MAKVb	1	1	0

Fig. 4. Score of clean tweets (10) about Prime Minister Modi.

4   Experimental Results and Discussion

In this segment, we deliberate the output obtained after calculating the score of all tweets. All the results are stored in tabular form which are converted into a csv file and merged into one final table (table_final$Score). The final table consist of positive, negative and score values which is represented in the form of a histogram. This compares the final table values (-2 to 2) and the frequency of the score occurrence (0 to 5) as shown in Fig. 5.

The range is small because we have taken a less number of tweets in our dataset. Some of parameters are not taken into consideration, as it will be more complex. For instance, the hybrid language "Hinglish". The result can be improve by considering above parameters and using new techniques. In future, we will work on these problems.

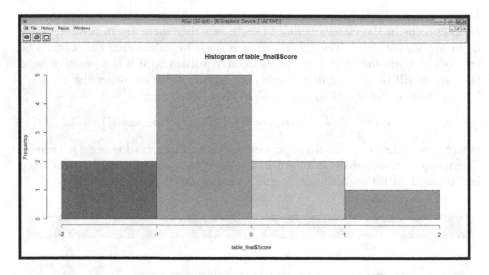

Fig. 5. Histrogram.

5   Conclusion

Sentiment analysis is the method of investigating the sentiments of the given text so that a good decision could be made for improvement. Mainly there are two approaches lexicon based and machine learning based. We have focused on lexicon based approach. In our experiment, we use a dataset of twitter and two dictionaries (Positive and Negative) which were manually designed. We have taken the support of R language for our experiments. Some of the twitter sentences are shown on Hon'ble Prime Minister Narendra Modi. The difference between positive word and negative word in a sentence was calculated which was stored in variable Score. Score states the polarity of the sentence, whether it is a positive or negative sentence. If the score has a positive value then the sentence is positive, otherwise negative. The result is shown in Fig. 5.

In the future, we will use machine learning approach to compare the result with the lexicon based approach. In addition, we will consider emoticons, discourse words and slang words used in tweets while expressing the feeling. Hybrid language and complex sentences will be considered too.

References

1. Thakkar, H., Patel, D.: Approaches for sentiment analysis on Twitter: a state-of-art study, arXiv preprint arXiv:1512.01043 (2013)
2. Bouazizi, M., Ohtsuki, T.: A pattern-based approach for sarcasm detection on Twitter. IEEE Access **4**, 5477–5488 (2016)
3. Joshi, A., Bhattacharyya, P., Carman, M.J.: Automatic sarcasm detection: a survey, arXiv preprint arXiv:1602.03426 (2016)
4. Xia, R., Xu, F., Zong, C., Li, Q., Qi, Y., Li, T.: Dual sentiment analysis: considering two sides of one review. IEEE Trans. Knowl. Data Eng. **27**, 2120–2133 (2015)
5. Hu, M., Liu, B.: Mining and summarizing customer reviews. In: Proceedings of the Tenth ACM SIGKDD International Conference on Knowledge Discovery and Data Mining, pp. 168–177. ACM (2004)
6. Ding, X., Liu, B., Yu, P.S.: A holistic lexicon-based approach to opinion mining, pp. 231–240. ACM (2008)
7. Taboada, M., Brooke, J., Tofiloski, M., Voll, K., Stede, M.: Lexicon-based methods for sentiment analysis. Comput. Linguist. **37**, 267–307 (2011)
8. Kanakaraj, M., Guddeti, R.M.R.: NLP based sentiment analysis on Twitter data using ensemble classifiers, pp. 1–5. IEEE (2015)
9. Rennie, J.D, Shih, L., Teevan, J., Karger, D.R.: Tackling the poor assumptions of naive bayes text classifiers. In: Proceedings of the 20th International Conference on Machine Learning (ICML-2003), pp. 616–623 (2003)
10. Schrauwen, S.: Machine learning approaches to sentiment analysis using the Dutch Netlog Corpus. Comput. Linguist. Psycholinguistics Res. Center, 30–34 (2010)
11. Bouazizi, M., Ohtsuki, T.: A pattern-based approach for multi-class sentiment analysis in Twitter. IEEE Access **5**, 20617–20639 (2017)
12. Boiy, E., Moens, M.-F.: A machine learning approach to sentiment analysis in multilingual Web texts. Inf. Retrieval **12**, 526–558 (2009)
13. Paltoglou, G., Thelwall, M.: Twitter, MySpace, Digg: unsupervised sentiment analysis in social media. ACM Trans. Intell. Syst. Technol. (TIST) **3**, 66 (2012)
14. Wilson, T., Wiebe, J., Hoffmann, P.: Recognizing contextual polarity: an exploration of features for phrase-level sentiment analysis. Comput. Linguist. **35**, 399–433 (2009)
15. Jain, A.P., Katkar, V.D.: Sentiments analysis of Twitter data using data mining. In: 2015 International Conference on Information Processing (ICIP), pp. 807–810. IEEE, December 2015
16. Parveen, H., Pandey, S.: Sentiment analysis on Twitter Data-set using Naive Bayes algorithm. In: 2016 2nd International Conference on Applied and Theoretical Computing and Communication Technology (iCATccT), pp. 416–419. IEEE, July 2016
17. Jha, V., Manjunath, N., Shenoy, P.D., Venugopal, K.R., Patnaik, L.M.: Homs: hindi opinion mining system. In: 2015 IEEE 2nd International Conference on Recent Trends in Information Systems (ReTIS), pp. 366–371. IEEE, July 2015

18. Boiy, E., Moens, M.F.: A machine learning approach to sentiment analysis in multilingual Web texts. Inf. Retrieval **12**(5), 526–558 (2009)
19. Ganeshbhai, S.Y., Shah, B.K.: Feature based opinion mining: a survey. In: 2015 IEEE International Advance Computing Conference (IACC), pp. 919–923 (2015)
20. http://rfunction.com/archives/1984

Twitter Based Event Summarization

Amrah Maryam[✉] and Rashid Ali

Department of Computer Engineering, Zakir Hussain College of Engineering and Technology,
Aligarh Muslim University, Aligarh 202002, UP, India
almas36912@gmail.com, rashidaliamu@rediffmail.com

Abstract. Twitter, a Social networking service produce a huge quantity of data daily for many trending real-world events. As hundreds of millions of Twitter users generate many posts on a daily basis, therefore it's very challenging to extract and summarize the user-generated content. Moreover, the Twitter API also provides only latest posts in a sequential order. This motivates the dire need for a new automatic event summarization system that provides the informative summaries of user-generated content that might help in making decisions supporting intelligence. In this paper, we intend to summarize the twitter posts corresponding to twitter hashtags to find a representative post among a set of posts that correspond to the same hashtag, with the intent to identify the strongly relevant post. We used two approaches Temporal TF-IDF and Temporal TF-IDF with keyword importance for finding the summary of the events. Then we evaluate and compare these approaches using a self-generated dataset of Twitter posts and show that our system automatically select posts that are more relevant.

Keywords: Event summarization · TF-IDF · Keywords · Twitter · Relevance

1 Introduction

Nowadays social networking sites like Twitter, Facebook, MySpace, Google+ etc. generate a huge quantity of data on a daily basis. Selecting the most relevant multimedia content about an event is a very exacting task because of the enormous and heterogeneous data content [2].

Twitter started in 2006 and has grown to one of the most popular websites on the Web. Presently, Twitter maintains over 328 million users that generate over 500 million tweets a day. Due to exponentially increasing user base, rich information content and an easily accessible public API, it has been a subject of various researchers in the near past.

Text Summarization is the process of summarizing a text document automatically with the intent that it would provide necessary information to the user. Generally, there are two methods of performing text summarization: Extractive text summarization and Abstractive text summarization. In Extractive methods, the summary is formed from the subsets of words, sentences or phrases from the original text. However, in abstractive methods, the summary is formed by rephrasing the original text.

© Springer Nature Singapore Pte Ltd. 2018
M. Singh et al. (Eds.): ICACDS 2018, CCIS 905, pp. 165–174, 2018.
https://doi.org/10.1007/978-981-13-1810-8_17

Twitter event summarization can be understood as the task of selecting the most relevant tweets from the set of tweets in a particular hashtag about an event. Moreover, this task can also be considered as a grading task where all tweets from the same hashtag are weighted according to their relevance measure.

In this work, we aim to summarize the twitter posts corresponding to twitter hashtags to find a representative post among a set of posts that correspond to the same hashtag, with the intent to identify the strongly relevant post. In addition, our method is able to satisfy the real-time requirement and is also applicable to a huge quantity of twitter dataset. We used two approaches Temporal TF-IDF [1] and temporal TF-IDF with keyword importance to selects posts with high relevance to form the summary of a particular event hashtag. Then we assess our proposed technique on the self-generated twitter dataset and proved that the system can automatically create the most relevant summary for an event.

2   Related Work

Summarizing micro blogs can be seen as a problem of automatically summarizing the given text by creating a concise form of the most relevant content from one or more text documents. During recent years there are various approaches developed for automatic text summarization for the social media content and some of the notables are discussed here.

In extractive summarization methods, a centroid-based method is very popular and MEAD [7] is one of its implementation. MEAD is a freely available, highly adaptable platform supporting many languages and summarizing many text documents automatically. It ranks sentences based on inter-sentence level and sentence level features including positions, cluster centroids etc. Similarly, Becker et al. [8] also proposed a centroid-based method in which they presented three approaches approach for selecting high-quality posts from a set of documents.

Feature-based methods include another form of text summarization methods. Sharifi et al. [9] have worked on the method that can summarize the whole twitter topic in one sentence indicating the highlights of the topic. LexRank is one of the implementations of the graph-based approach proposed by Erkan et al. [13]. The LexRank approach calculates the comparable importance of sentences in documents. They focused on proving that the graph-based methods are better than centroid based methods for summarizing the sentences.

3   Temporal TF-IDF with Keyword Based Importance

In this work, we have used two techniques Temporal TF-IDF based Event Summarization [1] and Temporal TF-IDF based Event Summarization with Keyword Importance that focuses on summarizing Twitter posts corresponding to Twitter event hashtags to provide for more precise and relevant event summary. These techniques are discussed in detail below:

3.1 Temporal TF-IDF Based Event Summarization

Temporal TF-IDF (Term Frequency–Inverse Document Frequency) creates the summary by considering the occurrence of a word in different timeframes. Temporal TF-IDF, like the TF-IDF approach, does not require the prior knowledge of entire documents for creating the summary of the document [1].

Generally, the frequency of each word (TF) occurring in the document and the total number of text documents where that particular word appeared at least once (DF) is required in the calculation of TF-IDF formula. However, the requirement of the prior knowledge of entire documents for creating the summary instigates a significant challenge of using TF-IDF in a place where the summary is required at the same time when the event took place.

Thus, to beat this problem we make use of temporal TF-IDF IDF considering all the posts in one-time frame in one document. After one timeframe, we take posts of the same hashtag from the antecedent timeframe in another document to add more relevance to our summaries generated. Accordingly, we employ the document frequencies of posts in two different timeframes in order to account for the dynamic and descriptive changing of real-time events. The TF-IDF formula is defined as follows:

$$w_{ji} = (1 \; / \; norm(d_i))f_{ji} \times \log(1 + N/N_j) \tag{1}$$

where f_{ji} is the number of times a word appears in the document d_i and N_j is the number of the document in which that word appears and N is the total number of documents in each hashtag. $norm(d_i)$ is the normalized length of each document.

3.2 Temporal TF-IDF Based Event Summarization with Keyword Importance

Keyword-based event summarization involves choosing specific terms from the text document that can describe the document in the best way on its own without any human involvement and then generate the summary of the top posts.

Keywords are like notions and topics that explain what the entire content is all about. In words of SEO (Search Engine Optimization), keywords are the terms or short sentences that web searchers type into search engines, also called "search queries". There are many ways to determine the keywords of a document but it has to be chosen with careful analysis of whether the keywords that are chosen fully describe the document.

Hashtags simply provide a way to classify a tweet's topic(s), which then makes easier for peoples searching for other tweets about those topics. Thus, considering the importance of hashtags we are extracting all the hashtags present in the document as the keywords (Fig. 1).

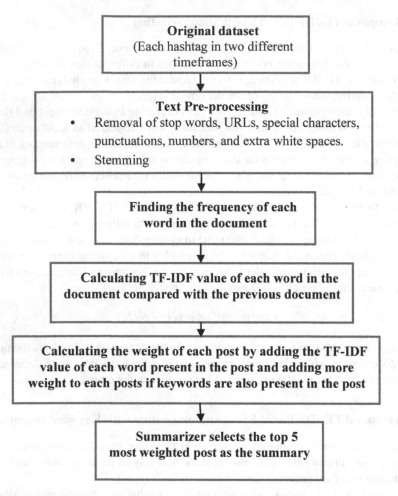

Fig. 1. Overall procedure for the keyword importance based Twitter event summarization.

4   Experiments

4.1   Dataset Generation

We have used the Twitter Search API to gather around 1.8 lakh tweets (180,000) of 120 hashtags posted from 6 September 2017 to 21 October 2017. We choose the top-10 most trending hashtags of different events each day, with approximately containing around 1000 posts per hashtags in two different timeframes (00:00 to 06:00 a.m and 06:00 a.m to 18:00 p.m). And in each hashtag, we choose top-5 posts using our technique (Temporal TF-IDF with Keyword Importance) as the summary generated by the system. The data corresponding to each hashtag is organized into 2 different CSV files representing the two different timeframes.

4.2 Implementation: Keyword-Based Event Summarization

(i) *Tweets Preprocessing:* A tweet has to be preprocessed so that it doesn't affect the accuracy of the model. We undertake following steps for preprocessing tweets:

Removal of stop words
Removal of ULRs
Identifying hashtags
Removal of special characters
Removal of punctuations
Stemming
Conversion to lowercase
Removal of extra white spaces

We also apply Stemmer to the words. Stemming involves the removal of the commoner structural and inflexional endings from words in English. For example, the word 'running' will become 'run': we won't count 'running' and 'run' separately in our dataset. It may improve the accuracy of our model [5].

(ii) *Term Frequency:* The frequency of each word occurring in the document i.e. term frequency is calculated. Term frequency (TF) is required for finding the TF-IDF value of each word occurring in the document.

(iii) *Term frequency-Inverse document frequency of each term:* The TF-IDF weighting formula is composed by two components: the first component is for computing the normalized Term Frequency and the second component computes the Inverse Document Frequency.

Here, we make use of temporal TF-IDF considering all the posts in the one-time frame as one document. After one timeframe, we take posts of the same hashtag from the antecedent timeframe in another document to add more relevance to our summaries generated. Accordingly, we employ the document frequencies of posts in two different timeframes in order to account for the dynamic and descriptive changing of real-time events.

For each event hashtag, there are a total of two documents representing the two different timeframes. Thus, temporal TF-IDF weighting formula (1) is given as:

$$w_{ji} = (1/norm(d_i))f_{ji} \times \log(1 + 2/N_j) \tag{2}$$

(iv) *Keyword Extraction:* In Keyword based event summarization method we are using all the hashtags present in the document as keywords. Thus first, we are extracting all the hashtags present in the document then, we are checking whether a particular tweet contains any of those hashtags. If any of those hashtags are present in the tweet then we are exceeding their weight by a factor of 0.5 for each new hashtag present.

(v) *Tweets Weight*: The total weight of each post is then learned by summing the TF-IDF value of each word occurring in the post and also incrementing the value of each post by a factor of 0.5 if that post contains the keyword.

(vi) *Event Summarization using Temporal TF-IDF with Keyword Importance:* The system then rank all the posts in decreasing order of their tweets weight and the resulted summary is the top-5 most weighted post.

5   Results

5.1   System Evaluation

We have done human evaluation to evaluate and compare the two approaches implemented (temporal tf-idf and temporal tf-idf with keyword importance based event summarization). We employed three different human annotators to label each post on the metric: Relevance.

1. *Evaluation Metric*

   For each post, the annotators have to label the relevance on a scale of 1–5, where the label 5 represents strongly relevant post and the label 1 represents a post with no relevance.

   Relevance signifies that whether the information contained by twitter posts is related to its associated event or not. Strongly relevant posts are the one that reflects clear information about its associated event.

2. *User Feedback based evaluation*

   The U-set table given to the annotators for human evaluation contains top 5 most weighted post generated from temporal TF-IDF method and also top 5 most weighted posts generated from temporal TF-IDF with the keyword importance based method. There are 10 maximum rows in each table where the first 5 rows are the result of temporal TF-IDF summarizer and the rest of the rows from 6 to 10 are the result of temporal TF-IDF with keyword importance. If any of the top 5 posts of temporal TF-IDF with keyword importance summarizer is same as the temporal TF-IDF based summarizer then that post is omitted from the U-set table. Therefore the U-set table has a maximum of 10 posts and a minimum of 5 posts (in case all the top 5 most weighted post of temporal TF-IDF with keyword importance summarizer is same as the top 5 posts of temporal TF-IDF summarizer). The U-set table of the #HurricaneIrma2017 is shown in Table 1.

   The annotators have to read the posts given in Table 1 and label the particular post on the scale of 1–5 on Table 2.

Table 1. U-set table for #HurricaneIrma2017

No.	Tweets	Date/Time
1	Ponce City Living: Georgia braces for a Category 5 Hurricane	07-09-2017 15:58:09
2	My beautiful #Miami today! We're getting ready #hurricane	07-09-2017 15:58:15
3	PBC Hurricane Irma 6 pm Update #WeAreWithYouPBC	07-09-2017 15:58:44
4	Be Prepared! Be Safe! Don't Panic! God Save us all	07-09-2017 16:02:59
5	Holy shit people are going crazy for water. Getting ready for #HurricaneIrma	07-09-2017 16:02:00
6	People from Northern Florida preparing for #Irma Vs. People from the Miami area!! #hurricaneirma2017	07-09-2017 15:57:12
7	#Hurricane #Irma cuts communication to Barbuda wreaks 'absolute devastation' #hurricaneirma2017	07-09-2017 16:02:00
8	Four deaths reported as #HurricaneIrma rakes Caribbean with Florida likely in crosshairs.	07-09-2017 15:37:42
9	Hope everyone in the caribbean islands are safe. this is so devastating	07-09-2017 16:34:10
10	Pray for Florida #Miami #hurricaneirma2017	07-09-2017 15:55:03

Table 2. Table for labeling posts

No.	Relevance
1	
2	
3	
4	
5	
6	
7	
8	
9	
10	

Now, we have to calculate the final labels in order to find out the aggregate between annotators. Since each annotator had given a different range of labels to each post, therefore, we have normalized the entire labels to avoid the bias caused by a different range of labels. Normalization of labels is performed using Eq. (3).

$$U_{norm} = (U - U_{min})/U_{max} - U_{min} \qquad (3)$$

Where, U_{norm} is the normalized value of label, U is the label whose normalization is to be done; U_{max} and U_{min} are the maximum and minimum label for relevance respectively.

3. Result

We report the result of the relevance of Temporal TF-IDF and Temporal TF-IDF with keyword importance method by calculating the average of precision at 5 of both these methods (table 3).

Table 3. Result of Relevance of the Event Summarization methods Evaluation

Average of P @ 5 for Temporal TF-IDF	Average of P @ 5 for Temporal TF-IDF with keyword importance method
4.68	4.68

Even if the relevance is coming equal for both these methods, it is quite possible that if we have increased the score of keywords by a factor of more than 0.5 (not just 0.5 say 1, 1.5, 2, 2.5 or more) then the Temporal TF-IDF with keyword importance method is more relevant (Fig. 2).

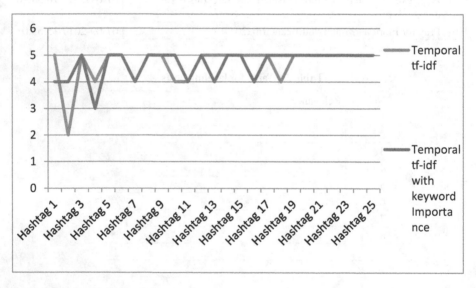

Fig. 2. Relevance of 25 hashtags on temporal tf-idf and temporal tf-idf with keyword importance method.

6   Conclusion and Future Work

With the increasing speed of information growth due to the vast amount of content generated by the social networking sites and the necessity of required tools for gathering relevant information from that multimedia content have called for a dire need for an efficient event summarization system. In this paper, we have implemented two summarization approaches Temporal TF-IDF, and Temporal TF-IDF with the Keyword Importance method to select posts or tweets that represent an event hashtag with strong relevance. We evaluate and compare these techniques using a self-generated dataset of

Twitter according to the metric relevance. The results showed that the temporal frequency based method and the temporal TF-IDF with the keyword importance based method are equally relevant in the human evaluation done by three annotators. However, if we increase the score of the keywords by some more factor (instead of only 0.5) then it is quite possible that the keyword importance method is more relevant.

There can be many fascinating ways for future work in this area. One could be to perform a pairwise evaluation of the two summarization techniques and perform further experiments on larger datasets.

References

1. Alsaedi, N., Burnap, P., Rana, O.: Temporal TF-IDF: a high-performance approach for event summarization in Twitter. In: IEEE/WIC/ACM International Conference on Web Intelligence (2016)
2. Shaifi, B.P.: Automatic microblog classification and summarization. B.S. thesis, University of Colorado, Colorado Springs (2015)
3. Becker, H., Naaman, M., Gravano, L.: Selecting quality twitter content for events. In: Proceedings of the Fifth International AAAI Conference on Weblogs and Social Media (2011)
4. Williams, G.: Data Mining with Rattle and R. Springer, New York (2011). https://doi.org/10.1007/978-1-4419-9890-3
5. Zhao, Y.: Twitter Data Analysis with R-Text Mining and Social Network Analysis. RDM, Canbera (2016)
6. http://blogs.lse.ac.uk/impactofsocialsciences/2015/09/28/challenges-of-using-twitter-as-a-data-source-resources/
7. Radev, D.R., Blair-Goldensohn, S., Zhang, Z.: Experiments in single and multi-document summarization using mead. In: First Document Understanding Conference (2001)
8. Becker, H., Naaman, M., Gravano, L.: Selecting quality twitter content for events. In: Proceedings of the 5th International AAAI Conference on Weblogs and Social Media (ICWSM 2011) (2011)
9. Sharifi, B., Hutton, M.-A., Kalita, J.: Summarizing microblogs automatically. In: Human Language Technologies: The 2010 Annual Conference of the North American Chapter of the Association for Computational Linguistics, ser. HLT 2010, pp. 685–688 (2010)
10. Nichols, J., Mahmud, J., Drews, C.: Summarizing sporting events using twitter. In: Proceedings of ACM International Conference on Intelligent User Interfaces, pp. 189–198 (2012)
11. Shen, C., Liu, F., Weng, F., Li, T.: A participant-based approach for event summarization using twitter streams. In: Human Language Technologies: Conference of the North American Chapter of the Association of Computational Linguistics, pp. 1152–1162 (2013)
12. Zubiaga, A., Spina, D., Amigó, E., Gonzalo, J.: Towards real-time summarization of scheduled events from twitter streams. In: Proceedings of the 23rd ACM Conference on Hypertext and Social Media, pp. 319–320 (2012)
13. Erkan, G., Radev, D.R.: Lexrank: Graph-based lexical centrality as salience in text summarization. J. Artif. Intell. Res. **22**(1), 457–479 (2004)
14. Mihalcea, R., Tarau, P.: TextRank: bringing order into texts. In: Proceedings of the 2004 Conference on Empirical Methods in Natural Language Processing (EMNLP), pp. 404–411 (2004)

15. Xu, W., Grishman, R., Meyers, A., Ritter, A.: A preliminary study of tweet summarization using information extraction. In: Workshop on Language in Social Media (LASM 2013), Conference of the Association of Computational Linguistics, ACL 2013, pp. 20–29 (2013)
16. Olariu, A.: Efficient online summarization of microblogging streams. In: Proceedings of the 14th Conference of the European Chapter of the Association for Computational Linguistics, EACL 2014, pp. 236–240 (2014)

Comparative Analysis of Fixed Valued Impulse Noise Removal Techniques for Image Enhancement

Rashmi Bisht[1]($\boxtimes$), Ritu Vijay[1], and Shweta Singh[2]

[1] Department of Electronics, Banasthali Vidyapith, Rajasthan 304022, India
rashmi.bisht2000@gmail.com
[2] Department of Electronics Engineering, KNIT Sultanpur,
Sultanpur 228118, India
shwetaknit.ec@gmail.com

Abstract. Various nonlinear image filters have been reported in the past years. But not a single study exhibits the performance of various filters for image enhancement analysis of image processing. This paper will show an exhaustive study and comparative analysis of Simple, Adaptive, and Decision based (DBMF), Decision-based untrimmed (DBUTM), Edge preserving median filtering techniques. This study is based on finding the parameter i.e. PSNR, MSE and IEF, Computational time. The above study will consider fixed valued impulse noise. For the analysis, the standard image of 512×512 size has been chosen. The simulation results have been calculated with fixed window size i.e. 3×3. For fixed valued noise, DBUTM and edge-preserving filters restoration results exceed other techniques. The image restoration performance of Simple Adaptive median filter exceeds counterpart at the high noise level. The DBMF is given optimized restoration in PSNR and computational time.

Keywords: FVIN · Median filter · Image filter

1 Introduction

Removal of noise is extreme demanded research domain in image processing. It is undesirable information which degrades image quality. Impulse noise is commonly encountered noise in digital images. It arises from the process of image acquisition and transmission. Fixed and Random valued are the two types of impulsive noise encountered. Fixed valued impulse noise (FVIN) has black/white dot appearance, also called Salt & Pepper noise. Random valued impulse noise (RVIN) can have any intensity pixel value. To remove these noises, it is necessary that the acquired image must pass through an image preprocessing stage defined as a filter. The primary task in noise removal is to depress the noise with preservation of fine details and edges. The fixed and random valued noise removal is two step processes. The noisy pixel detection is the first step, followed by replacement of corrupted pixel. The median filter is practiced as a foundation for removal of various kind of image noise. Here different algorithms of the modified median filter have been tested for test image and extensive results are presented and discussed for removal of impulsive noise.

© Springer Nature Singapore Pte Ltd. 2018
M. Singh et al. (Eds.): ICACDS 2018, CCIS 905, pp. 175–184, 2018.
https://doi.org/10.1007/978-981-13-1810-8_18

Image filters are classed into Linear and nonlinear filtering techniques. The linear filtering algorithm applies noise reduction formula to all pixels without identifying noisy pixels. The linear filter results, blurriness in edges and other image details. Averages, mean and median are some of the examples of linear filtering algorithms. The performance of median filter exceeds other linear filtering [1]. In median filter, a square window of odd size (3×3, 5×5, 7×7 etc.) are used. Window odd size is taken to get exactly the median and central pixel. The noisy pixel intensity is replaced by the median of its neighbor pixels coming inside the window. Recently various non linear techniques for noise reduction have been proposed. In all these techniques noise processing splits into two parts, detection followed by filtering. The efficiency of any noise reduction technique depends on both noise detection and noise replacement. As a result non linear filter can preserve edges and be very effective in removing impulsive noise.

Generally, all the filters give good results at low noise intensity (less than 50%) but they give poor result for high noise intensity. So, different algorithms are proposed to improve the range of noise reduction.

Satpathy et al. [1] have proposed Min-Max Median Filter (MMF), a nonlinear conditional filter. A window of 3×3 is used to scan image row and column wise. Every text pixel is checked by a condition. If it is found corrupted, median filter is applied, otherwise it kept unchanged. A weighted median filter (WMF) in the extension of the simple median filter which offers advantage of robustness and edge preservation capabilities has been presented by Brownrigg [2]. Ko and Lee [3] have proposed Center Weighted Median Filter (CWMF) which is the extension of WMF. It gave more weightage to central value of each window. Hwang and Haddad [4] have proposed adaptive median filter (AMF). It utilizes adaptive size window according to noise density of an overall image for noise reduction.

Wang and Zhang [5] have proposed Progressive Switching Median filter (PSMF). It performs better compared to already existing filter (Median, iterative median, CWM). Hsia [6] has presented adaptive filtering approach for image restoration at high noise level. It avoid edge remove by using adaptive size window.

The above discussed algorithms do not provide good restoration at high noise density. When the noise level of digital images increases, the estimated median value is noisy itself sometimes. To overcome, poor restoration at high noise density Srinivasan and Ebenezer [7] have proposed a Decision Based Median filter (DBMF) for removing impulse noise. Shekar and Srikanth [8] have proposed decision based unsymmetric trimmed median filter (DBUTM) for high density impulse noise removal. The algorithm estimates the pixel intensity by mean of all pixels in the selected window when all pixels are corrupted. Otherwise, noisy pixel is replaced by trimmed median.

The outline of the paper is as follows. The noise removing techniques are explained in Sect. 2. Simulation results, analysis and conclusions are presented in Sects. 3 and 4 respectively.

2   Fixed Valued Impulse Noise Removal Techniques

Spatial and frequency domain filtering are two basic types of image denoising. Spatial filters are the traditional method of image filtering. The traditional median filter is a basic nonlinear image filter. In recent years there are many improved median filters such as Simple Adaptive Median filter (AMF) [8], Decision Based Median Filter (DBMF) [7], Decision Based Untrimmed Median Filter (DBUTM) [9], edge Preserving Median Filter [10].

The classification of these filters is shown in Fig. 1 and detail analysis of these algorithms is done in a further section.

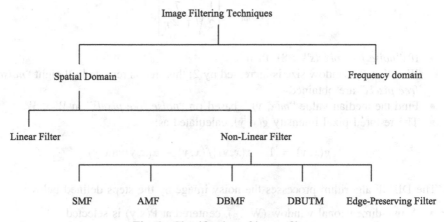

Fig. 1. Classification of image filters

The algorithm of the Simple median filter (SMF) given below:

- Check the processing pixel is noisy or not.
- Select a 2-D window W of size m × n, if the processed pixel found noisy.
- Determine median of m × n matrix and replace noisy pixel by the median.
- The above steps repeat until whole image processed.

When the noise percentage is high in image, then the number of non-noisy pixels is less at any window size to estimate correct value of the corrupted pixel. It is required to have an adaptive size of the window to restore image at high noise density. The algorithm of the AMF is as follows:

Stage 1: Noise detection and approximation of noise level

- A mask $\alpha(x, y)$ is defined:
$$\alpha(x,y) = \begin{cases} 1 : p(x,y) = 0, p(x,y) = 255 \\ 0 : otherwise \end{cases}, p(x,\ y) = \text{pixel intensity.}$$

- Total number of noisy pixel (k) is calculated: $k = \sum_{x=0}^{M-1} \sum_{y=0}^{N-1} \alpha(x,y)$

- Impulse noise level (η) is estimated using value of k. It is ration of k and total pixels contained in image.
  $\eta = \frac{k}{MN}$ (Should be between 0 and 1)

  Stage 2: Noise Cancellation

- Initialize the filter size:

$$W = 2R_{min} + 1$$

- Value of R_{min} is defined as:

$$R_{min} = \left\lfloor \frac{1}{2}\sqrt{\frac{7}{1-\eta}} \right\rfloor$$

- If (*"noise free pixels"* < 8); then
  W = W + 2; window size is increased by 2; this step is repeated till eight *"noise free pixels"* are obtained.
- Find the median value *"m(x, y)"*, based on *"noise-free-pixels"* in $W \times W$.
- The restored pixel intensity $g(x, y)$, calculated as:

$$g(x, y) = [1 - \alpha(x,y)\}f(x,y) + \alpha(x,y)m(x,y)$$

The DBMF algorithm processes the noisy image by the steps defined below:

- A two-dimensional window ($W_{3\times3}$), centered at P(x,y) is selected.
- Check, P(x, y) is corrupted or uncorrupted.
- If P(x, y) lies in between 0 and 255: noise free, else: noisy pixel
- If P(x, y) is noisy: calculate P_{med} of S_{xy}.
- If P_{med} is equal to 0 or 255: P_{med} is noisy and replace by P(x − 1, y).
- Repeat the above steps for entire image.

It is one step further of Simple median filter, results in performance enhancement in filtering operation. DBUTM algorithm is a modification of DBMF for digital image restoration. It works efficiently with highly impulse noise corrupted images. The filtering algorithm of the DBUTM Filter is as follows.

- Select two-dimension window ($W_{3\times3}$) centered at P_{ij}.
- If P_{ij} value lies between 0 and 25, it is an uncorrupted pixel.
- If P_{ij} is equal to 0 or 255 then P_{ij} is a corrupted pixel.
    Case i): If ("$W_{3\times3}$ contains only 0's and 255's")
  P_{ij} = mean ($W_{3\times3}$)
    Case ii): If ($W_{3\times3}$ contains not all elements as '0' and '255') remove 255's and 0's
  P_{ij} = median of the remaining pixels
- Repeat above steps until all pixels are processed.

In simple filter, sometimes the fine details or edge present in images is detected as noise. In the consequences, the fine details of images are also filtered. It results in the blur after filtering. An edge preserving technique has been developed to restore corrupted images. It gives superior restoration result with direction correlation dependent filtering. For each detected pixel, this method identifies edges in six directions and calculates the pixel intensity accordingly. Figure 2 shows the corrupted pixel P(x,y) and the surrounding pixel intensities.

a	b	c
d	P(x,y)	e
f	g	h

Fig. 2. Surrounding pixels of current pixel

The steps of edge preserving filter to find the output pixel intensity are given below:

- The eight direction difference D_1, D_2 ...... D_8 have been found as follows:

$$D_1 = |d - h| + |a - e|, \quad D_2 = |a - g| + |b - h|, \quad D_3 = |b - g|X2$$
$$D_4 = |b - f| + |c - g|, \quad D_5 = |c - d| + |e - f|, \quad D_6 = |d - e|X2$$
$$D_7 = |a - h|X2, \quad D_8 = |c - f|X2,$$

- Check whether the four pixels, e, f, g, h are equal to 0 or 255.
- If yes, the directional difference containing it, do not consider. The corresponding directional difference variable is set to maximum pixel intensity of 512.
- Finding the minimum among D_1, D_2 to D_8. This minimum value is denoted as D_{min}.
- The reconstructed value of noisy pixel is calculated as follow:

$$y_{i,j} = \begin{cases} \frac{(a+d+e+h)}{4}, D_{min} = D1 \\ \frac{(a+b+g+h)}{4}, D_{min} = D2 \\ \frac{(b+g)}{2}, D_{min} = D3 \\ \frac{(b+c+f+g)}{4}, D_{min} = D4 \\ \frac{(c+d+e+f)}{4}, D_{min} = D5 \\ \frac{(d+e)}{2}, D_{min} = D6 \\ \frac{(a+h)}{2}, D_{min} = D7 \\ \frac{(c+f)}{2}, D_{min} = D8 \\ \frac{(c+d)}{2}, D_{min} = 512 \end{cases}$$

- The last condition of D_{min} equal to 512 showing that all the pixels e, f, g, h are noisy and in this case the value of filter pixel is reconstructed by the mean of previously denoised pixels.

3 Simulation Results and Analysis

This section presents an exhaustive study of Fixed Valued Impulse Noise filters. For comparative analysis following parameters have been chosen:

- Window size: 3×3
- Standard image: Lena
- Image size: 512×512
- Noise density: 10% to 70%
- Noise type: Salt & Pepper impulse noise or FVIN.
- Image Filter: SMF, SAMF, DBMF, DBUTM, Edge Preserving Filter.
- Restoration Performance Parameter: PSNR, IEF, Computational Time.

The mean square error (MSE) indicates the average error of the pixels throughout the image. In general, a lower MSE indicates a less deviation between the original and filtered image. This means that there is a significant noise reduction. The MSE per pixel is calculated as per Eq. 1.

$$MSE = \frac{\sum_{i=1}^{M} \sum_{j=1}^{N} [Q'(i,j) - Q(i,j)]^2}{M \times N} \tag{1}$$

Where

i, j - pixel positioning coordinates
Q' and Q - Original and restored image respectively
$M \times N$ - size of image

For gray scale image, PSNR is defined as given in Eq. 2 and it's unit is decibel (dB)

$$PSNR = 10 \times \log_{10} \frac{255 \times 255}{MSE} \tag{2}$$

A Higher value of PSNR of restored image shows the better quality.

The IEF is a quantitative measure of the enhanced signal and is defined as the ratio of mean square error before filtering to the mean square error after filtering. The quality of the image is found to be enhanced if its edges are preserved and hence higher value of IEF denotes not only the higher noise reduction but also the greater enhancement of the image. It is given in Eq. 3.

$$IEF = \frac{\sum_{m,n} (Q'(i,j) - X(i,j))^2}{\sum_{m,n} (Q(i,j) - Q'(i,j))^2} \tag{3}$$

Where, Q' is noisy image, "X" denotes the original image and Q represents the denoising image. The IEF value is high; it indicates that the quality of the restored image is better.

Matlab (version 7.9.0.529) on PC equipped with 4GB RAM and 2.93 GHz CPU has been employed for the evaluation of computational time of all algorithms. Comparisons of performance are listed in Tables 1 and 2. A simple physical realization, as well as low computational time, has been obtained with fixed size 3 × 3 window. For quantitative analysis, performances of the filters are tested at different levels of noise densities and the results are shown in Figs. 3 and 4.

Table 1. Restoration results in PSNR (dB)

	Window size	Percentage of Noise Density						
		10	20	30	40	50	60	70
Median Filter	3 × 3	33.12	28.93	23.54	19.06	15.17	12.28	9.95
SAMF	3 × 3	41.38	37.67	31.19	29.68	28.55	27.56	29.51
DBMF	3 × 3	41.87	37.45	33.96	30.12	26.47	22.40	18.25
DBUTM	3 × 3	43.01	39.25	36.58	34.53	32.39	30.15	27.65
Edge Preserving	3 × 3	43.30	39.31	36.38	33.90	32.17	30.15	27.90

Table 2. Restoration results in MSE

	Window size	Percentage of Noise Density						
		10	20	30	40	50	60	70
Median Filter	3 × 3	27.03	68.277	259.334	770.502	1935	3791	6529
SAMF	3 × 3	4.01	10.33	21.56	35.87	55.45	85.26	152.51
DBMF	3 × 3	4.74	11.49	22.24	37.09	64.31	102.12	178.33
DBUTM	3 × 3	3.13	7.68	14.39	24.14	37.52	62.81	111.62
Edge Preserving	3 × 3	3.11	7.88	16.38	26.13	32.04	64.70	104.84

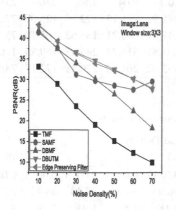 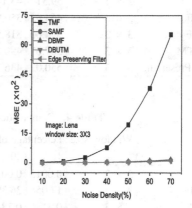

Fig. 3. Restoration results in PSNR (dB) and MSE

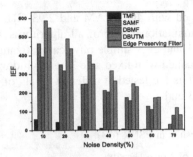 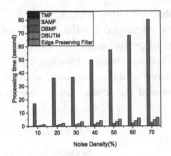

Fig. 4. Comparison of Restoration results in IEF and computational time (sec)

From the Tables 1 and 2, it can be observed that DBUTM and Edge preserving filters gives the highest value of PSNR and Lowest Value of MSE. It indicates the superiority of these filters over other median filters. At a noise level of 70% which can be considered as high noise level, the Simple Adaptive Median filter has the highest value of PSNR.

Tables 3, 4 and Fig. 4 are the test results in terms of IEF and computational time. A higher value of IEF shows good restoration of noisy images. DBUTM have highest IEF. At high noise level, DBUTM and Edge preserving filter have near about equal value of IEF. SAMF required maximum Computational time as compared to other algorithms. SMF needed minimum processing time but it is not fruitful as it results in poor restoration. DBMF have lowest computation time to process corrupted image with a significant good value of PSNR. DBMF results in the lowest value of time due to its less complex algorithm steps.

Table 3. Restoration results in IEF

	Window size	Percentage of Noise Density						
		10	20	30	40	50	60	70
SMF	3 × 3	59.51	43.14	20.17	9.04	4.80	2.92	2.00
SAMF	3 × 3	464.95	350.91	245.92	211.13	172.86	125.09	27.52
DBMF	3 × 3	394.60	318.50	247.01	203.21	155.62	107.16	75.37
DBUTM	3 × 3	587.67	490.29	403.81	316.24	245.53	169.85	116.80
Edge Preserving	3 × 3	550.02	436.31	353.62	261.94	230.21	172.17	78.50

Table 4. Computational time (sec) results

	Window size	Percentage of Noise Density						
		10	20	30	40	50	60	70
SMF	3 × 3	0.0013	0.0012	0.0012	0.0013	0.0013	0.0013	0.0014
SAMF	3 × 3	17.05	36.30	36.95	50.02	57.40	68.42	80.33
DBMF	3 × 3	0.41	0.78	1.18	1.55	1.93	2.28	2.72
DBUTM	3 × 3	0.77	1.50	2.07	2.69	3.34	4.01	4.68
Edge Preserving	3 × 3	1.460	2.38	3.35	4.24	5.19	6.01	6.51

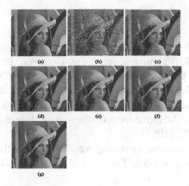

Fig. 5. Restoration results of noisy image "Lena" (a) original image, (b) corrupted image with 40% impulse noise, (c) traditional median filter, (d) AMF, (e) DBMF, (f) DBUTM, (g) Edge preserving Filter.

4 Conclusion

The results of the comparative analysis can be concluded in the following way.

I   The basic simple median filter has been studied with different window size, and it has been found that the filter gives the best restoration with a minimum size of the window, i.e. 3×3. As the window size increased further, the restored images have been found blurry.

II   The best restoration of noisy grayscale images in terms of PSNR has been achieved with DBUTM and edge-preserving filter for low noise level.

III The Simple Adaptive median filter gives the highest restoration in terms of PSNR at the high noise level. The increased restoration of SAMF has been achieved with increment in complexity and computational time. It has been proved that it is not a good option while moving for hardware implementation of real-time image enhancement filters.

IV   Best edge preservation has been obtained with DBUTM filter. The edge preservation is needed in real time edge detection system like medical imaging system, targeting any object in defense application etc.

V   The least computational time has been obtained with SMF filter but it has the least restoration in other terms. So it is not chosen over other filtering techniques when the low computational time is the main requirement. The best computational time with optimized restoration has been obtained with DBMF.

Figure 5(a)–(g) shows the results of filtering of the noisy image with 3×3 window. Comparison of these images clearly indicates that the advance version of median filter performance is good while the basic median filter performs worst.

References

1. Satpathy, S.K., Panda, S., Nagwanshi, K.K., Ardil, C.: Image restoration in non-linear filtering domain using MDB approach. Int. J. Inf. Commun. Eng. **6**, 45–49 (2010)
2. Brownrigg, D.R.K.: The weighted median filter. Commun. ACM **27**, 807–818 (1984)
3. Ko, S.-J., Lee, Y.H.: Center weighted median filters and their applications to image enhancement. IEEE transactions on circuits and systems **38**, 984–993 (1991)
4. Hwang, H., Haddad, R.A.: Adaptive median filters: new algorithms and results. IEEE Trans. Image Process. **4**, 499–502 (1995)
5. Wang, Z., Zhang, D.: Progressive switching median filter for the removal of impulse noise from highly corrupted images. IEEE Trans. Circ. Syst. II: Analog Digital Sig. Process. **46**, 78–80 (1999)
6. Hsia, S.-C.: A fast efficient restoration algorithm for high-noise image filtering with adaptive approach. J. Vis. Commun. Image Represent. **16**, 379–392 (2005)
7. Srinivasan, K.S., Ebenezer, D.: A new fast and efficient decision-based algorithm for removal of high-density impulse noises. IEEE Signal Process. Lett. **14**, 189–192 (2007)
8. Ibrahim, H., Kong, N.S.P., Ng, T.F.: Simple adaptive median filter for the removal of impulse noise from highly corrupted images. IEEE Trans. Consum. Electron. **54**, 1920–1927 (2008)
9. Esakkirajan, S., et al.: Removal of high-density salt and pepper noise through a modified decision based unsymmetric trimmed median filter. IEEE Signal Process. Lett. **18**, 287–290 (2011)
10. Chen, P.-Y., Lien, C.-Y.: An efficient edge-preserving algorithm for removal of salt-and-pepper noise. IEEE Signal Process. Lett. **15**, 833–836 (2008)

A Novel Load Balancing Algorithm Based on the Capacity of the Virtual Machines

S. B. Kshama$^{(\boxtimes)}$ and K. R. Shobha$^{(\boxtimes)}$

MSRIT, Bengaluru, Karnataka, India
Kshamasb08@gmail.com, shobha_shankar@msrit.edu

Abstract. Now a day's cloud computing has become a social phenomena by allowing users and enterprises to access the shared pools of configurable resources with the capacities of storing, managing and processing data in a privately owned cloud or a third-party datacenter sever. The major issues of this social phenomenon are security and performance. The better performance can be achieved by performing proper load balancing. Here, we have proposed a novel approach for load balancing in cloud computing environment using allocation of tasks to Virtual Machines (VMs) based on the capacity of the virtual machines. The proposed algorithm also utilizes the resources efficiently by distributing the workload among all the VMs.

Keywords: Cloud computing · Load balancing
Capacity based load balancing algorithm · Throttled load balancing algorithm
Virtual machines

1 Introduction

Cloud Computing [1] is the practice of using a remotely hosted network servers on the internet to store, process and manage data, instead of using a personal computer or a local server. In cloud computing the users can use the technologies without having dept knowledge or expertise about them, for instance using Facebook, checking bank balance etc. From this user can take benefits of those technologies like automatic software updates, disaster recovery, security, increased collaboration, work from anywhere, capital-expenditure free and document control. There are four deployment models in cloud computing:

Private: The cloud infrastructure is owned by a single organization having multiple consumers exclusively provisioned for its use and may exist on or off premises. It is operated and managed by the organization, third party, or combination of the two.

Community Cloud: The cloud infrastructure is exclusively provisioned for a specific community comprising of several organizations of common concerns like mission, policy, security, jurisdiction and compliance considerations. It may be operated and managed within the community or by a third party or some combination of them and it may be hosted on or off premises.

M. Singh et al. (Eds.): ICACDS 2018, CCIS 905, pp. 185–195, 2018.
https://doi.org/10.1007/978-981-13-1810-8_19

Public Cloud: This cloud infrastructure is provided for the general public for open use. It can be provided for free or based on pay-as-you-go model. The government organization, a private organization or combination of both may own, operate and maintain the public cloud, and it exist in the premises of the cloud provider.

Hybrid Cloud: This cloud infrastructure is the combination of either private, public or community cloud. Combined entities are bound together by proprietary technology for communication between them, but remains as unique entities. This gives more flexibility in the businesses.

In the cloud computing, users demand for varying usage of services. The cloud computing uses the pay-as-you-go model [2] for the payment in which user is charged only for their usage of the resources. The different services use different format of the pay-as-you-go model. There are three main categories of cloud computing services: Software as a Service (SaaS), Platform as a Service (PaaS) and Infrastructure as a Service (IaaS) [3–5].

Now a day's everyone is using services of cloud directly or indirectly. As cloud usage is increasing there is a need of computing and storage of resources. Plenty of user requesting at a single point of time may result in system break down or system imbalance i.e. a single virtual machine (a processing unit of cloud environment) with more work load while others with partially loaded or with no requests. The load balancing [6, 7] enables better resource utilization and system throughput by distributing workload among all the Virtual Machines (VMs). So the main objective of the load balancing method is to balance the system by distributing the work load among all the VMs and speed up the execution with minimum response time. Scalability is also major concern in cloud computing, can also be addressed by load balancing. There are basically two types of load balancing techniques namely static and dynamic.

Static load balancing [8] is one in which balancing of load is achieved by the prior information about the system during estimation of resource requirements. The static load balancing algorithms are easy to implement and have less overhead. The current state of the system is not considered in this technique while making allocation decision. The technique works properly only for low variation in the load for the VMs and are not flexible. In distributed system this has the major impact on the overall performance of the system due to varying load. So the static load balancing techniques are not suitable for the distributed cloud computing environment. Some static algorithms popularly used are Round Robin, Max-Min and Min-Min, suffrage Algorithms and Opportunistic Load Balancing (OLB).

In dynamic load balancing [9] the current state of the system is used to make allocation decisions Therefore dynamic load balancing is well suited for cloud computing environment in order to improve the performance and flexibility. The disadvantage of dynamic load balancing is that they are complex and difficult to implement as it requires monitoring of the system's current state. Some of the dynamic algorithms are throttled, ant colony optimization and honey bee foraging. The metrics that are considered for load balancing [10] are throughput, response time, make span, scalability, fault tolerance, migration time, degree of imbalance, performance, energy consumption and carbon emission. In the proposed algorithm we have considered the make span and average response time.

The remaining sections in the paper are organized as follows. The Sect. 2 contains the related work in which the classifications of load balancing algorithms and papers which are related to the proposed work are discussed. The proposed work is explained in the Sect. 3. The tool used and the experimental results are discussed in Sect. 4. In the Sect. 5 conclusion and the future work of the paper is specified.

2   Related Work

The existing load balancing algorithms can be classified into seven categories [10]:

1. General load balancing
2. Natural Phenomena-based load balancing
3. Hadoop Map Reduce load balancing
4. Application oriented load balancing
5. Agent-based load balancing
6. Workflow specific scheduling algorithms
7. Network-aware load balancing

The proposed algorithm falls under the General load balancing category. Some of the general load balancing algorithms are First-in-First-Out (FIFO), Throttled, Min-Min, Max-Min, and Equally Spread Current Execution Load (ESCEL). As specified earlier Min-Min and Max-Min are static algorithms and are not well suited for cloud computing environment. Hitherto many researchers have proposed modifications on throttled and ESCEL.

Maysoon et al. [11] proposed an algorithm by merging throttled and ESCEL algorithms. The proposed method maintains an index table of VMs with allocation status and count of allocated requests. During allocation, index table in searched for all available VMs. If available VM's size is equal to the user request then the request is allocated to that VM. Otherwise the VM with least load and suitable for user request is found and the request is allocated or else the request is queued for the VM. The disadvantage of this method is that it consumes more time to search a suitable VM, thus resulting in performance degradation.

Imtiyaz et al. [12] introduced a priority based enhanced throttled algorithm in which priority is calculated based on capacity of VMs, task count and size. The algorithm maintains an allocation table which stores VM id, VM capacity, Active task count, Status and Priority of VM. During task allocation the allocation table is searched for best suitable VM. Even though selection of VM is based on priority, the index table had to be scanned for selection of VM. Subalakshmi et al. [13] proposed an enhanced hybrid approach for load balancing in cloud computing environment. This approach is the advancement of hybrid algorithm which contains both Throttled and Equally Spread Current Execution algorithm. The algorithm maintains two lists: VMs index list and allocation list. The VMs index list maintains the allocation status i.e. it indicates whether a VM is available or not. The allocation list maintains the allocation count i.e. the count of allocated tasks to a VM. During allocation both the lists are compared. If VMs index list is greater than allocation list means that the VM is available then the request is allocated to available VM else the request is queued until a VM is available. When a new host is created and VMs are available, the requests in the queue are allocated to them and both the lists are updated. As authors have specified the algorithm is centralized and need to be combined with some other algorithm to make it distributed in nature.

A task scheduling algorithm has been proposed by Subhadra [14] to allocate the tasks among all VMs without overloading any of the VMs. The algorithm identifies the least loaded VM and checks the state of the VM. If VM state is available then the algorithm will return the VM id, else it finds the next least loaded VM which is available. Even though the algorithm utilizes all the resources properly it takes time to search for a least loaded VM. If the searched VM is busy the task is not allocated to that VM, again a new search is made to get the next least loaded VM, which is available. The previous search time gets wasted.

A Hybrid Approach of Round Robin, Throttle & Equally Spread Technique is proposed by Suman et al. [15] in which all the three techniques are combined in order to increase the response time and uniformly distribute the workload among all VMs. In this technique initially round robin is used to allocate the requesting user to the available server. Then the datacenter is allocated by using throttled algorithm. The process also consider the threshold (>75%) to consider other datacenters for the allocation. To distribute the load among active datacenters ESCE is used. If load of any active server is less than 25% then the load is transferred to another active server with required space and the former server is closed.

A Starvation Optimizer Scheduler is discussed by Ahmad et al. [16]. The scheduler is introduced in order to reduce waiting time, turnaround time of jobs and to increase throughput and CPU utilization of complete system. Initially a job pool is created with associated five characteristics (Arrival time, CPU execution time, CPU requirement, I/O resource requirement and job criticality). Based on these characteristics priority is calculated for each job. The higher priority jobs are assigned first to VMs. For remaining jobs VMs having least execution time is considered. The allocation of the job is based on the priority. The priority of a job is increased by one if waiting time of the job exceeds threshold value.

Shikha et al. [17] have enhanced the active monitoring load balancing (AMLB) algorithm in order to decrease the response time. AMLB finds the least loaded VM among all VMs. Along with least loaded VM the enhanced AMLB considers the recently allocated VM. This avoids continuous allocation to the same least loaded VM and allocates workload to all VMs. But the technique does not reduce the search time for the least loaded VM. A task based load balancing algorithm is proposed by Kaur et al. [18] in cloud computing using efficient utilization of VMs. In the initial phase the tasks are grouped into upper and lower class based on average length of cloudlets. Similarly, VMs are also classified into upper and lower class based on MIPS of VMs. In the next phase upper class tasks are submitted to upper class VMs and lower class tasks are submitted to both lower class and upper class (if available) VMs. During allocation utilization power of each VM is calculated.

Many researchers have worked on throttled load balancing algorithm and have proposed many enhanced throttled algorithm in order to improve the average response time of the cloudlets. Meanwhile they proclaimed that throttled algorithm performs better than other general algorithms like ESCEL [12, 13]. So, in the paper throttled algorithm is considered for the comparison with the proposed algorithm. The performance parameters that are used in load balancing algorithms are response time, turnaround time, make span, scalability, throughput, fault tolerance, the degree of imbalance and resource utilization [9, 18]. Here we have considered the average response time and make span as measuring parameters of the proposed algorithm. And also we have taken resource utilization into consideration while allocating cloudlets to virtual machines.

3 Proposed Work

The proposed algorithm is a novel approach for the load balancing in the cloud computing environment. The main goal of the algorithm is proper utilization of resources during allocation and to avoid the time to search for available VMs. To achieve this goal an array of lists of VMs is utilized. The array contains 0–10 positions; each position holds the list of VM/VMs based on the utilized capacity of the VMs. The reason for taking an array of size eleven is; utilized capacity will be in the range of 0%–100%. If VM is not utilized, that VM is stored in zeroth position. If half of the capacity of a VM is utilized then that VM is stored in 5th position of the array.

Initially the array contains NULL values which indicate that no VMs are created. Whenever the VMs are created, the list of those virtual machines are stored in the zeroth position of the array indicating that all the VMs are available with their complete capacity as shown in Fig. 1. During allocation of cloudlets, the cloudlets are allocated to the VMs which are in the list of first position of the array. Once a cloudlet is allocated to a VM, the VM is removed from current position list and moved to the other position of the array. The movement is decided based on the utilized capacity of the VM, which is calculated as follows:

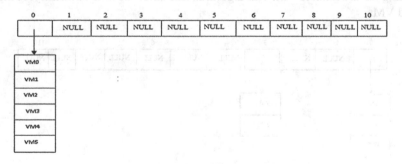

Fig. 1. Array representation of utilization of VMs

$$UC = L/((PE * MIPS) + BW) \quad [19] \tag{1}$$

Where,

UC - Utilized capacity
L   - Cloudlet length
PE - Number of processing elements of VM
MIPS - MIPS of VM
BW - Bandwidth

The Fig. 2 shows the movement of VMs. The position movement is done for VM0 and VM1 by allocating cloudlets to them one after the other. When a cloudlet is allocated to the first VM in the list at the first position of the array i.e. VM0, the utilized capacity of the VM0 is calculated using Eq. 1. Here in the figure the utilization capacity is assumed to be 0.3 for demonstrating the movement of VM. Therefore VM0 is removed from the zeroth position in the list and inserted into the 3rd position in the list at the end. If the position contains NULL value, a new list is created with that VM and stored in that position. When the next allocation is done to VM1 with UC = 0.3, the VM1 is removed from the 0th position list and added at the end of the 3rd position in the list. The allocation continues until there is no VM available in the first position. Whenever no VMs are left in the 0th position, the position holds the NULL value. Then the allocation is continued with next position that is having the list of VM/VMs. The process is repeated till last position. If the capacity of VM is filled then the VM is stored in the last i.e. 10th position of the array. Whenever all VMs are in the last position of the array, remaining cloudlets are kept waiting in the queue until a VM is freed up. Once the execution of a cloudlet is completed, again the position of the VM is changed. If a VM is finished with all the allocated cloudlets it is moved to the first position of the array. The first position of the array list holds all available VMs with complete capacity and the last position of the array list holds the completely allocated VMs. Therefore during the allocation of the cloudlets to VMs, there is no need to search for an available VM. It saves the time of searching for an available VM. This algorithm also saves the time of identifying the less loaded VMs.

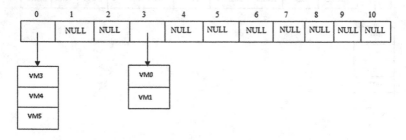

Fig. 2. Reallocation of VMs in the array based on their available capacity

The working of the proposed Capacity Based Load Balancing (CBLB) algorithm is shown in the form of flowchart in Fig. 3. The algorithm takes created VMs and cloudlets as input. In the first step array is initialized by inserting all created VMs at the zeroth position and NULL in the remaining positions. If there are no cloudlets waiting in the queue for allocation, stop execution. Else check for VMs' availability in array (Starts from zeroth position). A cloudlet is allocated to available VM; utilized capacity is calculated and based on utilized capacity VM is moved to new position. If no more VM is available in that array position, array position is increased by 1 and again allocation process repeats. Whenever position reaches tenth position cloudlets wait in queue until any VM is free. Whenever a VM gets free, its position is moved by calculating utilized capacity and allocation process continues.

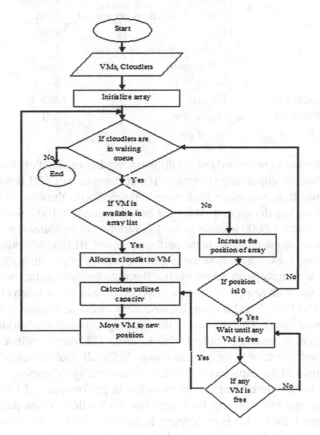

Fig. 3. Flow chart of proposed algorithm

4   Implementation

Nowadays many cloud computing open source simulators are available. Some of the simulators are CloudSim, CloudAnalyst, GreenCloud, iCanCloud, EMUSIM, GroudSim, DCSim. Among these simulators CloudSim is a java based tool kit which is highly generalized and extensible software framework for carrying out simulation in cloud environment. This toolkit enables seamless modeling, simulation and experimentation in cloud computing and application services [20, 21]. Therefore CloudSim [22] is chosen for the implementation of the proposed algorithm. The Table 1 shows the parameter setup for experiment.

Table 1. Experimental setup

No. of data centers	3	
VM parameters	Image size	10000 (MB)
	Memory	512 (MB)
	Million instructions per second	1000
	Band width	1000
	No. of processing elements (pes)	1
	VM monitor	Xen
	No. of VMs	50
Cloudlet parameters	File size	300
	Output size	300
	No. of pes	1

The experiments were carried out for different number of cloudlets from 100–1500 by keeping cloudlets length range constant. The performance of CBLB with respect to average response time and make span were compared with throttled algorithm. The different cloudlets length ranges used for the experiment are 0–1000, 0–2000, 0–3000, 0–4000, 0–5000 and 0–6000 in order to see the variation in performance.

The graphs are plotted to analyze the performance of CBLB and throttled algorithm. Figures 4, 5, 6 and Figs. 7, 8, 9 show the graphs for number of cloudlets against average response time and make span respectively. The deterioration in the performance of CBLB is observed with respect to average response time in Fig. 4 when cloudlets have short length. And Figs. 5 and 6 show improvement in the performance of CBLB for increased cloudlet length. This is because; throttled algorithm allocates a single cloudlet to a VM at a time. Whenever cloudlet length is short, VM completes its execution in a short duration and is available for next allocation. In CBLB, multiple cloudlets are allocated to a single VM for complete utilization of its capacity. Therefore when average response time is considered there is deterioration in performance of CBLB for short length cloudlets and improvement for longer length cloudlets. When parameter make span is considered, the CBLB is performing better than throttled for both short length and longer length cloudlets due to complete utilization of VMs' capacity, which is depicted in Figs. 7, 8 and 9.

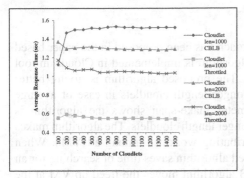

Fig. 4. Average response time for a fixed range of cloudlets lengths 1000 & 2000

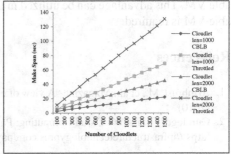

Fig. 5. Average response time for a fixed range of cloudlets lengths 3000 & 4000

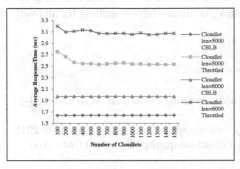

Fig. 6. Average response time for a fixed range of cloudlets lengths 5000 & 6000

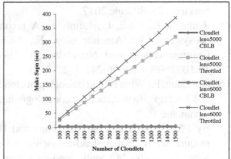

Fig. 7. Make Span for a fixed range of cloudlets lengths 1000 & 2000

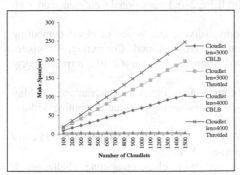

Fig. 8. Make Span for a fixed range of cloudlets lengths 3000 & 4000

Fig. 9. Make Span for a fixed range of cloudlets lengths 5000 & 6000

5   Conclusion and Future Work

A novel capacity based load balancing approach has been proposed in the paper based on the utilized capacity of the VMs. The algorithm is implemented in CloudSim tool and is compared with throttled algorithm. The proposed algorithm is giving better performance than throttled algorithm for longer length cloudlets in case of average response time. The analysis of the parameter make-span shows the algorithm is performing better for both short length and longer length cloudlets. The algorithm makes proper utilization of the resources by distributing workload among all VMs. When compared to throttled algorithm, the proposed algorithm saves time of searching for an available VM during allocation. The CBLB algorithm moves the freed up VM at the end of the respective positions list. During next allocation, the cloudlet will be allocated to the first VM in the list. This avoids allocation of cloudlet to the recently freed up VM. The major advantage of the CBLB algorithm is it avoids the time to search for an available VM. This advantage can be utilized in the algorithms where searching for an available VM is required.

References

1. Armbrust, M., et al.: Magazine "A view of cloud computing". Commun. ACM 53(4), 50–58 (2010)
2. Gundogdu, I.: PAYG Cloud Computing: Pay for Only what You Use!, 19 November 2015. https://infrastructuretechnologypros.com/payg-cloud-computing-pay-for-only-what-you-use/
3. Bhardwaj, S., Jain, L., Jain, S.: Cloud computing: a study of infrastructure as a service (IAAS). Int. J. Eng. Inf. Technol. 2(1), 60–63 (2010)
4. Zhang, S., Yuan, D., LiPan, Liu, S., Cui, L., Meng, X.: Selling reserved instances through pay-as-you-go model in Cloud Computing. In: IEEE 24th International Conference on Web Services, 25–30 June 2017
5. Rimal, B.P., Choi, E., Lumb, I.: A taxonomy, survey, and issues of cloud computing ecosystems. In: Antonopoulos, N., Gillam, L. (eds.) Cloud Computing, Computer Communications and Networks, pp. 21–46. Springer, London (2010). https://doi.org/10.1007/978-1-84996-241-4_2
6. Abraham, P.: What is load balancing in cloud computing and what are its advantages, 29 May 2017. https://www.znetlive.com/blog/what-is-load-balancing-in-cloud-computing-and-its-advantages/
7. By F5, "Load Balancing 101: Nuts and Bolts", 10 May 2017. Available:https://f5.com/resources/white-papers/load-balancing-101-nuts-and-bolts
8. Shah, N., Farik, M.: Static load balancing algorithms in cloud computing: challenges & solutions. Int. J. Sci. Technol. Res. 4(10), 365–367 (2015)
9. Milani, A.S., Navimipour, N.J.: Load balancing mechanisms and techniques in the cloud environments: systematic literature review and future trends. J. Netw. Comput. Appl. 71, 86–98 (2016)
10. Ghomi, E.J., Rahmani, A.M., Qader, N.N.: Load-balancing algorithms in cloud computing: a survey. J. Netw. Comput. Appl. 88(C), 50–71 (2017)

11. Alamin, M.A., Elbashir, M.K., Osman, A.A.: A load balancing algorithm to enhance the response time in cloud computing. Red Sea Univ. J. Basic Appl. Sci. **2**(2) (2017). ISSN: 1858-7658
12. Ahmad, E.I., Ahmad, E.S., Mirdha, E.S.: An enhanced throttled load balancing approach for cloud environment. Int. Res. J. Eng. Technol. (IRJET), **4**(6) (2017). e-ISSN: 2395-0056
13. Subalakshmi, S., Malarvizhi, N.: Enhanced hybrid approach for load balancing algorithms in cloud computing. Int. J. Sci. Res. Comput. Sci., Eng. Inf. Technol. IJSRCSEIT, **2**(2) (2017). ISSN: 2456-3307
14. Shaw, S.B.: Balancing load of cloud data center using efficient task scheduling algorithm. Int. J. Comput. Appl. (0975–8887) **159**(5), 1–5 (2017)
15. Rani, S., Saroha, V., Rana, S.: A hybrid approach of round robin, throttle & equally spaced technique for load balancing in cloud environment. Int. J. Innov. Adv. Comput. Sci. (IJIACS) **6**(8), 2347–8616 (2017)
16. Ahmad, E.S., Ahmad, E.I., Mirdha, E.S.: A novel dynamic priority based job scheduling approach for cloud environment. Int. Res. J. Eng. Technol. (IRJET), **4**(6) (2017). e-ISSN: 2395-0056
17. Garg, S., Gupta, D.V., Dwivedi, R.K.: Enhanced active monitoring load balancing algorithm for virtual machines in cloud computing. In: 5th International Conference on System Modeling & Advancement in Research Trends, 25–27 November 2016. ISBN: 978-1-5090-3543-4
18. Kaur, R., Ghumman, N.S.: Task-based load balancing algorithm by efficient utilization of VMs in Cloud Computing. In: Aggarwal, V., Bhatnagar, V., Mishra, D. (eds.) Advances in Intelligent Systems and Computing, vol. 654. Springer, Singapore (2018). https://doi.org/10.1007/978-981-10-6620-7_7
19. Kimpan, W., Kruekaew, B.: Heuristic task scheduling with artificial bee colony algorithm for virtual machines. In: 8th International Conference on Soft Computing and Intelligent Systems and 2016 17th International Symposium on Advanced Intelligent Systems (2016)
20. Nayyar, A.: The best open source cloud computing simulators (2016). Available:http://opensourceforu.com/2016/11/best-open-source-cloud-computing-imulators/
21. Calheiros, R.N., Ranjan, R., Beloglazov, A., De Rose, C.A.F., Buyya, R.: CloudSim: a toolkit for modeling and simulation of cloud computing environments and evaluation of resource provisioning algorithms. Softw: Pract. Exper. **41**, 23–50 (2011). https://doi.org/10.1002/spe.995
22. Goyal, T., Singh, A., Agrawal, A.: Cloudsim: simulator for cloud computing infrastructure and modeling. Procedia Eng. **38**, 3566–3572 (2012)

A Hybrid Approach for Privacy-Preserving Data Mining

NagaPrasanthi Kundeti[1]([⊠]), M. V. P. Chandra Sekhara Rao[2],
Naga Raju Devarakonda[3], and Suresh Thommandru[3]

[1] Department of CSE, Acharya Nagarjuna University,
Guntur, Andhra Pradesh, India
prasanthi.kundeti@gmail.com
[2] Department of CSE, RVR & JC College of Engineering,
Guntur, Andhra Pradesh, India
manukondach@gmail.com
[3] Department of IT, LBR College of Engineering,
Mylavaram, Krishna Dt., Andhra Pradesh, India
dnagaraj_dnr@yahoo.co.in,
sureshthommandru007@gmail.com

Abstract. In recent years, the growing capacity of information storage devices has led to increased storing personal information about customers and individuals for various purposes. Data mining needs extensive amount of data to do analysis for finding out patterns and other information which could be helpful for business growth, tracking health data, improving services, etc. This information can be misused for many reasons like identity theft, fake credit/debit card transactions, etc. To avoid these situations, data mining techniques which secure privacy are proposed. Data Perturbation, Knowledge Hiding, Secure Multiparty computation and privacy aware knowledge sharing are some of the techniques of privacy preserving data mining. A combination of these approaches is applied to get better privacy. In this paper we discuss in detail about geometric data perturbation technique and k-anonymization technique and prove that data mining results after perturbation and anonymization also are not changed much.

Keywords: Data mining · Privacy preserving data mining · Data perturbation
K-anonymization

1 Introduction

In current age, data plays an important role in extracting knowledge. From decades companies running software systems are flooded with lot of data which is of no use to them. Through Data Mining those large volumes of data can be processed and useful patterns can be identified. These patterns help managers to take decisions to improve their businesses. However, the collected information may contain some sensitive information which raises privacy concern.

Privacy does not has a benchmark definition [2]. Westin [4] defined privacy as "the assertion of individuals, groups or institutions to specify when, how and to what extent their information can be shared to others."

© Springer Nature Singapore Pte Ltd. 2018
M. Singh et al. (Eds.): ICACDS 2018, CCIS 905, pp. 196–207, 2018.
https://doi.org/10.1007/978-981-13-1810-8_20

Bertino [5] et al. gave a similar definition as "the security of data about an individual contained in an electronic repository from unauthorized disclosure."

Privacy preservation methods protect from information leakage by modifying the original data and protect owner's exposure.[6, 7]. But utility of data is reduced by data transformation. This data transformation results in inaccurate or infeasible knowledge extraction through data mining. Privacy preserving data mining (PPDM) methodologies are equipped with certain level of privacy, while not compromising data utility and still provide efficient data mining. PPDM is a collection of techniques that preserve privacy while extracting knowledge from data. While carrying out data mining, there is a chance for private data to be disclosed in the public and PPDM protects from this disclosure. PPDM is latest area of research and many algorithms are proposed for it. Different techniques preserve privacy in different levels of data mining process. There are three layers in PPDM framework namely Data Collection Layer(DCL) at lower level, Data Pre-process Layer(DPL) at middle level and Data Mining Layer(DML) at higher level.

2 PPDM FrameWork

According to the PPDM framework defined by Li et al. [1] the PPDM techniques are categorized based on data mining process stages. DCL has huge collection of data providers and sensitive information may be part of this data. Data can be collected without losing privacy. In DPL, the data that is collected in DCL layer is stored in data warehouses and later processed by data warehouse servers. There are two aspects of privacy preservation in this layer. (i) datapre processing in such a way that privacy is preserved for doing data mining later and (ii) security of data access. Actual data mining is performed by data mining servers and data miners and results are provided in third layer. There are two aspects for privacy preservation in this layer. They are (a) incorporating privacy features into data mining methods, (b) combining lot of data sets from different parties and carrying out collaborative data mining without any private information revelation (Fig. 1).

Privacy at Data Collection Layer:
In order to provide privacy at data collection time, raw data need to be randomized and stored. If original values are stored there is a chance of privacy leakage. So, randomization is performed for each value separately. According to statistical distribution, noise is calculated and added to data to modify data in randomization methods. Simple randomization approach is described as: if X is original data distribution, Y is noise distribution already known and Z is result of randomization then definition of Z can be given as

$$Z = X + Y \tag{1}$$

Later X is constructed as $X = Z - Y$. We can not reconstruct entire X as it is but only X distribution can be reconstructed. This is known as additive noise. There is another way

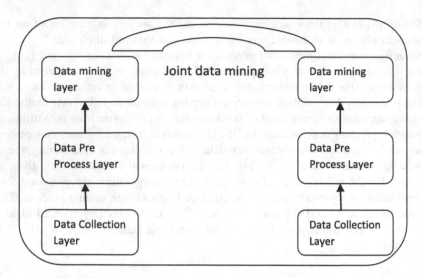

Fig. 1. A PPDM framework

of randomization that is perturbing the data i.e. modify original data into perturbed data. Data mining algorithms which are based on distribution of data rather than individual values are used. But there is loss of data readability. When compared to the privacy preservation, the data readability loss is negligible. So, this method is followed. Randomization is a subset of data perturbation.

Data Privacy: Data privacy is generally identified as a level of difficulty, an attacker has to face in approximately identifying the original data from the available perturbed data. PPDM Techniques are said to provide higher level of privacy if estimation of original data from perturbed data is more difficult. Geometric data perturbation provides moderate level of data privacy but is more efficient compared to other algorithms [3].

Data Utility: Based on quantity of important data that is preserved after perturbation the level of data utility is defined. In this paper we present the steps of geometric data perturbation based on [3]. Many data mining models can be applied with geometric data perturbation for privacy preservation and they also provide better utility.

Some of the data perturbation techniques are mentioned as following.

Noise Additive Perturbation: "It is an additive randomization which is a column based one. This kind of technique is based upon the two factors i.e. (1) Data owner does not require to secure all components in a record equally, this gives the freedom to apply column based distortion on some sensitive fields. (2) Individual records are not needed for Classification model. Chosen Classification models only require value distributions and assume that they are independent columns " [3]. The fundamental method adds the certain amount of noise to the columns, keeping the structure intact and can be easily recreated from bewildered data.

A classic random noise addition model is outlined as following. Let a variable K having some distributions, be described as (k1, k2, k3... kn). The random noise addition process changes its original value by adding some kind of noise R and generates perturbed value Y. Now Y will be K + R, resulting into(k1 + r1, k2 + r2, k3 + r3 ...kn + rn). Using this noise R, the original value K can be recovered by applying reconstruction algorithm on the perturbed values [3].

While this approach is simple, it has some cons. Several researchers have found that it is easy to perform reconstruction based attacks, which is major weakness of randomized noise addition approach. Also, resembling properties of the perturbed data can become handy to identify and remove noise from the perturbed data. Moreover, algorithms like association rule mining and decision tree are based on the autonomic columns assumption and work only on column distributions. These algorithms can be modified to reconstruct the column distributions from modified datasets [3].

Condensation-Based Algorithm: "This is a multi-dimensional data perturbation technique. This technique preserves the dispersion matrix for multiple columns. Decision boundary which is a geometric property is preserved well. This algorithm unlike the randomize approach, disturbs multiple columns at a time and generates the entire new dataset. Because of above mentioned properties, modified data sets can be directly used in many existing data mining algorithms without any change or need to develop new algorithms" [3].

"The approach is outlined as follows. Algorithm begins by partitioning the original dataset Dinto number of groups of records, say k-record groups. There are two parts in each group. One is a center of the group, selected randomly from the original dataset and the other part is of (k–1) members from original dataset, found using k-1 nearest neighbours. These chosen k records are first deleted from the original dataset. Then the remaining groups are materialized. Advantage of having small locality of the group, it is achievable to revive k records set to maintain the covariance and distribution.

The size of the locality is reciprocal of the preservation of covariance with regenerated k records. If in each group, size of locality is smaller, then it offers better quality of covariance preservation for regenerated k records" [3].

Rotation Perturbation: "For privacy preserving data clustering this technique is nominated. Geometric data perturbation has rotation perturbation as one of its major component. The definition of Rotation perturbation is given as $G(X) = R*X$ where $X_{d \times n}$ is the original dataset and $R_{d \times d}$ is rotation matrix which is randomly generated. Distance preservation is the unique benefit as well as major weakness of this method. This method is vulnerable to distance-inference attacks" [3].

Random Projection Perturbation: "In this technique data points from original multi-dimensional space are projected into another arbitrarily chosen multidimensional space. Let $Q_{k \times d}$ be a random projection matrix. Here, Q contains orthonormal rows.

$$G(x) = \sqrt{d}/kQX \tag{2}$$

The above formula is administered to ruffle the dataset C. According to Johnson – Lindenstrauss Lemma, projection perturbation approximately preserves the distance. A given data set in Euclidean space can be mapped into another space. This mapping should preserve the pairwise distance of any two points with least error. This results in model quality preservation" [3].

Privacy at Data Pre-process Layer

Data Anonymization is the most prevalent method used for preserving privacy at DPL (data pre-process layer). This data anonymization (k-anonymization) prevents the identity disclosure of data owners in public [10]. The k-anonymization technique works by specifying k-value so that there are k identical records in data.

In this, each record is identical toatleast k−1 other records. Table 1 shows an example data for a number of patients which is 4-anonymous. There are some distinctive attributes which identify a patient individually like age, country, disease, pincode. These attributes are categorized into two sets. They are attributes which are sensitive and non-sensitive attributes. Opponents should not be able to find these sensitive attributes ex. Ailment. Non-sensitive attributes like pincode, country and age are also called quasi-identifier attributes for the given data set.

Table 1. 4-anonymous data example

	Non-sensitive attributes			Sensitive attributes
	PinCode	Age	Country	Ailment
1	210**	≤ 30	*	Flu
2	210**	≤ 30	*	Flu
3	210**	≤ 30	*	Cancer
4	210**	≤ 30	*	orthoritis
5	250**	>40	*	Flu
6	250**	>40	*	Cardiomyopathy
7	250**	>40	*	Cancer
8	250**	>40	*	Diabetes
9	313**	≥ 55	*	Cancer
10	313**	≥ 55	*	Diabetes
11	313**	≥ 55	*	orthoritis
12	313**	≥ 55	*	cancer

According to L seweney's survey [12], we can not protect individual's privacy by simply eliminating explicit unique identifier. In the given table there are atleast 4 records which have identical values for every set of quasi-identifier attributes. K-anonymization is often performed by data generalization and suppression [11].

3 Geometric Data Perturbation

Translation transformation (Ψ), Multiplicative transformation (R) and distance per-turbation (Δ) are applied in a specific sequence to obtain geometric data perturbation.

$$G(X) = RX + \Psi + \Delta \qquad (3)$$

Multiplicative Transformation (R): Generally rotation matrix or random projection matrix are part of this. Distances are preserved exactly by rotation matrix. Exact distances are preserved by rotation matrix. Only Approximate distances are preserved by random projection. Rotation matrix protects the Euclidean distance. One of the crucial component of geometric perturbation is rotation perturbation.

Rotation perturbation protects ruffled data from naive estimation attacks. Rotation perturbation can be protected from more complicated attacks by using other compo-nents of geometric perturbation. The definition for random projection matrix $R_{k \times d}$ is given as R = sqrt((d/k)R$_0$). The Johnson- Lindenstrauss Lemma state that approximate Euclidean distances can be preserved by random projection when certain conditions are satisfied [3].

Translation Transformation ψ: In original space consider two points x and y, with translation the new distance will be $\| (x-t) - (y-t) \| = | x - y \|$. Therefore, distance is always preserved by translation. Translation perturbation alone can not furnish data protection.

Attacker can identify original data by cancelling translation perturbation if only it is applied alone. In order to resist attacks translation is combined with rotation perturbation.

Distance Perturbation: The distance relationship is preserved by above two com-ponents. However, distance-inference attacks can still be performed on distance preserving perturbation. The main aim of distance perturbation is to resist distance-inference attacks while preserving distances. Here, distance perturbation can be noise. As noise intensity is low, applying only other two components will not carry out privacy preservation.

The major issue of distance perturbation is a trade off between reduction of model accuracy and gain of privacy guarantee. The data owner may opt not to use distance perturbation with the assumption that data is secure and attacker does not know about the original data. Hence, distance-inference attacks are avoided.

The below graph will help summarizing about Random rotation, random projection and geometric dataperturbation (Table 2).

Table 2. Comparision of perturbation techniques

Random rotation	Geometric perturbation	Random projection
Y = R*X X is the original dataset for all three formulas Y is the perturbed dataset for all three formulas R is the random rotation matrix	Y = RX + T + D R is the secret rotation matrix (preserves Euclidean distances) T is the secret random translation matrix. D is the secret random noise matrix.	Y = A*X A is the random projection matrix.
Distances are preserved. Less secured [9].	Distances are approximately preserved [8].	Distance is not well preserved. Loss of Data [8].
Accuracy depends on the rotation matrix	Good accuracy than any other perturbation techniques.	Worse accuracy than geometric data perturbation

3.1 Algorithm: Geometric Data Perturbation

The idea behind using Geometric Data Perturbation algorithm is its simplicity. Geometric perturbation is nothing but the improvement to the rotation perturbation by coupling it with additional components like random translation perturbation and noise addition to the basic form of multiplicative perturbation Y = R £ X. Two additional components are added to normal rotation perturbation.

When compared to normal rotation based perturbation, geometric perturbation is more robust and efficient.

For each attribute of G(X), let T be the translation, random rotation R, D be a Gaussian Noise and X be the original dataset. The value of the attribute G(X) can be found using following formula.

$$G(X) = R * X + T + D \tag{4}$$

Procedure: Geometric transformation based Multiplicative data perturbation
Input: Dataset D, Sensitive attribute S.
Intermediate result: Perturbed dataset D'
Output: Classification result R and R' for dataset D and D' respectively (Fig. 2).

Now apply classification algorithm on data set D with sensitive attribute S and obtain results. Apply classification algorithm on perturbed data set D^1 and obtain results. Compare both the results and analyze the accuracy.

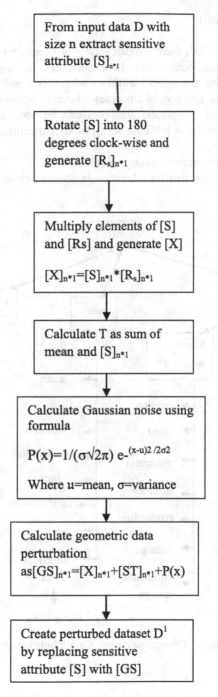

Fig. 2. Geometric data perturbation steps

4   K-Anonymization

In the perturbed data set, D^1, there are categorical attributes which can not be applied with geometric data perturbation. For those attributes we applied k-anonymization technique by generalizing the quasi identifiers wherever possible. The generalization hierarchy is followed for categorical attributes wherever necessary.

The generalization of categorical attributes can be obtained from the following hierarchical trees. In this the Adult data set from UCI machine learning repository is used for implementation.

The hierarchy tree for native-country is (Fig. 3).

Similarly the hieararchy tree for education is shown below (Fig. 4).

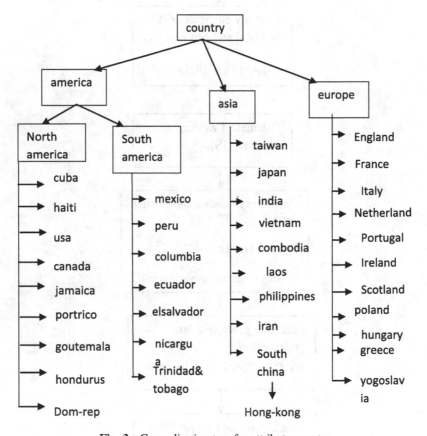

Fig. 3. Generalization tree for attribute country

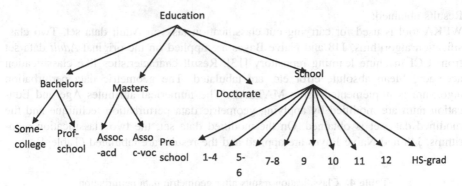

Fig. 4. Generalization tree for attribute education

5 Implementation

In this paper we have taken *Adult* data set from UCI Machine learning repository [13]. The data set contained 48,842 instances with 15 attributes. The Implementation part is carried out in two steps namely Step1: Applying geometric data perturbation and perform classification. Step2: Applying K-anonymization after perturbation and perform classification.

The geometric random perturbation technique can be applied on only numeric data. So this method is applied on attributes age and education-num. The data set is described as below (Table 3).

Table 3. Adult data set description

Attribute	Data type
Age	Numeric
Fnlwgt	Numeric
Work class	Text
Education	Text
Education num	Numeric
Marital Status	Text
Occupation	Text
Relationship	Text
Race	Text
Sex	Text
Capital gain	Numeric
Hours per week	Numeric
Native country	Text
Capital loss	Numeric
Class label	Text

Results obtained:
WEKA tool is used for carrying out classification task on Adult data set. Two classification algorithms, J48 and Naive Bayes are applied on the original *Adult* data set from UCI machine learning repository [13]. Result characteristics like classification accuracy, Mean absolute error etc. are tabulated. The geometric data perturbation algorithm is implemented using MATLAB. The numerical attributes Age and Education num are modified by applying geometric data perturbation technique and the modified data set is obtained. On the modified data set, the two classification algorithms, J48 and Naive Bayes are applied and the results are tabulated (Table 4).

Table 4. Classification results after geometric data perturbation

	Age				Education num			
	NB		J48		NB		J48	
	Original	Perturbed	Original	Perturbed	Original	Perturbed	Original	Perturbed
Correctly classified instances	0.8379	0.8363	0.8574	0.8550	0.8379	0.8272	0.8574	0.8542
Incorrectly classified instances	0.1620	0.1636	0.1425	0.1449	0.1620	0.1727	0.1425	0.1457
Kappa statistics	0.5191	0.4897	0.5732	0.5722	0.5191	0.4486	0.5732	0.5531
Mean absolute error	0.1704	0.1711	0.1917	0.1974	0.1704	0.1753	0.1974	0.2059
Root mean squared error	0.3655	0.3711	0.3191	0.3208	0.3655	0.3756	0.3191	0.3297
Relative absolute error	0.4641	0.4718	0.5286	0.5444	0.4641	0.4834	0.5286	0.5677

Since geometric data perturbation can be applied only to numerical attributes, for categorical attributes k-anonymization technique is applied. All the categorical attributes are generalized in such a way that atleast k records in perturbed data will have same values for the categorical quasi identifier attributes education, native country. The modified data set in step1 is applied with K-anonymization and final modified data set is obtained. The classification algorithms Naive Bayes and J48 are applied on final modified dataset. The results obtained after k-anonymization with k = 3 are shown below (Table 5).

Table 5. Final classification result after applying k-anonymization

	NB	J48
Correctly classified instances	0.8154	0.8488
Incorrectly classified instances	0.1845	0.1511
Kappa Statistics	0.4082	0.5477
Mean absolute error	0.1902	0.2087
Root mean squared error	0.3895	0.3312
Relative absolute error	0.5226	0.5735

6 Conclusion

In this paper, we proposed an effective hybrid perspective for preserving privacy during data mining. We applied geometric data perturbation technique for numerical data and for categorical data one of k-anonymization technique, specifically generalization method is applied. It is shown that even after applying privacy preserving methods, the data mining results do not vary much. In future, a different k-anonymization technique can be applied for better accuracy.

References

1. Li, X., Yan, Z., Zhang, P.: A review on privacy-preserving datamining. In: IEEE International Conference on Computer and Information Technology (2014)
2. Langheinrich, M.: Privacy in ubiquitous computing. In: Ubiquitous Computing Fundamentals, pp. 95–159. CRC Press (2009). ch. 3
3. Chen, K., Liu, L.: Geometric data perturbation for privacy preserving outsourced data mining. Knowl. Inf. Syst. **29**, 657–695 (2011)
4. Westin, A.F.: Privacy and freedom. Wash. Lee Law Rev. **25**(1), 166 (1968)
5. Bertino, E., Lin, D., Jiang, W.: A survey of quantification of privacy preserving data mining algorithms. In: Aggarwal, C.C., Yu, P.S. (eds.) Privacy-Preserving Data Mining. Advances in Database Systems, vol. 34, pp. 183–205. Springer, Boston (2008). https://doi.org/10.1007/978-0-387-70992-5_8
6. Aggarwal, C.C., Yu, P.S.: A general survey of privacy-preserving data mining models and algorithms. In: Aggarwal, C.C., Yu, P.S. (eds.) Privacy-preserving data mining. Advances in Database Systems, vol. 34, pp. 11–52. Springer, Boston (2008). https://doi.org/10.1007/978-0-387-70992-5_2
7. Aggarwal, Charu C.: Data Mining. Springer, Cham (2015). https://doi.org/10.1007/978-3-319-14142-8
8. Liu, K., Kargupta, H., Ryan, J.: Random projection based multiplicative data perturbation for privacy preserving distributed data mining. IEEE Trans. Knowl. **18**(1), 92–106 (2006)
9. Oliveria, S.R.M., Zaiane, O.R.: Data Perturbation by rotation for privacy preserving Clustering. Technical Report TR 04-17, August 2004
10. Agarwal, C.C.: On randomization, public information and the curse of dimensionality. In: IEEE 23rd International conference on Data engineering, pp. 136–145, April 2007
11. Samarati, P.: Protecting respondents' indentities in microdata release. IEEE Trans. Knowl. Data Eng. **13**, 1010–1027 (2001)
12. Sweeney, L.: Achieving k-anonymity privacy protection using generalization and suppression. Int. J. Uncertain. Fuzziness Knowl.-Based Syst. **10**(05), 571–588 (2002)
13. Kohavi, R., Becker, B.: UCI Machine Learning Repository (http://archive.ics.uci.edu/ml). Adult, CA: University of California, School of Information and Computer Science

Network Traffic Classification
Using Multiclass Classifier

Prabhjot Kaur[1][(✉)], Prashant Chaudhary[1], Anchit Bijalwan[1],
and Amit Awasthi[2]

[1] Department of Computer Science and Engineering,
Uttaranchal University, Dehradun, India
info.prabh@gmail.com, kmahil985@gmail.com,
anchit.bijalwan@gmail.com
[2] University of Petroleum and Energy Studies, Dehradun, India
aawasthi@ddn.upes.ac.in

Abstract. This paper aims to classify network traffic in order to segregate normal and anomalous traffic. There can be multiple classes of network attacks, so a multiclass model is implemented for ordering attacks in anomalous traffic. A supervised machine learning method SVM support Vector Machine has been used for multiclass classification. The most widely used dataset KDD Cup 99 has been used for analysis. Firstly, the dataset has been preprocessed using three way step and secondly the analysis has been performed using multi-classifier method. The results acquired exhibited the adequacy of the multiclass classification on the dataset to a fair extent.

Keywords: Multiclass classification · Normal traffic · Anomalous traffic

1 Introduction

Human has always aspired to develop techniques that could replace human efforts to a great extent. In this era, machine and deep learning is superseding other techniques. If one can train the machine using the data instead of explicitly programming the machine, that's where we need machine learning. Machine learning has empowered many domains such as web search, text recognition, speech recognition, medicine such as protein structure estimation, network traffic analysis and prediction, intrusion detection etc. Network traffic analysis is one of the emerging domains. An attack can be predicted from the current network traffic flow and it can held stop the intruders before actually attacking the network. This can be done using machine learning by training the network. There are three categories of machine learning: supervised, un-supervised and semi-supervised [1]. This paper focuses on Support Vector Machine (SVM) supervised machine learning technique for network traffic classification. Network traffic classification using SVM can include two approaches: binary or two-way classification and multi-class classification [2]. The first approach works simply by classifying the network between normal and anomalous traffic. The second approach can be applied using two sub-approaches i.e. (a) mapping multiple classes to individual binary classes;

© Springer Nature Singapore Pte Ltd. 2018
M. Singh et al. (Eds.): ICACDS 2018, CCIS 905, pp. 208–217, 2018.
https://doi.org/10.1007/978-981-13-1810-8_21

(b) directly solving multi-class problem. In this paper, first sub-approach is used to classify multi-class traffic classification [2].

The word classifier is a type of algorithmic technique used to implement classification [3]. The classification techniques can either be applied to the active data collected on site or passively on already built dataset. There are widely available network traffic collection tools such as: Iris, NetIntercept, tcpdump, Snort, Bro etc. [4, 5]. The online data stores of network traffic datasets are widely available for analysis of network traffic [6]. The network traffic files are generally stored in packet capture format (.pcap) which can subsequently be converted to desired format for analysis. These network files consist of features showing the type of traffic. For classification of network traffic, the most relevant features are selected out of the all features set. Then classification is performed on network traffic using the reduced feature set. Reducing the features may lessen the computation time and affirmatively affect the accuracy of the learning classification technique [7]. There are various models provided for feature selection: Wrapper and filter method [7], Correlation based feature selection (CFS) [8], INTERACT algorithm [9], The Consistency-based filter [10], gini covariance method [11], information gain, attribute evaluation etc. [12]. Wrapper method aims to select the feature subset with high extrapolative power that optimizes the classifier. Whereas in filter method, the best possible feature subset is selected from the data set irrespective of the classifier optimization. CFS technique aims to select the features that are highly correlated with the class and least correlated with remaining features of the class. INTERACT deals with inspecting the contribution of individual feature in the whole dataset and how its removal affects the consistency. The contribution is generated based on the ratio between entropy and information gain (IG) known as symmetrical uncertainty (SU) [13]. Information gain aims to determine the maximum information obtained from a particular feature. Gini covariance method aims at checking the variability of the feature and assigning respective ranks using spatial ranking method. The features within a particular threshold value are selected and beyond are rejected. Information gain attribute evaluation is to determine the best possible feature or attribute in the dataset.

Traditional binary classifiers work well with known patterns and their accuracy is fairly good. However, the drawback of these traditional binary classifiers is their inability to detect novel patterns in the data. This limitation has been removed for anomaly detection in wireless sensor networks by using a modified version of SVM for unknown traffic classification [14].

1.1 Related Work

Numerous studies have been conducted for traffic analysis using KDD Cup'99 dataset [6]. A computational efficient technique called novel multilevel hierarchical Kohonen net focuses on reduced feature and network size. The subset from KDD Cup'99 data is selected consisting of combination of normal and anomalous traffic records, which can be used to train the classifier. However, the test data consists of more attacks than available in train set, are used for testing the classifier [15]. Evolutionary neural networks based novel approach for intrusion detection has been proposed over the same KDD dataset. This approach takes way less time to find the higher neural networks than the conventional neural network approaches by learning system-call orders [16].

Another technique applied on KDD Cup data set is modified and improved version of C4.5 decision tree classifier. In this method new rules are derived by evaluating the network traffic data and thereby applied to detect intrusion in the real time [17]. Another technique applied on the modified version of KDD'99 data set named NSL-KDD that aims to decrease the false rate and increase the detection rate by optimizing the weighted average function [18]. A novel technique named Density peaks nearest neighbors (DPNN) is applied on KDD'99 cup data set to yield an improved accuracy over SVM method. This approach detects unknown attacks thus improving the sub categorical accuracy improvement of 15% on probe attacks and an overall efficiency improvement of 20.688% [23]. The authors used deep auto-encoder technique on KDD'99 cup dataset by constructing multilayer neurons showing improved accuracy over traditional attack identification techniques [24]. The authors performed a two way step on KDD'99 cup dataset: feature reduction using three different techniques i.e. gain ratio, mutual information, correlation and generated analysis score using Naïve Bayes, random forest, adaboost, SVM, bagging, kNN and stacking. Their results showed the maximum performance given by SVM with 99.91% score and closer performance score of 99.89 by random forest algorithm [25].

1.2 Data Set: KDD Cup 99

The full train dataset consists of 4,898,431 records out of which 972,781 are normal records and 3,925,650 are attack records. In this full train dataset vast numbers of records are redundant and after redundancy removal the total records, normal and attack records become 1,074,992, 812,814 and 262,178 respectively [19]. However the 10% train dataset consists of total of records 494,021 out of which record are 97,278 normal whereas are 396,743 attack records. The test dataset consists of 311,027 records out of which 60,591 are normal records and 250,436 are attack records. In this test dataset vast numbers of records are redundant and after redundancy removal the total records, normal and attack records become 77,289, 47,911 and 29,378 respectively. There were two invalid records found in the test dataset having record number 136,489 and 136,497 consisting of unacceptable value for service feature as ICMP, henceforth removed these two records from test dataset [19]. KDD CUP 99 dataset includes four different categories of attacks which are further subcategorized into twenty two categories shown in Fig. 1. The four classes of attacks present in train dataset are: Denial of Service (DoS), User to Root (U2R), Remote to Local (R2L) and Probe. DoS attack denies user's genuine access to the machine by either flooding the network with excess traffic or making the system resources over utilized. In U2R, the unauthorized user gains access to the system's root directory, thereby attaining all rights of the super user. R2L deals with getting local access of the machine from remote location by exploiting unknown vulnerability. Probe attack deals with gaining control of the system by security breach [19]. Sub categories of the aforementioned attacks are depicted in Fig. 1. The frequency of the number of attacks present in the particular train and test data set files are mentioned clearly. Though the redundancy has already removed from both train and test datasets. Test dataset has unknown traffic category as well. Therefore total number of reduced records after redundancy removal in train dataset and test dataset are: 1,074,992 and 77289 respectively.

Test Data

Category	Attack	Count
DoS	back.	386
	land.	9
	neptune.	20332
	pod.	45
	smurf.	936
	teardrop.	12
U2R	buffer_overflow.	22
	loadmodule.	2
	perl.	2
	rootkit.	13
R2L	warezmaster.	1002
	ftp_write.	3
	guess_passwd.	1302
	imap.	1
	multihop.	18
	phf.	2
Probe	nmap.	80
	portsweep.	174
	satan.	860
	ipsweep.	155
Unknown	apache2.	794
	httptunnel.	145
	mailbomb.	308
	mscan.	1049
	named.	17
	processtable.	744
	ps.	16
	saint.	364
	sendmail.	15
	snmpgetattack.	179
	snmpguess.	359
	sqlattack.	2
	udpstorm.	2
	worm.	2
	xlock.	9
	xsnoop.	4
	xterm.	13
*	normal.	47911

Test Dataset Traffic Statistics

DoS	21720
U2R	39
R2L	2328
Probe	1269
Unknown	4022
Normal	47911

Train Data

Category	Attack	Count
DoS	back.	968
	land.	19
	neptune.	242149
	pod.	206
	smurf.	3007
	teardrop.	918
U2R	buffer_overflow.	30
	loadmodule.	9
	perl.	3
	rootkit.	10
R2L	warezmaster.	20
	warezclient.	893
	ftp_write.	8
	guess_passwd.	53
	imap.	12
	multihop.	7
	phf.	4
	spy.	2
Probe	nmap.	1554
	portsweep.	3564
	satan.	5019
	ipsweep.	3723
*	normal.	812814

Train Dataset Traffic Statistics

DoS	247267
U2R	52
R2L	999
Probe	13860
* normal	812814

Fig. 1. Train and Test network traffic data statistics (KDD Cup'99)

1.3 Support Vector Machine

SVM is one of the most widely used classification techniques. A decade ago it was typically used for binary classification, however with the advent of its variants; multi-class classification is most frequently in use today. A hyper plane need to be selected in such a way that it precisely separates between two classes of data. The wider the hyper plane width, the better it is. The width points of the hyper plane are decided from the closest points to the hyper plane line known as support vectors. In context of network traffic data, there can be either normal traffic or anomalous traffic which comes under binary classification. Multiple subclasses of anomalous traffic can be determined using multi-class SVM. Binary classification is easy to implement as the classifier need to learn either the traffic is normal or anomalous. In order to perform multiple class classification, certain characterizations need to be considered i.e. One versus one (OvO) and one versus rest (OvR). In OvR, one class separates from other classes if binary characteristics of one class distinguish it from remaining set of classes. In OvO, here each classifier forms a pair with every other classifier and learns from the relationship formed [20]. Yet, there are many variants of SVM such as least squares SVM, v-SVM, nearly-isotonic SVM, Bounded SVM, NPSVM and Twin SVM, but this paper shall focus on multi-class categorization property of SVM [18].

2   Methodology

In order to perform the whole scenario, a formal step line has been followed. In general it must follow the four-steps: Data selection, Pre-processing, Analysis and result evaluation [21] as shown in Fig. 2. In nearly every data analytical domain, the generic flow model steps are followed meticulously. The steps may vary depending upon the unlike analysis requirements. Based on the generic model, the stair step followed in this paper is shown in Fig. 3. The four steps are: data selection, data preprocessing, analysis and result respectively which further consists of sub-steps. Data selection may either include the primary dataset collected in hand or the secondary datasets selection from online repository. Data preprocessing is subdivided into three parts: (1) *Removing redundancy*, (2) *Feature selection* and (3) *Data transformation*.

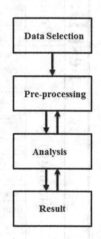

Fig. 2. Generic flow model

Data analysis step involves extracting the relevant information from vast amount of data. The researcher may use different methods for data analysis. In this paper, supervised machine learning technique SVM for multi class classification has been used. The final step is obtaining results and accuracy.

2.1   Experimental Setup

The firsthand experiment is run on an Intel Core i5-5200U CPU @ 2.20 GHz computer with 8.00 GB RAM running operating system Linux (Ubuntu 16.04 LTS). Python 3.6 has been used for programming with scikit learn libraries such as Pandas and NumPy [22].

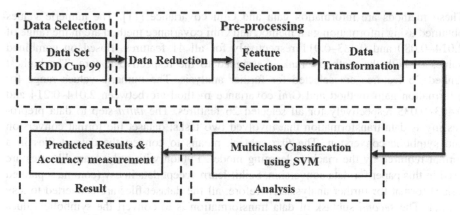

Fig. 3. Proposed step line for data analysis

2.2 Data Selection

In Data selection step, KDD CUP 99 is selected for data analysis. The brief detail about this dataset is already mentioned in second section. This first step could either be data collection or data selection. Data collection can be done by deploying network traffic collection tools such as tcpdump, NetIntercept, Snort, Bro etc. [4, 5]. The data collected using these methods are called primary data collection. The collected data is stored as datasets having specific extension such as .pcap. These datasets are most often available publicly to researchers. If a data set is selected from these publicly available data sets then it is called secondary dataset selection [6]. The data is selected based on researcher's area of interests.

2.3 Data Preprocessing

Data preprocessing means cleaning the data and making it readily available for further handling. In this step, the data in dataset is fine-tuned as per the input requirements to the model for processing. KDD Cup 99 dataset includes many redundant rows in training and testing datasets. There can be variant steps followed to preprocess the data. There is no generic step line for data pre-processing. In this paper three-step process is followed to preprocess data: (1) *Removing redundancy*, (2) *Feature selection* and (3) *Data transformation* [21]. KDD Cup 99 dataset has two sets of train data and test data: complete dataset and 10 percent of complete dataset. The size of complete train and test dataset is 4,898,431 rows X 41 features and 311,031 rows X 41 features respectively. Whereas the size of 10 percent of complete train dataset is 494,021 rows X 41 features. Both the above complete and 10 percent of complete data sets consist of redundant rows. After redundancy removal from 10 percent of complete train data set the records become 145586. The data redundancy may lead to the problem of biased results of the classifier towards frequently occurring records. Therefore, using a python script, the redundancy of training and testing dataset has been removed as a part of *first* step to data preprocessing. The *second* step to data preprocessing is feature extraction. Two widely used methods are used in combination and ranked the features accordingly.

These methods are information gain and Gini covariance [11]. The numeric values obtained using information gain method and Gini covariance method are in the range of 2.014–0.080 and 0.483–0.011 respectively for all 41 features. Based on combined values of both the methods, rank is assigned to the respective feature. The highest ranked 26 features are selected for further analysis. The numeric values range for information gain method and Gini covariance method are between 2.014–0.214 and 0.483–0.035 respectively for all selected 26 features. The *third* step to data preprocessing is data transformation that involved two tasks: dataset file format conversion and symbolic conversion. The *first* subtask means to convert the dataset files in a format required by the machine learning model. Python with scikit learn libraries are used in this paper for data conversion. Scikit-learn accept data in csv (comma separated value) format for further analysis. Therefore, all the dataset files are converted to .csv format. The *second* subtask of data transformation is to convert the symbolic values with numeric values. Python code has been written for symbolic value conversion in the train and test dataset. Therefore, data preprocessing step prepares the data for analysis in further steps. The authors have selected the subset of train set consisting of few attack sets from all four categories.

2.4   Analysis

Data analysis is the process of determining the relevant information by data modeling. In this paper, the authors have used Support Vector Machine (SVM) supervised machine learning technique for modeling the network traffic data. Since SVM can be implemented for both binary class and multiclass classification, thus multiclass SVM has been used in this paper. This has been implemented by using python programming with scikit learn libraries. A classifier known as Support Vector Classifier has been used requiring set of values to be passed as its parameters. The most relevant is the kernel which can take the values such as rbf, linear etc. but the default kernel is set to Radial Basis Function (rbf). Other parameters include C = 1.0, cache_size, coef, class_weight, kernel, degree, gamma and decision_function_shape, verbose etc. The parameter decision_function_shape can take either of two values: ovr or ovo. The results using One vs. One value of decision_function_shape obtained categorically [DoS, U2R, R2L, normal] is: 100, 66.66, 96, 98.12. The results using One vs. Rest value of decision_function_shape obtained categorically [DoS, U2R, R2L, normal] is: 100, 60, 96, 98.53. However the results are little improved when analysis is performed on the reduced feature dataset. In reduced feature dataset, the results using One vs. One value of decision_function_shape obtained categorically [DoS, U2R, R2L, normal] is: 100, 67.6, 96.1, 98.12. The results using One vs. Rest value of decision_function_shape obtained categorically [DoS, U2R, R2L, normal] is: 100, 60.37, 96, 98.79. The above values are obtained by using Eq. (1). Substantial amount of computational time has decreased due to analysis being performed on reduced feature set data.

3 Results and Discussion

The results aforementioned in the analysis part are calculated using the simple accuracy formula of:

$$\text{Accuracy} = (\text{CorrectPrediction}/\text{NumOfTestingSamplePerCatogry}) * 100 \quad (1)$$

The NumOfTestingSamplePerCatogry is implied as the number of testing samples per category. For experimental purpose the subset of the complete dataset is selected for analysis and NumOfTestingSamplePerCatogry list holds the number of attacks categorically in the selected subset. The outcome of the machine learning model is compared with the actual data label which is stored in the list named CorrectPrediction implied as correct predictions obtained.

However, the authors felt that its accuracy can be improved if the four notations are duly considered: True Positives (TPs), True Negatives (TNs), False Positive (FPs) and False Negatives (FNs). True positives are the correct predictions for correct traffic which is the most ideal case and focus remains on maximizing TPs. True negatives denotes appropriately labeled the network traffic data records as normal. False positives, label as an attack to the normal record. False negative means considering attack traffic records as normal traffic records [18]. Therefore, the measurement terms are [18, 25]:

$$\text{Accuracy} = (\text{TPs} + \text{TNs})/(\text{TPs} + \text{TNs} + \text{FPs} + \text{FNs}) \quad (2)$$

$$\text{ErrorRate} = (\text{FNs} + \text{FPs})/(\text{TPs} + \text{TNs} + \text{FPs} + \text{FNs}) \quad (3)$$

$$\text{Precision} = \text{TPs}/(\text{TPs} + \text{FPs}) \quad (4)$$

$$\text{Recall} = \text{TPs}/(\text{TPs} + \text{FNs}) \quad (5)$$

The Eq. (2) is preferred over Eq. (1) while calculating the accuracy of the proposed machine learning model. The error rate, precision and recall parameters are depicted in Eqs. (3), (4) and (5) respectively.

Using python programming, the values of TPs, TNs, FPs and FNs are calculated which are subsequently put in the Eqs. (2) to (4) to obtain the values of different metrics. The accuracy, error rate, precision and recall obtained categorically [DoS, U2R, R2L, normal] is: [1.0, 0.55, 1.0, 0.99], [0, 0.44, 0, 0.0020], [1.,1.,1.,1.] and [1., 0.99, 0.2, 1.] respectively. However emphasis is done on maximizing TPs and minimizing FNs.

4 Conclusion and Future Scope

In this paper, KDD cup dataset has been analyzed using multiclass SVM supervised machine learning technique. First of all the data preprocessing is done by removing the redundant rows, substituting the numeric values for columns consisting of text data and reducing the feature by applying appropriate feature selection technique. Thereafter the dataset is converted in the format desired by appropriate classification technique. Then a subset of train data set is selected to train the classifier. After analysis is done, the results obtained using reduced feature set showed substantial improvement over the results obtained with full 41 feature analysis. However, significant improvement in computational time has been seen. Furthermore, accuracy has been derived using two different approaches which do show greater variability in accuracy of R2L attacks. Thus the overall analysis work helps to understand and apply the multiclass problem to a fair extent. On account of the technical limitations of the current work is the handling of big dataset. It is computationally expensive to process the complete dataset in one go. Therefore, subsets of dataset are selected to perform analysis. On part of future scope, cross validation can be performed by taking various folds of the dataset. Learners rules can be derived which can subsequently be used in domain of intrusion detection systems. Also, the SVM multiclass model can be applied with kernel function to check its accuracy with the given dataset.

References

1. Chapelle, O., Schölkopf, B., Zien, A.: Semi-Supervised Learning. MIT Press, London England (2006)
2. Bolón-Canedo, V., Sánchez-Maroño, N., Alonso-Betanzos, A.: Feature selection and classification in multiple class datasets: an application to KDD Cup 99 dataset. Expert Syst. Appl. **38**, 5947–5957 (2011)
3. Kwon, D., Kim, H., Kim, J., Suh, S.C., Kim, I., Kim, K.J.: A survey of deep learning-based network anomaly detection. Cluster Comput. **20**, 1–13 (2017)
4. Pilli, E.S., Joshi, R.C., Niyogi, R.: Network forensic frameworks: survey and research challenges. Digital Invest. **7**, 14–27 (2010)
5. Kaur, P., Bijalwan, A., Joshi, R.C., Awasthi, A.: Network forensic process model and framework: an alternative scenario. In: Singh, R., Choudhury, S., Gehlot, A. (eds.) Intelligent Communication, Control and Devices. AISC, vol. 624, pp. 493–502. Springer, Singapore (2018). https://doi.org/10.1007/978-981-10-5903-2_50
6. KDD Cup 1999 Data. http://kdd.ics.uci.edu/databases/kddcup99/kddcup99.html
7. Kohavi, R., John, G.H.: Wrappers for feature subset selection. Artif. Intell. **97**, 273–324 (1997)
8. Doshi, M., Chaturvedi, S.k.: Correlation based feature selection (CFS) technique to predict student performance. Int. J. Comput. Netw. Com. (IJNC) **6**(3) 197–206 (2014)
9. Zhao, Z., Liu, H.: Searching for interacting features. In: Proceedings of international joint conference on artificial intelligence, 1156–1167 (2007)
10. Dash, M., Liu, H.: Consistency-based search in feature selection. Artif. Intell. **151**, 155–176 (2003)
11. Sang, Y., Dang, X., Sang, H.: Symmetric Gini Covariance and Correlation version. Can. J. Stat. **44**(3), 1–20 (2016)
12. Bajaj, K., Arora, A.: Dimension reduction in intrusion detection features using discriminative machine learning approach. Int. J. Comput. Sci. **10**(4), 324–328 (2013)
13. Forman, G.: An extensive empirical study of feature selection metrics for text classification. J Mach. Learn. Res. **3**, 289–1305 (2003)

14. Shilton, A., Rajasegarar, S., Palaniswami, M.: Combined multiclass classification and anomaly detection for large-scale wireless sensor networks. In: IEEE Eighth International Conference on Intelligent Sensors, Sensor Networks and Information Processing, pp 491–496. IEEE Press, New York (2013)
15. Sarasamma, S., Zhu, Q., Huff, J.: Hierarchical Kohonen net for anomaly detection in network security. IEEE Trans. Syst. Man Cybern. Part B (Cybern.) **35**(2), 302–312 (2005)
16. Han, S.J., Cho, S.B.: Evolutionary neural networks for anomaly detection based on the behavior of a program. IEEE Trans. Syst. Man Cybern. **36**(3), 559–570 (2005)
17. Rajeswari, L.P., Arputharaj, K.: An active rule approach for network intrusion detection with enhanced C4.5 algorithm. Int. J. Commun. Netw. Syst. Sci. **4**, 285–385 (2008)
18. Bamakan, S.M.H., Wang, H., Yingjie, T., Shi, Y.: An effective intrusion detection framework based on MCLP/SVM optimized by time-varying chaos particle swarm optimization. Neurocomputing **199**, 90–102 (2016)
19. Tavallaee, M., Bagheri, E., Lu, W., Ghorbani, A.A.: A detailed analysis of the KDD CUP 99 data set. In: Proceedings of the 2009 IEEE Symposium on Computational Intelligence in Security and Defense Applications. IEEE Press, New York (2009)
20. Yukinawa, N., Oba, S., Kato, K., Ishii, S.: Optimal aggregation of binary classifiers for multi-class cancer diagnosis using gene expression profiles. IEEE/ACM Trans Comput. Biol. Bioinform. **6**(2), 333–343 (2009)
21. Singh, R., Kumar, H., Singla, R.K.: Analysis of feature selection techniques for network traffic dataset. In: 2013 International Conference on Machine Intelligence and Research Advancement, pp. 42–46 (2013)
22. Scikit learn machine learning in python. http://scikit-learn.org/stable/auto_examples/svm/plot_rbf_parameters.html
23. Li, L., Zhang, H., Peng, H., Yang, Y.: Nearest neighbors based density peaks approach to intrusion detection. Chaos, Solitons Fractals **110**, 33–40 (2018)
24. Farahnakian, F., Heikkonen J.: A deep auto-encoder based approach for intrusion detection system. In: 20th International Conference on Advanced Communication Technology (ICACT), pp. 178–183 (2018)
25. Kushwaha, P., Buckchash, H., Raman, B.: Anomaly based intrusion detection using filter based feature selection on KDD-CUP 99. In: 2017 IEEE Region 10 Conference (TENCON), Malaysia (2017)

An Efficient Hybrid Approach Using Misuse Detection and Genetic Algorithm for Network Intrusion Detection

Rohini Rajpal and Sanmeet Kaur[✉]

CSED, Thapar Institute of Engineering and Technology, Patiala 147004, India
sanmeet.bhatia@thapar.edu

Abstract. In today's fast-changing Information Technology world, even the best available security is deficient for the latest vulnerabilities. In order to protect data and system integrity, Intrusion Detection is a preferred choice of researchers. In this paper, we have proposed a hybrid approach for intrusion detection that is based on misuse detection and genetic algorithm approach. Here, feature selection technique has been used for extracting important features and genetic algorithm is used for generating new rules. In this paper, we have detected ten different types of attacks that have high detection as well as low false positive rates.

Keywords: Intrusion detection · Genetic algorithm · Misuse detection

1 Introduction

With immense use of Internet, information has become valuable resource that needs to be protected from unauthorized access. In today's fast-changing Information technology world, even the best available security is deficient for the latest vulnerabilities, so network security and intrusion detection has become inevitable requirement. The research article suggests a hybrid approach for Intrusion Detection using misuse detection and genetic algorithm for efficient detection of attacks.

2 Backround

2.1 Intrusion Detection Techniques

Intrusion detection is process of detecting attacks within computer or networks to identify security breaches. Although there are numerous techniques but most important among them all are Misuse detection and Anomaly detection.

Misuse Intrusion Detection
Misuse detection compares observed events with prior known threat signatures that is incorporated to identify incidents. This proves efficient while detecting known threats; however, the detection system sometimes proves ineffective while detecting unknown

threats. There are various types of misuse intrusion detection methods like signature based, rule based, state transition and data mining based methods [11].

Anomaly detection
In anomaly based intrusion detection, detectors detect behaviors on a computer or computer network [9]. Anomaly detection relies on being able to define desired behavior of the system and then to distinguish between desired and anomalous behavior [8]. There are various types of anomaly intrusion detection methods like statistical approach, profiling, distance based, model based [13]. Anomaly detection methods prove to be very effective at detecting new threats. A common problem with anomaly-based detection is generating many false positives.

2.2   Related Work

Many researchers have proposed Intrusion Detection using genetic algorithms. Salah et al. (2014) presents a genetic algorithm approach with an improved initial population and selection operator to improve intrusion detection [1]. Fatemeh (2014) presented a hybrid approach for dynamic intrusion detection in MANET's to classify attacks such as flooding, wormhole and blackhole [16]. Padmadas et al. (2013) proposed layered based approach to detect attacks [18]. Jongsuebsuk et al. (2013), proposed real time intrusion detection using fuzzy genetic algorithm to classify attacks [2]. Senthilnayaki et al. (2013) proposed a system in which genetic algorithm was used for preprocessing and advanced J48 classifier was used for classifying attacks [19]. Fan Li (2010) had proposed combination of neural network and genetic algorithm to improve detection rates [20]. Wang(2009) presented expert fuzzy system based on genetic algorithm and fuzzy logic to improve detection rates with comparatively using less fuzzy rules [3]. Chang et al. (2009) proposed an algorithm which combines wavelet neural network with genetic algorithm to achieve network efficiency and low false positive rates [17].

Zorana et al. (2007) suggested a misuse detection system that was based on genetic algorithm approach [4]. Hui et al. (2005) presented a software implementation of genetic algorithm to obtain a set of classification rules for intrusion detection [5]. Khan (2011), proposed Network Intrusion Detection that was based on some pre-defined rules, that used genetic algorithm to classify DoS or Probing attack [6]. Balajinath et al. (2001) proposed an approach that was based on genetic algorithm to learn individual user behavior [7].

3   Materials and Method

The proposed hybrid approach in the study has two stages of detection, namely, Misuse detection and Genetic Algorithm. For the purpose of experimentation KDD Cup'99 dataset has been used. Figure 1 describes the methodology used in proposed work. In first stage, *i.e.* Misuse detection, the training data set attributes are compared with testing data attributes. The performing comparisons, the results obtained are stored in database. In second stage, *i.e.* Genetic Algorithm, rules with the highest fitness are inserted in training dataset and these rules are used for classifying attacks. The steps of hybrid intrusion detection are as follows:

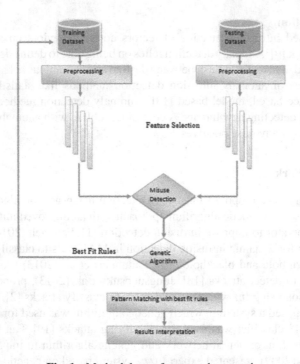

Fig. 1. Methodology of proposed approach

A. Preprocessing

   Preprocessing involves removal of redundant records from both datasets. If redundant data points are not removed, then result will be biased towards only few types of attacks. This step also includes conversion of categorical data to numerical data.

B. Feature Selection

   To improve performance, feature selection has been performed. For selection of attributes InfoGain measure has been used. There are total forty one features in KDD Cup'99 data set. Out of these, three features are selected for further evaluation to classify attacks. Features selected are src_bytes, service, and protocol_type.

C. Misuse detection

   In this phase, selected attributes from testing dataset are comparted with same selected attributes as given in training dataset. If there is a match, then system will find the corresponding class of the training data which is pre-existing in database and assigns it to testing on data record.

D. Genetic algorithm

   Genetic Algorithm is deployed to improve the functional capability of the system. This algorithm is used to input initial rules (population) and output best fit rules (best individuals). Every rule for classifying attack is if-then clause. Attributes from Table 1 are joined using AND (&&) function. Three attributes with two && function justifying it as the conditional part of a rule. If part of rule is conditional part and then part of rule is conclusion part. The outcome of every rule is the substantiation of an intrusion.In fitness function (1), α is the count of correctly detected attacks, β is the count of normal connections incorrectly identified as attacks, A is the total number of attacks in the training dataset, whereas B is the total number of connections which are normal in the training dataset [15].

Table 1. Detection rates of misuse approach

Attack names	Type of attack	Detection rate (%)	False positive rate
Smurf	DoS	100	
Normal	No Attack	74.3	0.35
Neptune	DoS	66.3	
Snmpgetattack	R2L	2	
Portsweep	Probe	0	
Ipsweep	Probe	2.8	
Nmap	Probe	0	
Xlock	R2L	0	
Multihop	R2L	0	
Worm	R2L	0	
Xterm	U2R	0	
Teardrop	DoS	100	
Sqlattack	U2R	0	
apache2	DoS	0	

For example, any rule could be:

if(src_bytes == 0 && service == "remote _job" && protocol_type = "tcp") then nepture

In order to determine a fitness value of each rule, following fitness functions can be used.

$$fitness = \frac{\alpha}{A} - \frac{\beta}{B} \qquad (1)$$

$$fitness = w1 * support + w2 * confidence \qquad (2)$$

where, $support = \frac{|A \, and \, B|}{N}$ and $confidence = \frac{|A \, and \, B|}{|A|}$

Scale of fitness values is [−1, +1], where −1 is the lowest value and +1 the highest value. High detection rate and low false-positives rate result in a high fitness value, while low detection rates and high false-positives rates result in a low fitness value. As per the previous fitness function (1) it is being able to find only of total number of intrusions and not of its exact type, as we have deployed a support-confidence framework [10] in order to determine precise type of attack. This can be done by calculating fitness of each rule by fitness function (2). In fitness function (2) described above, N represents the total number of connections within the training dataset.

Suppose the rule is

$$if(a = 0 \ \&\& \ b = 2) \ then \ d = 4$$

if part of this rule is considered as A and then part of this rule is considered as B. In fitness function (2), |A| is the count of connections matching if part of the rule, and |A and B| stands for the total number of connections that matched the complete rule i.e. (if A then B) complete rule is matched. The weights w1 and w2 were used to control the balance among support and confidence. Generating new rules form old one is the key process. In this process, initial population (set of rules) is made from the combination of selected attributes described above. Attributes act as genes for this algorithm. Each individual is a chromosome which is collection of genes. Initial population is collection of individuals, after every generation best fit individuals are obtained by the process of selection and crossover. After this step, initial population is being evolved into best fit individuals. The outcome or the result of the algorithm is best fit set of rules for intrusion detection. This algorithm generates the best fit rules which are also added to training database. In this approach, we found ten different types of attacks that has improved detection rate as well as low false positive rates.

E. Pattern matching

After applying genetic algorithm on random population of rules, system is allowed to match the selected features of training along with testing data. In this technique, the system is capable to classify attacks more accurately because of best fit rules in training dataset.

4 Implementation

Two experiments have been carried out for evaluation of detection rates with two different approaches. Subset of KDD Cup'99 dataset has been used for both training and testing of data. First experiment is carried out by making use of Misuse detection, is used for detecting intrusions from dataset using pattern matching. In second experiment, hybrid approach which is combination of misuse based and genetic algorithm is used for detecting intrusions with best fit rules and gives better detection rates. The goal of carrying out these experiments is to clearly identify the detection rates as well as false positive rates of both approaches and compare them. Figure 2 shows the flow diagram of both the experiments

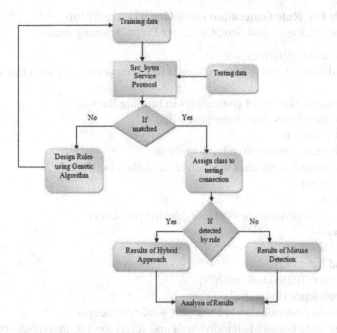

Fig. 2. Flow diagram of misuse detection and hybrid approach

Experiment 1: Misuse Detection

While carrying out the experimentation, training data attributes were matched with testing data attributes and incase if there is a complete matched, means all attributes which were selected for intrusion detection from training dataset, matched with same attributes of testing data, then training data class was to be assigned to a testing connection.

Algorithm 1: Misuse Detection

Step 1. Remove redundant data from training dataset.
Step 2. Select three features based on rank of their Info Gain Value.
Step 3. Load testing dataset.
Step 4. For each connection in testing dataset
Step 5. Match selected features of training data with same features of testing data.
Step 6. If (class is not assigned for this connection)
    6.1. if (all three attributes matched)
    6.2. assign training class attribute value to testing connection.
    6.3. else
    6.4. don't assign any class to testing connection.
Step 7. else
Step 8. Break(exit for outer loop, do these steps for next connection).
Step 9. End For.

Algorithm 2: For Rule Generation using Genetic Algorithm
Input: Population, Population Size, Crossover Point, Training dataset

Step 1. Initialize 350 Rules.
Step 2. Initialize w1 and w2 [range should be in between 0 to 1 such that w1 + w2 = 1.
Step 3. N = total number of connections in training dataset.
Step 4. For each individual in the population
Step 5. a = 0, ab = 0
Step 6. For each connection in training dataset
    6.1. if connection matches the individual(if-then both parts)
    6.2. ab = ab + 1;
    6.3. end if
    6.4. if connection matches the individual(if part only)
    6.5. a = a+1;
    6.6. end if
Step 7. End for
Step 8. Support (individual) = ab/N;
Step 9. Confidence (individual) = ab/a;
Step 10. Fitness (individual) = w1*support + w2*confidence;
Step 11. Calculate fitness of all individuals and select top 100 individuals out of them.
Step 12. End for.
Step 13. For each chromosome in new population
    13.1. Apply crossover operator to form new offspring and crossover point is 0.5.
Step 14. End for.

The proposed system is implemented in JAVA using MySql. Training and Test dataset are created in database. The classes in this system are Crossover, Individual, Fitness of Population, Training, Testing and main class.

5 Results and Discussion

The system is trained with 10000 records of KDD Cup'99 training datasets and then tested on 1400 records of KDD Cup'99 test dataset. Table 1 represents the results using misuse detection approach. Using this approach, we were able to find only four types of attacks: namely, smurf, neptune, teardrop and snmpgeattack.

Detection rate using Misuse and Hybrid approach is shown in Tables 1 and 2 respectively Weights (w1 and w2) play an important role to minimize false positive rates.

The proposed system has achieved a very less false positive rate of 0.30. Along with this, high detection rates of 100 percent of three attacks: namely, smurf, ipsweep and teardrop has been observed. In our approach, nearly all types of attacks present in training dataset were detected with low false positive rate, high detection rate and less time complexity.

Various researchers have worked on genetic algorithm for improving diminishing false positive rates and detection rates. Figure 3 specifically depicts the false positive rates of proposed approach and approaches used by various researchers. Results of their work and proposed approach are compared and below graph shows that proposed approach gives lesser false positive rates.

Table 2. Detection rates of hybrid approach using 200/350 rules and weights, w1 = 0/.4 & w2 = 1/.6

200/350 rules	w1 = 0/.4, w2 = 1/.6		
Attack names	Type of attack	Detection rate (%)	False positive rate (%)
Smurf	DoS	100/100	0.35
Normal	No Attack	89.6/89.6	
Neptune	DoS	97.9/23.3	
Snmpgetattack	R2L	0/0	
Portsweep	Probe	0/12.6	
Ipsweep	Probe	100/100	
Nmap	Probe	0/0	
Xlock	R2L	0/0	
Multihop	R2L	0/0	
Worm	R2L	0/0	
Xterm	U2R	0/0	
Teardrop	DoS	100/100	
Sqlattack	U2R	0/0	
apache2	DoS	0/0	

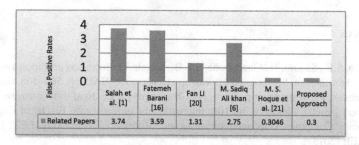

Fig. 3. Comparison of proposed approach along with existing approaches.

Table 3 shows the attacks detected by misuse and proposed approach. Figure 4 represents number of attacks detected by misuse and proposed approach.

Table 3. Attacks detected by misuse v/s proposed approach

	Misuse	Proposed
DoS	neptune, smurf, teardrop	neptune, smurf, teardrop, apache2
Probe	ipsweep	ipsweep, nmap, portsweep
R2L	snmpgetattack	snmpgetattack, multihop
U2R	--	Xterm

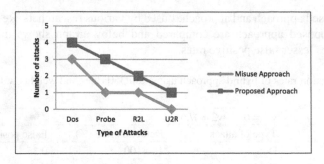

Fig. 4. Attacks detected by misuse v/s proposed approach.

6   Conclusion

In this paper, we a have implemented hybrid approach with feature selection for intrusion detection. In this approach, Misuse detection and Genetic Algorithm has been incorporated. Feature Selection has further been added to the study to identify the key features of network connections. Genetic Algorithm has been used to derive best fit rules among a large population of rules. Our system has ability to update new rules and it is easy to maintain. Therefore, the proposed system is able to classify connections as normal or intrusive along with the kind of attack. A clear classification of attack is important in order to perform recovery. Proposed system detects ten different types of attacks with only three features out of forty one resulting in lower time complexity.

References

1. Benaicha, S.E., Saoudi, L., Guermeche, S.E.B., Lounis, O.: Intrusion detection system using genetic algorithm. In: Science and Information Conference (SAI), pp. 564–568. IEEE (2014)
2. Jongsuebsuk, P., Wattanapongsakorn, N., Charnsripinyo, C.: Real time intrusion detection with fuzzy genetic algorithm. In: 10th International Conference on Electrical Engineering/ Electronics, Computer, Telecommunications and Information Technology (ECTI-CON), pp. 1–6. IEEE (2013)
3. Wang, Y.: Using fuzzy expert system based on genetic algorithms for intrusion detection system. In: International Forum on Information Technology and Applications, IFITA 2009, vol. 2, pp. 221–224. IEEE (2009)
4. Bankovic, Z., Stepanovic, D., Bojanic, S., Taladriz, O.N.: Improving network security using genetic algorithm approach. Comput. Electr. Eng. **33**(5), 438–451 (2007)
5. Gong, R.H., Zulkernine, M., Abolmaesumi, P.: A software implementation of a genetic algorithm based approach to network intrusion detection. In: Sixth International Conference on Software Engineering, Artificial Intelligence, Networking and Parallel/Distributed Computing, 2005 and First ACIS International Workshop on Self-Assembling Wireless Networks. SNPD/SAWN 2005, pp. 246–253. IEEE (2005)
6. Khan, M.S.A.: Rule based network intrusion detection using genetic algorithm. Int. J. Comput. Appl. **18**(8), 26–29 (2011)
7. Balajinath, B., Raghavan, S.V.: Intrusion detection through learning behavior model. Comput. Commun. **24**(12), 1202–1212 (2001)

8. Axelsson, S.: Intrusion detection systems: a survey and taxonomy, vol. 99. Technical report (2000)
9. Kumar, S.: Classification and detection of computer intrusions. Ph.D. thesis, Purdue University (1995)
10. Wei, L., Issa, T.: Detecting new forms of network intrusion using genetic programming. Comput. Intell. **20**(3), 475–494 (2004)
11. Kumar, S., Spafford, E.H.: A software architecture to support misuse intrusion detection. Technical report CSD-TR- 95-009 (1995)
12. Holland, J.H.: Adaptation in Natural and Artificial Systems (1992)
13. Teodoro, G., Pedro, J.D.V., Fernandez, G.M., Vazquez, E.: Anomaly-based network intrusion detection: techniques, systems and challenges. Comput. Secur. **28**(1), 18–28 (2009)
14. Pohlheim, H.: Genetic and evolutionary algorithms: principles, methods and algorithms (2006)
15. Hashemi, V.M., Muda, Z., Yassin, W.: Improving intrusion detection using genetic algorithm. Inf. Technol. J. **12**(5), 2167–2173 (2013)
16. Barani, F.: A hybrid approach for dynamic intrusion detection in ad hoc networks using genetic algorithm and artificial immune system. In: 2014 Iranian Conference on Intelligent Systems (ICIS), pp. 1–6. IEEE (2014)
17. Chang, N., He, Y., Huifang, L., Ren, H.: A study on GA-based WWN intrusion detection. In: International Conference on Management and Service Science, MASS 2009, pp. 1–4. IEEE (2009)
18. Padmadas, M., Krishna, N., Kanchana, J., Karthikeyan, M.:Layered approach for intrusion detection system based genetic algorithm. In: IEEE International Conference on Computational Intelligence and Computing Research, pp. 1–4 (2013)
19. Senthilnayaki, B., Venkatalakshmi, K., Kannan, A.: An intelligent intrusion detection system using genetic based feature selection and modified J48 decision tree classifier. In: 2013 Fifth International Conference on Advanced Computing (ICoAC), pp. 1–7. IEEE (2013)
20. Fan, L.: Hybrid neural network intrusion detection system using genetic algorithm. In: 2010 International Conference on Multimedia Technology (ICMT), pp. 1–4. IEEE (2010)
21. Hoque, M.S., Mukit, B., Naser, A.: An implementation of intrusion detection system using genetic algorithm. arXiv preprint arXiv: 1204.1336 (2012)

Ensemble Technique Based on Supervised and Unsupervised Learning Approach for Intrusion Detection

Sanmeet Kaur[✉] and Ishan Garg

Thapar Institute of Engineering and Technology, Patiala, India
sanmeetkaur@thapar.edu

Abstract. Security of networks within an organization is one of the most crucial issue for any organizations. Numerous techniques have either been developed or implemented to secure computer network and communication over the Internet. One method that has gathered attention under security domain over the years is the Intrusion detection method. This security technique analyzes information from various nodes within a network to identify possible threat. In this paper an ensemble technique using supervised and unsupervised learning approach has been proposed. At first Clustering is performed over data and then classification of data is performed. Clustering is used so as to detect unknown attacks in the networks and also to form clusters of same type of data. Then with the help of Classification algorithms classification of data into its appropriate classes is done and it is also used to measure the detection rate, false positive rate *etc*. NSL-KDD, KDD Cup'99 and Kyoto 2006+ datasets are used in this paper for experimentation purpose. The results of misuse-based intrusion detection and proposed system is compared on various parameters like detection rates, false positive rates, precision, true positive rate. Results prove that the proposed approach has better low false positive as well as detection rates, than misuse based intrusion detection. Proposed System detects various types of attacks with high percentage of detection as well as and low false positive rates. This system is also compared with existing systems which were described in research papers and results shows that our system gives less false positive rates than existing systems.

Keywords: Intrusion detection system · Supervised learning
Unsupervised learning · KDD cup 99 · NSL-KDD · KYOTO 2006+
Anomalies · Clustering · Classification · Intrusion

1 Introduction

With the advancement in technology and with the introduction of networks providing high exchange rates, the exchange of data between the people and various organizations for different purposes such as business, entertainment, education etc. keeps on increasing continuously over the internet. With this increase in data exchange, new types of anomalies, attacks have been introducing day-by-day which compromise the normal operation of the networks and also plays a major threat to the privacy of

© Springer Nature Singapore Pte Ltd. 2018
M. Singh et al. (Eds.): ICACDS 2018, CCIS 905, pp. 228–238, 2018.
https://doi.org/10.1007/978-981-13-1810-8_23

individuals. These attacks are normally targeted at stealing confidential information like passwords, banking details of the individuals. It is a big concern to find out these threats so as to alert the individual about the anomaly in the network and protect their data from intruders. For this purpose, Intrusion Detection System (IDS) plays a vital role *i.e.* combination of both hardware and software.

There are mainly two categories in which most of the IDS are categorized: Misuse or Signatures based intrusion detection (that identifies from what is known already) and Anomaly based intrusion detection (identify the new intrusion that is not known). In signature based intrusion detection, IDS monitors for the patterns or signatures in the networks and then compare it with the signatures of known threats that were already stored in the database. If there occur any known attack then the system alert the user about the intrusion. Signature based IDS, needs to be continuously updated with new signatures (attacks), as it is unable to detect unknown threats. The benefit of using this methodology is that it gives low false positive rate. Anomaly based IDS detects the pattern deviating from its normal behavior *i.e.* baseline and give alert to the users about the possibility of detecting a new anomaly. It is capable of detecting new attacks which are not been detected before. The main drawback of this system is that, it gives high false positive rate. It is also arduous to maintain the normal behavior baseline for anomaly based IDS. Both being conflicting in nature, share a common property that both require knowledge either in term of attack-signature or normal-operation profile provided by some external source so as to achieve their goals [1]. In this paper we also emphasize on ensemble techniques.

2 Related Work

Seong *et al.* [5] proposed a hybrid IDSthat supported Support Vector Machine (SVM) and genetic algorithm using KDD Cup'99 dataset. Lee *et al.* [7] proposed a hybrid mechanism for real time IDS for KDD Cup 99 dataset. Chang *et al.* [2], proposed a hybrid algorithm which integrate wavelet neural network with Genetic Algorithm to achieve efficiency and low false positive rates in networks. Muda *et al.* [8, 9] first applied k-means clustering algorithm so as to classify data and in the next following phase, the Naive Bayes algorithm is applied to classify the clustered data. Jain *et al.* [3], mainly focused on hybrid approach which increases the correctly classifying rate of the system.

3 Methodology and Implementation

To carry out the work two experiments have been performed. In first experiment the results are obtained using only classification algorithms whereas in second experiment the results are obtained using ensemble approach of anomaly based intrusion detection and misuse based intrusion detection. For the purpose of anomaly based intrusion detection clustering has been used whereas for misuse based intrusion detection various classification algorithms have been applied. The benefit of using this approach is that by performing anomaly based intrusion detection the probability of detecting unknown attacks increases, and on the other hand it also classified the data into various clusters according to their similar properties. Followed by a functional aspect that was based on intrusion detection, misuse based intrusion detection is performed which classifies the data into its specific belonging class. The advantage of using ensemble technique is that it increases the probability of detection some unknown attacks which is not possible in case of simple misuse detection.

3.1 Datasets

We have done our experimentation work on three datasets namely, NSL-KDD dataset (dataset 1), KYOTO 2006+ (dataset 2), KDD Cup'99 (dataset 3).1) KDD dataset: KDD Cup'99 [4] has been the most broadly used dataset for intrusion detection since 1999. This dataset is prepared by Stolfo*et al.* and is generated on the basis of data captured in DARPA'98 Intrusion Detection System evaluation program. KDD training dataset in total, has 41 features. These features are mentioned in Table 1. and F42 is class, which differentiates between normal and anomalous groups.

Table 1. List of features of KDD Cup 99 dataset (dataset 3) and NSL-KDD dataset (dataset 1)

Feature no	Feature name	Feature no	Feature name	Feature no	Feature name
F1	Duration	F15	Su attempted	F29	Same srv rate
F2	Protocol type	F16	Num root	F30	Diff srv rate
F3	Service	F17	Num filecreations	F31	Srv diff host rate
F4	Flag	F18	Num shells	F32	Dst host count
F5	Source bytes	F19	Num access files	F33	Dst host srv count
F6	Destinationbytes	F20	Num outbound cmds	F34	Dst host same srv rate
F7	Land	F21	Is host login	F35	Dst host diff srv rate
F8	Wrong fragment	F22	Is guest login	F36	Dst host samesrcport rate
F9	Urgent	F23	Count	F37	Dst host srv diff host rate
F10	Hot	F24	Srv count	F38	Dst host serror rate
F11	Number failed login	F25	Serror rate	F39	Dst host srvserror rate
F12	Logged in	F26	Srvserror rate	F40	Dst host rerror rate
F13	Num compromised	F27	Rerror rate	F41	Dst host srvrerror rate
F14	Root shell	F28	Srvrerror rate	F42	Class label

From KDD'99 new dataset has been formed named, NSL-KDD [8]. NSL-KDD is formed so as to solve some inherited problem of KDD'99. The total no. of records in NSL-KDD training as well as in testing set are reasonable as compared to KDD'99. This advantage makes the researchers able to do the experiment portion on whole of the dataset unlike picking some random portion of a dataset as in case of KDD'99. KYOTO 2006+ dataset: Kyoto [6] dataset is formed from three years of continuous analyzing of real time data traffic (from November 2006 to August 2009). The data is captured from different types of honeypots, sensors, Windows XP installation etc. in Kyoto University. The list of features of dataset 2 is shown in Table 2.

Table 2. List of features of KYOTO 2006+ dataset

Feature no.	Feature name	Feature no.	Feature name	Feature no.	Feature name
F1	Duration	F7	Serror rate	F13	Dst host srverror rate
F2	Service	F8	Srverror rate	F14	Flag
F3	Source bytes	F9	Dst host count	F15	Source port number
F4	Destination byte	F10	Dst host srv count	F16	Dst port no.
F5	Count	F11	Dst host samesrc port rate	F17	Label
F6	Same srv rate	F12	Dst host serror rate		

3.2 Experiment 1 - Misuse Based Intrusion Detection Using Supervised Learning

The schematic flow diagram of experiment 1 is shown in Fig. 1. In this experiment, the collected dataset is preprocessed. Then the classification of dataset is performed. Various classification algorithms used to perform experiments are namely, J-48, Random Tree, Random Forest, Naïve Bayes and Adaboost etc. This experiment has been performed on all the datasets step-by-step to obtain the results namely, correctly classified instances, false positive rate, roc area *etc*.

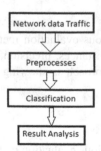

Fig. 1. Schematic flow diagram of steps involved in performing experiment 1

3.3 Experiment 2 - Misuse and Anomaly Based Intrusion Detection Using Ensemble Approach

The schematic flow diagram of experiment 2 is shown in Fig. 2.

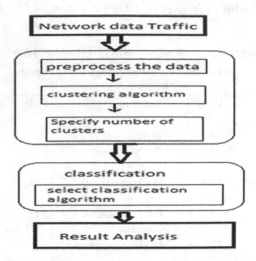

Fig. 2. Schematic flow diagram showing steps involved in performing experiment 2

In this experiment, an ensemble approach of classification and clustering has been used. Firstly, after uploading and preprocessing of data, clustering is performed. The number of clusters has been inputted and clustering algorithm has been chosen. After performing clustering, the classification has been performed on the clustered dataset. Some of the ensemble approaches that have been used are K-means + J-48, K-means + Adaboost, K-means + Random Tree, K-means + Random Forest, K-means (Manhattan distance) K-means + Naïve Bayes, Make Density Based Clustering + J-48 and Make Density Based Clustering + Naïve Bayes.

4 Results and Discussion

The results are compared on various evaluation metrics like false positive rate, true positive rate, correctly classified instances, precision, recall etc. After valuation it has been concluded that ensemble approach is showing better results compared to individual classification techniques.

4.1 Evaluation Metrics

To test the performance of IDS various evaluation metrics can be used. The best way to represent classification results of the IDS is in the form of confusion matrix (Table 3). The other evaluation metric include TPR, Accuracy, Precision, Recall, Accuracy and F-Measure.

Table 3. Confusion matrix for evaluation of IDS

	Predicted normal	Predicted attack
Actual Normal	TN	FP
Actual Attack	FN	TP

4.2   Results Obtained from Dataset 1, Dataset 2 and Dataset 3

In this section, the results of experimentation done on dataset 1 have been compared. Figures 3 and 4 represent the graphs of results obtained in terms of correctly classified instances and false positive rate respectively. Figures 5 and 6 presents the graphs of

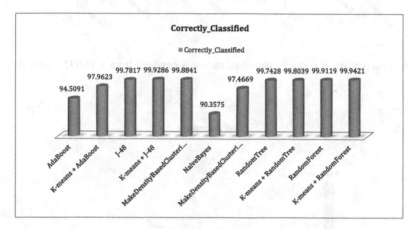

Fig. 3. Comparison of correctly classified instances obtained from NSL-KDD dataset

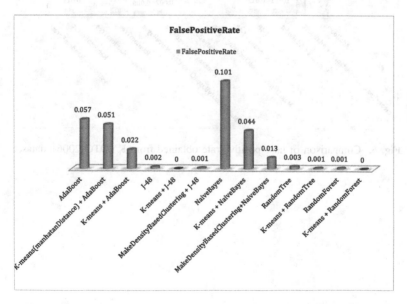

Fig. 4. Comparison of false positive rate obtained from NSL-KDD dataset

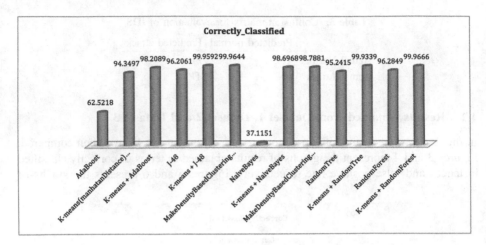

Fig. 5. Comparison of correctly classified instances obtained from KYOTO 2006+ dataset

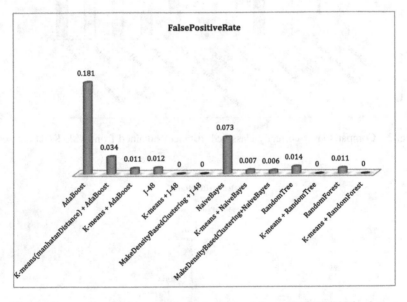

Fig. 6. Comparison of false positive rate obtained from KYOTO 2006+ dataset

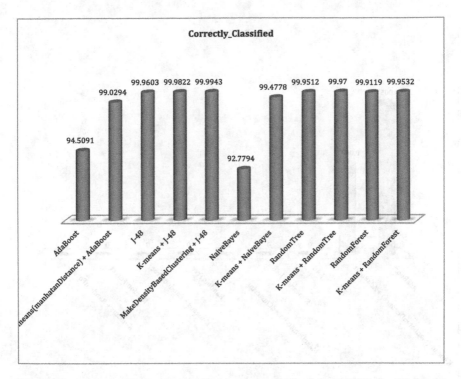

Fig. 7. Comparison of correctly classified instances obtained from KDD Cup 99 dataset

results obtained in terms of correctly classified instances and false positive rate for dataset 2, and Figs. 7 and 8 represents correctly instances for dataset 3. Table 4 depicts that for other parameters, K-means + RandomForest, K-means + J-48, MakeDensityBasedClustering + J-48 and K-means + RandomTree are the best ensemble approaches.

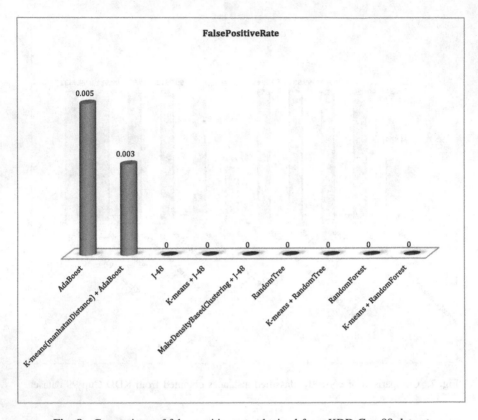

Fig. 8. Comparison of false positive rate obtained from KDD Cup 99 dataset

Table 4. Results of performance metric parameters for NSL-KDD/KYOTO 2006+/KDD Cup 99 dataset

Approach	TP rate	Precision	Recall	F-Measure	ROC area
Adaboost	0.945/.625/.979	0.945/.404/.96	0.945/.62/.97	0.945/.488/.97	.988/.79/.99
K-means + Adaboost	0.98/.982/.99	0.98/.98/.99	0.98/.98/.99	0.979/.98./99	.996/.99/.1
J-48	0.998/.96/1	0.998/.96/1	0.998/.96/1	0.998/.96/1	0.999/.99/1
K-means + J-48	0.999/1/1	0.999/1/1	0.999/1/1	0.999/1/1	1/1/1
Make density based clustering + J-48	0.999/1/1	0.999/1/1	0.999/1/1	0.999/1/1	0.999/1/1

(continued)

Table 4. (*continued*)

Approach	TP rate	Precision	Recall	F-Measure	ROC area
Naïve Bayes	0.904/ .372./92	0.904/ .724/.98	0.904/ .37/.92	0.903/ .39/.95	.966/ .83/1
Make density based clustering + Naïve Bayes	0.974/ .98/.99	0.975/ .98/.99	0.974/ .98/.99	0.975/ .98/.99	0.994/ .99/1
Random tree	0.997/ .95/1	0.99/ .95/1	0.997/ .95/1	0.997/ .95/1	0.998/ .98/1
K-means + Random tree	0.997/ .99/1	0.997/ .99/1	0.997/ .99/1	0.997/ .99/1	0.998/ .99/1
Random forest	0.999/ .96/1	0.999/ .96/1	0.999/ .96/1	0.999/ .96/1	1/.99/1
K-means + Random forest	0.999/1/1	0.999/1/1	0.999/1/1	0.999/1/1	1/1/1

5 Conclusion and Future Scope

In this paper, comparison of various ensemble and non-ensemble techniques have been done and concluded out that the ensemble techniques outperforms non-ensemble techniques. The comparison is done on different datasets so as to figure out whether a particular technique is showing promising results on all the datasets. From the above results we can easily interpret that the technique: K-means + J-48 and K-means + RandonForest are showing better results in case of each datasets. Out of all computed approaches, a model can be formed by utilizing the approach that shows best results and consistency and this model can also be used for detecting intrusions on live network traffic. The model can also be trained on new datasets so as to increase the detecting efficiency of the model regarding the new types of attacks.

References

1. Casas, P., Mazel, J., Owezarski, P.: Unsupervised network intrusion detection systems: detecting the unknown without knowledge. Comput. Commun. 35(7), 772–783 (2012)
2. Chang, N., et al.: A Study on GA-Based WWN intrusion detection. In: International Conference on Management and Service Science, MASS 2009. IEEE (2009)
3. Jain, P., Sardana, A.: Defending against internet worms using honeyfarm. In: Proceedings of the CUBE International Information Technology Conference. ACM (2012)
4. KDD, UCI The third international knowledge discovery and data mining tools competition dataset KDD Cup 1999 data. http://kdd.ics.uci.edu/databases/kddcup99/_kddcup99.html
5. Kim, D.S., Nguyen, H.N., Park, J.S.: Genetic algorithm to improve SVM based network intrusion detection system. In: 19th International Conference on Advanced Information Networking and Applications (AINA 2005), vol. 1, (AINA papers), vol. 2. IEEE (2005)
6. KYOTO 2006+ Traffic Data from Kyoto University's Honeypots. http://www.takakura.com/Kyoto_data/

7. Muda, Z., et al.: Intrusion detection based on K-Means clustering and Naïve Bayes classification. In: 2011 7th International Conference on Information Technology in Asia (CITA 11). IEEE (2011)
8. NSL-KDD (2009). http://nsl.cs.unb.ca/NSL-KDD/.Lee
9. Lee, S.M., Kim, D.S., Park, J.S.: A hybrid approach for real-time network intrusion detection systems. In: 2007 International Conference on Computational Intelligence and Security. IEEE (2007)

Recognition of Handwritten Digits
Using DNN, CNN, and RNN

Subhi Jain[1]([✉]) and Rahul Chauhan[2]([✉])

[1] Computer Science, and Engineering Department, Graphic Era Hill University, Dehradun, India
2510shubhijain@gmail.com
[2] Electronics and Communication Engineering Department, Graphic Era Hill University,
Dehradun, India
chauhan14853@gmail.com

Abstract. Deep learning is the domain of machine learning that implements deep neural architectures, with multiple hidden layers to mimic the functions of the human brain. The network learns from multiple levels of representation and accordingly responds to different levels of abstraction, where each layer learns different patterns. Handwritten digit recognition is a classic machine learning problem to evaluate the performance of classification algorithms. This paper focuses on the implementation of deep neural networks and deep learning algorithms. The NN algorithms such as DNN, CNN, and RNN are implemented for the classification of handwritten digits. The algorithms are implemented on various deep learning frameworks and the performance is evaluated in terms of accuracy of the models. The best accuracy is of CNN 99.6% model and the error rate of algorithms ranges from 0.2–3%.

Keywords: Deep learning · Convolutional neural networks
Recurrent neural networks · Deep neural networks · Shallow neural networks

1 Introduction

Handwritten digit recognition is a classic problem in the field of image recognition. It is an excellent way to evaluate the performance of algorithms on classification problems [1]. The shape of the digits and its features helps to identify the digit from the strokes and boundaries. There have been great achievements in recent years in the field of pattern recognition and computer vision, like in medical image analysis and other classification problems [2, 19]. Handwriting recognition is the ability of a device to take handwriting as input from sources and interpret it. The handwriting is fed as input can be to verify signatures, used to interpret text and OCR (optical character recognition) to read the text and transform it into a form which can be manipulated by computer [13, 15, 16]. The traditional machine learning algorithms are shallow learning algorithms and incapable of extracting multiple features. In the era of big data, deep learning algorithms have performed efficiently in digit recognition tasks on MNIST (Modified National Institute of Standards and Technology) dataset [12, 14]. Figure 1 shows a sample of digits in MNIST dataset.

© Springer Nature Singapore Pte Ltd. 2018
M. Singh et al. (Eds.): ICACDS 2018, CCIS 905, pp. 239–248, 2018.
https://doi.org/10.1007/978-981-13-1810-8_24

Fig. 1. A sample of handwritten digits in MNIST dataset

The neural networks with one hidden layer are called Shallow Neural Networks (SNN). The shallow neural networks are incapable of training datasets that require multiple feature extraction. Hence, Deep Neural Networks (DNN) was introduced. Deep neural networks are the neural networks with more than one hidden layers. In this, each hidden layer learns a different feature. The state of art neural networks recently evolved into Deep Learning Algorithms (DLA) which mimic the functions of human cerebral cortex in their implementation [17].

In this paper, Neural Network and DLA are implemented to perform handwritten digit recognition. The implementations discussed in this paper are of DNN and deep learning algorithms. The architectures of the neural networks are different and each algorithm performs differently on the dataset. The experiments were conducted and results are verified with algorithms and their performance is evaluated in terms of accuracy.

The paper has the following sections: Introduction is followed by the literature survey. In the next section, dataset and implementation of learning algorithms are discussed. The models implemented are DNN (4-layer), CNN (Convolutional neural networks) and Bidirectional RNN (Recurrent Neural networks). The results are in the next section in form of tabular data.

2 Literature Survey

Some of the works in the field of handwritten digit recognition have been listed below:

Alonso-weber et al. [3] in their work present an approach to combine the standard neural network backpropagation with input transformations. They achieve an error rate ranging between 0.3–0.4% for a number chosen at random, but the main issue is additive noise schedule for input and training pattern generations, which is the key factor in the fair performance of this approach.

Hamid et al. [16] have performed handwritten digit recognition over MNIST dataset using CNN, SVM (Support Vector Machines) and KNN (K-Nearest Neighbour) classifiers. In their work, KNN and SVM predicted the outcomes correctly on datasets but Multilayer perceptron fails to recognize the digit 9 due to non-convex function as it gets stuck in the local minima. It was concluded that the accuracy would improve by using CNN with Keras.

Chherawala et al. [5] in their article stated that the word image is used to extract features and then the handwriting is recognized from those features. They developed the model as an application of recurrent neural networks. The RNN classifier used a weighted vote combination, where the significance of feature sets is recognized by the weights and their combination.

Ilmi et al. [6] in their article use local binary patterns for feature extraction and KNN classifier for the recognition of handwritten digits. The testing result on MNIST data had an accuracy of 89.81% and the C1 form data has an accuracy of 70.91%. The C1 form data was used by the General Elections in Indonesia.

Abu Ghosh et al. [12] have performed a comparative study on digit recognition using neural networks. They implemented DNN, CNN and Deep Belief Networks (DBF). The maximum accuracy is of DNN i.e. 98.08% as evaluated by the model. They have also compared the execution time and shown the error rates with various digits that may appear similar.

Phạm [4] in his work built an online handwriting recognition model using C# as the programming base on UNIPEN dataset using multi CNN model. The recognizer recognized MNIST with an accuracy of 99% and UNIPEN at 97%. Further, a segmentation algorithm is given to segment handwriting and feed it to the input network.

LeCunn et al. [17] in their article explain the details of deep Learning. Deep learning is a form of Representation learning where the model learns the representations itself by the input which is fed. The article discusses deep learning applications and its algorithms like CNN and RNN. It also discusses the future scope of deep learning in reference to unsupervised learning approaches.

Deep learning algorithms like BLSTM RNN (bidirectional long short-term memory) have been implemented for gesture recognition in 3D [18] and the CNN models have been implemented in the field of medical image analysis for analyzing data from mammography [19], Computer vision problems, classifying low resolution images of handwritten digits using back propagation [20], Natural Language processing [17] and Speech Recognition [17].

3   Proposed Methods

3.1   Datasets

The handwritten digit recognition system uses the MNIST dataset [7]. It has 70,000 images that can be used to train and evaluate the system. The train set has 60,000 images and the test set has 10,000 images. It is the subset of NIST dataset (National Institute of Standards and Technology), having 28×28 size input images and 10 class labels from (0–9). Therefore, the size of the image is 28×28 pixel square i.e. 784 pixels.

The dataset is fed to the classification algorithms, namely: Deep neural networks (4-layer), Convolutional neural networks, and Bidirectional Recurrent neural networks and the performance is evaluated.

3.2 Classifiers

3.2.1 Deep Neural Networks

The Deep neural networks are implemented in form of a neural network. The 4-layer deep neural network uses a multilayer perceptron classifier or a deep neural network with 3 hidden layers and one output layer. A typical neural network has input neurons, hidden layer neurons, and an output layer. Each connection of one neuron to the other neuron has a weight, and every node is connected to every other node. "Weight" is defined as the power of connection between the nodes, which is equivalent to the firing capability from one neuron to another. The output node(nodes) passes the output through the activation function to define the output of the output node for the given input data. Generally, the activation function is taken as sigmoidal. There is a threshold value of the output in the activation function, i.e. if the output value is greater than or equal to the threshold, then only it is forwarded otherwise not. There are two phases in the neural network: Forward propagation phase and Back propagation phase.

(1) Forward propagation phase:

Each hidden units calculates the summation of the input weights and other factors and produces net input, which is then passed to the activation function.

$$h_{inj} = u_{0j} + \sum_{i=1}^{n} a_i u_{ij} \tag{1}$$

$$h_j = f\left(h_{inj}\right) \tag{2}$$

Similarly, each output(O) units do the summation of the values it receives and passes it to the activation function to calculate the net output depicted as:

$$O_{ink} = w_{0k} + \sum_{j=1}^{p} h_j w_{jk} \tag{3}$$

$$O_k = f\left(O_{ink}\right) \tag{4}$$

(2) Backpropagation of error:

The error correction term is calculated by the received target (t) pattern corresponding to the input training set and on the basis of this term, the weight(w) and bias(b) are updated.

$$\partial_k = \left(t_k - O_k\right) f'\left(O_{ink}\right) \tag{5}$$

$$\Delta w_{jk} = b \partial_k h_j \tag{6}$$

$$\Delta w_{0k} = b \partial_k \tag{7}$$

The summation of delta input units from the output units is done by each hidden layer and is multiplied with the function derivative of $f(h_{inj})$ for error term calculation. The weights and bias are updated based on the term ∂_j.

$$\partial_{inj} = \sum_{k=1}^{m} \partial_k w_{jk} \tag{8}$$

$$\partial_j = \partial_{inj} f'(h_{inj}) \tag{9}$$

$$\Delta u_{ij} = b\partial_j a_i \tag{10}$$

$$\Delta u_{0j} = b\partial_j \tag{11}$$

Weight and bias updation:

- Output units bias and weight updation:

$$w_{jk}(new) = w_{jk}(old) + \Delta w_{jk} \tag{12}$$

$$w_{0k}(new) = w_{0k}(old) + \Delta w_{0k} \tag{13}$$

- Hidden units bias and weight updation:

$$u_{ij}(new) = u_{ij}(old) + \Delta u_{ij} \tag{14}$$

$$u_{0j}(new) = u_{0j}(old) + \Delta u_{0j} \tag{15}$$

The hyperparameters for the model are: number of neurons in hidden layers is 200,150 and 100 respectively, learning rate 0.005, the batch size of 128 and number of epochs is 10. The number of neuron in the output layer is 10. The architecture uses Relu activation for the hidden layers and softmax activation for the output layer. Figure 2 Show the 4-layer architecture, Fig. 3(i) and (ii) show the calculated accuracy i.e. 97.8%. As depicted in the graph, the accuracy increases with every epoch and reaches a maximum accuracy of 97.8%, adding the number of layers results in learning the same features repeatedly which is not required.

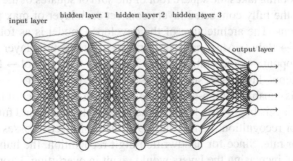

Fig. 2. 4-layer neural network architecture

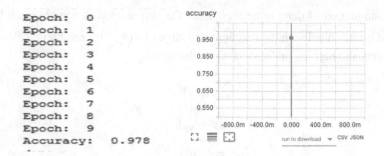

Fig. 3. (i) Accuracy of the deep neural network (4 layers), (ii) Accuracy graph

3.2.2   Convolutional Neural Networks

CNN deal with image data, typically 2D data and use convolution, pooling, and fully connected layers to classify the data and produce the output. The three main features of CNN are: Local Receptive field, shared weights, and biases and pooling. The convolution layers use the convolution operation between the input image and the filter or kernel. The filter or kernel is also a 2D matrix that is responsible for generating feature maps using the local receptive field. The local receptive field is a small localized field of the input image connected to a single neuron in the feature map. The number of feature maps is dependent on the number of features to be classified. The kernel acts as a weight matrix and learns the weights after the feature map detects the features. The shared weights and bias are connected to the local receptive field and the output is given as [8–10]:

$$O = \sigma\left(v + \sum_{i=0}^{4} \sum_{j=0}^{4} w_{i,j} h_{a+i,b+j}\right) \tag{1}$$

Here, O = output, σ = sigmoidal function, v = shared bias value, $w_{i,j}$ = 5 × 5 array of shared weights and $h_{x,y}$ is the input activation at position x,y. It means that first hidden layer neurons detect the same feature across the entire image. The pooling layers simplify the output after convolution. There are two types of pooling: Max pooling and L2 pooling. In max pooling the maximum activation output is pooled into a 2 × 2 input region and L2 pooling takes the square root of the sum of squares of the activation 2 × 2 region. Finally, the fully connected layers connect each layer of max pooling layer to the output neurons. The architecture of the developed model is as follows: Convolution_layer   1 → Relu → Max_pool → dropout → Convolution_layer   2 → Relu → Max_pool → dropout → Convolution_layer 3 → Relu → Max_pool → fully_connected → dropout → output_layer → Result. (Fig. 4 shows the structure.)

Since CNN is capable of high-end feature extraction the number of layers is 4 where the convolution layers begin with learning the low-level features and further learn high-level features for recognition. Increasing the number of layers crosses the Bayes error and human error rate. Since for handwritten digit recognition, the human error rate is not 0% therefore, increasing the layers would result in overfitting. Dropout is a regularization parameter that prevents overfitting of the data. It randomly deads some nodes depending on the probability. Keep_prob is the probability of the hidden nodes to be in the network. The 28×28 input image is taken by the model and passed to the various layers. The first filter is of size $5 \times 5 \times 1 \times 32$ (32 features to learn in the first hidden layer), $3 \times 3 \times 32 \times 64$ for the second convolution layer, $3 \times 3 \times 64 \times 128$ for the third layer, $(128 * 4 * 4,625)$ for the fourth layer and $(625,10)$ for the last layer. The stride is 1 for convolution layer and 2 for max-pooling layers. The padding is SAME.

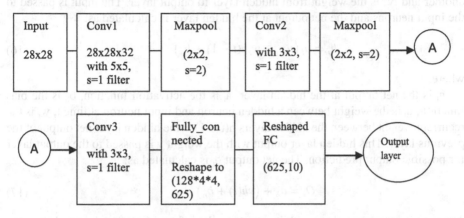

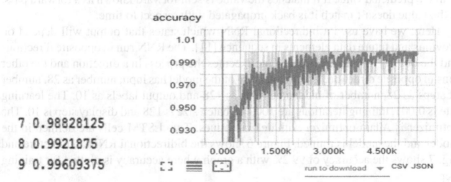

Fig. 4. Architecture of model

The optimizer used is RMS optimizer with a learning rate of 0.001 and the parameter β is 0.9. The keep_prob value is 0.8. The accuracy of this model is the highest amongst all i.e. 99.6% as depicted by the graph in Fig. 5(ii).

7 0.98828125

8 0.9921875

9 0.99609375

Fig. 5. (i) Accuracy of CNN model, (ii) Graph of accuracy at every training step.

3.2.3 Recurrent Neural Network

RNN allow the information to be continuous and lasting by using a loop. It processes the input one at a time in sequence and updates the state of the vector which has data about past elements. Traditionally, the neural networks give input simultaneously, are independent of one another and have different parameters. The recurrent neural networks process one input at a time, the weight and shared bias parameters are same and a dependent on one another.

'I' denote the input neurons, 'h' denotes the hidden layer neurons and 'o' denotes the output neurons. 't − 1' is the previous neuron layers, t is the present neuron layers and 't + 1' is the output neuron layers. 'U' is the weight between input neuron and hidden neuron, 'w' is the weight passed to the hidden layer neurons from one hidden layer to another and 'v' is the weight from hidden layer to output layer. The input is passed to the input neurons and the net output at the hidden layer is calculated as:

$$h_t = a_h \left(u_{i(t)} + w_r h(t-1) + b_h \right) \tag{16}$$

where,

h_t is the net output at the hidden layer, a_t is the activation function, b_h is the bias function, u_i is the weight between a hidden neuron and input neuron at time t, w_r is the recurrent weight between the hidden layers $h(t-1)$ is the hidden layer net output of the previous layer. This hidden layer output with the weight v is passed to the output layer for possible output prediction. The net output o_t is calculated as:

$$O_t = a_o + \left(vh(t) + b_o \right) \tag{17}$$

The next input neuron along with its input has the information of weight and previous layer parameters for the prediction of next value. a_o is the activation function generally, the softmax function and b_o is the shared bias. The weights u, v, w are shared and remain same. These weights are finalized through various training examples after which the system starts giving correct output values. When the values are obtained and matched with the predicted value if it matches the value is sent forward known as a forward pass. If the value doesn't match it is back propagated with respect to time.

Here, we have used a bidirectional RNN which states that output will depend on previous and future data elements in sequence [11]. The RNN run in opposite directions and the outputs of both are mixed. One executes the process in a direction and the other runs in opposite direction. The architecture of the model has input number as 28, number of steps as 28, number of hidden neurons as 128 and output labels as 10. The learning rate is 0.001, training iterations are 100000, batch size is 128 and display step is 10. The optimizer is Adam optimizer with default values. Two LSTM cells are defined in the model and the model is trained. Figure 6 shows the bidirectional RNN architecture and Fig. 7 shows the accuracy of 99.2% with a graph where accuracy is plotted for training steps.

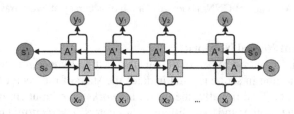

Fig. 6. Bidirectional RNN architecture

```
Iter 96000, Minibatch Loss= 0.102605, Training Accuracy= 0.98438
Iter 97280, Minibatch Loss= 0.112486, Training Accuracy= 0.95312
Iter 98560, Minibatch Loss= 0.088333, Training Accuracy= 0.96094
Iter 99840, Minibatch Loss= 0.082829, Training Accuracy= 0.98438
Optimization Finished!
Testing Accuracy: 0.9921875
```

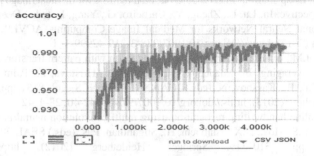

Fig. 7. (i) Accuracy of bidirectional RNN model, (ii) Graph of the accuracy of training steps

4   Results of Experiment

DNN, CNN, and Bidirectional RNN are implemented on MNIST dataset with varying accuracy. The accuracy and error rate of the algorithms is tabulated below in Table 1:

Table 1. Accuracy of algorithms

Algorithms	Accuracy	Error rates
4 Layer DNN	97.8%	2.2%
CNN	99.6%	0.4%
Bidirectional RNN	99.2%	0.8%

5   Conclusion

The results conclude that CNN performed has the best accuracy on MNIST dataset of 99.6%. Bidirectional RNN has the accuracy of 98.43% on the training dataset and 99.2% on the testing dataset. The 4-layer DNN has the least accuracy of 97.4%. This is because the convolution neural network use feature maps to learn the features from an image with kernels that identify strokes from digits, which help in recognizing important digit features. The features and stroke are more helpful in predicting the digits accuracy rather than the hidden layers in DNN. Bidirectional RNN also performs well as they use previous layer output as input. Thus, CNN classifies the model with the best accuracy and least error rate.

References

1. LeCun, Y., et al.: Comparison of learning algorithms for handwritten digit recognition. In: Fogelman-Soulié, F., Gallinari, P. (eds.) Proceedings of the International Conference on Artificial Neural Networks, Nanterre, France (1995)
2. Summers, R.M.: Deep learning and computer-aided diagnosis for medical image processing: a personal perspective. In: Lu, L., Zheng, Y., Carneiro, G., Yang, L. (eds.) Deep Learning and Convolutional Neural Networks for Medical Image Computing. ACVPR, pp. 3–10. Springer, Cham (2017). https://doi.org/10.1007/978-3-319-42999-1_1
3. Alonso-Weber, J.M., et al.: Handwritten digit recognition with pattern transformations and neural network averaging. In: Mladenov, V., Koprinkova-Hristova, P., Palm, G., Villa, A.E.P., Appollini, B., Kasabov, N. (eds.) ICANN 2013. LNCS, vol. 8131, pp. 335–342. Springer, Heidelberg (2013). https://doi.org/10.1007/978-3-642-40728-4_42
4. Phạm, D.V.: Online handwriting recognition using multi convolution neural networks. In: Bui, L.T., Ong, Y.S., Hoai, N.X., Ishibuchi, H., Suganthan, P.N. (eds.) SEAL 2012. LNCS, vol. 7673, pp. 310–319. Springer, Heidelberg (2012). https://doi.org/10.1007/978-3-642-34859-4_31
5. Chherawala, Y., Roy, P.P., Cheriet, M.: Feature set evaluation for offline handwriting recognition systems: application to the recurrent neural network. IEEE Trans. Cybern. **46**(12), 2825–2836 (2016)
6. Ilmi, N., Tjokorda Agung Budi, W., Kurniawan Nur, R.: Handwriting digit recognition using local binary pattern variance and k-nearest neighbor. In: 2016 Fourth International Conference on Information and Communication Technologies (ICoICT) (2016)
7. http://yann.lecun.com/exdb/mnist/ - MNIST database
8. Szegedy, C., et al.: Going deeper with convolutions. CoRR, abs/1409.4842 (2014)
9. Wei, Y., et al.: CNN: single-label to multi-label. CoRR, abs/1406.5726 (2014)
10. Zeiler, M.D., Fergus, R.: Visualizing and understanding convolutional networks. CoRR, abs/1311.2901 (2013). Published in Proceedings of ECCV (2014)
11. Schuster, M., Paliwal, K.K.: Bidirectional recurrent neural networks. IEEE Trans. Sig. Process. **45**(11), 2673–2681 (1997)
12. Abu Ghosh, M.M., Maghari, A.Y.: A comparative study on handwriting digit recognition using neural networks. IEEE (2017)
13. Liu, C.-L., Nakashima, K., Sako, H., Fujisawa, H.: Handwritten digit recognition: benchmarking of state-of-the-art techniques. Pattern Recogn. **36**, 2271–2285 (2003)
14. Lauer, F., Suen, C.Y., Bloch, G.: A trainable feature extractor for handwritten digit recognition. Pattern Recogn. **40**(6), 1816–1824 (2007)
15. LeCun, Y., Bottou, L., Bengio, Y., Ha®ner, P.: Gradient-based learning applied to document recognition. Proc. IEEE **86**(11), 2278–2324 (1998)
16. Hamid, N.B.A., Sjarif, N.N.B.A.: Handwritten recognition using SVM, KNN and neural network. www.arxiv.org/ftp/arxiv/papers/1702/1702.00723
17. LeCun, Y., Bengio, Y., Hinton, G.: Deep learning. Nature **521**, 436–444 (2015)
18. Lefebvre, G., Berlemont, S., Mamalet, F., Garcia, C.: BLSTM-RNN based 3D gesture classification. In: Mladenov, V., Koprinkova-Hristova, P., Palm, G., Villa, A.E.P., Appollini, B., Kasabov, N. (eds.) ICANN 2013. LNCS, vol. 8131, pp. 381–388. Springer, Heidelberg (2013). https://doi.org/10.1007/978-3-642-40728-4_48
19. Kuang, P., Cao, W., Wu, Q.: Preview on structures and algorithms of deep learning. IEEE (2014)
20. LeCun, Y., et al.: Handwritten digit recognition with a back-propagation network. In: Proceedings of Advances in Neural Information Processing Systems, pp. 396–404 (1990)

Evaluating Effectiveness of Color Information for Face Image Retrieval and Classification Using SVD Feature

Junali Jasmine Jena, G. Girish$^{(\boxtimes)}$, and Manisha Patro

Department of Computer Science and Engineering, National Institute of Science
and Technology, Berhampur 761008, Odisha, India
gandhamgirish@gmail.com

Abstract. LBP (Local Binary Pattern) algorithm has been a popular pattern matching technique used for various purposes such as image retrieval, image classification etc. But efficiency of the algorithm could be enhanced more by applying it over decomposed sub-images of the original image as it enables in extracting and identifying more prominent features and the accuracy could be increased. Thus, in this paper, SVD (Singular Value Decomposition) is applied to individual component of a color space followed by LBP. The individual feature vectors are merged to get the final feature vector. The combined process has been applied to RGB, YCbCr, HSV and La*b color spaces for image retrieval and their behavior is analyzed. The highest value of precision, recall and f-score was found to be 57.0,85.5 and 68.4 respectively for the technique LBP-S-YCbCr, in its optimal bin size 16. Behaviour of finally obtained feature vectors of all the techniques, has also been analyzed by classifying them using KNN. Highest accuracy of classification with a value of 90% was also found for the technique LBP-S-YCbCr.

Keywords: LBP · SVD · RGB · YCbCr · HSV · La*b · KNN

1 Introduction

Local pattern matching algorithms have performed extremely well in identifying the interim patterns of images from which suitable feature vectors could be extracted and used successfully in image retrieval and classification techniques. But the pattern matching could be done more accurate by pre-processing the image and decomposing it into sub-images where the hidden patterns become more distinct. Thus, applying local pattern matching algorithms upon suitable decomposed sub-images may give better results.

1.1 Background Study

Pattern matching process is a method for analyzing texture of an image. Materka et al. [13] had reviewed various texture analyzing techniques on basis of suitable classifications. Local binary pattern, proposed by Ojala et al. [2], has been a popular approach among other local pattern matching algorithms. The most significant factor is its

© Springer Nature Singapore Pte Ltd. 2018
M. Singh et al. (Eds.): ICACDS 2018, CCIS 905, pp. 249–259, 2018.
https://doi.org/10.1007/978-981-13-1810-8_25

simplified computational complexity. So, various other techniques have been devised in addition to LBP for efficient pattern matching. Iakovidis et al. [3], proposed a fuzzy LBP approach for pattern analysis of ultrasound images. Nanni et al. [4], have surveyed various LBP based texture descriptors in their paper. Similarly, Li et al. [5], proposed a LBP based machine-learning technique for classification of hyper-spectral images. Liu et al. [7] proposed another texture classification technique known as median robust extended LBP. Nosaka et al. [8] used invariant co-occurence based LBP for classification of HEp-2 cells. LBP technique has also been used over color images for patttern recognition. Choi et al. [9], in their paper have used LBP over color images for face recognition.

Decomposition of original image matrix to proper sub-image matrices could draw significant features from the original image. Applying pattern matching algorithms upon these sub-images has yielded better results. Haeffele et al. [6], used factorization of low rank matrix for decomposition. Dubey et al. [1] used singular value decomposition to obtain sub-images. SVD technique has got various applications in the field of image processing [20, 22, 24].

Performance of a classifier implemented on a technique, also reveals lots of its behavioral aspect. So estimating a suitable classifier according to the nature of generated data affects its efficiency to a great extent. Gao et al. [27], in their paper, proposed a semi-supervised classification for a face data which has insufficient labeled samples. Wang et al. [29] proposed a PCA and KNN based classification for facial expression detection. Face detection has been a widely used area for determining accuracy of a newly developed approach. Hassaballah et al. [14] discussed various features and challenges of automated face detection. Similarly, Huang et al. [17] and Ahonen et al. [18] discussed application of LBP to facial image analysis. Kim et al. [25] and Chander et al. [26] discussed about the applications of SVD technique for facial image detection. Chelali et al. [30], in their paper, discussed about the performance analysis of face recognition system in RGB and YCbCr color space.

In this paper, a combined approach of decomposition and pattern matching has been used for color face image retrieval and the performance has been analyzed by implementing the algorithm upon various color spaces. Finally performance of each technique has been evaluated by implementing KNN on them. Rest of the paper is organized as follows: Proposed approach, Results and Discussion and Conclusion.

2 Proposed Approach

The proposed approach is the combination of two techniques: Singular Value Decomposition (SVD) and Local Binary Pattern (LBP).

2.1 SVD

It is a technique proposed by Beltrami [10] and Jordan [11] in 1870s. In this technique a matrix S[mxn] is divided into three sub-matrices A is the diagonal matrix having values $(a_1, a_2 \ldots a_{x)}$, B[nxn] and C[mxm], relationship among which is described in equation,

$$S = BA'C^T$$

where, $A' = \begin{pmatrix} P & 0 \\ 0 & 0 \end{pmatrix}$

a_i = singular values of A obtained by positive square roots of the eigen values of $A^T A$.

A^T = Transpose of A.

m, n = dimension of matrix S

Suitable application of this method for image decomposition was proposed by Dubey et al. in [1], where from a 2×2 matrix another 2×2 SUVD matrix was derived capturing its embedded patterns. The derivation has been explained in Fig. 1.

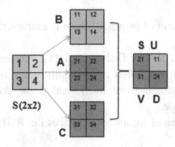

Fig. 1. Decomposition of S to S,U,V and D

2.2 LBP

Ojala et al. in [2] proposed an simple and efficient pattern matching algorithm known as LBP. This operator compares one pixel value with its eight neighbouring pixels and extracts a binary pattern among the nine-pixels and determines a single value for them. LBP operator can be described as follows,

$$LBP = \sum_{i=1}^{8} L(b_0 - b_i)2^{i-1}, \text{where } L(b_0, b_i) = \begin{cases} 1, if & b_i \geq b_0 \\ 0, if & b_i < b_0 \end{cases}$$

2.3 KNN

K-Nearest Neighbour classifier matches the features of testing data and training data and searches for most nearly matching samples of the testing data. Value of K specifies the number of nearly matching samples.

2.4 Procedure

Block diagram of the proposed approach is given in Fig. 2. Following are the steps undertaken to obtain the final feature vector.

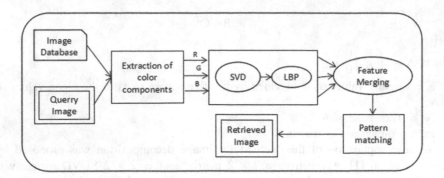

Fig. 2. Block diagram of the proposed approach

Individual color component of original image is extracted and SVD is applied upon it S, U, V and D sub-bands.

II. According results obtained by Dubey et al. [1], sub-image obtained by S-band is the efficient one, hence LBP is applied upon S-sub image only.

III. Feature vectors obtained from individual color components are merged to obtain the final feature vector.

IV. Same process is repeated for all color spaces i.e. RGB, YCbCr, HSV and La*b.

Table 1. Recall, Precision and F-Score value of the techniques

Techniques	Precision	Recall	F-Score
LBP	53.42	80.13	64.10
LBP-RGB	53.58	80.38	64.30
LBP-S-RGB	56.08	84.13	67.3
LBP-HSV	55.5	83.25	66.6
LBP-S-HSV	50.16	75.25	60.2
LBP-YCbCr	49.9	74.8	59.9
LBP-S-YCbCr	55.58	83.3	66.7
LBP-La*b	48.33	72.5	58.0
LBP-S-La*b	55.91	83.87	67.10

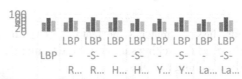

Fig. 3. Graph showing precision, recall and F-Score value of each technique

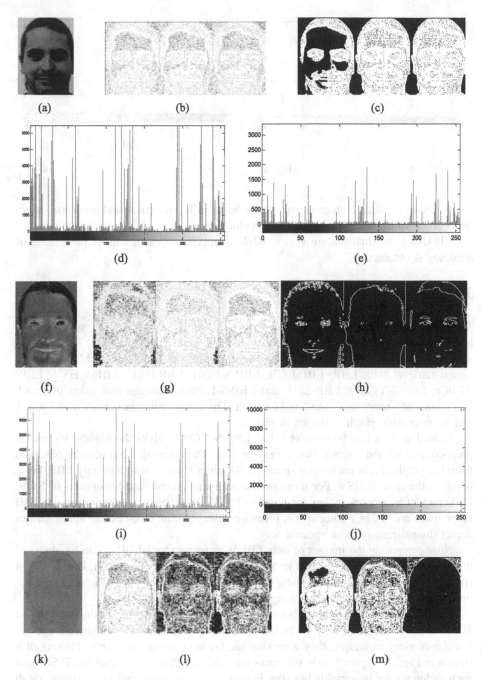

Fig. 4. (a), (f) and (k) are RGB, HSV and YCbCr images. (b), (g) and (l) are the images obtained by applying only LBP to their respective color spaces and (d), (i) and (n) are the histograms of images in respective order. (c), (h) and (m) are the images obtained by applying LBP to the S-sub image of their respective color spaces and (e), (j) and (o) are the histograms of images in respective order.

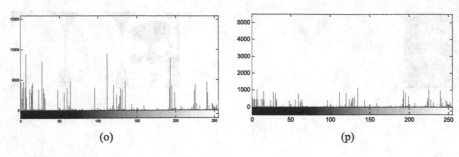

(o)   (p)

Fig. 4. (*continued*)

V. Using the final feature vector, image retrieval is performed and precision, recall and f-score values are obtained for each color spaces.

VI. Using the final feature vector, KNN is applied to each, and its percentage of accuracy is obtained.

3 Results and Discussion

The proposed approach was simulated on a 2.40 GHz i5-4210 CPU system using MATLAB 8.3 software. KNN was simulated using Ri386 3.4.3 software. The database used was FEI face database [28]. First the database was simulated in MATLAB for image retrieval with LBP, LBP-RGB, LBP-S-RGB, LBP-HSV, LBP-S-HSV, LBP-YCbCr, LBP-S-YCbCr, LBP-La*b and LBP-S-La*b techniques and value of recall, precision and f-score was calculated for each. The calculated data is shown in Table 1 and its respective graph is shown in Fig. 3.

From Fig. 3, it can be observed that, LBP-S-YCbCr, gives the highest values for precision, recall and f-score. But, a very peculiar characteristics can also be observed from the graph i.e. for each color space S-LBP gives better result than only LBP, but it is not in the case of HSV. For more precise analysis, images and histograms of RGB, HSV and YCbCr color spaces are given in Fig. 4. Now, compare the images of RGB color space and YCbCr color space. It can be observed that YCbCr color space images depict the patterns in more specific way.

Now comparing the images of only LBP with respect to S-LBP, it can be observed that the patterns are more specific in S-LBP, thus it yielded better result. But, in Fig. 4 (j), it can be observed that the histogram has highest number of zero intensity levels, thus it gave the least accuracy among all.

Implementation of the above discussed techniques was performed using the bin size of 256 in all cases. But it may not be the optimal bin size. Thus, to estimate the optimal bin size of every technique, they were simulated using variable bin size and the result is shown in Figs. 5. Figure 5(a) to (i) shows the values of Precision, recall and F-Score of each technique for its variable bin size. Figure 5(j) shows the graph of precision, recall and f-score values for each technique in its optimal bin size and from the graph it can be observed that LBP-S-YCbCr performed the best in the bin size 16.

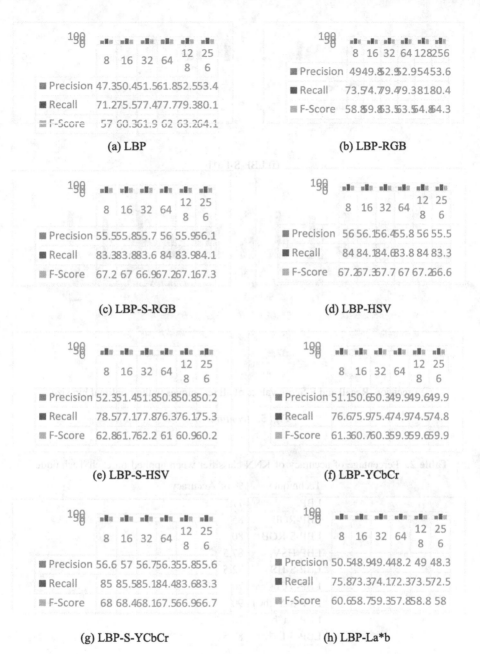

Fig. 5. (a) to (i) shows the graphs of precision, recall and f-score values of techniques for variable bin sizes. (j) shows the graph of precision,recall and f-score values of techniques in their optimal bin sizes.

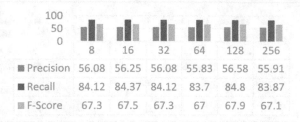

(i) LBP-S-La*b

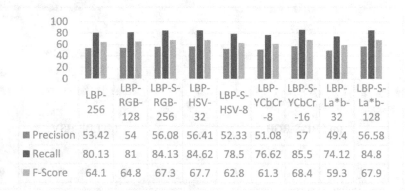

(j) Precision, Recall and F-Score values of all techniques in their optimal bin size

Fig. 5. (*continued*)

Table 2. Percentage of accuracy of KNN classifier when applied on each Technique

Techniques	% of Accuracy
LBP	77.5
LBP-RGB	85
LBP-S-RGB	80
LBP-HSV	87.5
LBP-S-HSV	72.5
LBP-YCbCr	70
LBP-S-YCbCr	90
LBP-La*b	75
LBP-S-La*b	87.5

Finally, the final feature vectors obtained from all the techniques in their optimal bin size were extracted and fed to the KNN classifier. KNN is the suitable classifier for this type of data, as it has more number of classes but less number of samples in each class. As the sample size in each class is 2, so value of K used in KNN was also set to

2. Table 2 gives the percentage of accuracy of the classifier in each technique and its respective graph is shown in Fig. 6. From the obtained values it can be observed that pattern also affects the process of classification in a similar manner, as it affected in case of image retrieval. The reason is that, performance of both the processes is depended on the feature vector. In, KNN classification also, LBP-S-YCbCr performed the best and LBP-S-HSV had the least performance.

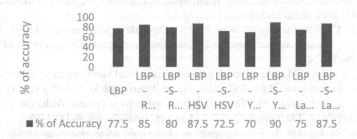

Fig. 6. Graph showing percentage of accuracy of KNN classifier when applied on each technique

4 Conclusion

From the analysis of the proposed approach it was observed that LBP-S-YCbCr performed most efficiently in image retrieval in its optimal bin size of 16, with the values of precision, recall and f-score were 57, 85.5 and 68.4 respectively, as well as, it performed best with KNN classification with a percentage accuracy of 90%. The least performance was recorded for LBP-S-HSV in both image retrieval and KNN-classification. Further work may be done in this field, by applying other decomposition methods which can depict the inherent patterns more minutely and may give better results.

References

1. Dubey, S.R., Singh, S.K., Singh, R.K.: Local SVD based NIR face retrieval. J. Vis. Commun. Image Represent. **49**, 141–152 (2017)
2. Ojala, T., Pietikainen, M., Maenpaa, T.: Multiresolution gray-scale and rotation invariant texture classification with local binary patterns. IEEE Trans. Pattern Anal. Mach. Intell. **24** (7), 971–987 (2002)
3. Iakovidis, D.K., Keramidas, E.G., Maroulis, D.: Fuzzy local binary patterns for ultrasound texture characterization. In: Campilho, A., Kamel, M. (eds.) ICIAR 2008. LNCS, vol. 5112, pp. 750–759. Springer, Heidelberg (2008). https://doi.org/10.1007/978-3-540-69812-8_74
4. Nanni, L., Lumini, A., Brahnam, S.: Survey on LBP based texture descriptors for image classification. Expert Syst. Appl. **39**(3), 3634–3641 (2012)
5. Li, W., Chen, C., Hongjun, S., Qian, D.: Local binary patterns and extreme learning machine for hyperspectral imagery classification. IEEE Trans. Geosci. Remote Sens. **53**(7), 3681–3693 (2015)

6. Haeffele, B., Young, E., Vidal, R.: Structured low-rank matrix factorization: optimality, algorithm, and applications to image processing. In: International Conference on Machine Learning, pp. 2007–2015 (2014)

7. Liu, L., et al.: Median robust extended local binary pattern for texture classification. IEEE Trans. Image Process. 25(3), 1368–1381 (2016)

8. Nosaka, R., Fukui, K.: HEp-2 cell classification using rotation invariant co-occurrence among local binary patterns. Pattern Recogn. 47(7), 2428–2436 (2014)

9. Choi, J.Y., Plataniotis, K.N., Ro, Y.M.: Using colour local binary pattern features for face recognition. In: 2010 17th IEEE International Conference on Image Processing (ICIP), pp. 4541–4544. IEEE (2010)

10. Beltrami, E.: Sulle funzioni bilineari. Proc. of Giornale di Mathematiche 11, 98–106 (1873)

11. Jordan, C.: Mmoire sur les formes trilinaires. Journal de Mathmatiques Pures et Appliques 19, 35–54 (1874)

12. Murala, S., Wu, Q.M.J.: Local mesh patterns versus local binary patterns: biomedical image indexing and retrieval. IEEE J. Biomed. Health Inform. 18(3), 929–938 (2014)

13. Materka, A., Strzelecki, M.: Texture analysis methods–a review. Technical University of Lodz, Institute of Electronics, COST B11 report, Brussels, pp. 9–11 (1998)

14. Hassaballah, M., Aly, S.: Face recognition: challenges, achievements and future directions. IET Comput. Vis. 9(4), 614–626 (2015)

15. Guo, Z., Zhang, D.: A completed modeling of local binary pattern operator for texture classification. IEEE Trans. Image Process. 19(6), 1657–1663 (2010)

16. Zhao, G., Ahonen, T., Matas, J., Pietikainen, M.: Rotation-invariant image and video description with local binary pattern features. IEEE Trans. Image Process. 21(4), 1465–1477 (2012)

17. Huang, D., Shan, C., Ardabilian, M., Wang, Y., Chen, L.: Local binary patterns and its application to facial image analysis: a survey. IEEE Trans. Syst. Man Cybern. Part C Appl. Rev. 41(6), 765–781 (2011)

18. Ahonen, T., Hadid, A., Pietikainen, M.: Face description with local binary patterns: Application to face recognition. IEEE Trans. Pattern Anal. Mach. Intell. 28(12), 2037–2041 (2006)

19. Konda, T., Nakamura, Y.: A new algorithm for singular value decomposition and its parallelization. Parallel Comput. 35(6), 331–344 (2009)

20. Andrews, H., Patterson, C.: Singular value decompositions and digital image processing. IEEE Trans. Acoust. Speech Signal Process. 24(1), 26–53 (1976)

21. Kakarala, R., Ogunbona, P.O.: Signal analysis using a multiresolution form of the singular value decomposition. IEEE Trans. Image Process. 10(5), 724–735 (2001)

22. Yang, J.F., Lu, C.L.: Combined techniques of singular value decomposition and vector quantization for image coding. IEEE Trans. Image Process. 4(8), 1141–1146 (1995)

23. Bhatnagar, G., Saha, A., Wu, Q.M.J., Atrey, P.K.: Analysis and extension of multiresolution singular value decomposition. Inf. Sci. 277, 247–262 (2014)

24. Singh, S.K., Kumar, S.: Singular value decomposition based sub-band decomposition and multi-resolution (SVD-SBD-MRR) representation of digital colour images. Pertanika J. Sci. Technol. 19(2), 229–235 (2011)

25. Kim, W., Suh, S., Hwang, W., Han, J.-J.: SVD face: illumination-invariant face representation. IEEE Signal Process. Lett. 21(11), 1336–1340 (2014)

26. Chandar, K.P., Chandra, M.M., Kumar, M.R., Swarnalatha, B.: Preprocessing using SVD towards illumination invariant face recognition. In: Proceedings of Recent Advances in Intelligent Computational Systems, pp. 051–056 (2011)

27. Gao, Y., Ma, J., Yuille, A.L.: Semi-supervised sparse representation based classification for face recognition with insufficient labeled samples. IEEE Trans. Image Process. **26**(5), 2545–2560 (2017)
28. The FEI face database. http://fei.edu.br/~cet/facedatabase.html
29. Wang, Q., Jia, K., Liu, P.: Design and implementation of remote facial expression recognition surveillance system based on PCA and KNN algorithms. In: 2015 International Conference on Intelligent Information Hiding and Multimedia Signal Processing (IIH-MSP), pp. 314–317. IEEE (2015)
30. Chelali, F.Z., Cherabit, N., Djeradi, A.: Face recognition system using skin detection in RGB and YCbCr color space. In: 2015 2nd World Symposium on Web Applications and Networking (WSWAN), pp. 1–7. IEEE (2015)

PDD Algorithm for Balancing Medical Data

Karan Kalra$^{(\boxtimes)}$, Riya Goyal$^{(\boxtimes)}$, Sanmeet Kaur, and Parteek Kumar

Department of Computer Science and Engineering, TIET, Patiala 147001, India
karankalra11@gmail.com, riyagoyal9328@gmail.com,
{sanmeet.bhatia,parteek.bhatia}@thapar.edu

Abstract. There can be various aspects that can affect the performance of a machine learning classifier, among which the unbalanced dataset is the most prominent. The unbalanced dataset is the one in which there is a disproportion among classes i.e. instances belonging to the one class heavily outnumber instances belonging to all other classes. This problem of the unbalanced dataset is more common in medical data as it is collected from the real world where the number of persons affected by the disease will always be less than the non-affected persons. Due to this disproportion among the classes, classifiers face difficulties in learning concepts related to the class in minority. Most of all data balancing techniques are created keeping general data in mind and are not viable for medical data. In this paper, a method is proposed that helps balance medical data more effectively and at the same time increase performance and decrease the leaning time for the classifier.

Keywords: Parallel data division · Unbalance dataset
Balancing medical dataset · Data balancing technique

1 Introduction

Data unbalancing is a typical problem in the field of supervised classification. The aim of the supervised classification is to categorize data points that are unknown considering a given set of known data points. Application of the supervised classifier over imbalanced data has become a matter of interest in the recent years. The unbalanced dataset is common among real word situation such as diagnosing gear faults [1], in diagnosis of medical data [2], detecting network intrusion [3, 4], classification of text [5, 6], detecting financial statement fraud [7] classification of streams of data [8]. These real-life classification problems mostly consist of a majority class that has a significantly larger number of instances than other minority classes and generally these minority classes depict occurrence of an event and is more relevant than majority class. Due to data unbalancing machine learning based classifiers face problems in learning minority classes as the weightage for misclassification of a data point belonging to minority class is very less than that of majority class. As a result, most machine learning classifiers

---

K. Kalra and R. Goyal—These authors contributed equally to this work.

© Springer Nature Singapore Pte Ltd. 2018
M. Singh et al. (Eds.): ICACDS 2018, CCIS 905, pp. 260–269, 2018.
https://doi.org/10.1007/978-981-13-1810-8_26

become biased towards classifying instances in majority class and tend to consider minority class instances as outliers. This type of classification prevents the system to be used in real case scenarios [9, 10].

Most researches in previous years have been focused on the classification of unbalanced binary data [11]. The problem of unbalanced datasets become more crucial in case of multi-class classification problems where multi-class data is converted into binary by selecting smallest class as minority class and merging all other classes into one majority class [12, 13]. These approaches face difficulty in selecting artificial minority class as two or more classes may have a similar number of data points. Many approaches try synthetic dataset creation to increase minority data using methods like SMOTE [14] but over sampling minority class by adding synthetic data points is not considered a novel and reliable approach in context to medical data as it raises a question on the authenticity of data.

In this paper parallel data division based method is proposed for efficient data balancing of medical data. This approach helps balance instance among majority and minority class utilizing each and every valuable data instance in the dataset. Without the creation of any synthetic data for over sampling the minority classes as well as losing valuable data by using under sampling techniques on majority class this approach proves to be very efficient in un-biasing the classifier, increasing the performance of the system and at the same time reducing the training time of the system.

2   Background

There are many approaches proposed to solve the problem of the unbalanced learning. Each of this approach tries to balance the dataset by using either under sampling or over sampling. To have a deep understanding, these approaches can be generalized as follows:

2.1   Random Sampling

This data balancing technique uses non-heuristic functions to balance data which can be further classified into two categories namely ROS and RUS.

Random Over Sampling. Random over sampling is a method that tries to balance disproportion among the classes by using a non-heuristic function to randomly replicate instances of a minority class. The main drawback of random over sampling is that it replicates instances of minority class without any alteration which increases the chances of occurrence of overfitting.

Random Under Sampling. Random under sampling is a method that tries to balance disproportion among the classes by using a non-heuristic function to randomly eliminate instances of majority class. The main shortcoming of random under sampling is that it affects the induction process by potentially discarding valuable data.

2.2 Tomek Links

It is an approach used for Under sampling in which Tomek links [15] belonging to majority class are eliminated. let I_a, I_b are instances that belong to two different classes, then (I_a, I_b) is a Tomek Link if there doesn't exist any instance I_c for which $D(I_a, I_c) < D(I_a, I_b)$ or $D(I_b, I_c) < D(I_a, I_b)$ where $D(x, y)$ represents distance between instances x and y. The disadvantage of this approach is that if there exists a majority class that represents more than 70% of data than Tomeks links are not an effective solution as they will not able to undersample the majority class to an extent where classes become balanced.

2.3 Neighborhood Cleaning Rule

It is an Under sampling technique used to remove majority class instances by using Edited Nearest Neighbor Rule (ENN) [16] proposed by Wilson. The principle behind the working of ENN is that it removes an instance I_a from the dataset if two of its three nearest neighbor instances differ from its class label. Neighborhood Cleaning Rule modifies ENN which can be explained as follows:

Given a binary classification problem where M and N represent majority class and minority class respectively. For each instance I_a, three nearest neighbors are identified. If $I_a \in M$ is an instance of majority class and any of its three nearest neighbors belong to class N then I_a is deleted from the dataset. If $I_a \in N$ and any of its three nearest neighbors belong to class M than those neighbors of I_a are deleted from the dataset.

2.4 Synthetic Instance Creation

Synthetic data creation is the production of new instances by using the already given instances. The three widely used approaches under this are as follows:

SMOTE. Synthetic Minority Over sampling Technique [17] is one of the most widely used over sampling methods. In this approach synthetic instances of a minority, the class is created to increase oversample the minority class. Instance creation in SMOTE uses a simple approach of taking k nearest instances of a minority class and interpolating them to create a new minority class instance. This approach helps spread boundaries of a minority class and also avoids overfitting.

Borderline SMOTE. Borderline SMOTE [18] method is also a type of Over-sampling method based on SMOTE. The main idea behind Borderline SMOTE is to create instances of using the borderline instances of a minority class. This approach achieves better true positive rates than SMOTE.

ADASYN. Adaptive synthetic sampling [19] approach is an Over-sampling Techniques which uses weights to increase the learning from unbalanced datasets. The main method behind ADASYN is to assign more weightage to the instances of minority class that are difficult to learn by the classifier than those instances of minority class that was learned more easily. So, more synthetic instances are created from data points that were harder to be classified by the classifier.

All the data balancing techniques discussed above have drawbacks that prevent them to be used in balancing Medical Data. Under sampling techniques don't take into account the cost of collecting medical data and try to eliminate valuable medical data instances [20]. Over sampling techniques create synthetic minority data which otherwise should include sample data points having significant information about disease affected patients. So over sampling the minority data affects the authenticity of data as well as the classifier.

3 Proposed Approach

The method proposed in this work helps balance unbalanced data without synthetically creating data or eliminating it. Generally in case of medical data majority class represents a class of non affected patients. If a classifier is biased towards this majority class then there is a high chance of an affected patient to be classified as not affected by the disease.

So this type of unbalancing becomes more catastrophic in case of such type of data. Figure 1 shows how the given methods create multiple balanced datasets from the single unbalanced dataset. Each of the created dataset is further fed parallely to the machine learning classifier. The output from these classifiers are then ensembled using majority voting to create the final set of predictions.

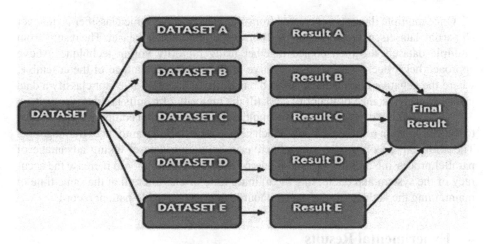

Fig. 1. Overview of the proposed method.

Let $D = \{M_1, M_2, M_3, \ldots M_n\}$ where M_i is the class of dataset D and $M_i > M_j$ if $i > j$. So in this method firstly the majority class (M_n) is identified. After identifying M_n it is divided in such a way that each subpart of the class M_n is in equal proportion with the class M_{n-1}. If there still exists high disproportion among class M_{n-1} and M_1 then M_n and M_{n-1} classes are divided in such a way that each subpart is in equal proportion with the class M_{n-2}.

After that, it is checked if there still exists high disproportion among M_{n-2} and M_1 class if yes, then the whole process is repeated again till all classes are balanced.

Table 1 shows the working of PDD. Let D be set containing all classes of dataset and S be an empty dataset Max(D) represents max function that outputs majority class from dataset, Count(X) counts number of instances in X, RoundOf (X) gives nearest integer value of X, Divide (S, P) divides every class in S in equal proportion to P.

Table 1. Working of PDD algorithm

Algorithm PDD (S, D)
S←Max (D)
D=D-S
X←Max (D)
Y←Max (S)
Z←Min (D)
If (Count(Y)/Count (Z)) >=2   then
P=RoundOf (Count(Y)/Count(X))
SubData←Divide(S, P)
For Each class A in SubData do
PDD(A, Di)
Else
return D

Once multiple datasets are created from single dataset the same classifier is run over all partial datasets and result is obtained corresponding to each dataset. The results from multiple datasets are then pooled together using majority voting technique. Above approach helps decrease the false negative rate by taking advantage of the ensemble, where the negative class is the class in the majority. Classifier does not classify a data instance as an instance of majority class till the majority of results are in favor of it.

As datasets are divided into parallel multiple datasets parallel computing can be used to run classifier on multiple datasets which help reduce the huge amount of training time. The above approach proves very effective in balancing dataset taking advantage of parallel processing architecture and modern ensemble technology to increase the accuracy of the system and decreasing the training time of classifier all at the same time of maintaining the authenticity of data without losing any valuable patient record.

4   Experimental Results

The approach proposed in this work was applied on a medical dataset containing 33,545 images for training the network and 3,576 images for testing the network. Table 2 shows the distribution of dataset with respect to each class.

Table 2. Training dataset

Class	Name	Number of images
0	Normal	25,810
1	Mild stage	5,292
2	Severe stage	2,443

The percentage distribution in Fig. 2 shows the highly unbalanced dataset with class 0 having 76.94% records, class 1 having 15.87% records and 7.28% records of the dataset. This kind of data distribution is very common in case of medical datasets where the numbers of people not affected by the disease are always greater than the people not affected by disease. In these case the PDD algorithm provides an efficient solution of balancing the data by increasing the response time and accuracy of the system without affecting the authenticity of data.

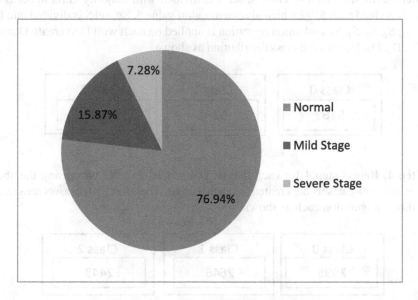

Fig. 2. Percentage distribution of dataset.

Initially, machine learning classifier was applied in a dataset without following any balancing approach. As classifier was applied to unbalanced dataset it showed biased results classifying every class into class "0". Table 3 shows the Confusion matrix for the output.

Table 3. Confusion matrix for the unbalanced dataset.

	0	1	2
0	25810	0	0
1	5292	0	0
2	2443	0	0

Now Parallel Data Division algorithm (PDD) is applied to the above dataset. The dataset is divided into 10 balanced datasets with the following steps.

Step 1: Firstly the Majority class from the dataset is identified and move to set S.

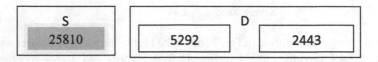

Step 2: After that, the majority class in set S is compared with the minority class in set D i.e. 25810 is compared with 2443. As 25810 is greater than twice of 2443 so, the dataset needs to be divided.

Step 3: So, the majority class in set S is divided with majority class in set D i.e. 25810 is divided with 5292 which gives a roundoff value 5. So, set S is divided into five parts S_1, S_2, S_3, S_4, S_5, and union operation is applied on each with D to create Datasets D_1, D_2, D_3, D_4, D_5 with the class distribution as shown.

Class 0	Class 1	Class 2
5162	5292	2443

Step 4: Repeat step 1 for each dataset D_i created. So after processing the above dataset, two sub-datasets are created for each dataset. Therefore, 10 datasets are created with this configuration each as shown.

Class 0	Class 1	Class 2
2596	2646	2443

The machine learning model is applied on these datasets and corresponding 10 confusion matrixes are generated to calculate the accuracy of the algorithm. Figure 3 shows the Confusion Matrixes for each dataset.

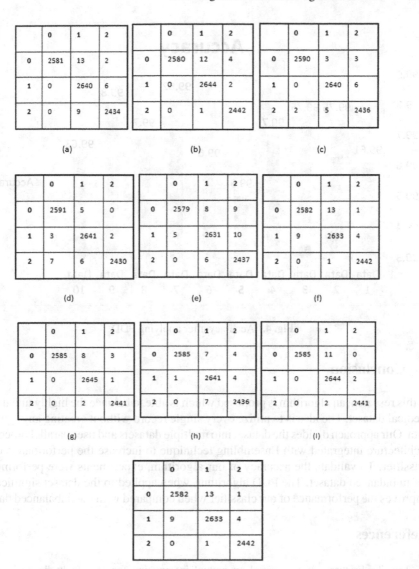

Fig. 3. Confusion matrix for balanced dataset (a) Data1 (b) Data2 (c) Data3 (d) Data4 (e) Data5 (f) Data6 (g) Data7 (h) Data8 (i) Data9 (j) Data10

The initial accuracy of the system was restricted 76.94% during unbalance dataset. The PDD algorithm helps scale up the accuracy as shown in Fig. 4 and generates a more unbiased output.

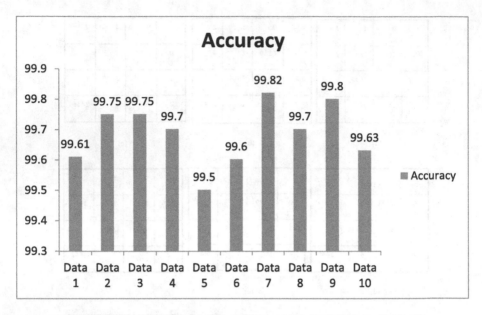

Fig. 4. Accuracy after applying PDD.

5 Conclusion

In this research, an algorithm is proposed which is able to balance the highly unbalanced medical dataset. The idea is to utilize every single record without creating any synthetic data. Our approach divides the dataset into multiple datasets and uses parallel processing architecture integrated with Ensembling technique to increase the performance of the classifier. To validate the accuracy of our algorithm, experiments were performed on the imbalanced dataset. The PDD algorithm, when applied to the dataset significantly, improves the performance of our classifier when compared with the unbalanced dataset.

References

1. Liu, T.: Feature selection based on mutual information for gear faultydiagnosis on the imbalanced dataset. J. Comput. Inf. Syst. **8**(18), 7831–7838 (2012)
2. Mena, L., Gonzalez, J.A.: Symbolic one-class learning from imbalanced datasets: application in medical diagnosis. Int. J. Artif. Intell. Tools **18**(02), 273–309 (2009)
3. Cieslak, D.A., Chawla, N.V., Striegel, A.: Combating imbalance in network intrusion datasets. In: GrC, pp. 732–737, May 2006
4. Thomas, C.: Improving intrusion detection for imbalanced network traffic. Secur. Commun. Netw. **6**(3), 309–324 (2013)
5. Zheng, Z., Wu, X., Srihari, R.: Feature selection for text categorization on imbalanced data. ACM SIGKDD Explor. Newsl. **6**(1), 80–89 (2004)

6. Li, Y., Sun, G., Zhu, Y.: Data imbalance problem in text classification. In: 2010 Third International Symposium on Information Processing (ISIP), pp. 301–305. IEEE, October 2010
7. Perols, J.: Financial statement fraud detection: an analysis of statistical and machine learning algorithms. Audit. J. Pract. Theory **30**(2), 19–50 (2011)
8. Ghazikhani, A., Monsefi, R., Yazdi, H.S.: Ensemble of online neural networks for non-stationary and imbalanced data streams. Neurocomputing **122**, 535–544 (2013)
9. Galar, M., Fernandez, A., Barrenechea, E., Bustince, H., Herrera, F.: A review on ensembles for the class imbalance problem: bagging-, boosting-, and hybrid-based approaches. IEEE Trans. Syst. Man Cybern. Part C (Appl. Rev.) **42**(4), 463–484 (2012)
10. Qian, Y., Liang, Y., Li, M., Feng, G., Shi, X.: A resampling ensemble algorithm for classification of imbalance problems. Neurocomputing **143**, 57–67 (2014)
11. Pearson, R., Goney, G., Shwaber, J.: Imbalanced clustering for microarray time-series. In: Proceedings of the ICML, vol. 3 (2003)
12. Sun, Y., Kamel, M.S., Wang, Y.: Boosting for learning multiple classes with imbalanced class distribution. In: Sixth International Conference on Data Mining, ICDM 2006, pp. 592–602. IEEE, December 2006
13. Chen, K., Lu, B.L., Kwok, J.T.: Efficient classification of multi-label and imbalanced data using min-max modular classifiers. In: International Joint Conference on Neural Networks, IJCNN 2006, pp. 1770–1775. IEEE, July 2006
14. Witten, I.H., Frank, E., Hall, M.A., Pal, C.J.: Data Mining: Practical Machine Learning Tools and Techniques. Morgan Kaufmann, Burlington (2016)
15. Tomek, I.: Two modifications of CNN. IEEE Trans. Syst. Man Cybern. **6**, 769–772 (1976)
16. Wilson, D.L.: Asymptotic properties of nearest neighbor rules using edited data. IEEE Trans. Syst. Man Cybern. **3**, 408–421 (1972)
17. Chawla, N.V., Bowyer, K.W., Hall, L.O., Kegelmeyer, W.P.: SMOTE: synthetic minority over-sampling technique. J. Artif. Intell. Res. **16**, 321–357 (2002)
18. Han, H., Wang, W.-Y., Mao, B.-H.: Borderline-SMOTE: a new over-sampling method in imbalanced data sets learning. In: Huang, D.-S., Zhang, X.-P., Huang, G.-B. (eds.) ICIC 2005. LNCS, vol. 3644, pp. 878–887. Springer, Heidelberg (2005). https://doi.org/10.1007/1153 8059_91
19. He, H., Bai, Y., Garcia, E.A., Li, S.: ADASYN: adaptive synthetic sampling approach for imbalanced learning. In: IEEE International Joint Conference on Neural Networks, IJCNN 2008. IEEE World Congress on Computational Intelligence, pp. 1322–1328. IEEE, June 2008
20. Drummond, C., Holte, R.C.: C4. 5, class imbalance, and cost sensitivity: why under-sampling beats over-sampling. In: Workshop on Learning from Imbalanced Datasets II, vol. 11, pp. 1–8. Citeseer, Washington DC, August 2003

Digital Mammogram Classification Using Compound Local Binary Pattern Features with Principal Component Analysis Based Feature Reduction Approach

Menaxi J. Bagchi[1(✉)], Figlu Mohanty[1], Suvendu Rup[1],
Bodhisattva Dash[1], and Banshidhar Majhi[2]

[1] Department of Computer Science and Engineering,
International Institute of Information Technology, Bhubaneswar, Odisha, India
menaxijbagchi@yahoo.in
[2] Indian Institute of Information Technology, Kancheepuram, India

Abstract. Breast cancer is the most identified reason for death among women worldwide. New developments in the field of biomedical image processing have enabled the early and effective diagnosis of breast cancer. Therefore, this article aims at developing an effective computer-aided diagnosis (CAD) system which can precisely label the mammograms as normal, benign or malignant. In the presented scheme, compound local binary pattern (CLBP) is used to obtain the texture features from the extracted regions of interest (ROI) of mammograms. Then, principal component analysis (PCA) is used to obtain the reduced feature set. Finally, different classifiers like support vector machine (SVM), k-nearest neighbors (KNN), C4.5, artificial neural network (ANN), and Naive Bayes are utilized for classification. The proposed model is validated on two standard datasets, namely, MIAS and DDSM. Further, the proposed model's performance is assessed in terms of different measures like classification accuracy, sensitivity, and specificity. From the result analysis, it is noticed that the proposed scheme achieves better classification accuracy as compared to the benchmark schemes.

Keywords: Breast cancer · Computer-aided diagnosis system
Compound local binary pattern · Principal component analysis

1 Introduction

Breast cancer is considered to be the major cause of death among women after lung cancer. It is the result of the unrestricted growth of breast cells. According to GLOBOCAN cancer survey [1] about 1.67 million new cases of breast cancer were diagnosed in the year 2012 which constituted about 25% of all the cancers. Moreover, an approximate figure of 266,120 new cases of breast cancer

© Springer Nature Singapore Pte Ltd. 2018
M. Singh et al. (Eds.): ICACDS 2018, CCIS 905, pp. 270–278, 2018.
https://doi.org/10.1007/978-981-13-1810-8_27

is anticipated in men and women in the year 2018. Early detection and treatment are necessary in order to combat the mortality rate due to breast cancer. Mammography is one of the most genuine methods for screening and detection of breast cancer as compared to other methods such as breast self-examination (BSE), surgery and clinical breast examination(CBE). It uses X-rays for analysis of breasts in order to locate suspicious lesions. It results in the formation of an X-ray image called a mammogram which is studied by a radiologist. Computer-aided diagnosis (CAD) systems assist the radiologists in the understanding of breast images in order to detect the suspicious regions. The CAD system helps in increasing the diagnostic accuracy and thus improves the mammogram interpretation rate.

Talha [2] used discrete wavelet transform (DWT) along with discrete cosine transform (DCT) for extracting features. The obtained features were classified as normal or abnormal using SVM. Beura et al. [3] used two dimensional DWT and gray level co-occurrence matrix (GLCM) for extracting the relevant features from the ROI, followed by the selection of a subset of the extracted features using F-test and t-test and used backpropagation neural network for classification. Pratiwi et al. [4] presented a classification of mammograms using radial basis function neural network (RBFNN) based on GLCM texture based features. A CAD system has been proposed by Mohamed et al. [5] wherein GLCM is used for feature extraction along with three different classifiers, namely, SVM, ANN, and KNN. Dong et al. [6] used dual contourlet transform for feature extraction and an improved KNN classifier. Reyad et al. [7] showed a comparison of statistical, local binary pattern (LBP) and multi-resolution features based on DWT and contourlet transform and SVM as a classifier. Wang et al. [8] presented a mass classification scheme which utilized hidden features of mass to expose the hidden distribution pattern. Phadke et al. [9] proposed a CAD system which utilized a combination of local and global features to find out the abnormalities in the mammograms with the help of SVM. Liu et al. [10] combined a support vector machine based recursive feature elimination technique along with normalized mutual information to eliminate singular disadvantages. Zhang et al. [11] developed an ensemble system for the classification of the region of interest as benign or malignant with the help of SVM by using mass shape features. Gedik [12] introduced a new method for extracting features based on fast finite shearlet transform and used SVM for classification. Elmoufidi et al. [13] used dynamic K-means clustering algorithm for regions of interest (ROI) detection on the mini-MIAS dataset. Hariraj et al. [14] used wiener filter for noise removal, GLCM for feature extraction and SVM and KNN for classification. From the literature, it is realized that the improvement in the modules like feature extraction, feature reduction and classification leads to improvement in the overall performance of a CAD system. There exists an enormous scope to develop an improved CAD system to correctly diagnose the mammograms. Hence, keeping this in mind, authors are motivated to propose a CAD system using the compound local binary pattern for feature extraction, principal component analysis for feature reduction and different classifiers like SVM, KNN, ANN, C4.5, and

Naive Bayes. Further, as per the best knowledge of the authors, this is the first attempt to propose a CAD system with this combination (CLBP+PCA+SVM, KNN, ANN, C4.5, and Naive Bayes).

2   Proposed CAD Framework

The proposed CAD system comprises of mainly three modules, namely, feature extraction using compound local binary pattern (CLBP), feature reduction using principal component analysis (PCA) and classification using SVM, KNN, ANN, C4.5, and Naive Bayes. The complete design of the presented scheme is represented in Fig. 1.

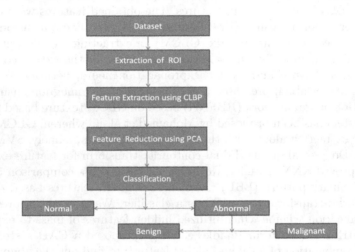

Fig. 1. Framework of CAD

2.1   Preprocessing and ROI Extraction

Noise and unwanted pectoral muscles are removed from the mammograms in the preprocessing stage. The mammograms are provided with information regarding the size of the abnormality. Hence to extract the ROI, a suitable cropping mechanism is used. Figures 2 and 3 represents the ROIs of the MIAS and DDSM databases respectively.

2.2   Feature Extraction Using Compound Local Binary Pattern

The output of a classifier is determined by the quality of the extracted features. The local binary pattern (LBP) is a simple and efficient texture feature extraction technique. However, it does not take into consideration the difference in magnitude between the center and neighboring pixel values. Therefore, this method produces conflicting results. In order to incorporate the magnitude

Fig. 2. ROI of MIAS dataset

Fig. 3. ROI of DDSM dataset

information along with the sign, a new technique called compound local binary pattern (CLBP) which is an extension of LBP is introduced [15,16]. CLBP allocates a code of 2P-bit to the middle pixel depending on the P number of neighboring pixels. Each of the P neighbors gets encoded with two bits. The first bit encodes the sign information while the second bit encodes the magnitude of difference with respect to a threshold value. This is illustrated in Eq. (1).

$$s(i_n, i_m) = \begin{cases} 00 & i_n - i_m < 0, \quad |i_n - i_m| \leq Avg \\ 01 & i_n - i_m < 0, \quad |i_n - i_m| > Avg \\ 10 & i_n - i_m \geq 0, \quad |i_n - i_m| \leq Avg \\ 11 & \text{otherwise} \end{cases} \tag{1}$$

where, i_m is the pixel intensity of the middle pixel, i_n is the pixel intensity of the surrounding pixel and Avg is the average magnitude of the difference between i_n and i_m in the local neighborhood.

For example, in a 3×3 neighborhood with 8 neighboring pixels, the center pixel is assigned a 16-bit code. This increases the number of features. Thus the two 8 bit patterns which are obtained by dividing the 16-bit pattern helps in reducing the number of features. The first one is generated by joining the bit values in the up, right, down, and left directions of the center pixel, respectively

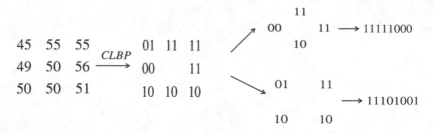

Fig. 4. CLBP example

and the other one is formed by combining the bit values in the north-east, south-east, south-west, and north-west directions of the center pixel respectively. Figure 4 illustrates a CLBP example. Therefore, each pixel gets two 8-bit binary codes after the application of the CLBP operator on all pixels followed by dividing the obtained 16-bits into two 8-bits. Thus, two encoded images are obtained for an image from which two histograms are generated. These two histograms are then combined to obtain a histogram which serves as a feature vector for the whole image.

2.3   Feature Reduction Using Principal Component Analysis

PCA converts the features into a set of linearly uncorrelated variables called principal components [17]. It helps in reducing the dimensionality of the original feature set. It maps the data from a higher dimensionality space to a lower dimensionality space thus reducing the number of redundant features. The obtained reduced set contains maximum variability of the original data.

2.4   Classification

SVM is a supervised learning model which is used for classification and regression purposes [5]. It constructs a hyperplane that has the maximum distance from the data. ANN imitates the biological neural networks. It has an input layer, one or more hidden layers, and an output layer [5]. It is a supervised learning model. The generated output is compared with the actual output and an error (difference) is generated. Based on this error, the weights are adjusted unless and until the desired output is obtained. KNN is used for classification and regression [5]. The unknown sample is given a label which is most common among its k neighbors. C4.5 is used for generating decision trees [18]. It is an extension of ID3. It is also called a statistical classifier as the decision tree generated by it can be used for classification. Naive Bayes is based on Bayes' theorem and is used in medical imaging [19]. It belongs to a family of probabilistic classifiers. Based on training, it classifies features and gives them labels taken from a finite set. In all the above classifiers, training is carried out with 70% data and the rest 20% data is utilized for testing.

In the proposed scheme, SVM, KNN, ANN, C4.5, and Naive Bayes are used for segregating the images into normal, benign or malignant.

3   Results

MATLAB 2017a environment is used for carrying out the experiments. All images are taken from Mammographic Image Analysis Society (MIAS) [20] and Digital Database for Screening Mammography (DDSM) [21] repositories. MIAS dataset comprises of 319 images out of which 207 are normal, 64 are benign and 48 are malignant ones. A total of 291 images are collected from DDSM dataset out of which 180 are normal, 55 are benign and 56 are malignant images. The ROIs are extracted by cropping the original images and resizing them to 256×256. Then from each of the ROIs, texture features are extracted using CLBP. A feature vector consisting of 512 features is generated. It may be possible that all the 512 features which are extracted do not contribute towards the overall performance of the proposed model. Hence, to reduce the feature set and to curb the curse of dimensionality problem, PCA is applied which reduces the feature vector length to 20 keeping 95% variance of the original data. The reduced feature set is thus fed to different classifiers to classify the mammograms.

Table 1 lists the values of different performance metrics like accuracy (Acc), sensitivity (Sn) and specificity (Sp) obtained with the proposed model for different classifiers for MIAS dataset.

Table 1. Performance measure of MIAS dataset (A-Abnormal, N-Normal, B-Benign, M-Malignant)

MIAS(N-A)				MIAS(B-M)		
Classifier	Acc (%)	Sn	Sp	Acc (%)	Sn	Sp
SVM	100	1	1	100	1	1
C4.5	95.9248	0.9614	0.9554	91.0714	0.8750	0.6250
ANN	88.1	0.7767	0.9371	80.4	0.8125	0.7916
KNN	83.3856	0.6607	0.9275	76.7857	0.8750	0.6250
Naive Bayes	83.3856	0.9227	0.6696	71.4286	0.5417	0.8438

From the table, it is noticed that SVM has the highest accuracy of 100% followed by C4.5 with an accuracy of approximately 95.92%, ANN with 88.1%, and KNN and Naive Bayes both with an accuracy of 83.3856% for normal and abnormal images. In the case of Benign-Malignant, SVM has an accuracy of 100%, followed by C4.5 with an accuracy of approximately 91.07%, ANN with 80.4%, KNN with an accuracy of 76.7857%, and Naive Bayes with an accuracy of 71.4286%. Similarly, the results obtained for DDSM dataset are shown in Table 2.

Table 2. Performance measure of DDSM dataset

DDSM (N-A)			DDSM (B-M)		
Classifier	Acc (%)	Sn	Sp	Acc (%)	Sn	Sp
SVM	100	1	1	100	1	1
C4.5	98.9691	0.9910	0.9889	95.4955	0.9643	0.9455
ANN	100	1	1	93.7	0.9454	0.9285
KNN	99.66	0.9944	1	81.08	0.7818	0.8393
Naive Bayes	98.6254	1	0.9778	80.18	0.9286	0.6727

It is observed that SVM and ANN both have an accuracy of 100% followed by KNN with an accuracy of 99.66%, C4.5 with an accuracy of 98.9691%, and Naive Bayes with an accuracy of 98.6254% for normal and abnormal images. In the case of Benign-Malignant, SVM has an accuracy of 100%, followed by C4.5 with an accuracy of 95.4955%, ANN with an accuracy of 93.7%, KNN with an accuracy of 81.08%, and Naive Bayes with an accuracy of 80.18%. The performance of the proposed scheme is matched with some of the recent approaches with respect to accuracy as depicted in Table 3.

Table 3. Comparison of Accuracy of Diferent Models (A-Abnormal, N-Normal, B-Benign, M-Malignant)

Reference	Dataset	Classifier	Accuracy (%)	
			N-A	B-M
[5]	MIAS	SVM	70	70
		KNN	68	68
[8]	DDSM	SVM	-	92.74
[9]	MIAS	SVM	-	93.17
[10]	DDSM	SVM	-	93
[11]	DDSM	SVM	-	72
		SVM	100	100
		C4.5	98.9691	95.4955
Proposed model (CLBP + PCA)	DDSM	ANN	100	93.7
		KNN	99.66	81.08
		Naive Bayes	98.6254	80.18
		SVM	100	100
		C4.5	95.9248	91.0714
	MIAS	ANN	88.1	80.4
		KNN	83.3856	76.7857
		Naive Bayes	83.3856	71.4286

4   Conclusion

Detection and diagnosis of breast cancer at an early stage helps in reducing the fatality rate to a greater extent. Hence, it becomes utmost important to develop an efficient and reliable CAD system which can classify the mammograms accurately. In this article, a model CAD system (CLBP+PCA+SVM, KNN, ANN, C4.5, and Naive Bayes) is proposed. In the presented scheme, compound local binary pattern (CLBP) which is a texture feature extraction technique is used. A total of 512 features are extracted which are then converted to a reduced feature set of size 20, with the help of PCA. The reduced feature set is fed to various classifiers like SVM, KNN, ANN, C4.5 and Naive Bayes to evaluate the performance measures.

It has been observed that SVM obtains the highest accuracy rate among all the classifiers for both Normal-Abnormal and Benign-Malignant classification. Further, it has also been observed that in the majority of the cases, the proposed model achieves better results than that of the competent schemes.

The proposed work can be extended towards the formulation of alternative feature extraction, feature reduction, and classification schemes to obtain an improved classification accuracy.

References

1. The International Agency for Research on Cancer: Globocan 2012: estimated cancer incidence, mortality and prevalence worldwide in 2012 (2012)
2. Uppal, M.T.N.: Classification of mammograms for breast cancer detection using fusion of discrete cosine transform and discrete wavelet transform features. Biomed. Res. **27**(2) (2016)
3. Beura, S., Majhi, B., Dash, R.: Mammogram classification using two dimensional discrete wavelet transform and gray-level co-occurrence matrix for detection of breast cancer. Neurocomputing **154**, 1–14 (2015)
4. Pratiwi, M., Harefa, J., Nanda, S.: Mammograms classification using gray-level co-occurrence matrix and radial basis function neural network. Procedia Comput. Sci. **59**, 83–91 (2015)
5. Mohamed, H., Mabrouk, M.S., Sharawy, A.: Computer aided detection system for micro calcifications in digital mammograms. Comput. Methods Programs Biomed. **116**(3), 226–235 (2014)
6. Dong, M., Wang, Z., Dong, C., Mu, X., Ma, Y.: Classification of region of interest in mammograms using dual contourlet transform and improved KNN. J. Sens. (2017)
7. Reyad, Y.A., Berbar, M.A., Hussain, M.: Comparison of statistical, LBP, and multi-resolution analysis features for breast mass classification. J. Med. Syst. **38**(9), 100 (2014)
8. Wang, Y., Li, J., Gao, X.: Latent feature mining of spatial and marginal characteristics for mammographic mass classification. Neurocomputing **144**, 107–118 (2014)
9. Phadke, A.C., Rege, P.P.: Fusion of local and global features for classification of abnormality in mammograms. Sādhanā **41**(4), 385–395 (2016)

10. Liu, X., Tang, J.: Mass classification in mammograms using selected geometry and texture features, and a new SVM-based feature selection method. IEEE Syst. J. 8(3), 910–920 (2014)
11. Zhang, Y., Tomuro, N., Furst, J., Raicu, D.S.: Building an ensemble system for diagnosing masses in mammograms. Int. J. Comput. Assist. Radiol. Surg. 7(2), 323–329 (2012)
12. Gedik, N.: A new feature extraction method based on multi-resolution representations of mammograms. Appl. Soft Comput. 44, 128–133 (2016)
13. Elmoufidi, A., El Fahssi, K., Jai-Andaloussi, S., Sekkaki, A.: Detection of regions of interest in mammograms by using local binary pattern and dynamic k-means algorithm. Int. J. Image Video Process. Theory Appl. 1(1), 2336-0992 (2014)
14. Hariraj, V., Wan, K., Zunaidi, I., et al.: An efficient data mining approaches for breast cancer detection and segmentation in mammogram (2017)
15. Doshi, N.P.: Multi-dimensional local binary pattern texture descriptors and their application for medical image analysis. Ph.D. thesis (2014). Niraj P. Doshi
16. Tyagi, D., Verma, A., Sharma, S.: An improved method for facial expression recognition using hybrid approach of CLBP and Gabor filter. In: 2017 International Conference on Computing, Communication and Automation (ICCCA), pp. 1019–1024. IEEE (2017)
17. Buciu, I., Gacsadi, A.: Directional features for automatic tumor classification of mammogram images. Biomed. Signal Process. Control. 6(4), 370–378 (2011)
18. Martens, D., De Backer, M., Haesen, R., Vanthienen, J., Snoeck, M., Baesens, B.: Classification with ant colony optimization. IEEE Trans. Evol. Comput. 11(5), 651–665 (2007)
19. Yang, M.C., Huang, C.S., Chen, J.H., Chang, R.F.: Whole breast lesion detection using Naive Bayes classifier for portable ultrasound. Ultrasound Med. Biol. 38(11), 1870–1880 (2012)
20. Suckling, J., Parker, J., Dance, D., Astley, S., Hutt, I., Boggis, C., Ricketts, I., Stamatakis, E., Cerneaz, N., Kok, S.: The mammographic image analysis society digital mammogram database. Exerpta Medica. Int. Congr. Series. 1069, 375–378 (1994)
21. Heath, M., Bowyer, K., Kopans, D., Moore, R., Kegelmeyer, P.: The digital database for screening mammography. In: Digital mammography, pp. 431–434 (2000)

Assessing the Performance of CMOS Amplifiers Using High-k Dielectric with Metal Gate on High Mobility Substrate

Deepa Anand(✉), M. Swathi(✉), A. Purushothaman,
and Sundararaman Gopalan

Department of Electronics and Communication Engineering,
Amrita Vishwa Vidyapeetham, Amritapuri, India
deepa.anand89@gmail.com, swathi.prakashan@gmail.com

Abstract. With the increase in demand for high-performance ICs for both memory and logic applications, scaling has been continued down to 14 nm node. To meet the performance requirements, high-k dielectrics such as HfO_2, ZrO_2 have replaced SiO_2 in the conventional MOS structure for sub-45 nm node. Correspondingly, the polysilicon gate electrode has been replaced by metal gate electrode in order to enable integration with high-k. Furthermore, the standard silicon substrate has been replaced by high mobility substrate in order to obtain desired transistor performance. While the fabrication technology for CMOS has advanced rapidly the traditional design tools used for designing circuits continues to use conventional MOS structure and their properties. This paper aims to analyze frequency response of CMOS common source amplifier(CSA) and differential amplifier by simulating in MATLAB using metal gate/high-k/Ge structure and to compare with traditionally used amplifier design using standard MOS structure.

Keywords: CMOS - Complementary Metal Oxide Semiconductor
EOT - Effective Oxide Thickness · CSA - Common Source Amplifier
UGB - Unity Gain Bandwidth
High-k dielectrics based amplifier design

1 Introduction

In accordance with Moore's law, the transistor density on a chip has been increasing exponentially over the last several decades [1], which leads to continuous scaling of the device. This continued scaling has resulted in improvement in functionality and performance of the chip while reducing the power consumption and cost. One of the fundamental components of an IC for any application (memory, logic, telecommunications etc.) is the CMOS transistor, which accounts for more than 95% of transistors used by the industry [2,3]. Traditionally, the MOS structures are made up of polysilicon gate electrode, SiO_2 gate dielectric and conventional silicon substrate. However, scaling of device dimensions leads

© Springer Nature Singapore Pte Ltd. 2018
M. Singh et al. (Eds.): ICACDS 2018, CCIS 905, pp. 279–289, 2018.
https://doi.org/10.1007/978-981-13-1810-8_28

to the subsequent reduction in gate oxide thickness which in turn has led to very high leakage current especially for 45 nm node and below [4,5]. This has been overcome by use of hafnium-based and zirconium-based dielectrics which have higher dielectric constant ($\approx$22–25) [8,19] than the conventional SiO$_2$. Since the high-k dielectrics are not thermodynamically stable with polysilicon and due to poly depletion effect which reduces the overall gate capacitance, polysilicon has to be replaced with suitable metal gate electrodes [4,5]. The gate capacitance needs to be maintained high for better performance of the device. The gate capacitance is given by the Eq. 1,

$$\frac{C_{ox}}{A} = \epsilon_0 \frac{k}{t_{ox}} \tag{1}$$

where, C_{ox} is the oxide capacitance, ϵ_0 is the permittivity, k is the dielectric constant, A is the area, and t_{ox} is the oxide thickness. As the MOSFET width and length are decreasing, C_{ox} has come down. For all these years this was countered by decreasing t_{ox}. However as SiO$_2$ thickness reduces below 4–5 nm, direct tunneling between the gate electrode and substrate takes place which causes high leakage and reliability issues [5]. But this leakage was found acceptable for high-performance applications down to 65 nm node, however, for the 45-nm node and below the t_{ox} requirement goes below 1 nm which causes unacceptably high leakage current [4,5,19]. Therefore, in order to reduce the leakage current high-k dielectrics were used. In accordance with Eq. 1, for the same oxide capacitance, a thinner SiO$_2$ film can be replaced with a much thicker high-k film which will cause a significant reduction in leakage, which will also improve the reliability. Equation 2 gives the thickness of the high-k film which is equivalent to 1 nm SiO$_2$. The EOT (equivalent to 1 nm SiO$_2$ thickness) is calculated using the k values 17 for ZrO$_2$, 22 for HfO$_2$ and 5 for nitrided oxide (SiON) obtained from fabricated results [13,15,17].

$$EOT = t_{High-k}\left(\frac{k_{SiO2}}{k_{High-k}}\right) \tag{2}$$

where, t_{High-k} and k_{High-K} are the thickness and relative dielectric constant of the high-k material. The thickness of ZrO$_2$, HfO$_2$, and nitrided oxide (SiON) are obtained as 4.35 nm, 5.64 nm, 1.6 nm respectively for EOT, equivalent to 1 nm SiO$_2$ thickness. As further scaling continues a lower EOT is preferred [6] and using high-k would ensure lower leakage compared to SiO$_2$. For 1 nm EOT, the leakage current is found to be in the range of $\approx$10^{-3} A/cm^2 for ZrO$_2$ and HfO$_2$ which is very much less compared to SiO$_2$ which has a leakage current of 100 A/cm^2 [19]. After the rigorous study on high-k materials for over two decades, HfO$_2$ and ZrO$_2$ were chosen as suitable candidates based on their high-k value ($\approx$ 22–25), compatibility with the substrate, good band offset, high thermal stability etc [19].

Poly-crystalline silicon (polysilicon) was used as gate material since it has same chemical composition as the silicon channel beneath the gate oxide, due to its high melting point, easiness to fabricate etc. But because of dopant penetration, poly depletion effect, Fermi level pinning, thermodynamic stability issue with high-k [5] etc, polysilicon had to be replaced with the metal gate in the 45 nm node. It was found that high-k/ metal gate is much better than high-k/poly w.r.t above mentioned issues. There are many candidates such as TaN, TiN, Pt etc which can be used for the gate electrode, based on the work function and thermal stability [5, 7, 9, 10].

It was observed that upon the integration of high-k dielectrics into CMOS it leads to mobility degradation of the carrier at high electric field in the channel region due to columbic scattering [14]. In 45 nm node, this issue was addressed by using 'strained silicon' in the substrate/channel region which improves the mobility of the carriers [5]. However, since 45 nm node, scaling of high-k continues even further, leading to further mobility degradation (due to increase in the vertical electric field). This may be resolved by using high mobility substrates such as Germanium or Gallium Arsenide in the channel region for the sub-22 nm nodes [5, 16, 19].

While the fabricated technology has changed drastically since 2007, IC designs and design tools continue to use basic MOS structure and their characteristics. Despite the fact that there are a lot of studies on high k/metal gate transistors, not much study is available for CMOS amplifier design circuits using high-k and metal gates. Since the technology is progressed for conventional MOS structure, it will be better if high-k/metal gate/Ge combination is used. By using this combination in the designing stage itself we can get a more accurate prediction of the VLSI circuit. In this work, CMOS single stage common source amplifier (CSA) circuits (R Load, Active load) and the differential amplifier is designed with metal gate/high-k/Ge transistor using MATLAB. With the simulation results, the impact of various combinations of gate stack on frequency response is studied and this is being compared with traditionally used MOS transistor.

2   Methodology

An amplifier is one of the essential and critical circuit which have a wide range of applications [2, 3]. Gain and bandwidth are two main parameters in the amplifier. Amplifier performance can be improved by increasing these two parameters. The effect of proposed gate stacks such as $TaN/HfO_2/Ge$, $Pt/ZrO_2/Ge$ and strained-Si is studied on the above parameters and compared with traditional gate stack ($Polysilicon/SiO_2/Si$).

The frequency response of CMOS single stage amplifier primarily depends on trans conductance and output resistance. Transconductance, g_m, is defined as the change in current to change in voltage by keeping V_{DS} constant [12]. Increase in g_m will increase the gain (amplification) and bandwidth of the amplifier. Transconductance g_m is given as,

$$g_m = u_n C_{ox} \left(\frac{W}{L} \right) \left(V_{GS} - V_{TH} \right) \tag{3}$$

where μ_n - electron mobility, C_{ox} - oxide capacitance, W - width, L - length, V_{GS} - Gate source voltage, V_{TH} - threshold voltage.

From the above Eq. 3, it is clear that g_m is dependent on mobility, gate oxide thickness, width, length, current, V_{GS}, and V_{TH}. Mobility, gate oxide thickness and threshold voltage depends on the materials used in the gate stack whereas width, length, current, and V_{GS} are design parameters.

Mobility varies with channel length and adds second order effects on transistor parameters. For conventional MOS structure the effective mobility for fabricated device is $260\,cm^2/Vs$ [19], but upon using strained silicon extracted mobility obtained from fabricated result is $450\,cm^2/Vs$ [17]. For smaller gate length using metal gate/high-k/G, we can obtain higher mobility compared to the metal gate/high-k/Si gate stack [5,11]. As transconductance depends directly on mobility (Eq. 3) it is obvious that we can achieve an increase in transconductance upon using strained-Si and metal gate/high-k/Ge gate stack combination.

Since the saturation current also depends directly on the mobility (Eq. 4), increase in mobility by using strained-Si and Germanium can also result in the increase of drive current which makes the device to perform better. The saturation current is given as,

$$I_D = \frac{1}{2}u_n C_{ox}\left(\frac{W}{L}\right)\left(V_{GS} - V_{TH}\right)^2 \tag{4}$$

where I_D - saturation current

The transistor parameters for proposed gate stacks is obtained for EOT of 1 nm. As discussed in the above section by using high-k materials, same gate capacitance as that of SiO_2 can be obtained with higher gate oxide thickness. As a result of which gate leakage will get reduced.

2.1 Frequency Response of Single Stage CSA (R Load and Active Load):

A single stage CSA with the resistive load and active load are considered in the paper (Fig. 1: A and B). Gain and bandwidth (UGB) for proposed combinations of gate stacks are analyzed and compared with traditional gate stack (Polysilicon/SiO_2/Si).

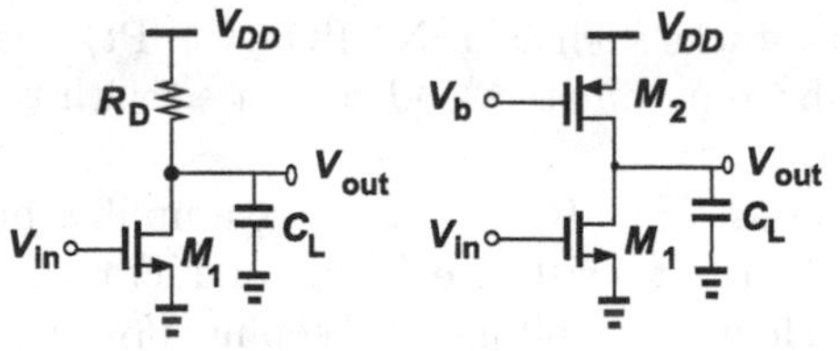

Fig. 1. (A) Common source amplifier with R load. (B) Common source amplifier with Active load

The open loop transfer function of CSA with R load is obtained as [12],

$$A(S) = \frac{g_m R_D}{1 + sR_D C_L} \tag{5}$$

Where, R_D is load resistance, C_L is load capacitance, r_{01} saturation resistance of nMOS. Since R_D is very much smaller in size than r_{01} and both are in parallel, r_{01} can be neglected. As a result, the channel length coefficient does not affect the gain of R load CSA. From the Eq. 5, it is clear that gain depends on trans conductance. As g_m increases gain will be increased.

CSA with resistive load has got trade-offs between voltage swing, gain, and bandwidth hence resistor has to be replaced with active load [12]. The open loop transfer function of CSA with the Active load is obtained as,

$$A(S) = \frac{g_m(r_{01}\|r_{02})}{1 + s(r_{01}\|r_{02})C_L} \tag{6}$$

Where r_{01} and r_{02} are saturation resistances of nMOS and pMOS.

Care has to be taken to address the device parameter λ, which affects the gain in Active load. This is because saturation resistances r_{01} and r_{02} depend inversely on this parameter. λ is channel length modulation coefficient. It is predominant in short channel devices. Channel length modulation is a phenomenon which results in a non-zero slope in I_D- V_{DS} characteristics and hence drain current never saturates [12].

Often, the channel-length modulation coefficient λ is expressed as early voltage V_A, which is the inverse of λ. Early voltage is obtained from output characteristics of MOSFET, by extrapolating the graph to the x-axis [14] (Fig. 2).

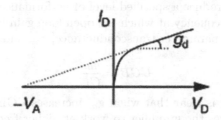

Fig. 2. Obtaining early voltage

Device parameter, λ for various combinations in the paper, is obtained from output characteristics of the fabricated device with the respective combinations from works of literature [13,15,17]. For traditional MOS structure output characteristics is obtained from Cadence simulations. Substituting the obtained values of λ, the gain obtained from the frequency response of CSA with the active load of various combinations is compared with CSA with traditional MOS structure.

The work is extended to study on differential amplifier Fig. 3. The differential input is given to the two transistor M1 and M2. V_b is applied in such a way that, the transistor M3, M4, M_T will be in saturation. M_T is the tail transistor, which acts as a constant current source. Current has to be maintained constant to avoid DC voltage shift [12].

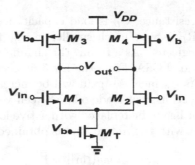

Fig. 3. Differential amplifier

Frequency response of the differential amplifier is obtained as,

$$A(S) = \frac{2g_m(r_{01}\|r_{03})}{1 + s(r_{01}\|r_{03})C_L} \tag{7}$$

Where r_{01} and r_{03} are saturation resistances of nMOS and pMOS.

Using the Eq. 7, frequency response of the differential amplifier is analyzed and gain for different gate stacks is compared.

Finally, the study on Unity Gain Bandwidth (UGB) is done. UGB also determines the amplifier performance. Bandwidth is the range of frequencies over which amplifier can produce a specified level of performance. Unity Gain Bandwidth (UGB) is the frequency at which the open loop gain becomes unity. UGB depends on transistor parameter transconductance, g_m, and load capacitance. It is given as:

$$UGB = \frac{g_m}{C_L} \tag{8}$$

From the Eq. 8, it is clear that when g_m increases UGB will get increased. Increase in UGB makes the amplifier to work at higher frequencies also, which is much advantageous for many applications. In this work, UGB for various combinations is obtained using the Eq. 8 and compared.

3   Results and Discussions

The effect of Strained-Si, TaN/HfO$_2$/Ge and Pt/ZrO$_2$/Ge gate stacks on transistor parameters is studied first and compared with traditional gate stack Polysilicon/SiO$_2$/Si. TaN/HfO$_2$/Ge and Pt/ZrO$_2$/Ge gate stacks are used because there is fabricated data in various literatures. For all simulations except for active load CSA and differential amplifier design W/L ratio is taken as 125μ/5μ, $V_{gs} = 1.2$ V, $V_{th} = 0.3$V. The extracted electron mobility at 0.6 MV/cm for TaN/HfO$_2$/Ge is 215 cm^2/Vs [18], Pt/ZrO$_2$/Ge is 275 cm^2/Vs [13], polysilicon/SiO$_2$/Si is 260 cm^2/Vs [19] and for strained-Si is 450 cm^2/Vs [17]. The effect of Strained-Si, TaN/HfO$_2$/Ge and Pt/ZrO$_2$/Ge gate stacks on transistor parameters is studied first and compared with traditional gate stack Polysilicon/SiO$_2$/Si.

The transistor parameters such as saturation current, transconductance which effect CSA characteristics are compared and tabulated (Table 1) for various combinations of gate stack (Fig. 4) whose thickness is taken with respect to 1 nm EOT of SiO$_2$. The effect of the increase in mobility can be clearly observed from this simulation. Increase in transconductance and saturation current is tremendous compared with traditional MOS structure. From the Table 1, it can be found that as thickness is reduced and mobility is increased, transistor performance can be improved.

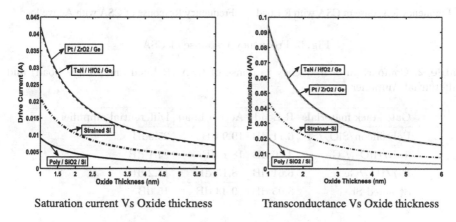

Saturation current Vs Oxide thickness   Transconductance Vs Oxide thickness

Fig. 4. Transistor parameter analysis

Table 1. Analysis on Transistor Parameters with respect to oxide thickness

Gate stack materials	g$_m$ (mA/V)	I$_d$ (mA)
Polysilicon/SiO$_2$/Si	20.2	9.1
TaN/HfO$_2$/Ge	16.7	7.5
Pt/ZrO$_2$/Ge	21.4	9.6
Strained-Si	28	13.1

The frequency response of common stage amplifier (CSA) is done with the resistive load and active load (Fig. 5) and compared (Table 2). Depending on gain and bandwidth, R load is taken as 100 ohms. From the Table 2 it can be observed that for smaller R load, gate stacks under consideration can give gain which is comparable with traditional gate stack. It can be observed that by using germanium substrate and strained-Si, and with the incorporation of high-k/metal gate as the gate oxide and gate electrode, we can obtain gain which is comparable with traditional device. From the Table 2, it can be observed that for R load, strained-Si gives higher gain than traditional gate stack. It is because

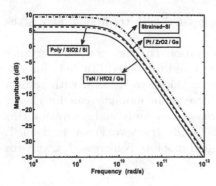
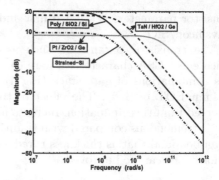

Frequency Response of CSA with R Load   Frequency Response of CSA with Active load

Fig. 5. Frequency response of CSA

Table 2. Comparison of frequency response of CSA (R Load and Active Load) and Differential Amplifier

Gate stack materials	R Load	Active Load	Differential amplifier
Polysilicon/SiO$_2$/Si	6.11 dB	19.9 dB	25.9dB
TaN/HfO$_2$ / Ge	4.46 dB	18.1 dB	24.1 dB
Pt/ZrO$_2$/Ge	6.61 dB	8.15 dB	14.2 dB
Strained-Si	8.95 dB	9.43 dB	15 dB

of higher mobility. TaN/HfO$_2$/Ge combination gives lesser gain compared with traditional gate stack because of lower mobility as compared to traditional one.

The frequency response of CSA with active load depends on device parameter as discussed in the above section. By curve fitting method, lambda values for nMOS and pMOS are obtained from the fabricated results of $I_d - V_{ds}$ characteristics of strained-Si [17], TaN/HfO$_2$/Ge gate stack [15], Pt/ZrO$_2$/Ge [13] and Polysilicon/SiO$_2$/Si from Cadence result. Lambda values obtained for nMOS and pMOS devices with TaN/HfO$_2$/Ge are $0.185\,V^{-1}$ and $0.0925\,V^{-1}$ for W/L ratio $400\,\mu/10\,\mu$, for Pt/ZrO$_2$/Ge are $0.58\,V^{-1}$ and $0.29\ V^{-1}$ with W/L ratio $320\mu/2\mu$, for strained-Si are $0.5\,V^{-1}$ and $0.25\,V^{-1}$ with W/L ratio $0.3\,\mu/70\,nm$ and for traditional device $0.15\,V^{-1}$ and $0.075\,V^{-1}$ with W/L ratio $125\,\mu/10\,\mu$. From the results of λ it can be observed that as length decreases λ value increases (Strained-Si and Pt/ZrO$_2$/Ge) which affects the gain. Also, as Ge substrate is showing higher λ value because of short channel effect compared with traditional gate stack, gain for poly/SiO$_2$/Si is higher compared to gate stacks under consideration (Table 2).

From the above results, it can be observed that strained-Si gives better results for transistor characteristics such as saturation current, transconductance compared to traditional substrate because of its higher mobility. The gain of CSA (R load) with strained-Si gives a better result. But in active load TaN/HfO$_2$/Ge gives better result compared to all other proposed combinations. The gain for TaN/HfO$_2$/Ge gate stack is slightly lesser than Poly/SiO$_2$/Si, it is because of channel length modulation coefficient λ. Gate stack using Pt/ZrO$_2$/Ge gives good results but active load gain is less compared to other combinations because of high channel length coefficient.

As done in the above section, frequency response of differential amplifier for different gate stacks is obtained (Fig. 6). From the results (Table 2), it is observed that TaN/HfO$_2$/Ge gate stack can give better gain for differential amplifier design comparing with traditional gate stack even under the high short channel effect (λ). As length is getting decreased short channel effect gets increased in Ge substrate compared to Si substrate. Even under this high short channel effect, the gate stack using Ge substrate is giving better gain.

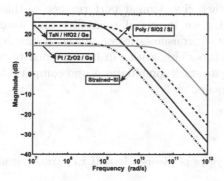

Fig. 6. Frequency response of differential amplifier

UGB is obtained for various combinations and tabulated (Table 3). It can be observed that the gate stack which gives higher g_m gives higher UGB. The UGB obtained for strained-Si is higher than traditional gate stack. But as gain and bandwidth become key parameters for amplifier applications, TaN/HfO$_2$/Ge gate stack outperformed all other proposed stacks.

When power consumed for various gate stacks were calculated it was found that TaN/HfO$_2$/Ge gate stack consumes less power (Table 3).

From all the above results it can be concluded that TaN/HfO$_2$/Ge gives better frequency response for active load and differential amplifier under less

Table 3. Comparison of Unity Gain Bandwidth and power consumption for various gate stacks

Gate stack materials	UGB	Power
Polysilicon/SiO$_2$/Si	20.2 GHz	10.92 mW
TaN/HfO$_2$/Ge	16.7 GHz	9 mW
Pt/ZrO$_2$/Ge	21.4 GHz	11.52 mW
Strained-Si	29.13 GHz	15.72 mW

power consumption and low leakage current compared to traditional gate stack and other gate stacks under consideration.

4 Conclusion

Transistor parameters such as transconductance, saturation current, oxide capacitance using different metal gate/high-k with Ge substrate and strained-Si has been analyzed and compared with traditional gate stack Polysilicon/SiO_2/Si. Simulation results for the frequency response of CMOS CSA (R load and Active load) using different metal gate/high-k with Ge substrate and strained-Si has been analyzed and compared with traditional gate stack Polysilicon/SiO_2/Si. The work has been extended to differential amplifier design and found that TaN/HfO_2/Ge gate stack gives similar performance as that of traditional gate stack while maintaining an improved reliability and lower leakage. Also, as TaN/HfO_2/Ge gate stack consumes lesser power, it can be a good option for future design of amplifiers. This work can be extended to fabrication of amplifiers using the above gate stack combinations and compare the simulation results with the fabricated results.

References

1. Mack, C.A.: Fifty years of Moore's law. IEEE Trans. Semicond. Manuf. **24**(2), 202–207 (2011)
2. Ravindran, A., Balamurugan, K., Jayakumar, M.: Design of cascaded common source low noise amplifier for s-band using transconductance feedback. Indian J. Sci. Technol. **9**(16) (2016)
3. Vinod, B., Balamurugan, K., Jayakumar, M.: Design of CMOS based reconfigurable LNA at millimeter wave frequency using active load. In: ICACCCT 2014, IEEE-Explore, pp. 713–718 (2014)
4. Seshan, K.: Limits and hurdles to continued CMOS scaling. In: Handbook of Thin Film Deposition. 4th edn. Science Direct (2018)
5. He, G., Zhu, L., et al.: Integrations and challenges of novel high-k gate stacks in advanced CMOS technology. In: Progress in Materials Science. Elsevier (2011)
6. Gardner, M.I., Gopalan, S., et al.: EOT Scaling and Device Issues for High-k Gate Dielectrics. IEEE (2003)
7. Gopalan, S., Onishi, K.: Electrical and physical characteristics of Ultrathin Hafnium Silicate films with polycrystalline silicon and TaN gates. Appl. Physics Lett. **80**(23), 4416–4418 (2002)
8. Wilk, G.D., Wallace, R.M., Anthony, J.M.: Hafnium and zirconium silicates for advanced gate dielectrics. J. Appl. Phys. **15**(1), 484 (2000)
9. Nam, S.-W.: Characteristics of ZrO2 films with Al and Pt gate electrodes. J. Electrochem. Soc. **150**, G849–G853 (2003)
10. Frank, M.M.: High-k/metal gate innovations enabling continued CMOS scaling. In: Solid-State Device Research Conference (ESSDERC) (2011)
11. Pillarisetty, R.: Academic and industry research progress in germanium nanodevices. Nature **479**(7373), 324 (2011)
12. Razavi, B.: Design of Analog CMOS ICs. McGraw-Hill (2001)

13. Chui, C.O., et al.: A Sub-400°C Germanium MOSFET Technology with High-K Dielectric and Metal Gate. IEEE (2002)
14. Chau, R.: High-k/metal-gate stack and its MOSFET characteristics. IEEE Electron. Dev. Lett. **25**(6), 408–410 (2004)
15. Whang, S.J., et al.: Germanium'p- and n-MOSFETs Fabricated with Novel Surface Passivation (plasma-PH3 and thin AIN) and TaN/HfO2 Gate Stack. IEEE (2004)
16. Del Alamo, J.A.: Nanometre-scale electronics with III-V compound semiconductors. Nature **479**, 317–323 (2011)
17. Hwang, J.R., et al.: Performance of 70 nm strained-silicon CMOS devices. In: Symposium on VLSI Technology Digest of Technical Papers (2003)
18. Wu, N., et al.: Characteristics of Self-Aligned Gate-First Ge p- and n-Channel MOSFETs Using CVD HfO2 Gate Dielectric and Si Surface Passivation. IEEE (2007)
19. Robertson, J., Wallace, R.M.: High-K materials and metal gates for CMOS applications. In: Materials Science and Engineering R. Elsevier (2015)

The Impact of Picture Splicing Operation for Picture Forgery Detection

Rachna Mehta$^{(\boxtimes)}$ and Navneet Agrawal

Maharana Partap University of Agriculture and Technology,
Udaipur 313001, India
er.rachnamehta10@gmail.com, navneetctae@gmail.com

Abstract. In the time of the present world, analyze of pictures accept a fundamental part. Some picture editing software are open in the market which can change the photo in particular ways. By abusing these software's, we can adjust the photo by splicing which is difficult to distinguish by human eyes. The electronic pictures have a no. of applications like in criminal and legalistic examination, military, news and so on. So we required some strong strategy for a picture to identify the forgery. This paper proposes a forgery detection technique with Markov Procedure and ensemble classifier, It focuses on splicing detection which extricates Markov-features in spatial and DCT-domain to recognize the antiquated rarities exhibited by the splicing operation and classify them with the ensemble classifier. Not at all like the earlier work, for reducing the computational complexity of SVM with PCA, is an ensemble classifier with an Adaboost algorithm is utilized to classify the photos as being altered or original. The suggested system is surveyed on a straightforwardly available picture splicing data file by using the cross-verification. The results exhibited that the suggested strategy eclipse in inactive splicing identification method.

Keywords: Forgery detection · Splicing detection · PCA · Spatial
DCT · SVM · Ensemble classifier · Adaboost algorithm · Markov-features

1 Introduction

While the bigger piece of research work disseminated on picture examination and concentrate on picture splicing detection by making energetic steps for recognizing modifying operations. Thusly, we note here that experts working in legitimate sciences imaging have either classification perspective or the confinement perspective [2–4].

In this paper, we propose the forgery detection of the picture splicing in light of Markov-features and ensemble classifier. We are not just calculating Markov-features in DCT-domain and Spatial-domain, we additionally classify them with an ensemble classifier. After combining these features from two spaces has driven its distinguishing proof to achieve better results in terms of accuracy, TPR and TNR, unlike to earlier work, e.g. [1, 7, 8, 12, 13]. The huge difference of this work from earlier work is that we are using ensemble classifier [24–28] without using PCA with SVM classifier [22] and accomplish the best accuracy then earlier work.

© Springer Nature Singapore Pte Ltd. 2018
M. Singh et al. (Eds.): ICACDS 2018, CCIS 905, pp. 290–301, 2018.
https://doi.org/10.1007/978-981-13-1810-8_29

The relationship of the paper is according to the accompanying. Sect 2 gives the literature review from existing techniques. Sect. 3 shows suggested work with feature extraction and classification. In Sect. 4, test work is represents results. Finally, Sect. 5 completes the paper with the conclusion.

2 Literature Review for Splicing Detection

Most of the research into splicing location relies upon the way that the photo splicing procedure can cause disconnection along boundary and corners. These unpredictable advances are a fundamental sign in the check of picture's validity. Early undertakings to distinguish altered pictures concentrate on diversity in the overall quantifiable qualities caused by sudden disconnection in the altered pictures [5–8].

One of these systems is the run length-based splicing recognizable proof approach [9–11]. Using this methodology, we can take out neighborhood changes caused by splicing distortion. Run length-based splicing Identification procedures have achieved surprising recognizable proof sign with few elements. Regardless, the acknowledgment rates of these computations are not impeccable in light of the way that the finishing up elements are isolated from the snapshots of various run length frameworks.

Other promising splicing acknowledgment systems that use neighborhood changed elements are Markov techniques. Markov-features are sensibly useful for the distinguishing proof of changed pictures that have been altered. In 2012, He et al. [12] show Markov-features in both discrete cosine transform (DCT) and discrete wavelet transform (DWT) domain, and they perceive picture splicing as demonstrated by the cross-space Markov-features. This procedure achieved a accuracy of 93.55% on Colombia picture data set [13]. Regardless, this strategy required up to 7290 features. In this way, a dimension decreasing strategies, for instance, recursive component end (REF) was indispensable. An enhanced Markov state decision procedure [14] was represented decreasing the number of elements. This approach analyzes the anticipated coefficients for change area and maps endless coefficients with limited expresses that have coefficients in light of various inferred work models. In any case, to diminish the number of elements, this procedure surrendered the recognizable proof execution.

El-Alfy et al. suggested a forgery location strategy for picture splicing by using Markov-features that incorporate into both spatial and DCT-domain [15]. They furthermore utilized Principle Component Analysis (PCA) to pick the most vital elements. They achieved a precision rate of 98.82% with a more straightforward testing condition (they utilized ten times cross-verification, while most extremes utilized six times cross-verification). In 2015, a photo grafting perceiving system [16] using a two-dimensional (2D) noncausal Markov technique was introduced. In this technique, a 2D Markov demonstrate was associated in the DCT area and the discrete Meyer wavelet transform domain and the cross area elements were considered as the closed elements for classification. This technique achieved an acknowledgment rate of 93.36% on Colombia gray scale picture data file; nevertheless, up to 14,240 elements were required.

3 Suggested Work

The suggested work uses a pre-named data file to assemble a computational model prepared for perceiving picture for splicing operations. It starts with partition of image into blocks and then we find the difference arrays for each domain. After that we set the values of difference arrays in between threshold values which is helpful in the reduction of dimensionality and then we extract the features in both domain by using Markov process. After combining the markov features in both domain we classify them with an efficient ensemble classifier by considering the two class classification problem, One is original image and other spliced image. For classification we preferred Adaboost algorithm opposed to using support vector machine with PCA [22, 23] and accomplish best outcomes in terms of Accuracy, TPR and TNR then earlier work [9, 12, 14–16] The purposes of enthusiasm of these methods are cleared up in the going with sections.

3.1 Markov-Features Extraction

A key issue in picture forgery detection is feature extraction and its classification which should outfit a gathering of particular elements with low association with each other. We extract elements from Spatial-domain and union them with coefficients of DCT-domain, In each space, we show the quantifiable changes through a Markov process.

3.1.1 Partition of Picture in 8 × 8 Blocks
The photo is first divided into non-overlapping pieces and the DCT-coefficients are registered for each square. The DCT-coefficients are then abbreviate to absolute values and arrange in BDCT 2D array D(r, c) ∀ r, c which has an same size from the original picture I(r, c).

3.1.2 Spatial and DCT Difference Array
Splicing recognition methods are generally in light of getting the curios displayed in the boundary and pixels. Hence, the edge pictures are figured in horizontal, vertical, minor minor diagonal and major diagonal. Any sensible edge detection techniques can be used yet here for ease we needed to subtract the pixel esteem from its neighboring pixel esteem in each position to get the edge pictures by using Eqs. (1–4). One of its examples is shown in Fig. 1 in horizontal direction. Similarly we can find difference arrays in each direction.

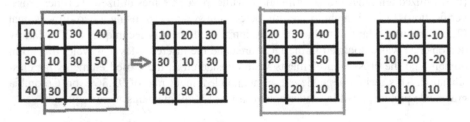

Fig. 1. Horizontal difference array

$$S_h(r,c) = I(r,c) - I(r+1,c); \qquad 1 \leq r \leq U_r - 1, 1 \leq c \leq U_c \qquad (1)$$

$$S_v(r,c) = I(r,c) - I(r,c+1); \qquad 1 \leq r \leq U_r, 1 \leq c \leq U_c - 1 \qquad (2)$$

$$S_{md}(r,c) = I(r,c) - I(r+1,c+1); \qquad 1 \leq r \leq U_r - 1, 1 \leq c \leq U_c - 1 \qquad (3)$$

$$S_{mj}(r,c) = I(r+1,c) - I(r,c+1); \qquad 1 \leq r \leq U_r - 1, 1 \leq c \leq U_c - 1 \qquad (4)$$

where I(r, c) $\forall$r, c is the source picture in the spatial domain and Ur, Uc denotes the dimensionality of the spatial picture. For DCT based Markov-features, contrast array for DCT-coefficients is shortened to fixed values and processed in all by Eqs. (5–8).

$$D_h(r,c) = D(r,c) - D(r+1,c); \qquad 1 \leq r \leq U_r - 1, 1 \leq c \leq U_c \qquad (5)$$

$$D_v(r,c) = D(r,c) - D(r,c+1); \qquad 1 \leq r \leq U_r, 1 \leq c \leq U_c - 1 \qquad (6)$$

$$D_{md}(r,c) = D(r,c) - D(r+1,c+1); \qquad 1 \leq r \leq U_r - 1, 1 \leq c \leq U_c - 1 \qquad (7)$$

$$D_{mj}(r,c) = D(r+1,c) - D(r,c+1); \qquad 1 \leq r \leq U_r - 1, 1 \leq c \leq U_c - 1 \qquad (8)$$

where D(r,c)$\forall$r, c is the fixed value of BDCT 2D array.

3.1.3 Thresholding Technique for Minimizing Dimensionality

To minimize the dimension of transition probability matrix (TPM), to be computed in the following section, an threshold E is assumed and the values of the difference array are set between -E and E respectively using Eq. (9)

$$E(r,c) = \begin{cases} +E & H(r,c) \geq +E \\ -E & H(r,c) \leq -E \\ H(r,c) & Otherwise \end{cases} \qquad (9)$$

To reduce the features, an Threshold E is accepted and the estimations of the distinction array are set between $-E$ and E individually utilizing Eq. (9). where H(r, c) speaks to for S_h(r, c), S_v(r, c), S_{md}(r, c), S_{mj}(r, c), and D_h(r, c), D_v(r, c), D_{md}(r, c), D_{mj}(r, c). Henceforth, the estimations of the distinction array of spatial and DCT-coefficients are compelled to the range ($-E$, E) with only (2E + 1) possible esteems. This is a basic step to limit the feature vector space dimensionality and furthermore the computational figuring. Special care must be taken in picking the threshold esteem E, which should not be too small or too huge. As E increases, the number of elements in the TPM matrix increases along with calculation count increases. For the selection of the threshold value we can check the performance parameter which is shown in Table 2. There it shows that as the value of threshold increase our accuracy goes decreases. This increasing value of threshold increases the no. of features also and reduces the accuracy.

3.1.4   Markov Based Transition Probability Matrix (TPM)

In the wake of thresholding, the qualities are at present entire numbers among [−E, E] and can be composed as a Finite state machine (FSM) to get between pixel connection in DCT and Spatial-domain. The Markov methodology can be depicted by a transition probability matrix (TPM) outlined from the threshold esteems. Thus, we utilized the one stage TPM. Along these lines, this matrix has (2E + 1) * (2E + 1) values for each direction. We utilized these values as features; accordingly, the total number of Markov-features incorporates each direction for a spatial picture is 4 * (2E + 1) * (2E + 1) and equivalent number for DCT Markov-feature. One stage TPM in each position is figured by given underneath Eq (10–13)

$$Pr\{E_h(r+1,c) = m|E_h(r,c) = n\}$$
$$= \frac{\sum_{r=1}^{U_{r-2}} \sum_{c=1}^{U_c} \delta(E_h(r,c) = m, E_h(r+1,c) = n)}{\sum_{r=1}^{U_{r-2}} \sum_{c=1}^{U_c} \delta(E_h(r,c) = m)} \quad (10)$$

$$Pr\{E_v(r,c+1) = m|E_v(r,c) = n\}$$
$$= \frac{\sum_{r=1}^{U_r} \sum_{c=1}^{U_{c-2}} \delta(E_v(r,c) = m, E_v(r,c+1) = n)}{\sum_{r=1}^{U_r} \sum_{c=1}^{U_{c-2}} \delta(E_v(r,c) = m)} \quad (11)$$

$$Pr\{E_{md}(r+1,c+1) = m|E_{md}(r,c) = n\}$$
$$= \frac{\sum_{r=1}^{U_{r-2}} \sum_{c=1}^{U_{c-2}} \delta(E_{md}(r,c) = m, E_{md}(r+1,c+1) = n)}{\sum_{r=1}^{U_{r-2}} \sum_{c=1}^{U_{c-2}} \delta(E_{md}(r,c) = m)} \quad (12)$$

$$Pr\{E_{mj}(r,c+1) = m|E_{mj}(r,c) = n\}$$
$$= \frac{\sum_{r=1}^{U_{r-2}} \sum_{c=1}^{U_{c-2}} \delta(E_{mj}(r+1,c) = m, E_{mj}(r,c+1) = n)}{\sum_{r=1}^{U_{r-2}} \sum_{c=1}^{U_{c-2}} \delta(E_{mj}(r+1,c) = m)} \quad (13)$$

Where

$$\delta(F = m, G = n) = \begin{cases} 1 & F = m, G = n \\ 0 & otherwise \end{cases}$$

$$\forall F, G \in \{-E, -E+1, \ldots\ldots\ldots -0, E-1, E\}$$

3.2   Classification

A standout amongst the unique areas of research in supervised learning has been to think about methodologies for building an incredible group of classifiers. Ensemble classifier [25–29] are learning algorithm that fabricates a course of action of classifiers whose individual decisions are united and after that arrange new data concentrates on taking a weighted vote of their forecasts. The essential divulgence is that ensembles are oftentimes significantly more correct than the individual classifiers like Support Vector Machine (SVM) [22] that impact them to up.

SVMs are extremely restrictive on account of the multifaceted nature of SVM will be extended rapidly with the dimensionality of feature space developing. Generally for feature reduction authors preferred Principal component analysis but they have some disadvantages one drawback is that the new elements can be difficult to interpret, along these lines making it hard to relate the events to the first feature. A minute inconvenience of the element diminishing frameworks like PCA is the gigantic computational counts while ascertaining the covariance matrix of feature vectors with an enormous number of elements. The ensemble classifier is the answer to these challenges. We are looked into that the ensemble classifier [25] can give execution relative to that of a Support Vector Machine (SVM) even without utilizing the principle component analysis (PCA) for picture examination of tremendous databases with large feature vectors. Here we favored one of the sorts of boosting algorithm is an AdaBoost algorithm. Which is more precise and appropriate for paired classification and furthermore it is quick and less memory utilization than others. Here we investigate how AdaBoost ensemble classifier functions.

The ensemble classifier, $h_f(x) = \sum_i w_i h_i(x)$, is worked by a weighted estimation of the single classifiers and every classifier is weighted by (w_i) according to its accuracy on the weighted training set that it was trained. To reduce this error function, assume that each training features are named as +1 for altered pictures or then again - 1 for genuine pictures identifying with the positive and negative pictures, Then the sum $m_i = y_i h(x_i)$ is exact if h accurately classifieds xi and negative in another case. This sum mi is known as the margin of classifier h on the training of features. AdaBoost [23] can be seen as endeavoring to

$$\sum_l -\exp\left(-y_1 \sum_i w_i h_i(x_1)\right),\qquad(14)$$

Minimize the error, it is the negative exponential of the margin of the weighted voted classifier.

4 Evaluation and Experimental Results

4.1 Testing Frame Work and Classification

The structure for detection of splicing by using features and its classification is showed up in Fig. 2

To confirm the execution of the suggested splicing discovery technique, we initially utilized the Columbia Picture Splicing Detection Evaluation Data file (DVMM) [13]. This grayscale data file comprises of 933 original pictures and 912 altered pictures, The majority of the pictures in this dataset are in BMP arrange with a size of 128×128. The we find the difference arrays in both domain. After finding the difference array we set the values of arrays between −E and +E with the help of hard thresholding technique. Then we extract the features in both spatial and DCT domain with the help pf

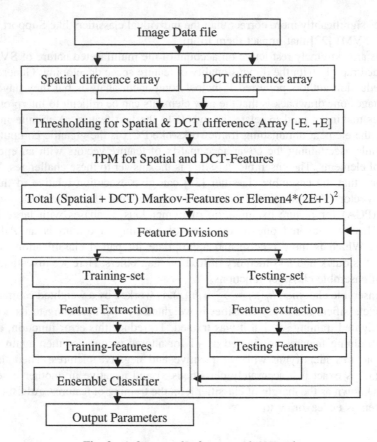

Fig. 2. A framework of suggested approach

one step Markov transition probability matrix. After extracting the features we combine them and we classify them with the help of ensemble classifier with Adamost Algorithm by considering the binary class problem with 100 iterations. The aggregate quantities of Markov feature for spatial and additionally DCT-domain for certain threshold value is shown in Table 1 for different value of E.

Table 1. Total markov-features are computed by using Eq. 4 $(2E + 1)^2$.

Domain	E = 1	E = 2	E = 3	E = 4	E = 5
DCT	36	100	196	324	484
Spatial	36	100	196	324	484
DCT + Spatial	72	200	392	648	968

4.2   Performance Parameters

To assess the execution, we compute the true positive rate (TPR), the true negative rate (TNR), and the accuracy (ACC). The TPR is the rate of precisely distinguished credible pictures and the TNR is the rate of accurately distinguished altered pictures. The ACC speaks to the discovery rate, which is the normal of the TPR and TNR esteems. We likewise utilized the Receiver Operating Curve (ROC) and the Area Under the Curve (AUC) to plot the progressions in TPR and FPR.

4.3   Experimental Results

For our experimental results, We first extract the Markov-features by utilizing the TPM for both DCT and spatial domain then we combine these features or elements and classify them with an efficient ensemble classifier [25].by using an AdaBoost algorithm and 100 number of 'Tree' weak learners. Instead of using six-fold cross-verification [9, 12], we utilized tenfold cross-verification to assess the ensemble model parameters. In ten-fold cross-verification, we haphazardly separated each of the authentic pictures and the altered pictures into ten equivalent group. In every cycle, we utilized nine groups each from the authentic pictures and the altered pictures for training, while the remaining was utilized for testing. In this way, towards the ending with no. of ten iterations, all the ten groups have been tried. There is no over-fitting problem has been found between the training set and the testing set in an emphasis which is generally presented in SVM classifier. Table 2 demonstrates the execution of the suggested technique on the Columbia gray DVMM data file [13] and it demonstrates the ten times cross validation comes about for E = 1, 2, 3 and E = 4 for various dimensions D = 72; 200; 392; and 648 in terms of accuracy, TPR, TNR. The outcomes demonstrate that when the two areas are joined, the outcomes have enhanced essentially and as it appeared in Table 2 we accomplish 99.63% of recognition accuracy when the no. of features or elements was 72 at the threshold value of E = 1 and then accuracy decreases to 99.52% when the quantity of elements is 200 at threshold value of E = 2 and further it reduces to 99.46% and 98.36% when the no. of features or elements increased by 392 and 648 at threshold value of E = 3 and E = 4 even without using SVM with PCA in comparison to other methods [9, 12, 14–16]. The noticing point is that we achieved maximum accuracy at threshold E = 1, 2, 3 and E = 4 as compared to other techniques [9, 12, 14–16]. The ROC curve describe the progressions of the FPR versus TPR are appeared in Fig. 3 for combined Spatial and DCT based Markov-features. The ROC

Table 2. Examination of accuracy for the suggested work with the threshold value and dimensionality

Threshold	Dimension	TPR (%)	TNR (%)	Accuracy (%)	AUC
E = 1	72	99.99	92.0	99.65	0.9895
E = 2	200	99. 97	90.68	99.51	0.9893
E = 3	392	99.94	84.45	99.46	0.9890
E = 4	648	99.90	77.85	98.36	0.9888
E = 5	968	99.83	65.70	98.15	0.9885

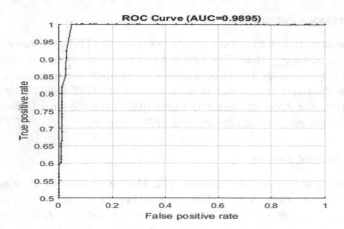

Fig. 3. ROC curves for total Markov-features in Spatial and DCT domain with threshold E = 1 and D = 72

curve for combined feature is near the upper corner demonstrating the most elevated execution with area under the curve more like 1.

As appeared in Table 3, the existing splicing detection approach with our updated ensemble classifier shows prevalent accuracy in comparison to the traditional methods which are utilized SVM classifier with PCA. Our splicing detection process was executed in MATLAB R2016a with *fit ensemble* command.

Table 3. Examination of Accuracy for the our work in comparison to other techniques

Methods	Elements	TPR (%)	TNR (%)	Accuracy (%)
Suggested	72	99.99	92.0	99.65
Suggested	200	99.97	90.68	99.51
Suggested	392	99. 94	84.45	99.46
Suggested	648	99.90	77.85	98.36
[9]	30	82.3	78.9	78.9
[15]	150	98.89	98.49	98.69
[15]	100	99.06	98.60	98.81
[15]	50	99.05	98.59	98.82
[15]	30	98.94	98.01	98.47
[12]	150	93.0	94.0	93.5
[12]	100	93.3	93.8	93.5
[12]	50	92.3	93.1	92.6
[14]	64	87.5	87.6	87.5
[16]	14,240	93.0	93.8	93.4

5 Conclusion

The passive forgery detection technique for picture splicing identification and its classification is suggested and assessed in this paper. The thought is to classify the combined Markov-features computed from boundary pictures in the Spatial-domain and DCT domain with an efficient ensemble classifier have achieved best accuracy and perfectly classified then others. An improved ensemble classifier with AdaBoost algorithm and 'Tree' weak learner has demonstrated a proficient classification with combined Markov-features. The outcomes demonstrate that recognition accuracy is enormously expanded with ensemble classifier for combined Spatial-Features and DCT based-features. The test outcomes approve the execution of existing strategy with Ensemble classifier achieved best outcomes when contrasted with the most astounding detection accuracy achieved up till now from existing altering recognition techniques which utilized SVM classifier with PCA on the same data file and with the main 72 features or elements. The execution is evaluated and looked at as far as recognition accuracy, true positive rate and true negative rate, and ROC curve. With 72 features or elements, the consolidated approach with ensemble classifier can accomplish 99.65% exactness, 99.99% TPR, 92.0% TNR and 98.95% AUC at threshold E = 1. Like wise other paper achieved this comparable accuracy at E = 3 and E = 4.

References

1. Mehta, R., Agarwal, N.: Splicing detection for combined DCT, DWT and spatial markov-features using ensemble classifier. Procedia Comput. Sci. **132**, 1695–1705 (2018)
2. Farid, H.: A survey of picture forgery detection. IEEE Signal Process. Mag. **26**, 6–25 (2009)
3. Mahdian, B., Saic, S.: A bibliography on blind methods for identifying Picture forgery. Signal Process. Picture Commun. **25**(6), 389–399 (2010)
4. Farid, H.: A picture tells a thousand lies. New Sci. **2411**, 38–41 (2003)
5. Ng, T.T., Chang, S.F., Sun, Q.: Blind detection of photomontage using higher order statistics. In: Proceedings of IEEE International Symposium on Circuits and Systems (ISCAS). pp. 688–691 (2004)
6. Fu, D., Shi, Y.Q., Su, W.: Detection of image splicing based on hilbert-huang transform and moments of characteristic functions with wavelet decomposition. In: Shi, Y.Q., Jeon, B. (eds.) IWDW 2006. LNCS, vol. 4283, pp. 177–187. Springer, Heidelberg (2006). https://doi.org/10.1007/11922841_15
7. Chen, W., Shi, Y.Q., Su, W.: Picture splicing detection using 2-D phase congruency and statistical moments of characteristic function. In: SPIE Electronic Imaging: Security, Steganography, and Watermarking of Multimedia Contents. pp. 65050R.1–65050R.8 (2007)
8. Shi, Y.Q., Chen, C., Chen, W.: A natural Picture model approach to splicing detection. In: Proceedings of ACM Multimedia and Security (MM&Sec), pp. 51–62 (2007)
9. He, Z., Sun, W., Lu, W., Lu, H.: Digital picture splicing detection based on approximate run length. Pattern Recognit. Lett. **32**(12), 591–1597 (2011)

10. He, Z., Lu, W., Sun, W.: Improved run length based detection of digital image splicing. In: Shi, Y.Q., Kim, H.-J., Perez-Gonzalez, F. (eds.) IWDW 2011. LNCS, vol. 7128, pp. 349–360. Springer, Heidelberg (2012). https://doi.org/10.1007/978-3-642-32205-1_28

11. Moghaddasi, Z., Jalab, H.A., Noor, R.: Improving RLRN picture splicing detection with the use of PCA and kernel PCA. Sci. World J. (2014). Article ID 606570, https://doi.org/10.1155/2014/606570

12. He, Z., Lu, W., Sun, W., Huang, J.: Digital Picture splicing detection based on Markov features in DCT and DWT domain. Pattern Recog. **45**(12), 4292–4299 (2012)

13. Ng, T.T., Chang, S.F.: A data set of authentic and spliced Picture blocks. Technical report 203–2004, Columbia University (2004). http://www.ee.columbia.edu/ln/dvmm/downloads/

14. Su, B., Yuan, Q., Wang, S., Zhao, C., Li, S.: Enhanced state selection Markov model for Picture splicing detection. Eurasip. J. Wirel. Comm. **2014**(7), 1–10 (2014)

15. El-Alfy, M., Qureshi, M.A.: Combining spatial and DCT based Markov features for enhanced blind detection of Picture splicing. Pattern Anal. Appl. **18**(3), 713–723 (2015)

16. Zhao, X., Wang, S., Li, S., Li, J.: Passive Picture-splicing detection by a 2-D noncausal Markov model. IEEE Trans. Circuits Syst. Video Technol. **25**(2), 185–199 (2015)

17. Moghaddasi, Z., Jalab, H.A., Md Noor, R.: Improving RLRN picture splicing detection with the use of PCA and kernel PCA, Sci. World J. (2014). Article ID 606570, https://doi.org/10.1155/2014/606570

18. Muhammad, G., Al-Hammadi, M.H., Hussian, M., Bebis, G.: Picture forgery detection using steerable pyramid transform and local binary pattern. Mach. Vis. Appl. **25**(4), 985–995 (2014)

19. Hussain, M., Qasem, S., Bebis, G., Muhammad, G., Aboalsamh, H., Mathkour, H.: Evaluation of picture forgery detection using multi-scale weber local descriptors. Int. J. Artif. Intell. Tools **24**(4), 1540016 (2015). https://doi.org/10.1142/s0218213015400163

20. Han, J.G., Park, T.H., Moon, Y.H., Eom, I.K.: Efficient Markov feature extraction method for Picture splicing detection using maximization and threshold expansion. J. Electron. Imaging **25**(2), 023031 (2016)

21. Nissar, A., Mir, A.H.: Classification of steganalysis techniques: a study. Digit. Signal Process. **20**, 1758–1770 (2010)

22. Chang, C.C., Lin, C.J.: LIBSVM—a library for support vector machines. ACM Trans. Intell. Syst. Technol. **2** (2011). https://doi.org/10.1145/1961189.1961199

23. Kambhatla, N., Leen, T.K.: Dimension reduction by local principal component analysis. Neural Comput. **9**(7), 1493–1516 (1997)

24. Dietterich, T.G.: Ensemble methods in machine learning. In: Kittler, J., Roli, F. (eds.) MCS 2000. LNCS, vol. 1857, pp. 1–15. Springer, Heidelberg (2000). https://doi.org/10.1007/3-540-45014-9_1

25. Kodovský, J., Fridrich, J.: Steganalysis in high dimensions: Fusing classifiers built on random subspaces. In: IS&T/SPIE Electronic Imaging. International Society for Optics and Photonics, USA, California, pp. 78800L–78800L (2011)

26. Kodovsky, J., Fridrich, J., Holub, V.: Ensemble classifiers for steganalysis of digital media. IEEE Trans. Inf. Forensics Secur. **7**, 432–444 (2012)

27. Duda, R.O., Hart, P.E., Stork, D.G.: Pattern Classification. Wiley (2012)

28. Polikar, R.: Ensemble learning, Ensemble Machine Learning. Springer, New York (2012). https://doi.org/10.1007/978-1-4419-9326-7

29. Tao, H., Ma, X., Qiao, M.: Subspace selective ensemble algorithm based on feature clustering. J. Comput. **8**, 509–516 (2013)

30. Fridrich, J., Kodovsky, J.: Rich models for steganalysis of digital Pictures. Inf. Forensics Secur. **7**, 868–882 (2012)
31. Shi, Y.Q., Chen, C., Chen, W.: A natural image model approach to splicing detection. In: Proceedings of the 9th Workshop on Multimedia and Security, pp 51–62 (2007)
32. Zhao, X., Wang, S., Li, S., Li, J.: A comprehensive study on third order statistical features for image splicing detection. In: Shi, Y.Q., Kim, H.-J., Perez-Gonzalez, F. (eds.) IWDW 2011. LNCS, vol. 7128, pp. 243–256. Springer, Heidelberg (2012). https://doi.org/10.1007/978-3-642-32205-1_20

LEACH- Genus 2 Hyper Elliptic Curve Based Secured Light-Weight Visual Cryptography for Highly Sensitive Images

N. Sasikaladevi[✉], N. Mahalakshmi, and N. Archana

Department of CSE, School of Computing, SASTRA Deemed University,
Thanjavur, TN, India
sasikalade@gmail.com,
maha.naga.97@gmail.com, archananarayanan223@gmail.com

Abstract. Various data checks and threats prevails in today's digital environment, as a result of which one's details get compromised. Existing data encryption techniques are either vulnerable (RSA 256,512,2 K,4 K bits) or exploit the available resources (ECC-160 bits: the size of the encrypted data is significantly more than the actual evidence). In this paper, we provide a new line of sight on extending the available ECC methods, i.e. Genus-2 **H**yper **E**lliptic **C**urve Based Light-weight **C**ryptographic technique. Experimental results show that HECC offers enhanced security with Perfect Recovery Schemes and limited utilization of additional space compared to existing ECC methods.

Keywords: HyperElliptic curve · Visual cryptography

1 Introduction

Image security is an active process, on which most data representation relies on. Specific standardized cryptographic algorithms have failed at times to provide the required protection, which puts-forth the need to come up with algorithms that are highly secure and computationally infeasible to break down. One such concept is HyperElliptic Curve based Cryptography. It is well-known that cryptographic implementations based on Elliptic and Hyper-Elliptic Curves require group order of size $\approx 2^{160}$. More specifically, Hyper-Elliptic Curves of Genus-2 will need Jacobi field F_q with $|F_q| \approx 2^{80}$ which outperforms ECC. These key-features of HECC include robustness to the proposed system. Based on the above Idea, HECC emerges as one of the best technique for highly sensitive data encryptions especially Medical Images.

The remaining part of this paper includes the followings: a literature review of Curve-Based Cryptography which is explained in Sect. 2. Section 3 introduces the proposed system, while Sect. 4 provides the detailed analysis of the system. Section 5 verifies the effectiveness of the projected algorithm compared with the similar techniques and justifies the projected idea.

© Springer Nature Singapore Pte Ltd. 2018
M. Singh et al. (Eds.): ICACDS 2018, CCIS 905, pp. 302–311, 2018.
https://doi.org/10.1007/978-981-13-1810-8_30

2 Related Work

Going digital has a drawback of being vulnerable, which has led to the emergence of the full range of cryptographic techniques for securing the data. Currently, Curve based cryptography is widespread due to its high-security aspects. Many researchers have developed novel ideas for achieving data especially based on pairing based cryptography.

Li et al. [1] proposed image encryption based on curve and discrete logarithms based cryptography for grayscale images. Cyclic elliptic curve based image scrambling technique is recommended in [2]. Keystream with the size of 256 bit is created and assorted with critical patterns from the points in the elliptic curve. Dolendro et al. [3] recommended image scrambling based on curve based cryptography. Shukla et al. [4] suggested image scrambling technique based on paring based crypto system. Kumar et al. [5, 6] suggested color coded image scrambling technique based on DNA computing and pairing based cryptography. The color coded image scrambling method using diffusion process coupled with the chaotic map is proposed. Dolendro et al. [7] proposed Elgamal elliptic curve based medical image encryption. Shahryar et al. [8] suggested elliptic curve pseudo-random number based image encryption. Dolendro et al. [9] suggested chaotic image scrambling techniques using elliptic curve finite field. Dolendro et al. [7] discussed explicitly Medical image encryption using enhanced ElGamal scheme.

Above mentioned work focused on various image encryption techniques using ECC. Due to the performance gap between ECC and HECC [11], here we propose medical image encryption using HECC- Genus 2 curve. It is an improved version of ECC.

3 Proposed LEACH Crypto System

LEACH cryptosystem is based on genus 2 HyperElliptic Curve (HEC). Selecting the cryptographically suitable curve is a tedious issue in curve based cryptography. This paper is based on genus 2 HEC over GF(P) where p is the 256 bits prime number. The suitable curve is selected based on Complex Multiplication(CM) method. In HECC, group elements are divisors. Cantor algorithm is used for divisor addition and doubling.

F: The HyperElliptic Curve with genus two is given by

$$f = x^5 + 15384295433461683634059 * x^3 + 150354294764347319629935$$
$$* x^2 + 139071402580455445358068 * x$$
$$+ 79099282479987590526969$$

e1: A randomized divisor is obtained from the curve which acts as a generator.

d = Private Key of Receiver.

e2: e2 is computed using the equation $e2 = d * e1$. (Using cantor algorithm for Addition and Doubling of Divisors)

r = Private Key of the Sender.

c1: c1 is computed using the equation $c1 = r * e1$. (Using cantor algorithm for Addition and Doubling of Divisors)

Algorithm1: LEACH Encryption Algorithm

step 1.   2 Points$(x1, x2)$ are taken, and their corresponding Y coordinates$(y1, y\,2)$ are calculated using the equation of the curve.

step 2.   2 Pair of Points $P1[x_1, y_1]$, $P2[x_2, y_2]$ is taken, and corresponding divisor D $(U, V)$is obtained using Mumford algorithm, which is the Message to be encrypted.

step 3.   The Cipher Text c2 is generated using the formula $c2 = D + r * E$ (Using Cantor Algorithm for Addition and Doubling)

step 4.   The points from the encrypted divisor are obtained using completing square method using *sqrtmodp( )* function in MATLAB.

The corresponding X coordinates are represented as the Cipher Text (Fig. 1).

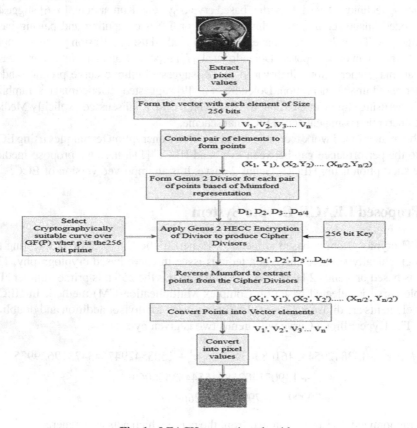

Fig. 1.   LEACH encryption algorithm

Algorithm2: LEACH Decryption Algorithm

step 1. From the encrypted Image, Obtain the points and map it to the curve to get the cipher points $(x_1, y_1)(x_2, y_2)\ldots (x_n, y_n)$ which are manipulated to obtain the divisors using Mumford representation.

step 2. The decrypted divisor is retrieved using the formula $p = c2 - d * c1$ (Using Cantor Algorithm for Addition and Doubling).

step 3. The Image Points are obtained using *reverse Mumford representation* (Fig. 2).

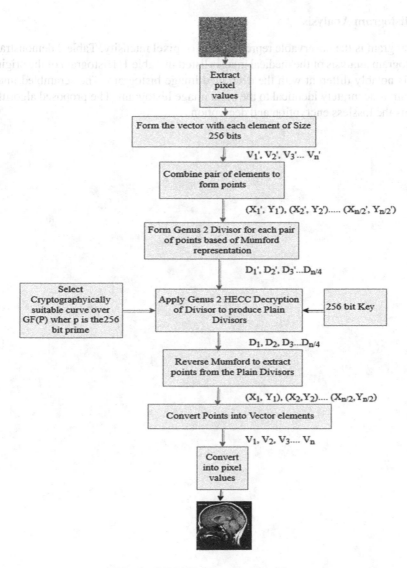

Fig. 2. LEACH decryption algorithm

4 Experimental Analysis

The experiment was performed on an Intel Core i7 @ 2.20 GHz laptop with 4 GB RAM. The proposed algorithm is implemented and tested using Matlab R2016b. The hyper-elliptic curve components used are given in Table 4. The suggested technique is performed on benchmark medical images. Experimental results are shown in this section. Medical images are downloaded from various medical image databases in [10].

4.1 Histogram Analysis

The histogram is the observable representation of pixel intensity. Table 2 demonstrates the histogram analysis of the medical images listed in Table 1. Histogram of the original image is notably different with the decrypted image histogram. The scrambled image histogram is accurately identical to the plain image histogram. The proposed algorithm performs the lossless encryption and decryption.

Table 1. Original medical images with its encrypted and decrypted version

Img	Original Image	Encoded Image	Decoded Image
Img 1			
Img 2			
Img 3			
Img 4			
Img 5			
Img 6			

Table 2. Histogram analysis of medical images

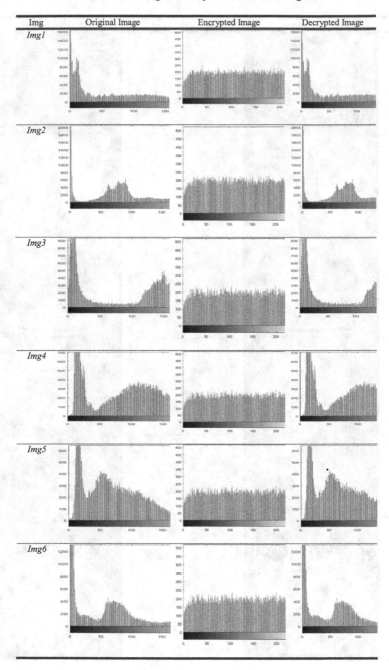

4.2 Mean Square Error (MSE) Analysis

Mean Square Error (MSE) and Peak Signal to Noise Ratio is estimated for the benchmark images.

$$MSE = \frac{1}{N * M} \sum_{n=1}^{N} \sum_{m=1}^{M} \left[\lfloor f(i,j) - f_0(i,j) \rfloor^2 \right]$$

Where f and f_0 are the intensity functions of scrambled and plain images. (i, j) is the location of the pixels. (N*M) Is the dimension of the image. Table 3 depicts the MSE value of plain and scrambled image. It shows that the MSE of the decrypted image concerning its original image is 0. Table 3 shows the MSE of the plain image and recovered image. It shows that the MSE of the encrypted image concerning its original image is high.

Table 3. MSE of original, encrypted and decrypted images

Image ID	BW original and encrypted	BW original and decrypted
Img1	1.46E + 04	0
Img2	1.29E + 04	0
Img3	1.23E + 04	0
Img4	1.00E + 04	0
Img5	1.16E + 04	0
Img6	1.10E + 04	0

Table 4. PSNR of Original, Encrypted and Decrypted Images

Image ID	BW original and encrypted	BW original and decrypted
Img1	6.4999	Infinity
Img2	7.0123	Infinity
Img3	7.2202	Infinity
Img4	8.1235	Infinity
Img5	7.4906	Infinity
Img6	6.6577	Infinity

4.3 Peak Signal to Noise Ratio (PSNR) Analysis

PSNR is the ratio between the square of the maximum intensity of a pixel with the square root of the mean square error. Larger the PSNR then higher the quality of the image.

$$PSNR = 20 * log \frac{255^2}{\sqrt{MSE}}$$

PSNR value is calculated for the decrypted images concerning its original images. It is infinite. PSNR value is calculated for red, blue and green component separately for Lena image, baboon image, and pepper image.

5   Conclusion

Genus 2 Hyperelliptic curve visual cryptography for medical images is proposed in this paper. Genus 2 Hyperelliptic curve is based on degree 5 equations. And it is complicated as compared to ECC as it involved degree 3 equation. Cryptography suitable curve is selected over large prime to eliminated brute force attack and cryptanalytic attacks. Medical images are correctly encrypted using genus 2 HECC. The perks of HECC is, the cryptographical aspects such as Confidentiality, Integrity, Authentication depends on the selected curve and the prime field but independent of Key size,i.e., Computation points are highly scattered even for tiny key size. This unique feature enables the algorithm to provide defense against cryptanalysis. Rigorous security analysis is performed to verify the security strength of the proposed algorithms. Statistical investigations prove that the proposed LEACH algorithm yields ideal MSE and PSNR values as compared other visual cryptography methods.

Acknowledgment. The part of this research work is supported by Department of Science and Technology (DST), Science and Engineering Board (SERB), Government of India under the ECR grant (ECR/2017/000679/ES)

References

1. Li, L., El-Latif, A.A.A., Niu, X.: Elliptic curve ElGamal based homomorphic image encryption scheme for sharing secret images. Signal Process. **92**(4), 1069–1078 (2012)
2. El-Latif, A.A.A., Niu, X.: A chaotic hybrid system and cyclic elliptic curve for image encryption. AEU-Int. J. Electron. Commun. **67**(2), 136–143 (2013)
3. Singh, L.D., Singh, K.M.: Image encryption using elliptic curve cryptography. Procedia Comput. Sci. **54**, 472–481 (2015)
4. Shukla, A.: Image encryption using elliptic curve cryptography. Int. J. Students Res. Technol. Manag. **1**(2), 115–117 (2015)
5. Kumar, M., Iqbal, A., Kumar, P.: A new RGB image encryption algorithm based on DNA encoding and elliptic curve Diffie-Hellman cryptography. Signal Process. **125**, 187–202 (2016)
6. Kumar, M., Powduri, P., Reddy, A.: An RGB image encryption using diffusion process associated with the chaotic map. J. Inf. Secur. Appl. **21**, 20–30 (2015)
7. Laiphrakpam, D.S., Khumanthem, M.S.: Medical image encryption based on improved ElGamal encryption technique. Opt.-Int. J. Light. Electron Opt. **147**, 88–102 (2017)
8. Toughi, S., Fathi, M.H., Sekhavat, Y.A.: An image encryption scheme based on elliptic curve pseudo-random and advanced encryption system. Sig. Process. **141**, 217–227 (2017)
9. Laiphrakpam, D.S., Khumanthem, M.S.: A robust image encryption scheme based on chaotic system and elliptic curve over the finite field. Multimed. Tools Appl., 1–24 (2017)

10. SampleMedicalImages (2015). http://www.dicomlibrary.com/, https://eddie.via.cornell.edu/cgi-bin/datac/signon.cgi. Accessed 24 June 2015

11. Pelzl, J., Wollinger, T., Guajardo, J., Paar, C.: Hyperelliptic curve cryptosystems: closing the performance gap to elliptic curves. In: Walter, C.D., Koç, Ç.K., Paar, C. (eds.) CHES 2003. LNCS, vol. 2779, pp. 351–365. Springer, Heidelberg (2003). https://doi.org/10.1007/978-3-540-45238-6_28

HEAP- Genus 2 HyperElliptic Curve Based Biometric Audio Template Protection

N. Sasikaladevi[1(✉)], A. Revathi[2(✉)], N. Mahalakshmi[1], and N. Archana[1]

[1] Department of CSE, School of Computing, SASTRA Deemed University, Thanjavur, TN, India
sasikalade@gmail.com, maha.naga.97@gmail.com, archananarayanan223@gmail.com
[2] Department of ECE, School of EEE, SASTRA Deemed University, Thanjavur, TN, India
revathi@ece.sastra.com

Abstract. Increasing evolution of technology demands the innovative applications. E-commerce, e-banking, e-health, and e-payment, etc. being carried out by mobile devices. Mobile device-based speaker authentication is one of the predominant biometric-based authentication schemes. As the mobile devices are vulnerable to physical attacks, speech template stored in the mobile devices may be compromised. To protect the speech template, it should be stored in the encrypted form. Audio templates produce the large bitstream that leads to long encryption phase. Hence, there is a need for lightweight cryptosystem for audio template protection. In This paper, a light weight cryptographic algorithm based on Genus-2 Hyper-Elliptic Curves in Jacobi field is proposed. Genus-2 curves are deployed over a field F such that $|F| \approx 2^{80}$. With these features, improved security is provided for the stored data.

Keywords: HyperElliptic curve · Audio cryptography

1 Introduction

Today, prevalently utilized data representation formation is the audio signals, which are extensively exploited by the today's society for various kinds of the communication. In the model world, secret audio communications are transmitted over public medium. Audio is acknowledged as the proof in the judicial cases. Digital speech requires to be secured against illegal usage. However speech signals are completely special categories of signals as evaluated to data and pictures, which are depicted as wave signals and have been classified by different factors like frequency, amplitude, and phase. The majority of the offered cryptographic techniques are well applicable for text representation of information. It is not ideal for speech signals, due to its format. In particular, speech signals are huge in size and have greatly redundant samples. Therefore, well-organized cryptographic techniques are necessary to protect the perceptive speech

© Springer Nature Singapore Pte Ltd. 2018
M. Singh et al. (Eds.): ICACDS 2018, CCIS 905, pp. 312–320, 2018.
https://doi.org/10.1007/978-981-13-1810-8_31

signals for backup and scrambling before spreading the signal over the community network in particular Internet and mobile application.

In this proposal, we have introduced a new approach for encrypting the data to be stored and transmitted, using Curve-Based Cryptography. Cryptographically suitable Hyper-Elliptic Curve is chosen for the process. The audio signals used for implementing the idea is obtained from an open-source database *time*. Audio signals from both Male and Female jacks from an acoustic environment are tested for the accuracy of the suggested method. Experimental results show that the suggested system provides chaotic encryption with reliable data recovery. This article is organized with Sect. 2 putting forth the works related to the idea proposed. Sect. 3 explains the working of the algorithm, providing the expected results which are depicted in Sects. 4 and 5 concludes the work with perks of the ideas that were put forth.

2   Related Work

Speech scrambling constructed on LFSR is suggested in [1]. Dengre et al. [2] proposed speech scrambling for sensitive audio signals. Discriminatory speech scrambling for multimodal supervision scheme is suggested in [3]. Datta et al. [4] proposed fractional scrambling and watermarking techniques for speech data with the compromise on quality. Bahram et al. [5] suggested an FPGA based AES scrambling techniques for a speech signals. Bio metric speech authentication and real-time speech scrambling technique is suggested in [6]. Kulkarni et al. [7] suggested a well-built scrambling method for speech signal hiding in images for enhanced protection. Ashok et al. [8] depicted a protected cryptographic method for speech data. Iyer et al. [9] suggested multimedia scrambling using fusion technique. Context-aware multimedia scrambling is suggested in [10]. Washio et al. [11] depicted an speech covert distribution method. Zhao et al. [12] suggested a dual key audio scrambling technique using under resolute BSS. Scrambling based audio protection based on compressed sensing is suggested in [13]. Lu et al. [14] depicted speech signal hiding based on AT and dual random phase encryption techniques.

In the present times, numerous secret profitable speeches required to be secured. In various real-time scenarios, digital speech requires to be secured from malevolent exploits, and this consciousness of privacy defense aggravates the swift growth of security method. Speech scrambling has requested an immense deal of attention from researchers. Speech is measured as one of the necessary illustration types; it has been largely employed in current society. In a few cases for instance susceptible business discussion, audio evidence is good enough in court. Hence, the digital audio require be obscured as secret data. In particular, increasing awareness of individual privacy defense activates the immediate expansion of audio scrambling methods. Therefore, audio scrambling has gained a immense deal of consideration from researchers.

3   Proposed HEAP Crypto System

HEAP cryptosystem is based on genus 2 Hyper Elliptic Curve (HEC). Selecting the cryptographically suitable curve is a tedious issue in curve based cryptography. This paper is based on genus 2 HEC over GF(P) where p is the 256 bit prime number. Suitable curve is selected based on Complex Multiplication (CM) method. In HECC, group elements are divisors. Cantor algorithm is used for divisor addition and doubling (Figs. 1 and 2).

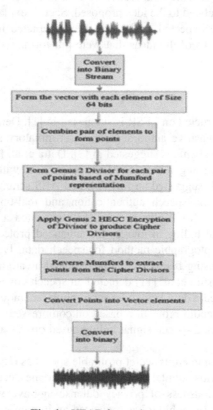

Fig. 1. HEAP forward process

f: The Hyper Elliptic Curve with genus two is given by

$$f = x^5 + 153834295433461683634059 * x^3 + 150354294776434731962 9935$$
$$* x^2 + 193071402580455445358006 8 * x$$
$$+ 790992824799875905266969$$

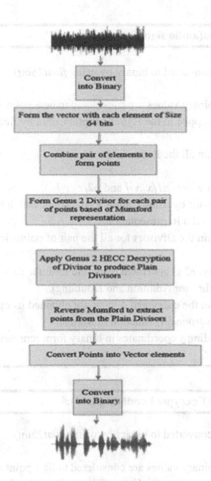

Fig. 2. HEAP reverse process

e1: A randomized divisor is obtained from the curve which acts as a generator.
d = Private Key of Receiver.
e2: *e2* is computed using the equation $e2 = d * e1$. (Using cantor algorithm for Addition and Doubling of Divisors)
r = Private Key of the Sender.
c1: *c1* is computed using the equation $c1 = r * e1$ (Using cantor algorithm for Addition and Doubling of Divisors)

HEAP Forward Process(audio signal):

---

1. The input signal is converted to binary by using *float2bin()*
2. Points Formation:
   - 2.1. The first 256 binary values are considered to be a point x.
   - 2.2. This point is mapped to the Hyper-Elliptic Curve by finding the corresponding y.
   - 2.3. Similarly, obtain all the Points in the curve.
3. Divisor Formation:
   - 3.1. Select a pair of points $p1[x_1,y_1]$ and $p2[x_2,y_2]$.
   - 3.2. Obtain the Divisor by using Cantor's Algorithm which is represented in the form of Mumford's Representation.
   - 3.3. Similarly, obtain the Divisors for all the pair of points in the curve.
4. Encryption:
   - 4.1. The Cipher Text $c2$ is generated using the formula $c2 = D + r * e2$ (Using Cantor Algorithm for Addition and Doubling).
   - 4.2. The points from the encrypted divisor are obtained using completing square method using *sqrtmodp()* function in Matlab.
   - 4.3. The corresponding x coordinates in binary form represents the encrypted audio signals.

HEAPReverse Process(Encrypted audio signals):

---

5. The input signal is converted to binary by using *float2bin()*
6. Points Formation:
   - 6.1. The first 256 binary values are considered to be a point x.
   - 6.2. This point is mapped to the Hyper-Elliptic Curve by finding the corresponding y.
   - 6.3. Similarly, obtain all the Points in the curve.
7. Divisor Formation:
   - 7.1. Select a pair of points $p1[x_1,y_1]$ and $p2[x_2,y_2]$.
   - 7.2. Obtain the Encrypted Divisor by using Cantor's Algorithm which is represented in the form of Mumford's Representation.
   - 7.3. Similarly, obtain the Encrypted Divisors for all the pair of points in the curve.
8. Decryption:
   - 8.1. The Plain Text p is generated using the formula $p = c2 - d * c1$ (Using Cantor Algorithm for Addition and Doubling).
   - 8.2. The points from the decrypted divisor p are obtained using completing square method using *sqrtmodp()* function in Matlab.
   - 8.3. The corresponding x coordinates in binary form represents the original audio signals.

4 Experiments and Analysis

This is because the original and decrypted speech utterances and their spectrograms are same. Figures 3 and 4 give the details about the correlation between the original and decrypted speech utterance for the female speech regarding sample values and set of frequency components present in them.

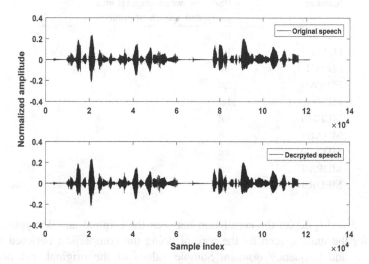

Fig. 3. Sample speech (Female)– Original and decrypted

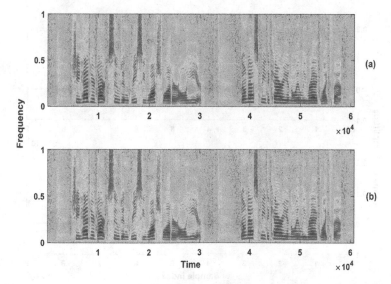

Fig. 4. Spectrogram (Female speech) (a) Original speech (b) Decrypted speech

Table 1 indicates the comparison between original and decrypted speech utterances regarding computing PSNR between them. It is shown that decrypted speech utterances are exactly similar as that of original speech utterances. PSNR values being infinity indicates that mean squared error between the set of original speech and decrypted speech utterances is zero.

Table 1. Comparison concerning PSNR values

Speaker	PSNR between original and decrypted speech utterances
FAKS0	Inf
FCJF0	Inf
FDAC1	Inf
FDAW0	Inf
FDML0	Inf
MCPM0	Inf
MDAB0	Inf
MDAC0	Inf
MDPK0	Inf
MEDR0	Inf

Figures 5 and 6 depict the correlation between the original and decrypted speech utterance for the male speech by the way of doing the comparison between them in time-domain and frequency domain. Sample values of the original and decrypted speech utterance are same leading to PSNR being infinity. A concentration of energy in the frequency band remains same between original and decrypted speech utterances.

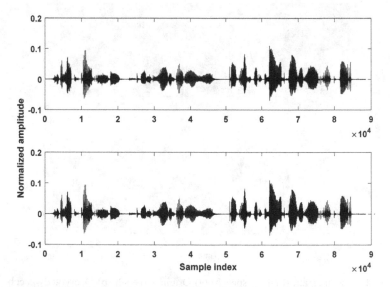

Fig. 5. Sample speech (Male)– Original and decrypted

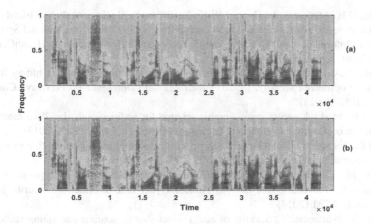

Fig. 6. Spectrogram (Male speech) (a) Original speech (b) Decrypted speech

5 Conclusion

Audio Signals has a higher rate of including noise over the channels. On processing encryption with Genus 2 Hyper elliptic curve audio cryptography, 100% of the noise can be removed, which acts as an added advantage for this scheme. The above-proposed algorithm can be molded according to the application required. Rigorous security analysis is performed to verify the security strength of the proposed algorithms. Statistical analyses prove that the proposed algorithm yields exemplary MSE and PSNR values as compared other visual cryptography methods.

Acknowledgment. The part of this research work is supported by Department of Science and Technology (DST), Science and Engineering Board (SERB), Government of India under the ECR grant (ECR/2017/000679/ES).

References

1. James, S.P., George, S.N., Deepthi, P.P.: An audio encryption technique based on LFSR based alternating step generator. In: 2014 IEEE International Conference on Electronics, Computing and Communication Technologies (IEEE CONECCT). IEEE (2014)
2. Dengre, Amit, Gawande, A.D.: Audio encryption and digital image watermarking in an uncompress video. Int. J. Adv. Appl. Sci. **4**(2), 66–72 (2015)
3. Cichowski, J., Czyzewski, A.. "Sensitive audio data encryption for multimodal surveillance systems. In: Audio Engineering Society Convention, vol. 132. Audio Engineering Society (2012)
4. Datta, K., Gupta, I.S.: Partial encryption and watermarking scheme for audio files with controlled degradation of quality. Multimedia tools Appl. **64**(3), 649–669 (2013)
5. Rashidi, B., Rashidi, B.: FPGA based a new low power and self-timed AES 128-bit encryption algorithm for encryption audio signal. Int. J. Comput. Netw. Inf. Secur. **5**(2), 10 (2013)

6. Nguyen, H.H., Mehaoua, A., Hong, J.W.K.: Secure medical tele-consultation based on voice authentication and realtime audio/video encryption. In: 2013 First International Symposium on Future Information and Communication Technologies for Ubiquitous HealthCare (Ubi-HealthTech). IEEE (2013)
7. Kulkarni, S.A., Patil, S.B.: A robust encryption method for speech data hiding in digital images for optimized security. In: 2015 International Conference on Pervasive Computing (ICPC). IEEE (2015)
8. Asok, S.B., et al.: A secure cryptographic scheme for audio signals. In: 2013 International Conference on Communications and Signal Processing (ICCSP). IEEE (2013)
9. Iyer, S.C., Sedamkar, R.R., Gupta, S.: A novel idea on multimedia encryption using hybrid crypto approach. Procedia Comput. Sci. **79**, 293–298 (2016)
10. Fazeen, M., Bajwa, G., Dantu, R.: Context-aware multimedia encryption in mobile platforms. In: Proceedings of the 9th Annual Cyber and Information Security Research Conference. ACM (2014)
11. Washio, S., Watanabe, Y.: Security of audio secret sharing scheme encrypting audio secrets with bounded shares. In: 2014 IEEE International Conference on Acoustics, Speech and Signal Processing (ICASSP). IEEE (2014)
12. Zhao, H., et al.: Dual key speech encryption algorithm based underdetermined BSS. Sci. World J. 2014 (2014)
13. Zeng, L., et al.: Scrambling-based speech encryption via compressed sensing. EURASIP J. Adv. Signal Process. **2012**(1), 257 (2012)
14. Lu, X., et al.: Digital audio information hiding based on Arnold transformation and double random-phase encoding technique. Optik-Int. J. Light Electron Optics **123**(8), 697–702 (2012)

Greedy WOA for Travelling Salesman Problem

Rishab Gupta[1(✉)], Nilay Shrivastava[1], Mohit Jain[2], Vijander Singh[2], and Asha Rani[2]

[1] COE Division, Netaji Subhas Institute of Technology, University of Delhi, Sec-3,
Dwarka, New Delhi, India
rishab0611@gmail.com, nilayshrivastava1729@gmail.com
[2] ICE Division, Netaji Subhas Institute of Technology, University of Delhi,
Dwarka, New Delhi, India
nsit.mohit@gmail.com, vijaydee@gmail.com, ashansit@gmail.com

Abstract. Travelling salesman problem (TSP) is an NP-hard combinatorial problem and exhaustive search for an optimal solution is computationally intractable. The present work proposes a discrete version of Whale optimization algorithm (WOA) to find an optimal tour for a given travelling salesman network. Further, a greedy technique is incorporated in WOA (GWOA) to generate new tours which avoid the creation and analysis of non-optimal tours during successive iterations. Standard TSPLIB dataset is used for validation of the proposed technique. Further robustness of GWOA is evaluated on random TSP walks. It is observed from the results that proposed GWOA provides near optimal solution in less number of iterations as compared to WOA and Genetic algorithm (GA) for a given network of TSP.

Keywords: Evolutionary algorithms · Nature-Inspired algorithms
Whale optimization algorithm · Travelling salesman problem

1 Introduction

TSP is a classic optimization problem which aims to create the shortest path by visiting each city once and returning to the source city. It is an NP-hard problem having a non-polynomial complexity which means that an increase in number of cities, increases the computational time exponentially. Classic TSP (CTSP) considers a symmetric path between each pair of cities and fixed distance between them. It is useful in the study of crystal structure, order picking in warehouses for distribution [1], vehicle routing [2, 3], gas guidance in turbine engines of an aircraft [4] and wiring in computer components for efficient data transmission [5] etc. These applications work well with a near optimal solution with reasonable cost. Attempts are made for solving TSP by presenting deterministic algorithms like dynamic programming [6], branch-bound algorithm [7] and stochastic algorithms like genetic algorithm [8], ant colony optimization [9] and simulated annealing [10–12]. The deterministic algorithms produce optimal solutions with the least cost but they are limited to small number of cities. In case of a large number of cities, these algorithms are found computationally very expensive. On contrary, non-deterministic methods provide a quality-time trade-off by presenting better sub-optimal tours with larger number of cities in the TSP network.

© Springer Nature Singapore Pte Ltd. 2018
M. Singh et al. (Eds.): ICACDS 2018, CCIS 905, pp. 321–330, 2018.
https://doi.org/10.1007/978-981-13-1810-8_32

WOA is one of the recently proposed meta-heuristic based on hunting methodology of whales [13]. It is successfully applied to various complex optimization problems like economic dispatch problem [14], work flow planning of construction sites [15] and neural network training [16] etc. These problems are defined for continuous search space [17, 18, 21]. In the present work, WOA is developed for discrete search domain to address the complex problem of CTSP. Further, the performance of WOA is improved by incorporating a guiding mechanism based on greedy search leading to GWOA. Main contributions of the present work are as follows:

1. A maiden attempt is made to develop the discrete version of WOA for solving CTSP.
2. Greediness is used for agent generation with a better tour and local optimization.

Organization of the paper is as follows. Section 2 presents the details of Whale optimization algorithm. Section 3 explains the implementation of GWOA. Section 4 discusses a comparative analysis of GWOA, WOA and GA on TSPLIB dataset. Finally, the work is concluded in Sect. 5.

2   Overview of Whale Optimization Algorithm

WOA imitates the intelligent and magnificent bubble-net feeding technique of humpback whales [13]. Baleen humpback whales hunt in groups and explore the ocean for prey i.e. school of small fish or krill. Once the prey is located, a leader whale dives down about 12 m and starts the process of forming bubbles around it. As the leader whale moves up, a spiral of bubbles constraints the movement of fishes towards a common point. Finally, the group of whale attacks on this location to get food [19, 22].

2.1   Exploration in WOA

Whales search the ocean (n-dimensional search space) for prey and perform random walks without following any leader whale. This phase is mathematically modelled as [13]:

$$\vec{P}(t+1) = \vec{P}_{rand}(t) - \vec{A}.\vec{D} \tag{2.1}$$

$$\vec{D} = |\vec{C}.\vec{P}_{rand}(t) - \vec{P}(t)| \tag{2.2}$$

where $\vec{P}$ is position vector of size $1 \times n$, $\vec{P}_{rand}$ is a randomly selected position vector from the current population, t is current iteration, $\vec{A}$ and $\vec{C}$ are calculated as follows:

$$\vec{A} = 2.\vec{a}.\vec{r} - \vec{a} \tag{2.3}$$

$$\vec{C} = 2.\vec{r} \tag{2.4}$$

where

$$\vec{a} = 2 - 2.\frac{Current\ Iteration}{Total\ Iterations} \tag{2.5}$$

and $\vec{r}$ is a uniformly distributed random vector in the range [0, 1]. The value of $\vec{A}$ controls the movement of whales. $\left|\vec{A}\right| \geq 1$ enables whales to explore the search space, while $\left|\vec{A}\right| < 1$ promotes them to exploit around the best solutions.

2.2 Exploitation (Bubble-Net Attack)

In this phase, the leader whale guides other whales towards the location of prey. Therefore, whales move closer to the leader and encircle the prey. This encircling phenomenon is mathematically modelled by following equations [13]:

$$\vec{P}(t+1) = \vec{P}_{leader}(t) - \vec{A}.\vec{D} \tag{2.6}$$

$$\vec{D} = |\vec{C}.\vec{P}_{leader}(t) - \vec{P}(t)| \tag{2.7}$$

where $\vec{P}_{leader}$ is the best position vector in the current iteration of WOA, $\vec{A}$ is dependent on $\vec{a}$ (Eq. 2.3) which decreases linearly from 2 to 0 over the course of iterations (Eq. 2.5). This simulates shrinking behavior of whales while hunting in groups. Further, the leader's created a spiral wall of bubbles on which other whales attack for food is modeled as follows:

$$\vec{P}(t+1) = \vec{D}e^{bl} \cos(2\pi l) + \vec{P}(t) \tag{2.8}$$

where $\vec{D} = |\vec{C}.\vec{P}_{leader}(t) - \vec{P}(t)|$, b is a constant and l is a random number in the interval $[-1, 1]$. WOA uses the following probabilistic exploitation strategy based on the above equations:

$$\vec{P}(t+1) = \begin{cases} \vec{P}_{leader}(t) - \vec{A}.\vec{D} & \text{if } p < 0.5 \\ \vec{D}e^{bl} \cos(2\pi l) + \vec{P}(t) & \text{if } p \geq 0.5 \end{cases} \tag{2.9}$$

where p is a uniformly distributed random number between 0 and 1.

3 Greedy Whale Optimization Algorithm (GWOA)

Permutation of nodes (cities) is required to solve a complex CTSP problem using meta-heuristic approach. Therefore, an initial solution matrix (P) based on random permutation of cities is generated (Fig. 1).

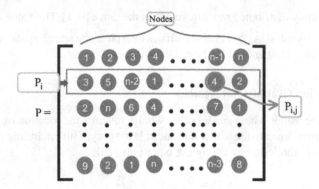

Fig. 1. Initial population matrix P

where $P_{i,j}$ refers to the jth city visited by i^{th} whale. The elements of solution matrix are updated using Eq. (3.1).

$$P_{i,j}(t+1) = \begin{cases} swap(P_{rand,j}(t), P_{rand,k}(t)) & if \ A \geq 1 \\ swap(P_{leader,j}(t), P_{leader,k}(t)) & if \ A < 1 \end{cases} \tag{3.1}$$

where i varies from 1 to m and j varies from 1 to n, k is the node to be swapped and evaluated using following equations:

$$k = \left| j + \left\lfloor \frac{C}{A}.n \right\rfloor \right| - n. \left\lfloor \frac{\left| j + \left\lfloor \frac{C}{A}.n \right\rfloor \right|}{n} \right\rfloor + 1 \tag{3.2}$$

$$k = \left\lfloor D_{leader} e^{bl} \cos(2\pi l) + j \right\rfloor + \left\lfloor \frac{D_{leader} e^{bl} \cos(2\pi l) + j}{n} \right\rfloor + 1 \tag{3.3}$$

Equations (3.2) and (3.3) are the discrete version of Eqs. (2.1) and (2.8) respectively.

The discretization of search domain increases the probability of getting trapped in local minima. This problem is overcome by incorporation of greedy swap technique in WOA called as GWOA. Greedy selection helps in reduction of generation as well as path calculation of inefficient routes. The effect of greedy swap for a P_i at $j = 3$ and $k = 5$ is depicted in Fig. 2. If the distance covered by neighbors of j before swap $(10 + 2 = 12$ in Fig. 2(b)) is greater than the distance after swap $(7 + 2 = 9$ in Fig. 2(c)), algorithm updates P_i (Fig. 2(d)). Swapping results in reduced neighboring distance and therefore overall length of the route is decreased.

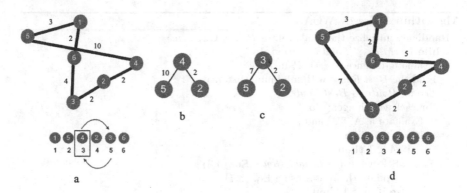

Fig. 2. Greedy Swap: (a) P_i before swap (b) Neighbors of j before swap (c) Neighbors of j after swap (d) P_i after swap

Figure 3 shows the path followed by an artificial whale while solving CTSP. The pseudocode of proposed GWOA is provided in Algorithm 1.

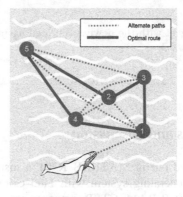

Fig. 3. Whale finding an optimal tour while solving CTSP

Algorithm 1 Greedy WOA

Randomly initialize the whale routes $P_i (i = 1, 2, ..., m)$
while $Iteration \leq Total\ Iteration$ **do**
  Evaluate distance of each P_i in P
  Find the *Best Route* with minimum distance
  Leader Route $\leftarrow$ *Best Route*
  for each search agent **do**
    Evaluate a, A, C, l and p
    if $p < 0.5$ **then**
      if $A < 1$ **then**
        Select k using *Leader Route* Eq. (3.3)
        Update the routes using Eq. (3.1)
      else if $A \geq 1$ **then**
        Select k using random route Eq. (3.2)
        Update the routes using Eq. (3.1)
      end if
    else if $p \geq 0.5$ **then**
      Select k using *Leader Route* Eq. (3.2)
      Update the routes using Eq. (3.1)
    end if
  end for
  Update the current agent with the newly generated agent
  $Iteration \leftarrow Iteration + 1$
end while
return *Leader Route*

---

4 Simulation Results and Discussion

The experiments are carried out in MATLAB R2017a installed on a HP Pavillion computer having a 64-bit operating system with Intel Core I5 CPU 5200U having 2.20 GHz frequency and 8 GB RAM. CTSP instances are considered from standard TSPLIB dataset [20]. A typical instance of city locations (Sgb128) with their corresponding distances is shown in Fig. 4.

The performance of implemented algorithms is evaluated with identical parametric settings for fair comparison i.e. 1000 iteration with 100 agents over 30 independent runs. The statistical mean and standard deviation (SD) of the recorded results are presented in Table 1. It is observed from results that GWOA shows superior performance in comparison to GA and WOA on all datasets except Gr17 and Wgg22. GWOA outperforms both the algorithms as it provides optimal solution with less number of iterations. The convergence rate comparison of algorithms (Fig. 5) also depicts the excellent performance of GWOA.

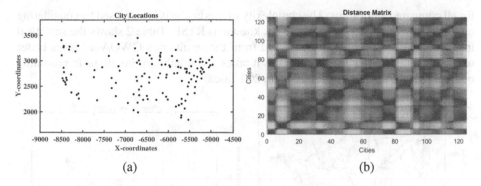

Fig. 4. City locations in Sgb128 (**b**) Distance matrix in Sgb128

Table 1. Comparative analysis of GA, WOA and GWOA

Dataset	No. of cities	GA Distance		WOA Distance		GWOA Distance	
		Mean	SD	Mean	SD	Mean	SD
Uk12	12	1872.78	0	1910.20	50.1033	**1872.78**	0
Gr17	17	1504.65	304.21	1504.65	654.5	1553.42	276.85
Wgg22	22	806.142	22.84	947.15	189.3	861.3911	23.021
Kn57	57	15101.72	353.88	27478.8	3258.7	**15097.72**	337.13
Eil76	76	711.3718	29.74	2015.24	86.7895	**710.4366**	33.7714
Sgb128	128	36752.4	1818.7	145950.54	5401.3	**3436.45**	2536.26

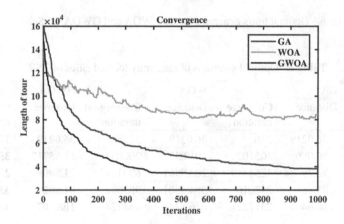

Fig. 5. Convergence rate comparison of algorithms while solving CTSP

Figure 6 shows the optimal routes generated by all the implemented algorithms for Sgb128. The robustness of proposed algorithm is also evaluated in unconstrained environment i.e. unlimited number of iterations with 100 agents. Further 500 iterations without any improvement in tour length is considered as the common stopping criterion for all compared algorithms. The complexity of this analysis is increased by considering randomly located cities of TSP network known as RTSP. Table 2 shows the statistical mean of recorded results. It is observed from the results that GWOA achieves better results than the compared algorithms as it takes less number of iterations in providing optimal tour for all cases of RTSP up to 200 cities.

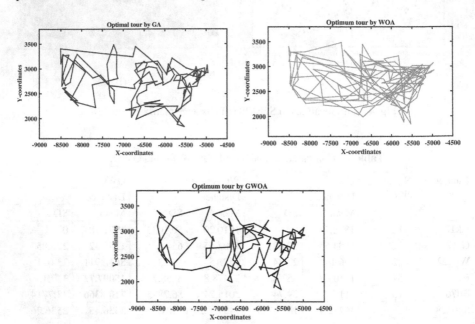

Fig. 6. Optimal tours generated by GA, WOA and GWOA for Sgb128

Table 2. Optimal solutions of randomly located cities of TSP

No. of cities	GA		WOA		GWOA	
	Distance	Converge at iteration	Distance	Converge at iteration	Distance	Converge at iteration
20	36.0219	356	36.0219	31288	**36.0219**	**173**
50	56.086	305102	101.037	200033	**55.95717**	**35473**
80	73.29784	3254499	203.9961	679126	**71.8008**	**226593**
120	83.46	2420169	384.4681	983082	**81.882**	**359428**
200	110.6401	2317221	416.54	884724	**108.1075**	**454667**

5   Conclusion

A discrete version of WOA is proposed for travelling salesman problem. Incorporation of greedy approach with WOA leads to GWOA with improved convergence characteristics while solving TSP network. The proposed technique is evaluated on standard

TSPLIB datasets and compared with WOA and GA. Further, the robustness of GWOA is analyzed using RTSP under unconstrained conditions. It is revealed from the results that GWOA provides more accurate results with better convergence rate in comparison to GA and WOA. Hence it is concluded that the proposed algorithm can be applied to other discrete NP-hard problems.

References

1. Warren, R.: Special cases of the traveling salesman problem. Appl. Math. Comput. **60**, 171–177 (1994)
2. Marinakis, Y., Marinaki, M., Dounias, G.: A hybrid particle swarm optimization algorithm for the vehicle routing problem. Eng. Appl. Artif. Intell. **23**, 463–472 (2010)
3. Savla, K., Frazzoli, E., Bullo, F.: Traveling salesperson problems for the Dubins vehicle. IEEE Trans. Autom. Control **53**, 1378–1391 (2008)
4. Plante, R., Lowe, T., Chandrasekaran, R.: The product matrix traveling salesman problem: an application and solution heuristic. Oper. Res. **35**, 772–783 (1987)
5. Lenstra, J., Kan, A.: Some simple applications of the travelling salesman problem. Oper. Res. Q. **26**(717), 1970–1977 (1975)
6. Bellman, R.: Dynamic programming treatment of the travelling salesman problem. J. ACM **9**, 61–63 (1962)
7. Langevin, A., Desrochers, M., Desrosiers, J., Gélinas, S., Soumis, F.: A two-commodity flow formulation for the traveling salesman and the makespan problems with time windows. Networks **23**, 631–640 (1993)
8. Yang, J., Wu, C., Lee, H., Liang, Y.: Solving traveling salesman problems using generalized chromosome genetic algorithm. Prog. Nat. Sci. **18**, 887–892 (2008)
9. Yang, J., Shi, X., Marchese, M., Liang, Y.: An ant colony optimization method for generalized TSP problem. Prog. Nat. Sci. **18**, 1417–1422 (2008)
10. Lo, C.-C., Hsu, C.-C.: An annealing framework with learning memory. IEEE Trans. Syst. Man Cybern.-Part A: Syst. Hum. **28**, 648–661 (1998)
11. Meer, K.: Simulated annealing versus metropolis for a TSP instance. Inf. Process. Letters **104**, 216–219 (2007)
12. Wang, L., Tian, F., Soong, B., Wan, C.: Solving combinatorial optimization problems using augmented lagrange chaotic simulated annealing. Differ. Equ. Dyn. Syst. **19**, 171–179 (2011)
13. Mirjalili, S., Lewis, A.: The whale optimization algorithm. Adv. Eng. Softw. **95**, 51–67 (2016)
14. Bhesdadiya, R., Parmar, S., Trivedi, I., Jangir, P., Bhoye, M., Jangir, N.: Optimal active and reactive power dispatch problem solution using whale optimization algorithm. Indian J. Sci. Technol. **9** (2016)
15. Kaveh, A., Rastegar Moghaddam, M.: A hybrid WOA-CBO algorithm for construction site layout planning problem. Sci. Iran. (2017)
16. Aljarah, I., Faris, H., Mirjalili, S.: Optimizing connection weights in neural networks using the whale optimization algorithm. Soft Comput. (2016)
17. Jain, M., Singh, V., Rani, A.: A novel nature-inspired algorithm for optimization: squirrel search algorithm. Swarm Evol. Comput. (2018)
18. Jain, M., Maurya, S., Rani, A., Singh, V.: Owl search algorithm: a novel nature-inspired heuristic paradigm for global optimization. J. Intell. Fuzzy Syst. **34**, 1573–1582 (2018)
19. Goldbogen, J., Friedlaender, A., Calambokidis, J., McKenna, M., Simon, M., Nowacek, D.: Integrative approaches to the study of baleen whale diving behavior, feeding performance, and foraging ecology. Bioscience **63**, 90–100 (2013)

20. Reinelt, G.: Tsplib95. Interdisziplinäres Zentrum für Wissenschaftliches Rechnen (IWR), Heidelberg (1995)
21. Singh, M., Srivastava, V.M., Gaurav, K., Gupta, P.K.: Automatic test data generation based on multi-objective ant lion optimization algorithm. In: Pattern Recognition Association of South Africa and Robotics and Mechatronics (PRASA-RobMech), Bloemfontein, pp. 168–174 (2017)
22. Akay, B., Karaboga, D.: A modified Artificial Bee Colony algorithm for real-parameter optimization. Inf. Sci. Int. J. **192**, 120–142 (2012)

Deterministic Task Scheduling Method in Multiprocessor Environment

Ranjit Rajak[✉]

Department of Computer Science and Applications,
Dr. Harisingh Gour Central University, Sagar, M.P., India
ranjit.jnu@gmail.com

Abstract. Task Scheduling is one of the thrust areas of the research in parallel computing where tasks are allocated in the available processors. The objective of the task scheduling method is to minimize the overall execution time in multi-processor environment. A new task scheduling technique is presented in the paper that is extended version of previous developed method: Static Task Scheduling Algorithm with Minimum Distance for multiprocessor system (STMD). The proposed algorithm modified the priority attribute method of STMD algorithm and omitted the communication delay among the tasks during the allocation of the tasks and also excluded duplication of an entry task among the all processors. This method also gives better results as compare to STMD and heuristics algorithms such as HLFET and MCP algorithms. The performance study has been done on the basis of some metrics such as efficiency, load balancing, scheduling length, speedup, and normalized scheduling length

Keywords: Speedup · Task scheduling · Efficiency · Scheduling length
DAG

1 Introduction

Parallel computing [1] is composed of hardware and software and it can be formally defined as the collection of sequential computers which are inter-connected and solve the complex problem in high speed. There are number research areas in parallel computing and task scheduling is one of them. The main goal of any task scheduling algorithm is to identify the optimal schedule which will be reduced the cost of the entire process. Task scheduling problem is generally considered as NP- hard problem [2].

Task scheduling in the multiprocessor environment can be explained as the process of allocating the tasks on the idle processors in order to get minimum scheduling length.

There are various scheduling methods has been developed and their primary goal is to minimize the overall scheduling length.

Every task scheduling problem having mainly three components [3] such as *processor performance, tasks mapping onto available processors and order of execution of the tasks*. Two types of task scheduling are present in multiprocessor environment such as *deterministic and non-deterministic task scheduling*. Deterministic task scheduling can be defined as the information related to scheduling such as number

© Springer Nature Singapore Pte Ltd. 2018
M. Singh et al. (Eds.): ICACDS 2018, CCIS 905, pp. 331–341, 2018.
https://doi.org/10.1007/978-981-13-1810-8_33

processors, number of tasks and the precedence constraints among the tasks are known in advanced. This scheduling is also known as static task scheduling or compile time task scheduling. Minimization of parallel execution time and communication time between the tasks are the two primary objectives [1] of this scheduling. Whereas *non-deterministic task scheduling* can be defined as the information related to scheduling are not known in advanced [1].

Task scheduling is denoted by a well known graph that is Directed Acyclic Graph (DAG) and this graph is basically used to denote of an application. Fig. 1. Shows mapping of an application program to available processors with satisfying precedence constraints among the tasks.

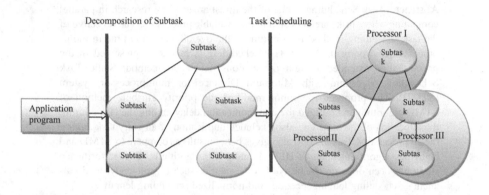

Fig. 1. Processors mapping application program [4]

This paper proposed deterministic task scheduling method that is modified version of Static Task Scheduling Algorithm with Minimum Distance for Multiprocessor System (STMD) [5] and it does not use in the allocation of the tasks onto the available processors. This method provides the minimum scheduling length as compared to STMD and two well known heuristic algorithms HLFET and MCP algorithms [6].

2   Task Scheduling Model

This section is divided into four components such as *Platform Model, Application Model, Task Attributes and Objective function.*

2.1   Platform Model

Platform model can be defined by a graph $Gp = (PE, CL)$ which has two tuples such as PE and CL. That is PE = {PE_1, PE_2,…., PE_n} finite number of processing elements and CL is communication links between the processors. Figure 2 shows the platform model for n = 4 i.e. Four processing elements $PE = \{PE_1, PE_2, PE_3, PE_4\}$.

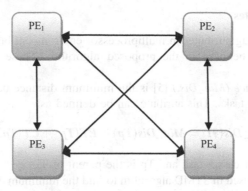

Fig. 2. Platform Model

2.2 Application Model

Consider weighted Directed Acyclic Graph (DAG) represents an application program in task scheduling

It can be defined using 4-tuples as $G = (V, E, CT, ET)$ where $V = \{ T_1, T_2, \ldots T_n\}$ finite set of n tasks of DAG, E is set of edges between the tasks, CT is the communication time between the tasks i.e. CT (T_i, T_j) where T_i and T_j are two different tasks and ET is the execution time of a task T_i on available processor. It is denoted by $ET(T_i)$. Every DAG model having an entry task and an exit task. An entry task T_{entry} is a task which has no parent whereas an exit task T_{exit} is a task which has no children. An example of application model with six tasks is depicted in Fig. 3.

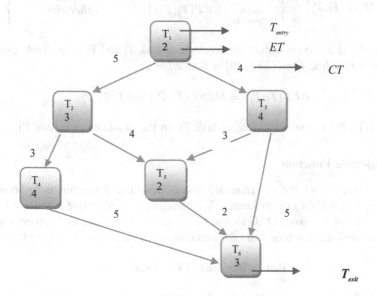

Fig. 3. Application Model [7]

2.3   Task Attributes

Lot of task scheduling attributes in multiprocessor environment but Here, using some attributes that will be used in the proposed algorithm. These are the followings attributes:

Minimum Distance (Min_Dis.) [5] is the minimum distance between the an entry task to its successor tasks. This attribute can be defined as

$$Min\_Dis(Ti) = Min\_Dis(Tp) + ET(Tp) + CT(Tp, Ti)$$

Where Ti is a successor task and Tp is the parent of Ti

This attribute is used in STMD algorithm to find the minimum distance of tasks and as per the priority, sorted the tasks and allocated in the available processors. The proposed algorithm is modified this attribute by excluding communication time between the tasks Tp and Ti. The new attribute is known as *Modified Minimum Distance Attribute (MMin_Dis)*. This can be rewritten as

$$MMin\_Dis.(ti) = \begin{cases} ET(tj) & if\ tj = Tentry \\ MMin\_Dis.(tj) + ET(tj) & Otherwise \end{cases}$$

Where tj is parent task of ti which has minimum distance

The proposed algorithm also not uses the communications time during the allocation of the tasks on to the available processors. For this purposed, *Modified Earliest Start Time (MEST)* [8] *attribute* is used. It can be defined as

$$MEST(T_i, P_j) = \begin{cases} 0 & if\ T_i = T_{entry} \\ \max_{T_j \in pred(T_i)} \{EFT(T_j, P_j)\}, & otherwise \end{cases}$$

where *pred (T_i)* is the immediate predecessor of task T_i and Pj is available processor. *Earliest Finished Time (EFT)* [9] is defined as

$$EFT(T_i, P_j) = MEST(T_i, P_j) + ET(T_i, P_j)$$

where ET(Ti, Pj) is execution time of task Ti on the available processor Pj.

2.4   Objective Function

The key objective of the deterministic task scheduling algorithm is to minimalize scheduling length *(Slen)* i.e. makespan. We can define the objective function can define as an exit task of the given DAG should be allocate onto the available processor which takes minimum starting time and take maximum of execution time of the last task i.e.

$$Slen = Min[Max\{EFT(Texit, Pa)\}]$$

Where *Texit* is an exit task of the given DAG and *Pa* is available processor.

3 Algorithm Design

The proposed algorithm is modified version of previous developed algorithm namely as Static Task Scheduling Algorithm with Minimum Distance for Multiprocessor System (STMD) [5].

The new algorithm has been changed three parameters such as communication time during computing minimum distance attribute is excluded, an entry task as duplicate is not allocated to the processors and third parameter the communication time between the tasks during allocation onto the processors are excluded.

This algorithm proposed a new priority attribute without communication time and the new attribute name as modified minimum distance (MMin_Dis). It can be defined as follows:

$$MMin\_Dis.(ti) = \left\{ \begin{array}{ll} ET(tj) & \textit{if } tj = Tentry \\ MMin\_Dis.(tj) + ET(tj) & \textit{Otherwise} \end{array} \right\}$$

where tj is parent task of ti which has minimum distance

The proposed algorithm will minimize the scheduling length and gives better result compared to STDM algorithm and heuristic algorithms such as HLFET and MCP algorithms. Details of the proposed is shows in the Table 1.

4 Performance Evaluation

An analysis of proposed algorithm and heuristic algorithms has been done based on some performance metrics [6, 10–12] such as

$$Scheduling\ Length(Slen) = Min[Max\{Texit, P\}] \qquad (1)$$

$$Speedup(S) = \frac{\sum_{i=1}^{n} ET(T_i)}{Slen} \qquad (2)$$

$$Efficiency(Eff) = \frac{S}{PEn} \qquad (3)$$

$$Load\ Balancing(Lb) = \frac{Slen}{Average} \qquad (4)$$

$$Normalized\ Scheduling\ Length(NSL) = \frac{Slen}{Critical\ Path} \qquad (5)$$

Table 1. Proposed Algorithm

Step1.   *Application Program as DAG of finite number of tasks {T: t_1, t_2, t_3... t_n}*
Consider T_{entry} is the starting or entry task of given DAG.

Step2.   *Find Minimum distance of all the tasks of given DAG using*

$$MMin\_Dis.(ti) = \begin{cases} ET(tj) & if\ tj = Tentry \\ MMin\_Dis.(tj) + ET(tj) & Otherwise \end{cases}$$

Where tj is parent task of ti which has minimum distance .

Step 3.   *Sorting the tasks in increasing order as per the value of Minimum distance attribute of each task.*

Step 4.   *Allocate the sorted tasks in a Priority Queue Task(PQT)*

Step 5.   **While***(PQT is not empty)* **then**
    Select task ti from PQT
    For *k=1 to PE$_n$ processors* **do**
      If *ti is an entry task* **then**
        ti is allocated to PE$_1$(first processor)
      Else if *ti   is not entry tasks and does not satisfied the Precedence Constraint(PC)***then**
        ti will be inserted into PQT for next turn.
      Else
        ti will be allocated to the available processor as per minimum value of MEST and
        find EFT
    End For
    End While

Step 6.   *Compute Scheduling length i.e. Slen = Min[Max{EFT(Texit, Pa)}]*

Step 7.   **End**

4.1   Numerical Examples

Two DAG1 [6] with nine tasks and DAG2 [13] with twelve tasks models are taken to measure the performance of proposed and heuristic algorithms,. Here, considering four homogenous processors (Figs. 4, 5, 6, 7, 8, 9, 10).

The observation find here that the scheduling length of proposed algorithm is minimum as compared to STDM algorithm and heuristic algorithms such HLFET and MCP algorithms. Other performance metrics such as *Speedup (S)], Efficiency (Eff), Load Balancing (Lb)* and *Normalized Scheduling Length (NSL)* are also better results (Tables 2, 3, 4, 5, 6).

Table 2. Compute MMin_Dis for DAG 1

Task (Ti)	MMin_Dis. From entry task
T1	0
T2	2
T3	2
T4	2
T5	2
T6	5
T7	2
T8	5
T9	6

Table 3. Compute MMin_Dis for DAG 2

Task (Ti)	MMin_Dis. From entry task
T1	0
T2	4
T3	4
T4	4
T5	4
T6	10
T7	8
T8	8
T9	8
T10	15
T11	13
T12	17

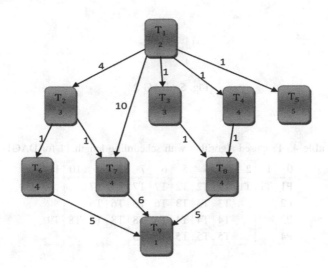

Fig. 4. DAG1

PQT is the list of the tasks which consists of tasks as sorted form as per MMin_Dis. Attribute value of the tasks. The order of the tasks in PQT will be T1, T2, T3, T4, T5, T7, T6, T8, T9. Now allocating the tasks from PQT onto the processor and excluding duplication of an entry task on to all the processors and communication time between the tasks.

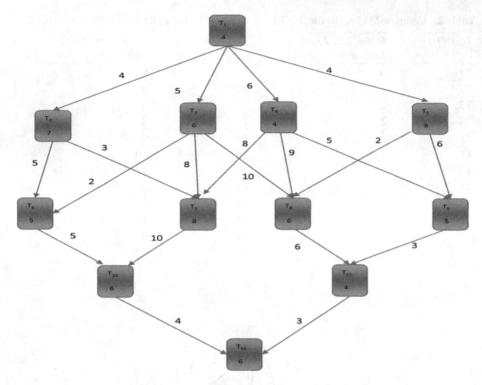

Fig. 5. DAG 2.

Table 4. Proposed algorithm with scheduling length 11 for DAG1

0	1	2	3	4	5	6	7	8	9	10	11
P1	T1	T1	T2	T2	T2	T7	T7	T7	T7		
P2			T3	T3	T3	T6	T6	T6	T6		
P3			T4	T4	T4	T4	T8	T8	T8	T8	T9
P4			T5	T5	T5	T5	T5				

Table 5. Proposed algorithm with scheduling length 31 for DAG2

0	1	2	3	4	5	6	7	8	9	10	11	12	13	14	15	16	17	18	19	20	21	22	23	24	25	31
P1	T1	T1	T1	T1	T2	T2	T2	T2	T2	T2	T2	T7	T7	T7	T7	T7	T7	T7	T7	T10	T10	T10	T10	T10	T10	T12
P2					T3	T3	T3	T3	T3	T3	T8	T8	T8	T8	T8	T8										
P3					T4	T4	T4	T4			T6	T6	T6	T6	T6											
P4					T5	T5	T5	T5	T5	T5	T5	T5	T9	T9	T9	T9	T9	T11	T11	T11	T11						

Table 6. Performance Analysis Result

Scheduling algorithms	DAG1: performance metrics					DAG2: performance metrics				
	Slen	S	Eff	Lb	NSL	Slen	S	Eff	Lb	NSL
Proposed algorithm	11	2.73	68%	1.22	0.48	31	2.23	56%	1.49	0.54
STMD	16	1.87	46%	1.56	0.69	39	1.77	44%	1.43	0.76
HLFET	19	1.57	39%	1.58	0.83	44	1.57	40%	1.50	0.77
MCP	20	1.50	37%	1.50	0.69	42	1.64	41%	1.42	0.73

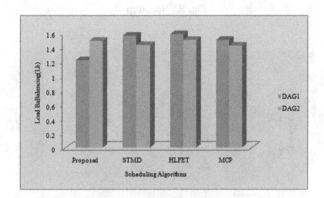

Fig. 6. Load Balancing

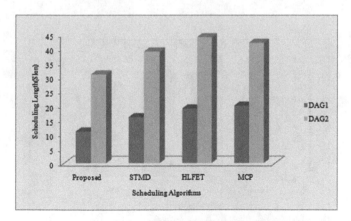

Fig. 7. Scheduling Length

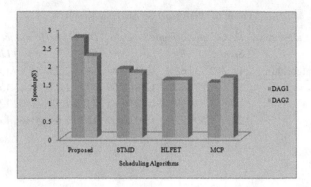

Fig. 8. Speedup

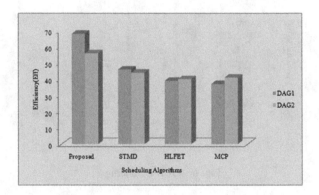

Fig. 9. Efficiency

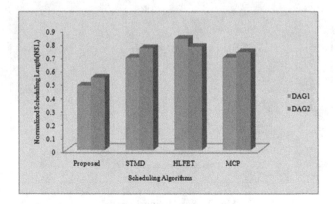

Fig. 10. Normalized Scheduling Length (NSL)

5   Conclusion

The content of proposed algorithm is modified version of STMD algorithm and it has excluded communication time and duplication of an entry task to all the processor. The performance analysis of proposed has been done based on two different models of DAGs and four homogenous processors, it is found that new algorithm reduces the scheduling algorithm. Other performance metrics such as speedup, efficiency, load balancing and normalized scheduling length are also used to compared the proposed and heuristic algorithms such as HLFET and MCP.

References

1. Rajaraman, V., Ram Murthy, C.S.: Parallel Computers Architecture and Programming. PHI Publication (2012)
2. Pinedo, M.L.: Scheduling: Theory, Algorithms and Systems, 3rd edn. Springer, Berlin (2008). https://doi.org/10.1007/978-1-4614-2361-4
3. Singh, J.: Improved task scheduling on parallel system using genetic algorithm. Int. J. Comput. Appl. 39(17) (2012)
4. Sinnen, O.: Task Scheduling for Parallel Systems. Wiley-Interscience Publication (2007)
5. Rajak, R., Katti, C.P.: Static task scheduling algorithm with minimum distance for multiprocessor system (STMD). J. Smart Comput. Rev. South Korea 5(2), 113–125 (2015)
6. Kwok, Y.K., Ahmad, I.: Static scheduling algorithms for allocating directed task graphs to multiprocessors. ACM Comput. Surv. 31(4) (1999)
7. Rajak, R.: Comparison of BNP class of scheduling algorithms based on metrics. GESJ Comput. Sci. Telecomun. 34(2), 35–44 (2012)
8. Rajak, R., Shukla, D., Alim, A.: Modified critical path and top-level attributes (MCPTL)-based task scheduling algorithm in parallel computing. In: Pant, M., Ray, K., Sharma, T.K., Rawat, S., Bandyopadhyay, A. (eds.) Soft Computing: Theories and Applications. AISC, vol. 583, pp. 1–13. Springer, Singapore (2018). https://doi.org/10.1007/978-981-10-5687-1_1
9. Zhou, G., Xu, Y., Tian, S., Zhao, H.: A genetic-based task scheduling algorithms on heterogeneous computing systems to minimize makespan. J. Converg. Inf. Technol. (JCIT) 8 (5), 547–555 (2013)
10. Quinn, M.J.: Parallel Programming in C with MPI and Open MP. Tata McGraw-Hill (2003)
11. Topcuoglu, H., Wu, M.Y.: Performance effective and low complexity task scheduling for heterogeneous computing. IEEE Trans. Parallel Distrib. Comput. 13(3), 260–274 (2002)
12. Omara, F.A., Arafa, M.M.: Genetic algorithm for task scheduling problem. J. Parallel Distrib. Comput. 70, 13–22 (2010)
13. Zhou, L., Shi-xin, S.: A genetic scheduling algorithm based on knowledge for multiprocessor system. In: Proceedings of International Conference on Communications, Circuits and Systems, Kokura, pp. 900–904 (2007)

Performance Comparison of Measurement Matrices in Compressive Sensing

Kankanala Srinivas[✉], Nagapuri Srinivas, Puli Kishore Kumar, and Gayadhar Pradhan

Department of Electronics and Communication Engineering,
National Institute of Technology, Patna 800005, India
{kankanala.ec16,ns,pulikishorek,gdp}@nitp.ac.in

Abstract. Compressive sensing is a new method of signal acquisition and reconstruction through which one can greatly reduce the cost of processing, transmission and storage requirements as compared with the conventional sampling rates. This facilitates the accurate reconstruction of the signals even at sub-Nyquist rates. The role of measurement matrix is indispensable in loyal reconstruction. If the measurement matrix is more obtuse then it takes large computational time for signal reconstruction. This paper mainly focuses on different measurement matrices which are used in compressive sensing. The performance of these measurement matrices for compression and reconstruction of 4 GHz Gaussian modulated sinusoidal pulse are compared in this paper.

Keywords: Compressive sensing · OMP · Measurement matrix

1 Introduction

The conventional digital signal processing is based on the Nyquist criteria which states that any band-limited signal can be exactly reconstructed if it is sampled at least twice the maximum signal frequency [1]. Most of the signal processing systems are using the same criteria. According to this theory, it is not possible to reconstruct the signal if it is sampled at sub-Nyquist rates. Compressive sensing (CS) is a new revolutionary technique in signal processing by which one can do signal acquisition and reconstruction without the limits on the sampling frequency [2]. It can reconstruct the signals based on numerical optimization algorithm.

In the traditional communication, the data is first sampled and then the compression is applied to reduce the storage and transmission costs. Instead, if we combine these two steps into a single step i.e., compressing the signal at the time of sensing itself leads to a new method called compressive sensing. This will reduces the demand of high speed data acquisition systems and also enhances the efficient utilization of resources.

In radar imaging applications higher frequencies are required for good resolution. Designing Analog to Digital Converters (ADC) at that higher sampling

© Springer Nature Singapore Pte Ltd. 2018
M. Singh et al. (Eds.): ICACDS 2018, CCIS 905, pp. 342–351, 2018.
https://doi.org/10.1007/978-981-13-1810-8_34

rates may not be possible with the current day ADC technology. Different beam-forming methods are used to extract the radar images from the radar array. In-order to achieve the higher resolution images large number of array elements and Ultra Wide Band (UWB) signals are required. This results in a huge data collection, storage and high computational complexity. As the processing of data takes more time the targets may change their positions which causes blurred images. Compressive Sensing is the promising technology to acquire reliable, high resolution radar images with fewer data samples and less number of computations.

Emmanuel Candès et al., in the year 2004, proposed a new method in which an original image was reconstructed with less number of data samples that does not follow the Nyquist criterion [3,4]. With the application of CS, Professors of Rice University developed the "single-pixel" camera. Since then compressive sensing has seen many applications in industry.

Compressive Sensing can be applied to the signals which have sparse representation. Most of the natural signals are sparse in one or other domain and are suitable for compressive sensing. Currently, CS is applied in many fields like image processing [5], radar signal processing [6] and communications [7] etc. In CS, the high dimensional signal is converted to low dimension space using measurement matrix. During the re-construction process in CS, the measurement matrix plays a vital role. The measurement matrix and basis matrix should follow the Restricted Isometric Property (RIP) [2]. A great deal of work is going ahead to outline a proficient measurement matrix which will lead to lower computational cost and storage space.

In the remaining part of the paper, the Compressive Sensing framework is presented in Sect. 2. A Gaussian modulated sinusoidal pulse of 4 GHz frequency is used as a test signal for compressive sensing. Different sensing matrices were introduced in Sect. 3. Reconstruction quality and results are discussed in Sect. 4. The paper concludes by summarizing the significance of different measurement matrices for compressive sensing.

2   Compressive Sensing

Compressive sensing is a new technology by which one can reconstruct the original signal with lesser number of random samples [2,8]. The framework of the CS is divided into three major categories: (i) sparse representation, (ii) compression and (iii) reconstruction. The framework of CS is applicable to a signal if it sparse. Most of the natural or man-made signals are sparse in native domain or transform domain. The sparse signal can be compressed to a lower dimensional signal using the measurement matrix. This process is called the compression. These compressed signals are used to recover the original sparse signal using the sparse recovery algorithms. This comes under the solving of under-determined system of linear equations.

CS relies mainly on two principles: sparsity and incoherence. A signal is said to be sparse if most of its components are zeros. In other words the signal should have a fewer non-zero components in its representation. A signal may be sparse in its native domain or can be made sparse in the transformed domain. Coherence is a quality measure of the measurement matrix, lower coherence leads to better performance of the recovery algorithm.

Most common and man-made signals are compressible or can have compact representations when expressed in a favorable basis. Let x represents a signal of length N. If the signal $x \in \mathcal{R}^N$ is assumed to have S-sparse representation in the complete dictionary set of Ψ ($N \times N$ matrix), then x can be expressed as

$$x = \Psi\alpha \tag{1}$$

where α is a sparse signal with S non-zero entries. If a signal y is acquired using M number of random measurements, from the linear combination of the points in x, then it can be written as

$$y = \Phi x = \Phi\Psi\alpha \tag{2}$$

where, Φ is a measurement matrix with dimension $M \times N$. Measurement matrix can be framed by the random measurements or by using different transformations or the combination of the two. If $M << N$ it is not possible to restore the signal accurately from less number of measurements. Such cases are treated as underdetermined system of equations and can be solved using linear algebra but leads to infinite solutions. However, if the signal has the sparse nature, with only S nonzero positions and satisfies the condition $S < M$, then we can pick one exact solution from many by using linear programming [9].

There exists several algorithms to solve this sparse recovery problem. Few among them are Convex optimization, Greedy approach and Bayesian methods. In convex category, a solution is obtained using optimization algorithms like basis pursuit, gradient descent. These are complex in nature and require high recovery time. Greedy techniques which are iterative in nature provides the result in a faster manner whereas bayesian based procedures requires prior information about the sparse signal. In general, the existence of a unique solution is dependent on the measurement matrix. This paper uses greedy based Orthogonal Matching Pursuit (OMP) algorithm [10] for signal reconstruction and analyses the effect of different measurement matrices in compressive sensing.

3   Measurement Matrices

Measurement matrix plays a vital role in compressive sensing. Particularly for faithful signal reconstruction the compressed signals should contain all the significant information. Otherwise it is not possible to reconstruct the the original signal back. Measurement matrix takes the prominent role both in signal compression and reconstruction. Choosing an efficient measurement matrix is very much necessary for CS.

The quality of measurement matrix is decided by the following conditions: Coherence and Restricted Isometric Property (RIP). If the measurement matrix follows the above two properties, it ensures the uniqueness of the reconstructed signal. Coherence of a matrix measures the most extreme connection between any two columns of the matrix. Smaller the coherence better the reconstruction, which means that with fewer samples perfect recovery is possible for sparse signal.

If Φ is a measurement matrix of $M \times N$ having normalized column vectors $\Phi_1, \Phi_2, \Phi_3, ...\Phi_N$. Then the mutual coherence constant is defined as

$$\mu(\Phi) = \max_{i \neq j} \frac{| < \Phi_i . \Phi_j > |}{||\Phi_i||_2 . ||\Phi_j||_2} \tag{3}$$

Restricted Isometric Property (RIP) is also called as the uniform uncertainty principle. It assures the success of sparse recovery algorithms. The restricted isometric constant of order s involves all s-tuples of columns of measurement matrix, unlike coherency which takes pairs of columns. With the coherence, smaller restricted isometric constants are desired. The formal definition of the RIP is as follows.

$$(1 - \delta_k)||x||_2^2 \leq ||\Phi x||_2^2 \leq (1 + \delta_k)||x||_2^2 \tag{4}$$

The measurement matrix Φ satisfy the RIP property if there exist a constant δ_k satisfying the above equation [11]. The $\delta_k \in [0, 1]$ is called the restricted isometric constant of Φ and the value should be smaller than 1.

A number of measurement matrices which follows the above properties has been already proposed. These can be comprehensively partitioned into two classes: random and deterministic.

Random matrices are produced using random functions. They are easy to generate and satisfy the RIP with higher probabilities. These are again divided into two types: structured and unstructured. Structured random matrices are generated by selecting the random rows of generated random functions. Examples are partial hadamard matrix and random partial Fourier matrices. Matrices of unstructured type are generated using the given distribution function. Examples are Gaussian and Bernoulli which are generated using the Gaussian and Bernoulli distributions.

Unlike the random matrices which are generated in random form, deterministic matrices are constructed deterministically that satisfy the RIP and coherency properties. These are additionally of two sorts: semi-deterministic and full deterministic. Semi-deterministic matrices are generated in two stages. In the initial step, entries of the first column are generated randomly based on some functions. In the second stage, remaining columns of the matrix are generated by applying a straight forward change on the first column. Examples are Circulant and Toeplitz frameworks. Full-deterministic matrices have an unadulterated deterministic development. Examples of these type include Chirp sensing, second-order Reed-Solomon and Quasi-Cyclic Low-Density Parity-Check code (QC-LDPC).

This paper selects the Gaussian random matrices, Random Bernoulli matrices, random partial Fourier matrix, partial orthogonal random matrices, partial hadamard matrices, Toeplitz matrices and chaotic random matrices [12–16] as measurement matrices for radar pulse compression and reconstruction using CS.

3.1 Gaussian Random Measurement Matrix

The probability density function of a random variable x in Gaussian distribution is given as

$$f(x) = \frac{1}{\sqrt{2\pi\sigma^2}} e^{-\frac{(x-\mu)^2}{2\sigma^2}} \qquad (5)$$

where μ is the expectation or the mean, and σ^2 is the variance of the distribution. The elements of the Gaussian random matrix $\Phi_{i,j}$ are independent random variables which obey the Gaussian distribution with mean of 0 and variance 1. It can be written as

$$\Phi_{i,j} = N(0,1) \qquad (6)$$

The random matrix Φ ($M \times N$) satisfies the RIP with probability of at least $1 - \varepsilon$ provided

$$M \geq \frac{Cs}{\varepsilon^2} log(\frac{N}{\varepsilon^2 s}) \qquad (7)$$

where C is a common constant ($C > 0$), M indicates the number of measurements to take out from N, which is the length of the input signal and s is the sparsity level [17]. This accurately reconstruct the signal and is most commonly used. But the problem with this matrix is that all the elements are uncertain and need to be stored. That means this matrix requires large storage and high computational complexity which indicates difficult hardware implementation.

3.2 Random Bernoulli Matrix

Each element in this matrix follows Bernoulli distribution which is a discrete probability distribution and a special case of binomial distribution. If X is a random variable with this distribution, we have:

$$Pr(X = 1) = p = 1 - q = 1 - Pr(X = 0) \qquad (8)$$

The probability mass function f of this distribution, over k possible outcomes, is

$$f(k;p) = \begin{cases} p, & \text{if } k = 1 \\ 1-p, & \text{if } k = 0 \end{cases} \qquad (9)$$

Bernoulli matrix $B \in R^{M \times N}$ is having the entries of $+1$ or -1 and is given by

$$\Phi_{i,j} = \begin{cases} 1, & \text{if } p = 1/2 \\ -1, & \text{if } 1 - p = 1/2 \end{cases} \qquad (10)$$

where p denotes the probability of the value.

The condition to satisfy RIP for random Bernoulli matrix is same as the Gaussian random matrix [12].

3.3 Random Partial Fourier Matrix

Partial Fourier matrix is formed using the Fourier matrix of size $N \times N$. In this case first we will generate a Fourier matrix of size $N \times N$ whose entries are given by the equation

$$\Phi_{m,n} = \exp^{2\pi imn/N} \tag{11}$$

where $m, n = 1, 2, 3.....N$. From this $N \times N$ matrix, an $M \times N$ measurement matrix is constructed by selecting M random rows. If $M \geq C.s.log(N/\varepsilon)$, [18] this matrix follows the RIP with a probability of at least $1 - \varepsilon$.

3.4 Partial Orthogonal Random Matrix

Matrix Φ is said to be orthogonal, if it satisfies the condition $\Phi^T \Phi = I$. Thus the column vector of a matrix Φ is a standard orthogonal vector. The method of constructing a partial orthogonal matrix includes the generation of an $N \times N$ orthogonal matrix Φ, and selecting M random rows from that matrix.

3.5 Partial Hadamard Matrix

Hadamard matrix is a square matrix composed by elements $+1$ and -1 and satisfies the orthogonality condition. The method of generating the partial hadamard matrix is same as the partial orthogonal matrix except for the generation of hadamard matrix in place of orthogonal matrix. This matrix follows RIP with probability of at least $1 - \frac{5}{N} - e^{-\beta}$, if $M \geq C_0(1 + \beta)SlogN$, where β and C_0 are constants.

3.6 Toeplitz Matrix

This matrix is generated by using the successive shift of a random variable t where $t = (t1, t2.....t_{Q+M-1})\varepsilon R^{Q+M-1}$. The vector t is generated by using the Bernoulli distribution function whose entries are $+1$ or -1. This is a circulant matrix with constant diagonal i.e. $t_{m,n} = t_{m+1,n+1}$. The matrix is framed in the following form

$$\Phi = \begin{bmatrix} t_Q & t_{Q-1} & \cdots & t_1 \\ t_{Q+1} & t_Q & \cdots & t_2 \\ \vdots & \vdots & \ddots & \vdots \\ t_{Q+M-1} & t_{Q+M-2} & \cdots\cdots & t_Q \end{bmatrix} \tag{12}$$

After forming the $N \times N$ matrix, a random $M \times N$ matrix is selected such that the Toeplitz matrix follows the RIP with probability at least $\delta_k < \delta$ if $M \geq C\delta S^2 log(N/S)$. The (m,n)th entry of t is given by $t_{m,n} = t_{m-n}$. The structural characteristics of this matrices reduce the randomness of elements, which impacts in reducing the memory and hardware complexity. But this matrix does not correlate with all the signals and is used only with some special signals.

3.7   Chaotic Random Matrices

The chaotic random matrices can be derived from the logistic map function which can be expressed as $x_n + 1 = \mu x_n(1 - x_n)$ where $\mu \varepsilon(0, 4)$ and $x_n \varepsilon(0, 1)$. For the special case of $\mu = 4$, the solution of the system is given by $x_n = (1/2)(1 - cos(2pi\theta 2^n))$, where $\theta \varepsilon [0, pi]$ which satisfies $x_0 = (1/2)(cos2pi\theta)$ [14]. It is well known that chaotic system can produce very complex sequences. The chaotic matrix is given by

$$\Phi = \sqrt{\frac{2}{M}} \begin{bmatrix} x_0 & \cdots & x_{M(N-1)} \\ x_1 & \cdots & x_{M(N-1)+1} \\ \vdots & \ddots & \vdots \\ x_{M-1} & \cdots\cdots & x_{MN-1} \end{bmatrix} \tag{13}$$

where the scalar $\sqrt{2/M}$ is for normalization. Chaotic matrix follows the RIP for constant $\delta > 0$ with good probability providing that $s \leq O(M/log(N/s))$.

4   Simulation and Analysis

Figure 1(a) shows the Gaussian modulated sinusoidal pulse of 4 GHz frequency which is used as input signal for compressive sensing. The Gaussian pulse itself is treated as a sparse representation because it has more number of zeros. The compresssion is performed using different measurement matrices as discussed

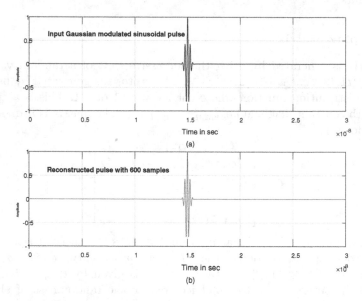

Fig. 1. (a) Input Gaussian modulated sinusoidal pulse (b) Reconstructed Pulse with 600 Samples

in Sect. 3. Finally, the Gaussian pulse is successfully recovered using OMP algorithm and the recovered signal is shown in Fig. 1(b). PSNR (Peak Signal to Noise Ratio) and recovery time is taken as the key parameters to evaluate the measurement matrix performance for faithful signal reconstruction. The simulations are carried out on MATLAB R2015a software with Intel I7 octa core processor.

During simulation, the length of the original signal is taken as 3600 samples. The value of M, which is the number of compressed measurements from the input samples, is varied from 1 to 600 with a displacement of 30. Peak Signal to Noise Ratio (PSNR) is calculated to show the difference between the recovered and original signal and the equation used is $PSNR = 20log\frac{MAX(x)}{\sqrt{MSE}}$, $MSE = \frac{1}{N}\sum(\hat{x} - x)^2$ where x and $\hat{x}$ are the original and recovered signals respectively.

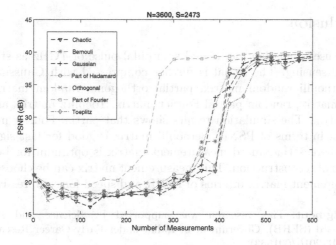

Fig. 2. Plot of PSNR for different measurements

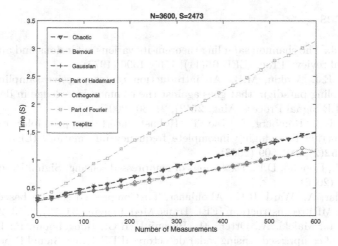

Fig. 3. Plot of reconstruction time for different measurements

Figures 2 and 3 shows the graphs of PSNR and execution time of the reconstructed signal for different lengths of the compressed signal respectively. From the figures it can be concluded that partial Fourier matrix is giving the highest PSNR for almost all measurements as compared with the other matrices. However, it fails interms of execution time. As the number of measurements increases the execution time increases, and is the highest comparing with other measurement matrices. In the case of signal recovery time Bernoulli matrix is taking the lowest computation time as compared with other matrices. However, interms of PSNR value it is not the lowest compared with the other measurement matrices. On the other hand Hadamard matrix gives good performance in terms of both PSNR and recovery times. Hence, this matrix is preferred as measurement matrix for signal reconstruction using CS.

5   Conclusion

This paper uses Gaussian modulated sinusoidal pulse of 4 GHz as stimulus for compressive sensing. The signal is further compressed with Gaussian random matrix, Bernoulli random matrix, partial orthogonal random matrix, partial hadamard matrix, random partial Fourier matrix, Toeplitz matrix, and chaotic random matrix. The simulation results shows that partial Fourier matrix performs better in terms of PSNR, Bernoulli matrix is good for fast signal reconstruction whereas Hadamard measurement matrix is optimum for both PSNR and fast signal reconstruction. This measurement matrix can be choosen as optimum measurement matrix interms of PSNR and speed for compressive sensing.

Acknowledgment. This research was supported by Science and Engineering Research Board (SERB), Government of India, under Early Career Research Award scheme (ECR/2016/001563).

References

1. Jerri, A.J.: The shannon sampling theorem-its various extensions and applications: a tutorial review. Proc. IEEE **65**(11), 1565–1596 (1977)
2. Candes, E.J., Wakin, M.B.: An introduction to compressive sampling: a sensing/sampling paradigm that goes against the common knowledge in data acquisition. IEEE Signal Process. Mag. **25**(2), 21–30 (2008)
3. Candès, E.J., Romberg, J., Tao, T.: Robust uncertainty principles: exact signal reconstruction from highly incomplete frequency information. IEEE Trans. Inf. Theory **52**(2), 489–509 (2006)
4. Tsaig, Y., Donoho, D.L.: Extensions of compressed sensing. Signal Process. **86**(3), 549–571 (2006)
5. Majumdar, A., Ward, R.K., Aboulnasr, T.: Compressed sensing based real-time dynamic MRI reconstruction. IEEE Trans. Med. Imaging **31**(12), 2253–2266 (2012)
6. Anitori, L., Maleki, A., Otten, M., Baraniuk, R.G., Hoogeboom, P.: Design and analysis of compressed sensing radar detectors. IEEE Trans. Signal Process. **61**(4), 813–827 (2013)

7. Yang, X., Tao, X., Dutkiewicz, E., Huang, X., Guo, Y.J., Cui, Q.: Energy-efficient distributed data storage for wireless sensor networks based on compressed sensing and network coding. IEEE Trans. Wirel. Commun. **12**(10), 5087–5099 (2013)
8. Candes, E.J., Tao, T.: Near-optimal signal recovery from random projections: universal encoding strategies? IEEE Trans. Inf. Theory **52**(12), 5406–5425 (2006)
9. Candès, E.J., Romberg, J.K., Tao, T.: Stable signal recovery from incomplete and inaccurate measurements. Commun. Pure Appl. Math. **59**(8), 1207–1223 (2006)
10. Tropp, J.A., Gilbert, A.C.: Via orthogonal matching pursuit. IEEE Trans. Inf. Theory **53**(12), 4655–4666 (2007)
11. Candès, E.J.: The restricted isometry property and its implications for compressed sensing. Comptes Rendus Math. **346**(9–10), 589–592 (2008)
12. Zhang, G., Jiao, S., Xu, X., Wang, L.: Compressed sensing and reconstruction with Bernoulli matrices. In: 2010 IEEE International Conference on Information and Automation, ICIA 2010, pp. 455–460 (2010)
13. Wipf, D.P., Rao, B.D.: Sparse Bayesian learning for basis selection. IEEE Trans. Signal Process. **52**(8), 2153–2164 (2004)
14. Yu, L., Barbot, J.P., Zheng, G., Sun, H.: Compressive sensing with chaotic sequence. IEEE Trans. Signal Process. **17**(8), 731–734 (2010)
15. Applebaum, L., Howard, S.D., Searle, S., Calderbank, R.: Chirp sensing codes: deterministic compressed sensing measurements for fast recovery. Appl. Comput. Harmon. Anal. **26**(2), 283–290 (2009). https://doi.org/10.1016/j.acha.2008.08.002
16. Haupt, J., Bajwa, W.U., Raz, G., Nowak, R.: Toeplitz compressed sensing matrices with applications to sparse channel estimation. IEEE Trans. Inf. Theory **56**(11), 5862–5875 (2010)
17. Mendelson, S., Pajor, A., Tomczak-Jaegermann, N.: Uniform uncertainty principle for Bernoulli and subgaussian ensembles. Constr. Approx. **28**(3), 277–289 (2008)
18. Yu, N.Y., Li, Y.: Deterministic construction of Fourier-based compressed sensing matrices using an almost difference set. Eurasip J. Adv. Signal Process. **2013**(1), 1–14 (2013)

A Novel Approach by Cooperative Multiagent Fault Pair Learning (CMFPL)

Deepak A. Vidhate[1]([⊠]) and Parag Kulkarni[2]

[1] Department of Computer Engineering, College of Engineering, Pune, Maharashtra, India
dvidhate@yahoo.com
[2] iKnowlation Research Laboratory Pvt. Ltd., Pune, Maharashtra, India
parag.india@gmail.com

Abstract. The paper gives the novel approach by cooperative multiagent fault pair learning (CMFPL) for dynamic decision making in the retail shop application based on proposed improved Nash Q learning using Fault Pair Algorithm. The novel move considers three retailer shops in the retail market. Shops must support each other to gain maximum revenue from cooperative knowledge via learning their own policies. The suppliers are the intelligent agents to utilize the cooperative learning to train in the situation. Assuming significant theory on the shop's storage plan, restock time, arrival process of the customers, the approach is formed as Markov decision process model that makes it feasible to develop the learning algorithms. The proposed algorithm obviously learn changing market situation. In addition, the paper demonstrate results of cooperative reinforcement learning algorithms. Results obtained by two approaches i.e. Nash Q Learning and improved Nash Q leaning by Fault Pair are compared. An agent keeps Q-functions containing joint actions and carries out modifications depending on Nash equilibrium performance for the present Q-values. Paper discovers that the agents are intended to attain a joint best possible path with Nash Q-learning. The performance of both agents enhanced after using Fault pair Nash Q-learning.

Keywords: Cooperative learning · Fault pair learning · Reinforcement learning Multi-agent learning · Nash Q learning

1 Introduction

Multiagent reinforcement learning (MARL) is a practical move towards the implementation of multi-agent cooperation jobs, like cooperation in multi-robot system and controlling the traffic signal [1]. However, MARL has difficulty with developing high-quality results because the nature of the agents is very complicated to permit for cooperation through other agents. Especially, the cooperative nature of agents is hardly developed for any diagnostic applications. Most of the methods given in the literature, [2], put forward that agent to cooperate with one another by getting the data of other agents during the conversation. This data is helpful for cooperation between the agents. Therefore, it is significant to discover approaches to accomplish multi-agent cooperation for diagnostic applications [3]

© Springer Nature Singapore Pte Ltd. 2018
M. Singh et al. (Eds.): ICACDS 2018, CCIS 905, pp. 352–361, 2018.
https://doi.org/10.1007/978-981-13-1810-8_35

The objective of predicting the sales business is to assemble data from different stores and investigate it by reinforcement learning algorithms. The capable consequences of the real data by simple methods are not actually possible since the data is tremendously huge [4]. The association between the customers and the retail stores is calculated and the changes that need obtaining extra profit are prepared. Moreover, the history of the sale of each product in each shop and section is retained. By investigating these, the sales are forecasted that make possible the accepting of profit and loss occur in one year [5]. In Christmas festival, the transactions are increased in particular stores like clothing, footwear, jewelry etc. During summer period the sale of cotton clothing is increased. The sale of products varies as by the season. By investigating the history of sale, the purchases can be predicted for the future [6].

Retail shop prediction has many issues. Particularly, retailers are ineffective to approximate the market situation [7]. Retailers do not consider the seasonal changes. The retailers face the problem in inventory management of the stop. As a result, they could not concentrate on the competition or cooperation in the business. Retailers should develop a proper plan that must helpful towards the successful business [8].

Generally, the profit received from the sale of a particular item is considered for predicting the highest potential of the number of purchases for given time period in dynamic conditions. It creates an impact on the upcoming purchase of items in a particular store [9]. Items to purchase and sell, storage management, and warehouse management are the critical tasks in the designing the shop. Accordingly, observing the previous records of the shop supports to propose a model of the sale and create the required alteration in the scheme to become the maximum commercial [10].

Wedding scenario is considered for the development. Starting with the selection of a spot, invitations, beautification, the catering arrangement, purchase of clothes, jewelry and accessories for bride and groom. Moreover, such seasonal scenarios must realistically implement as: Person purchasing clothing must go to buy jewellery, footwear, and other accessories. Consequently, the seller of various products must come together in cooperation to satisfy customer need. In addition to this, seller declares smart ideas like a festive offer, concession on selected products, 'Buy one Get one free' to attract the consumers. Under the situations, the seller must forecast and maintain their inventory updated. As a result, it should enhance the total products sell giving the more profit for each shop [10, 11].

2 Related Work

A multiagent system (MAS) has become more & more popular because of its wide application outlook, which has numerous research avenues containing formation [11], foraging [12], prey-pursuing [13], and robot soccer [14]. Robot soccer is connected with robot design, decision making, planning and communication, which possess all the important characteristics of the multi-agent system. The robot soccer system is explained as a standard in the paper [15].

Q- learning concept from reinforcement learning [16] has straight use in a multiagent system for decision making. It disobeys the stationary surroundings hypothesis of

Markov Decision Process (MDP) [17]. In multi-agent, action selection of the learning agent is certainly challenged by actions of other agents, so multi-agent reinforcement learning concerning joint state and joint action is further appropriate and capable approach [18].

Multi-agent reinforcement learning depend on Stochastic Game (SG) that can be also called Markov game (MG) has a firm conceptual base, which has expended into various subdivision for example Mini-Max Q learning [19], Nash [20], FF [21], and CE [22] Q learning algorithms. These algorithms study joint action values which are fixed and in some situations ensure that these values can lead to Nash equilibrium (NE) values or correlated equilibrium (CE) values [23].

Fault pairing has been implemented both in game theory [24] and computer science. Fault pair calculates how much bad an algorithm achieve compare with the best static policy whose aim is to ensure at least zero standard faults. Fault pairing [25] ensures that the joint action will asymptotically lead towards a set of points of no-fault that can be considered to as common connected equilibrium in Markov Games [26]. Because Nash equilibrium is in fact coarse correlated equilibrium [27], it can be conditional that fault pairing that converges to joint action points of coarse correlated equilibrium can successfully enhance the convergence rate of original Nash Q learning algorithm [28, 29].

3   Proposed Fault Pair Learning Algorithm

To obtain the Nash Equilibrium $\pi^1(s_t)$..... $\pi^k(s_t)$ ....$\pi^n(s_t)$ agent i require to identify Q functions $Q_t^1(s_t)$ .....$Q_t^k(s_t)$ ....$Q_t^n(s_t)$. Agent i should have imagined regarding Q values at the starting. As the event progress, agent i monitor another agents' direct reinforcements and earlier actions. Accordingly, this data is utilized for modification of agents i's assumption upon another agents' Q function. Agent i update its actions about agent j's Q values as per the following equation [30, 31].

$$Q_{t+1}^j\left(s_t, a_t^1 \dots a_t^k \dots a_t^n\right) = \left(1 - \alpha_t\right)Q_t^j\left(s_t, a_t^1 \dots a_t^k \dots a_t^n\right) + \alpha_t\left[r_t^j + \gamma \operatorname{Nash} Q_t^j\left(s_{t+1}\right)\right] \tag{1}$$

However, this equation does not modify each & every content of the Q table. It modifies simply the contents related current situation of the agents. That means there is need of backtracking or repairing of fault made by an agent [31, 32]. Hence the new approach is projected. The approach is inspired by the decision-making problem solving of a human being. If a decision went wrong, a person feels sorry for it. A human can understand better through past experience and feeling apologetic. So he then tries to improve the action taken in a situation and enhance the learning efficiency. Feeling disappointed drives him toward better strategy and to build development rapidly. Joint action will convey each one better reward if people accept such thought [33]. A no-fault point characterizes a case for which the average reward which an agent actually obtained is as much as the counterpart that the agent "would have" obtained had the agent used a dissimilar permanent policy at all earlier time episodes [34, 35].

A new algorithm Nash-Q learning with backtracking or fault pair is projected to enhance the speed of convergence in multi-agent systems. In the given algorithm, backtracking or fault pair is utilized to choose the action in each state to improve the convergence speed toward Nash equilibrium strategy [35, 36].

$$F_i^{ai}(s,t) = \frac{1}{N} \sum_{m=0}^{N-1} \left(r_i\left(s, a_i a_{-i}(m)\right) - r_i(s, a(m)) \right) \tag{2}$$

According to the above notation,

We define the average fault $F_i^{ai}(s,t)$ of agent i at time t and in state s as where

a_{-i} denotes the collective $(a_1, \ldots, a_{i-1}, a_{i+1}, \ldots a_n)$, of agents' action except agent i,

a represents the joint actions $(a_1, \ldots, a_n)$ of all agents, and

N represents the number of state s visited.

Above equation shows that average fault pair for $a_i \in A_i$ of agent i presents the normal increase in the reward if it had preferred $a_i \in A_i$ in all previous episodes and all other agents' actions had stay unchanged up to time t. Fault pairing based each agent i computes $F_i^{ai}(s,t)$ for every action $a_i \in A_i$ using the following iterative equation [37]:

$$F_i^{ai}(s,t) = \frac{t-1}{t} F_i^{ai}(s, t-1) + \frac{1}{t} \left(r_i\left(s, a_i a_{-i}(t)\right) - r_i(s, a(t)) \right) \tag{3}$$

At every time stage $t > 0$, agent i updates all entries included in his average fault collect $F_i(s,t) = \left[F_i^{ai}(s,t) \right]$. In fault pairing after agent i calculated its average fault collected $F(s,t)$, action $a_i(s,t)$ is selected according to the probability distribution $p_i(t)$, as shown in the following equation [38, 39]:

$$P_i^{ai} = \Pr\left[a_i(s,t) = a_i \right] = \frac{F_i^{ai}(s,t)}{\sum \left[F_i^{ai'}(s,t) \right]} \tag{4}$$

where $p_i(t)$ is the uniform distribution over A_i.

In other words, an agent using fault pair/backtracking selects a specific action at any time episode with possibility relative to the normal backtrack for not selecting that specific action in the previous time episodes [39].

4   Results of Fault Pair Learning Algorithm

4.1   Agent 1

Figure 1 shows yearly analysis for shop agent 1. The graph indicates profit margin vs months for three methods i.e. simple Q learning, Nash Q learning and Fault Pair. Proposed Fault Pair method leads to considerable enhancement in income as compared to simple Q learning and Nash Q learning methods.

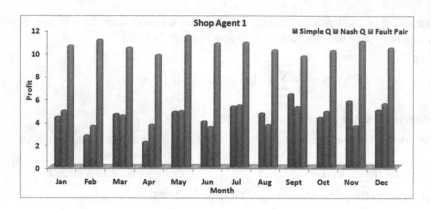

Fig. 1. Yearly analysis for agent 1

Figure 2 shows reward analysis for shop agent 1. The graph indicates average reward vs months for two methods i.e. Nash Q learning and Fault Pair learning. The average reward per month is increased as agent obtained more experience of cooperating. Highest average reward obtained by shop agent 1 using proposed Fault Pair method and Nash Q learning method are 8.86 and 8.36 correspondingly and the lowest average reward obtained are 4.93 and 4.31 respectively. A greater average reward signifies that the agents employed good cooperation strategies to obtain more profit.

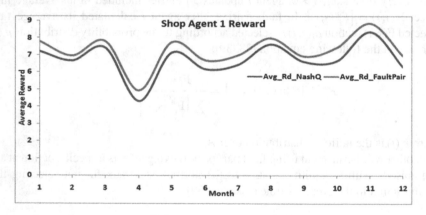

Fig. 2. Agent 1 reward

4.2 Agent 2

Figure 3 shows yearly analysis for shop agent 2. The graph indicates profit margin vs months for three methods i.e. simple Q learning, Nash Q learning and Fault Pair. Proposed Fault Pair method leads to considerable enhancement in income as compared to simple Q learning and Nash Q learning methods. It is detected from the graph that there is the very minimum difference between the profit obtained by simple Q learning and Nash Q learning methods for agent 2.

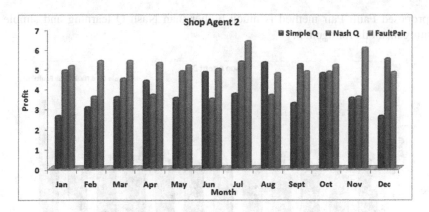

Fig. 3. Yearly analysis for agent 2

Figure 4 shows reward analysis for shop agent 2. The graph indicates average reward vs months for two methods i.e. Nash Q learning and Fault Pair learning. The average reward per month is increased as agent obtained more experience of cooperating. Highest average reward obtained by shop agent 2 using proposed Fault Pair method and Nash Q learning method are 4.98 and 4.54 correspondingly and the lowest average reward obtained are 3.58 and 3.29 respectively. A greater average reward signifies that the agents employed good cooperation strategies to obtain more profit.

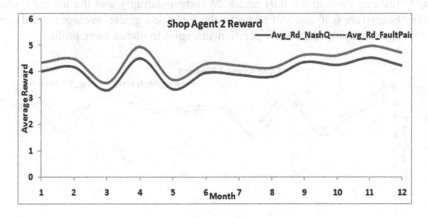

Fig. 4. Agent 2 reward

4.3   Agent 3

Figure 5 shows yearly analysis for shop agent 3. The graph indicates profit margin vs months for three methods i.e. simple Q learning, Nash Q learning and Fault Pair Proposed Fault Pair method leads to considerable enhancement in income as compared to simple Q learning and Nash Q learning methods. It is also detected that profit gained by proposed Fault Pair method is much higher than Nash Q learning and simple Q learning methods for agent 3.

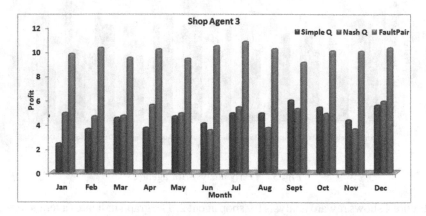

Fig. 5. Yearly analysis for agent 3

Figure 6 shows reward analysis for shop agent 3. The graph indicates average reward vs months for two methods i.e. Nash Q learning and Fault Pair learning. The average reward per month is increased as agent obtained more experience of cooperating. Highest average reward obtained by shop agent 3 using proposed Fault Pair method and Nash Q learning method are 8.91 and 8.29 correspondingly and the lowest average reward obtained are 6.36 and 5.91 respectively. Because a greater average reward signifies that agents employed good cooperation strategies to obtain more profit.

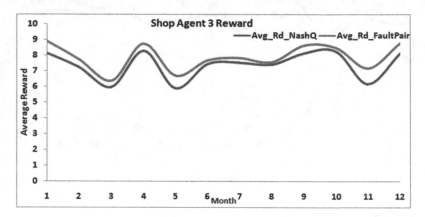

Fig. 6. Agent 3 reward

4.4   Multiagent System Analysis

Evaluation of three agents with reference to profit and reward for simple Q learning, Nash Q learning and Fault Pair learning for multiagent system i.e. for all three agents for the one-year is shown in the graph in Fig. 7. It indicates average profit gained by the multiagent system in one-year by using Nash Q learning and Fault Pair learning. Profit gained by the multiagent system by using proposed Fault Pair learning method is much more than the profit obtained by the state-of-the-art methods.

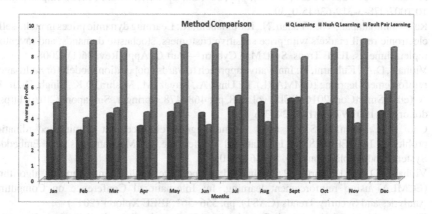

Fig. 7. Average profit analysis for multiagent system

5 Conclusion

The paper presents a new reinforcement learning approach combing Nash-Q with Fault Pair learning algorithm to enhance the convergence rate of existing Nash-Q algorithm. It has higher learning efficiency than the original Nash-Q learning algorithm. In particular, the new algorithm Nash-Q learning with fault pair takes less time to convergence as compared to Nash-Q equilibrium. The paper presents a new multi-agent reinforcement learning approach combining Nash-Q learning with fault pair to increase the convergence rate of an original Nash-Q learning algorithm that learns Nash-Q equilibrium values by random action selection in a multi-agent system. Paper investigates how to make improved action selection in original Nash-Q learning algorithm through fault pair. Examining with the existing Nash-Q learning approach, the results of proposed experiments validate that Nash-Q learning with Fault Pairing algorithm has better achievements in terms of reinforcements received, and strategy convergence for getting the Nash equilibrium strategy.

References

1. Park, K.-H., Kim, Y.-J., Kim, J.-H.: Modular Q-learning based multi-agent cooperation for robot soccer. Robot. Auton. Syst., 3026–3033 (2015)
2. Camara, M., Bonham-Carter, O., Jumadinova, J.: A multi-agent system with reinforcement learning agents for biomedical text mining. In: Proceedings of the 6th ACM Conference on Bioinformatics, Computational Biology and Health Informatics, BCB 2015, pp. 634–643. ACM (2015)

3. Iima, H., Kuroe, Y.: Swarm reinforcement learning methods improving certainty of learning for a multi-robot formation problem. In: CEC, pp. 3026–3033, May 2015
4. Vidhate, D.A., Kulkarni, P.: Expertise based cooperative reinforcement learning methods (ECRLM) for dynamic decision making in retail shop application. In: Satapathy, S.C., Joshi, A. (eds.) ICTIS 2017. SIST, vol. 84, pp. 350–360. Springer, Cham (2018). https://doi.org/10.1007/978-3-319-63645-0_39
5. Raju Chinthalapati, V.L., Yadati, N., Karumanchi, R.: Learning dynamic prices in multi-seller electronic retail markets with price sensitive customers, stochastic demands, and inventory replenishments. IEEE Trans. Syst. Man Cybern.—Part C: Appl. Rev. 36(1) (2008)
6. Vidhate, D.A., Kulkarni, P.: Innovative approach towards cooperation models for multi-agent reinforcement learning (CMMARL). In: Unal, A., Nayak, M., Mishra, D.K., Singh, D., Joshi, A. (eds.) SmartCom 2016. CCIS, vol. 628, pp. 468–478. Springer, Singapore (2016). https://doi.org/10.1007/978-981-10-3433-6_56
7. Choi, Y.-C., Ahn, H.-S.: A survey on multi-agent reinforcement learning: coordination problems. In: IEEE/ASME International Conference on Mechatronics and Embedded Systems and Applications, pp. 81–86 (2010)
8. Vidhate, D.A., Kulkarni, P.: Enhanced cooperative multi-agent learning algorithms (ECMLA) using reinforcement learning. In: International Conference on Computing, Analytics and Security Trends (CAST), pp. 556–561. IEEE Xplorer (2017)
9. Gosavi, A.: Simulation-based Optimization: Parametric Optimization Techniques and Reinforcement Learning. Kluwer Academic Publishers, Norwell (2003)
10. Vidhate, D.A., Kulkarni, P.: Performance enhancement of cooperative learning algorithms by improved decision-making for context-based application. In: International Conference on Automatic Control and Dynamic Optimization Techniques IEEE Xplorer, pp. 246–252 (2016)
11. Wang, P.K.C.: Navigation strategies for multiple autonomous mobile robots moving in formation. J. Rob. Syst. 8(2), 177–195 (1991)
12. Matari, M.J.: Reinforcement learning in multirobot. Auton. Robot. 4(1), 73–83 (1997)
13. Tan, M.: Multi-agent reinforcement learning: Independent versus cooperative agents. In: Proceedings of the 10th International Conference on Machine Learning, pp. 330–337. Morgan Kaufmann (1993)
14. Uchibe, E., Nakamura, M., Asada, M.: Co-evolution for cooperative behavior acquisition in a multiple mobile robot environments. In: Proceedings of the IEEE/RSJ International Conference on Intelligent Robots and Systems, vol. 1, pp. 425–430, October 1998
15. Kim, J.H., Vadakkepat, P.: Multi-agent systems: a survey from the robot-soccer perspective. Intell. Autom. Soft Comput. 6(1), 3–18 (2000)
16. Harmon, M.E., Harmon, S.S.: Reinforcement Learning: A Tutorial, Wright Lab, Wright-Patterson AFB, Ohio, USA (1997)
17. Wang, Y.: Cooperative and intelligent control of multi-robot systems using machine learning [thesis]. The University of British Columbia (2008)
18. Duan, Y., Cui, B.X., Xu, X.H.: A multi-agent reinforcement learning approach to robot soccer. Artif. Intell. Rev. 38(3), 193–211 (2012)
19. Littman, M.L.: Markov games as a framework for multi-agent reinforcement learning. In: Proceedings of the 11th International Conference on Machine Learning, pp. 157–163 (2000)
20. Hu, J., Wellman, M.P.: Nash Q-learning for general-sum stochastic games. J. Mach. Learn. Res. 4(6), 1039–1069 (2004)
21. Littman, M.L.: Friend-or-foe Q-learning in general-sum games. In: Proceedings of the 18th International Conference on Machine Learning (ICML 2001), pp. 322–328 (2001)

22. Greenwald, A., Hall, K.: Correlated-Q learning. In: Proceedings of the 20th International Conference on Machine Learning, pp. 242–249, August 2003
23. Bowling, M.: Convergence and no-regret in multi-agent learning. Adv. Neural. Inf. Process. Syst. **17**, 209–216 (2005)
24. Hart, S., Mas-Colell, A.: A simple adaptive procedure leading to correlated equilibrium. Econometrica **68**(5), 1127–1150 (2000)
25. Auer, P., Cesa-Bianchi, N., Freund, Y., Schapire, R.E.: Gambling in a rigged casino: the adversarial multi-armed bandit problem. In: Proceedings of the 36th IEEE Annual Symposium on Foundations of Computer Science, pp. 322–331, October 1995
26. Marden, J.R.: Learning in Large-Scale Games and Cooperative Control. University of California, Los Angeles (2007)
27. Vidhate, D.A., Kulkarni, P.: New approach for advanced cooperative learning algorithms using RL methods (ACLA). In: Proceedings of the Third International Symposium on Computer Vision and the Internet, ACM DL, VisionNet 2016, pp. 12–20 (2016)
28. Ichikawa, Y., Takadama, K.: Designing internal reward of reinforcement learning agents in multi-step dilemma problem. J. Adv. Comput. Intell. Intell. Inform. (JACIII) **17**(6), 926–931 (2013)
29. Elidrisi, M., Johnson, N., Gini, M., Crandall, M.: Fast adaptive learning in repeated stochastic games by game abstraction. Auton. Agents Multi-Agent Syst., 1141–1148 (2014)
30. Vidhate, D.A., Kulkarni, P.: Multi-agent cooperation models by reinforcement learning (MCMRL). Int. J. Comput. Appl. **176**(1), 25–29 (2017)
31. Vidhate, D.A., Kulkarni, P.: Enhancement in decision making with improved performance by multi-agent learning algorithms. IOSR J. Comput. Eng. **1**(18), 18–25 (2016)
32. Liu, Q., Ma, J., Xie, W.: Multi-agent reinforcement learning with regret matching for robot soccer. J. Math. Probl. Eng. 2013, Article ID 926267
33. Vidhate, D.A., Kulkarni, P.: Implementation of multi-agent learning algorithms for improved decision making. Int. J. Comput. Trends Technol. (IJCTT) **35**(2) (2016)
34. Junling, H., Wellman, M.P.: Nash Q-learning for general-sum stochastic games. J. Mach. Learn. Res. **4**, 1039–1069 (2003)
35. Vidhate, D.A., Kulkarni, P.: To improve association rule mining using new technique: multilevel relationship algorithm towards cooperative learning. In: International Conference on Circuits, Systems, Communication and Information Technology Applications. IEEE Explorer (2014)
36. Abbasi, Z., Abbasi, M.A.: Reinforcement distribution in a team of cooperative q-learning agent. In: Proceedings of the 9th ACIS International Conference on Artificial Intelligence (2012)
37. Vidhate, D.A., Kulkarni, P.: Design of multi-agent system architecture based on association mining for cooperative reinforcement learning. Spvryan's Int. J. Eng. Sci. Technol. (SEST) **1**(1) (2014)
38. Vidhate, D.A., Kulkarni, P.: Single agent learning algorithms for decision making in diagnostic applications. SSRG Int. J. Comput. Sci. Eng. (SSRG-IJCSE) **3**(5), 46–52 (2016)
39. Vidhate, D.A., Kulkarni, P.: Multilevel relationship algorithm for association rule mining used for cooperative learning. Int. J. Comput. Appl. (0975 – 8887) **86**(4), 20–27 (2014)

Novel Technique for the Test Case Prioritization in Regression Testing

Mampi Kerani[✉] and Sharmila

Department of CSE, Krishna Engineering College, Ghaziabad, India
mampi7889.happy@gmail.com, sharmila1ece@gmail.com

Abstract. The process that is applied to verify the modified software within the maintenance phase is called regression testing. The test case prioritization is the technique of regression testing in which test cases are prioritized according to the changes which are done in the project. This work is based on manual slicing and automated slicing for test case prioritization to detect maximum number of faults from the project in which some changes are done for the new version release. The best fitness value is calculated based on mutation value which will be the importance of the particular function. To test the performance of proposed and existing algorithm MATLAB tool is being used by considering the dataset of ten projects. It is analyzed that proposed automated multi-objective algorithm performs well in terms of percentage of fault detection and execution time as compared to the manual multi-objective system.

Keywords: Regression testing · Manual slicing · Bio-inspired

1 Introduction

The complete process that is conducted while production of software is known as software engineering. In order to organize the gathered data and instructions related to a system, software is generated. There are two broader categories of the software which are system software and application software. The hardware components are handled by the system software such that the functional unit can be viewed by the other software or user. There is operating system available within the software along with many utilities. Some particular tasks are achieved with the help of application software which might or might not include within it one program. The collection of programs generates software. A software is dissimilar from a program is various manners [1]. There are programs, their documentations, procedures to initialize the software and its various operations included within software. It can also be said that a program is a subset of software. The need of software has been incrementing with each day due to which the production of good quality software is very important. Software engineering is the technology which is utilized in order to provide good quality software. The concepts, strategies and practices of software engineering are acquired by the software developer such that within the development process any kind of problems can be eliminated [2]. The development, maintenance and operation of software are known as software engineering mechanism. Within software engineering, the development of software is an important

© Springer Nature Singapore Pte Ltd. 2018
M. Singh et al. (Eds.): ICACDS 2018, CCIS 905, pp. 362–371, 2018.
https://doi.org/10.1007/978-981-13-1810-8_36

step to be performed. In order to build up the software, there are numerous techniques needed [3–5]. The collection of requirements and demands of clients is the most important and initial step within the development process. Good quality software might not be possible to generate in case if the developer does not fulfill the requirements of the clients. In case if the software provides complete satisfaction to the requirements of clients, it is considered to be of good quality [6].

In terms of quality, cost and design of the software, the client's satisfaction can rely. In order to build up the software, there are numerous systematic and organized scientific procedures are acquired by the developers [7]. A software development process is used to interpret the software product, in which the customer transcribe all the needs to the developers that what kind of changes a customer requires [8]. A test case is set of procedure use to test the software. In order to determine whether the application is performing in correct manner or not, a set of condition is provided by the software tester which is known as test case. To design a test case for specific software the designer must design positive or negative test case for the software. Positive test cases are planned to check software under ordinary condition and negative test case are design to examine software at maximal condition. The time that is required to complete the objective of testing is influenced by the order of test case execution. The delay occurring in bug fixing activity and delivering the software is resultant of the improper execution. The fault rate is known with the help of fault detection process involved here [9]. Regression testing is a testing that refers to that components of the test cycle in which programs are tested to make sure that modifications do not influence features that are not believed to be affected.

The process of verifying the customized software within the maintenance stage is known as Regression testing. Due to the higher complexity of process, the major disadvantages are caused due to the time and cost constraints. The numbers of subset of tests that are already conducted are re-executed in order to perform regression testing. There is an increment in the number regression tests as integration of testing is done within regression testing. The re-execution of each test is not practical as well as effective for every program function during any kinds of modifications observed [10, 11].

The main contribution of the work as follows,

1. To study and analyze various regression testing and test case prioritization techniques
2. To proposed improvement in recovery traceability link module for test case prioritization in multi-objective technique.
3. To implement proposed technique and compared with existing multi-objective technique in terms of accuracy and execution time.

2   Literature Review

Khanna (2016) explained fault occurs due to alterations done in maintenance stage. Modification of software requires re-execution of all the test cases to validate that changes in one module have not modified the correct functionalities of other modules in software [1]. It is not possible to re-run all the test cases as it will consume time therefore it requires to prioritize the test cases intelligently in order to facilitate effective regression testing by genetic algorithm.

Rajal and Sharma (2015) explained that regression testing is required to enhance software code in accordance to the changes done by customer end, functionality of software, fixing the defects after modifications and removal of out-dated functionalities [2].

Catal [3] discussed the ten best practices for test case prioritization and their role in booming software testing. The paper explains importance of software testing in software development and significance of regression testing by test case prioritization in maintenance phase when changes are done in accordance to customer requirement.

Shivanandam (2012) the book on principles of soft computing explains the genetic algorithm is an intelligent search technique and is used to solve optimization problem. The book explains neural networks [4], various types of learning, fuzzy logic, genetic algorithm and programming and other applications of soft computing.

Suri et al. (2012) presented in this paper [12] that in order to examine the test case selection, Bee Colony Optimization (BCO) is used to propose a hybrid technique. A new tool is created and Test suite is minimized as per the results acquired by applying proposed technique. Along with the reduction in cost, the test suite is also minimized. The BCO and genetic algorithm are joined in order to propose a hybrid approach. In comparison to the Ant Colony Optimization (ACO) technique, the proposed hybrid technique provides better results. In order to result the least number of subsets of test cases, the designed tool provides results at higher speed. In each execution, different results are provided by this tool.

2.1 Problem Formulation

The regression testing is the types of testing which is applied to test the software after certain updation are made in the software. The regression testing has two techniques which are test case generation and test prioritization. In the test case prioritization, the test cases are prioritized or ordered according to the changes done in the software. The test case prioritization leads to detect maximum number of faults from the software and detected faults are technical faults. The test case prioritization also reduces the execution cost of the test cases for fault detection in the software. In the existing paper, the multi-objective based approach is proposed for test case prioritization which automatically detects faulty portion of the software. In the multi-objective technique, the weight is calculated corresponding to each test case. The weight is calculated based on the maintainability index which is calculated using the four steps. They are recovering the traceability links, computing matrix and estimating maintainability index. In this work, the improvement in the step of recovering the traceability link will be proposed to detect maximum number of faults for test case prioritization.

3   Proposed Methodology

The Regression testing is the testing which is applied to test the software when some changes are done in the already developed project. The test case prioritization is the technique of regression testing which prioritizes the test cases according to the changes which are done in the developed project. This work is based on automated test case prioritization techniques. In the existing technique the manual test case prioritization is been implemented to detect faults from the project. In the manual test case prioritization two parameters are considered which are number of times function encountered and number of functions associated with the particular function. To increase the fault detection rate of the test case prioritization, automated test case prioritization is being implemented in this work.

In the first step of the algorithm, the population values are taken as input which is the number of times function encountered and number of functions associated with a particular function. In the second step, the algorithm will start traversing the population values and error is calculated after every iteration. The iteration at which the error is maximum at that point the mutation value is calculated as the best mutation value of the function. The function mutation value will be the function importance from where the test cases are prioritized according to the defined changes. The automated technique of hill-climbing algorithm is used to generate best test cases and each test case is assigned a fitness value on the basis of fault coverage criteria which leads to detect more faults than the manual technique (Fig. 1).

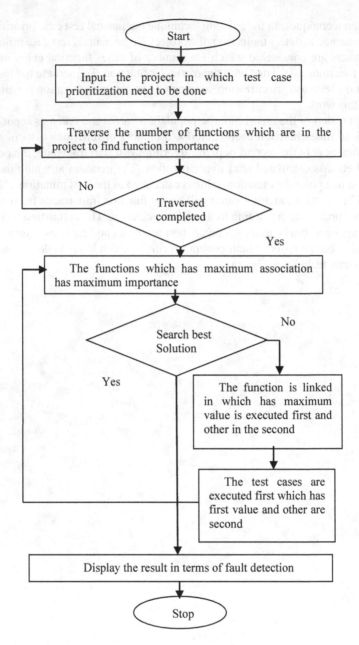

Fig. 1. Flowchart of proposed automated multi-objective algorithm in regression testing.

Proposed Algorithm

Input: Test cases = P(i)
Number clicks on each function = F(i)
Output: prioritized test cases
I ← Consider value of F(i) for the each test case
 Test case F(i) value < − i
while (fault value of each test case is calculated)
a = F(i)
calculate number of links L(i) = F(i)′/F(i)
if(L(i) > L(i + 1)
b = L(i)
else
b = L (i + 1)end
Calculate fault value
Fault (i + 1) = fault(i)/L(i)
if Fault(i) > Fault(i + 1)
best_so_far < −Fault(i)
i < − generate an individual randomly end

Steps of the Proposed Automated Multi-objective Algorithm

Following are the various steps of proposed multi-objective algorithm,

1. In the improved multi-objective algorithm, the function importance is also calculated on the basis of number of functions associated. The function which has maximum association is considered as the most important function.
2. To calculate the number of functions associated, the technique of automated slicing is been applied which traverse the Data Flow Diagram (DFD) and generate final result as Function Traverse Value (FTV).
3. The automated slicing will work in the iterative manner and search the best value of the test case as which maximum number of errors get detected from the project.

4   Experimental Results and Discussion

The proposed algorithm and existing algorithms are implemented in MATLAB for the ten project and in each project 10 to 15 test cases are considered. The fault detection rate is increased and execution time is reduced as illustrated the figures shown below. The fault detection rate is increased and execution time is reduced as illustrated the figures shown below.

As shown in Fig. 2, the proposed algorithm and existing algorithm are compared in terms of fault detection rate. It has been analyzed proposed algorithm performs well in terms of fault detection rate. As shown in Fig. 3, the execution time of the proposed algorithm is less as compared to the existing algorithm.

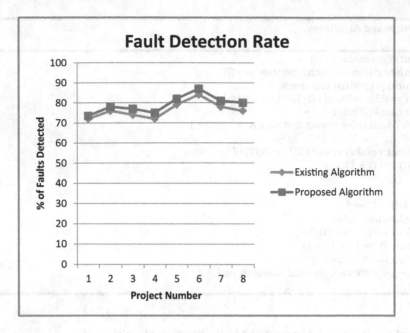

Fig. 2. Fault detection rate

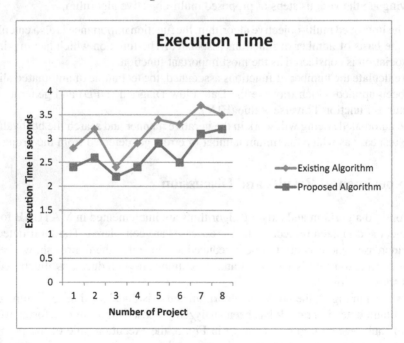

Fig. 3. Execution time

4.1   Comparison of Performance of Existing and Proposed Multi-objective

The proposed algorithm enhances the rate of fault detection by running the test cases in automated manner with the help of function traverse values calculated with respect to changes done during regression testing in software development. In order to achieve expected simulation results 10 projects have been taken to verify the output as enhanced rate of fault detection. The following Tables depicts the four changes done in the one of the projects to show the comparative study that how the fault rate values get enhanced efficiently.

Table 1 shows the fault detection rate by multi-objective approach with respect to each change for Online Shopping Project.

Table 1.   Fault detected by multi-objective approach.

Online Shopping Project					
Functions	Function execution value	Attached functions	Function importance	Fitness value	Fault detection rate
Show products	3	6	0.5	According to Change 1: 3.309524	According to Change 1: 5.913
Show category	8	7	1.1429		
Check availability	1	6	0.16667	According to Change 2: 3.166667	According to Change 2: 5.4046
Request order	6	4	1.5		
Shipping	9	3	3	According to Change 3: 3.292857	According to Change 3: 6.0006
Payment accept	2	5	0.4		
Cancel order	7	4	1.75	According to Change 4: 8.459524	According to Change 4: 17.8968

Table 2 shows the Fault Detection Rate by Enhanced multi-objective Approach with respect to each change for Online Shopping Project.

Table 2. Fault detected by enhanced multi-objective approach.

Online Shopping Project

Functions	Function execution value	Attached functions	Function importance	Fitness value	Fault detection rate of proposed method
Show products	3	6	0.5	According to Change 1: 3.309524	According to Change 1: 6.7022
Show category	8	7	1.1429		
Check availability	1	6	0.16667	According to Change 2: 3.166667	According to Change 2: 12.428
Request order	6	4	1.5		
Shipping	9	3	3	According to Change 3: 3.292857	According to Change 3: 14.4892
Payment accept	2	5	0.4		
Cancel order	7	4	1.75	According to Change 4: 8.4595	According to Change 4: 20.258

5   Conclusion

In this work, it is concluded that regression testing is the type of testing which is applied to test the project after some changes are being done for future release. The test case prioritization is the technique of regression testing which is being applied to prioritize the test cases according to the defined changes. The multi-objective algorithm is being applied to implement the test case prioritization in the automated manner. To analyze the performance of proposed and existing algorithm simulation is being done in MATLAB by considering ten projects with four changes. It has been analyzed that fault detection rate is increased and execution time is reduced by applying automated test case prioritization as compared to manual test case prioritization in regression testing. The limitation of the research is that it detects the faults by local search by mutation operation. In future the research paves the way so as to have comparative study of other greedy or heuristic search algorithms to deliver the best of all search algorithms for efficient test case prioritization in regression testing for enhancing rate of fault detection.

References

1. Khannan, E.: Regression testing based on genetic algorithms. Int. J. Comput. Appl. **154**(8), 43–46 (2016)
2. Rajal, J.S., Sharma, S.: A review on various techniques for regression testing and test case prioritization. Int. J. Comput. Appl. **116**(16), 8–13 (2015)
3. Catal, C.: The ten best practices for test case prioritization. In: Skersys, T., Butleris, R., Butkiene, R. (eds.) ICIST 2012. CCIS, vol. 319, pp. 452–459. Springer, Heidelberg (2012). https://doi.org/10.1007/978-3-642-33308-8_37

4. Shivvanandan, S.N., Deepa, S.N.: Principles of Soft Computing, 2nd edn. Wiley, New Delhi (2012)
5. Pressman, R.S.: Software Engineering: A Practioner's Approach, 3rd edn. McGraw-Hill Higher Education, New York (2005)
6. Raju, S., Uma, G.V.: Factors oriented test case prioritization technique in regression testing using genetic algorithm. Eur. J. Sci. Res. **74**(3), 123–131 (2012)
7. Ruchika, M., Arvinder, K., Yogesh, S.: A regression test selection and prioritization technique. J. Inf. Process. Syst. **6**(2), 321–412 (2010)
8. Siripong, R., Jirapun, D.: Test case prioritization techniques. J. Theor. Appl. Inf. Technol. **18**(2), 45–60 (2010)
9. Hyunsook, D., Siavash, M., Ladan, T., Gregg, R.: The effect of time constraint on test case prioritization. IEEE Trans. Softw. Eng. **36**, 593–617 (2010)
10. Paolo, T., Paolo, A., Angelo, S.: Using the case-based ranking methodology for test case prioritization. In: 22nd IEEE International Conference on Software Maintenance, pp. 123–133 (2006)
11. Zheng, L., Mark, H., Robert, M.H.: Search algorithms for regression test case prioritization. IEEE Trans. Softw. Eng. **33**(4), 225–237 (2007)
12. Suri, B, Mangal, I.: Analyzing test case selection using proposed hybrid technique based on BCO and genetic algorithm and a comparison with ACO. Int. J. Comput. Appl. 41–46 (2012)

Extreme Gradient Boosting Based Tuning for Classification in Intrusion Detection Systems

Ashu Bansal[(⊠)] and Sanmeet Kaur

CSED, Thapar Institute of Engineering and Technology, Patiala 147004, India
ashubansal8@gmail.com, sanmeet.bhatia@thapar.edu

Abstract. In a fast-growing digital era, the increase in devices connected to internet have raised many security issues. For providing security, varieties of the system are available in the IT sector, Intrusion Detection system is one of such system. The design of an efficient intrusion detection system is an open problem to the research community. In this paper, various machine learning algorithms have been used for detecting different types of Denial-of-Service attack. The performance of the models have been measured on the basis of binary and multi-classification. Furthermore, parameter tuning algorithm has been discussed. On the basis of performance parameters, XGBoost performs efficiently and in robust manner to find an intrusion. The proposed method i.e. XGBoost has been compared with other classifiers like AdaBoost, Naïve Bayes, Multi-layer perceptron (MLP) and K-Nearest Neighbour (KNN) on recently captured network traffic by Canadian Institute of Cybersecurity (CIC). In this research, average class error and overall error have been calculated for the multi-classification problem.

Keywords: Intrusion detection system (IDSs) · Machine learning
XGBoost · Denial-of-Service · MLP · KNN

1 Introduction

In modern era, the techno-savvy workers, high-end devices are growing at a very high pace. Over the past decade, the new technology and the fast-growing internet have brought people together, but also raised a number of security issues. The vulnerabilities in network or devices attract hackers to perform malicious activities, by which the organization and the end users have to bare a huge loss. These malicious activities can be performed by a number of attacks including MITM, DDoS, spoofing. But DoS is the most significant among all. To defend these attacks there are various types of Intrusion Detection System (IDS) available in the cyber sector. Basically, intrusion detection is the monitoring process of network traffic or events occurred in the network and examine them for finding malicious activities. It also analyses the attempts made by a hacker to compromise the Confidentiality, Integrity, and Availability (CIA). In simple words, IDSs are the software or hardware product that automate the monitoring process [1].

An IDS has become an important security measure and act as a second line of defense. The number of IDS faces common challenges i.e. low detection rate and high

© Springer Nature Singapore Pte Ltd. 2018
M. Singh et al. (Eds.): ICACDS 2018, CCIS 905, pp. 372–380, 2018.
https://doi.org/10.1007/978-981-13-1810-8_37

false positive rates, by which normal action is classified as an attack and thus, obstructs legitimate user access to network resources [2].

Most IDS use various machine learning approaches to obtain high accuracy for detecting an intrusion, cut the overall error and unstable architecture due to the large volume of high-dimensional data-values. To overcome these challenges, this paper presents gradient approach for finding an intrusion, which enhances the detection rate and stability of IDS. During the initial phase of Extreme Gradient boosting, the selection of sample and weight distribution has been done intelligently to classify intrusion. Experiments were carried out on CICIDS intrusion dataset [3, 4] over the existing classifiers such as AdaBoost [7], Naïve Bayes [8], Multi-layer perceptron (MLP) [9] and KNN [10] using Weka [11] tool with respect to classifier accuracy and detection rate. This paper represents both multi-classification and binary classification results on the basis of data.

The rest of the paper is structured as follows: Sect. 2 describe the related work Sect. 3 provides details of methods and material used in model building. Section 4 highlights the discussion about the experimental results and a comparison with other classifiers. Finally, Sect. 5 concludes the paper and future work.

2 Related Work

Boosting models is popularly used in supervised learning algorithm. However, many boosting model like Adaboost and Stochastic gradient boosting. Many researches [13, 14] have been used these type of boosting model for find the better results. Steve *et al.* [7] describe the Adaboost algorithm for find the network intrusion by using simple over fitting. Chen *et al.* [15] proposed an ensemble technique which is the combination of Adaboost and Incremental Hidden Markov model to improve the detection rate for UNM dataset. Schapire [16] describe the approach which can turn a weak learner to a strong learner by combining classifiers. Boro *et al.* [17] proposed a meta- ensemble technique by combining the weights to determine the output. Weighted Majority Voting has been chosen to specific class. Emad *et al.* [18] proposed a boosting Anti-Colony optimization algorithm for find an intrusion. This algorithm is used for generating classification rules and it is improved version of Anti-Miner algorithm. There are various researches on IDS based on rule-based approach, which has difficulty to detect new attack patterns [19].

3 Methods and Materials

For predictive modeling, there are various types of machine learning algorithm like, AdaBoost, KNN, MLP, Naïve-Bayes, and Extreme Gradient Boosting classifier (XGBoost) [6] has been used and in all these methods XGBoost is highly sophisticated and powerful enough to deal with the irregularities in the network traffic data. XGBoost has several features: fast processing, takes several types of input data, sparsity, built-in cross-validation, tree pruning, highly flexible. Over-fitting is controlled by XGBoost model for better performance which makes this model better than the other boosting models. The steps involved in XGBoost-IDS are shown in Fig. 1.

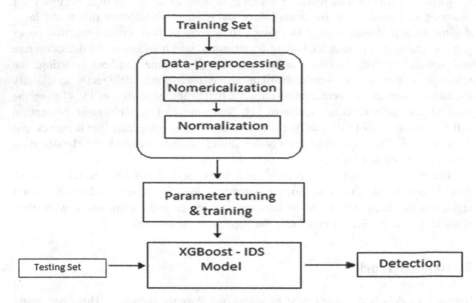

Fig. 1. Proposed XGBoost-IDS model

In the above figure, training set has been processed through data-preprocessing phase. Afterward, parameter tuning and training step has done and model has been built on the basis of XGBoost classifier. Finally the testing set has been arrived, where detection of malicious activities has been detected.

3.1 Dataset Description

The CICIDS 2017 dataset [3, 4] generated in 2017 has been used in this research and it covers necessary and updated attacks such as DoS, DDoS, Brute Force, XSS, SQL injection, Infiltration, Port scan, and Botnet. The previous publically available datasets lacks traffic diversity, volumes, anonymized packet information payload, constraints on the variety of attacks, lack of the feature set and metadata. So, CICIDS 2017 overcome these issues like various protocols such as HTTP, HTTPS, FTP, SSH and email protocol are present, which were not available in the previous dataset. The dataset recorded on Wednesday has been selected which contains a different type of DoS Attack. After capturing the network traffic, the.pcap file has been converted into CSV file through CICFlowMeter [5]. Denial-of-Service attacks have been classified into five categories:

DoS Slow Loris: It is the type of attack which tries to keep open many connections to the target web server and hold them open as long as possible. This opening session has been done through periodically sent HTTP headers, adding to but never completing the request. The affected server will never shut the connection and deny additional connection attempts from the client.

DoS Slowhttptest: This kind of malicious activity relies on HTTP protocol configuration, expects solicitations to be totally gotten by the server before they are handled. If the HTTP request isn't finished, the server keeps its resources busy for remaining data, this happens continuously and implies that DoS Slowhttptest has been abused.

DoS Hulk: The main idea behind this attack is to develop an identical connection for each and every request generated, thus avoiding/bypassing engine caching and effecting directly on the server's load itself.

DoS Goldeneye: It is an HTTP/S-Layer 7 Denial-of-Service Testing Tool. It utilizes KeepAlive (and Connection: keep-alive) combined with Cache-Control alternatives to hold on socket association busting through reserving (when conceivable) until the point when it devours every single accessible socket on the HTTP/S server.

Heartbleed: This sort of assault is generally executed in transport layer security (TLS) protocol. It is ordinarily misused by sending a twisted heartbeat request with the little payload, so as to trigger the victim's reaction.

The dataset contains 80 features proposed by Canadian Institute of Cybersecurity (CIC) [5] shown in Table 1.

Table 1. Listed feature

No.	Feature	No.	Feature	No.	Feature
1	Source Port	28	Bwd IAT Total	55	Average Packet Size
2	Destination Port	29	Bwd IAT Mean	56	Avg Fwd Segment Size
3	Protocol	30	Bwd IAT Std	57	Avg Bwd Segment Size
4	Flow Duration	31	Bwd IAT Max	58	Fwd Avg Bytes/Bulk
5	Total Fwd Packets	32	Bwd IAT Min	59	Fwd Avg Packets/Bulk
6	Total Backward Packets	33	Fwd PSH Flags	60	Fwd Avg Bulk Rate
7	Total Length of Fwd Pck	34	Bwd PSH Flags	61	Bwd Avg Bytes/Bulk
8	Total Length of Bwd Pck	35	Fwd URG Flags	62	Bwd Avg Packets/Bulk
9	Fwd Packet Length Max	36	Bwd URG Flags	63	Bwd Avg Bulk Rate
10	Fwd Packet Length Min	37	Fwd Header Length	64	Subflow Fwd Packets
11	Fwd Pck Length Mean	38	Bwd Header Length	65	Subflow Fwd Bytes
12	Fwd Packet Length Std	39	Fwd Packets/s	66	Subflow Bwd Packets
13	Bwd Packet Length Max	40	Bwd Packets/s	67	Subflow Bwd Bytes
14	Bwd Packet Length Min	41	Min Packet Length	68	Init_Win_bytes_fwd
15	Bwd Packet Length(avg)	42	Max Packet Length	69	act_data_pkt_fwd
16	Bwd Packet Length Std	43	Packet Length Mean	70	min_seg_size_fwd
17	Flow Bytes/s	44	Packet Length Std	71	Active Mean
18	Flow Packets/s	45	Packet Len. Variance	72	Active Std
19	Flow IAT Mean	46	FIN Flag Count	73	Active Max
20	Flow IAT Std	47	SYN Flag Count	74	Active Min
21	Flow IAT Max	48	RST Flag Count	75	Idle Mean
22	Flow IAT Min	49	PSH Flag Count	76	Idle packet
23	Fwd IAT Total	50	ACK Flag Count	77	Idle Std
24	Fwd IAT Mean	51	URG Flag Count	78	Idle Max
25	Fwd IAT Std	52	CWE Flag Count	79	Idle Min
26	Fwd IAT Max	53	ECE Flag Count	80	Label
27	Fwd IAT Min	54	Down/Up Ratio		

3.2 Data Preprocessing

(1) Numericalization: There are 80 numeric feature and one non-numeric feature in the CICIDS 2017 dataset. The input value in the XGBoost-IDS should be in the numeric matrix, so it is necessary to convert the label value in the numeric vector. For instance, the six different attributes in the label feature, 'BENIGN', 'DoS Slowloris', 'Dos Slowhttptest', 'DoS Hulk', 'DoS Goldeneye', 'Heartbleed' are converted into 1, 2, 3, 4, 5, 6 respectively.

2) Normalization: There are some values in the dataset such as 'Flow Duration', 'Fwd Packet Length Std', 'Flow Bytes/s', 'Flow Packets/s', 'Flow IAT Mean', 'Flow', where the difference between the maximum and minimum values has a very large scope. To normalize them the logarithmic method for scaling has been applied to get the values in the range [0, 1].

3.3 Parameter Tunning and Boosting Algorithm

The machine learning algorithm XGBoost model works on numeric vectors, so conversion of categorical variables into the numeric vector. For this work, the sparse matrix using flags on every possible value has been used. XGBoost follows a format which has training samples $x_i (i = 1, 2, 3, \ldots\ldots, n)$ and sequence of prediction $y_i\, i(1, 2, 3, \ldots., n)$. Basically, XGBoost rely on assigning weights to the observation. Uniform distribution assumption has been used for assigning weights. Let the supposed distribution is D_1 which $1/n$ for all n observation. α (Learning rate) and $h()$ is the weak classifier.

> Algorithm 1: Parameter tuning algorithm
> Inputs: $x_i\ (i = 1,2,3, \ldots\ldots, n)$
> Initializations: α_t, h_t
> Output: $y_i (i = 1,2,3, \ldots, n)$
> 1. Update the uniform distribution for step 2
>
> $$D_{t+1}(i) = \frac{D_t \exp(-\alpha_t\, y_i\, h_t\, (x_i))}{Z_t}$$
>
> $$where\ Z_t = \sum_{i=1}^{n} D_t\,(i)\, \exp(-\alpha_t y_i h_t(x_i))$$
>
> 2. Use step-1 to find new Distribution for next learner.
> 3. Iterate step-1 and step-2, until no hypothesis is found for better nature.
> 4. Take a weighted average (α values).

For learning parameters logistic and sotftMax objectives has been used for binary and multi-classification problem respectively.

3.4 Confusion Matrix Representation

In this entire work intrusion detection is the most critical part, so accurately detection of intrusion by the classifier has been considered as most important factor. Moreover, two other metrics i.e. Average Class Error and Overall Error for the multi-classification problem have been introduced. Apart from that, four other metrics have also been measured in our research for binary classification such as True positive (TP), False positive (FP), True negative (TN), False negative (FN). The True Positive rate is the correctly find the projected attacks, for instance, number of intrusion record identified as an intrusion. The FP denotes the benign traffic as an intrusion. The TN means benign records identifies as benign and FP equivalent to the number of intrusions are identifies as benign traffic. We have following notation:

$$\text{ACCURACY (ACC)} = \frac{TP+TN}{TP+TN+FP+FN},$$

$$\text{True Positive Rate (TPR)} = \frac{TP}{TP+FN},$$

$$\text{False Positive Rate (FPR)} = \frac{FP}{FP+TN}.$$

Confusion matrix has been shown in Table 2.

Table 2. Confusion Matrix

Actual	Predicted	
	Intrusion	Benign
Intrusion	TP	FN
Benign	FP	TN

4 Results and Discussion

In this research, the best machine learning framework i.e. Rstudio [12] has been used. The experiment is done on a personal laptop Dell Inspiron 7000 series two in one which has the configuration of Intel i7 core @ 2.3 GHz, 8 GB memory. To study the performance of XGBoost model the two experiments for binary classification (Benign, Intrusion) and the multi-classification of DoS attacks, such as DoS Slowloris, DoS Slowhttptest, DoS Hulk, DoS GoldenEye, heartbleed and Benign (normal network traffic) has been examined. By contrasting them, the performance of AdaBoost [7], Naïve Bayes [8], Multi-layer perceptron (MLP) [9] and KNN [10] has been studied.

Multiclass Classification
In multi-classification, 79 input nodes and one output node have been considered. This output have six types of attributes, the accuracy given by the trained model is as high as 99.54% on CICIDS 2017 dataset at 0.5 learning rate. In order to compare the performance of this multi-classification problem through other machine learning algorithms such as KNN, AdaBoost, MLP, Naïve Bayes with the help of data mining open source software Weka [11]. Table 3 describes the comparison of accuracy with other machine learning algorithms. Furthermore, in this experiment other metrics for categorical classification through the confusion matrix which has been described in

Table 4. The experimental result of XGBoost-IDS like Accuracy, Average Class Error, and Overall Error have been shown in Table 5. The error matrix has been described in Table 6.

Table 3. Accuracy comparison

Model	Accuracy (%)
KNN	96.54
AdaBoost	78
MLP	94.7
Naïve-Bayes	96.07
XGBoost	**99.54**

Table 4. Confusion matrix for multi-classification

Actual	Predicted						
	1	2	3	4	5	6	Error (%)
1	**63700**	0	3	93	0	0	0.15
2	69	**754**	0	0	0	0	8.3
3	36	2	**681**	0	2	0	5.5
4	27	0	0	**33131**	0	0	0.08
5	6	0	1	4	**1490**	0	0.73
6	0	0	0	0	0	**1**	0

Table 5. Accuracy, overall error, average class error for multi-classification

Accuracy (%)	Overall error (%)	Average class error (%)
99.54	**0.237**	**2.46**

Table 6. Error matrix

Actual	Predicted					
	1	2	3	4	5	Error (%)
1	0	0	0.003	0.09	0	0.15
2	0.069	0	0	0	0	8.3
3	0.036	0.002	0	0	0.002	5.5
4	0.027	0	0	0	0	0.08
5	0.006	0	0.001	0.004	0	0.73
6	0	0	0	0	0	0

Binary Classification

The above multi-classification problem has been reduced to binary classification in which two label i.e. intrusion as 1 and benign as 0 has been considered and the models are trained same dataset and has a learning rate of 0.01. Table 7 shows the confusion matrix of the XGBoost-IDS on one lac records taken from CICIDS 2017 dataset in the binary classification. The experiment shows that the model gives the better performance with the accuracy of 91.36%, True Positive Rate (TPR) and False Positive Rate (FPR) is 0.974 and 0.12 respectively. Table 8 shows TPR against different model respectively.

Table 7. Confusion matrix binary classification

Actual	Predicted	
	Intrusion	Benign
Intrusion	35209	923
Benign	7719	56149

Table 8. TPR rates

Model	TPR rates
KNN	0.96
AdaBoost	0.77
MLP	0.77
Naïve-Bayes	0.88
XGBoost	**0.97**

5 Conclusion

IDS plays a significant role in network defense which helps the business organization to keep eyes on security breaches and their vulnerability. This research directed towards the design of an efficient and robust Intrusion Detection System. However, the performance of the learning models depends on nature of the dataset. To solve this problem the dataset which is diversified in nature (CICIDS 2017) has been chosen and Extreme Gradient Boosting algorithm has been performed to find an intrusion. The XGBoost-IDS model not only resulting in the high accuracy as compared to traditional approaches but also performs efficiently as compared to others. Besides this, new evaluation metrics for the multi-classification problem has been discussed in this research i.e. Average class error and Overall error. In future, the performance of the algorithm can be enhanced through feature extraction and deep learning.

References

1. Scarfone, K., Mell, P.: Guide to intrusion detection and prevention systems (IDPS). NIST special publication 800.2007, p. 94 (2007)

2. Sommer, R.: Viable Network Intrusion Detection: Trade-Offs in High-Performance Environments. VDM Verlag, Saarbrücken (2008)
3. Sharafaldin, I., Gharib, A., Habibi Lashkari, A., Ghorbani, A.A.: Towards a reliable intrusion detection benchmark dataset. Softw. Netw. **2018**(1), 177–200 (2018)
4. Shiravi, A., et al.: Toward developing a systematic approach to generate benchmark datasets for intrusion detection. Comput. Secur. **31**(3), 357–374 (2012)
5. CICFlowMeter: Canadian Institute for Cybersecurity (CIC) (2017)
6. Dieci, L., Friedman, M.J.: Continuation of invariant subspaces. Numer. Linear Algeb. Appl. **8**(5), 317–327 (2001)
7. Hu, W., Hu, W., Maybank, S.: Adaboost-based algorithm for network intrusion detection. IEEE Trans. Syst. Man Cybern. Part B (Cybern.) **38**(2), 577–583 (2008)
8. Panda, M., Patra, M.R.: Network intrusion detection using naive Bayes. Int. J. Comput. Sci. Netw. Secur. **7**(12), 258–263 (2007)
9. Tsai, C.-F., et al.: Intrusion detection by machine learning: a review. Exp. Syst. Appl. **36**(10), 11994–12000 (2009)
10. Li, W., et al.: A new intrusion detection system based on KNN classification algorithm in a wireless sensor network. J. Electr. Comput. Eng. (2014)
11. Frank, E., Hall, M.A., Witten, I.H.: The WEKA Workbench. Online Appendix for "Data Mining: Practical Machine Learning Tools and Techniques", 4th edn. Morgan Kaufmann (2016)
12. RStudio Team: RStudio: integrated development for R. RStudio, Inc., Boston (2015). http://www.rstudio.Com
13. Vezhnevets, A., Barinova, O.: Avoiding boosting overfitting by removing confusing samples. In: Kok, Joost N., Koronacki, J., Mantaras, RLd, Matwin, S., Mladenič, D., Skowron, A. (eds.) ECML 2007. LNCS (LNAI), vol. 4701, pp. 430–441. Springer, Heidelberg (2007). https://doi.org/10.1007/978-3-540-74958-5_40
14. Polikar, R.: Ensemble based systems in decision making. IEEE Circ. Syst. Mag. **6**(3), 21–45 (2006)
15. Chen, Y.-S., Chen, Y.-M.: Combining incremental Hidden Markov Model and Adaboost algorithm for anomaly intrusion detection. In: Proceedings of the ACM SIGKDD Workshop on Cybersecurity and Intelligence Informatics. ACM (2009)
16. Schapire, R.E.: The strength of weak learnability. Mach. Learn. **5**(2), 197–227 (1990)
17. Boro, D., Nongpoh, B., Bhattacharyya, D.K.: Anomaly based intrusion detection using meta-ensemble classifier. In: Proceedings of the Fifth International Conference on Security of Information and Networks, pp. 450–455. ACM (2012)
18. Soroush, E., Abadeh, M.S., Habibi, J.: A boosting ant-colony optimization algorithm for computer intrusion detection. In: Proceedings of the 2006 International Symposium on Frontiers in Networking with Applications (FINA 2006) (2006)
19. Mukkamala, S., Janoski, G., Sung, A.H.: Intrusion detection using neural networks and support vector machines. In: Proceedings of IEEE International Joint Conference on Neural Networks, pp. 1702–1707 (2002)

Relative Direction: Location Path Providing Method for Allied Intelligent Agent

S. Rayhan Kabir[2], Mirza Mohtashim Alam[1],
Shaikh Muhammad Allayear[1,2], Md Tahsir Ahmed Munna[1(✉)],
Syeda Sumbul Hossain[2],
and Sheikh Shah Mohammad Motiur Rahman[2]

[1] Department of Multimedia and Creative Technology,
Daffodil International University, Dhaka, Bangladesh
{mirza.mct,drallayear.swe,tahsir411}@diu.edu.bd
[2] Department of Software Engineering, Daffodil International University,
Dhaka, Bangladesh
{rayhan561,syeda.swe,motiur.swe}@diu.edu.bd

Abstract. The most widely recognized relative directions are left, right, forward and backward. This paper has presented a computational technique for tracking location by learning relative directions between two intelligent agents, where two agents communicate with each other by radio signal and one intelligent agent helps another intelligent agent to find location. This proposed method represents an alternative approach to GSM (Global System for Mobile Communications) for the AI (Artificial Intelligence), where no network may not be available. Our research paper has proposed Relative Direction Based Location Tracking (RDBLT) model for understanding how one intelligent agent assists another intelligent agent to find out the location by learning and identifying relative directions. Moreover, three proficient algorithms have been developed for constructing our proposed model.

Keywords: Artificial General Intelligence (AGI) · Multi-agent system
Relative direction · Magnetic Navigation Compass · Radio signal

1 Introduction

Constant or real-time location finding processes are utilized to consequently recognize and track the area. Difficulties in left-right segregation are typically experienced in ordinary every day of real life [1]. Contrasting aspects of relative direction is a regular event in human life, for example, "go forward", "turn left" or "turn right". Sometimes these moves or directions are needed for helping find a place or location, for example, "there is a market on your left side". If we think these aspects from any device's perspective, where one computational device wants to find a location by using left, right, forward, and backward directions, it is very vital to four relative directions for both perspectives.

© Springer Nature Singapore Pte Ltd. 2018
M. Singh et al. (Eds.): ICACDS 2018, CCIS 905, pp. 381–391, 2018.
https://doi.org/10.1007/978-981-13-1810-8_38

Relative directions are an auxiliary matter for individuals to locate the cardinal directions. A study displays an investigation regarding the contrasting point of landmark-based guidelines with relative directions over people on foot in genuine city conditions [2] and mentioned relative direction work well than the landmark [3]. A paper tended to an energy proficient routing algorithm, which based on the relative direction [4]. A new research introduces a computation to take in human's relative directions [5], where one intelligent device can take in any human's relative directions. Another new research demonstrates a communication technique for rescuers where data transmit by the signal and estimate the relative localization [6]. In our paper, we displayed a new mapping system, where an intelligent agent wants to help another intelligent agent for finding a particular location by using relative directions; two agents are communicated by radio signal [7, 8]. To keep up with this situation, we have done this research where two intelligent agents help each other for finding a location by using right, left, forward and backward directions.

2 Proposed RDBLT Model

2.1 Handoff–Agent and Tracking–Agent

A recent examination utilized Handoff UAV and Tracking UAV for the hypothesis of the relative attitude between two unmanned flying aircrafts [9]. In our experiment, we utilized two intelligent agents those are Tracking–Agent and Handoff–Agent [10]. Handoff–agent contains the location data. On the other hand, tracking–agent needs to find the location by using relative directions. Figure 1 represents the relative directions and direction points (a, b, c and d) of handoff–agent and also illustrates direction points (a1, b1, c1 and d1) of tracking–agent [11, 12]. In our experiment, handoff– agent's direction points of relative directions are constant but for tracking–agent, direction points depend on several 2D aspects of tracking–agent [13, 14]. In Fig. 1 we have shown the tracking–agent and the various 2D position of tracking–agent.

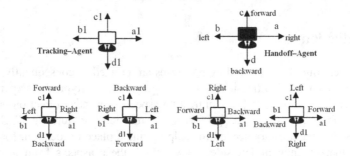

Fig. 1. Relative directions and direction points of two intelligent agents.

2.2   Structure of RDBLT Model

Our research showed Relative Direction Based Location Tracking (RDBLT) model which have demonstrated how one intelligent system assists another intelligent system for finding out the desired location. In this method, there are two intelligent agents are situated in the different area. Imagine a tracking–agent is located in Area-1 and wants to find a specific location. A handoff–agent is located in Area-2 and knows the target location of Area-1. Now tracking-agent communicates with handoff-agent by signal for finding out the desired target place. For that reason, handoff-agent learns and identifies tracking–agent's relative directions by using cardinal directions (North, South, East and West). Then handoff–agent provides a location path to tracking-agent. Afterward, tracking–agent tracks the location. Figure 2 illustrates this scenario.

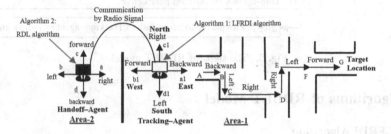

Fig. 2. A scenario of RDBLT model.

In this research, we have used the array structure for learning and identifying relative directions, where directions contain numerical values (See Table 1). The basis of the values depends on specific relative directions of two agents.

Table 1. Numerical value and array index of relative directions

Relative directions of handoff-agent	Relative directions of tracking-agent	Array index and contain values
Right	Right	0
Left	Left	1
Forward	Forward	2
Backward	Backward	3

2.3   Steps of RDBLT Model

Here, we show the structure of Relative Direction Based Location Tracking (RDBLT) model in Artificial General Intelligence (AGI) point of view.

At first, tracking-agent gives a request to handoff–agent by a radio signal for finding target location path. Handoff-agent collects data from the database and learns the location path for tracking–agent's 2D aspects (See Fig. 1 and Fig. 2), where handoff–agent uses the Location Finder's Relative Direction Identification (LFRDI) algorithm,

Relative Direction Learning (RDL) algorithm and RDBLT algorithm (See Algorithms 1, 2 and 3). Then the handoff–agent provides a location path to the tracking–agent. Consequently, tracking–agent can get the relative direction based path of target location. The steps of RDBLT model have been shown in Fig. 3.

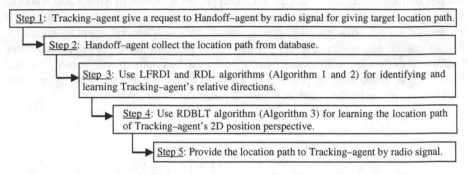

Step 1: Tracking–agent give a request to Handoff–agent by radio signal for giving target location path.

Step 2: Handoff–agent collect the location path from database.

Step 3: Use LFRDI and RDL algorithms (Algorithm 1 and 2) for identifying and learning Tracking–agent's relative directions.

Step 4: Use RDBLT algorithm (Algorithm 3) for learning the location path of Tracking–agent's 2D position perspective.

Step 5: Provide the location path to Tracking–agent by radio signal.

Fig. 3. The steps of RDBLT model.

3   Algorithms of RDBLT Model

3.1   LFRDI Algorithm

Before providing the location path, handoff–agent needs to know the 2D position of tracking–agent. Handoff–agent can identify tracking agent's relative directions by using cardinal directions such as north, south, east, and west. A Magnetic Navigation Compass helps for knowing these directions. The approach of the LFRDI algorithm by the idea of programming perspective is as follows:

- An array *trackingAgent* is created which contains relative directions (*Right, Left, Forward* and *Backward*) of tracking-agent and respectively containing 0, 1, 2 and 3 direction values (See Table 1). We also declared direction points ($a1, b1, c1$ and $d1$) of tracking-agent (See Fig. 1).
- Cardinal Directions (*North, South, East* and *West*) also declared which are being obtained by a Magnetic Navigation Compass (See Fig. 2).
- A loop has occurred where variable $k = 0$ to 3. If particular cardinal direction (*North, South, East* and *West*) is coordinated by the specific relative directions (*Right, Left, Forward* and *Backward*). Subsequently, specific direction points ($a1, b1, c1$ and $d1$) contain specific relative directions values.
- Upon completion of this loop tracking–agent returns the value of these direction points to handoff–agent by radio signal.

We have exhibited LFRDI algorithm for this issue which is based on Eq. 1. Let North, South, East and West directions are defined as N, S, E and W respectively. Tracking–agent is defined as T.

$$\forall_k \in \{0,1,2,3\} f(N,S,E,W) := \begin{cases} a1 \leftarrow k \; \textit{if} \; N = T_k \\ b1 \leftarrow k \; \textit{if} \; S = T_k \\ c1 \leftarrow k \; \textit{if} \; E = T_k \\ d1 \leftarrow k \; \textit{if} \; W = T_k \end{cases} \tag{1}$$

Here, we are assigning each of the k (ranges from 0 to 3) based on certain inputs of the cardinal directions N, S, E and W. Whatever the Tracking–agent's direction matches with the Handoff–agent's direction, we are assigning the k's value to the direction point (a1, b1, c1, d1) (See Eq. 1). The formation of LFRDI algorithm for the programming point of view is as per the following algorithm 1:

Algorithm 1. LFRDI Algorithm

```
1: function LFRDI():
2:    trackingAgent[] ← [Right, Left, Forward, Backward];
3:    Right ← 0; Left ← 1; Forward ← 2; Backward ← 3;
4:    direction points: a1; b1; c1; d1;
5:    Cardinal direction: North; South; East; West;
6:    /* directions are get by Magnetic Compass */
7:    for k := 0 to 3
8:        if North == trackingAgent[k] then, a1 ← k;
9:        else if South == trackingAgent[k] then, b1 ← k;
10:       else if East == trackingAgent[k] then, c1 ← k;
11:       else if West == trackingAgent[k] then, d1 ← k;
12:   end for
13:   return a1, b1, c1, d1; /* fixed direction points
14:   are returned to caller in Algorithm 2 and 3 */
```

3.2 Relative Direction Learning Algorithm

In this section, we demonstrate Relative Direction Learning (RDL) algorithm for learning tracking–agent's relative directions. Through this algorithm, handoff–agent can give relative direction based location tracking instruction to the tracking-agent. The statement of RDL algorithm by the idea of programming standpoint is as follows:

- Array *handoffAgent* is created which contains handoff–agent's relative directions (*right, left, forward* and *backward*) and respectively containing 0, 1, 2 and 3 direction values (See Table 1). Moreover, direction points (*a, b, c* and *d*) of handoff–agent contains relative directions (See Fig. 1).
- Another array *trackingHuman* is created which also contains relative directions (*Right, Left, Forward* and *Backward*). Their direction point variables (*a1, b1, c1* and *d1*) have been declared accordingly. These points can be identified by calling LFRDI function (See Algorithm 1). These points contain values (See Table 1) which depend on the 2D aspects of tracking–agent (see Fig. 1).
- A loop has been created where variable $i = 0$ to 3. We have declared j, where $j = 0$, 1, 2, 3. When i is equal to direction point (*a1, b1, c1* and *d1*) of tracking-agent then

the value of j changes and j index of the *handoffAgent* array is assigned to i index of the *trackingAgent* array. Through this loop, handoff–agent can learn tracking–agent's relative directions.

- Upon completion of this loop, learning directions are returned to *getLocation (Location)* function of *HandoffAgent* class for routing location which can be easily perceived by seeing Algorithm 3.

Let the direction points be defined as a1, b1, c1 and d1. The Handoff–agent is defined as H and Tracking-agent as T. We are assigning Handoff–agent's indices to certain values (0 to 3) based on function's input values (a1, b1, c1, d1) for each i from 0 to 3 (See Eq. 2). Subsequently, each of the indexed values of handoff–agent also have been assigned to tracking-agent's index values (See Eq. 3).

$$\forall_i \in \{0,1,2,3\}f := \begin{cases} H_{j\leftarrow 0} & \text{if } i = a1 \\ H_{j\leftarrow 1} & \text{if } i = b1 \\ H_{j\leftarrow 2} & \text{if } i = c1 \\ H_{j\leftarrow 3} & \text{if } i = d1 \end{cases} \tag{2}$$

$$T_i := H_j \tag{3}$$

The formation of RDL algorithm for programming perspective is according to Algorithm 2:

Algorithm 2. RDL Algorithm

```
1:  Function RDL ():
2:      handoffAgent[] ← [right, left, forward, backward];
3:      directions points: a; b; c; d;
4:      right ← 0; left ← 1; forward ← 2; backward ← 3;
5:      a ← right; b ← left; c ← forward; d ← backward;
6:      trackingAgent[] ← [Right, Left, Forward, Backward];
7:      directions points: a1, b1, c1, d1 ← LFRDI ();
8:      /* Call Procedure LFRDI () of Algorithm 1*/
9:      int j;
10:     for i:= 0 to 3
11:         if i == a1 then, j ← 0;
12:         else if i == b1 then, j ← 1;
13:         else if i == c1 then, j ← 2;
14:         else if i == d1 then, j ← 3;
15:         trackingAgent[i] ← handoffAgent[j];
16:     end for
17:     return trackingAgent[];
18:     /*learning directions are returned to HandoffAgent
19:     Class of Algorithm 3*/
```

3.3   Structure of RDBLT Algorithm

The procedure of RDBLT algorithm by the idea of the programming perspective is as follows

- At first two class *TrackingAgent* and *HandoffAgent* are created, for representing tracking–agent and handoff–agent
- Tracking–agent wants to get location path from handoff–agent. For that reason, another array *Path* can acquire the target location path by calling *getLocation (Location)* function of *HandoffAgent* class.
- In our experiment handoff–agent contains the location data in the database. An array *LocationPath* of class *HandoffAgent* collects the data of target location.
- An array *Direction* is created which contains handoff–agent's relative directions (*right, left, forward* and *backward*) and respectively contained 0, 1, 2 and 3 direction values (See Table 1).
- For providing the relative direction based mapping, array *LearningDirection* can get of the learning relative directions of tracking–agent by calling RDL() function (See Algorithm 2). For the same reason, handoff–agent need to know the tracking–agent's direction points (*a1, b1, c1* and *d1*) which is called by LFRDI() function (See Algorithm 1).
- A variable *h* has been declared, where *h* = 0. Then declare an array *PathSegment* for understanding the segmentation of *LocationPath* (See Fig. 4).

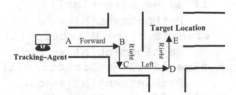

Fig. 4. Figure shows that, a *LocationPath* which is A→E, where have several path segments, which are A→B = Forward = 2, B→C = Right = 0, C→D = Left = 1 and D→E = Right = 0 (See Table 1). In order that, *PathSegment[]* =[2, 0, 1, 0, 1].

- A while loop is finished before the competition of *LocationPath* array length. Another inner loop appears, where variable *i* = 0 to 3.
- If *h* index of *LocationPath* is equal to *i* index of *LearningDirection* then, another inner four conditional statements (if-else if) have occurred where handoff–agent is checking the *LocationPath* for tracking–agent's 2D aspects (See Fig. 1)
- If specific tracking–agent's direction point (*a1, b1, c1* and *d1*) is equal to *i* index of *Direction* array, then the specific direction point is assigned into *PathSegment* array. So handoff–agent can estimate the path for tracking–agent's 2D position.
- Upon completion of these loops, handoff–agent is provided the *PathSegment* to tracking-agent. As a result, tracking-agent gets the location path.

The formation of RDBLT algorithm for programming viewpoint is according to Algorithm 3:

```
Algorithm 3. RDBLT Algorithm
1: TrackingAgentclass:
2:     Location ← Tracking or target location;
3:     HandoffAgent HA = new HandoffAgent();
4:     Path[] ← HA.getLocation(Location);
5:
6: HandoffAgentclass:
7:     getLocation(Location):
8:         LocationPath[] ← Data(Location);
9:         Direction[] ← [right, left, forward, backward];
20:         right ← 0; left ← 1; forward ← 2; backward ← 3;
10:         LearningDirection[] ← RDL();
11:         /* Call Procedure RDL() of Algorithm 2 */
12:         directions points: a1, b1, c1, d1 ← LFRDI();
13:         /* Call Procedure LFRDI()of Algorithm 1 */
14:         PathSegment[];
15:         h ← 0;
16:         While(LocationPath[].length() not complete)
17:             for i:= 0 to 3
18:                 if LocationPath[h] == LearningDirection[i]
19:                     if a1 == Direction[i]
20:                         PathSegment[h] ← a1;
21:                     else if b1 == Direction[i]
22:                         PathSegment[h] ← b1;
23:                     else if c1 == Direction[i]
24:                         PathSegment[h] ← c1;
25:                     else if d1== Direction[i]
26:                         PathSegment[h] ← d1;
27:                 end if
28:             end for
29:         h++;
30:         end while
31:         return PathSegment[]; /*Return to Tracking-agent*/
```

4 Conceptual Result and Analysis

Figure 5 represents a test case where tracking–agent and handoff–agent are situated in isolated area and their relative direction positions are also different. Now tracking–agent communicates with handoff–agent for getting target location path.

In (A) section of Fig. 5, tracking–agent gives a request to handoff–agent for getting target location path. Handoff–agent contains the location path in the database. Assume that, for handoff–agent's 2D perspective, the Location Path = [right, left, right] = [0, 1, 0] (See Table 1). In the (B) section, by using LFRDI, RDL and RDBLT algorithms,

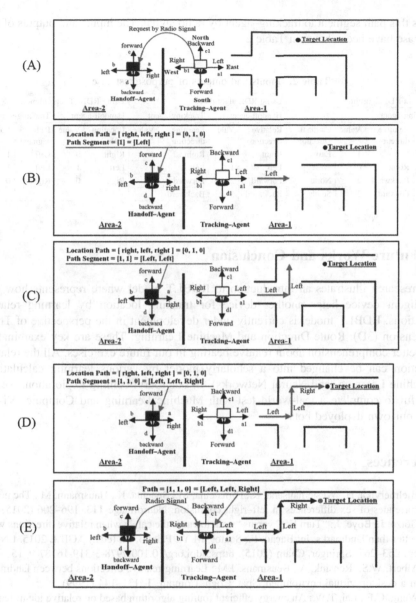

Fig. 5. A simple test case of RDBLT model.

handoff–agent can track the first path which is left. The coordination of tracking agent's Left direction and handoff–agent's right direction is the same. By using these three algorithms full path is achieved, which have shown in (C) and (D) section of Fig. 5. Learning direction values can not follow the Table 1, because these values depend on the distinct 2D position of two agents. After using loop of RDBLT algorithm, the Path Segment = [1, 1, 0] = [Left, Left, Right] is acquired (See Table 1). Finally, handoff–agent sends this path segment to tracking–agent by radio signal. The inputs and outputs of this test case have been shown in Table 2.

Table 2. Inputs and outputs of purpose test case

Using LFRDI algorithm				Using RDL algorithm				Using RDBLT algorithm			
Tracking-agent				Handoff-agent		Tracking-agent		Handoff-agent		Tracking-agent	
Point	Relative direction	Value	Cardinal Direction	Relative direction	Value	Learning direction	Value	Location path	Value	Path segment	Value
a1	Left	1	East	Right	0	Right	1	Right	0	Left	1
b1	Right	0	West	Left	1	Left	0	Left	1	Left	1
c1	Backward	3	North	Forward	2	Forward	2	Right	0	Right	0
d1	Forward	2	South	Backward	3	Backward	3				

5 Future Works and Conclusion

The research illustrates an introduction to RDBLT model where represents how one intelligent device helps another device for tracking location by learning relative directions. RDBLT model is currently under development in the perspective of Three Dimension (3D), Route Direction and Machine Learning. These are key examination for better comprehension about relative bearing in our future exercises. All the relative direction can be changed into a scholarly model by various learning calculations (Machine Learning, and Neural Networks). In our fourth coming exploration, we are hopeful to complete a real-world test with Machine Learning and Computer Vision with our own deployed bots.

References

1. Hjelmervika, H., Westerhausena, R., Hirnsteina, M., Spechta, K., Hausmann, M.: The neural correlates of sex differences in left–right confusion. NeuroImage **113**, 196–206 (2015)
2. Götze, J., Boye, J.: "Turn left" versus "walk towards the café": when relative directions work better than landmarks. In: Bação, F., Santos, M.Y., Painho, M. (eds.) AGILE 2015. LNGC, pp. 253–267. Springer, Cham (2015). https://doi.org/10.1007/978-3-319-16787-9_15
3. Albert, W.S., Rensink, A., Beusmans, J.M.: Learning relative directions between landmarks in a desktop virtual environmen. Spat. Cogn. Comput. **1**, 131–144 (1999)
4. Weng, C.E., Lai, T.W.: An energy-efficient routing algorithm based on relative identification and direction for wireless sensor networks. Wirel. Pers. Commun. **69**, 253–268 (2013)
5. Kabir, S.R., Allayear, S.M., Alam, M.M., Munna, M.T.A.: A computational technique for intelligent computers to learn and identify the human's relative directions. In: International Conference on Intelligent Sustainable Systems, pp. 1036–1039. IEEE Xplore, India (2017)
6. Lurz, F., Mueller, S., Lindner, S., Linz, S., Gardill, M., Weigel, R., Koelpin, A.: Smart communication and relative localization system for firefighters and rescuers. In: 2017 IEEE MTT-S International Microwave Symposium (IMS), pp. 1421–1424. IEEE Xplore, USA (2017)

7. Lowrance, C.J., Lauf, A.P.: Direction of arrival estimation for robots using radio signal strength and mobility. In: 2016 13th Workshop on Positioning, Navigation and Communications (WPNC). IEEE Press (2016)
8. Kolster, A.F., Dunmore, F.W.: The Radio Direction Finder and Its Application to Navigation, Washington (1921)
9. Mahmood, A., Wallace, J.W., Jensen, M.A.: Radio frequency UAV attitude estimation using direction of arrival and polarization. In: 11th European Conference on Antennas and Propagation, pp. 1857–1859. IEEE Press, France (2017)
10. Kabir, S.R.: Computation of multi-agent based relative direction learning specification. B.Sc. thesis, Daffodil International University, Bangladesh (2017)
11. Mossakowski, T., Moratz, R.: Qualitative reasoning about relative direction of oriented points. Artif. Intell. **180–181**, 34–45 (2012)
12. Moratz, R.: Representing relative direction as a binary relation of oriented points. In: 17th European Conference on Artificial Intelligence, pp. 407–411. IOS Press, Netherlands (2006)
13. Hahn, S., Bethge, J., Döllner, J.: Relative direction change - a topology-based metric for layout stability in treemaps. In: 12th International Conference on Information Visualization Theory and Applications, pp. 88–95. Portugal (2017)
14. Lee, J.H., Renz, J., Wolter, D.: StarVars—effective reasoning about relative directions. In: Twenty-Third International Joint Conference on Artificial Intelligence (IJCAI 2013), pp. 976–982. AAAI Press, California (2013)

FPGA Implementation for Real-Time Epoch Extraction in Speech Signal

Nagapuri Srinivas[✉], Kankanala Srinivas, Gayadhar Pradhan,
and Puli Kishore Kumar

Department of Electronics and Communication Engineering,
National Institute of Technology, Patna 800005, India
{ns,kankanala.ec16,gdp,pulikishorek}@nitp.ac.in

Abstract. During the production of a speech, the instant of significant excitation's are called epochs. In speech processing, epochs plays a significant role and used in many applications. Accurate detection of epochs from the speech is a challenging task due to time varying nature of the vocal-tract system and excitation source. To detect the epochs from the speech signal several algorithms are already proposed. Zero Frequency Filter (ZFF) approach is one among the different techniques which gives better performance. This method is based on the impulse nature of the excitation source and not affected by the vocal-tract system characteristics. The original filter design of ZFF realized as Infinite Impulse Response (IIR) filter followed by two detrenders. Due to the unstable nature of IIR filter, later the ZFF is realized as the Zero-Band Filter (ZBF). In this paper, we have designed the hardware architectures for IIR and ZBF realization of ZFF. The hardware architectures of ZFF are verified by implementing it on FPGA (ZedBoard Zynq Evaluation and Development Kit $xc7z020clg4841$) using Xilinx system generator-2016.2.

Keywords: Epochs · Zero-Band Filter (ZBF)
Zero Frequency Filter (ZFF) · Hardware architecture · FPGA

1 Introduction

The speech signals are produced by exciting the vocal-tract systems. This excitation might be because of: 1. Glottal vibration, 2. Burst, 3. Frication [1]. In the case of voice speech, the excitement for the vocal tract system is glottal vibration. It is nothing but closing and opening of the glottis. The agitation of the vocal tract system is present during speech production. But it is more significant at the moments of glottal closure. These are called epochs. These excitation's at the instants are like impulse nature, as the energy at the epochs are more comparing to the energy of the neighboring instants. Because of the time changing nature of both excitation source and vocal tract framework identification of precise location of epochs stayed as a challenging area of research. Throughout the years, a few strategies have been proposed for the precise recognition of epochs.

© Springer Nature Singapore Pte Ltd. 2018
M. Singh et al. (Eds.): ICACDS 2018, CCIS 905, pp. 392–400, 2018.
https://doi.org/10.1007/978-981-13-1810-8_39

Linear prediction (LP) analysis is performed to extract the LP residual signal [2,3]. It is assumed that the LP residual signal mostly contains the excitation source information. The epoch detection methods relay implicitly and explicitly on processing of LP residual signal assume that the higher energy is present around the epoch locations [1]. However such assumption may not hold all the times. Furthermore, several methods based on the properties of minimum phase signals and group-delay function [4], the maximum-likelihood theory [5] and the dynamic programming projected phase-slope algorithm (DYPSA) [6] were also explored for the detection of epochs. During the generation of voiced speech a train of impulse like excitation with time fluctuating amplitude and interval is convolved with a time fluctuating vocal tract channel. Because of time fluctuating nature of excitation and vocal tract channel, source channel separation is basically a blind deconvolution issue. Since, during the production of voiced signals the excitation is like impulse nature, the frequency response of such impulses is spread through out the frequency domain of speech signal including the *zero* Hz frequency component. To extract the *zero* Hz frequency component a resonator is designed and termed as zero frequency filter (ZFF) [1]. The initially proposed ZFF realized as, an infinite impulse response (IIR) filter supplanted by two detrenders. The output of the IIR filter aggressively increasing or decreasing function of time depending on the polarity of speech signal which makes filter unstable. Afterward, a stable ZBF realization of ZFF is proposed in [7].

The Epoch detection has many applications in speech processing like speech synthesis [8], foreground speech segmentation [9], detection of vowel-like regions in a speech sequence [10], segmentation of speech into voiced and unvoiced regions [11], extraction of pitch contours [12] and many other. We have implemented IIR and ZBF realization of ZFF on the ZedBoard Zynq Evaluation and Development Kit ($xc7z020clg4841$) FPGA using Xilinx system generator-2016.2. The theoretical hardware requirement and hardware utilization on FPGA for hardware implementation of IIR and ZBF realization of ZFF is also presented.

The rest of the paper is arranged as: Sect. 2 describes the implementation of ZFF using IIR and ZBF realizations. Section 3 deals with the experimental results. Finally Sect. 4 concludes the paper.

2   Hardware Architecture of Zero Frequency Filter

The following subsections present the IIR and ZBF realization architectures of ZFF.

2.1   IIR Realization of Zero Frequency Filter

The block diagram representation of ZFF using IIR realization [1] is shown in Fig. 1. It consists of three types of sub-blocks known as first order difference

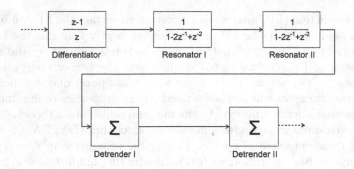

Fig. 1. Block diagram representation of IIR realization of ZFF.

filter, zero frequency resonator and detrender. The process of extracting epochs from a speech signal using IIR realization of ZFF is as follows:

- The first order difference is calculated for the input speech signal $s(n)$, to remove the low frequency fluctuation, and is given as

$$x[n] = s[n] - s[n-1] \qquad (1)$$

- The difference signal $x(n)$ is processed through a cascade of two ideal resonators at *zero* Hz. The output of the cascade resonators is a exponentially increasing or decreasing function of time. As the length of the output signal increases, the number of bits required to store the above polynomial increases. So, the IIR filter is marginally stable. The zero frequency resonator is given as

$$r[n] = x[n] + 2r[n-1] - r[n-2] \qquad (2)$$

The data flow graph of Eq. 2 is shown in Fig. 2. The element D represents the unit delay.

- Remove the exponential trend from the cascade resonators output $y(n)$ by subtracting the local mean computed over a window of length $2N + 1$. This process helps in highlighting the discontinuities in the filtered signal due to impulse type of excitation. The value of window length is not critical as long as it lies in the range of one to two pitch periods.

$$\hat{y}[n] = y[n] - \frac{1}{(2N+1)} \sum_{m=-N}^{N} y[n-m] \qquad (3)$$

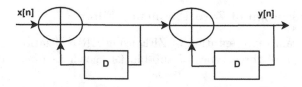

Fig. 2. Data flow graph of zero frequency resonator

– The Eq. 3, the present output depends on future samples which makes it non−causal. For real time implementation the detrender output is delayed by N samples to make causal as follows.

$$\bar{y}[n - N] = y[n - N] - \frac{1}{(2N + 1)} \sum_{m=0}^{2N} y[n - m] \qquad (4)$$

The data flow graph of Eq. 4 is shown in Fig. 3 with latency N clock cycles. In the present work the value of N is considered as 64 samples (8 ms duration for speech signal sampled at 8 kHz) for better roll-off. As suggested in the original work [1], deviation of N from 50 to 100 samples will not affect the performance significantly.

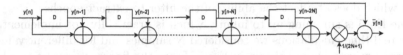

Fig. 3. Data flow graph of detrender.

2.2   ZBF Realization of Zero Frequency Filter

The IIR realization of ZFF have the poles on the unit circle, which makes the filter marginally stable. To overcome this problem, a modified method based on stable IIR resonant filter has been proposed in [7]. This method employs a different filter which allows a narrow band of frequencies around the *zero* Hz to pass through, and this filter is called a zero-band filter. By placing the poles inside unit circle, this task can be achieved and it is realized as ZBF. The output of this ZBF is neither increasing nor decreasing function of time. Therefore, the removal of trend from the output of the ZBF is not necessary for obtaining the exact locations of the epochs. These locations are indicated directly by the positive zero crossings of the output of zero-band filter. Block diagram for ZBF realization for ZFF is shown in Fig. 4. As suggested in [7], the ZBF output $y(n)$ is realised from differenced speech signal $x(n)$ as follows.

$$y[n] = \sum_{k=0}^{\infty}(k + 1)r^k x(n - k) \qquad (5)$$

If r = 1, then y[n] is diverging and called the zero-frequency filter. If r < 1, then y[n] is converging and called the zero-band filter.

From the Eq. 5, it can be observed that as the value of r increases from 0 to 1, the magnitude response of the ZBF becomes sharper increasing the value of gain at 0 Hz compared to other frequency components. As the value of r reaches one the gain of the filter becomes infinity at 0 Hz and the filter behaves as ideal resonator at zero frequency. This ideal 0 Hz resonator is called zero-frequency

Fig. 4. Block diagram representation of the ZBF realization of ZFF.

filter and it is marginally stable. The output of the ZFF is unstable. Hence, a stable filter called the ZBF whose poles lie within the unit circle is used instead of zero-frequency filter. The output of the zero-band filter is stable. The stability of the output of zero-band filter is achieved at the cost of finite gain at 0 Hz and a narrow increase in the bandwidth of the filter. As the magnitude response of the filter is sufficiently narrow and allows a band of frequencies close to zero Hertz which doesn't affect the ability of the filter to extract epochs.

The Eq. 5 is summing up to infinity which is practically not implementable. So for real-time calculations we considered N samples and for different values of N, output waveforms are shown in Fig. 5. From the figure, it can be concluded that by increasing the value of N from 20 to 40 the curve has got smoothed and no large difference is seen from $N = 40$ to $N = 100$. Here, we consider N = 40 for optimum results. The positive zero crossings in ZBF output represents the epochs. The value of r = 0.99 is taken for maintaining the system stable. The DFG of ZBF is shown in Fig. 6.

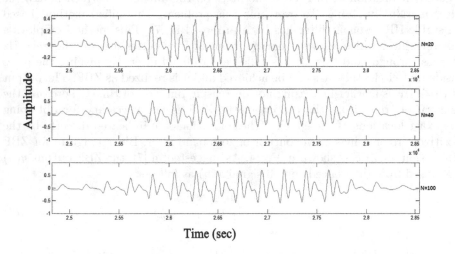

Fig. 5. Matlab analysis of the ZBF for different filter orders

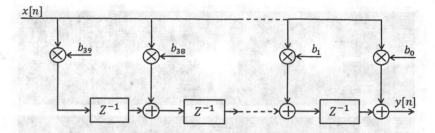

Fig. 6. Data flow graph of zero band filter

3   Hardware Implementation and Results Discussion

High-level synthesis tools are used for hardware implementation of digital system due to the following advantages:

– Easy to alter the design hardware architecture.
– Rapid hardware prototyping time of algorithms.
– Automatic generation of the target HDL codes.
– Flexibility and re-usability.

High-level synthesis tools facilitate the introduction of designs at a much higher level of abstraction. Although C/C++ are the most common in describing complex systems, high-level tools such as the Xilinx System Generator (XSG) offer the above advantages. The XSG is a system-level design tool for plug-in Xilinxs line of FPGAs to MATLAB-Simulink. It consists of a set of Intellectual Property (IPs) for basic combinational, sequential and control logic blocks. The architecture of proposed method is modeling by integrating the IPs. Each of the blocks in XSG are configured to use a fixed point notation by specifying the bit precision, latency and implementation option (to optimize speed or area) by altering properties of the corresponding blocks. The XSG tool successfully used to implement digital hard of various algorithms and controllers [13–25] for real time applications on FPGA

Xilinx system generator (XSG) 2016.2 is used for system level modeling of the IIR and FIR realization of ZFF as DFGs discussed earlier. The IIR and ZBF realization of ZFF are implemented with input and output of 24-bit precision with 23-bit fractional signed fixed-point data type. The XSG gives fast-tracked simulation through hardware co-simulation. The XSG will automatically generates a hardware simulation token for a design conquered in the Xilinx DSP blockset that will run on validated hardware platforms. Here we used the Zed board for hardware co-simulation. After generating the hardware co simulation tokens of IIR and ZBF realization of ZFF, we supplied the speech samples taken from the TIMIT database from the MATLAB work and observe the hardware co-simulated output on scope as shown in Fig. 7.

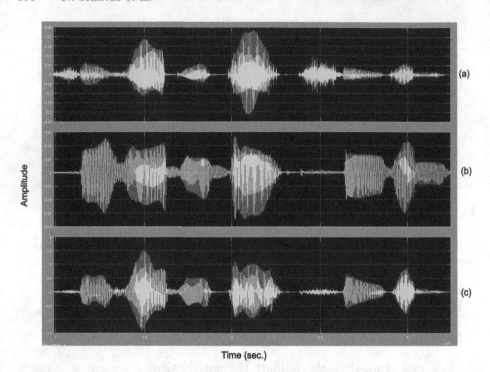

Fig. 7. Hardware co-simulation results of ZFF (a) Speech samples taken from the TIMIT database, (b) IIR realization of ZFF output, (c) ZBF realization of ZFF output.

The comparison of hardware requirement(theoretically calculated from respected DFGs) of ZBF and IIR realization is given in Table 1. The hardware utilization, Power consumption and operating clock frequency on FPGA (Zed-Board Zynq Evaluation and Development Kit $xc7z020clg4841$) for ZBF and IIR realizations of ZFF is summarized in Table 2.

Table 1. Comparison of theoretically calculated hardware requirement for IIR and ZBF realizations of ZFF.

No. of	ZBF realization	IIR realization
Adders	39	263
Multipliers	40	0
Delays	39	261

Table 2. The hardware utilization, Power consumption and operating clock frequency on FPGA (ZedBoard Zynq Evaluation and Development Kit $xc7z020clg4841$) for ZBF and IIR realizations of ZFF.

Design	LUT	Flip flop	DSP slices	Power	Frequency
ZBF realization	1150	2290	40	0.344 W	72 MHz
IIR realization	17232	16704	0	0.188 W	16 MHz

4   Conclusions

The IIR and ZBF realizations of ZFF are implemented on FPGA for detection of epochs in real-time speech signal. The theoretical hardware requirement and hardware utilization on FPGA (ZedBoard Zynq Evaluation and Development Kit $xc7z020clg4841$) are presented. It observed that ZBF realization of ZFF can operate with high clock frequency with more power consumption when compared with IIR realization of ZFF.

References

1. Murty, K.S.R., Yegnanarayana, B.: Epoch extraction from speech signals. IEEE Trans. Audio, Speech, Lang. Process. **16**(8), 1602–1613 (2008)
2. Atal, B.S., Hanauer, S.L.: Speech analysis and synthesis by linear prediction of the speech wave. J. Acoust. Soc. Am. **50**(2B), 637–655 (1971)
3. Ananthapadmanabha, T., Yegnanarayana, B.: Epoch extraction from linear prediction residual for identification of closed glottis interval. IEEE Trans. Acoust. Speech Signal Process. **27**(4), 309–319 (1979)
4. Smits, R., Yegnanarayana, B.: Determination of instants of significant excitation in speech using group delay function. IEEE Trans. Speech Audio Process. **3**(5), 325–333 (1995)
5. Strube, H.W.: Determination of the instant of glottal closure from the speech wave. J. Acoust. Soc. Am. **56**(5), 1625–1629 (1974)
6. Kounoudes, A., Naylor, P.A., Brookes, M.: The DYPSA algorithm for estimation of glottal closure instants in voiced speech. In: 2002 IEEE International Conference on Acoustics, Speech, and Signal Processing (ICASSP), vol. 1, p. I-349. IEEE (2002)
7. Deepak, K.T., Prasanna, S.R.M.: Epoch extraction using zero band filtering from speech signal. Circuits, Syst. Signal Process. **34**(7), 2309–2333 (2014). https://doi.org/10.1007%2Fs00034-014-9957-4
8. Prasanna, S.R.M., Govind, D., Rao, K.S., Yenanarayana, B.: Fast prosody modification using instants of significant excitation. In: Proceedings of Speech Prosody (2010)
9. Deepak, K., Sarma, B.D., Prasanna, S.M.: Foreground speech segmentation using zero frequency filtered signal. In: Thirteenth Annual Conference of the International Speech Communication Association (2012)
10. Pradhan, G., Prasanna, S.M.: Speaker verification by vowel and nonvowel like segmentation. IEEE Trans. Audio, Speech, Lang. Process. **21**(4), 854–867 (2013)
11. Dhananjaya, N., Yegnanarayana, B.: Voiced/nonvoiced detection based on robustness of voiced epochs. IEEE Signal Process. Lett. **17**(3), 273276 (2010)

12. Seshadri, G., Yegnanarayana, B.: Performance of an event-based instantaneous fundamental frequency estimator for distant speech signals. IEEE Trans. Audio Speech Lang. Process. **19**(7), 1853–1864 (2011)
13. Monmasson, E., Cirstea, M.: FPGA design methodology for industrial control systems—a review. IEEE Trans. Ind. Electron. **54**(4), 1824–1842 (2007)
14. Jimenez-Fernandez, A., Linares-Barranco, A., Paz-Vicente, R., Lujan-Martenez, C.D., Jimenez, G., Civit, A.: AER and dynamic systems co-simulation over Simulink with Xilinx System Generator. In: Proceedings of the 15th IEEE International Conference on Electronics, Circuits and Systems, ICECS 2008, pp. 1281–1284 (2008)
15. Rabah, H., Amira, A., Mohanty, B.K., Almaadeed, S., Meher, P.K.: FPGA implementation of orthogonal matching pursuit for compressive sensing reconstruction. IEEE Trans. Very Large Scale Integr. (VLSI) Syst. **23**(10), 2209–2220 (2015)
16. Kasap, S., Redif, S.: Novel field-programmable gate array architecture for computing the eigenvalue decomposition of para-hermitian polynomial matrices. IEEE Trans. Very Large Scale Integr. (VLSI) Syst. **22**(3), 522–536 (2014)
17. Prince, A.A., Ganesh, S., Verma, P.K., George, P., Raju, D.: Efficient implementation of empirical mode decomposition in FPGA using Xilinx system generator. In: IECON Proceedings (Industrial Electronics Conference), pp. 895–900 (2016)
18. Athar, S., Ieee, M., Siddiqi, M.A., Masud, S., Member, S.: Teaching and research in FPGA based digital signal processing using Xilinx system generator, pp. 2765–2768 (2012)
19. Selvamuthukumaran, R., Gupta, R.: Rapid prototyping of power electronics converters for photovoltaic system application using Xilinx system generator. Power Electron. IET **7**(9), 2269–2278 (2014)
20. Parmar, C.A., Ramanadham, B., Darji, A.D.: FPGA implementation of hardware efficient adaptive filter robust to impulsive noise. IET Comput. Digit. Tech. **11**(3), 107–116 (2017). https://doi.org/10.1049/iet-cdt.2016.0067
21. Pinto, S.J., Panda, G., Peesapati, R.: An implementation of hybrid control strategy for distributed generation system interface using xilinx system generator. IEEE Trans. Ind. Inform. **13**(5), 2735–2745 (2017)
22. Vayada,M.G., Patel, H.R., Muduli, B.R.: Hardware software co-design simulation modeling for image security concept using Matlab-Simulink with Xilinx system generator. In: Proceedings of 2017 3rd IEEE International Conference on Sensing, Signal Processing and Security, ICSSS 2017, pp. 134–137 (2017)
23. Bahoura, M., Ezzaidi, H.: FPGA-implementation of a sequential adaptive noise canceller using Xilinx system generator. Proc. Int. Conf. Microelectr. ICM **4**, 213–216 (2009)
24. Ownby, M., Mahmoud, W.H.: Dr. Wagdy H. Mahmoud, pp. 404–408
25. Bahoura, M., Ezzaidi, H.: FPGA-implementation of discrete wavelet transform with application to signal denoising. Circ. Syst. Signal Process. **31**(3), 987–1015 (2012)

Privacy-Preserving Random Permutation of Image Pixels Enciphered Model from Cyber Attacks for Covert Operations

Amit Kumar Shakya[✉], Ayushman Ramola, Akhilesh Kandwal, and Vivek Chamoli

Department of Electronics and Communication, Graphic Era (Deemed to Be University),
Clement Town, Dehradun 248002, Uttrakhand, India
xlamitshakya.gate2014@ieee.org

Abstract. We all are aware from the fact that 21st century is the era of space technology, IoT (Internet of Thing), advanced robotics and extreme weaponry, each and every country of the world wishes to progress at a rapid rate. This intention gives rise to a new situation where own national interest becomes the top priority, so less developed countries are destabilised by adopting policies like cyber-attacks & state sponsored terrorism. Many countries are nowadays involved in such activities, so the challenges become more tenacious for the intelligence agencies to tackle such sought of the problem. Problem-related to data theft while transmission, pre-planned hacking, cyber attacks etc., are some common modes of data robbery. The data that is transmitted can be in form of images, documents, codes, etc. Here we are proposing an image encipher scheme based on strong encryption and random permutation of image pixels for intelligence agencies by which even if any particular information gets leaked out, the probability of extracting useful information from the hacked data is not possible for an unknown hacker, organization or any country.

Keywords: National interest · State sponsored terrorism · Image encipher
Hacking · Cyber attacks · Random permutation

1 Introduction

Today computer technology has reached an extent that was not even imagined in the past decades. This development has made the human life more comfortable and effortless but at the same time created new challenges in the field of security and defence. It is a fact that countries with better software skills will dominate the technological warfare [1]. Cyber-attack is the first step towards data robbery, it is defined as the action directed towards electronic gadgets like computers, personal laptops, telecommunication devices, etc., with the objective to disrupt and steal vital information, change processing control and damage operating software [2]. There are several types of cyber-attacks with the motive to stole personal or professional data, these are categorized as indiscriminate attacks [3], cyber warfare [4], destructive attacks [5], corporate espionage [6], government espionage [7], stole email address and login credentials [8], stole credit cards and financial data [9], stole medical data [10] etc. In cryptography, encryption is defined as

© Springer Nature Singapore Pte Ltd. 2018
M. Singh et al. (Eds.): ICACDS 2018, CCIS 905, pp. 401–410, 2018.
https://doi.org/10.1007/978-981-13-1810-8_40

a process through which message, data and images are coded in a manner that they are only decoded only by the authorized person [11]. Houas [12] developed an encipher scheme to encrypt binary or bi-valued images. Pareek [13] proposed an encipher scheme with an external secret key having 80 bits and two chaotic logistics (CL) maps. Askar [14] developed an image encipher scheme in which both encryption and decryption operations can be performed on the images with the same security key. Wu et al. [15] proposed an image encipher scheme based on the colour map lattice (CML) and fractional order chaotic systems (FOCS). There are several types of malware's from which we have to protect our vital data from the cyber mugging (Fig. 1).

Fig. 1. Pictorial representation of the software-based computer malware

There are several images encipher schemes and models for the data hiding and recovery. These include content-based image retrieval (CBIR), and its advanced version private content-based image retrieval (PCBIR). The main motive of these encryption schemes is to secure the information that is transmitted from 'one' end to 'other' end. In the proposed privacy preserving random permutation of the image pixels enciphered model (RPIPEM), one end is the 'sender' and the other end is the 'receiver'. The sender end collects data, images, codes, etc. based on ground conditions and uses the RPIPEM model to transmit information to the receiver end. This scheme contains two steps. In the first step, sender end performs the random pixel arrangement encryption and evaluation of the statistical parameters for the original dataset. In the second step statistical parameters are computed for the enciphered images, histogram matching of the original and enciphered images is performed and finally, the parameters matching are done to identify the original images.

2   Mathematical Imitation of the Proposed Privacy Preserving (RPIPEM) Model

2.1   Generation of New Enciphered Image

Digital images contain pixels in a matrix format these pixels are located at a specific position to produce a useful representation of a scene, event, location etc. Let a digital image 'i' contain 'r' number of rows and 'c' numbers of columns, then the total number of pixels contained in the image is $i = r \times c$. These pixels are arranged in specific positions to optically represent a meaningful image. Here $(r \times c)$ image pixels distributed in an image are represented in matrix notation, where each and every pixel carries a specific pixel value or digital number (DN) (Fig. 2).

$$i = \begin{bmatrix} i(1,1) & i(1,2) & & i(1,r-1) & i(1,r) \\ i(2,1) & i(2,2) & \cdots & i(2,r-1) & i(2,r) \\ \vdots & & \ddots & & \vdots \\ i(c-1,1) & i(c-1,2) & \cdots & i(c-1,r-1) & i(c-1,r) \\ i(c,1) & i(c,2) & & i(c,r-1) & i(c,r) \end{bmatrix}$$

Fig. 2.   Matrix notation of the digital image

Now we are arranging the pixels in the random order, and then we have taken only 10% (Ten-percent) of the total pixels to create a new image i^i which contains r_{new} numbers of rows and c_{new} numbers of columns.

Now, these 10% (Ten-percent) pixels are arranged in a random order in a vector of a single row.

$$V = \begin{bmatrix} p_1, p_2, p_3, p_4, p_5, \cdots \cdots \cdots \cdots \cdots p_k \end{bmatrix} \tag{1}$$

Here p1 to p_k represents the pixel intensity of the 10% (Ten-percent) pixels. The pixels in the vector V are arranged in the random order of $(r_{new} \times c_{new})!$ combinations, which represents the total combination of the pixel arrangements. The new image will contain randomly selected pixel in an unplanned order. The matrix notion of the randomly arranged image pixels in shown below (Fig. 3).

$$i^i = \begin{bmatrix} i(1,4) & i(c-4,r-4) & & i(2,8) & i(9,0) \\ i(c_{new}-1, r_{new}-1) & i(c,r-2)) & \cdots & i(5,9) & i(c-2,r-3) \\ \vdots & & \ddots & & \vdots \\ i(c-1,r-1) & i(9,8) & & i(1,1) & i(2,2) \\ i(4,1) & i(c-3,r-7) & \cdots & i(8,6) & i(8,4) \end{bmatrix}$$

Fig. 3.   Matrix notation of the unplanned pixel arrangement image

2.2 Retrieving Original Image from a Enciphered Image

A digital image contains various pixels intensity values, these values are expressed as $(0 - 2^n)$ where n = number of bits in an image. For $n = 8$, 8 bit image bit image intensity values are expressed as $i_v = \{0,1,2,3\ldots\ldots\ldots255 - 1\}$. Now, the probability of occurrence of the specific intensity value in the new enciphered image is expressed as $(0 - 2^n)$ where n = number of bits in an image. The probability of occurrence of the specific intensity value in the new image is expressed as under.

$$p_{i_v} = \{n(i_v)/(r \times c)\} \tag{2}$$

Where $n(i_v)$ is the occurrence time of the intensity value in the original image. Now the first order image statistical parameters mean μ_0, variance σ_0^2, and standard deviation $\sqrt{\sigma_0^2}$ are computed for the original image.

$$Mean(\mu_0) = \sum_{i_v=0}^{i_v=256-1} i_v \times p(i_v) \tag{3}$$

$$Variance(\sigma_0^2) = \sum_{i_v=0}^{i_v=256-1} (i_v - \mu_0)^2 \times p(i_v) \tag{4}$$

$$Standard\ Deviation = \sqrt{\sigma_0^2} \tag{5}$$

Now for the encipher image, we have also calculated statistical parameters mean $\mu_{encipher}$, variance $\sigma_{encipher}^2$ and standard deviation $\sqrt{\sigma_{encipher}^2}$.

$$Mean(\mu_{encipher}) = \sum_{i_v=0}^{i_v=256-1} i^i \times p(i)^i \tag{6}$$

$$Variance\left(\sigma_{encipher}^2\right) = \sum_{i_v=0}^{i_v=256-1} (i^i - \mu_{encrypt})^2 \times p(i^i) \tag{7}$$

$$Standard\ Deviation = \sqrt{\sigma_{encipher}^2} \tag{8}$$

Experimental studies conclude that Eq. 3 $\cong$ Eq. 6, Eq. 4 $\cong$ Eq. 7 and the Eq. 5 $\cong$ Eq. 8. Here RPIPEM model suggests that the mean, variance and standard deviation for the original and enciphered image have obtained approximately same values having less than 1% error.

2.3 Histogram Matching of the Original and Enciphered Image

Now we have performed the histogram matching for both original and encipher images, both the histograms are converted to histogram signatures (HS) to visually confirm the similarity in the statistical property of the both original and encipher images.

2.4 Proposed Algorithm

In the proposed algorithm we will proceed in a stepwise manner as follows.

a. Take an input image of any dimension say $(r \times c)$.
b. Arrange pixels of the original image in a vector of single row 'V'.
c. Randomly arrange only 10%, pixels obtained from the original image.
d. Store pixels obtained from the above step into a newly created matrix 'i'$^{i.}$
e. Calculate statistical parameters for the original image.
f. Calculate statistical parameters for the encipher image.
g. Equate the statistical parameters of the original image and the image obtained after random pixel arrangement (encipher image).
h. Perform histogram signature matching for the original and encipher image.
i. Calculate error percentage between statistical parameters of both original and encipher images.

3 Experimental Result

In this experiment, we have randomly arranged pixel of the original image into a new position through random permutation. The images obtained look like a noisy picture which does not reveal any useful information. We have titled this image as random pixel arrangement (RPA) coded image or encipher images. This image is transmitted during covert operations. All categories of the images like grayscale, multi-spectral, synthetic aperture radar (SAR) images have shown satisfactory results from our model. During covert operations, satellite location, weaponry, bunker photographs, road and bridges, maps, etc. are some of the most important assets of the enemy camps, pre- information about these assets give an upper edge to any counterforce. We have performed this operation over 100 images, here we are presenting nine samples categorized in missile defence system, border army & weaponry, SAR satellite images. The result proves that from the RPA images, information about the original images can be obtained easily. During the experiment we have used MATLAB 2013 (a) with core i7 processor and CPU enabled with 4 GB RAM and 2 TB hard disk for the practical work. The images are categorized into three different groups. The group 1, 2, 3 contains Missile defence systems, border army and weaponry and Terra SAR images of different crucial border locations (Figs. 4, 5 and 6).

1. **Group A: Missile Defence Systems (MDS)**
2. **Group B: Border Army & Weaponry (BAW)**
3. **Group C: Terra SAR images of the crucial locations (SAR_ICL)**

Fig. 4. (a) Patriot MDS, USA (b) S-400 MDS, Russia (c) Iron Dome MDS, Israel

Fig. 5. (a) US BAW (b) Japan BAW (c) India BAW

Fig. 6. (a) Tucson, Arizona SAR_ICL (b) Astravets Nuclear Plant SAR_ICL (c) Waterkloof SAR_ICL

Now we have arranged only 10% (Ten Percent) pixels of the original image in a random manner so the resultant images do not reveal any information and look like a noisy image (Fig. 7).

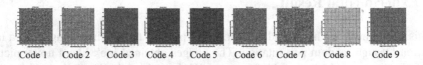

Code 1   Code 2   Code 3   Code 4   Code 5   Code 6   Code 7   Code 8   Code 9

Fig. 7. Random pixel arrangement (RPA) coded images

Now the first order statistical parameters of the original and the RPA coded images are calculated, which are shown in Tables 1 and 2 respectively.

Table 1. First order statistical parameters mean, variance and standard deviation for the original images

S.No	Original image	Original image dimension	Mean μ	Variance σ	Standard deviation $\sqrt{\sigma}$
1	MDS, Patriot, USA	2889696	111.307	9.91599	3.148966
2	MDS, S 400, Russia	364665	134.07	10.6898	3.269525
3	MDS, Iron Dome, Israel	921600	123.081	7.09546	2.663730
4	BAW, USA	768240	147.318	12.5092	3.53683
5	BAW, Japan	731724	128.646	16.2534	4.03155
6	BAW, India	270000	88.8954	9.83766	3.13650
7	SAR, Tucson, Arizona	8400000	68.9754	8.90386	2.98393
8	SAR, Astravets	10667500	82.3608	12.0023	3.46443
9	SAR, Waterkloof Airstrip	2510000	92.0351	9.63284	3.10368

Table 2. First order statistical parameters mean, variance and standard deviation for the RPA coded images

S. No.	Original image	RPA image dimension	Mean μ	Variance σ	Standard deviation $\sqrt{\sigma}$
1	MDS, Patriot, USA	288970	111.283	9.91791	3.14927
2	MDS, S 400, Russia	36467	133.833	10.6993	3.27097
3	MDS, Iron Dome, Israel	92160	123.062	7.09517	2.66367
4	BAW, USA	76824	147.657	12.5095	3.53687
5	BAW, Japan	73173	128.524	16.0138	4.00172
6	BAW, India	27000	88.5491	9.81466	3.13283
7	SAR, Tucson, Arizona	840000	68.8936	8.89448	2.98236
8	SAR, Astravets	1066750	82.3706	12.0041	3.46469
9	SAR, Waterkloof Air strip	251000	92.0075	9.62142	3.10184

Now for the original and RPA coded image histogram matching is done by sub-plotting histogram signatures for the both original and the RPA coded images.

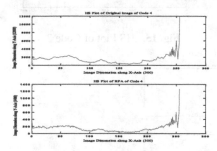

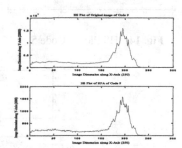

Fig. 8. HS Plot of Code 4

Fig. 9. HS Plot of Code 9

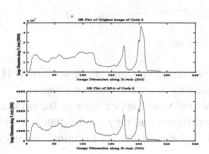

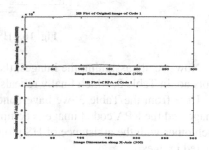

Fig. 10. HS Plot of Code 6

Fig. 11. HS Plot of Code 1

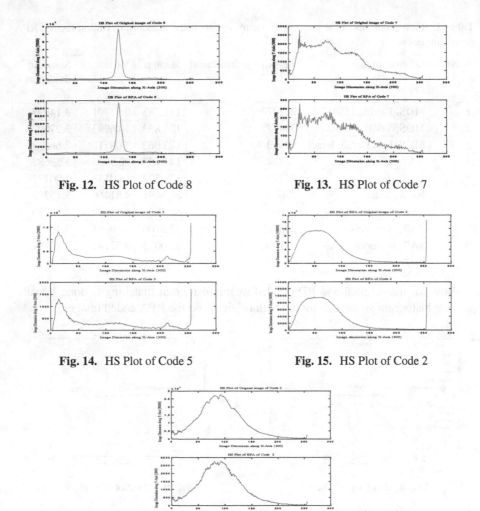

Fig. 12. HS Plot of Code 8   **Fig. 13.** HS Plot of Code 7

Fig. 14. HS Plot of Code 5   **Fig. 15.** HS Plot of Code 2

Fig. 16. HS Plot of Code 3

Now we are assigning the images, their RPA coded versions, along with their HS plots no. in Table 3, which finally reveals the identity about the original images.

Here from the Table 3, we have concluded that visual appearance of the original image and the RPA coded image is completely different and they can be matched with each other with the assistance of HS plots and statistical features of original and enciphered images.

The overlay bar plots shown in Figs. 17 and 18 represents that the statistical parameters on comparison have obtained approximately same values. The error in statistical parameters between the original and RPA coded images is less than 1% (one percent) i.e. 0.120894% for mean and 0.229024% for standard deviation on an average through this RPIPEM scheme.

Table 3. Image identification from the RPA coded image with HS plot

S.No	Groups	Original Image	RPA Coded Image	HS Plot Code
1	Missile Defence Systems	Patriot,USA	Code 6	Fig. 10
2	(MDS)	S 400,Russia	Code 4	Fig. 8
3		Iron Dome, Israel	Code 8	Fig. 12
4	Border Army &	USA	Code 9	Fig. 9
5	Weaponry (BAW)	Japan	Code 5	Fig. 14
6		India	Code 7	Fig. 13
7	SAR images of the crucial	Tucson, Arizona	Code 2	Fig. 15
8	locations (SAR_ICL)	Astravets	Code 1	Fig. 11
9		Waterkloof Airstrip	Code 3	Fig. 16

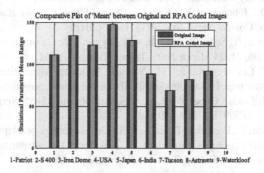

Fig. 17. Overlay plot between original and RPA coded image for statistical parameter 'Mean'

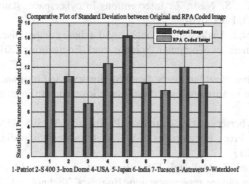

Fig. 18. Overlay plot between original and RPA coded image for statistical parameter 'Standard Deviation'

4   Conclusion

The proposed RPIPEM scheme is quite a useful scheme for data hiding during covert operations. The most important advantage of this algorithm is the transmission of data of extreme importance from sender end to the receiver end with privacy and security.

One of the limitations of this algorithm is if two images develop same statistical parameter then one can get confused in recognizing the original image. The solution to this situation can be an inclusion of some more statistical parameters like skewness and kurtosis, which can narrow the range of wrong interpretation.

Acknowledgment. Authors will like to pay sincere tribute and salute brave Indian Defence Forces who are continuously protecting our borders from all kinds of global threats. Their constant endeavour is the only inspiration behind this research work.

References

1. Geers, K., Kindlund, D., Moran, N., Rachwald, R.: World War C: understanding Nation-State motives behind today's advanced cyber attacks, pp. 1–20 (2013)
2. Guo, Z., Shi, D., Johansson, K., Shi, L.: Optimal linear cyber-attack on remote state estimation. Trans. Control Netw. Syst. **4**(1), 1–10 (2016)
3. Barreno, M., Nelson, B., Sears, R., Joseph, A.D., Tygar, J.D.: Can machine learning be secure? In: ASIACCS 2006, 21–24 March 2006, Taipei, Taiwan. ACM
4. Elder, Robert J., Levis, Alexander H., Yousefi, Bahram: Alternatives to cyber warfare: deterrence and assurance. In: Jajodia, Sushil, Shakarian, Paulo, Subrahmanian, V.S., Swarup, Vipin, Wang, Cliff (eds.) Cyber Warfare. AIS, vol. 56, pp. 15–35. Springer, Cham (2015). https://doi.org/10.1007/978-3-319-14039-1_2
5. Lakhno, V., Tkach, Y., Petrenko, T., Zaitsev, S.: Developement of adaptive expert system of information security using a procedure of clustering the attributes of anomalies and cyberattacks. East. Eur. J. Enterp. Technol. **94**(6), 32–44 (2016)
6. Gandhi, R., Sharma, A., Mahoney, W., Sauson, W.: Dimensions of cyber attacks: Social, political, economical and cultural. Technol. Soc. Spring (11), 28–38, 8 March 2011
7. Shamsi, J., Zeadally, S., Nasir, Z.: Interventions in cyberspace: status and trends. IT Pro Comput. Soc. **18**(1), 1–9 (2016)
8. Mirante, D., Cappos, J.: Understanding password database compromise. Polytechnic Institute of NYU, Department of Computer Science and Engineering 2013. Report no.: TR-CSE-2013-02
9. Choo, K.K.R.: Cyber threat landscape faced by financial and insurance industry. Canberra: Australian Institute of Crimonology, Australian Government; Feburary 2011. Report No.: ISSN 0817-8542
10. Perakslis, E.D.: Cybersecurity in health care. Perspective **31**, 395–397 (2014)
11. Wikipedia: The Free Encylopedia (2017). https://en.wikipedia.org/wiki/Encryption. Accessed 8 Aug 2017
12. Houas, A., Mokhtari, Z., Melkemi, K.E., Boussaad, A.: A novel binary image encryption algorithm based on diffuse representataion. Eng. Sci. Technol. Int. J. **12**(19), 1887–1894 (2016)
13. Pareek, N.K., Patidar, V., Sud, K.K.: Image encryption using chaotic logistic map. Image Vis. Comput. **24**, 926–934 (2006)
14. Askar, S.S., Karawia, A.A., Alshamrani, A.: Image encryption algorithm based on chaotic economic model. Math. Probl. Eng. (Article ID 341729), p. 1–10, 24 December 2014 (2015)
15. Wu, X., Li, Y., Kurths, J.: A new color image encryption scheme using CML and a fractional-order chaotic system. PLoS ONE **10**(3), e0119660 (2015)

MIDS: Metaheuristic Based Intrusion Detection System for Cloud Using k-NN and MGWO

Jitendra Kumar Seth[1](✉) and Satish Chandra[2]

[1] Department of Information Technology, Ajay Kumar Garg
Engineering College, Ghaziabad, India
mrjkseth@gmail.com
[2] Department of Computer Science and Engineering, Jaypee Institute
of Information Technology, Noida, India
satish.chandra@jiit.ac.in

Abstract. This paper presents an efficient metaheuristic based intrusion detection system (MIDS) in cloud. The proposed scheme incorporates a modified grey wolf optimization (MGWO) method for relevant feature selection from input dataset whereas the k-Nearest Neighbor (k-NN) is utilized for binary classification of input dataset. The training and evaluation of the scheme are performed over the cloud specific intrusion dataset (CSID) which is generated by the mapping between the system audit logs and corresponding tcpdump data. The key benefits of using MGWO is that it provides the low dimensional space with high efficiency for classifier training and classification. The k-NN classifier is useful for low dimension dataset therefore k-NN is chosen for classification in the scheme. The comparative performance of the proposed scheme is observed better than the existing models in terms of both accuracy and false alarm rate.

Keywords: Intrusion · Metaheuristic · GWO · K-NN · Cloud
Machine learning · Security

1 Introduction and Related Literature Review

Cloud computing provides unlimited IT resource provisioning on pay per use basis, where the IT resources include network, storage, service and application. Cloud can be deployed with least management interaction of service provider [1]. Different from the traditional computing model, the cloud computing takes advantage of virtual computing technology. The users store their sensitive data on cloud either for processing or simply for later access. The attackers may access the cloud services which may cause the loss of user data, data leakage or difficulty in accessing cloud services. These attackers can be an external entity or it may be a user of cloud services. They may harm the cloud services intentionally or unintentionally and such abnormal behaviors of users should be identified and stopped. To detect the abnormal behavior in cloud environment we have proposed an efficient intrusion detection model using k Nearest Neighbor (k-NN) through key feature selection using MGWO. A number of meta-heuristic algorithms proposed by many researchers in the past few of them are Particle

© Springer Nature Singapore Pte Ltd. 2018
M. Singh et al. (Eds.): ICACDS 2018, CCIS 905, pp. 411–420, 2018.
https://doi.org/10.1007/978-981-13-1810-8_41

Swarm Optimization (PSO) [2], Artificial Bee Colony Optimization (ABCO) [3], Ant Colony Optimization (ACO) [4] and Grey Wolf Optimization (GWO) [14]. Meta-heuristics are designed to find and generate a heuristic (search algorithm) that found a good solution of a given optimization problem [5]. The researchers [6, 7] found that GWO performs better in optimization problems than other existing optimization techniques. Intrusion Detection System (IDS) uses one of the two intrusion detection approaches [8] namely signature based or misuse based intrusion detection and anomaly based intrusion detection system. Many feature selection and classification algorithms were proposed in past to classify intrusion dataset. We discussed few of them in this section that encouraged us to pursue the research work in this area.

Fatemeh Amiri et al. [9] proposed a Modified Mutual Information based Feature Selection (MMIFS) algorithm for intrusion detection. Mutual information measures the mutual dependence of two variables and used to quantify both relevance and redundancy. The MMIFS is modified to avoid selection of irrelevant features into the selected feature subset. However, this problem has not been fully solved yet. Snort and Decision Tree classifier are used to implement the Intrusion detection framework by Modi et al. [10]. Nodes of decision tree presents attribute of packet and leaf represents the class label. ID3 decision tree classifier is used for classification of user behavior. Out of 41 features in dataset, 17 features were selected to train the classifier. The experiment results demonstrated that more than 95% intrusions were detected correctly. The method detects unknown attacks also but the detection accuracy of the work can be further improved. Hisham Kholidy et al. [11] proposed a framework for Intrusion Detection in cloud systems in which detection using Snort is a part of all nodes in the system. It detects the known attacks but it has a high computational complexity and fails to detect unknown attacks at the network layer. Additionally, this model is not sufficient for detecting large scale distributed attacks. Bahaweres et al. [19] has tested the functions of private cloud and measures the quality of service. After the installation of Cloud Server using own cloud, authors test it for its efficiency. The throughput of the server in terms functionality reduces on occurrence of DOS attack. Increasing the resources to retain the computing performance is not a good solution [20] as attacker can add more computers to attack on victim host. Manthira Moorthy et al. [12] discussed Cloud Intrusion Detection Dataset (CIDD) and proposed a virtual host based Intrusion Detection System. Genetic algorithm was applied for generating rules from the datasets to detect intrusion in dataset. The genetic algorithms faced the problem of inter communication with different agents. This model predicts the result over 400 packets and obtained a true positive ratio of 80% only on CIDD which needs to be improved by using other optimization and classification method. Later, A. Kannan et al. [13] used feature selection on CIDD dataset and improved the detection accuracy over the model proposed by Manthira-Moorthy et al. [12]. They have used Information Gain Ratio (IGR) for feature selection based on pre-defined threshold. The threshold based selection may not be optimal which may cause wrong feature selection. Further the accuracy of the classifier produced can be improved. The next section discussed the GWO methodology and classifier used in the proposed scheme.

2   The GWO Algorithm

Grey wolf optimization (GWO) is one of the nature inspired meta-heuristic algorithm that mimics the leadership hierarchy of grey wolves [14]. The grey wolves live in a pack. The pack size is usually of 5 to 12. There are four types of wolves living in the pack. The alpha (α) wolves are at the top of the hierarchy, beta (β) wolves are next to the α wolves. They help alpha in decision making. The third level wolves in the hierarchy are delta (δ) wolves. Delta wolves submit to alpha and beta, but dominate omega (ω) wolves. The last category is Omega (Ω) wolves. They are allowed to eat last in the pack.

2.1   Mathematical Model of GWO

The mathematical model of hunting behavior of grey wolves is completed in three parts- Encircling the prey, Hunting the prey and Attacking the prey which are as follows:

Encircling the Prey
During the hunt the grey wolves encircle the prey and this behavior is shown using Eqs. (1) and (2).

$$\vec{D} = \left| \vec{C}. \overrightarrow{Xp}(k) - \vec{X}(k) \right| \tag{1}$$

$$\vec{X}(k+1) = \overrightarrow{Xp}(k) - \vec{A}.\vec{D} \tag{2}$$

$$\vec{A} = 2.a.\vec{r_1} - a \tag{3}$$

$$\vec{C} = 2.\vec{r_2} \tag{4}$$

Where k is the current iteration, A and C are coefficient vectors. X_p is the position vector of prey and X is position vector of grey wolf. r_1 and r_2 are random vectors.

Hunting the Prey
The wolves follow the alpha in hunting. Alpha, Beta and Delta wolves have better knowledge about the position of prey, remaining wolves follow them in hunting, this behavior is presented by Eq. (5).

$$\vec{X}(k+1) = \frac{\sum_{u=1}^{3} \overrightarrow{Xu}}{3} \tag{5}$$

where $u = 1, 2, 3$
   The values of X_1, X_2 and X_3 are given by Eq. (6) below-

$$\overrightarrow{X_u} = \left| \overrightarrow{X_v} - \overrightarrow{A_u}.\overrightarrow{D_v} \right| \tag{6}$$

where $u = 1, 2, 3$ and $v = \alpha, \beta, \delta$.

X_α, X_β, and X_δ are the positions of alpha, beta and delta wolves. D_α, D_β and D_δ are given in Eq. (7) below-

$$\overrightarrow{D_v} = |\overrightarrow{C_u}.\overrightarrow{X_v} - \vec{X}| \tag{7}$$

where $u = 1, 2, 3$ and $v = \alpha, \beta, \delta$.

Attacking the Prey

The grey wolves attack the prey when it stops moving. The value of variable a is decreasing in each iteration of algorithm and the wolves are approaching near to the prey. The value of a is decreasing from 2 to 0 as given in Eq. (8) below.

$$a = 2 - \frac{2.k}{\max\_k} \tag{8}$$

Where k is current iteration and max_k is the maximum number of iterations.

2.2   k-Nearest Neighbor Classifier (k-NN)

The k nearest neighbor (k-NN) is used in classification and regression problems. k-NN is a supervised learning algorithm that classifies an unknown instance using distance between the instance and k selected neighbors, then majority of voting of neighbors decides the class of instance.

3   Formation of CSID

Security dataset of cloud is not publicly available for research. Most of the researchers have been used KDD'99 dataset [15] in their research for intrusion detection in cloud. KDD'99 dataset is not a real cloud intrusion dataset. CIDD [16] is the first cloud intrusion dataset available for research. CIDD is using a systematic approach to generate cloud dataset [13]. The CIDD consists of two parts – The first part is collection of Solaris audit logs and their corresponding tcpdump data and the second part is collection of Windows audit logs and their corresponding tcpdump data. The audit data and their corresponding tcpdump data are available to download from the website in [17]. We have mapped both (Solaris and Windows) audit logs with their corresponding tcpdump data using common SourceIP address and time. After mapping and merging, we get the cloud specific intrusion dataset (CSID) which contains the attributes from audit logs and tcpdump data. The CSID is formed into two datasets one for Solaris and other for Windows. The attributes of CSID for Solaris is shown in Table 1 and for Windows in Table 2. In the process of mapping between audit logs and tcpdumb data more than 1 million of records were produced. The datasets are sampled for experiments using Reservoir Sampling [18] which preserves 50,000 records from Solaris and 50,000 records from Windows dataset.

Table 1. CSID dataset features for Solaris.

1.Order, 2.Real order, 3.User ID, 4.User Name, 5.Time, 6.System Call, 7.Source IP, 8.Session ID, 9.Effective User ID, 10.Session Start-End, 11.Category, 12.VM Audit Part No., 13.VM Name, 14.Date, 15.Duration, 16.Service Name, 17.Source Port, 18. Destination Port, 19.Destination IP, 20.Attack, 21.Attack description

Table 2. CSID dataset features for windows.

1.Order, 2.Real Order, 3.Users, 4.Target, 5.Type, 6.Time, 7.Event, 8.Audit Action, 9.Domain\User, 10.Source Machine, 11.VM Name, 12.Date, 13.Duration, 14.Service Name, 15.Source Port, 16.Destination Port, 17.Destination IP,

4 Modified GWO for Feature Selection – MGWO

The number of attributes in our dataset is D, therefore the number of columns in position matrix of grey wolves must be D. The number of grey wolves are N therefore the number of rows (vectors) in position matrix must be N therefore the size of position matrix is $N \times D$. Each index of a row X_n in position matrix of grey wolves is correspond to an attribute in our dataset. Each row is of size $1 \times D$ and must contains only binary value 0 and 1 for feature selection. The attributes in dataset corresponding to value 1 in a row vector are selected for training and evaluation of the classifier and corresponding to value 0 are not selected. To binarize the position matrix we have modified the original GWO algorithm and formed MGWO. Let each element of a row X_n ($n = 1,2....N$; where N is number of grey wolves) is denoted by X_{nd} ($d = 1,2,....D$; where D is number attributes in dataset). Each element X_{nd} in X_n is a decimal value by using the Eq. (5) in original GWO. To binarize the decimal value of each element X_{nd} in a row X_n we have used two methods proposed in Eqs. (9) and (10).

$$\forall n \forall d : X_{nd} = \frac{X_{nd}}{max(x_n)} \tag{9}$$

By using Eq. (9) each element X_{nd} of a row X_n in position matrix transformed into decimal values which are less than or equal to 1. Now we have used another method given in Eq. (10) below to transform the each value X_{nd} into binary values 0 and 1.

$$\forall n \forall d : X_{nd} = \begin{cases} 0 \, , & if \ X_{nd} \leq 0.5 \\ 1 \, , & otherwise \end{cases} \tag{10}$$

The position matrix which is obtained after transformation by using Eq. (9); now contains all the values between [0,1]. The values in position matrix which are less than or equal to 0.5 are replaced by 0 and greater than 0.5 are replaced by 1 by using Eq. (10).

5 Proposed MIDS

The proposed scheme MIDS detects the intrusion in cloud environment. The system takes input from network packets (tcpdump) and the host (audit logs) of the same user session to detect the intrusion. The training phase of MIDS finalize the best feature subset (BFS) using MGWO. In classification only BFS is extracted from the network and the host to classify the user behavior i.e. normal or intrusion. The MIDS may be installed on cloud host or any other network computer that can capture the features from the host and network to detect intrusion in cloud environment. In our case we have installed MIDS on host. Figure 1 depicts the working of the proposed scheme. The proposed MIDS is integration of k-NN and MGWO. In the first phase of MIDS, the classifier is trained and evaluated on different feature subsets of CSID selected by MGWO. For evaluation of classifier k-fold cross validation is used. Phase 1 of the proposed scheme returns the BFS that gives the best accuracy of the classifier. In MIDS the maximum number of iteration is set to 20. In each iteration of the algorithm MGWO selects the different feature subsets to train and evaluate the classifier.

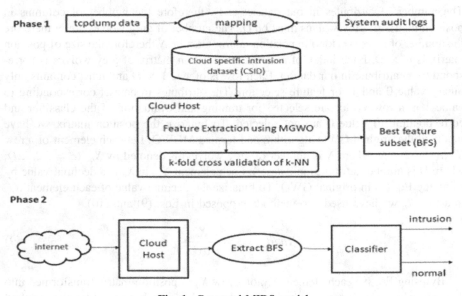

Fig. 1. Proposed MIDS model

At the end of the 8th iteration of algorithm it returns the BFS and accuracy beyond that no further improvement is observed. In k-fold cross validation k is set to 10. The 10-fold cross validation means the dataset is partitioned into 10 equal parts and the classifier is trained by the 9 parts and tested by one part termed as validation part. This practice is iterated for ten times with ten different training and validation part and finally returns the best accuracy that the classifier can achieved on given dataset. Once the features are finalized in phase 1; classifier is trained with BFS and finally it is deployed on cloud host that classifies the users as shown in phase 2 of Fig. 1. The classifier predicts the users in phases 2 by extracting only the BFS.

The MIDS Algorithm

1. Initialize the position matrix, A and C.
2. Transform and binarize the positions matrix using Eqs. (9) and (10) respectively.
3. *k=1*
4. **while** *k< max_k*
   for each wolf in the pack
       Select the features from position vector correspond to value 1.
       Train and evaluate the classifier with selected features.
   end for
   Record first three best accuracies and their corresponding positions; these are α, β and δ wolves positions.
   for each wolf in the pack
       Update a, A and C using Eqs. (8), (3) and (4).
       Calculate X_u using Eq. (6).
       Update the position of grey wolves in position matrix using Eq. (5).
   end for
   Transform and binarize the positions matrix using Eqs. (9) and (10) respectively.
   k=k+1
5. **end while**
6. Output: BFS (alpha position) with best classification accuracy (alpha_score).

In each iteration of algorithm, Eq. (9) transform the position matrix into the decimal values in the interval [0,1] then Eq. (10) checks the values and transform them into binary values 0 and 1. Here accuracy is used as the fitness function. The algorithm terminates after max_k number of iterations and returns the best accuracy (alpha_score) and BFS (alpha_position).

6 Experiment and Results

The machine configuration used to perform various experiments of the proposed scheme is as follows: 2.4 GHz intel core i3 processor, 6 GB RAM and 500 GB HDD. A series of experiments are conducted and best observed values of various parameters are found which are as follows; max_k = 20, number of grey wolves = 12 and the number of neighbors = 3. In addition, 10-fold cross validation is used to evaluate MIDS. The classification of user behavior is categorized into five classes i.e. DOS, Probing, U2R, R2L and normal. The separate experiments for binary classification are performed in each category i.e. [*normal, attack*] where class *attack* includes DOS, Probing, R2L and U2R attacks, [*normal, DOS*], [*normal, probing*] and [*normal, Others*] where *Others* include R2L & U2R attacks. The performance of MIDS is

Table 3. Experiment results on solaris and windows dataset.

Classification category	Selected features using MGWO	Selected features	Accuracy	Sensitivity	Specificity
[*normal, attack*]	Solaris = 8	1, 5, 7, 9, 10, 14, 16, 19	99.87	99.84	99.96
	Windows = 11	2, 4, 5, 6, 7, 8, 10, 11, 12, 13, 17	98.94	98.8	99.91
[*normal, DOS*]	Solaris = 8	1, 5, 7, 9, 10,14, 16, 19	99.87	100	100
	Windows = 7	1, 6, 7, 10, 11, 13, 17	98.97	99.71	100
[*normal, Probing*]	Solaris = 9	1, 5, 6, 7, 8, 9, 10, 16, 19	99.83	99.81	100
	Windows = 11	2, 4, 5, 6,7, 8, 10, 11, 12, 13, 17	98.94	99.9	99.16
[*normal, Others*]	Solaris = 8	1, 5, 7, 9, 10, 14,16, 19	99.87	100	93.75
	Windows = 9	1, 2, 6, 10, 11, 12, 13, 15, 17	98.69	99.5	100

measured in terms of *accuracy, sensitivity* and *specificity*. The experiments are conducted to train and evaluate the classifier. Table 3 shows the results of experiment
conducted on Solaris and Windows dataset.

We have 21 features in Solaris dataset and by using MGWO the features are
reduced by approximately 60% in all category of attacks. The selected features are
numbered in Table 3; these numbers are the serial numbers of the features given in
Table 1. We have 19 features in Windows dataset and by using MGWO the features
are reduced by approximately 40% in all category of attacks. The selected features are
numbered in Table 3; these numbers are the serial numbers of the features given in
Table 2. The classifications in both the cases, Solaris and Windows datasets, are performed in low dimensional space with minimal computing resources using MGWO.
Table 4 shows the performance comparison of MIDS with other existing cloud
Intrusion detection systems. MIDS is compared with Genetic Algorithm based IDS
termed GAID [12] and decision tree based IDS termed MHDT [13].

From Table 4, it can be observed that the accuracy of MIDS is improved by 1.64%
for Solaris dataset and 0.71% for Windows dataset when compared with MHDT. It also
shows the sensitivity of MIDS is improved by 19.84% for Solaris dataset and 18.8% for
Windows dataset when compared with GAIDS. The specificity of MIDS is closed to
GAIDS. The experiment results shown the improved *accuracy* and *sensitivity* of the
proposed scheme. As the *specificity* is very high in MIDS hence it has a very low false
alarm rate for both Solaris and Windows.

Table 4. Comparison of MIDS with other existing cloud IDS.

IDS type	Selected features using MGWO	Accuracy (All category)	Sensitivity (All category)	Specificity (All category)
MIDS	Solaris = 8 Windows = 11	Solaris = 99.87 Windows = 98.94	Solaris = 99.84 Windows = 98.8	Solaris = 99.96 Windows = 99.91
MHDT [13]	13	98.23	–	–
GAIDS [12]	–	–	80	100

7 Conclusion and Future Work

The objectives of designing an intrusion detection system are to increase the correct detection rate and decrease the false positive rate. To fulfill the objectives, we have eliminated the irrelevant features from dataset using MGWO. We obtained the BFS in CSID for both Solaris and Windows based virtual machines that gives the best accuracy of classification. The MGWO has reduced the dataset features approximately by 60% on Solaris dataset and more than 40% on Windows dataset. The accuracy of proposed MIDS has improved significantly over the other existing IDS methods in cloud. The results also shown a very low false alarm rate on both datasets. For future work the proposed model can be tested on real cloud intrusion dataset. The intrusion dataset of a private cloud network can be implemented to run MIDS and observation can be made to analyze the differences in results and feature subsets produced. The observations can be used to improve the proposed model.

References

1. Peng, J., Zhang, X., Lei, Z., Zhang, B., Zhang, W., Li, Q.: Comparison of several cloud computing platforms. In: 2009 Second International Symposium on Information Science and Engineering (ISISE), pp. 23–27 (2009)
2. Kennedy, J., Eberhart, R.: Particle swarm optimization. In: IEEE Conference Neural Networks, pp. 1942–1948, December 1995
3. Karaboga, D., Akay, B.: A comparative study of artificial bee colony algorithm. Appl. Math. Comput. 214(1), 108–132 (2009)
4. Dorigo, M., Birattari, M., Stutzle, T.: Ant colony optimization. IEEE Comput. Intell. Mag. 1 (4), 28–39 (2006)
5. Lones, M.A.: Metaheuristics in nature-inspired algorithms. In: Proceedings of the Companion Publication of the 2014 Annual Conference on Genetic and Evolutionary Computation, pp. 1419–1422 (2014)
6. Gupta, P., Kumar, V., Rana, K.P.S., Mishra, P.: Comparative study of some optimization techniques applied to Jacketed CSTR control. In: 2015 4th International Conference on Reliability, Infocom Technologies and Optimization (ICRITO) (Trends and Future Directions), pp. 1–6 (2015)

7. Islam, M.J., et al.: A comparative study on prominent nature inspired algorithms for function optimization. In: 2016 5th International Conference on Informatics, Electronics and Vision (ICIEV), pp. 803–808 (2016)
8. Qian, Q., Cai, J., Zhang, R.: Intrusion detection based on neural networks and Artificial Bee Colony algorithm. In: 2014 IEEE/ACIS 13th International Conference on Computer and Information Science (ICIS), pp. 257–262 (2014)
9. Amiri, F., et al.: Mutual information-based feature selection for intrusion detection systems. J. Netw. Comput. Appl. **34**(4), 1184–1199 (2011)
10. Modi, C., Patel, D., Borisanya, B., Patel, A., Rajarajan, M.: A novel framework for intrusion detection in cloud. In: Proceedings of the Fifth International Conference on Security of Information and Networks, pp. 67–74 (2012)
11. Kholidy, H., Baiardi, F.: CIDS: a framework for intrusion detection in cloud systems. In: 2012 Ninth International Conference on Information Technology: New Generations (ITNG), pp. 379–385. IEEE (2012)
12. Moorthy, M., Rajeswari, S.: Virtual host based intrusion detection system for cloud. IACSIT Int. J. Eng. Technol. **5**(6), 5023–5029 (2014)
13. Kannan, A., Venkatesan, K.G., Stagkopoulou, A., Li, S., Krishnan, S., Rahman, A.: A novel cloud intrusion detection system using feature selection and classification. Int. J. Intell. Inf. Technol. (IJIIT) **11**(4), 1–15 (2015)
14. Mirjalili, S., Mirjalili, S.M., Lewis, A.: Grey wolf optimizer. Adv. Eng. Softw. **69**, 46–61 (2014)
15. http://kdd.ics.uci.edu/databases/kddcup99/kddcup99.html
16. Kholidy, H.A., Baiardi, F.: CIDD: a cloud intrusion detection dataset for cloud computing and masquerade attacks. In: 2012 Ninth International Conference on Information Technology: New Generations (ITNG), pp. 397–402 (2012)
17. http://www.di.unipi.it/~hkholidy/projects/cidd/
18. Vitter, J.S.: Random sampling with a reservoir. ACM Trans. Math. Softw. (TOMS) **11**(1), 37–57 (1985)
19. Bahaweres, R.B., Alaydrus, J.S.M.: Building a private cloud computing and the analysis against DoS (Denial of Service) attacks: case study at SMKN 6 Jakarta. In: International Conference on Cyber and IT Service Management, pp. 1–6 (2016)
20. Xiao, L., et al.: A protocol-free detection against cloud oriented reflection DoS attacks. Soft. Comput. **21**(13), 3713–3721 (2017)

An Improved RDH Model for Medical Images with a Novel EPR Embedding Technique

Jayanta Mondal, Debabala Swain$^{(\boxtimes)}$, and Devee Darshani Panda

School of Computer Engineering, KIIT, Bhubaneswar, India
jayantamondal777@gmail.com, debabala.swain@gmail.com,
deveedarshani288@gmail.com

Abstract. An improved RDH scheme is proposed in this paper for medical images that can overcome the challenges in implementing secure online medical system. Security of the medical images and privacy of the medical report and patient information remains a big hurdle. This approach aims at solving the security problem through two level security mechanism: encryption and data embedding. For privacy preservation EPR embedding technique is introduced to hide sensitive patient data into the medical image itself. The experimental results shows that the proposed method is highly efficient in embedding capacity and lossless recovery for grey-scale medical images. Based on PSNR values it outperforms the existing RDH methods for medical images.

Keywords: Reversible data hiding · Electronic patient record
Medical images

1 Introduction

Security is the ultimate concern in this digitized era. Service oriented architecture has evolved immensely in the last decade through cloud computing and huge availability of internet. Every system is going online and so does medical service. The digitization of medial system needs utmost attention to solidify the privacy and security concern. Sensitive images, like medical or military imagery, needs special care during transmission. A minimal distortion can make the image completely unfit for the purpose. Same as the medical image, the medical report holds highly sensitive information and needs full confidentiality and security.

There are several ways for secure medical image digitization, like several encryption standards, watermarking techniques, digital signature implementation and so on. Reversible data hiding (RDH) is the best solution for digitization of sensitive images. RDH was first proposed by Barton in a US patient in 1997 [1]. Since then different improvements happened and RDH has evolved to be the most efficient method for data hiding in sensitive cover images. Several mechanisms are available for implementing RDH technique that suits for medical imagery. RDH in encrypted domain is the best possible way for medical image digitization as it includes encryption for cover image security, data embedding for marking the cover image and providing authentication and a second level of security, and finally additional data hiding for privacy preservation. RDH offers maximum reversibility which is essential for medical

© Springer Nature Singapore Pte Ltd. 2018
M. Singh et al. (Eds.): ICACDS 2018, CCIS 905, pp. 421–430, 2018.
https://doi.org/10.1007/978-981-13-1810-8_42

images for right diagnosis. In 2011 Zhang proposed an RDH scheme for encrypted images [2]. Several different methods have been proposed in last few years in encrypted domain. Any conventional RDH scheme for encrypted images consists of three actors: the content owner, the data hider, and the receiver. The content owner encrypts the original cover image and sends it to the data hider for data embedding. The data hider sends the marked-encrypted image to the receiver. If the receiver has both the data-embedding and the encryption key then the additional data can be extracted and the original image can be recovered losslessly. In 2017 J Mondal et al proposed a LSB based RDH scheme [3] that outperformed the previous methods for grey-scale images in encrypted domain.

In this paper we have tried to enhance the previously proposed RDH method [3] with additional electronic patient data (EPR) embedding in medical images. This process is conceptualized for secure online medical service. The primary challenges in offering medical treatment as an online service are security of medical data and privacy preservation of patient data. The proposed architecture can solve these problems. The experimental results shows good potential in terms of image recovery and additional EPR recovery. A brief summary on RDH in encrypted domain for medical images is given in Sect. 2. In Sect. 3 the proposed work is presented with the working architecture and algorithms. Section 4 shows the experimental results and finally we conclude in Sect. 5.

2 Related Works

In this section three RDH schemes has been discussed in detail that are quite efficient for medical images. In 2013, T Ahmad et al proposed a quad and reduced difference expansion based RDH method for medical data hiding in medical images [4]. Difference expansion (DE) is a widely used mechanism for RDH implementation. In 2004, AM Alattar proposed a reversible watermarking method using DE of quads [5]. T Ahmad et al improved Alattar's method and implemented it in medical images. This proposed method increased the image quality and embedding capacity remarkably than the previous method. The experimental results shows better visual quality in terms of peak signal to noise ratio (PSNR) values. Figure 1 shows the basic difference between this proposed method and Alattar's proposed method.

In 2015, HT Wu et al proposed contrast enhancement capability based RDH method for medical images [6]. HT Wu et al proposed previously method an RDH method with contrast enhancement [7] for normal standard images and [6] in the improved implementation of [7] in medical image domain. Instead of directly applying the algorithm in this method a mechanism is proposed to select the region of interest (ROI) for embedding additional medical information. An automatic background segmentation is done for the ROI selection. The additional bits embedding is carried out by histogram modification of the enhanced ROI region. The experimental results shows improvement in PSNR and SSIM values. The data hiding process is described in Fig. 2.

In 2016, Qian et al. proposed a joint reversible data hiding which is the improved version of [2, 9, 10]. In this paper a two-step LSB-based RDH scheme is proposed and

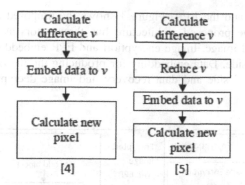

Fig. 1. Basic difference in the working principle between [4, 5].

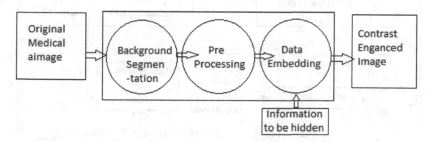

Fig. 2. Data hiding process in [6].

successfully implemented in medical images. In the data embedding phase a combination of cyclic shifting and LSB swapping is carried out for generating the marked image. This process works in encrypted domain and thus much more secure than other methods.

In 2017, Chandrasekaran and Sevugan applied RDH method for medical images [11] using histogram modification in hybrid domain. It uses the pixel difference of neighboring pixel histograms. The payload is embedded in the frequency domain through a 2D DWT haar transform. The experimental results are compared to [7, 12, 13] and it shows huge improvement in image quality.

3 Proposed Work

This RDH scheme aims at securing medical images and preserving privacy of patient data during online treatment service. Suppose a patient from India wants to consult a doctor in the US through an online medical system. In this scenario, according to the proposed approach, the patient encrypts the medical image and embeds EPR into the encrypted medical image and sends it to the cloud service. In the cloud, the data hider with the help of data hiding key generates the marked image, which provides authentication and an extra level of security and sends it to the doctor. The doctor needs to have the encryption key, the EPR hiding key and the data embedding key to recover the image losslessly and the EPR. Figure 3 shows the proposed architecture. It evidently shows that the proposed architecture has three actors as a traditional RDH method for encrypted image. Image encryption and EPR embedding is carried out in the content owners' side. Data embedding for producing the marked image is carried out in the data hiders' side and data recovery and image decryption is done in the receivers' side.

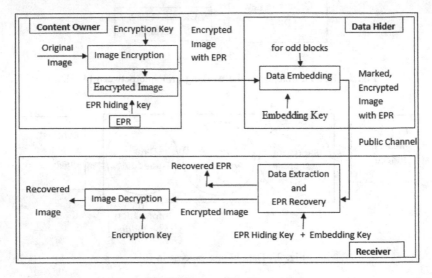

Fig. 3. Proposed architecture.

3.1 Proposed Algorithm

A novel EPR embedding scheme is proposed which is carried out at content owner's end after image encryption. Conventional encryption method is carried out at the beginning. An LSB based data embedding algorithm for producing the marked image is performed at the data hiders' side. This proposed scheme can be divided into 4 parts. Image encryption for generating the encrypted image, EPR hiding into the encrypted image using the EPR hiding key, data embedding using the data embedding key for generating the marked encrypted image and finally decryption and image recovery.

Encryption: Suppose that the size of the original image I is M × N and the gray value of each pixel in I can be represented by

$$I(i,j) = I_{gray}(i,j) \times (a+b) \tag{1}$$

Where $2^a = M$ and $2^b = N$ and $I_{gray}(i,j)$ = grayscale weight generated from the RGB scale.

Now the encrypted image can be formulated as

$$I_{E(i,j)} = I_{(i,j)} \oplus K_{(i,j)} \qquad (2)$$

Where K (i,j) is the key matrix generated using any asymmetric random function of order M $\times$ N.

EPR Hiding:
    Step-1: Here we divide the encrypted image I_e into non overlapping image blocks of order Z $\times$ Z. Let the total number of blocks are n.
    Step-2: For all even number of blocks (block 2 to block n) the last LSB of the last pixel of the block is subjected for EPR embedding. We are assuming the worst case and flipped all of them.

Data Embedding: For all alternatives block B_q starting from q = 1 to n–1, i.e. for all odd counting blocks are subjected for generating marked image, now embedding into a pixel can be made as follows:

    Step-1: Let the 1st row be unchanged.
    Step-2: Perform the XOR operation between the three LSB bits of the consecutive rows x and y.
    Step-3: If the XOR result is 000, then the pixel will remain unchanged.
        Else
        Left rotate the 3 LSB of row x and flip the 4th LSB.
        Continue step 2 for all marked blocks.
    Finally combine the blocks to form the embedded image I'_E.

EPR Recovery and De-Embedding: The same process is needed to be executed. The EPR can be read from the even blocks and then flipped back. The encrypted image can be recovered or de-embedded by going through the embedding process once again.

Decryption: Decrypted image can be obtained through XOR-ing the de-embedded image with the encryption key.

4 Experimental Result Analysis

To prove the efficiency of the proposed RDH technique, experiments were conducted on two standard gray-scale images i.e., Lena and Lake, and two medical images each of size 512 $\times$ 512. Experiments are carried out on a computer with 2.00 GHz AMD-A10 processor, 8 GB ram, Windows 8 operating system, and the programming environment was Matlab 13. Results are basically compared with other existing methods in terms of peak signal to noise ratio (PSNR), structural similarity index (SSIM) values and number of bits for embedding capacity. PSNR and SSIM are calculated as-

$$PSNR = 10.\log_{10}\left(\frac{MAX_I^2}{MSE}\right)$$

$$= 20.\log_{10}\left(\frac{MAX_I}{\sqrt{MSE}}\right)$$

$$= 20.\log_{10}(MAX_I) - 10.\log_{10}(MSE)$$

$$SSIM(x,y) = \frac{(2\mu_x\mu_y + c1)(2\sigma_{xy} + c_2)}{\left(\mu_x^2 + \mu_y^2 + c_1\right)\left(\sigma_x^2 + \sigma_y^2 + c_2\right)}$$

Where μ, σ denotes the average value and variance.

Figure 4 shows the original test images taken for experiments. Figures 5, 6, 7, and 8 shows different states of the images during implementation for Lena, Lake, CT and MR, where (a), (b), (c), (d), (e), (f), and (g) consecutively represents original image, encrypted image, EPR embedded image, marked EPR embedded image, de-embedded image, decrypted image, and EPR recovered image. Here CT refers to CT scan image of a brain and MR refers an MRI image of a brain. Figure 9 shows a graphical view of the PSNR values for different block sizes for the test images, and Fig. 10 graphically depicts the SSIM comparisons of decrypted image for different block sizes for 4 test images.

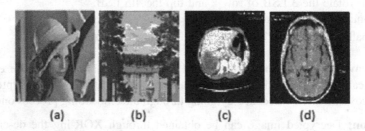

(a)   (b)   (c)   (d)

Fig. 4. Original test images Lena, Lake, CT, and MR.

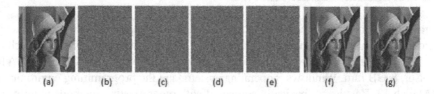

(a)   (b)   (c)   (d)   (e)   (f)   (g)

Fig. 5. Different experimental phases of Lena image.

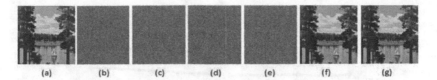

Fig. 6. Different experimental phases of Lake image.

Fig. 7. Different experimental phases of CT image.

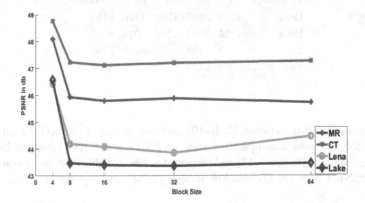

Fig. 8. Different experimental phases of MR image.

Table 1 shows the PSNR and SSIM values of directly decrypted images and decrypted images after de-embedding and EPR recovery for the 4 test images for 4 × 4 block size.

To prove better efficiency and capability of this method we have given some comparative analysis with the existing methods. Table 2 shows a comparison table on

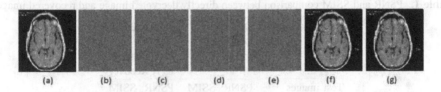

Fig. 9. PSNR comparisons of directly decrypted image for different block sizes for 4 test images.

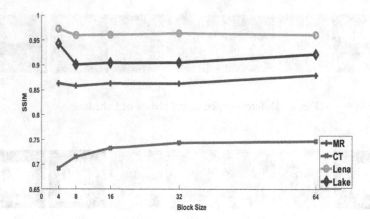

Fig. 10. SSIM comparisons of decrypted image for different block sizes for 4 test images.

Table 1. PSNR and SSIM comparison between directly decrypted image and recovered image.

Block size 4 × 4	Directly Decrypted Image		Decrypted after de-embedding & EPR Recovery	
Test images	PSNR	SSIM	PSNR	SSIM
Lena	44.40	0.9584	63.60	0.9996
Lake	43.67	0.8977	63.50	0.9986
CT	47.41	0.6883	67.38	0.9933
MR	46.08	0.8514	65.27	0.9972

Table 2. Comparison table on EPR embedding bits between [2, 8–10] and the proposed method.

Test image	[2]	[8]	[9]	[10]	Proposed
Lena	1156	3897	1296	1296	8192
Lake	1024	2094	1296	1024	8192
CT	9	8439	9	9	8192
MR	9	8439	9	9	8192

embedding rate in bits between [2, 8–10] and the proposed method for all the test images. Table 3 shows a comparative view on PSNR and SSIM values of brain CT-scan image between [6, 7, 11–13] and proposed method. Table 4 shows a comparative view on PSNR values for CT and MR images [4, 5] and proposed method.

Table 3. Comparison table on PSNR and SSIM of brain CT-scan image between [6, 7, 11–13] and proposed method.

Method	PSNR	SSIM
[6]	29.83	0.9788
[7]	60.98	0.9899
[11]	62.81	0.9982
[12]	60.82	0.9941
[13]	61.28	0.9891
Proposed	67.38	0.9933

Table 4. Comparison table between [4, 5] and proposed method on PSNR for CT and MR images.

Test Image	[4]	[5]	Proposed
CT	40.98	36.24	67.38
MR	41.12	35.97	65.27

5 Conclusion

This paper proposes an efficient model for RDH implemented on medical images. We implemented an LSB-based RDH method with a novel EPR embedding technique for medical images in encrypted domain. To provide adequate security encrypted domain is the safest option. Marked image is generated through a combination of LSB modification techniques and additional EPR data is embedded into the encrypted medical image using last LSB substitution method. The experimental method shows great potential in terms of embedding capacity, visual quality and recovery. In terms of PSNR the proposed method outperforms the existing methods and the SSIM values denotes almost lossless recovery.

References

1. Barton, J.M.: U.S. Patent No. 5,646,997. U.S. Patent and Trademark Office, Washington, DC (1997)
2. Zhang, X.: Reversible data hiding in encrypted image. IEEE Sig. Process. Lett. **18**(4), 255–258 (2011)
3. Mondal, J., Swain, D., Singh, D.P., Mohanty, S.: An improved LSB-based RDH technique with better reversibility. Int. J. Electron. Secur. Digit. Forensics **9**(3), 254–268 (2017)
4. Ahmad, T., Holil, M., Wibisono, W., Muslim, I.R.: An improved Quad and RDE-based medical data hiding method. In: 2013 IEEE International Conference on Computational Intelligence and Cybernetics (CYBERNETICSCOM), pp. 141–145. IEEE, December 2013
5. Alattar, A.M.: Reversible watermark using difference expansion of quads. In: 2004 Proceedings of IEEE International Conference on Acoustics, Speech, and Signal Processing, (ICASSP 2004), vol. 3, pp. iii–377. IEEE, May 2004

6. Wu, H.T., Huang, J., Shi, Y.Q.: A reversible data hiding method with contrast enhancement for medical images. J. Vis. Commun. Image Represent. **31**, 146–153 (2015)
7. Wu, H.T., Dugelay, J.L., Shi, Y.Q.: Reversible image data hiding with contrast enhancement. IEEE Sig. Process. Lett. **22**(1), 81–85 (2015)
8. Qian, Z., Dai, S., Jiang, F., Zhang, X.: Improved joint reversible data hiding in encrypted images. J. Vis. Commun. Image Represent. **40**, 732–738 (2016)
9. Hong, W., Chen, T.S., Wu, H.Y.: An improved reversible data hiding in encrypted images using side match. IEEE Sig. Process. Lett. **19**(4), 199–202 (2012)
10. Liao, X., Shu, C.: Reversible data hiding in encrypted images based on absolute mean difference of multiple neighboring pixels. J. Vis. Commun. Image Represent. **28**, 21–27 (2015)
11. Chandrasekaran, V., Sevugan, P.: Applying Reversible Data Hiding for Medical Images in Hybrid Domain Using Haar and Modified Histogram
12. Sachnev, V., Kim, H.J., Nam, J., Suresh, S., Shi, Y.Q.: Reversible watermarking algorithm using sorting and prediction. IEEE Trans. Circuits Syst. Video Technol. **19**(7), 989–999 (2009)
13. Gao, G., Shi, Y.Q.: Reversible data hiding using controlled contrast enhancement and integer wavelet transform. IEEE Sig. Process. Lett. **22**(11), 2078–2082 (2015)

Machine Learning Based Adaptive Framework for Logistic Planning in Industry 4.0

Krista Chaudhary[1(✉)], Mayank Singh[3], Sandhya Tarar[2],
D. K. Chauhan[1], and Viranjay M. Srivastava[3]

[1] Department of Computer Science and Engineering,
Noida International University, Greater Noida 203201, India
krista2330@gmail.com, prof.dkchauhan@gmail.com
[2] School of Information and Communication Technology,
Gautam Buddha University, Greater Noida 203201, India
tarar.sandhya@gmail.com
[3] Department of Electrical, Electronic and Computer Engineering,
Howard College, University of KwaZulu-Natal, Durban 4041, South Africa
{dr.mayank.singh,viranjay}@ieee.org

Abstract. A drastic change occurs in the logistics business from over the past 20 years. In today's scenario, a novel logistic approach is a requirement. Due to the difficulties in integrating the information and dynamic changes in the situation, the logistic approach planning becomes more challenging. The logistics planning process can be useful if the data can be integrated from various partners to generate the combined knowledge. This paper presents a machine learning based adaptive framework for logistics planning and digital supply chain the new industrial revolution is useful to Logistics Processes like Cyber-Physical System. It is explained which are the technical components of digital logistics and supply chain. The proposed system will grow, acclimate and expand as its knowledge grows to provide a generalized solution to all kinds of logistics and supply chain activities.

Keywords: Logistic planning · Industry 4.0 · Supply chain management
Procurement 4.0

1 Introduction

The economy of a country depends on the industries which produce the materials and goods. Every enterprise wants its production process should be automated and effective. A lot of work is carried out in this area for every type of industries. For effective, efficient and mass production, a new approach is required which should be based on cutting-edge technologies like the Internet of Things, Cyber-Physical Systems (CPS), Cloud computing and big data analysis. The techniques will contribute to the industrial revolution [1, 2].

The extensive use of information and communication technologies and increasing globalization are effective every part of our life. Industries are now focusing on customer relationship management by using these technologies in logistics or supply chain

© Springer Nature Singapore Pte Ltd. 2018
M. Singh et al. (Eds.): ICACDS 2018, CCIS 905, pp. 431–438, 2018.
https://doi.org/10.1007/978-981-13-1810-8_43

management. With better customer relationship, companies are competing with the fast-growing market. Logistic of the company is the process to realize the right product at the right place at the right time in proper condition [3].

Logistics can be defined as a large organization and execution of complex processes. In supply chain management, the logistics management plays an essential role in planning and implementation of logistic strategies. It also effectively and efficiently controls the flow of goods, services, and related information. This information is helpful for the appropriate steps to be taken according to the customer's requirements.

Significant changes and improvements in the logistics industry are being suggested and implemented on a daily basis. RFIDs, AIDCs, Omni-Channel Solutions and other IoT (Internet of Things) - based Technologies are making their way into logistics, and their usage will proliferate in the coming years.

The biggest shortcoming the logistics industry faces today is the lack of intellectual frameworks or systems that could help analyze vast amounts of data & information to derive reliable decisions. Decision-making on operational and tactical levels of logistics has the higher level of uncertainty and complexity compared to other functional areas of an organization. Current systems that assist in decision making still rely on humans to quite an extent. This paper proposed an intelligent logistics framework that will reduce human involvement in decision making to a minimal, refining the logistics of an organization to its maximum potential. The logistics planning shown in form of triangle in Fig. 1.

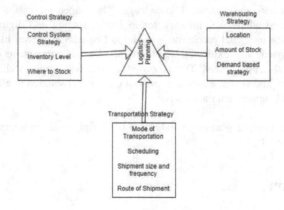

Fig. 1. The logistics planning triangle

2 Related Work

The manufacturing plays a vital role in the growth of a country's economy. It can be achieved by the better optimization of the production processes. That can only be possible with the use latest technologies that adopt the customer requirements and changes accordingly. Every industry has its type of customers and their characteristics, but in general, the manufacturing process demands the flexibility, real-time responses, adoption of customer requirements and forecast the market to change the strategy in advance [3].

The current situation in manufacturing is to set up the integration networks between enterprises so that they can collaborate and produces goods on time as per the market needs. This can be achieved only through the effective supply chain between enterprises to complete the operation within the given time [4]. The information should also have flowed in real time with the help of internet for the logistic planning and execution without any human intervention. The use of technologies heavily will also increase the infrastructural cost which needs to be catered by the enterprises to make it Industry 4.0 [5].

Hermann defines the industry 4.0 along with the keywords associated with it. The author explains that the machine to machine is not considered as the independent component in Industry 4.0. [6]. The cloud computing, big data, and data analytics are used to gather and generate the information for Industry 4.0. [7]

There are five main components of Industry 4.0. i.e., Internet of Things, Cyber-Physical Systems, Big Data, Data Analytics, and smart factories. The intelligent logistic and digitized supply chain are the processes used in to make industry 4.0. Sundmaeker defines the use of internet of things in various domains to make the logistics and supply chain efficiency. [8] CPS is another essential component of industry 4.0 stated by Kagermann [9]. CPS integrates the virtual and physical processes with computation [10]. Big data can be defined the collection of extensive data which cannot be handled by the database software. It can be used to gather all the related data and process thoroughly to get the information and make logistic forecasting automatically.

To process such huge data, the functional data analytic tools are required which can collect, organize and analyze the data to get the information for decision-makers. In recent trends of logistics, the system automatically takes decisions for the supply chain of goods or raw material in collaboration of partnering enterprises.

3 Industry 4.0, Logistics and Supply Chain

Every industry expects to deliver the products to the customer within the time frame using standard process. In the general method, marketing executives analyze the current and past data to predict the market demand for the product. By that analysis, industry orders the raw material and other related components to the partnering agencies so that the expected market demand can be achieved. Accordingly, the shipping is also instructed to ship the goods effectively to the customer. If the predicts goes well, the gap between demand and supply will be small at every point in time in the system [11].

However, it rarely happens because forecasting is an inexact science. In general, the data may be inconsistent and incomplete to gather the information and predict market forecast. The harsh reality is that the internal departments are also not in line and don't have the transparency in the communication. Manufacturing is independent of marketing, suppliers, partners, and customers. This transparency lack will reflect in the supply chain and customer satisfaction [12].

In the coming year, it is going to change as the change in the supply chain. The first change is the integration between internal departments further with the partners and customers by digitization of supply chain. To prepare an integrated automated network between all stakeholders is the goal of the digital supply chain [13].

Industry can achieve success in procurement, supply chain, and customer satisfaction by implementing the following four essential elements of the digital supply chain [14]:

- Smart Logistics
- Integrated data collection and analysis
- Automated procurements
- Smart warehousing

With these four essential elements, the industry can reduce the cost, be flexible, and effective market prediction with customer satisfaction. The evolution of Industry 4.0 shown in Fig. 2 where we can see that how each aspect of the business will be transformed through the vertical integration of several operations [15].

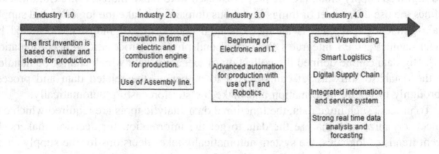

Fig. 2. The evolution of Industry 4.0

The ecosystem of Industry 4.0, smart logistics, warehousing, and procurement will be based on the implementation of several digital technologies like Cloud computing [16], Internet of Things, Machine Learning, AI, etc. If we put together all the techniques, it will create a new horizon for better customer satisfaction and sustain in the competitive market. The heart of all these activities is digital supply chain. It integrated vertically in all the dimensions of an industry. It combines with the supplier of raw material, manufacturing, distributing, warehousing to the customer [17]. This integration will work automatically by the data analytics and decision-making tools without any intervention of a human. The digitally integrated supply chain model is Fig. 3.

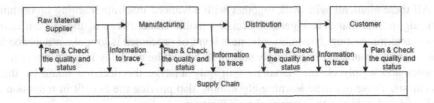

Fig. 3. Digitally integrated supply chain

4 Proposed Logistic Framework

The success of supply chin depends on the useful information exchanges. The traditional supply chain is lacking flowing the information timely and consistently. There are a lot of issues like lack of raw material in case of sudden change in the demand or disrupt the delivery or procurement process in natural calamities.

Due to this, the digitization of supply chain and logistics is required with smart warehousing and procurement. With this digitization, Business-to-Business (B2B) network will get the information timely for their raw material, the supply of intermediate and final goods and shipment. Customer will be also happy in getting the real-time status of their product in shipment. These processes will lead to customer satisfaction.

To achieve this, we have proposed a novel framework for logistics and supply chain, which are shown in Fig. 4.

This framework has different elements that are:

- Data collection from all sources, i.e., external and internal
- Integration with other available
- Analysis of data to get the cross-referral information
- Optimization of supply chain and logistics process with additional analysis
- Identify the risk and prepare the mitigation plan for all operations in the industry
- Forecasting the market trends and develop a plan accordingly.

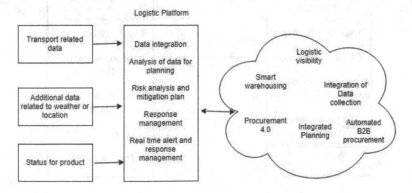

Fig. 4. Logistic framework

All these elements will work together with advanced machine learning algorithms. Such algorithms make managers or decision maker more aware of the system information and forecasting. Nowadays the next level of processes is to make a decision by these algorithms and act accordingly so that there will be no delay in the procurement, logistics and supply chain. Managers will only analyze the decision taken by these algorithms. These machine-learning algorithms also provide the benefit in reduction of workload and enhance the supply chain efficiency.

The requirement of tools and qualified skills have been changed drastically in the digital procurement. In the digital supply chain system, the integration of information and collaborating agencies are the most crucial process. A transparent building block is required for such integration with latest technologies like cloud computing, big data, and several big data analytics tools. The result of such combination is reducing the cost and on time delivery.

5 Prescriptive Supply Chain Analytics

The objective of the digital supply chain is the integration of various manufacturing processes and create a transparent system. Big data analytics is the essential element to achieve this integration and transparent system. Currently, several industries are using the analytics tools to identify the time of demand for the specific product and the time to deliver. Companies have also started the automated prediction of requirements of the particular good, ensuring the production capabilities, delivery of goods in warehouses for fast delivery to the customer and act on the customer feedback.

The next aim of supply chain analytics is to define the working operations of the supply chain. The goal is not only related to optimizing the demand planning or

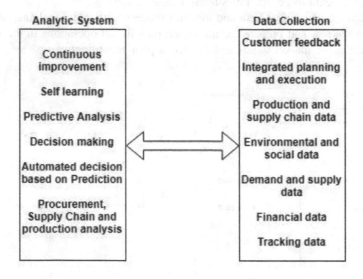

Fig. 5. Proposed academic centric cloud computing adoption model

inventory management or logistics planning. Instead of working on all aspects or processes involved in the complete chain of product manufacturing, delivery, and feedback. The perspective analytics system provides the automated decision support to the managers. Manager's role is to check the quality of the decision taken by the automated system and identify the area of improvement for usefully automated determination. The proposed analytics from big data and algorithm are shown in Fig. 5.

6 Benefits and Challenges of Industry 4.0

The possible benefits of Industry 4.0 are countless. It is benefitted in all aspects of any industry. The most important benefits are:

- Increase in efficiency
- Cost Reduction
- Revenu growth
- Increase Productivity
- Better customer service

None of the technology or improvement can be done with our facing challenges. Industry 4.0. is also having difficulties in the implementation. These challenges are:

- Excessive investments
- Lack of standard, regulations, and form of certifications
- Unclear legal situations for the use of external data
- Lack of prioritization
- Lack of qualified employees
- Insufficient network stability
- Data Security risk

7 Conclusion and Future Work

This paper presents frameworks for procurement 4.0, supply chain and adaptive system for analytics. The digital supply chain is the requirement of every industry to sustain in the competitive market. We have also proposed a novel approach to develop the automated system for analytics that can analyze the collected data, get the information about the supply chain and market demand, and automatically make decisions for procurement of raw material, and delivery of final goods to the warehouse. This process will revolutionize the industrial manufacturing and logistics processes. Integration of collaborative partners is possible with the digital supply chain. It also integrated the various latest technologies to make supply chain and logistics more effective and efficient. In future, the primary concern will be the security of external data integration and effective decision making by automated systems without any biasing in the decision.

References

1. Schelechtendal, J., Keinert, M., Kretschmer, F., Lechler, A.: Making existing production system Industry 4.0-ready. Prod. Eng. Res. Dev. **9**(1), 143–148 (2015)
2. Brettel, M., Friederichsen, N., Keller, M., Rosenberg, M.: How virtualization, decentralization and network building change the manufacturing landscape: an Industry 4.0 perspective. Int. J. Inf. Commun. Eng. Technol. **8**(1), 37–44 (2014)
3. Uckelmann, D.: A definition approach to smart logistics. In: Balandin, S., Moltchanov, D., Koucheryavy, Y. (eds.) NEW2AN 2008. LNCS, vol. 5174, pp. 273–284. Springer, Heidelberg (2008). https://doi.org/10.1007/978-3-540-85500-2_28
4. The state of Logistics Outsourcing, 20th Annual Third-Party Logistics Study (2016)
5. Seitz, K.-F., Nyhuis, P.: Cyber-physical production systems combined with logistic model – a learning factory concept for an improved production planning and control. In: Procedia CIRP for 5th Conference on Learning Factories, vol. 32, pp. 92–97. Elsevier (2015)
6. Hermann, M., Pentek, T., Otto, B.: Design principles for industrie 4.0 scenarios. In: 2016 49th Hawaii International Conference on System Sciences (HICSS), Koloa, HI, pp. 3928–3937 (2016)
7. Bauernhansl, T., Hompel, M.T., Vogel-Heuser, B.: Industrie 4.0 in Produktion, Automatisierung und Logistik: Anwendung, Technologien, Migration. Springer, Abraham-Lincoln-Strasse (2014)
8. Sundmaeker, H., Guillemin, P., Friess, P., Woelffl'e, S.: Vision and challenges for realising the Internet of Things. In: CERP-IoT – Cluster of European Research Projects on the Internet of Thing, vol. 20 (2010)
9. Kagermann, H., Wahlster, W., Helbig, J.: Recommendations for implementing the strategic initiative Industry 4.0. Technical report, Acatech National Academy of Science and Engineering, Lyoner Strasse (2013)
10. Lee, J., Bagheri, B., Kao, H.: A cyber-physical systems architecture for Industry 4.0-based manufacturing systems. Manufact. lett. **3**, 18–23 (2014)
11. Bücker, I., Hermann, M., Pentek, T., Otto, B.: Towards a methodology for industrie 4.0 transformation. In: Abramowicz, W., Alt, R., Franczyk, B. (eds.) BIS 2016. LNBIP, vol. 255, pp. 209–221. Springer, Cham (2016). https://doi.org/10.1007/978-3-319-39426-8_17
12. Norta, A., Ma, L., Duan, Y., Rull, A., Kolvart, M., Taveter, K.: eContractual choreography-language properties towards cross-organizational business collaboration. J. Int. Serv. Appl. **8**(8), 1–23 (2015)
13. Bunse, B.: Industrie 4.0 and the smart service world (2016). https://industrie4.0.gtai.de/INDUSTRIE40/Navigation/EN/industrie-4-0,t=industrie-40-and-the-smart-service-world, did=1182536.html. Accessed 1 May 2018
14. Norta, A., Grefen, P., Narendra, N.C.: A reference architecture for managing dynamic inter-organizational business processes. Data Knowl. Eng. **91**, 52–89 (2014)
15. Jeschke, S., Brecher, C., Meisen, T., Özdemir, D., Eschert, T.: Industrial internet of things and cyber manufacturing systems. In: Jeschke, S., Brecher, C., Song, H., Rawat, Danda B. (eds.) Industrial Internet of Things. SSWT, pp. 3–19. Springer, Cham (2017). https://doi.org/10.1007/978-3-319-42559-7_1
16. Wegener, D.: Industry 4.0-Opportunities and challenges of the industrial internet. Industry 4.0 - vision and mission at the same time (2014)
17. Schmidt, R., Möhring, M., Härting, R.-C., Reichstein, C., Neumaier, P., Jozinović, P.: Industry 4.0 - potentials for creating smart products: empirical research results. In: Abramowicz, W. (ed.) BIS 2015. LNBIP, vol. 208, pp. 16–27. Springer, Cham (2015). https://doi.org/10.1007/978-3-319-19027-3_2

An Analysis of Key Challenges for Adopting the Cloud Computing in Indian Education Sector

Mayank Singh[✉] and Viranjay M. Srivastava

Department of Electrical, Electronic and Computer Engineering,
Howard College, University of KwaZulu-Natal, Durban 4041, South Africa
{dr.mayank.singh,viranjay}@ieee.org

Abstract. The education sector is facing the major challenge for the quality and extent of education to the distant part of the nation. In the developing countries, the adoption of cloud computing in education is an opportunity to achieve the literacy target and provide quality education to every part of India with minimum investments. It also helps the government or private educational institutions in reducing the cost of educational setup. In this paper, we have explored the factors which are playing significant roles in the adoption of cloud in Indian educational sector. We have surveyed with higher management, dean, directors, teachers, and students of private and government institutions to evaluate their knowledge about cloud computing, its benefits, possible challenges and readiness for its adoption. A total of 1538 responses were received for the analysis. Seven hypothesis developed that affect the cloud computing adoption in the education sector and tested by using statistical analysis tools, i.e., SPSS. The cloud adoption rate is much higher in higher educational universities then small or medium level educational institutions. The finding shows that 87.77% of respondent are interested in adoption of cloud computing in their schools or colleges, while 54% supported the issue of security and privacy in the adoption of cloud computing. The security issue must be taken care by the cloud service providers for the implementation and best utilization of cloud computing in Indian education sector.

Keywords: Cloud adoption · Indian education sector
Cloud adoption challenges · Cloud computing

1 Introduction

In today's scenario, information technology is the backbone to get the growth in any business. But it comes with specific challenges like finding the business-related software; establish the computer hardware; networking and other IT infrastructures. An initial establishment of IT or other infrastructure requires substantial investments, which is a burden on any educational institutions. Cloud computing allows educational institutions to access the services and IT infrastructure with affordable cost [1]. In past few years, the cloud computing is having exponential grown of adoption all around the world [2]. This growth is irrespective of company size or business type. Almost all

© Springer Nature Singapore Pte Ltd. 2018
M. Singh et al. (Eds.): ICACDS 2018, CCIS 905, pp. 439–448, 2018.
https://doi.org/10.1007/978-981-13-1810-8_44

types of industries like retail, education, healthcare, and manufacturing are transforming toward cloud services to enhance the scope of availability, scalability, and performance. Today every organization is intended to implement the cloud computing for expending the business without any geographic barriers [3]. By 2020, a no-cloud policy will be rare for any organization [4]. According to a survey, in 2017 the significant share of investment will be in cloud computing [5].

Across the globe, the demand for cloud computing services is rising day by day, and the compound annual growth rate is expected to be double – digit of the year 2018 according to Sharon Ford, Office of Industries [6]. The early innovators in cloud computing and currently who dominate this market are the US firms. Based on the revenue generated, the United States owns the world's largest cloud computing industry. Most of the firms in the U.S. are already cloud-based now, and eventually, the most awaited part of the U.S. has already started, i.e., leaving the private sectors behind the U.S. government is winning the race in moving to cloud computing [7].

In education, the teaching and learning method is transforming faster than ever from the blackboard to online. Colossal cloud computing service providers are looking forward to incorporating Cloud computing with emerging technologies such as artificial intelligence, virtual reality and big data with conventional methods to augment the learning experience of students. Moreover, growing need for implementation of experiential and project-based learning in essential subjects such as science, mathematics, and engineering is driving the demand for cloud computing in the education sector [8].

Online learning resources and their adoption is growing day by day across various educational institutes worldwide to increase the demand for education technology market. The cloud computing is changing the way of learning and teaching method across the world. The teacher can record the lecture at any time, and that will be available for students. The students can access the best quality lecture from anywhere according to their convenience. With cloud computing, faculty can concentrate on quality education and research. Educational institutions are facing various challenges concerning teaching resources and infrastructure, which can easily be solved by the cloud computing [9].

This paper attempts to address the challenges and need of adopting cloud computing in Indian education sector. The identified factors have an impact on the adoption of cloud computing. A survey was conducted with various government and private institutions to determine the intent of cloud adoption. We have also identified the primary concern for cloud adoption. Furthermore, this research will help the students, educationist, researchers, and faculties to adopt the cloud computing. Section 2 represents the status of Indian education sector. Advantages of cloud computing adoption are presented in Sect. 3. Factors for the adoption of cloud computing and proposed model for Indian education sector is given in Sects. 4 and 5 respectively. Section 6 presents the research model and hypothesis. Analysis and results are explained in Sect. 7. Conclusion and future scope are given in Sect. 8.

2   Status of Indian Education Sector

For the development of socio-economic, the education industry plays a vital role. Education also plays an essential role in the building of a nation and improve its economic growth and living standards. The employment and social development can be possible with the national economic growth. Vision India 2020 documents stated that India's technological and economic evolutions would be accompanied by a multidimensional political transformation that will have a philosophical effect on the effective working of government [10]. The literacy will be the bare minimum privileges of every India citizen [11].

Education sector pressurized with the growth of Indian economy to enhance the quality of education, develop industry-specific world-class curriculum and affordable learning for all. The private players along with government are putting a lot of effort and money to make it a success, but their primary focus is to enhance the traditional methods of education without much emphasis on technology involvement.

Higher Education Universities and Colleges are the backbones of the country through its innovation, research, and development. The highest use of cloud computing can be done in higher education to access and use of the books, research papers, thesis, etc. anytime anywhere with low cost of hardware and software [12]. It revealed that many renowned universities in the world saved millions of dollars of its budget by adopting cloud computing in their universities.

The Indian government has been taken the initiatives to harness the internet in higher education like NPTEL which is a joint initiative by IISc and IITs. It broadcast the classroom teaching over the web in the field of humanities, engineering, and sciences [13]. Such efforts can be further explored using the cloud for broadcasting dedicated classroom teaching remotely.

3   Advantages of Cloud Adoption in Education Sector

The innovative use of cloud computing can significantly strengthen and change the Educational sector through e-learning, e-portals, Virtual labs, and classrooms. We can transform the education process by using of advanced technological tools for any stage of learning/study. The adoption of these methods could be possible at minimum cost so that we can drive the nation into becoming a "Knowledge Superpower." Transformation of the educational process using advanced technological techniques and tools for all stage shown in Fig. 1.

The state-of-the-art use of cloud in education solves the three critical challenges of quality, impartiality, and access. The implementation of cloud computing in education enables the improvement of system accessibility for online learning. It also improves the transparency and teaching quality for educational institutions especially across remote locations. With cloud computing, the analysis of student's performance, behavior, and involvement can be monitored and analyze efficiently. Using this analysis, teachers can modify their content delivery pattern, course content and teaching methodology to improve the student performance and learning [14].

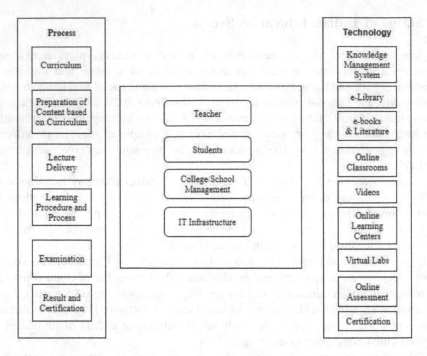

Fig. 1. Process and technology for the transformation of Indian education system

Furthermore, for the benefits of all stakeholders, the cloud computing can perform several roles in the education sector. Faculty can deliver a lecture as per their convenience and students can choose the lectures from available pools and study at any time from anywhere. Cloud computing provides a platform for researchers to perform the research activities in collaboration with various experts from external agencies or organizations. We can achieve all the benefits mentioned above without massive investment for IT infrastructure and its maintenance [15].

4   Factors for Adoption of Cloud Computing

Internal and external factors will be used to understand the overview of cloud computing adoption. These factors have a significant effect on the choice of cloud computing adoption approaches. The external factors are associated with the external societal situation, both globally and locally while internal factors related to the technical and internal societal environment. Based on the above two factors, we have proposed a new cloud computing adoption model. The proposed model is the extension of technological, organizational and environmental (TOE) model with the addition of two new factors named student-educator and cost especially for Indian education sector. Figure 2 presents the suggested cloud computing adoption model with identified factors.

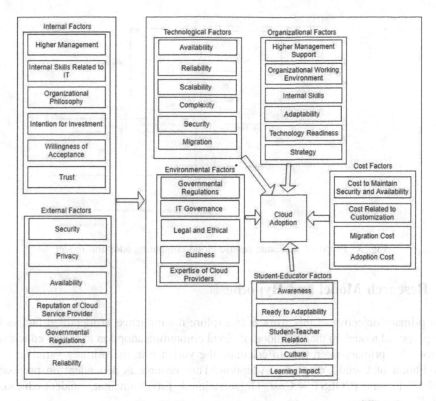

Fig. 2. Factors for cloud adoption

5 Proposed Cloud Adoption Model for Indian Education Sector

Cloud-based services help the education system to transform a collaborative, comprehensive and well-organized system.

Cloud also supports the education system in spreading the quality education to a large population in an effective manner with low cost. The quality of learning will also improve through this futuristic cloud-based model. The student-teacher collaboration will be highest with the help of cloud. From any geographical locations, students can learn from quality online teaching and clear their doubts by interactive with teachers just like a classroom learning.

The proposed academic centric cloud computing model presented in Fig. 3. Using this model, the teacher can primarily focus on quality contents for teaching and research instead of fundamental teaching issues. The students can learn the quality education from anywhere as per their convenient time. With this proposed model, students, teacher, and university or college can gain regarding quality education, adequate learning resources at low cost.

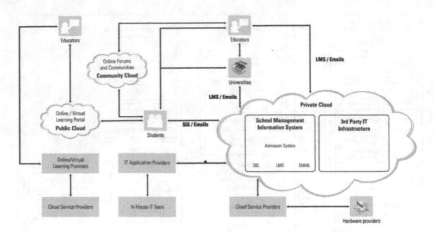

Fig. 3. Proposed academic centric cloud computing adoption model

6 Research Model and Hypothesis

The primary objective of this work is to explore the influence of identified factors in our proposed model on the likelihood of cloud computing adoption in Indian education sector. Our primary interest is to calculate the variance in the primary variable, i.e., Likelihood of Cloud Computing Adoption. This variable is dependent on proposed COEST factors. (COEST – Cost, Organizational, Environmental, Student-educator, and Technological).

Table 1 shows the research factors and their statistical analysis. The descriptive statistical analysis of each factor was carried out to measure the responses of the participants in the cloud adoption issues or hypothesis. After inserting quantitative data in the statistical analysis tool, i.e., IBM SPSS, descriptive results were generated to get statistics about the entered data.

Table 1. Research factors.

S. No.	Variables	No of factors
1	External	7
2	Internal	5
3	Cost	5
4	Organizational	6
5	Environmental	7
6	Student-Educator	5
7	Technological	6

We have used five points Likert scale system to examine our hypothesis for the likelihood of cloud computing adoption. Scale varies between strongly disagree = 1 and strongly agree = 5. Multi co-linearity test and regression analysis were lead to validate the studies and test hypothesis respectively.

The following hypotheses were developed and tested based on the proposed research factors:

H1: Internal factor an influences the likelihood of cloud adoption.

H2: External factor influences the likelihood of cloud adoption.

H3: Cost factor has a direct influence to the likelihood of cloud adoption.

H4: Organizational factor has a direct influence to the likelihood of cloud adoption.

H5: Environmental factor has a direct influence to the likelihood of cloud adoption.

H6: Student-Educator factor has a direct influence to the likelihood of cloud adoption.

H7: Technological factor has a direct influence to the likelihood of cloud adoption.

7 Results and Analysis

Reliability and validity are the two essential methods for determining the usefulness and quality and usefulness of collected data. Validity refers the accuracy of the measuring of instruments according to its intention, while reliability indicates the stability and consistency of the results obtained.

In this research, to assess the convergent validity, we use the loading of factors, Cronbach's alpha coefficient, composite reliability and the average variance inflation factor (AVIF). Composite reliability shows the degree to which the construct indicators indicate the latent construct and average variance inflation factor reflects the overall amount of variance in the factors accounted for by the latent construct. The loading value of all factors and average variance inflation factor should be higher than 0.5, the value of Cronbach's alpha coefficient should be above 0.6, and the value of composite reliability should be higher than 0.7 [16]. Table 2 represents the results of convergent validity for all factors, which shows that all measures in this research sufficiently meet the validity.

Table 2. Convergent validity results for all factors.

S. No.	Variables	Average loading	Cronbach's alpha	Composite reliability	Average variance inflation factor
1	External	0.895	0.813	0.862	0.716
2	Internal	0.851	0.788	0.837	0.769
3	Cost	0.835	0.789	0.868	0.820
4	Organizational	0.896	0.842	0.921	0.852
5	Environmental	0.898	0.905	0.933	0.798
6	Student-Educator	0.759	0.959	0.956	0.772
7	Technological	0.902	0.827	0.873	0.832

This research assessed the structural model for the hypothesis testing by t-test. The multiple correlation coefficients R is fixed on a nearly moderate associate that is 0.512 for evaluating the result, then the value of R2 will be 0.262. Also, the value of F = 22.986 is significant which shows that the regression model significantly predicts the dependent variables. Table 3 presents the testing results of seven hypotheses.

Table 3. Hypothesis Testing Results.

Hypothesis	β	t	Decision
H1: External	0.419	4.218	Supported
H2: Internal	0.132	1.627	Supported
H3: Cost	0.141	1.829	Supported
H4: Organizational	0.272	2.921	Supported
H5: Environmental	0.325	3.597	Supported
H6: Student-Educator	0.118	1.483	Supported
H7: Technological	0.407	4.201	Supported

If other predictors are constant, then β indicates to the distinct contribution of each predictor to the model. The positive values of β means hypotheses are supported. The β value represents the level of effect on the dependent variable, i.e., higher value means higher impact. The external factor has the highest contribution to the decision of cloud adoption because it has highest β value.

To in-depth analysis from the survey, we have identified the top ten issues of likelihood of cloud computing adoption in Indian education sector. Security is the major obstacle to the adoption of cloud computing in the education section. A total of 54% respondent voted for this issue. Figure 4 shows the top ten issues in the adoption of cloud computing in Indian education sector.

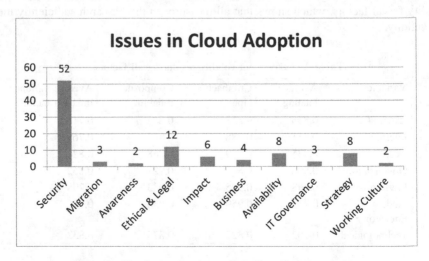

Fig. 4. Cloud adoption issues in Indian education sector

8   Conclusion and Future Work

This study targets a large population of colleges or universities in India. The response rate was relatively on higher side; therefore, the external validity is high. The Indian education institutions should invest in future technologies that help in focusing the quality of education and enhance core values and business. Cloud computing has high potential in the coming future for the education sector. In this paper, we have identified the factors which have a high impact on the adoption of cloud computing in Indian education sector. The hypothesis was tested to analyze the impact of cloud adoption. From the survey, a degree of privacy and security concern was identified for cloud computing adoption. Trust on the service provider is another concern in the adoption of cloud. Cloud service providers should play a significant role in establishing the trust on these services and provide a high degree of security and service quality.

References

1. Sultan, N.: Cloud computing: a democratizing force. Int. J. Inf. Manage. **31**(3), 810–815 (2013)
2. Sultan, N.A.: Reaching for the cloud: how SMEs can manage. Int. J. Inf. Manage. **31**(3), 272–278 (2011)
3. Venters, W., Whitley, E.A.: A critical review of cloud computing: researching desires and realities. J. Inf. Technol. **27**(3), 179–197 (2012)
4. http://www.varindia.com/news/1529256#sthash.2PO4NnR4.dpbs. Accessed 3 Mar 2018
5. https://www.entrepreneur.com/article/287021. Accessed 3 Mar 2018
6. Office in Education. Microsoft. http://products.office.com/en-us/student/office-in-education. Accessed 3 Mar 2018
7. Thakkar, P.: India becoming a second cloud computing hub. https://services.siliconindiamagazine.com/viewpoint/ceo-insights/india-becoming-a-second-cloud-computing-hub-nwid-8114.html. Accessed 3 Mar 2018
8. Katz, R.N., Goldstein, P.J., Yanosky, R.: Demystifying cloud computing for higher education. Educause Center Appl. Res. Bull. **19**, 1–13 (2009)
9. Marinela, M., Anca, A.: Using cloud computing in higher education: a strategy to improve agility in the current financial crisis. Commun. IBIMA **2011**, 1–15 (2011). http://web.msu.ac.zw/elearning/material/1327058884AgilityInHigherEducation.pdf
10. India vision document 2020, Technical report, Planning commission, Government of India (2002)
11. Online Education Market in India 2017–2021. A technical report by RNCOS (2017)
12. Ercan, T.: Effective use of cloud computing in educational institutions. Procedia Soc. Behav. Sci. **2**(2), 938–942 (2010)
13. Ibrahim, M.S., Salleh, N., Misra, S.: Empirical studies of cloud computing in education: a systematic literature review. In: Gervasi, O., et al. (eds.) ICCSA 2015. LNCS, vol. 9158, pp. 725–737. Springer, Cham (2015). https://doi.org/10.1007/978-3-319-21410-8_55
14. Karim, F., Rampersad, G.: Cloud computing in education in developing countries. Comput. Inf. Sci. **10**(2) (2017)

15. Kaur, R., Sawtantar, S.: Exploring the benefits of cloud computing paradigm in education sector. Int. J. Comput. Appl. **115**(7), 1–3 (2015)
16. Singh, M., Gupta, P.K., Srivastava, V.M.: Key Challenges in implementing cloud computing in indian healthcare industry. In: 2017 Pattern Recognition Association of South Africa and Robotics and Mechatronics International Conference (PRASA-RobMech), Bloemfontein, South Africa, pp. 162–167 (2017)

Texture Image Retrieval Based on Block Level Directional Local Extrema Patterns Using Tetrolet Transform

Ghanshyam Raghuwanshi and Vipin Tyagi[✉]

Jaypee University of Engineering and Technology, Guna, Raghogarh 473226, MP, India
dr.vipin.tyagi@gmail.com

Abstract. This paper introduces a novel texture image retrieval technique based on block level processing using Tetrolet and optimized directional local extrema patterns. Texture image categorization is performed for uniform and non-uniform distribution of the intensities within the image. Texture features are extracted by using Tetrolet transform and directional local extrema pattern. Image is processed at block level for extracting these features. The main concept of this approach is to analyze the image at block level to get better results in retrieval process. During image search, each block is compared with the corresponding block of another image. Categorization of the images reduces the search space. Proposed approach uses spatial and spectral domain analysis of the image. Performance of proposed retrieval system is tested on the Brodatz and VisTex benchmark databases. Retrieval results show that the proposed technique performs better in terms of average retrieval rate in comparison to other state-of-the-art techniques.

Keywords: Image search · Tetrolet transform · Content based image retrieval
Texture image search

1 Introduction

Image retrieval has been an issue of concern from last two decades. The rapid growth of image data influences the researcher to provide the better image retrieval system. The concept of Text-based image retrieval (TBIR) [2, 29, 30] came into existence for retrieving the relevant images according to the text in the query. Problems of huge annotation, semantic gap and query formulation are associated with this approach. These issues are better addressed by the content-based image retrieval system (CBIR). Instead of the text only, the content of the image is used for search in CBIR. Detailed description of CBIR and issues related to it, are are presented in [5, 26, 28, 30, 35]. Yao et al. [32] performed image retrieval by combining the CBIR and TBIR approaches. Initially images are retrieved on the basis of visual contents and then re-ranking of retrieved images is performed by textual information. Feature extraction is the key step in a CBIR system. Low level features like shape, texture, and color are generally used by the CBIR systems to index the images. These features can be local or global. Local feature extraction at region level is presented in [20, 25]. Global description of an image neither justifies the semantics of the image in the better way nor produces satisfactory results of the image retrieval like in medical domain as given in [27]. Most of the work has been done in the extraction of global features and only a few attentions have been paid to the feature extraction at the block level.

Feature extraction methods are categorized into spatial and spectral methods. Spatial domain methods deal with arrangement of pixel intensities and their relation with pixels surrounding to it. Local binary pattern (LBP) [16], Center Symmetric LBP (CS_LBP) [12], Directional Local Extrema Pattern (DLEP) [21], Block based LBP (BLK-LBP) [19] are technique used in spatial domain. There are various methods [24, 31] proposed in the spatial domain that are using the concepts presented in [12, 16, 19]. Spectral domain analysis of the image deals with frequency components and multi-resolution analysis of the image. Dual tree rotated complex wavelet filter (DT-RCWF), Dual tree complex wavelet transform (DT- CWT) [22], Gabor Wavelet (GT) [14], DT-RCWF + DT-CWT [9] and Tetrolet transform [10] are used in the spectral domain analysis of texture features. In spectral domain wavelet and its variants are used for calculating the texture descriptors [11, 13]. The method proposed in [14] used Gabor filter, [15] used wavelet decomposition. [9] used DT-CWT and DT-RCWF, which makes texture image retrieval invariant in twelve directions. More directional selectivity is provided by the methods [1, 4, 29] in the frequency domain. [7] proposed a method that constructs image signatures from the bit planes of decomposed wavelet subbands. [18] proposed a content-based image retrieval system that works both for texture and natural images. This approach updates the directional local extrema pattern by adding the oppugnant color space of RGB in combination with the value part of HSV model. Retrieved results are much better in this approach than other variants of the wavelets. [6, 10] proposed the concept of Tetrominoes. Raghuwanshi and Tyagi [17] used this concept by applying Tetrolet transform [10] for decomposing the images.

In the proposed method, instead of analyzing the complete image at once, better semantics are identified by processing the image at the block or region level. The image is divided into multiple regions and each region is processed separately. The approaches in which region information is employed to extract semantic concepts of images are known as region-based image retrieval (RBIR). In proposed work, we have processed the texture images using texture classification and texture feature. Texture categorization is performed with the help of second moment of the image and texture features are extracted using Tetrolet transform and directional local extrema pattern.

The proposed technique encapsulates the spectral and spatial approaches for achieving higher accuracy in texture image retrieval system. Local extrema pattern is used for structural approach and Tetrolet transform is used for extracting the texture features in the frequency or periodic domain.

1.1 Block Based LBP (BLK-LBP)

Due to the higher computation time taken by LBP, Block based LBP was developed [19]. BLK-LBP is having high region description power and computational time is reduced as well by dividing the image into the non-overlapping blocks of equal sizes and performs the LBP calculation at each block. Hence, at each block, boundary pixels get eliminated during LBP computation. This reduces the size of the histogram. LBP at block level reduces the complexity by greater than one-fourth. Image of size 16×16 is processed at the blocks of size 8×8. BLK-LBP calculates the binary pattern for 144 pixels. If complete image is taken at once then 196 pixels are used for pattern creation. BLK-LBP reduces the number of pixels nearly by half used in pattern generation phase.

BLK_LBP is calculated as:

$$\text{BLK\_LBP}_{P,R}(bl) = \sum_{bl=1}^{BL} \sum_{a=1}^{P} 2^{(a-1)} \times f_1\big(I(g_a) - I(g_c)\big) \tag{1}$$

Here bl represents the block number to be processed, BL is the total number of blocks. P and R the neighboring pixels and radius respectively. LBP is calculated for each block separately. It reduces the number of pixels to be used for pattern creation.

1.2 Directional Local Extrema Pattern (DLEP)

Local binary pattern [21] is not able to get direction related information from the image. Sometimes direction of the edge is important if the image is a complex one. DLEP describes the spatial structure of the local texture using the local extrema of the center gray pixel. In this method pattern is calculated in four different directions. DLEP for a given image is calculated by computing the difference between the center pixel and its neighbors in $0°$, $45°$, $90°$, and $135°$ directions.

1.3 Texture Categorization

Texture images are categorized as uniform and non-uniform. If the distribution of the intensities is in such a way that gap between successive pixels is not too high then images are uniform, otherwise non-uniform texture images. We have used second order moment or variance of the image for categorization.

$$m = \sum_{i=0}^{L-1} z_i \times p(z_i) \tag{2}$$

$$\mu_n(z) = \sum_{i=0}^{L-1} (z_i - m)^n p(z_i) \tag{3}$$

Where μ_n is the nth order moment of the image. The mean is calculated using Eq. 2. z_i is the intensity of the pixels present in the image and $p(z_i)$ is the gray level histogram. L represents the discrete intensity levels represent and n represent the order of the moment. If the variance of the image is very high then it shows the non-uniformity of the pixels within the image. Texture descriptor can be derived with the help of variance as:

$$R = 1 - \frac{1}{1 + \sigma^2(z)} \left\{ \begin{array}{l} 0 \; for \; uniform \; images \\ 1 \; for \; non - uniform \; images \end{array} \right\} \tag{4}$$

Here $\sigma^2(z)$ is the variance of the image. The value of R describes the roughness of the image. After performing multiple operations on the images for different values of

$\sigma^2(z)$, it is found that values greater than 0.18 for R categorize the texture in non-uniform class while less than this categorize the texture in uniform texture class.

2   Proposed Technique

Proposed technique emphasizes on achieving less retrieval time and less feature extraction time with higher accuracy in image retrieval. For achieving this goal, image is initially divided into non-overlapping sub-blocks. At each block, local geometry analysis is performed separately. Tetrolet and directional local extrema pattern are calculated at each block. A threshold (Th) is set to categorize the texture image on the basis of uniformity level. Each image is categorized in uniform and non-uniform category using Eqs. 2, 3, and 4. Search space for each query image is reduced by this categorization. Feature extraction is performed by taking both spectral and spatial analysis of the texture image into consideration. Block level DLEP is used for minimizing the number of patterns in the feature extraction process and Tetrolet at block level is applied to make the system adaptive at each block.

2.1   Proposed Block Based Directional Local Extrema Pattern (BLK_DLEP)

Proposed method introduces a new texture descriptor, BLK_DLEP, that extracts better texture feature and also reduces the feature extraction time. This descriptor works on blocks rather than the whole image as given in previous approaches [17–19]. This descriptor provides more directional selectivity than others. In BLK_LBP reduction in the time complexity is done but it does not meet the requirement for direction sensitivity. BLK_DLEP introduces the LBP with the directional information in the binary code. This binary code exhibits the directional property. At each block there are patterns of 3 × 3. This pattern is not calculated for boundary pixels. Each image is divided into non-overlapping blocks of M × M size and then DLEP is calculated for each block. Here a local pattern is generated for each pixel within a block. Instead of calculating only the differences between the center pixel with its neighborhoods, it checks the direction of the edge. If there exist any edge in between the center and its two consecutive pixels then set the value to 1 otherwise 0. DLEP code is created in the fixed order of neighboring pixels. If this order changes then DLEP code will be changed. This order must be fixed for all pixels and all blocks.

Processing at block level limits the number of pixels involved in the pattern generation process. NUP, the number of pixels, not used in pattern generation process can be calculated as:

$$NUP = R_{upper} + R_{lower} + \left(C_{leftmost} - 2\right) + \left(C_{rightmost} - 2\right) \tag{5}$$

R and C represent the number of rows and columns respectively. If number of rows and columns are equal then Eq. 5 will become:

$NUP = N + N + (N - 2) + (N - 2)\{R = C = N\}$, N is dimension of a block.

$\quad = 4N - 4$.

If the image is of size 64×64 then the total number of pixels not used is 248. But if the Local extrema is generated at block level by dividing the image into sixteen non-overlapping blocks then number of NUP is calculated as:

$$NUP_b = 16 \times (4 \times 16 - 4) = 960$$

Here NUP_b is the number of unused pixels at each block. It can be understood by the above explanation that 708 fewer pixels are compared at the whole image using this block based concept. It will decrease the feature extraction time approximately three-fourth of the time in comparison to calculation of DLEP on the complete image at once. Relation of time complexity among the variants of LBP is as follows:

$$LBP > CS - LBP > BLK - LBP > BLK - DLEP$$

Although less time complexity is achieved by BLK-DLEP, yet there is a challenge in the block based approach in choosing the appropriate size of the block that can enhance the performance of retrieval as well. Block of small size results in so many blocks if the image size is too large. The size of the block must be proportional to the size of the image.

$$blksize \propto imgsize \text{ i.e. } blksize = \frac{imgsize}{k}$$

Here $blksize$ is the size of the block and $imgsize$ is the size of the image and k is any coefficient. The value of k is determined using the assumption that image size will always be the multiple of 2. If the dimension of image is M and μ is any coefficient then value of k can be determined as:

If the image dimension is less than 7, then it is not divided in the sub-blocks and whole image is considered as a block. DLEP is calculated in four directions. Each pixel is compared with its neighbors in the four directions and BLK_DLEP is calculated as:

$$D(g_i) = I(g_c) - I(g_i) \text{ for } i = 1, 2 \ldots\ldots\ldots 8$$

$$2^M = 2^{k+\mu} \begin{cases} \mu = 3, 5 & \text{if } M = 7 \\ \mu = 4, 6 & \text{if } M = 8 \\ \mu = 1, 4, 7 & \text{if } M = 9 \\ \mu = 2, 6, 8 & \text{if } M = 10 \end{cases} \tag{6}$$

$$BLK\_DLEP = \sum_{p=1}^{BL} \{D_\alpha(g_c); D_\alpha(g_1); D_\alpha(g_2); \ldots\ldots.D_\alpha(g_8)\} \tag{7}$$

Where, $\alpha = \{0°, 45°, 90°, 135°\}$, BL is the total number of blocks and $D(g_i)$ is the difference between the center and neighboring pixels in α direction.

2.2 Block Based Tetrolet Transform

Tetrolet transform is used for extracting the texture features as given in [17]. In proposed work, we have refined the level of adaptability at block level. Each image is initially divided into four non-overlapping subparts. Now local geometry is considered at each level by applying 64 possible combinations of tetros at each block. Let A is a digital image with the index set $I = \{(i,j): i, j = 0, 1.....N-1\}$ with $N = 2^J$, $J \in N$. One to one and onto relation is maintained by applying bijective mapping. One dimensional index set $B(I)$ is prepared by taking the bijective mapping in the following way:

$$B:I \rightarrow 0, 1, 2......N^2 - 1 \text{ with } B((i,j)) := jN + i.$$

Initially block is divided in four equal parts. Then $(1:N/2, 1:N/2)$ part will be considered as initial low pass part. Low pass low^{r-1} of each subband is divided into blocks $P_{i,j}$ of size 4×4, i, j = 0, ... $\frac{N}{2^{r+1}} - 1$, where r is the decomposition level. All 64 possible coverings are applied to each block. Twelve high pass and four low pass coefficients are obtained at each block. Low pass coefficients at each decomposition level for each block are extracted as follows:

$$U^{r,(c)} = \left(low^{r,(c)}[s]\right)^3_{s=0} \tag{8}$$

$$low^{r,(c)}[s] = \sum_{(m,n)\in I_s^{(c)}} \mathcal{E}[0, B(m,n)]low^{r-1}[m,n] \tag{9}$$

Where $low^{r-1}[m,n]$ is the pixel value at the location, s is the value of subset, c is the covering index and r is the decomposition level. Three high pass coefficients for l = 1, 2, 3 at each level of decomposition are extracted as follows:

$$H_l^{r(c)} = \left(h^{r(c)}[s]\right)^3_{s=0} \tag{10}$$

$$h^{r,(c)}[s] = \sum_{(m,n)\in I_s^{(c)}} \mathcal{E}[l, B(m,n)]low^{r-1}[m,n] \tag{11}$$

$$G = (\mathcal{E}[l,m])^3_{l,m=0} = \frac{1}{2}\begin{pmatrix} 1 & 1 & 1 & 1 \\ 1 & 1 & -1 & -1 \\ 1 & -1 & 1 & -1 \\ 1 & -1 & -1 & 1 \end{pmatrix} \tag{12}$$

where the coefficients $\mathcal{E}[l, L(m,n)]$ is weight matrix as defined in Eq. 12 and L is the mapping relating the four index pairs (m, n) of $I_s^{(c)}$ with the values 0, 1, 2 and 3 in descending order. Selection of best tile is performed as follows

$$K^* = \arg\min(c) \sum_{l=1}^3 \left\|H_l^{r,(c)}\right\|_1 = \arg\min(c) \sum_{l=1}^3 \sum_{s=0}^3 \left|H_l^{r,(c)}[S]\right| \tag{13}$$

where K^* is the arrangement of the tetrominoes in best possible way such that l^1 -norm of the twelve high pass Tetrolet coefficients is minimum for that particular block. Hence in this way collection of corresponding low pass coefficients at each block becomes the new block for further Tetrolet decomposition.

Standard deviation α_k and Energy E_k of the Kth subband is computed as follows:

At each level of decomposition, standard deviation and energy is calculated for each subband.

$$\alpha_k = \left[\frac{1}{P \times Q} \sum_{i=1}^{Q} \sum_{j=1}^{P} \left(Z_x(i,j) - \mu_x \right)^2 \right]^{\frac{1}{2}} \tag{14}$$

$$E_k = \frac{1}{P \times Q} \sum_{i=1}^{Q} \sum_{j=1}^{P} |Z_x(i,j)| \tag{15}$$

where $Z_x(i,j)$ is the kth Tetrolet decomposed subband, P $\times$ Q is the size of Tetrolet decomposed subband and μ_x is the mean of the kth subband.

A feature vector is constructed by E_k and α_k as feature components, using a combination of standard deviation and energy.

$$f_B = [\alpha_1, \alpha_2, \dots \alpha_n, E_1, E_2 \dots E_n] \tag{16}$$

f_B represents the features of one block only for spectral domain. Feature vector of complete image in spectral domain is represented by the following way:

$$f = [f_{B1}, f_{B2}, f_{B1}, \dots f_{Bn}] \tag{17}$$

where f is the feature vector of the complete image using Tetrolet transform.

2.3 Experimental Results and Discussion

The performance of the image retrieval system has been tested by conducting the experiments on images taken from database D1 and database D2. Database D1 contains 109 images from Brodatz database [23] and 7 images from USC database [33] while database D2 contains 40 images from VisTex database [34]. Database D1 contains the images from two different databases to increase the diversity in the database. Images in the both the databases are of 512 $\times$ 512 size. Each image is divided into sixteen non overlapping sub images. Total number of images in database D1 is 1856 and in database D2 is 640. Image search is performed by taking each image of the database as a query image. Proposed Retrieval system selects the desired n images I = (I1, I2. ... In), according to the query image by computing the shortest distance using Eq. 18.

$$D(Q, I_j)_x = \sum_{x=1}^{M} \left[\sum_{i=1}^{N} \frac{|f_{DB_i} - f_{Q_i}|}{|f_{DB_i}| + |f_{Q_i}|} \right] \tag{18}$$

Comparison is performed with the existing methods (Gabor wavelet [14], DT-CWT [22], DT-RCWT [9], DT-CWT + DT-RCWT [9], CS_LBP [12], BLK_LBP [19], and LBP [16]) of texture image retrieval in terms of Average Retrieval Rate (ARR). ARR is the average percentage of the number of patterns relating to the same image as the query pattern in the top retrieved images.

Image feature extraction time, searching time and Database feature extraction time is compared with the variants of wavelet as shown in Table 1. Feature extraction time of proposed method is less among the other variants of wavelet. Although database is divided into two parts yet similarity matching time is higher than other methods, due to the block by block matching procedure. But total time complexity of the retrieval system is less.

Table 1. Feature extraction time, Retrieval time and Retrieval accuracy

	Standard DWT [17]	Gabor Wavelet [14]	KLD & GGD [3]	Tetrolet transform [17]	Proposed method
Feature Extraction Time	0.469 s	3.48 s	0.38 s	0.453 s	**0.292 s**
Total Retrieval Time	0.529 s	0.44 s	0.43 s	0.543 s	0.402 s
Database (**VisTex**) Feature extraction time	5.002 m	3.712 m	4.053 m	4.832 m	**3.114 m**
Retrieval Accuracy	69.9	80.2	84.7	85.9	**88.20%**

ARR of Proposed method (83.7%) improves the Retrieval efficiency on the variants of wavelets by 9.51% from Gabor wavelet (GT), 9.57% from DT-CWT, 12.53% from DT-RCWT, 5.95% from the combination of DT-CWT + DT-RCWT, and 5.6% from Tetrolet transform.

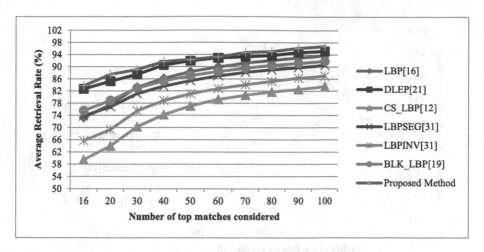

Fig. 1. Performance evaluation on top retrieved images with the variants of LBP in terms of ARR on database D1

Retrieval results are shown in Fig. 1. Proposed method also outperforms in comparison to variants of LBP (CS_LBP, BLK-LBP, DLEP) on database D1 as shown in Fig. 2. Performance of proposed method improves by 24.26% from CS_LBP, 8.16% from BLK_LBP, 10.44% from LBP, 1.02% from DLEP and 9.95% from LBPSEG.

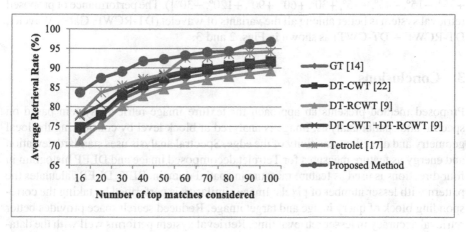

Fig. 2. Retrieval performance of proposed method with the variants of wavelets in terms of ARR on database D1

It is clear from Figs. 1, 2 and 3 that the combination of spectral and spatial analysis of texture properties of the proposed method outperforms other state-of-the-art methods.

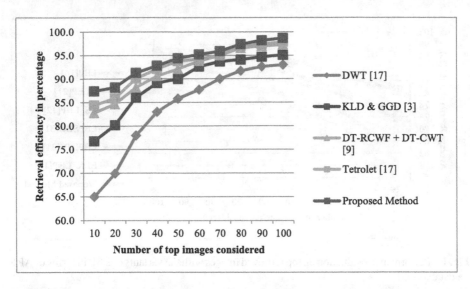

Fig. 3. Retrieval performance of proposed method with the variants of wavelets in terms of ARR on database D2

Texture image retrieval performed using the combination of DT-CWT and DT-RCWF [9] retrieves the texture feature in twelve different directions ({$0°$, $+15°$, $+45°$, $+75°$, $-15°$, $-45°$, $-75°$, $+30°$, $+60°$, $+90°$, $+120°$, $-30°$}). The performance of proposed retrieval system is better among all the variants of wavelet (DT-RCWF, Gabor Wavelet, DT-RCWF + DT-CWT) as shown in Figs. 2 and 3.

3   Conclusions

Proposed method presents an approach for texture image retrieval system based on spectral and spatial analysis. Image is analyzed at block level by considering the local geometry and direction sensitivity of the edge. Spectral analysis uses standard deviation and energy as feature measures for Tetrolet decomposed image and DLEP histogram in four directions is used as feature measure in spatial domain. BLK_DLEP calculates the pattern with lesser number of pixels. Image similarity is performed by taking the corresponding block of query image and target image. Reduced search space provides better retrieval accuracy in lesser retrieval time. Retrieval system performs well with the databases having high diversity. Images taken from VisTex and Brodatz benchmark databases are used for testing the performance of the retrieval system with the other existing methods. Experimental results show that the proposed method performs better in comparison to other state-of-the-art methods.

References

1. Candès, E.J., Donoho, D.L.: New tight frames of curvelets and optimal representations of objects with piecewise C2 singularities. Commun. Pure Appl. Math. **57**, 219–266 (2004)
2. Chang, S.K., Hsu, A.: Image information systems, where do we go from here? IEEE Trans. Knowl. Data Eng. **4**, 431–442 (1992)
3. Do, M.N., Vetterli, M.: Wavelet-based texture retrieval using generalized Gaussian density and Kullback-leibler distance. IEEE Trans. Image Process. **11**, 146–158 (2002)
4. Do, M.N., Vetterli, M.: The contourlet transform: an efficient directional multiresolution image representation. IEEE Trans. Image Process. **14**, 2091–2106 (2005)
5. Long, F., Zhang, H., Feng, D.D.: Fundamentals of content-based image retrieval. In: Feng, D.D., Siu, W.C., Zhang, H.J. (eds.) Multimedia Information Retrieval and Management. SCT, pp. 1–26. Springer, Heidelberg (2003). https://doi.org/10.1007/978-3-662-05300-3_1
6. Golomb, S.W.: Polyominoes: puzzles, patterns, problems, and packings, 2nd edn. Princeton University Press, Princeton (1994)
7. Pi, M.H., Tong, C.S., Choy, S.K., Hong, Z.: A fast and effective model for wavelet subband histograms and its application in texture image retrieval. IEEE Trans. Image Process. (2006). https://doi.org/10.1109/tip.2006.877509
8. Jain, P., Tyagi, V.: An adaptive edge preserving image denoising technique using Tetrolet transform. Vis. Comput. **31**, 657–674 (2015)
9. Kokare, M., Biswas, P.K., Chatterji, B.N.: Rotation invariant texture image retrieval using rotated complex wavelet filters. IEEE Trans. Syst., Man Cybern., Part-B. **36**, 1273–1282 (2006)
10. Krommweh, J.: Tetrolet transform: a new adaptive Haar wavelet algorithm for sparse image representation. J. Vis. Commun. Image Represent. **21**, 364–374 (2010)
11. Lasmar, N.-E., Berthoumieu, Y.: Gaussian copula multivariate modeling for texture image retrieval using wavelet transforms. IEEE Trans. Image Process. **23**, 2246–2261 (2014)
12. Heikkil, M., Pietikainen, M., Schmid, C.: Description of interest regions with local binary patterns. Pattern Recognit. **42**, 425–436 (2009)
13. Malik, F., Baharudin, B.: Analysis of distance metrics in content-based image retrieval using statistical quantized histogram texture features in the DCT domain. J. King Saud Univ. Comput. Inf. Sci. **25**, 207–218 (2013)
14. Manjunath, B.S., Ma, W.Y.: Texture features for browsing and retrieval of image data. IEEE Trans. Pattern Anal. Mach. Intell. **18**, 837–842 (1996)
15. Mao, J., Jain, A.K.: Texture classification and segmentation using multiresolution simultaneous autoregressive models. Pattern Recognit. **25**, 173–188 (1992)
16. Ojala, T., Pietikainen, M., Harwood, D.: A comparative study of texture measures with classification based on feature distributions. Pattern Recognit. **291**, 51–59 (1996)
17. Raghuwanshi, G., Tyagi, V.: Texture image retrieval using adaptive Tetrolet transforms. Digit. Signal Process. **48**, 50–57 (2016)
18. Reddy, A.H, Chandra, N.S.: Local oppugnant color space extrema patterns for content based natural and texture image retrieval. Int. J. Electron. Commun. (AEÜ) **69**, 290–298 (2015)
19. Takala, V., Ahonen, T., Pietikäinen, M.: Block-based methods for image retrieval using local binary patterns. In: Kalviainen, H., Parkkinen, J., Kaarna, A. (eds.) SCIA 2005. LNCS, vol. 3540, pp. 882–891. Springer, Heidelberg (2005). https://doi.org/10.1007/11499145_89
20. Mikolajczyk, K., Schmid, C.: A performance evaluation of local descriptors. IEEE Trans. Pattern Anal. Mach. Intell. **27**, 1615–1630 (2005)

21. Murala, S., Maheshwari, R.P., Balasubramanian, R.: Directional local extrema patterns: a new descriptor for content based image Retr. Int. J. Multimed. Inf. Retrieval **1**, 191–203 (2012)

22. Kingsbury, N.G.: Image processing with complex wavelet. Philos. Trans. R. Soc. Lond. Ser. A Math. Phys. Eng. Sci. **357**, 2543–2560 (1999)

23. Brodatz, P.: Textures: A Photographic Album for Artists and Designers. Dover, New York (1996)

24. Murala, S., Maheshwari, R.P., Balasubramanian, R.: Local tetra patterns: a new feature descriptor for content-based image retrieval. IEEE Trans. Image Process. **21**, 2874–2886 (2012)

25. Vikhar, P.A.: Content-based image retrieval (CBIR) State-of-the-art and future scope of research. IUP J. Inf. Technol. **6**(2), 64–84 (2010)

26. Rui, Y., Huang, T.S.: Image retrieval: current techniques, promising directions, and open issues. J. Vis. Commun. Image Represent. **10**, 39–62 (1999)

27. Shyu, C.R., Brodley, C.E., Kak, A.C., Kosaka, A., Broderick, A.L.: Local versus global features for content based image retrieval. In: IEEE Workshop on Content-Based Access of Image and Video Libraries, pp. 30–34 (1998)

28. Vassilieva, N.S.: Content-based image retrieval methods. Program. Comput. Softw. **35**, 158–180 (2009)

29. Velisavljevic, V., Beferull-Lozano, B., Vetterli, M., Dragotti, P.L.: Directionlets: anisotropic multi-directional representation with separable filtering. IEEE Trans. Image Process. **17**, 1916–1933 (2006)

30. Smeulders, A.W.M., Worring, M., Santini, S., Gupta, A., Jain, R.: Content-based image retrieval at the end of the early years. IEEE Trans. Pattern Anal. Mach. Intell. **22**, 1349–1380 (2000)

31. Yao, C.-H., Chen, S.-Y.: Retrieval of translated, rotated and scaled color textures. Pattern Recognit. **36**, 913–929 (2003)

32. Yao, T., Mei, T., Ngo, C.: Co-reranking by mutual reinforcement for image search. In: Proceedings of the ACM International Conference on Image and Video Retrieval, CIVR 2010, pp. 34–41 (2010). https://doi.org/10.1145/1816041.1816048

33. http://sipi.usc.edu/database/

34. http://vismod.media.mit.edu/pub/VisTex/VisTex.tar.gz

35. Tyagi, V.: Content-Based Image Retrieval. Springer, Singapore (2017). https://doi.org/10.1007/978-981-10-6759-4

Development of Transformer-Less Inverter System for Photovoltaic Application

Shamkumar B. Chavan[1(✉)], Umesh A. Kshirsagar[1], and Mahesh S. Chavan[2]

[1] Department of Technology, Shivaji University, Kolhapur, India
sbc_tech@unishivaji.ac.in
[2] Department of Electronics Engineering, KIT's College of Engineering, Kolhapur, India

Abstract. Efficiency improvement, optimization issues are important in power processing circuits of renewable energy applications. This article presents design, implementation and experimental results of a transformer less photovoltaic inverter system without batteries. The system converts PV DC voltage into AC sinusoidal waveform without using transformer. Batteries are omitted to reduce overheads on maintenance. In the developed inverter system P&O MPPT algorithm is implemented in boost converter stage. During day time load is operated on PV source while at night and in cloudy atmospheric conditions load is operated on domestic AC mains supply.

Keywords: PV-AC conversion · PV inverter · Transformer less PV inverter
Boost converter

1 Introduction

Nowadays focus of researchers is on development of highly efficient and optimized power processing circuits for non-renewable energy applications. A transformer less inverter is a recent trend in photovoltaic power processing systems. It offers advantages like lighter weight, economy, compactness etc. According to Rahim et al. [1] inverters should be water and dust proof with 5 to 10 years warranty and with features of condition monitoring, logging, cooling etc. Batteries are troublesome, they need maintenance, require more space and are bulky. Considering these aspects, in this work prototype of PV inverter system is developed without transformer and batteries.

Many researchers have valuable contribution in development of transformer less inverters. Single phase inverter topology based on ISPWM technique is presented along with simulation results [2] in this work mechanism to eliminate common mode leakage current is implemented. New method to design optimum transformer less inverter for PV system is presented [3], while designing the optimized inverter the parameters like component failure rates, maintenance cost, reliability etc. are considered, this design focuses on generation of more electricity in less cost. Hybrid clamped 3 level inverter topology without transformer has been developed and analyzed which omits problems of capacitor voltage unbalance and leakage current [4]. Three transformer-less inverter topologies are proposed and compared which avoids leakage current. Author reported good performance by 5L-ANPC inverter for PV systems [5]. Transformer-less inverter

© Springer Nature Singapore Pte Ltd. 2018
M. Singh et al. (Eds.): ICACDS 2018, CCIS 905, pp. 461–470, 2018.
https://doi.org/10.1007/978-981-13-1810-8_46

topology based on buck boost converter principle and extracting maximum power from two separate PV panels is presented. It also reduces leakage current [6]. Transformer-less inverter with integration of boost converter and H bridge converter has been experimented [7]. To reduce common mode leakage current single phase 3 level transformer-less topology using six switches is proposed. Authors reported reduction in leakage current below 300 mA [8]. Transformer-less inverter for low voltage PV modules is designed. In this buck boost converter is used. It uses current mode control and harmonic compensation strategies [9]. Multiple transformer-less inverter topologies and challenges are discussed. Authors depicted merits of transformer-less inverters [10]. Simulation model of transformer-less inverter in Matlab environment is developed [11].

2   PV Inverter Configuration

Circuit configuration for transformer-less inverter system is shown in Fig. 1. H-bridge inverter and LC filter is used to convert PV voltage into an AC voltage. IGBTs of H-bridge are triggered using SPWM waveforms. LC filter ensures sine waveform of desired amplitude and frequency.

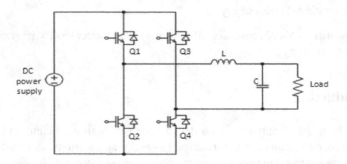

Fig. 1. H-bridge inverter without transformer

Generalized block diagram of system is shown in Fig. 2. Two boost converters are cascaded to raise the voltage up to desired level of 325 V which is fed to H-bridge inverter. Monitoring and controlling circuitry monitors input and output power and depending upon availability of sufficient power it switches load to transformer-less inverter system or to AC mains supply. By default load is connected to PV inverter system, if PV power is less than threshold then load is switched to AC mains supply.

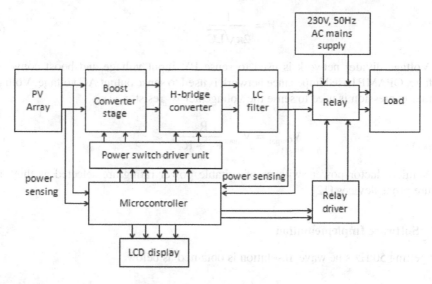

Fig. 2. System block diagram

3 System Development

3.1 Hardware Implementation

Cascaded boost stage boosts the input voltage to desired level of 325 V. Duty cycle of boost stage is set by expression 1. Reference [13] discusses boost converter stage design.

$$\text{Duty cycle} = 1 - \frac{V_{input}(min) \times \text{Efficiency}}{V_{output}} \tag{1}$$

Experimental results showed that duty cycle of 78% yields efficiency of 70%. Input inductor of 3.49 mH is designed using expression 2 for a switching frequency of 10 kHz with 2A ripple current [13].

$$L = \frac{V_{input} \times (V_{output} - V_{input})}{\Delta I_L \times f_{sampling} \times V_{output}} \tag{2}$$

Output capacitor is selected [13] using Eq. (3)

$$C_{filter}(min) = \frac{I_{output(max)} \times \text{Duty cycle}}{f_{sampling} \times \Delta V_{output}} \tag{3}$$

Output of boost converter with sufficient power is applied to H-bridge inverter. Sampling frequency of 10 kHz is used to generate SPWM signal for switching IGBTs. Output LC filter is designed using expression 4 to get 230 V, 50 Hz sine wave.

$$F = \frac{1}{2\pi\sqrt{LC}} \tag{4}$$

Voltage divider network is used to sense PV input voltage and boost converter voltage. OPAMP based impedance network is used to sense output AC voltage. Voltage divider expression is used to sense the voltage across resistor.

$$V_{Output} = V_{input}\frac{R_2}{R_1 + R_2} \tag{5}$$

Semiconductor power switches of suitable power rating are selected as they are failure prone devices [12].

3.2 Software Implementation

For getting 50 Hz sine wave, resolution is obtained as below.

$$T = \frac{1}{50} = 20\,\text{ms} \tag{6}$$

$$T = \frac{20\,\text{ms}}{200} = 100\,\mu\text{s} \tag{7}$$

Look up table is used to generate sine waveforms. The PWM Channels are configured to generate 10 kHz frequency with variable duty cycle using sine lookup table. Duty cycle of boost converter is varied according to MPPT algorithm. Figure 3 shows program flow chart.

Load is connected to PV inverter system but when PV power falls below threshold level load is switched to AC mains supply. System monitors PV power level, if it is above threshold level load is switched back to PV inverter. For sufficient PV power level system activates MPPT algorithm, till the boost converter output reaches the desired level. Then controller generates SPWM pulses which are fed to H-bridge inverter via power switch driver. System displays PV power, converter and inverter output power levels. When inverter power drops below threshold power, system monitors PV power level, if PV power level is below threshold level, system disconnects load from inverter and switches the load to AC mains supply.

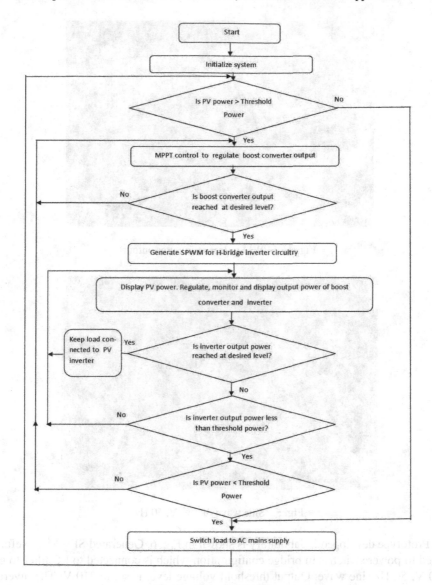

Fig. 3. System flow chart

4 Results and Discussions

In this section experimental results are presented and discussed. Figure 4 shows H-bridge inverter SPWM output of 320 V, 50 Hz and 10 kHz sampling frequency.

Fig. 4. SPWM pulses at inverter output

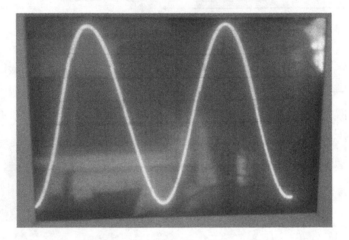

Fig. 5. Sine wave of 230 V, 50 Hz

Prototype developed in laboratory is shown in Fig. 6. Generated SPWM waveform is fed to power switches in bridge configuration which is connected to LC filter to get 230 V, 50 Hz sine wave. Output threshold voltage level is set to 210 V. The inverter performance is tested for a bulb of 230 V, 50 Hz frequency. Due to absence of transformer, isolation is poor and power switches may undergo electrical stress. Considering this reliability improvement aspects should be focused during design stage [14, 15]. Overrated components are preferred for reliability improvement. Design of gate driver circuitry is important to avoid damage of gate drivers and power switches. Expenditure required to be incurred on battery bank can be eliminated resulting in lowered system cost. Precise values of filter components and proper design of inductor is essential to get sine wave of 230 V, 50 Hz. Design of cascaded boost converter is important stage as input PV voltage is required to be boosted to 325 V. This leads electrical stress on power switches, which may get damaged. While designing cascaded boost converter stage thermal and reliability aspects should be considered. Effect of sampling frequency on output voltage can be understood from the Figs. 7 and 8. Output distortion can be minimized using higher sampling frequency. During night time, cloudy and rainy season, PV output lowers; therefore load is required to be switched on AC mains supply.

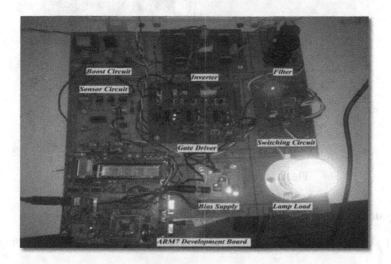

Fig. 6. Transformer less inverter prototype developed in laboratory

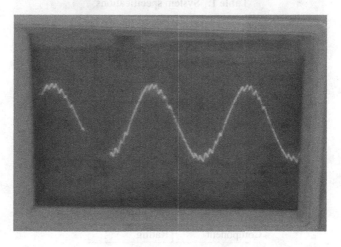

Fig. 7. Distorted output at 1 kHz sampling frequency

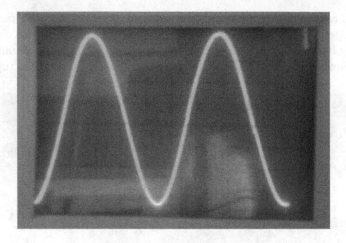

Fig. 8. Output at 10 kHz sampling frequency

4.1   System Specifications

Table 1 shows system specifications while Table 2 shows power stage component ratings.

Table 1. System specifications

Parameter	Value
Maximum PV Voltage	132 V
Minimum PV Voltage	102 V
PV Short circuit Current (I_{sc})	7A
Maximum PV Power	924 W
Boost Output Voltage	325 V
Output AC Voltage (V_{AC})	230 V
Output AC Current (I_{AC})	4 A
Maximum Output Power (P_{out})	920 W

Table 2. Component ratings

Component	Rating
Boost stage	
Inductor	3.4 mH
capacitor	1 uF, 400 V
Output filter	
Inductor	2.5 mH
Capacitor	820 uF, 400 V

5   Conclusions and Future Work

In the presented work PV inverter without transformer and batteries is developed. Experimental results have shown that transformer less inverter is able to generate sine waves of desired frequency and amplitude. Further few merits like lowered cost, compactness and lowered weight can be achieved due to the absence of transformer. Problem of power loss associated with transformer can be omitted. Batteries are costly and require maintenance; cost associated with batteries can be omitted. Due to absence of batteries the system power depends upon availability of sunlight, therefore in cloudy environment and at night time the load is required to switch on alternate source. Poor isolation is the demerit and future work can be extended to get a better isolation without using transformer. Consideration of reliability improvement aspects at design stage will be meritorious.

Acknowledgment. The presented work is completed in the Embedded systems and VLSI design laboratory of Department of Technology, Shivaji University, Kolhapur. Authors are thankful to Shivaji University, Kolhapur for providing necessary facilities for completion of this work.

References

1. Rahim, N.A., Saidur, R., Solangi, K.H., Othman, M., Amin, N.: Survey of grid connected photovoltaic inverters and related systems. Clean Techn. Environ. Policy **14**, 521–533 (2012)
2. Chacko, G., Scaria, R.: An improved transformer less inverter topology for cost effective PV Systems. In: Proceedings of 7th IRF International Conference, Bengaluru, pp. 170–177 (2014)
3. Koutroulis, E., Blaabjerg, F.: Design optimization of transformer less grid-connected PV inverters including reliability. IEEE Trans. Power Electron. **28**(1), 325–335 (2013)
4. Chen, L., Zhang, Q., Jiang, Z., Sun, C.: Transformerless photovoltaic inverter system based on multilevel voltage. In: IEEE Conference on Industrial Electronics and Applications, pp. 1663–1666 (2011)
5. Iturriaga-Medina, S., et al.: A comparative analysis of grid tied single phase transformerless five level NPC based inverters for photovoltaic applications. In: IEEE 13th International Conference on Power Electronics, pp. 323–328 (2016)
6. Debnath, D., Chatterjee, K.: Maximising power yield in a transformerless single phase grid connected inverter servicing two separate photovoltaic panels. IET Renew. Power Gener. **10**(8), 1087–1095 (2016)
7. Vazquez, J., Vazquez, N., Vaquero, J., Mendez, I., Hernandez, C., Lopez, H.: An integrated transformerless photovoltaic inverter. In: 41st Annual Conference of IEEE Industrial Electronics society, pp. 1333–1338 (2015)
8. San, G., Qi, H., Guo, X.: A novel single phase transformerless inverter for grid connected photovoltaic systems. Przegląd Elektrotechniczny **88**, 251–254 (2012)
9. Nunes, H., Pimenta, N., Fernandes, L., Chaves, P., Dores Costa J.M.: Modular buck boost transformerless grid tied inverter for low voltage solar panels. In: International Conference on Renewable Energies and Power Quality (2014)
10. Schimpf, F., Norum, L.E.: Grid connected converters for photovoltaic, state of the art, ideas for improvement of transformerless inverters. In: Nordic Workshop on Power and Industrial Electronics (2008)

11. Kshirsagar, U., Chavan S., Chavan, M.: Design and simulation of transformer less single phase photovoltaic inverter without battery for domestic application. IOSR J. Electr. Electron. Eng. **10**(1), 88–93 (2015)
12. Chavan, S., Chavan, M.: Power switch faults, diagnosis and tolerant schemes in converters of photovoltaic systems-a review. Int. J. Adv. Res. Electr. Electron. Instrum. Eng. **3**(9), 11729–11737 (2014)
13. Hauke, B.: Basic calculation of a boost converter's power stage application report, SLVA372C–November 2009–Revised January 2014. http://www.ti.com/lit/an/slva372c/slva372c.pdf. Accessed 02 Dec 2015
14. Chavan, S.: Reliability analysis of transformer less DC/DC converter in a photovoltaic system. Acta Electrotehnica **57**(5), 579–582 (2016)
15. Chavan, S., Chavan, M.: Web-based condition and fault monitoring scheme for remote PV power generation station. In: Mishra, D., Nayak, M., Joshi, A. (eds.) Information and Communication Technology for Sustainable Development. LNNS, vol 10. Springer, Singapore (2017). https://doi.org/10.1007/978-981-10-3920-1_14

English Text to Speech Synthesizer Using Concatenation Technique

Sai Sawant$^{(\boxtimes)}$ and Mangesh Deshpande

Department of Electronics and Telecommunication Engineering,
Vishwakarma Institute of Technology, Pune, India
{sai.sawant16,mangesh.deshpande}@vit.edu

Abstract. Text to speech synthesis (TTS) system is used to produce artificial human speech for input text. Any language text can be converted into speech signal using TTS system. This paper presents a method to design a text to speech synthesis system for English language. Container map data structure is used to design the TTS system. Phoneme concatenation is performed to get speech signal for input text. Phonetically rich 42 words in English language are recorded then phonemes are extracted from these recorded words using PRAAT tool. The extracted phonemes are compared with input text phonemes and then concatenated sequentially to reconstruct the desired words. Implementation of this method is simple and requires less memory usage.

Keywords: Text to speech · Speech synthesis · Phonetic concatenation

1 Introduction

Text to speech system transforms linguistic information present in the form of data or text into speech signal. TTS acts as an interface between digital content and people with literacy difficulties, learning disabilities and reduced vision. It is helpful for those people who are looking for simple ways to access digital content. It is also useful for telecommunication, industrial and educational applications.

Synthesized speech is produced by the imitation of natural human speech with the help of computer system. Speech synthesis can be performed by using different techniques depending upon the intended use of the system. A good quality synthesized speech is natural i.e., similar to human speech and intelligible in nature.

A lot of work has been done by many researchers in the field of text to speech synthesis using different synthesis techniques and for different languages. A fraction based waveform concatenation technique for different Indian languages has been implemented. This technique needed very less storage and computation overhead to produce intelligible speech segments from a small footprint speech database [1]. The work presented in [2] gives a multilingual text to speech system based on inductive learning algorithm called ILATalk. This system provides high performance with the least number of general letters to phoneme rules. Authors of [3] presented the development of a speech synthesis system for Indian English language using hidden markov models. This method has used trajectories of speech parameters which are obtained from the trained context dependent three state hidden markov models (HMMs). Output

© Springer Nature Singapore Pte Ltd. 2018
M. Singh et al. (Eds.): ICACDS 2018, CCIS 905, pp. 471–480, 2018.
https://doi.org/10.1007/978-981-13-1810-8_47

speech waveform is synthesized from these speech parameters. HMM based TTS is capable of producing adequately natural speech in terms of intelligibility and intonation. Implementation of natural prosody generation in English TTS using the phonetics integration has been done [4]. This method is simple to implement and involves much lesser use of memory space. Authors of [5] have presented a text to speech synthesis system for Kannada language using unit selection synthesis. Kannada text needs to be converted into English form for its segmentation into the smallest units of the word. This method achieves high degree of accuracy. Implementation of a vowel synthesizer using cascade formant technique is discussed in [6]. Authors found that implementation of cascade formant synthesis made it easier to generate speech waveforms. The speech output obtained was more robotic and unnatural in nature. The research presented in [7], describes an effort taken to modify the existing English grapheme to phoneme dictionary by implementing specific rules for Assamese English. This method of dictionary modification is applied at the front end of the Indian English TTS, developed using unit selection synthesis and statistical parametric speech synthesis frameworks. Unrestricted TTS for Bengali language has been implemented using Festival framework and syllable based concatenative synthesis [8]. Design and development of an Auto Associative Neural Network (AANN) based unrestricted prosodic information synthesizer for Tamil language is presented in [9]. It is a corpus based text to speech system based on the syllable concatenation. Five layers auto associative neural network is used for prosody prediction. Mel-LPC smoothing technique is used to remove discontinuities present at the unit boundaries. Authors of [10] have addressed the problem of audible discontinuities at the concatenation points of diphones in Bengali speech synthesizer. TDPSOLA algorithm is used to solve this problem.

The overall work is summarized as follows: Sect. 2 gives the brief description of concatenative synthesis and its subtypes. Section 3 provides the flow diagram and implementation of the proposed TTS system. Section 4 discusses experimental results and performance evaluation. Section 5 concludes the discussion by summarizing the findings and explaining the future direction of the work.

2 Concatenative Synthesis

Concatenative synthesis is the concatenation of the segments of recorded speech. This synthesis technique is simple to implement as it doesn't involve any mathematical model. Speech is synthesized using natural human speech. Concatenation of prerecorded speech utterances produces understandable and natural sounding synthesis speech. Concatenation can be done using different size of the stored speech units. There are four subtypes of this synthesis method, depending upon the speech unit size and use [11]:

1. Unit selection synthesis
2. Domain specific synthesis
3. Diphone synthesis
4. Phoneme based synthesis

Selection of correct speech unit length is important in concatenative synthesis. With selection of longer speech unit, high naturalness and less concatenation points are achievable on the verge of increase in the amount of required units and memory. For shorter speech unit, less memory is required but collecting samples and their labeling become difficult and complex [12]. The proposed system is implemented using phonemes as speech units.

2.1 Phoneme Based Speech Synthesis

In this synthesis technique, sequential combination of phonemes is used to synthesis desired continuous speech signal. Phoneme is one of the distinct units of sound in any specified language that distinguishes one word from another. For extraction of phonemes, different words need to be recorded that contain all possible phonemes of desired TTS system language. From these recorded word utterances, phonemes of particular duration are extracted. It creates database of extracted phoneme sounds. Whenever the word is to be synthesized, corresponding phonemes are fetched from the database and concatenated to obtain required word sound. Figure 1 shows how phoneme based synthesis is performed.

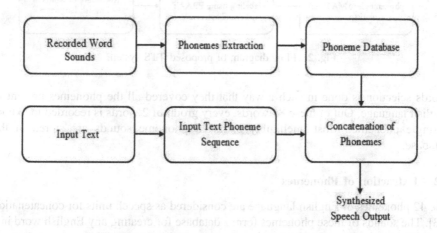

Fig. 1. Flow diagram of phoneme based synthesis

3 Proposed Text to Speech System Implementation

Figure 2 shows the block schematic of the proposed text to speech synthesis system. Various parts of the system are discussed as follows.

3.1 Recording of Words

Phonetically rich 84 English words are recorded by a single female speaker using Voice Recorder application for android phones. Sampling frequency and number of bits used are 44 kHz and 16 bits respectively. These words are recorded at room environment.

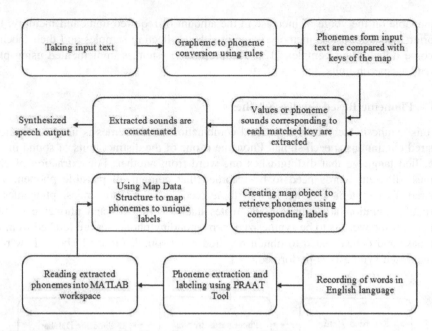

Fig. 2. Flow diagram of proposed TTS system

Words selection is done in such a way that they covered all the phonemes present in English language. Out of these 84 words, every group of 2 words is recorded to extract a single phoneme. Most intelligibly extracted phoneme sounds are stored in the database.

3.2   Extraction of Phonemes

The 42 phonemes of English language are considered as speech units for concatenation [13]. The sounds of these phonemes form a database for creating any English word in a standard lexicon. Therefore, these phoneme sounds are extracted from recorded words using PRAAT tool. The TextGrid editor of PRAAT tool is used for segmenting recorded sounds into constituent phonemes and labeling the segments [14]. Figure 3 shows extraction and annotation of phoneme /k/ using TextGrid editor. Table 1 shows some English phonemes and their examples.

3.3   Mapping of Phoneme Labels and Sound Files

MATLAB has Containers package with a Map class. It is a data structure that allows fetching values using a corresponding key. Keys can be real numbers or character vectors and must be positive integers. Values can be in the form of scalar or non-scalar arrays. Map object (an instance of Map class) is used to map values to unique keys.

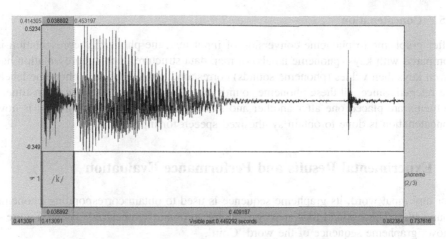

Fig. 3. Extraction of phoneme /k/ from word Cat

Table 1. English phonemes with examples

Phonemes	Example words
/a/	H*a*t, M*a*p, C*a*t
/ae/	Tr*ai*n, *Ei*ght, D*ay*
/ee/	K*ey*, Sw*ee*t
/oy/	T*oy*, C*oi*n

Using this object, extracted phoneme sounds are taken as values and their labels are considered as the keys. Therefore, every unique label or annotation corresponds to a particular phoneme sound. This forms the key-value pair of phonemes and their respective annotations.

3.4 Grapheme to Phoneme Conversion

This process is used to convert a letter string like 'Toy' into a phoneme string as [t oy] using certain rules. Position of a letter in the given word is considered to design these rules [15]. The input word is processed from left to right and a sequence of phoneme labels is selected. Every time when the match is occurred between input letters and phoneme labels then the phonemic representation is stored in another variable. The decision for every letter is taken before proceeding to the next letter. Table 2 shows some of the phonemes and their graphemes representations with examples.

Table 2. Phoneme and grapheme representation

Phoneme	Grapheme	Example words
/b/	b, bb	*B*ag, Ru*bb*er
/sh/	sh, ss	*Sh*ip, Mi*ss*ion
/e/	e, ea	B*e*d, H*ea*d
/zh/	ge, si	Gara*ge*, Divi*si*on

3.5 Concatenation

After grapheme to phoneme conversion of input text, the phonemic representation is compared with keys (phoneme labels) of map data structure. If this representation has given keys then values (phoneme sounds) corresponding to respective phoneme labels are fetched. Since, all these phoneme sounds are just column vectors, their constituent elements are placed one after another and stored in another vector [16]. This is how concatenation is done to obtain synthesized speech for input word.

4 Experimental Results and Performance Evaluation

For any input word, its grapheme sequence is used to obtain corresponding phoneme sound files. These sound files are concatenated to obtain synthesized speech. Figure 4 shows grapheme sequence of the word 'Coin'.

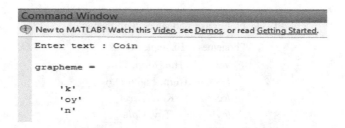

Fig. 4. Graphemes of input text - Coin

Figure 5 shows the phoneme waveforms of the word 'Coin'. Figure 6 shows the waveforms of concatenated speech signal and original utterance of the word 'Coin'.

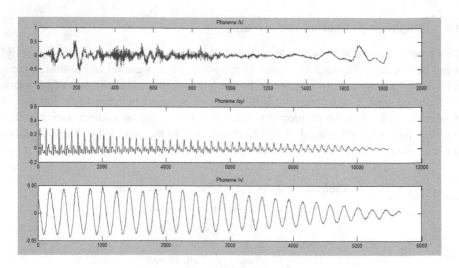

Fig. 5. Phoneme waveforms of input text - Coin

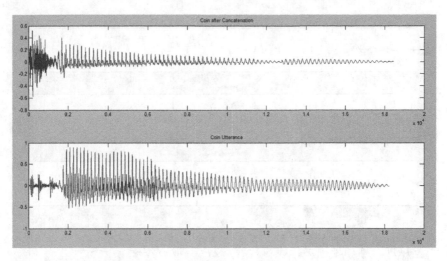

Fig. 6. Concatenated and original utterance waveforms of input text - Coin

Figures 7 and 8 show grapheme sequence and phoneme waveforms of the word 'Mirror' respectively. Figure 9 shows the waveforms of concatenated speech signal and original utterance of the word 'Mirror'.

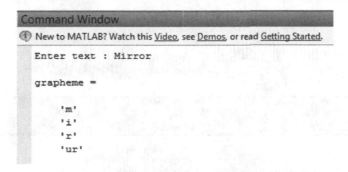

Fig. 7. Graphemes of input text - Mirror

From Figs. 6 and 9 it is observed that, for both the input words, concatenated and originally uttered speech waveforms have some similarities. The concatenated sound is close to the original sound. The degree of similarity increases with the precision in extracting the phonemes.

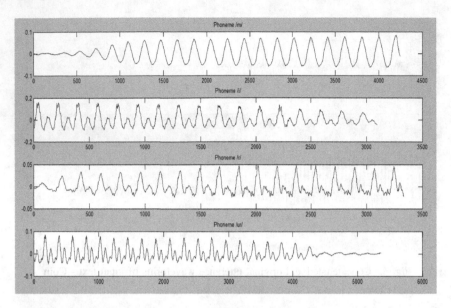

Fig. 8. Phoneme waveforms of input text - Mirror

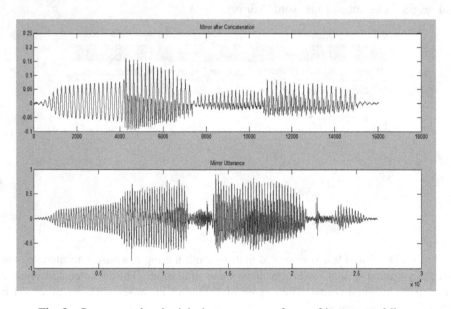

Fig. 9. Concatenated and original utterance waveforms of input text - Mirror

5 Conclusion

In this work, English text to speech synthesis system using phoneme based concatenative synthesis is developed. The system is implemented by the use of MATLAB map data structure and simple matrix operations. It can be seen that the proposed method is simple and efficient to implement unlike other methods that involve complex algorithms and techniques. As English phonemes are used as speech units, less memory is required. In order to bring more naturalness in the synthesized speech output, text analysis and prosody need to be improved.

References

1. Panda, S.P., Nayak, A.K.: A waveform concatenation technique for text-to-speech synthesis. Int. J. Speech Technol. **20**(4), 959–976 (2017)
2. Abu-Soud, S.M.: ILATalk: a new multilingual text-to-speech synthesizer with machine learning. Int. J. Speech Technol. **19**(1), 55–64 (2016)
3. Mullah, H.U., Pyrtuh, F., Singh, L.J.: Development of an HMM-based speech synthesis system for Indian English language. In: 2015 International Symposium on Advanced Computing and Communication (ISACC), Silchar, pp. 124–127 (2015). https://doi.org/10.1109/ISACC.2015.7377327
4. Suryawanshi, S.D., Itkarkar, R.R., Mane, D.T.: High quality text to speech synthesizer using phonetic integration. Int. J. Adv. Res. Electron. Commun. Eng. (IJARECE) **3**(2), 133–136 (2014)
5. Joshi, A., Chabbi, D., Suman, M., Kulkarni, S.: Text to speech system for Kannada language. In: 2015 International Conference on Communications and Signal Processing (ICCSP), Melmaruvathur, pp. 1901–1904 (2015). https://doi.org/10.1109/ICCSP.2015.7322855
6. Lukose, S., Upadhya, S.S.: Text to speech synthesizer-formant synthesis. In: 2017 International Conference on Nascent Technologies in Engineering (ICNTE), Navi Mumbai, pp. 1–4 (2017). https://doi.org/10.1109/ICNTE.2017.7947945
7. Mahanta, D., Sharma, B., Sarmah, P., Prasanna, S.R.M.: Text to speech synthesis system in Indian English. In: 2016 IEEE Region 10 Conference (TENCON), Singapore, pp. 2614–2618 (2016). https://doi.org/10.1109/TENCON.2016.7848511
8. Narendra, N.P., Rao, K.S., Ghosh, K., Vempada, R.R., Maity, S.: Development of syllable-based text to speech synthesis system in Bengali. Int. J. Speech Technol. **14**, 167 (2011)
9. Sangeetha, S., Jothilakshmi, S.: Syllable based text to speech synthesis system using auto associative neural network prosody prediction. Int. J. Speech Technol. **17**(2), 91–98 (2014)
10. Swarna, K., Naser, A.: A TDPSOLA based concatenation technique for Bengali text to speech synthesis system Subachan. In: 2016 9th International Conference on Electrical and Computer Engineering (ICECE), Dhaka, pp. 102–105 (2016). https://doi.org/10.1109/ICECE.2016.7853866
11. Apte, S.D.: Speech and Audio Processing, Wiley-India, New Delhi (2012)
12. Kumari, R.S.S., Sangeetha, R.: Conversion of English text to speech (TTS) using Indian speech signal. IJSET **4**(8), 447–450 (2015)

13. Orchestrating Success in Reading by Dawn Reithaug (2002)
14. Boersma, P., Weenink, D.: Praat: doing phonetics by computer [Computer program] (2013). http://www.praat.org
15. Shirbahadurkar, S.D., Bormane, D.S.: Marathi language speech synthesizer using concatenative synthesis strategy (spoken in Maharashtra, India). In: 2009 Second International Conference on Machine Vision, Dubai, pp. 181–185 (2009). https://doi.org/10.1109/ICMV. 2009.52
16. Patra, T.K., Patra, B, Mohapatra, P.: Text to speech conversion with phonematic concatenation. Int. J. Electron. Commun. Comput. Technol. (IJECCT) 2(5), 223–226 (2012)

Text Translation from Hindi to English

Ira Natu[✉], Sahasra Iyer, Anagha Kulkarni, Kajol Patil, and Pooja Patil

MKSSS's Cummins College of Engineering for Women, Pune, Maharashtra, India
{ira.natu,sahasra.iyer,anagha.kukarni,kajol.patil,
pooja.u.patil}@cumminscollege.in

Abstract. There exist numerous systems and applications that facilitated translation from English to numerous other global and Indian languages. For many in the Indian populace habited in the remote regions, a basic fluency in the English language, which is now a global necessity, is challenging. Furthermore, for many tourists visiting the country, a translation mechanism becomes essential, especially when it comes to signboards and banners on the roadside. Hence, there is plenty of research and work that has been carried out in this field. There exist many Transfer based machine translation systems such as the MANTRA MT system, Shakti MT system, MATRA MT system, etc. However there is no significant work undertaken when it comes to the Hindi script, and its translation to the English language. This paper places its focus on developing a translation tool using the transfer based MT mechanism. The system takes an input sentence in the Hindi language, analyses individual word tokens within the structure of the sentence and uses grammar rules to generate the final translated sentence in English. For rule-based/corpus-based machine translation elaborate knowledge of language is required. For the proposed technique knowledge of lexicons is not required. Instead knowledge of source and target language is required.

Keywords: Hindi-English translation · Transfer-based machine translation
Defined grammar · Hidden Markov Model · POS tagging

1 Introduction

1.1 Motivation

English, being the dominant global language that it is today, finds the requirement of its knowledge in a variety of domains. However, since Hindi is the national language within the country, there exists a vast population that is unaware of the linguistics and semantics of the English language. Thus, there is a necessity to develop a machine translation application that will bridge the gap between these two languages.

1.2 Existing Work

Machine translation, as a domain, reflects extensive and exhaustive work. MANTRA, [1] an application developed by CDAC Pune, is used to translate documents from English to Hindi. MANTRA translates from English to Hindi in the domain of Office

© Springer Nature Singapore Pte Ltd. 2018
M. Singh et al. (Eds.): ICACDS 2018, CCIS 905, pp. 481–488, 2018.
https://doi.org/10.1007/978-981-13-1810-8_48

Orders, Personal Administration, Office Memorandums and Circulars. Word-by-word or rule based strategy is not used in this application. This application uses translation based on lexical trees. A Lexicalized Tree Adjoining Grammar (LTAG) algorithm is used to represent the Hindi and English grammar. There is also Shakti [2], an application by Bharati, R Moona, B Sankar et al., which is used to translate English text to any Indian language. It combines statistical approach and linguistic rule based approach. Another existing system is the Bengali-to-Hindi Machine Translation system [3] developed by Chatterji S, Roy D et al., which is a MT system [4] which uses multiple machine translation approaches(statistical machine translation with a lexical transfer based system) also called hybrid system. The performance of hybrid system has a BLEU score is 0.2275. BLEU is an algorithm used to evaluate how close is the machine translation to the human translation for the same text. Perfect BLEU score is 1. Furthermore, there is also the VAASAANUBAADA [6], developed by Vijayanand, Choudhury and Ratna. It is an Automatic Machine Translation system for Bengali-Assamese News Texts. It includes sentence level translation for Bengali text to Assamese language. It involves preprocessing and post-processing tasks. The corpus consisting of these two languages has been created and arranged manually by supplying real-world examples.

1.3 Proposed System

This paper intends to elaborate on a method to take as input, a set of sentences in Hindi, execute the necessary semantics and output their syntactically correct English translations. This stems from the observation that, while there exist various tools for translation from Hindi to other regional languages and vice-versa, as well as from English to Hindi, there is no system that exists that carries out translation from Hindi to English seamlessly.

1.4 Organization

Thus far, this paper elaborated the motivation to develop the system and the work undertaken in similar endeavours. The Literature Survey details in brief, the various approaches to machine translation and the different systems in existence. The Methodology details the precise work undertaken to develop the system. The Experiments and Results section details an example that demonstrates the same.

2 Literature Survey

Machine translation (MT), falls within the domain of computational linguistics that explores the utilization of software systems that carry out translation tasks from language A to language B. On a basic level, MT systems carry out word-for-word translations from source language to target language. This, however, does not complete the requirement of a machine translation system, as only word-for-word translations do not suffice.

The following are the various approaches to machine translation:

1. Rule-based machine translation:
   Rule-based machine translation (RBMT) [7] is a machine translation approach that primarily studies the constituent morphemes, the grammar syntax and the semantic adherence of a sentence to both the source and target languages to generate a sentence. An example of a system adopting this approach is the English-Hindi MT System.

2. Direct, Transfer and Inter-lingual machine translation:
   The direct, transfer-based machine translation [7] and inter-lingual machine translation methods all take their root cause from RBMT systems but they show distinguishable properties in the levels of analysis that is carried out on the source language. The dissimilarities that distinguish each approach can be observed through the Vauquois Triangle (Fig. 1), which illustrates these levels of analysis. The Direct MT approach has been adopted by the Punjabi-Hindi MT system, the transfer MT approach by the ManTra and the interlingua MT approach by UNL-based (Universal Networking Language) English-Hindi MT System.

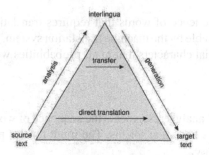

Fig. 1. Vauquois triangle

3. Statistical and example-based machine translation:
   Statistical machine translation (SMT) [7] carries out a detailed examination of text corpora that contains bilingual data. This study results in a set of parameters that is passed onto a statistical model to ultimately formulate a sentence. The initial model of SMT, based on Bayes Theorem, operates under the belief that translation of a sentence can be executed from any source language to any target language and that the most suitable translation will be that which is allocated the highest probability by the system. There is also the Example-based machine translation (EBMT) which carries out translation by taking into consideration analogies. To implement this, such systems use bilingual corpus with parallel texts as principal knowledge source. The statistical approach methodology has been adopted by the Shakti MT system and the example based methodology has been adopted by the VAASAANU-BAADA [6].

The approach undertaken for the research of this paper is the Transfer-based approach. Amongst all the prevalent machine translation approaches, this approach stands as the most widely adopted one. In contrast to the simpler direct model of MT, transfer MT breaks translation into three steps: analysis, transfer and generation. The system analyzes the text of the source language in order to deduce its grammatical structure. Post this, a transfer is carried out of the structure determined in the analysis phase to a structure that is suitable for finally generating target language text. Transfer based systems carry out their machine translation facilities thus: by using the knowledge of the source and target languages. Such a facility supports the proposed application and hence, makes this approach the most suitable.

3   Methodology

The primary step for the translation process is to carry out a word-for-word translation from individual Hindi word token to their corresponding English counterparts. This sequence of word tokens is then passed on for being tagged with their specific part-of-speech within the structure of the sentence. To effectively formulate a syntactically correct sentence, the following operations need to be carried out [8]:

1. Pre-processing

In this phase, the sequence of words that requires translation should be polished, such that they are executable by the machine translation system. This includes treatment of punctuation and special characters that in all probabilities would not requires translation.

2. Tokenizer

Tokenizer, or lexical analyzer, segments the sequence of words that require part-of-speech tagging into units known as tokens. The input for this phase will be the output of the preprocessing phase.

3. Part-of-Speech Tagging

The output from the above operations results in a word token sequence which will be required to be tagged with its specific part-of-speech [9] which will be used as a primary operative for formulating a sentence according to the provided grammar rules.

Knowing part-of-speech of a word in a sentence is important because of the huge amount of information provided by it about the word and its neighboring words as well. If we know whether a word is a noun or a verb, then it tells the likelihood of its adjacent words being a determiner or adjectives (precedes noun) or a noun (precedes verbs) which also hints about the syntactic structure around the word. This makes part-of-speech tagging a crucial part of syntactic parsing. This task is accomplished with the employment of the Hidden Markov Model. The Hidden Markov Model [9] is based on random probability distribution or pattern that are analyzed statistically which is used to describe a sequence of possible events where probability of each event is determined only by the state achieved in the previous event. A popular implementation of the HMM is the Viterbi algorithm [10]. In the scope of this paper, the Viterbi algorithm is employed to assign a sequence of part-of-speech tags for a sequence of translated words. The Viterbi algorithm is a dynamic programming algorithm that essentially uses a sequence of observable states in order to determine an underlying source of hidden states (often, called the Viterbi path). The Viterbi algorithm used for the reference of this paper follows a bi-gram model, i.e. the part-of-speech tag assigned to a word will only depend on the part-of-speech tag assigned to one previous word.

4. Translation

Individual words are processed to find their corresponding translation in the English script which is fetched from a database. Another task that is executed within this phase is known as Transliteration. For proper noun, transliteration is used instead of translation as entire scope of the proper noun set cannot be incorporated into the database.

5. Grammar check

The individual, translated word tokens, along with the tags assigned to them are used to determine the final structure of the translated sentence. This involves employing a predefined grammar, which will be used as a reference for syntactically arranging the words.

4 Experiments and Results

A sentence passed for translation will be pre-processed to make it void of any components that do not pass the parameters for making it necessary for translation (e.g. punctuation marks, special symbols, etc.).

Once this is done, the original sentence (Fig. 2) will proceed for tokenization. The sentence will go through the tokenization phase to obtain individual word tokens such as below (Fig. 3).

Fig. 2. Original sentence

Fig. 3. Tokenized sentence

This collection of tokenized words, will then be passed onto the part-of-speech tagging module.

Each tokenized word will now be passed on to the part-of-speech tagging module to tag it to create the most appropriate sequence of tags (as in Fig. 4). As the Viterbi algorithm being used within the scope of this paper follows a bi-gram model [11], there is no reference for the first word in the sequence, i.e. water. Hence a pseudo-state named START is used as a reference for the first word for every sequence. Another pseudo-state being used is known as END which will indicate the completion of the determined tag sequence. The motive of this algorithm is to find the most suitable tag sequence for the word sequence "he shop into went". This can be determined as shown in the figure below (Fig. 5).

```
The sentence was:
वह दुकान में गय ।

The best tag sequence is:
['START', u'PRP', u'NN', u'PREP', u'VFM', 'END']
```

Fig. 4. Tagged words

probability_of_tagSequence = P(START) * P(PRP|START) * P(वह | PRP) *
    P(NN | PRP) * P(दुकान |NN) *
    P(PREP | NN) * P(में | PREP) *
    P(VFM | PREP) * P(गया| VFM) *
    P(END | VFM)   [P(START)=1]

Fig. 5. Tagging words

To put it simplistically, the probability of the current word have tag PRP(pronoun) given that the previous tag is START is multiplied by the probability that the current word is वह given the current tag is PRP (refer Table 1) is calculated to decide upon PRP being the tag for this word. However, this probability is not estimated only for the PRP tag. This probability calculation takes place for all of the tags present within the Hindi corpus that is referenced for this paper and the tag having maximum probability is assigned to the current word. This assigned tag for the first word will be used as a backward reference for the second word till a tag sequence is estimated for the entire word sequence.

Table 1. Reference table

NN	Singular noun
PRP	Personal pronoun
PREP	Preposition
VFM	Verb

A diagrammatic representation of the Viterbi algorithm would be as follows (Fig. 6).

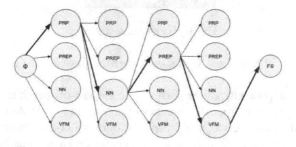

Fig. 6. Viterbi algorithm for tag sequence

Once the tag sequence has been obtained, the words will proceed to the translation module. Translation is carried out in a word-by-word fashion, wherein every word's corresponding English counterpart will be fetched, as shown in Fig. 7.

```
The sentence was:
यह दुकान में गया ।

The best tag sequence is:
['START', u'PRP', u'NN', u'PREP', u'VFM', 'END']
```

Fig. 7. Word-for-word translations

After the translated word sequence is obtained, it needs to be checked for its accordance with the grammar that is predefined. The grammar that was defined is as follows (Fig. 8).

```
Grammar with 18 productions (start state = S)
    S -> NP VP
    S -> Det NP VP
    NP -> PRP
    NP -> N
    NP -> PP NP
    NP -> AP NP
    NP -> A NP
    PP -> P
    PP -> P NP
    VP -> V
    VP -> V NP
    VP -> Aux VP
    VP -> V RB
    N -> 'shop'
    PRP -> 'he'
    V -> 'went'
    V -> ' '
    P -> 'into'
```

Fig. 8. Defined grammar

The word translations along with the part-of-speech tag assigned to them are used to determine which sequence of words are most appropriate with the above defined grammar. All of the tokenized words are placed into their appropriate part-of-speech array for processing. The primary rule that will always be followed is S -> NP VP. Post this the NP (noun phrase) is analyzed for rule check. For NP, the only rule fitting the criteria is NP -> N. Thus, the noun phrase analysis ends with water being processed as a noun. Moving on to VP (verb phrase), the rule that will be used will be VP -> V NP, for "is" and the consequent words to be processed. This processing will continue till all the word arrays are empty. The final sentence that will be obtained after restructuring it with proper grammar is as in Fig. 9.

```
Word-to-word translation
['he', 'shop', 'into', 'went']
```

Fig. 9. Final translated sentence

5   Conclusion

In this paper, a transfer based machine translation approach which is based on a rule-based approach of machine translation has been discussed. This system, translates text from Hindi to English which is not done by other systems. Furthermore, it checks for syntactic relevance of the translated sentence as well. A basic set of grammar rules has been incorporated to check the same. To improve quality of translation gender, tense and number will be taken into consideration.

References

1. Nair, L.R., David Peter, S.: Machine translation systems for Indian languages. Int. J. Comput. Appl. **39**, 24–31 (2012)
2. Dwivedi, S.K., Sukhadeve, P.P.: Machine translation system in Indian perspectives. J. Comput. Sci. **6**(10), 1082–1087 (2010)
3. Garje, G.V., Kharate, G.K.: Survey of machine translation system in India. Int. J. Nat. Lang. Comput. (IJNLC) **2**(4), 47 (2013)
4. Nair, J., Krishnan, K.A., Deetha, R.: An efficient English to Hindi machine translation system using hybrid mechanism. In: 2016 International Conference on Advances in Computing, Communications and Informatics (ICACCI) (2016)
5. Ananthakrishnan, R., et al.: MaTra: a practical approach to fully-automatic indicative English-Hindi machine translation. Centre for Development of Advanced Computing (formerly NCST), Juhu, Mumbai, India (2018)
6. Vijayanand, K., Choudhury, S.I., Ratna, P.: VAASAANUBAADA automatic machine translation of bilingual Bengali-Assamese news texts. In: Proceedings of the Language Engineering Conference (2002)
7. Antony, P.J.: Machine translation approaches and survey for Indian languages. The Association for Computational Linguistics and Chinese Language Processing (2013)
8. Gehlot, A., Sharma, V., Singh, S., Kumar, A.: Hindi to English transfer based machine translation system. Int. J. Adv. Comput. Res. **5**(19), 198 (2015)
9. Joshi, N., Darbari, H., Mathur, I.: HMM based PoS tagger for Hindi. Department of Computer Science. Banasthali University, Center for Development of Advanced Computing, Pune, India (2013)
10. Ye, Z., Jia, Z., Huang, J., Yin, H.: Part-of-speech tagging based on dictionary and statistical machine learning. In: Proceedings of the 35th Chinese Control Conference, 27–29 July 2016, Chengdu, China (2016)
11. Singh, J., Garcha, L.S., Singh, S.: A survey on parts of speech tagging for Indian. Int. J. Adv. Res. Comput. Sci. Softw. Eng. (2017)

Optical Character Recognition (OCR) of Marathi Printed Documents Using Statistical Approach

Pritish Mahendra Vibhute[✉] and Mangesh Sudhir Deshpande

E&TC Department, Vishwakarma Institute of Technology, Pune, India
vibhutepm@gmail.com, mangesh.deshpande@vit.edu

Abstract. Optical Character Recognition (OCR) of local languages is an important research area as the techniques developed for one language cannot apply directly to other languages. The paper presents the development of a new statistical method based on template matching and modified template matching used for recognition of a local language of the State of Maharashtra Marathi. It is noted that proposed method not only gives good recognition rate but also have offered good CPU and memory efficiency. Along with system accuracy, average CPU consumption and memory utilization is also analyses and found the acceptable minimum. The proposed algorithm for Marathi OCR is optimized for speed compared with the existing algorithm and hence permits porting on handheld devices with low processing power like Mobile phones. The algorithm is robust in terms of characters size and style of writing.

Keywords: Devanagari Marathi character recognition · OCR
Statistical feature extraction

1 Introduction

India is a multi-lingual as well as a multi-script country. Indian uses 12 different scripts for documentation. More than 500 million people in India make use of Devanagari script from Indo-Aryan family of languages for the sake of documentation. Hindi, an official language of the Republic of India, is the 3rd most popular language in the world. Hindi uses Devanagari script for written communication [13]. The same script is also used for documentation and communication of many other Indian languages like Marathi, Konkani, Sindhi, Nepali and Sanskrit including Hindi. Marathi, one of the most popular versions of the Indo-Aryan language, is known as the official language of State of Maharashtra and it exists since 1000AD. The Marathi language has more than 75 million speakers around the globe. As the language is quite old, the massive amount of written documentation is available which is yet to be digitized.

Optical Character Recognition (OCR) of any script is the process of automated recognition of characters, numbers, and symbols from the scanned or captured an image and extracting a text from the captured image [4]. Recognition of local language script is offering enormous applications. Marathi OCR is a relatively difficult task than English script, due to the existence of the compound character and different types and places of the modifiers used to form modified character. The compound characters, also known

© Springer Nature Singapore Pte Ltd. 2018
M. Singh et al. (Eds.): ICACDS 2018, CCIS 905, pp. 489–498, 2018.
https://doi.org/10.1007/978-981-13-1810-8_49

as conjunct character, are generated when two basic half characters touch or overlap in some cases. वक्क is an example of the compound character where two half 'क' touches each other to form the compound character. When vowels following consonants take a modified shape, then that the modified hybrid character is called as a modified character. Eg. कृ where 'क' along with 'उकार' arrives. Two characters may be in the shadow of each other due to their shapes and writing styles like 'क' and 'फ' which makes the job significantly difficult for recognition and classification algorithm. Isolation or segmentation of characters in Marathi is comparatively more difficult than English due to modifiers, compound characters, shirorekha alike characters etc. Incorrect segmentation not only misguides the classification step but also increases the execution time of algorithm significantly [1, 9].

Paper presents an efficient method for OCR of complicated Marathi script. Section 2 presents findings of the literature review. Section 3 presents system design of proposed method with simple template matching based approach and modified template matching based approach for the Marathi Optical Character Recognition (MOCR). Section 4 share the findings of the proposed algorithm, whereas Sect. 5 comments on the conclusion.

2 Literature Review

Several potential approaches have been presented by the researchers and developers in the field of OCR towards recognition of characters since starting of the computer era. Numerous recognition systems for segmented handwritten as well as printed numerals and characters of English and Roman are available in the literature. Significant work can also be found for Devanagari optical character recognition; however, contribution towards Marathi OCR is almost negligible. Detailed literature is reviewed and mentioned below. The existing OCR engines designed for Devanagari handwritten characters are actually fine-tuned for Hindi. Redesigning the said algorithm with respect to Marathi character and its occurrence frequency will surely increase the accuracy. The existing algorithm works on either printed data or handwritten data but not on both and hence combine OCR engine which deals with both are highly in need [2].

Existing OCR engines concentrate more on isolated characters of the word. State-of-art work is under implementation at Technology Development for Indian Languages (TDIL) a project of Ministry of Information Technology of Government of India. Centre for Development of Advance Computing (CDAC) is also actively involved in the development of tools for Marathi and other Indian languages. CDAC and team have successfully developed projects like 'Chitrankan' and other translators in collaboration with IIT Kanpur. I2IT Hyderabad, ISI Kolkata and many others institutes and private companies are working on the problem statement of DevanagriOCR [5].

Till today the maximum accuracy obtained for handwritten or printed Devanagari optical character recognition algorithm is 95.19% using standard ISI database of more than 36172 images of segmented characters [11, 12]. Further, no emphasis is given on recognition time even if it is one of the most important factors for real-time applications. With increasing popularity of handheld devices, there is a wide scope for the number of real-life applications using Marathi OCR based on mobile platforms, like mobile phones or tablet PCs. However, it is a very challenging task because of limited resources like computational power, inadequate primary storage memory, processor speed etc. Considering all these aspects this research work will focus on improving the accuracy of recognition at optimized speed [19].

3   Proposed System Design

Basic Marathi OCR implemented passes through different phases as shown in Fig. 1. Data acquisition process may accept an input either from camera or Scanner, ideally flatbed scanner with minimum 300 dpi resolution.

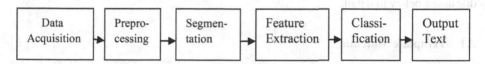

Fig. 1. Different phases of marathi optical character recognition

Preprocessing consists of the collection of algorithms working together to improve and enhance a quality of raw input image and to suppress different types of noises being captured by the system in the step of data acquisition. e.g. cropping, reshaping, filtering etc. [6]. It also converts an image in binary using proper thresholding techniques like Otsu's method or histogram based threshold detection [17].

Segmentation is most important phases of Marathi or Devanagari OCR and it will directly impact on the performance of character recognition algorithm [10]. This step subdivides preprocessed input image into its constituent areas representing a character available in the database. Modifiers and compound characters also need to be separated in this phase as shown in Fig. 2 [15]. If input image consists of any images, equation, graph etc. then same need to be removed in the phase of segmentation [7]. For implementation of proposed algorithm pre-segmented characters are used and hence segmentation is not performed.

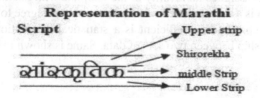

Fig. 2. Striping and segmentation

In feature extraction important and distinguished features of input images are identified. An optional step of feature vector size reduction will be performed if features are not independent [8, 16].

Classification/identification step classifies the unknown character given in the preprocessed form and the information from the known database. There are different statistical approaches given in the literature to determine similarity measure, distance measure or a discriminate function with respect to the database [18].

Each stage mentioned above has a different effect on overall performance of the algorithm, like pre-processing and segmentation in Devanagari decides robustness of algorithm even in the presence of compound characters, noise & blur occurred in the phase of data acquisition. Classification and feature extraction indirectly affects the accuracy, memory requirement (due to huge size to training database) and computational complexity of recognition algorithm

The two methods of classification used for recognition of Marathi characters named template matching and statistical approach combined with template matching are discussed below in detail.

3.1 Template Matching

Template matching is one of the most common and popular feature extraction and classification methods. These techniques are different from the others in that no features are actually extracted and hence the technique is much fast and trivial on execution platform.

The distance between the test pattern and each prototype in the database is computed, and the class of the prototype giving least distance is assigned to the pattern. The technique is simple and easy to implement in hardware and has been used in many commercial OCR engines. However, this technique is sensitive to noise style variations and has no inbuilt solution for handling rotated characters. But a proper preprocessing technique and normalization algorithms can help to overcome these limitations.

In template matching, individual image pixels are used as features. Classification is performed by comparing an input character image with a set of templates from each character class. Each comparison results in a similarity measure between the input character and the template. One measure increases the amount of similarity when a pixel in the observed character is identical to the same pixel in the template image. After successful comparison of input character image with the entire template in the database, character's identity is assigned an identity of the template with maximum similarity.

Cross-correlation is a standard method of estimating the degree to which two series are correlated. The correlation coefficient is a statistical calculation that is used to examine the relationship between two sets of data. Same is shown in Fig. 3.

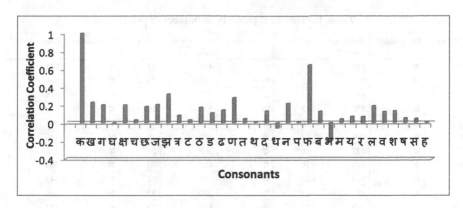

Fig. 3. Graphical representation of correlation coefficient analysis

The value of the correlation coefficient s(I, Tn) notifies about the strength and the nature of the relationship. The database consists of at least one template for all possible input characters. If I(i, j) is the input character and Tn(i, j) is the template of nth character, then the matching function s(I, Tn) will return a value indicating how well template-n matches with the input character I(i, j). Matching functions is based on the Eq. (1) shows normalized cross-correlation (−1 to 1) [1, 6]. |I| and |Tn| shows mean intensity of input image and template image.

$$s(I, Tn) = \frac{\sum_{i=0}^{w} \sum_{j=0}^{h} (I(i,j) - |I|)(Tn(i,j) - |Tn|)}{\sqrt{\sum_{i=0}^{w} \sum_{j=0}^{h} (I(i,j) - |I|)^2} \sqrt{\sum_{i=0}^{w} \sum_{j=0}^{h} (Tn(i,j) - |Tn|)^2}} \tag{1}$$

Correlation coefficient has the value;

- s(I, Tn) = 1 if the two images are absolutely identical. Perfect positive
- s(I, Tn) = 0 if the two images are completely uncorrelated.
- s(I, Tn) = −1 if the two images are completely anti-correlated. Perfect negative

3.2 Statistical Approach with Template Matching

In this method, statistical information is considered as one of the features of an image. The main aim of proposed method is to reduce the number of comparisons and correlations per recognition which in result increases performance of the system. Statistical method acts as the preprocessing step which considers pixels count as feature to perform pre-classification. Table 1 includes pixel count as a statistical feature. Based on said statistics characters are grouped in four different groups based on pixel count.

Table 2 shows said groups [3, 14]. In the traditional template matching based method, 33 correlation operations are performed for recognizing a consonant whereas in proposed method only one comparison and 9 correlation operations are performed.

Table 1. Statistical property as number of pixels

Sr. No.	Consonants	Pixels with value '1'	Sr. No.	Consonants	Pixels with value '1'	Sr. No.	Consonants	Pixels with value '1'
1	क	529	12	ठ	482	23	ब	574
2	ख	503	13	ड	416	24	भ	581
3	ग	481	14	ढ	517	25	म	608
4	घ	538	15	ण	531	26	य	509
5	क्ष	408	16	त	497	27	र	397
6	च	490	17	थ	516	28	ल	486
7	छ	527	18	द	388	29	व	536
8	ज	470	19	ध	488	30	श	503
9	झ	514	20	न	497	31	ष	543
10	ञ	483	21	प	500	32	स	456
11	ट	402	22	फ	544	33	ह	517

Table 2. Groups based on number of black pixels

Group	First	Second	Third	Fourth
# of pixels 1	<482	482 to 502	503 to 530	>530
Consonants	3, 5, 8, 11, 13, 18, 27, 32	6, 10, 12, 16, 19, 20, 21, 28,	1, 2, 7, 9, 14, 17, 26, 30, 33	4, 15, 22, 23, 24, 25, 29, 31

4   Performance Evaluation

Experimental Setup:-   For thorough performance evaluation of proposed algorithm an experimental setup was created on a system having the following specification. In software Windows 7 OS with MATLAB 2012b installed and in hardware Pentium IV processor with 2 GB RAM, 2 Mega Pixel USB web-cam, 80 GB HDD considered. Pre-segmented character's image of size 32×32 pixels (1024 pixels) is considered.

Timing Analysis:-   Reduction in the number of correlation operations helps to improve the performance of the proposed algorithm by reducing processing time. The rigorous experimentation demonstrates that performance of the proposed method is 8 times better than a traditional template matching approach. Figure 4 shows performance analysis of two methods in terms of elapsed time.

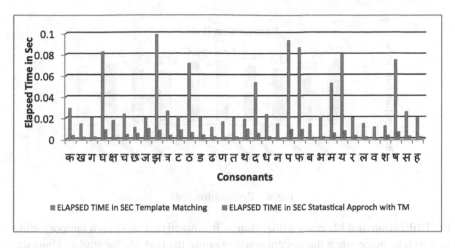

Fig. 4. Performance analysis of proposed methods in terms of elapsed time

Effect of font styles:- The main limitation of template matching based approach is its dependency on template structure and inability to ignore any minute change in the character template. Figure 5 shows the correlation coefficient of Marathi character 'क' for six different most popular font styles which are widely used in newspaper and books. As each font is having its own way and unique style to represent a consonants, corresponding correlation coefficient varies in predicted range of the values. The said drawback can be easily overcome by properly redesigning the template by taking average of templates of all possible fonts used in the system design.

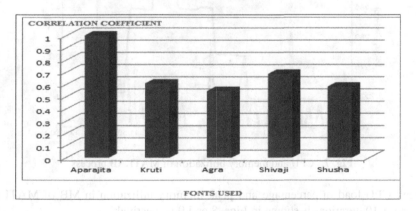

Fig. 5. Analysis of correlation coefficients for 5 fonts

Recognition rate:- The proposed system is tested thoroughly for recognition rate. Normalized ratio of the number of characters successfully identified in a dataset image captured to the number of characters present in the said image is used for calculating recognition rate in the application of OCR. Average success rate achieved is 88%. Same is shown in Fig. 6.

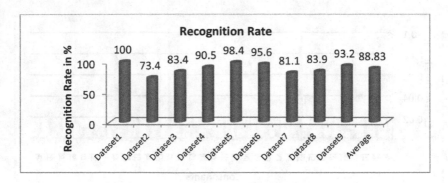

Fig. 6. Recognition Rate

CPU Utilization and Memory utilization:- It is noted that maximum memory utilization will take place when the system starts opening the text file for storing Unicode of Marathi character recognized. Also, it has been noted that maximum CPU utilization takes place at the end of the algorithm when MATLAB invokes Graphical User Interface (GUI) as well as Notepad application to demonstrate the result of recognition. Output of the MATLAB script to detect Peak CPU and peak memory utilization is demonstrated in Fig. 7.

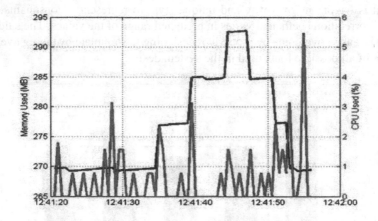

Fig. 7. CPU and memory utilization of MATLAB process

Peak CPU load in percentage and peak memory utilization in MB of MATLAB process for 10 iterations is shown in Figs. 8 and 9 respectively.

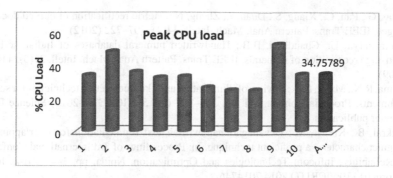

Fig. 8. Peak CPU load of MATLAB process

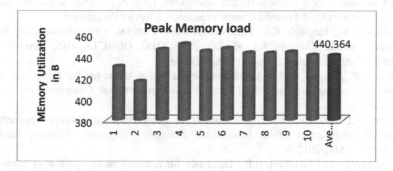

Fig. 9. Peak memory utilization of MATLAB process

5   Conclusion

The proposed method demonstrated good recognition rate of 88% with improved resource utilization. Even if template matching approach is font dependent but said drawback can be easily overcome by creating a template by averaging templates of different fonts. The template matching based method is efficient with respect to CPU and memory. Statistical approach combined with template matching further improved average CPU consumption and memory utilization. Recognition rate is also analyzed for statistical approach combined with template matching and found enhanced.

References

1. Jayadevan, R., Kolhe, S.R., Patil, P.M., Pal, U.: Offline recognition of devanagari script: a survey. IEEE Trans. Syst. Man Cybern. Part C Appl. Rev. **41**(6), 782–796 (2011)
2. Kompalli, S., Setlur, S., Govindaraju, V.: Devanagari OCR using a recognition driven segmentation framework and stochastic language models. IJDAR **12**, 123–138 (2009)
3. Ait-Mohand, K., Paquet, T., Ragot, N.: Combining structure and parameter adaptation of HMMs for printed text recognition. IEEE Trans. Pattern Anal. Mach. Intell. **36**(9), 1716–1732 (2014)

4. Meng, G., Pan, C., Xiang, S., Duan, J., Zheng, N.: Metric rectification of curved document images. IEEE Trans. Pattern Anal. Mach. Intell. **34**(4), 707–722 (2012)
5. Bhattacharya, U., Chaudhuri, B.B.: Handwritten numeral databases of Indian scripts & multistage recognition of numerals. IEEE Trans. Pattern Anal. Mach. Intell. **31**(3), 444–457 (2009)
6. Verma, R.N., Malik, L.G.: Review of illumination and skew correction techniques for scanned documents. Procedia Comput. Sci. **45**, 322–327 (2015). (ICACTA-2015) Science Direct, Elsevier publication
7. Thakral, B., Kumar, M.: Devanagari handwritten text segmentation for overlapping and conjunct characters- a proficient technique. In: Proceedings of 3rd International Conference on Reliability, Infocom Technologies and Optimization, Noida, pp. 1–4 (2014). https://doi.org/10.1109/ICRITO.2014.7014746
8. Surintan, O., Karaaba, M.F., Schomaker, L.B.R., Wiering, M.A.: Recognition of handwritten characters using local gradient feature descriptors. Eng. Appl. Artif. Intell. **45**, 405–414 (2015). Science Direct Procedia Computer Science, Elsevier Publication
9. Kamblea, P.M., Hegadib, R.S.: Handwritten marathi character recognition using R-HOG Feature. Procedia Comput. Sci. **45**, 266–274 (2015). (ICACTA-2015) Science Direct Procedia Computer Science, Else-vier Publication
10. Dhaka, V.P., Sharma, M.K.: An efficient segmentation technique for Devanagari offline handwritten scripts using the Feed-forward Neural Network. Nat. Comput. Appl. **26**, 1881–1893 (2015)
11. Dongre, V.J., Mankar, V.H.: Development of comprehensive devnagari numeral and character database for offline handwritten character recognition. Hindawi Publishing Corporation, May 2012
12. Bhattacharya, U., Chaudhuri, B.B.: Databases for research on recognition of handwritten characters of Indian scripts. In: ICDAR 2005, Seoul, Korea, vol. II, pp. 789–793 (2005)
13. Hanmandlu, M., Ramana Murthy, O.V., Madasu, V.K.: Fuzzy model based recognition of handwritten hindi characters. In: Digital Image Computing Techniques and Applications, vol. 2, no. 7, pp. 454–461. IEEE computer society, February 2007
14. Aharrane, N., El Moutaouakil, K., Satori, K.: A comparison of supervised classification methods for a statistical set of features: Application: Amazigh OCR. In: 2015 Intelligent Systems and Computer Vision (ISCV), Fez, pp. 1–8 (2015). https://doi.org/10.1109/ISACV.2015.7106171
15. Sahu, N., Raman, N.K.: An efficient handwritten devanagari character recognition system using neural network. IEEE J. PR, 173–177 (2013)
16. Hassan, E., Chaudhury, S., Gopal, M.: Word shape descriptor-based document image indexing: a new DBH-based approach. IJDAR **16**, 227–246 (2013)
17. Dhingra, K.D., Sanyal, S., Sharma, P.K.: A robust OCR for degraded documents. In: Huang, X., Chen, Y.S., Ao, S.I. (eds.) Advances in Communication Systems and Electrical Engineering. LNEE, vol. 4, pp. 497–509. Springer, Boston (2008). https://doi.org/10.1007/978-0-387-74938-9_34
18. Das, N., Sarkar, R., Basu, S., Saha, P.K., Kundu, M., Nasipuri, M.: Handwritten Bangla character recognition using a soft computing paradigm embedded in two pass approach. Pattern Recognit. **48**, 2054–2071 (2015)
19. Bhattacharya, U., Chaudhuri, B.B.: Databases for research on recognition of handwritten characters of Indian scripts. In: Proceedings of the 8th International Conference on Document Analysis and Recognition (ICDAR-2005), Seoul, Korea, vol. II, pp. 789–793 (2005)

Multi View Human Action Recognition
Using HODD

Siddharth Bhorge[✉] and Deepak Bedase

Department of Electronics and Telecommunication,
Vishwakarma Institute of Technology, Pune, Maharastra, India
{siddharth.bhorge,deepak.bedase16}@vit.edu

Abstract. Human action recognition from video is an important research area
in the field of computer vision. It is an integral part of surveillance systems,
human–computer interactions and various real-world applications. This paper
presents a method to automatically identify view invariant human activity from
input video stream using Motion History Image (MHI) and Histogram of Directional Derivative features (HODD). The proposed system uses Multi View
Human Action Video (MuHAVi) dataset for training and testing and the Support
Vector Machine (SVM) classifier for classification.

Keywords: MHI · HODD · SVM · MuHAVi

1 Introduction

Human Action Recognition is one of the promising research area in computer vision
community. Action recognition mainly divided into three main stages they are: Human
object segmentation, feature extraction, activity classification. Human Activity Recognition (HAR) is having many application such as video-surveillance, sports monitoring,
Artificially Intelligence [1]. Basically Activity is categorized into four different levels
viz. gesture, action, interaction and group activity. Gestures are elementary movements
of a person's body part which describe the meaningful action of a person. Stretching an
arm comes under the gesture category. Actions are single person activity such as
"walking", "hand waving". Interactions are activity that involves two or more human/
object. Group activity composed of group of people such as two groups are fighting [2].

The major issue of current the HAR system is view point-variation during testing
and training phase. In real life scenario for HAR, a person is observed from different
viewing angles by a camera, and hence HAR must be robust against view-point variation.
Otherwise the system fails to recognize the desired actions.

Recently, several methods have been proposed for the single view i.e. assuming the
same angle during training and testing. The main drawback of such system is that it fails
if one gives different view as input for testing. This drawback can be overcome by using
action videos captured from multiple cameras with varying angles.

In this proposed system we used the MuHAVidataset containing total 17 actions
such as kick, punch, WalkTurnBack, etc. These actions are performed by seven people.

M. Singh et al. (Eds.): ICACDS 2018, CCIS 905, pp. 499–508, 2018.
https://doi.org/10.1007/978-981-13-1810-8_50

Actions are recorded by 8 different closed circuit television (CCTV) cameras to achieve multi-view recording of the each action. This MuHAVi dataset is distinguished by the parameter such as Action/Actor/view. In this dataset a particular action is repeated three to four times by every actor [3].

The rest of the paper organized is as follows Sect. 2 describe the literature survey. Section 3 gives the proposed methodology for the system about proposed. Section 4 demonstrates the experimental results of proposed system on MuHAVi dataset. Section 5 concludes with some ideas for future work.

2 Related Work

Video is sequence of images and action is a set of small movement. In the past decades, many action recognition methods are proposed. Bobick et al. [4] extract the human shape mask from the images and he calculated the differences between the two frames. On the basis of this differences, Motion Energy Image(MEI) and Motion History Image(MHI) is computed. Then they proposed temporal templates against stored action. Yomato et al. [5] has proposed an idea of action recognition using Hidden Markov Models based on silhouette images and features. Weinland et al. [6] introduced the Action recognition using exemplar based embedding. They used Weizamn-dataset. Classification is done by Bayes classifier with Gaussian model. Niebles et al. [7] proposed unsupervised learning approach using Bag of Word representation of video. With the help of space time interest point detector they first extract local space-time regions which represented motion patterns. These local regions are clustered into code-block. They used SVM classifier for classification.

Willemset et al. [8] proposed method which uses determinant of 3D Hessian Matrix. This helps to combine point localization and scale selection. Further they have developed an implementation scheme using integral video, which allows the efficient computation for scaled-invariant spatio-temporal features. Shao et al [9] proposed a system in which they represent the spatio-temporal interest points using transformed based technique such as Fourier Transform and Wavelet Transform. Bhorge et a l [11] proposed a Histogram of Directional Derivative (HODD) as a spatio-temporal descriptor. Ikizler et al. [12] present a new descriptor called as Histogram od oriented gradient. Murtaza et al. [13] proposed multi view action recognition using MHI and HOG descriptor. They used NN classifier to classify test action video. Recently various methods are proposed to recognize human action recognition [14, 15].

3 Proposed Methodology

The proposed methodology for Multi view action recognition is mainly divided into four steps: noise removal, MHI estimation, Feature descriptor based on HODD descriptor, classifier to classify the testing action. The block diagram of proposed methodology is as shown in Fig. 1.

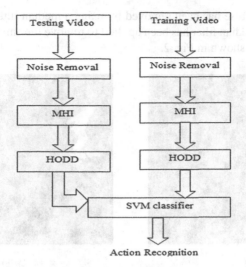

Fig. 1. Block diagram of proposed methodology

In the proposed system, first step is noise removal from the background subtracted silhouette. Output of first block is given to the MHI where we computed the MHIs of given noise removed input. [4] Feature extraction of every MHI is computed by using HODD descriptor [10]. Finally Support Vector Machine (SVM) is trained with the HODD descriptor which will going to classify the testing video. Following subsection explain complete methodology in details.

3.1 Shadow and Noise Removal

In our experiment we have used MuHAVi-uncut dataset [19]. This dataset is challenging due to, it is captured in following scenarios:

- Varying Lighting condition
- Non-uniform background
- Self shadow
- Fluctuating illumination and cast

Shadow may act as foreground and it very difficult to model background to remove it since it move with object.

The MuHAVi-uncut dataset is silhouette image dataset obtained by Self-adaptive Gaussian mixture model (SAGMM). The SAGMM was proposed by Chen and Ellis [16] and they used dynamically changing learning rate to model global illumination changes in the background. However, due to the different scenarios the silhouette image dataset consist of following different type of noises:

- shadow
- salt and pepper noise (small blobs)

Salt and pepper noise has been removed by using a median filtering. In our implementation 15×15 median filter has been applied to remove the small blob from silhouette image dataset as shown in Fig. 2.

(a)   (b)

Fig. 2. Background subtracted image frame (a) with noise (b) without noise removal

To remove the potential shadows we applied the method explained by Murtaza [21]. Authors applied fixed threshold to remove the noise from the MuHAViuncut dataset. The small holes are filled using binary closing operation.

3.2 MHI

Bobick and Davis [4] first introduced concept of motion based a representation for action recognition. They represent the video sequence using a single image template of motion history image (MHI). It represents the location of motion in video sequences. The intensity in MHI represents the recent motion in video sequence. The major advantages of MHI template it encode the temporal information in a single image. It is 2D static template obtained using a space time sequence of images.

It is constructed by assigning fixed intensity value to a foreground pixel and that constitutes the duration of an action. It decreased by a little constant value over time when the pixel begins to merge into background point. In 2D MHI the intensity value indicates of motion history of pixels at that location, where a high intensity value represents the more recent motion.

The MHI for a given video sequence can be computed by using following equation

$$MHI_\tau = \begin{cases} \tau, & if \ D(x,y,t) = 1 \\ \max(0, MHI_\tau(x, y, t-1) - 1), & otherwise \end{cases} \tag{1}$$

Where $D(x, y, t)$ is current motion image which is having value 1 if there is change in two consecutive time frames. MHI at time t is computed from MHI at time $(t-1)$ and current motion image. By using MHI at previous time frame $(t-1)$ and current motion image we can computed MHI at time t. The construction of MHI is shown in

Fig. 3. The representative frames of action 'run' and it constructed MHI is presented in Fig. 3.

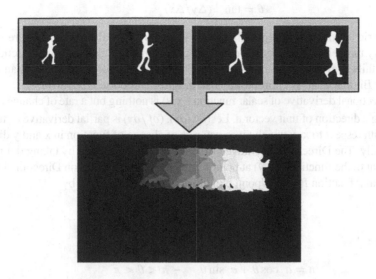

Fig. 3. MHI representation of Run action

To make it view independent we applied a method proposed by [20]. It makes use of multiple HOG-MHI images obtained from different views to train the classifier. While testing an arbitrary sequence is given to the learned model and it will predict the best match. In our implementation we have used the method proposed in [21]. It does not require the fusion of multiple view obtained by different camera. Authors used multiple view to train the model and it has been incorporated using manifold learning. It can improve the accuracy at the cost of computation cost.

3.3 Feature Descriptor

In this work, Histogram of directional derivative (HODD) [REF} based feature descriptor is used to describe the MHIs. Histogram of Oriented gradient (HOG) is widely used in human detection and action recognition. Murtaza et al. [21] applied HOG on MHIs for view independent action recognition. The major short coming of HOG is that it gives the information in only one direction which is normal to edge.

The gradient of function a 2-dimensional function f(x, y) is given by:

$$\Delta x = f(x+1, y) - f(x, y) \tag{2}$$

$$\Delta y = f(x, y+1) - f(x, y) \tag{3}$$

Above Eq. (2), (3) represents the gradient in x-direction and gradient in y direction respectively.

Magnitude and orientation is given by:

$$M_G = \sqrt{\Delta x^2 + \Delta y^2} \qquad (4)$$

$$\theta = \tan^{-1}(\Delta y / \Delta x) \qquad (5)$$

The orientation of gradient will always points in normal direction. There may be possibility that relevant information may be present in other than normal direction. The gradient fails to give this information [14]. To obtain the information other than normal direction Bhorge et al. [11] proposed Histogram of Direction Derivative.

A directional derivative of scalar function f(x,y) is nothing but a rate of change of function along a direction of unit vector u. Let $(\partial f / \partial x)$, $(\partial f / \partial y)$ is partial derivative of function f(x, y) with respect to x, y which gives you rate of change of function in x and y direction respectively. The Direction Derivative of the function is calculated by taking dot product of gradient of the function f(x, y) at point b and unit vector u. function Directional derivative of scalar function f(x, y) at point b in the direction of n is given by

$$D_n f(b) = \ <\nabla f(b), n> \qquad (6)$$

Where

$$n = a_x \cos\theta + a_y \sin\theta \quad -\pi < \theta < \pi \qquad (7)$$

3.4 Action Recognition

In our implementation we used Support Vector Machines (SVM) classifier for action recognition. Muratza et al. [21] applied a simple Nearest Neighbor based classifier. Even though, it does not require the prior knowledge of training samples its computational cost increases as the number of training samples increases. Also the classification accuracy is less as compared to other machine learning techniques such as SVM.

SVM is widely used by computer vision community for object recognition and classification task. It is a binary classifier and classifies the data by drawing an optimal hyperplane in higher dimensional space. In classification problem it works on training data $\{x_k, y_k\} \in \{-1, 1\}$ and testing dataset. x_k represent the training sample and y_k is the corresponding label. The objective of SVM to built a model which can predict the class label for a given testing sample.

Binary SVM find the a linear separating hyperplane in higher dimensional space with maximum margin. Figure 4 shows the two different possible hyperplane and margin between the hyperplane.

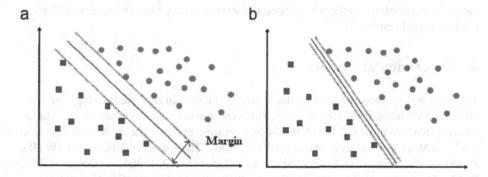

Fig. 4. Representative planes for classification of data points.

SVM solve the following constraint optimization problem

$$\min_{w,b,\xi} \frac{1}{2} w^T w + c \sum_{i=1}^{l} \xi_i, \tag{8}$$

$$\text{Subject to}: y_i(w^T \varphi(x_i) + b \geq 1 - \xi_i(\xi_i > 0) \tag{9}$$

The Eqs. (8) and (9) can be solved by using Lagrangian theory. The details of the solutions are discussed in [REF]. The solution of the above equations depends on the particular kernel function. Following are the different kernel functions widely used by computer vision community.

- Linear kernel
- Polynomial Kernel
- Sigmoid kernel
- Radial Basis Kernel

Because of non linear characteristics in feature space, we used radial basis function (RBF) which is given by

$$K(\chi_i, \chi_j) = \exp\left(-\gamma \|\chi_i - \chi_j\|^2\right) (\gamma > 0) \tag{10}$$

In our experiment we applied a non-linear RBF kernel function due to following advantages.

- It can handle the non-linear data in feature space
- It is computationally efficient as compared to other non-linear kernel.

The optimal solution for Eq. (10) can be obtained by finding optimal values of unknown parameters C and γ. Since these parameters are unknown and can be obtained by model selection method. A k-fold cross validation is widely used to obtain these parameters. Chang et al. [18] introduces a grid search based method to obtain the best values of parameters. Authors suggested that exponentially growing values of C and γ produces good results.

4   Experimental Results

The proposed method is tested on the MuHAvi-dataset. In this methodology we used HODD descriptor as of block 8×8 size. This experimental result is computed on Matlab 14 on system having 4 GB RAM and 64 bit operating system. There are total 10 action has been MuHAvi dataset contains total 17 actions. These are WalkTurnBack (WTB), RunStop (RS), Punch (PC), Kick, ShotGunCollapse (SGC), PullHeavyObject (PHO), PickUpThrowObject (PUTO), WalkFall (WF), LookInCar (LIC), CrawlOnKnees (COK), WaveArms (WA), DrawGraffitti (DG), JumpOverFence (JOF), DrunkWal1k (DW), ClimbLAdder (CL), SmashObject (SO), JumpOverGap (JOG). The resolution of the video sequence is 720 * 576 with frame rate 25 frames per second. Leave one sequence out (LOSO) cross-validation scheme is used for classification.

In LOSO cross validation scheme, the SVM classifier is trained with sixteen actions and remaining one is used for the testing. The resultant confusion matrix of LOSO is as shown in Table 1. The confusion matrix shows that draw graffiti action is having less accuracy and it is wrongly recognize with pull heavy object and smash object as these actions are having similar poses.

Table 1.   Confusion matrix for MuHAVi dataset actions using LOSO.

	WTB	RS	PC	Kick	SGC	PHO	PUTO	WF	LIC	COK	WA	DG	JOF	DW	CL	SO	JOG
WTB	1.00	0.00	0.00	0.00	0.00	0.00	0.00	0.00	0.00	0.00	0.00	0.00	0.00	0.00	0.00	0.00	0.00
RS	0.00	0.99	0.00	0.00	0.00	0.00	0.00	0.00	0.00	0.00	0.00	0.00	0.00	0.00	0.00	0.01	0.00
PC	0.00	0.00	0.98	0.00	0.00	0.00	0.00	0.02	0.00	0.00	0.00	0.00	0.00	0.00	0.00	0.00	0.00
Kick	0.00	0.00	0.00	0.97	0.00	0.00	0.00	0.00	0.00	0.00	0.03	0.00	0.00	0.00	0.00	0.00	0.00
SGC	0.00	0.00	0.00	0.00	1.00	0.00	0.00	0.00	0.00	0.00	0.00	0.00	0.00	0.00	0.00	0.00	0.00
PHO	0.00	0.02	0.00	0.00	0.00	0.98	0.00	0.00	0.00	0.00	0.00	0.00	0.00	0.00	0.00	0.00	0.00
PUTO	0.00	0.00	0.02	0.00	0.00	0.00	0.98	0.00	0.00	0.00	0.00	0.00	0.00	0.00	0.00	0.00	0.00
WF	0.00	0.00	0.00	0.00	0.00	0.00	0.00	1.00	0.00	0.00	0.00	0.00	0.00	0.00	0.00	0.00	0.00
LIC	0.00	0.00	0.00	0.00	0.00	0.00	0.00	0.00	1.00	0.00	0.00	0.00	0.00	0.00	0.00	0.00	0.00
COK	0.00	0.01	0.00	0.00	0.00	0.00	0.00	0.00	0.00	0.99	0.00	0.00	0.00	0.00	0.00	0.00	0.00
WA	0.00	0.00	0.00	0.00	0.00	0.00	0.00	0.00	0.00	0.00	1.00	0.00	0.00	0.00	0.00	0.00	0.00
DG	0.00	0.00	0.00	0.00	0.00	0.08	0.00	0.00	0.00	0.03	0.00	0.80	0.00	0.00	0.00	0.09	0.00
JOF	0.00	0.00	0.00	0.00	0.00	0.00	0.00	0.00	0.00	0.00	0.00	0.00	1.00	0.00	0.00	0.00	0.00
DW	0.02	0.00	0.00	0.00	0.00	0.01	0.01	0.00	0.00	0.00	0.00	0.00	0.00	0.95	0.00	0.00	0.01
CL	0.00	0.00	0.00	0.00	0.00	0.00	0.00	0.00	0.00	0.00	0.00	0.00	0.00	0.00	1.00	0.00	0.00
SO	0.00	0.00	0.00	0.00	0.00	0.00	0.00	0.00	0.00	0.00	0.00	0.00	0.00	0.00	0.00	1.00	0.00
JOG	0.00	0.00	0.00	0.00	0.00	0.00	0.00	0.00	0.00	0.00	0.00	0.00	0.02	0.02	0.00	0.00	0.96

5 Conclusion

In the proposed methodology, firstly MHI of each action sequence is computed. We used HODD descriptor which helps to improve the recognition rate. SVM classifier is used to classify the human action. In the proposed system we used multi view human action recognition dataset which consist of 17 actions. With the help of proposed system we achieved 97.64% recognition rate.

In the future scope, one can used NN classifier to classify the actions and check the recognition rate improves or not.

References

1. Poppe, R.: A survey on vision-based human action recognition. Image Vis. Comput. **28**, 976–990 (2010)
2. Aggarwal, J.K., Ryoo, M.S.: Human activity analysis: a review. ACM Comput. Surv. (CSUR) **43**, 16 (2011)
3. MuHAVi–MAS Multicamera Human Acion Video data set. http://dipersec.king.ac.uk/MuHAVi-MAS/
4. Bobick, A.F., Davis, J.W.: The recognition of human movement using temporal templates. IEEE Trans. Pattern Anal. Mach. Intell. **23**, 257–267 (2001)
5. Yamato, J., Ohya, J., Isshi, K.: Recognition of human action in timesequential images using hidden Morkov model. In: Proceedings of the Computer Vision and Pattern Recongnition, CVPR 1992, IEEE Computer Society Conference, pp. 379–385 (1992)
6. Weinland, D., Boyer, E.: Action recognition using exemplar-based embedding. In: IEEE Conference on Computer Vision and Pattern Recognition, pp. 1–7 (2008)
7. Nieble, J., Wang, H., Fei-Fei, L.: Unsupervised learning of human action categories using spatial-temporal words. Int. J. Comput. Vis. **79**, 299–318 (2008)
8. Willems, G., Tuytelaars, T., Van Gool, L.: An efficient dense and scale-invariant spatio-temporal interest point detector. In: Forsyth, D., Torr, P., Zisserman, A. (eds.) ECCV 2008. LNCS, vol. 5303, pp. 650–663. Springer, Heidelberg (2008). https://doi.org/10.1007/978-3-540-88688-4_48
9. Shao, L., Gao, R., Lui, Y., Zhang, H.: Transform based spatiotemporal descriptor for human action recognition. Int. J. Neurocomputing **74**, 962–973 (2011)
10. Tsai, D.M., Chiu, W., Lee, M.H.: Optical motion history image (OFMHI)for action recognition. Signal Image Video Process. **9**, 1897–1906 (2015)
11. Bhorge, S., Manthalkar, R.: Histogram of directional derivative based on spatio-temporal descriptor for human action recognition. In: ICDMAI 2017 (2017)
12. Ikizler, N., Duygulu, P.: Histogram of oriented rectangles: a new pose descriptor for human action recognition. Image Vis. Comput. **27**, 1515–1526 (2009)
13. Murtaza, F., Yousaf, M.H., Velastin, S.A.: PMHI: proposals from motion history images for temporal segmentation of long uncut videos. IEEE Signal Process. Lett. **25**, 179–183 (2018). ISSN 1070-9908
14. Bhorge, S.B., Manthalkar, R.R.: J. Ambient. Intell. Hum. Comput. (2017). https://doi.org/10.1007/s12652-017-0632-z
15. Klaser, A., Marszalek, M., Schmid, C.: A spatio-temporal descriptor based on 3d-gradients. In: British Machine Vision International Conference (2008)

16. Sepulveda, J., Velastin, S.A.: Evaluation of background subtractionalgorithms using MuHAVi, a multicamera human action video dataset. In: Sixth Chilean Conference on Pattern Recognition, Talca, Chile, 10–14 November 2014, pp. 10–14 (2014)
17. Chen, Z., Ellis, T.: Self-adaptive Gaussian mixture model for urban traffic monitoring system. In: 2011 IEEE International Conference on Computer Vision Workshops (ICCV Workshops), pp. 1769–1776 (2011)
18. Chang, C.-C., Lin, C.J.: LIBSVM: a library for support vector machine. ACM Trans. Intell. Syst. Technol. 2(3), 1–27 (2011)
19. Singh, S., Velastin, S.A., Ragheb, H.: MuHAVi: a multicamera human action video dataset for the evaluation of action recognition methods. In: Seventh IEEE International Conference on Advanced Video and Signal Based Surveillance (AVSS), pp. 48–55 (2010)
20. Weinland, D., Ronfard, R., Boyer, E.: A survey of vision-based methods for action representation, segmentation and recognition. Comput. Vis. Image Underst. 115(2), 224–241 (2011)
21. Murtaza, F., Yousaf, M., Velastin, S.: Multi-view human action recognition using 2D motion templates based on MHIs and their HOG description. IET Comput. Vis. 10, 758–767 (2016)
22. Cristianini, N., Shawe-Taylor, J.: An Introduction to Support Vector Machines. Cambridge University Press, Cambridge (2000)

Segmental Analysis of Speech Signal
for Robust Speaker Recognition System

Rupali V. Pawar[1(✉)], R. M. Jalnekar[2], and J. S. Chitode[2]

[1] Sinhgad College of Engineering, Pune, India
rupalipawar.scoe@sinhgad.edu
[2] Vishwakarma Institute of Technology, Pune, India
rajeshjalnekar@yahoo.com, j.chitode@gmail.com

Abstract. This paper discusses the implementation of four stages of speaker recognition system: Pre-Emphasis, Segmentation techniques, Feature Extraction and Recognition techniques. The paper elaborates on various segmentation techniques like sub segmental, segmental and supra segmental analysis of speech signal. The comparison of the results obtained using these techniques are presented. The features like pitch, MFCC and duration addressing the excitation source, vocal tract and prosodic features of the speaker are extracted. The results for different segmentation techniques and corresponding features using Gaussian Mixture Model and Expectation maximization are acquired. The system has shown higher accuracy for spectral features modelled using GMM.

Keywords: Pre-emphasis · Pitch · Duration · Segmentation
Gaussian mixture model

1 Introduction

Speaker Recognition is an important arena of Speech Processing and is a process of recognizing who is speaking based on features embedded in the speech wave. Researchers have explored various approaches of noise removal, feature extraction and recognition. Certain unanswered challenges in this field such as speaker variability, emotional states of the speaker, microphone characteristics, channel mismatch and room acoustics need to be addressed. An attempt to overcome these practical issues and challenges in speaker recognition system is an impetus behind this Research Work. The paper discusses the proposed methodology, experimentation details and the results obtained.

2 Methodology

The system is implemented using combination of sub segmental, segmental and supra segmental analysis. The algorithms used in Pre-Emphasis, Speech Analysis, Feature Extraction and Recognition stage are as shown in the Fig. 1 below.

The research work attempts to implement a robust speaker recognition system, the system has two phases - Training Phase and Testing Phase. In each phase, the system

© Springer Nature Singapore Pte Ltd. 2018
M. Singh et al. (Eds.): ICACDS 2018, CCIS 905, pp. 509–519, 2018.
https://doi.org/10.1007/978-981-13-1810-8_51

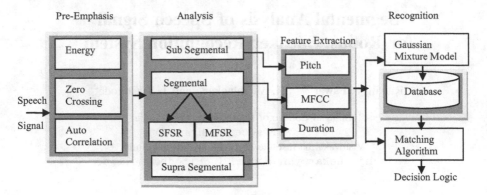

Fig. 1. System architecture

implements four stages: the pre-emphasis, Speech Analysis, Feature Extraction and Recognition. The system uses recorded speech signal and standard database.

In the pre-emphasis stage energy, zero crossing count and auto correlation algorithms are used to separate noise, unvoiced and silence from the speech signal. In the analysis phase, the speech signal is segmented into small size frames. The current research has implemented this stage using three techniques: Sub Segmental, Segmental and Supra Segmental analysis. Segments of 3 to 5 ms, 10 to 30 ms and 100 to 300 ms respectively. The features contributing to excitation source, vocal tract and prosodic characteristics are extracted [1, 2].

In the feature extraction phase the features Pitch, MFCC (Mel frequency Cepstral coefficient) and Duration are used. These features extracted are modeled using Gaussian Mixture Model (GMM), a probabilistic method of classification.

3 Experimentation

3.1 Database Used

The necessity of proper data selection in any Speaker Recognition System is to reduce the time required for further pre-processing. Depending on the necessity of the application and the research area, many researchers use standard database and native language database [4]. The current research work has used recorded speech, clean speech and noisy speech database. The recorded data for 8 speakers has paragraphs of approximately 50 s. These are divided into 3 parts and labeled as initial, intermediate and end paragraphs, having total 24 samples of speech for 8 speakers. The standard database from speech corpus: ELSDSR (English Language Speech Database for Speaker Recognition) and NOIZEUS is used. The current research work has used noise introduced by airport 5 db & 15 db [5]. System works as text dependent and text independent speaker recognition.

3.2   Pre-emphasis

This stage is implemented using energy, zero crossing and autocorrelation algorithms. The result of the wave file whose short time energy and zero crossing count (ZCC) are calculated is shown in the Fig. 2a below.

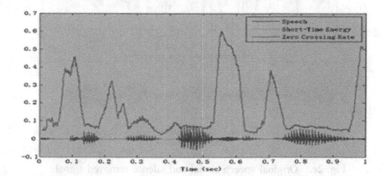

Fig. 2a.   Energy and ZCC of the speech wave form calculated

The voiced signal has high energy compared to unvoiced signal or noise. The ZCC is high for unvoiced speech signal while ZCC is low for voiced speech signal. Figure 2b shows Autocorrelation and formants of voiced and unvoiced speech. The autocorrelation exhibits the periodicity for voiced speech and is non-periodic for unvoiced speech. For voiced speech, the magnitude of lower frequencies is successively larger than the magnitude of the higher formant frequencies i.e. it enhances low frequency components & suppresses high frequency and vice-versa for unvoiced speech.

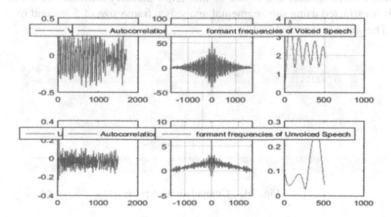

Fig. 2b.   Autocorrelation and formants of voiced and unvoiced speech

Figure 2c shows the original speech signal and the silence removed speech signal.

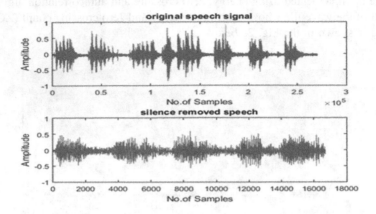

Fig. 2c.   Original speech signal and silence removed signal.

3.3   System Implementation

The research work uses sub segmental, segmental and supra segmental approach of analysis of speech. The segmental analysis further uses Fixed Frame Size and Rate (FFSR) or Multiple Frame Size and Rate (MFSR) approach [2].

Features characterizing uniqueness of a speaker is extracted in speaker recognition applications. The current work has extracted Pitch, MFCC and duration as features.

Pitch corresponds to the perceived fundamental frequency (F0) of a sound along with loudness and quality. The fundamental frequency has a different range for a male, female and a child speaker and is one of the major auditory attributes of sound.

Pitch is extracted using sub segmental analysis a frame size of 5 ms and overlap of 2.5 ms. The same is depicted in Fig. 2d.

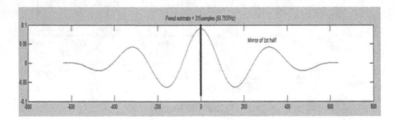

Fig. 2d.   Computation of pitch

The occurrence of maximum frequency between 50 Hz and 500 Hz is computed which is the normal frequency range for human voice. The time between the occurrences of first two peaks is considered as pitch.

MFCC is the most widely used feature extraction technique. This method is considered to be the best available approximation of human ear. The Mel frequency cepstral coefficient is computed using the steps shown in the Fig. 2e below

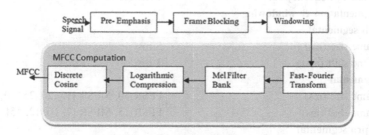

Fig. 2e. Computation of MFCC

Speech signal is framed using segmental analysis technique and signal is windowed using hamming window before computing Fast Fourier Transform (FFT) of the signal.

Mel scale filter bank consists of a series of triangular band pass filter banks which are arranged in such a way that the lower boundary of one filter is located at the centre frequency of the previous filter and the upper boundary of the same filter is situated at the centre frequency of the next filter The Mel scale is logarithmic scale that resembles the human ear perception of sound. Mel scale filter bank maps the powers of the spectrum obtained above onto the Mel scale by using triangular overlapping window. The Mel scale is represented by the following formula:

$$Melf = 2595 \ln\left(1 + \frac{f}{700}\right) \qquad (1)$$

Where *Melf* is Mel frequency in Mel and *f* is linear frequency in Hertz.

The signal passes through the filter banks; log energy at the output of each filter bank is calculated. The natural logarithm transforms the signal into cepstral domain. Finally, DCT is applied to each Mel spectrum (filter output) to convert the values back to real values in time domain [6, 7].

Average word duration, silence between words, average of voiced and unvoiced durations can be used as parameters of duration for analysis [8]. The features like standard deviation, range, variance, mean, maximum, minimum, range of energy, and pitch are important prosodic information [9].

The computation of duration in this work is similar to pitch computation except that the segmentation technique is supra segmental hence the segment size is considered to be 200 ms with an overlap of 100 ms

Table 1 gives the detail specifications of the implementation at every stage

3.4 Modelling

The features extracted are modelled using Gaussian Mixture Model. GMM has the ability to represent the spectral properties of the signal.

Table 1. System implementation

Parameter	Value
Database used	Recorded/ELSDSR/NOIZEUS
Sampling frequency Hz	44100/16000/8000
Segmentation & windowing	
Sub segmental	
Frame size (ms)	5 ms
Frame shift (ms)	3 ms
Segmental	
Frame size (ms)	FFSR 30, MFSR [15, 20, 25, 30]
Frame shift (ms)	FFSR 15, MFSR [7, 10, 12, 15]
Supra segmental	
Frame size (ms)	200
Frame shift (ms)	100
Window type	Hamming/Rectangular window
Pitch feature extraction	**50–500 Hz**
Number of coefficients	13×4
MFCC feature extraction	
FFT	512 point
Number of filters	20
Number of MFCC coefficients	13
Size of feature matrix for signal	$13 \times$ number of frames
Duration feature extraction	50–500 Hz
Number of Coefficients	$13 \times$ number of frames
GMM recognition	
Number of gaussian components	12
Size of mean vector for each component	13×1
Size of variance matrix for each component	13×13
Type of variance matrix	Diagonal matrix

It is a probabilistic model used for isolated as well as continuous word recognition. GMM provides a speaker representation immune to noise even for corrupted and unconstrained or text independent speech (Fig. 3).

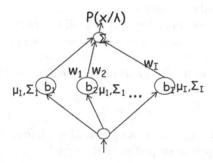

Fig. 3. Gaussian mixture component

A Gaussian mixture model is represented as

$$\lambda = (w_i, \ \mu_i, \ \Sigma_i)$$

Where –
w_i - mixture weights.
μ_i - mean vector (expected feature vectors)
Σ_i - variance matrix (covariance of elements of feature vectors) [3, 10].
bi - Component densities

For speaker identification, a group of S speakers, if $Sp = 1, 2, \ldots s$, is represented by GMM models $\{\lambda_1, \lambda_2, \ldots, \lambda_S\}$. The aim here is to compute the speaker model which has the maximum probability for a given feature vectors. The speaker identification system calculates the closest probability using the formula.

$$P = max_{1 \leq k \leq s} \sum_{t=1}^{T} P(x_t|\lambda_k) \tag{2}$$

The above equation gives the model which has the maximum probability for the given set of feature vectors.

The training of GMM is accomplished using the Expectation-maximization (EM) algorithm. The individual speaker models generated after training have components which represent certain general speaker dependent features. The individual Gaussian components of a GMM represent some general speaker-dependent spectral characteristics. These characteristics prove to be good representatives to model the speaker identity. Speaker model obtained from GMM attains greater identification accuracy compared to other speaker modelling techniques [11, 12]. The number of Gaussians used in this work is 12. The parameters modelled for the speaker to be recognized are compared with stored database decision of the best matched/recognized speaker is given [3, 13].

4   Results

The result for the research work are put forth: Table 2 gives the result of accuracy of the system using different algorithms tested for standard and recorded database. The system recognition using MFSR_MFCC algorithm outperforms the recognition using SFSR_MFCC and pitch for the standard database. Table 3 puts forth the results for recognition accuracy of the system using noisy database with airport noise of 5, 10 and 15 dB. Pitch, MFSR_MFCC, SFSR_MFCC and Duration are the algorithms used for extracting features.

The graph below represent the accuracy for the standard and recorded database (Fig. 4).

The Fig. 5 below depicts the graph for Accuracy using various Algorithms for Noisy Database.

The research work has used pitch of the speaker to recognise gender of the speaker, the database used is the noisy database. The system is tested for standard noisy

Table 2. Accuracy for different algorithms tested for standard and recorded database

ELSDSR data & Recorded data					
Speakers	Speech files	Database used	% Accuracy of recognition		
			MFSR_MFCC	SFSR_MFCC	Pitch
22	154	ELSDSR	95.45%		
	90.90%	68.18%			
8	8	Recorded paragraph 1	62.50%	62.50%	75.00%
8	8	Recorded paragraph 2	87.50%	87.50%	75.00%
8	8	Recorded paragraph 3	62.50%	62.50%	62.50%

Table 3. Accuracy for different algorithms tested for noizeus database for airport noise

SNR noizeus database	% Accuracy of recognition			
	Pitch	MFSR-MFCC	SFSR-MFCC	Duration
5 dB	33.33%	66.66%	66.66%	41.66%
10 dB	33.33%	91.66%	75%	75%
15 dB	33.33%	100%	83.33%	83.33%

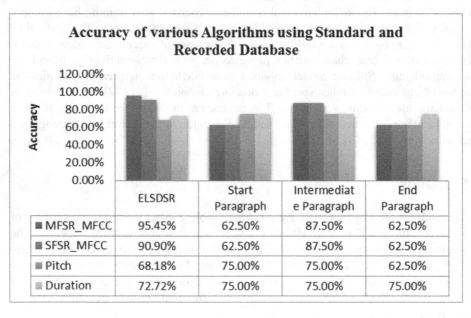

Fig. 4. Graph for accuracy for the standard and recorded database

database Noiszeus with SNR level 5 dB, 10 dB and 15 dB for added SNR level of airport noise. Table 4 gives the result of Gender Recognition using Pitch for Noisy database. The results show that gender recognition accuracy improves for added noise of 15 db SNR level compared to 5 dB SNR level.

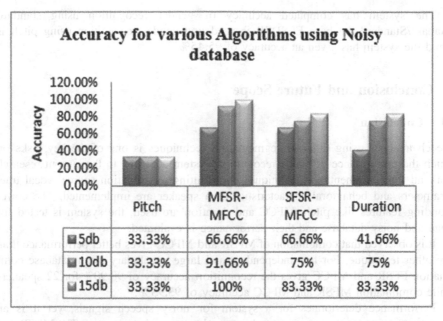

Fig. 5. Graph for accuracy using various algorithms for noisy database

Table 4. Gender recognition using pitch for noizeus database

Noizeus database (SNR)	Gender recognition using pitch
5 db	75%
10 db	75%
15 db	83.3%

The graphical representation for the same is depicted in Fig. 6 below.

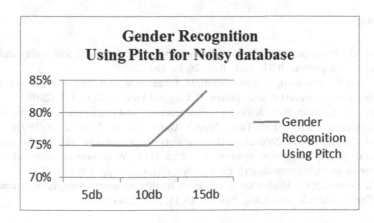

Fig. 6. Graph of gender recognition using noisy database for different SNR levels

The system has computed accuracy of gender recognition using standard database/Standard database ELSDSR is used and gender recognition using pitch is found the system has given an accuracy of 95.45%.

5   Conclusion and Future Scope

5.1   Conclusion

Speech analysis using different segmentation techniques is one of the key tasks on which the performance of whole recognition system depends. In the current research work all three segmentation techniques contributing to excitation source, vocal tract parameters and behavioral characteristics of a speaker are implemented. The corresponding features like pitch, MFCC and duration are used, the system is tested for clean and noisy database and their performance is evaluated.

It is observed that combination of MFSR and MFCC gives better performance than any other technique. For text independent and large vocabulary clean database combination FFSR and MFCC gives the recognition accuracy of 90.90% for 22 speakers while combination MFSR and MFCC accuracy of **95.95%**.

Performance deteriorates for a system for noisy speech signals, yet it is an important performance measure for robust speaker recognition system. The MFSR and MFCC have given result for recognition 66.66% for 5db added airport noise.

The gender recognition using pitch has given 95.45% accuracy for clean text independent large vocabulary database while minimum of 75% accuracy for noisy database at 5 dB SNR.

5.2   Future Scope

Future Scope: The MFSR and MFCC along with GMM have proved to recognize a speaker accurately. However this combination becomes less reliable and ineffective in the presence of noise. In future there is need to increase the performance of system in noisy environment to increase the speaker recognition accuracy.

References

1. Jayanna, H., Prasanna, S.M.: Analysis, feature extraction, modeling and testing techniques for speaker recognition. IETE Tech. Rev. **26**(3), 181 (2009)
2. Jayanna, H.S., Prasanna, S.R.M.: Multiple frame size and rate analysis for speaker recognition under limited data condition. IET Signal Process. **3**(3), 189 (2009)
3. Reynolds, D.A., Rose, R.C.: Robust text-independent speaker identification using Gaussian mixture speaker models. IEEE Trans. Speech Audio Process. **3**(1), 72–83 (1995)
4. Nagroski, A., Boves, L., Steeneken, H.: In search of optimal data selection for training of automatic speech recognition systems. In: 2003 IEEE Workshop on Automatic Speech Recognition and Understanding (IEEE Cat. No. 03EX721), pp. 67–72 (2003)
5. Hu, Y., Loizou, P.C.: Evaluation of objective quality measures for speech enhancement. IEEE Trans. Audio Speech Lang. Process. **16**(1), 229–238 (2008)

6. Singh, S., Rajan, E.G.: Application of different filters in Mel frequency Cepstral coefficients feature extraction and fuzzy vector quantization approach in speaker recognition. Int. J. Eng. Res. Technol. 2(6), 3171–3182 (2013)
7. Dabbaghchian, S., Sameti, H., Ghaemmaghami, M.P., BabaAli, B.: Robust phoneme recognition using MLP neural networks in various domains of MFCC features. In: 2010 5th International Symposium on Telecommunications, pp. 755–759 (2010)
8. Ashish, B.I., Chaudhari, D.S.: Speech emotion recognition. Int. J. Soft Comput. Eng. 2(1), 235–238 (2012)
9. Mary, L.: Prosodic features for speaker recognition. In: Neustein, A., Patil, H. (eds.) Forensic Speaker Recognition, pp. 365–388. Springer, New York (2012). https://doi.org/10.1007/978-1-4614-0263-3_13
10. Reynolds, D.A.: An overview of automatic speaker recognition technology. In: Proceedings of the ICASSP, vol. 4, pp. 4072–4075 (2002)
11. Shinozaki, T., Kawahara, T.: GMM and HMM training by aggregated EM algorithm with increased ensemble sizes for robust parameter estimation. In: 2008 IEEE International Conference on Acoustics, Speech and Signal Processing, pp. 4405–4408 (2008)
12. Campbell, J.P., Reynolds, D.A.: Corpora for the evaluation of speaker recognition systems. In: Proceedings of the 1999 IEEE International Conference on Acoustics, Speech, and Signal Processing, ICASSP 1999 (Cat. No. 99CH36258),vol. 2, pp. 829–832 (1999)
13. Memon, S., Lech, M., Maddage, N.: Information theoretic expectation maximization based Gaussian mixture modeling for speaker verification. In: 2010 20th International Conference on Pattern Recognition, pp. 4536–4540 (2010)

Multimicrophone Based Speech Dereverberation

Seema Vitthal Arote$^{(\boxtimes)}$ and Mangesh Sudhir Deshpande

E&TC Department, Vishwakarma Institute of Technology, Pune, India
seema.arote@gmail.com, mangesh.deshpande@vit.edu

Abstract. Speech signal received by distant microphones in real environments contains reverberation and noise. This deteriorates the quality of received signal. However to improve the speech quality, it is essential to remove reverberation and noise. The process of removing reverberation and reproducing original speech is called dereverberation. Generalized Sidelobe Canceller (GSC) is one of the speech dereverberation techniques focused by many researchers. This paper presents a method for removal of reverberation and noise using GSC which is one of beamforming technique. The proposed approach enhances speech quality in noisy environment for different source to array distances and signal to noise levels. It is also experimentally verified.

Keywords: Reverberation · Beamforming · Dereverberation
Generalized Sidelobe Canceller (GSC)

1 Introduction

In hands free applications signal received by microphone is not only desired signal. But multiple reflections from partitions and different objects available in the enclosure, this phenomenon is known as reverberation [1]. The reverberation deteriorates performance of speech processing systems. Which are part of hands free applications such as mobile phone, hearing aids, teleconferencing and automatic speech recognition [2, 3]. Dereverberation is process of eliminating reverberations from reverberant speech and is important in hands free speech processing systems where microphone is placed at a distance from talker. In this work dereverberation is achieved using beamforming. Beamforming refers to design of a spatio-temporal filter that operates on microphone array outputs. Microphone array beamforming is most widely used algorithm for reverberation suppression and background noise removal. In beamforming, microphone signals are filtered and outputs are combined to extract desired signal by rejecting interfering signals as per their spatial location.

Based on number of microphones used speech dereverberation can be categorized into single channel and multi-channel methods. Multi-channel systems are preferred for hands free and video conferencing applications. Generalized Sidelobe Canceller (GSC) is most widely used Linearly Constrained Minimum Variance (LCMV) beamforming technique. This separates adaptive beamformer into two paths namely, fixed beamformer and adaptive blocking matrix. However various approaches for spatial filtering, including GSC are summarized in [4]. Thus, variety of linearly

© Springer Nature Singapore Pte Ltd. 2018
M. Singh et al. (Eds.): ICACDS 2018, CCIS 905, pp. 520–529, 2018.
https://doi.org/10.1007/978-981-13-1810-8_52

constrained adaptive array processors can be implemented using beamforming structure presented in [5]. An alternative implementation of Frost's linearly constrained adaptive beamforming algorithm is GSC structure. Transfer Function Generalized Sidelobe Canceller (TF-GSC) is proposed in [6]. Convolutive Transfer Function Generalized Sidelobe Canceler is proposed for multichannel speech enhancement in reverberant environments [7]. Dual-microphone speech dereverberation algorithm is proposed in [8] and GSC structure is used to improve desired speech signal. Minimum Variance Distortionless Response (MVDR) beamformer and a single-channel Minimum Mean-Square Error (MMSE) estimator is used to reduce late reverberation in [9]. Two stage approach for joint suppression of reverberation and noise is presented in [10]. Ofer Schwartz et al. implemented multi-channel MVDR beamformer with wiener as a post filter for removing reverberation and noise in [11]. Spatial filtering techniques for multi-microphone speech dereverberation are proposed in [12]. In this paper speech dereverberation has been achieved using beamforming with generalized sidelobe canceller.

This paper is organized as follows. Section 2 presents generalized sidelobe canceller for speech dereverberation. Section 3, presents the performance evaluation of proposed technique. Section 4, presents conclusion of the paper.

2 Generalized Sidelobe Canceller for Speech Dereverberation

2.1 Beamformer

A beamformer is a spatial filter, splits signal and interference according to their spatial characteristics. The weighted combination of signals from M elements of sensor array produces beamformer output, as Eq. (1) (Fig. 1).

$$y(n) = \sum_{m=1}^{M} w_m^* x_m(n)$$ (1)

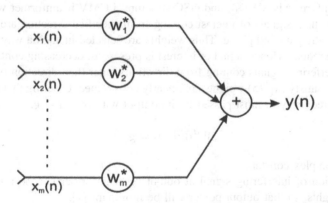

Fig. 1. A basic beamformer [4].

The beamformer is multiple inputs and single output system, considering signal at each individual sensor is observed as an input. Hence Eq. (1) has been represented in matrix form as follow,

$$Y(n) = W^H X(n) \tag{2}$$

where W represents weight vector and $X(n)$ is data vector.

In beamforming operation, sensor signals are combined with weights on each sensor signals, like an FIR filter. This produces an output as weighted sum of time samples. Frequency-selective FIR filter extract signal at its frequency of interest. Similarly beamformer seeks to emphasize signals with certain spatial frequency. Hence beamformer is viewed a as a spatial frequency-selective filter. Thus beamformer response can be viewed as FIR filter frequency response and is interpreted as amplitude and phase. Assuming signal is complex plane wave with direction of arrival θ and frequency ω. The beamformer response $r(\theta, \omega)$ in vector form is as below.

$$r(\theta, \omega) = W^H d(\theta, \omega) \tag{3}$$

The elements of $d(\theta, \omega)$ are expressed as Eq. (4).

$$d(\theta, \omega) = \left[1 e^{j\omega\tau 2(\theta)} \, e^{j\omega\tau 3(\theta)} \ldots e^{j\omega\tau N(\theta)} \right]^H \tag{4}$$

where $\tau i(\theta)$, $2 \leq i \leq N$ are the time delays. The $d(\theta, \omega)$ is array response or direction vector. Weights of statistically optimum beamformer are selected according to array data received statistics. At beamformer output signal-to-noise ratio is increased by rejecting signals from interfering sources [4]. As per statistical properties of the desired and interference signals, statistically optimal beamformers are designed for improving desired signal, discarding interference signal. As reverberation consists of multipath reflections and strength of the desired signal is unknown therefore linear constraints are applied to all weight vectors. Constraints beamformer include LCMV, its special structure beamformer is MVDR, and GSC structure. LCMV beamformer works under the constraints that, signals of interest coming from specified direction are allowed to pass with specific gain and phase. Thus weights are selected in such a way that output power will be reduce. Hence signal of interest is preserved, decreasing contributions of noise and interfering signals coming from directions other than direction of interest at the output. To satisfy Eq. (5) weights are linearly constrained, ensuring that signal from angle θ and frequency ω must passed to the output with response g.

$$W^H d(\theta, \omega) = g \tag{5}$$

where g is complex constant.

Contribution of interfering signal at output of beamformer can be minimized by selecting weights, so that output power will be minimum [4].

$$\min_w \quad W^H R_x w \quad \text{subject to} \quad d^H(\theta, \omega)w = g^* \tag{6}$$

Using Lagrange multipliers, we obtain

$$w = g^* \; \frac{R_x^{-1}d(\theta, \omega)}{d^{H(\omega, \theta)}R_x^{-1}d(\theta, \omega)} \tag{7}$$

where Rx = Array correlation matrix. If $g = 1$ then Eq. (7) is often called as MVDR beamformer. An alternative formulation of LCMV is GSC [4].

2.2 Generalized Sidelobe Canceller (GSC)

GSC is special type of LCMV beamformer that transforms constrained optimization problem into an unconstrained form. GSC consists of delay and sum beamformer (DSB), blocking matrix and adaptive noise canceller. DSB is fixed beamformer passes desired signals. In DSB output signal of each microphone is delayed to make up arrival time difference of speech signal for each microphone. Blocking matrix blocks desired signal and pass all other signals. Noise canceller cancels noise and other interference signal. Thus, GSC removes reverberation and noise of input reverberant signal (Fig. 2).

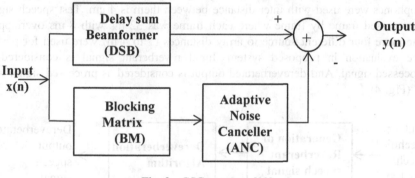

Fig. 2. GSC structure [11].

2.3 Proposed System

Proposed system consists of preprocessing, in which time domain reverberant input speech signal is transform in frequency domain, applying short time fourier transform (STFT) [15]. GSC is a spatial filtering technique used for multi-microphone speech dereverberation (Fig. 3).

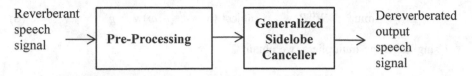

Fig. 3. Schematic representation of proposed system

3   Performance Evaluation of Proposed System

Performance evaluation of proposed algorithm is carried using two objective quality measures namely, Perceptual Evaluation of Speech Quality (PESQ) and Log Spectral Distance (LSD). Perceptual evaluation of speech quality is standardized as ITU-T recommendation P. 862 [14].

3.1   Experimental Set-up and Simulation Parameters

TIMIT database has been used in this work to evaluate proposed approach. The reverberant speech signal is generated, convolving anechoic speech signal with Room Impulse Response (RIR). RIR was generated using image method adding white noise [13]. Room dimensions were set to [6.1 × 5.3 × 2.7] m, reverberation time RT60 was set to 0.5 s, RIR were simulated at sampling rate of 16 kHz. The array of three microphones were used with inter distance between them is 4 cm. Test speech signal was processed frame by frame where each frame was 32 ms with 8 ms overlapped. Furthermore four different source to array distances (1 to 4 m) were used for performance evaluation in proposed system. Input reverberant signal is considered as unprocessed signal. And dereverberated output is considered as processed signal with GSC (Fig. 4).

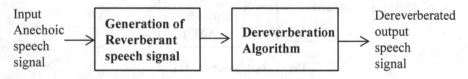

Fig. 4. Experimental setup of proposed method

3.2   Experimental Results

Figure 5 shows anechoic speech signal waveform. Figure 6 shows reverberant speech signal. Figure 7 shows dereverberated speech signal. Tables 1, 2, 3 and 4 illustrates results of PESQ and LSD obtained for various source to array distance with additive white noise. However, results obtained for PESQ and LSD using proposed approach is improved compared to unprocessed signal as illustrated in Tables 1, 2, 3 and 4.

Figures 8 and 9 illustrates plots of PESQ for unprocessed and processed with GSC (dereverberated) with source to array distance 1 to 4 m and various signal to noise ratios. Figures 10 and 11 shows plots of LSD for unprocessed and processed with GSC

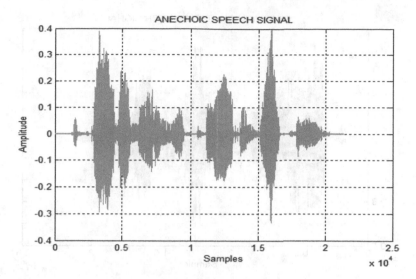

Fig. 5. Anechoic speech signal

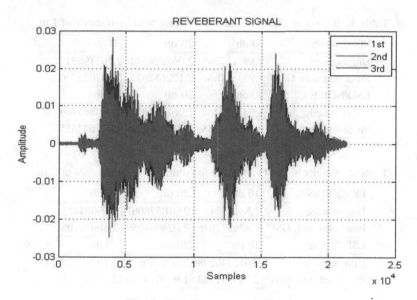

Fig. 6. Reverberant speech signal

(dereverberated) having source to array distance of 1 to 4 m, with different signal to noise ratios.

Results of Tables 1, 2, 3 and 4 shows that proposed GSC method gives better quality of speech signal in terms of PESQ and LSD. It also reduces reverberation and noise. The speech quality of dereverberated (processed with GSC) signal is improved in comparison with unprocessed signal for different source to array distance (1 to 4 m)

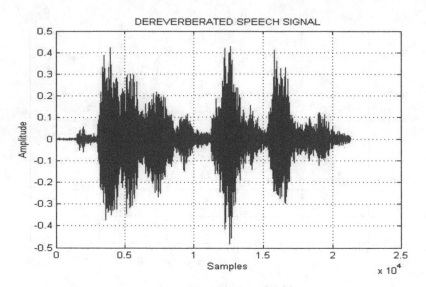

Fig. 7. Dereverberated speech signal

Table 1. Results of PESQ and LSD for source to array distance of 1 m.

PESQ/NOISE	10 db	20 db	30 db
Unprocessed	1.893117245	2.067824344	2.10719631
Processed with GSC	1.953511066	2.122682671	2.147025276
LSD/NOISE	10 db	20 db	30 db
Unprocessed	1.943870462	1.961221817	2.004865769
Processed with GSC	2.466663335	1.974948294	1.715647655

Table 2. Results of PESQ and LSD for source to array distance of 2 m.

PESQ/NOISE	10 db	20 db	30 db
Unprocessed	1.8612374	2.010578007	2.05084413
Processed with GSC	1.876577676	2.024044959	2.10970106
LSD/NOISE	10 db	20 db	30 db
Unprocessed	2.012748898	2.079760812	2.14247779
Processed with GSC	2.389541953	1.945014776	1.71071766

and different signal to noise ratios demonstrating that proposed method gives better results in noisy conditions.

Figures 8 and 9 illustrate effectiveness of GSC algorithm in reverberant environment. PESQ of dereverberated (processed with GSC) signal is improved compared to unprocessed signal, though distance between source to array is increased.

Table 3. Results of PESQ and LSD for source to array distance of 3 m.

PESQ/NOISE	10 db	20 db	30 db
Unprocessed	1.908953466	2.005125683	1.937277754
Processed with GSC	1.916153274	2.126690584	2.173254866
LSD/NOISE	10 db	20 db	30 db
Unprocessed	2.070754968	2.15476418	2.247486329
Processed with GSC	2.342971463	1.923348092	1.705490179

Table 4. Results of PESQ and LSD for source to array distance of 4 m.

PESQ/NOISE	10 db	20 db	30 db
Unprocessed	1.761303361	1.964960207	2.015182295
Processed with GSC	1.891523026	2.076221554	2.097449977
LSD/NOISE	10 db	20 db	30 db
Unprocessed	2.102770032	2.210201653	2.300927191
Processed with GSC	2.321478453	1.92704119	1.727455419

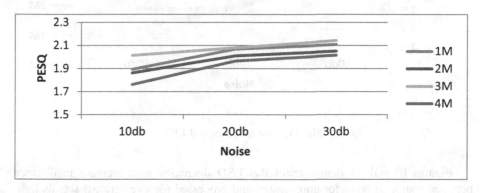

Fig. 8. Plot for unprocessed PESQ

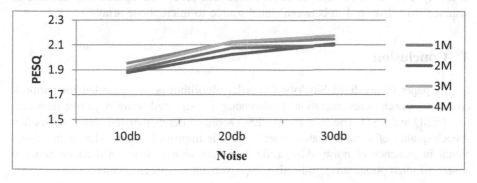

Fig. 9. Plot for processed PESQ

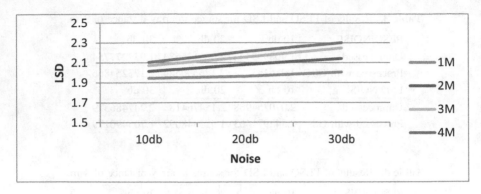

Fig. 10. Plot for unprocessed LSD

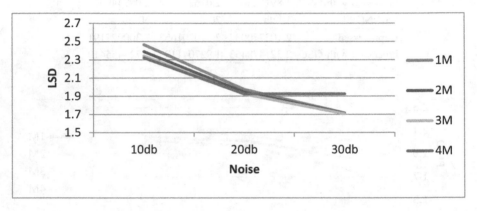

Fig. 11. Plot for processed LSD

Figures 10 and 11 demonstrates that LSD decreases with increase in distance between source to array for unprocessed and processed (dereverberated) signals indicating speech quality is improved. Improved speech quality demonstrates that, decrease in log spectral distance between unprocessed and processed signals with increase in distance from 1 m to 4 m between signal source to microphone array.

4 Conclusion

In this paper Generalized Sidelobe Canceller algorithm is implemented for multimicrophone speech dereverberation. Performance is evaluated using objective measures like PESQ and LSD. The increase in PESQ score of dereverberated signal shows that speech quality of dereverberated speech signal is improved compared to unprocessed signal in presence of noise. Also, LSD decreases with increase in distance between source to microphone array indicating improvement in speech quality.

References

1. Naylor, P.A., Gaubitch, N.D.: Speech Dereverberation. Spinger, London (2010)
2. Benesty, J., Sondhi, M.M., Huang, Y.A.: Springer Handbook of Speech Processing. Springer, New York (2008)
3. Habets, E.A.P.: Single and multi-microphone speech dereverberation using spectral enhancement. Ph.D. dissertation, Eindhoven University of Technology, Eindhoven, The Netherlands, June 2007
4. Van Veen, B.D., Buckley, K.M.: Beamforming: a versatile approach to spatial filtering. IEEE Acoust. Speech Signal Process. Mag. 2(5), 4–24 (1988)
5. Griffiths, L.J., Jim, C.W.: An alternate approach to linearly constrained adaptive beamforming. IEEE Trans. Antennas Propag. 30(1), 27–34 (1982)
6. Gannot, S., Burshtein, D., Weinstein, E.: Signal enhancement using beamforming and non stationarity with applications to speech. IEEE Trans. Sig. Process. 8(49), 1614–1626 (2001)
7. Talmon, R., Cohen, I., Gannot, S.: Convolutive transfer function generalized sidelobe canceler. IEEE Trans. Audio, Speech, Lang. Process. 7(17), 1420–1434 (2009)
8. Habets, E.A.P., Gannot, S.: Dual-microphone speech dereverberation using a reference signal. In: Proceedings of IEEE International Conference on Acoustics, Speech, Signal Processing, vol. 4, pp. 901–904 (2007)
9. Habets, E.A.P.: Towards multi-microphone speech dereverberation using spectral enhancement and statistical reverberation models. In: Proceedings of Asilomar Conference on Signals, Systems and Computers, pp. 806–810 (2008)
10. Habets, E.A.P., Benesty, J.: A two-stage beamforming approach for noise reduction and dereverberation. IEEE Trans. Audio, Speech, Lang. Process. 5(21), 945–958 (2013)
11. Schwartz, O., Gannot, S., Habets, E.A.P.: Multi-microphone speech dereverberation and noise reduction using relative early transfer functions. IEEE Trans. Audio, Speech, Lang. Process. 2(23), 240–251 (2015)
12. Deshpande, S.R., Deshpande, M.S.: Multi-microphone speech dereverberation using spatial filtering. In: IEEE International Conference on Advances in Signal Process, pp. 340–343 (2016)
13. Allen, J.B., Berkley, D.A.: Image method for efficiently simulating small-room acoustics. J. Acoust. Soc. Amer. 4(65), 943–950 (1979)
14. ITU-T Perceptual evaluation of speech quality (PESQ), an objective method for end-to-end speech quality assessment of narrowband telephone networks and speech codecs. In: International Telecommunication Union (ITU-T) Recommendations, p. 862 (2001)
15. Vikhe, P.S., Nehe, N.S., Thool, V.R.: Heart sound abnormality detection using short time fourier transform and continuous wavelet transform. In: IEEE International Conference on Emerging Trends in Engineering and Technology, pp. 50–54 (2009)

Modeling Nonlinear Dynamic Textures Using Isomap with GPU

Premanand Ghadekar[✉]

Department of Information Technology,
Vishwakarma Institute of Technology, Pune, India
ppghadekar@gmail.com

Abstract. Several methods exist to model a nonlinear dynamic texture like Mixture of Principal Component Analysis (MPCA), Time series analysis, Kernel Principal Component Analysis (KPCA), etc. The proposed method is a Hybrid DWT-DCT transform and Isomap with YC_bC_r color coding to model the nonlinear dynamic texture. To extract and remove the spatial redundancy, the Hybrid DWT-DCT transform coding is used. It provides better results than the standalone methods. YC_bC_r color coding is used to capture and remove chromatic redundancy. The modified Isomap method is used to model the nonlinearity and the temporal redundancy. The proposed algorithm is parallelized by using GPU to reduce the execution time. From the different experiments, it is observed that the proposed method provides better results.

Keywords: MPPCA · KPCA · YCbCr · Hybrid DWT-DCT transform
GPU · Isomap

1 Introduction

A dynamic texture is a sequence of images that shows spatial in addition to temporal stationarity [1]. This stationarity exhibits redundancy. A dynamic texture shows spatial as well as temporal redundancy. From their nature, dynamic texture broadly categorized into two types viz linear dynamic texture and non-linear dynamic texture. The motion in a linear dynamic texture is linear and changes smoothly. Hence, a linear dynamic texture is predictive in nature i.e. the next state can be predicted from the previous one. The modeling of a linear dynamic texture is easy, and there exist many methods for this purpose. A Non-linear dynamic texture is the representation of the real-world nonlinear dynamic system. Nonlinear dynamical systems have irregular and unpredictable behavior, but they are fundamentally deterministic up to a certain limit. A Nonlinear dynamic system has a nonlinear motion in which the direction of motion is always changing. Different methods exist to model the nonlinear dynamic texture like MPPCA [2] Time series analysis [3], KPCA [4, 5], etc.

Different transform coding techniques are used to capture and remove the spatial redundancy present in the dynamic texture. The transforms like Discrete Cosine Transform (DCT), Discrete Fourier transform (DFT), Discrete Wavelet Transform (DWT), etc. are being used for this purpose. Out of which DCT and DWT provide better results. However, these transforms have some pros and some cons. DCT has high

© Springer Nature Singapore Pte Ltd. 2018
M. Singh et al. (Eds.): ICACDS 2018, CCIS 905, pp. 530–542, 2018.
https://doi.org/10.1007/978-981-13-1810-8_53

energy compaction as it stores most of the information in few DC components. It has less computational complexity than DWT. However, it provides a less compression ratio as compared to that of DWT. Whereas DWT has less energy compaction, but it provides a high compression ratio and better visual quality as compared to DCT. So, to get the advantages of both the methods and to remove the limitations the Hybrid DWT-DCT transform is used [6, 7].

In the case of a linear dynamic texture, to capture the linear motion linear methods like PCA, and Multidimensional Scaling (MDS), etc. are used. These methods capture the linear motion from the dynamic texture and represent the dynamic texture in a compact form. However, they cannot capture the nonlinearity present in a nonlinear dynamic texture. So, in the case of nonlinear dynamic textures, some nonlinear methods like MPPCA, Nonlinear Principal Component Analysis (NLPCA), and the Chaos theory, etc. are used. These methods capture the nonlinearity present in a dynamic texture, but they have some disadvantages. So instead of using the above methods, the modified Isomap is used to capture the nonlinearity present in the non-linear dynamic texture. The Isomap method [8] is based on the MDS process, which is linear in nature and uses Euclidean distance for the relationship. However, in Isomap, geodesic distance is used, which helps to capture the nonlinearity. It is a global approach, which works in global space to capture the nonlinear motion. The Isomap can model nonlinear and non-stationary dynamic textures having irregular, random, and chaotic motion. The concept of Isomap is to preserve the geometry at all scales, mapping the nearby points on the manifold to the nearby points in low dimensional space and faraway points to far away points. The paper is organized as follows. Section 2 contains previous work; the proposed algorithm is discussed in Sect. 2.1, Sect. 3 provides experimental results, and Sect. 4 comprises of the conclusion.

2 Related Work

The methods like PCA [9], SVD [1], MDS [10], and HOSVD [11] capture the linear motion in a dynamic texture. So, they model the dynamic texture. However, as they cannot capture the nonlinear motion, they cannot model the dynamic texture. Nowadays many methods to model the nonlinear dynamic texture are present. These approaches are based on the nonlinear dimensionality reduction approach. These methods have some advantages and some limitations.

The time series analysis and attractors are used in the Chaos theory [3] to capture the nonlinearity. Here, the data is mapped to the attractor, and then the attractor is used to predict the data. Strange attractors are being used for this purpose. The limitations of this approach are that the data with only a small duration can be predicted, time and computational complexities are very high.

The extensions of PCA-like MPPCA and NLPCA are also used to model the nonlinear dynamic texture. In MPPCA [2], the method mixture of different PCAs has been used. Here, first, the different PCAs are trained to model the data. However, these PCAs have different coordinates. So the mixture of PCA is mapped to the global coordinate system. The global system models the nonlinear data. To synthesize the data, one point on the global system is taken, and the trajectory path is traced according to the local properties. The best PCA that represents the point is to be found out. Then the PCA is used to reconstruct the data. The MPPCA method has high time as well as computational complexity and is complex in nature.

The other extension NLPCA has two approaches. The first is by using a neural network and the second is by using the kernel function. In this approach, an auto-associative neural network [12] is trained for the dynamic texture. Here, the auto-associative neural network consists of many layers of neurons. The compact representation of the dynamic texture is achieved in the bottleneck layer. It captures the nonlinearity present in the dynamic texture and provides a better compact representation for the dynamic texture, but it has high computational complexity. Apart from that, it takes an enormous amount of time for the training of the network.

The other approach that NLPCA uses is the kernel function to capture the nonlinearity present in the dynamic texture. Hence, it is also called as KPCA [5]. There are three kernel functions that exist. These are simple kernel, polynomial kernel, and the Gaussian kernel function. The KPCA approach captures the nonlinearity and model the non-linear textures. In the KPCA method, first, the data is to be mapped to a higher dimensional space and then the nonlinearity is captured. The KPCA method provides better results when the kernel function is known previously.

A method like Local Linear Embedding (LLE) [13], embeds the observed data of high-dimensional input space into the low-dimensional hidden space. However, the limitation with the LLE method is that it uses the local space, so sometimes in the case of high variation; it does not capture the nonlinear motion correctly. In the case of very high dimensional data, it fails [14].

2.1 The Proposed Algorithm

As shown in Fig. 1, the proposed method consists of six steps. Out of, which the first three are analysis steps and the remaining three are the synthesis steps.

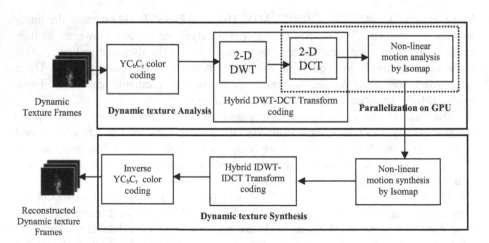

Fig. 1. Block diagram of the proposed research work

(1) Input the dynamic texture sequence [Y1, Y2...., YN] where Yi$\in$ R$_k$ and 'N' is the number of frames in a texture.
(2) Apply RGB to YC$_b$C$_r$ conversion frame by frame.
(3) Use the hybrid 2D DWT-DCT transform frame by frame.
   (i) Apply the DWT transform on each frame. It generates LL, LH, HL, HH components. Consider only the LL part of each frame.
   (ii) Down-sample C$_b$ and C$_r$ components.
   (iii) Apply the DCT transform on 16 × 16 blocks. Apply quantization on Y and C$_b$, C$_r$ components using the 16 × 16 quantization table.
   (iv) Construct a matrix by aligning Y, C$_b$, and C$_r$ components in one column for each frame.
(4) Compute the mean for each row.
(5) Normalize the matrix by subtracting the mean [14].

$$y_t \leftarrow y_t - \bar{y}, \forall t \tag{1}$$

(6) Apply Isomap for nonlinear motion analysis,
   (i) Construct the neighborhood graph by using the Euclidean distance formula given by

$$d_{ij} \leftarrow \sqrt{\sum (y_i - y_j)^2}, \forall i, j \tag{2}$$

   (ii) Estimate the geodesic distance by computing the shortest path

$$D^2 = \left[d_{ij}^2 \right] \tag{3}$$

   (iii) Normalize the matrix D^2 by using the following equation

$$k(D^2) = -\frac{1}{2} * H * D^2 * H \tag{4}$$

Where

$$H = I - \frac{1}{N} * e * e^t$$

and

$$e = [11.....1]^t$$

   (iv) Compute the largest eigen value c of the matrix $k(D^2)$ and construct the kernel matrix by using

$$K = k(D^2) + 2 * c * k(D) + \frac{1}{2} * c^2 * H \tag{5}$$

(v) Calculate the Eigen Value and Eigen vector using

$$K.\alpha = n.\lambda.\alpha \tag{6}$$

(7) Consider eigen vectors 'V' having high eigen values
(8) Calculate the Final Data D_t by projecting the Raw Eigen vector V on Y_t.

$$D_t = Y_t * V. \tag{7}$$

(9) Store D_t and V or transmit to a receiver as these components contain the entire information of a dynamic texture.

To capture the chromatic or spectral correlationship and to remove this correlationship, different color codings are used. There are many color coding techniques that exist like YC_bC_r, YIQ, YUV, etc. These methods separate out the luminance and chrominance parts, so the conversion from RGB to any other color space is necessary. Human visual system is more sensitive to the luminance part, this part is kept intact, but the chrominance part is down-sampled as per the requirement. The compression is achieved without much loss of information. It is found that the YC_bC_r color coding techniques provide better results as compared with the other coding techniques.

A. Hybrid DWT-DCT transform coding

To capture and remove the spatial redundancy between the pixels transform coding isused. However, each of these transforms has some advantages and some disadvantages. The advantages of the techniques are represented in Table 1. To get the advantages of both techniques, the hybrid DWT-DCT transform coding is used. It is found that the hybrid transform coding provides better results than the standalone techniques.

Table 1. Comparison between SVD and DWT-DCT with Isomap

Dynamic texture	Model components	SVD		Hybrid DWT-DCT with Isomap (proposed)	
		CR (%)	PSNR (dB)	CR (%)	PSNR (dB)
Flame	15	75.50	27.61	96.66	27.61
Wheel	10	46.54	18.96	91.77	20.97
Candle	20	49.39	23.95	96.88	35.02

1-level 2D-DWT is applied on each frame. It gives four components like LL, LH, HL, HH out of, which only LL components are considered. Then down-sampling of C_b, C_r parts are done as per the requirements. All Y, C_b, C_r parts are then divided into blocks of size 16 * 16. Further 2D-DCT is applied on these blocks of each plane. Quantization is applied on these blocks by using 16 * 16 quantization matrixes. Then all Y, C_b, C_r data of a frame is aligned in one column of a matrix. This procedure is to be applied for each frame, and a matrix is to be constructed where each column of a matrix represents an individual frame of a dynamic texture.

B. Nonlinear motion capture by modified Isomap

Isomap model a dynamic texture which shows chaotic, irregular, and random motions. The simple concept of Isomap is instead of mapping the data on the linear Euclidean distance it maps the data on nonlinear geodesic distance. The main idea of Isomap [8] is to preserve the geometry of the original data by mapping the nearby points on the manifold to the nearby points on the low dimensional space and far-away points on the manifolds to the far-away points in the low dimensional space.

The matrix of frames, which is the output of the Hybrid DWT-DCT coding method i.e. $Y = \{y_i \in R^n / i = 1,..., N\}$ is given as an input to the Isomap. This data is then normalized by using the step-5 of the proposed algorithm. In the next step neighbors of each pixel are calculated by using the Euclidean distance between each of the pixels as follows.

$$d_{ij} \leftarrow \sqrt{\sum (y_i - y_j)^2}, \forall i,j \tag{8}$$

From this data, a neighborhood graph is constructed. The shortest paths D^2 are computed from the neighborhood graph for all the pairs of pixels to approximate the geodesic distance between all pairs of pixels. To calculate the shortest paths Dijkstra's algorithm was used in the basic Isomap algorithm [8]. As the complexity of Dijkstra's algorithm is high, here, in the proposed algorithm the fast Floyd's algorithm is used to reduce the computational and time complexity. It provides the geodesic distance matrix, which is further centered to reduce the variation by using the following equations.

$$k\left(D^2\right) = -\frac{1}{2} * H * D^2 * H \tag{9}$$

Where $H = I - \frac{1}{N} * e * e^t$ and $e = [11.....1]^t$

Here, the concept of the Kernel Isomap [8] is used where the largest eigen value c of the following matrix is calculated.

$$\begin{bmatrix} 0 & 2k(D^2) \\ -I & -4k(D) \end{bmatrix} \tag{10}$$

However, the complexity of finding the largest eigen value of the following equation is high. So in the proposed algorithm, the largest eigen value of the above matrix k(D2) is calculated as the largest eigen values of both the matrices comes approximately same. It reduces the computational as well as time complexity of the algorithm.

In the further steps, the mercer kernel matrix K is calculated by using the largest eigen value c and the following equation.

$$K = k(D^2) + 2*c*k(D) + 1/2*c^2*H \qquad (11)$$

Then, MDS is applied on this kernel matrix K that finds the eigen vectors V and the corresponding eigen values λ ($\lambda \geq 0$) that satisfies

$$K.V = \lambda.V \qquad (12)$$

This subspace consists of eigen vectors and the corresponding eigen values. These eigenvectors form an orthogonal basis for Y and Eigen values represent the relevance of corresponding Principal Components (PC).

C. Dimensionality Reduction in Isomap

The matrix V contains temporal information in the form of eigen vectors or principal components of the input data. The corresponding eigen values are contained in the matrix λ represents the relevance of eigen vectors. The eigen vectors are sorted according to the corresponding eigen values in decreasing order. The vectors with high eigen values are also called as principal components are important and hence, retained. From the matrix V of dimension N * N, some columns that have high principal components are retained, and the vectors with small or zero eigen values are discarded. From N components, k components are selected, so the new dimension of V is N * k. To get more quality, more number of principal components are to be considered and vice-versa. The matrix Y_t contains the spatial information and has the dimension m*N where N<<m, which requires high space to store. The Row_Eigen_Vector V is projected on the data matrix Y_t, i.e., the multiplication of V and Y_t as shown in step-7and get the Final_Data matrix D_t. This final data will have the dimension m * k, which is very less than the original data and requires very low memory space as compared to the original data.

D. Synthesis using modified Isomap

The basic Isomap method is an irreversible technique [8] i.e. the original data cannot be reconstructed from the compressed or reduced components. In the analysis part of the basic Isomap algorithm, the k-nearest neighbors are selected in a forward manner for each pixel and the remaining data is skipped. In this strategy, a problem occurs due to the skipped data. In the proposed algorithm, the neighborhood matrix is generalized and let the algorithm select the neighbors for each pixel. So in the proposed algorithm synthesis is possible i.e. the original data can be reconstructed from the stored and compressed components.

The eigen vector matrix V is orthogonal in nature i.e. it possesses the property $V * V^T = I = V*V^{-1}$, and hence, it satisfies $V^T = V^{-1}$.

$$D_t = Y_t * V \Leftrightarrow D_t * V^{-1} = Y_t \Leftrightarrow D_t * V^T = Y_t$$

Some components of the eigen vector matrix V are discarded. So the coefficients of the reconstructed data will be slightly different from the original data Y_t and is called as

Y'$_t$. After getting Y'$_t$, to calculate the original data the subtracted mean is added to Y'$_t$. The evolution of the synthesis takes place as follows.

$$Y'_t = D_t * V^T \tag{13}$$

$$Y'_t \leftarrow Y'_t + \bar{y} \tag{14}$$

E. Parallelization on GPU

To reduce the time complexity parallelization of the proposed algorithm is done by using GPU. The part of the proposed algorithm, which is parallelized using GPU, is shown in Fig. 1 with dotted lines [14, 15]. As shown in the Fig. 1, 2D-DCT and the nonlinear motion analysis by Isomap are parallelized on GPU as their working methods are independent of their previous and current data. The loops in the DCT algorithms and that in the Isomap algorithms are parallelized on GPU as the data in the previous and the current states are independent. However, this is not true in the case of DWT. Hence, DWT is not implemented on GPU. It is observed that the parallelization on GPU reduces the time complexity of the proposed algorithm.

3 Experimental Results

For the experimentation the size of textures varies from 128×128 to 352×288. The total number of frames varies from 32 to 255. Different dynamic textures are taken with different resolutions, frames size, frames per seconds, etc.

Table 1 clearly shows that the proposed method Hybrid DWT-DCT with Isomap provides better Compression Ratio (CR) and the PSNR as compared to SVD is independent of whether it is a linear or non-linear dynamic texture.

Table 2 provides a comparison of both the proposed algorithms with SVD for a Flag dynamic texture. The comparison is done by considering different components for model coefficients, model size, and PSNR for different dynamic textures. It is observed that as the components are increased PSNR increases accordingly for both linear as well as nonlinear dynamic textures.

Table 2. Comparison of SVD & proposed methods by model coefficients for Flag sequence.

Model components	SVD			Hybrid DWT-DCT and Isomap (proposed)			Hybrid DWT-DCT and Isomap using YC_bC_r coding (proposed)		
	Model coefficient	Model size (MB)	PSNR	Model coefficient	Model size (MB)	PSNR	Model coefficient	Model size (MB)	PSNR
50	6622100	23.41	21.51	1855450	2.98	22.71	933850	1.06	22.18
100	13114600	46.49	23.48	3711150	6.035	25.31	1867950	2.13	24.24
150	19607100	69.57	25.83	5566850	9.02	27.30	2802050	3.20	25.64

Table 3 shows the comparison of both the proposed methods between the model size and PSNR for but the proposed method with YC_bC_r color coding provides better results than that without color coding. It is observed that the proposed methods provide better PSNR for a less number of model coefficients than the SVD. The proposed method with YC_bC_r color coding provides even better results than that without the color coding process.

Table 3. Relation between model size and PSNR for the proposed methods.

Dynamic texture	Size (MB)	Frames	Components	Hybrid DWT-DCT and Isomap (proposed)		Hybrid DWT-DCT and Isomap with YC_bC_r (proposed)	
				Model size (MB)	PSNR (dB)	Model size (MB)	PSNR (dB)
Steps	17.5	80	10	0.76	25.35	0.23	24.32
			20	1.40	25.50	0.47	24.44
			30	2.12	25.55	0.71	24.48
Wheel	21.7	75	10	1.62	20.75	0.52	20.66
			30	4.99	23.19	1.62	22.99
			50	8.34	23.63	2.70	23.37
Flag2	36.26	125	50	4.82	29.54	1.61	28.79
			75	7.35	31.39	2.42	30.24
			100	9.78	33.06	3.23	31.40

Table 4 shows the comparison of different methods like SVD, HOSVD, KPCA and the proposed methods between PSNR and compression ratio for the dynamic texture flame. From the table, it is clear that the proposed methods provide a higher compression ratio with comparatively better PSNR than the existing methods.

Table 4. Comparison of different methods for the dynamic texture Flame.

Model components	SVD		HOSVD		Hybrid DWT +DCT and KPCA with color coding		Hybrid DWT +DCT and Isomap		Hybrid DWT +DCT and Isomap with color coding	
	PSNR (dB)	CR (%)	PSNR (dB)	CR (%)	PSNR (dB)	CR (%)	PSNR (dB)	CR (%)	PSNR (dB)	CR (%)
15	27	75	27	98	27	96	27	96	27	98
30	30	50	30	90	29	93	30	93	29	97
50	33	20	31	70	31	89	32	89	31	95

The graph in Fig. 2 shows the comparison of HOSVD, SVD, KPCA, and the proposed algorithms for model size and PSNR. From the graph, it can be concluded that the proposed algorithms result are better than HOSVD, SVD, and KPCA.

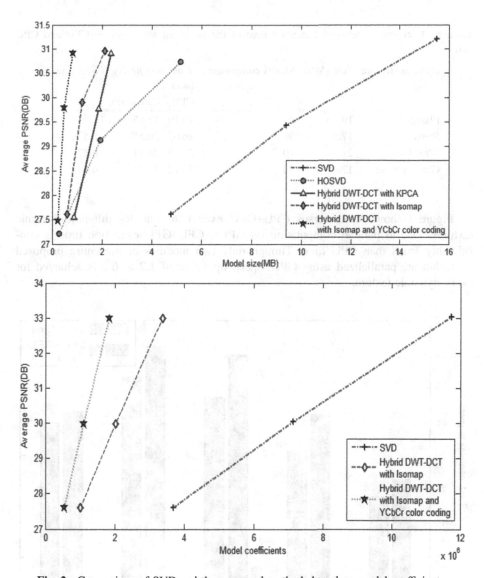

Fig. 2. Comparison of SVD and the proposed methods based on model coefficients.

A comparison of SVD and the proposed methods for model coefficients shown in Fig. 2. The graph is plotted against the model coefficients and the average PSNR. The SVD method requires higher model coefficients than the proposed methods to get the same PSNR as that of the proposed algorithms. From the graph, it is observed that the proposed methods beat the SVD method.

The proposed algorithm requires a large number of computations and time. To decrease time complexity of the proposed algorithm, GPU is used. It speeds up the execution of the proposed algorithm, which includes Isomap is shown in Table 5.

Table 5. Comparison between execution time of the proposed algorithm on CPU and CPU +GPU

Dynamic texture	Size (MB)	Model components	Time complexity (sec)		Speed up
			CPU	CPU+GPU	
Flame	19.56	30	16.10	13.45	2.65
Steps	17.5	30	26.07	20.55	5.52
Wheel	21.7	10	34.78	28.51	6.27
Grass &water	17.4	50	36.12	31.51	4.61

Figure 3 shows CPU versus CPU+GPU execution time for different dynamic textures. Due to parallel computation on GPUs, CPU+GPU execution time is considerably small than CPU time. Though only two modules of the entire proposed algorithm are parallelized using GPU, speed up factor of 1.2 to 6.2 is achieved for every dynamic texture.

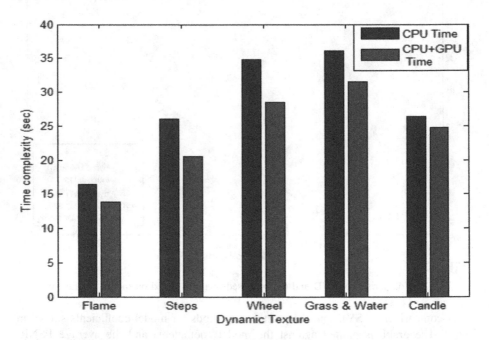

Fig. 3. Comparison of CPU and CPU+GPU execution time for different dynamic textures.

Visual perception of a synthesized dynamic texture is very important for the end user. In several cases objective quality assessment measures do not give proper information about the quality of a synthesized dynamic texture. So in such cases, it is important to analyze the synthesized dynamic texture by using subjective quality assessment measures. Here, 20 different people are shown the original and reconstructed dynamic textures and are asked to judge and give one of the quality measurements for that reconstructed video. The measurements are taken by different parameters like clearance, blurriness, edges of the reconstructed videos, color quality, etc. The following Table 6 shows the number of people who gave the measurements for different dynamic textures.

Table 6. Subjective quality assessment using different measurements

Dynamic textures	Quality measurements				
	Excellent	Good	Fair	Poor	Bad
Flame	5	14	1	0	0
Flag	4	12	3	1	0
Steps	3	15	2	0	0
Wheel	4	15	1	0	0
Grass & Water	5	13	2	0	0
Candle	3	16	1	0	0
Bird	4	15	1	0	0

From the Table 6, it is observed that maximum people have given the excellent and useful measurements to the reconstructed videos.

4 Conclusion

The proposed algorithm consists of the YC_bC_r color coding method, Hybrid DWT-DCT transform techniques and the Isomap approach. It is proved from the experimental results that the Isomap method is able to analyze and synthesize a nonlinear dynamic texture. Hence, it works better than the SVD, HOSVD, and KPCA. The proposed algorithm outperforms all the other existing methods as it analyzes and synthesizes the dynamic textures proficiently, and represents it with a less number of model coefficients and small model size. The proposed algorithm also provides better results regarding compression ratio and PSNR than the other existing methods. All the objectives are fulfilled by implementing the proposed algorithm on GPUs. Running the algorithm on GPU broadly decreases the execution time of the algorithm.

References

1. Soatto, S., Doretto, G., Wu, Y.: Dynamic textures. In: Proceedings of IEEE International Conference on Computer Vision, vol. 3, pp. 439–446 (2001)
2. Liu, C.-B., Lin, R.-S., Ahuja, N., Yang, M.-H.: Dynamic textures synthesis as nonlinear manifold learning and traversing. In: Proceedings of BMVC (2006)

3. Basharat, A., Shah, M.: Time Series Prediction by Chaotic Modeling of Nonlinear Dynamical Systems
4. Fauvel, M., Chanussot, J., AtliBenediktsson, J.: Kernel principal component analysis for feature reduction in hyperspectrale images analysis. EURASIP J. Adv. Sig. Process. (2009)
5. Mika, S., Scholkopf, B.: Kernel PCA and De-Noising in Feature Spaces
6. Kekre, H.B., Sarode, T., Natu, P.: Efficient image compression technique using full, column and row transforms on colour image. Int. J. Adv. Eng. Technol. (2013)
7. Singh, Satish K., Kumar, Shishir: Mathematical transforms and image compression: a review. Maejo Int. J. Sci. Technol. **4**(02), 235–249 (2010)
8. Choi, H., Choi, S.: Kernel Isomap. Proc. Electr. Lett. **40**(25), 1612–1613 (2004)
9. Roweis, S.: EM Algorithms for PCA and SPCA. roweis@cns.caltech.edu; Computation & Neural Systems, California Institute of Technology
10. Jaworska, N., Chupetlovska-Anastasova, A.: A review of multidimensional scaling (MDS) and its utility in various psychological domains. Tutorials Quant. Methods Psychol. **5**(1), 1–10 (2009)
11. Costantini, R., Sbaiz, L., Susstrunk, S.: Higher order SVD analysis for dynamic texture synthesis. IEEE Trans. Image Process. **17**(1), 42–52 (2008)
12. Scholz, M., Fraunholz, M.: Nonlinear Principal Component Analysis: Neural Network Models and Applications
13. Roweis, S.T., Saul, L.K.: Nonlinear dimensionality reduction by locally linear embedding. Proc. Am. Assoc. Adv. Sci. **290**(5500), 2323–2326 (2000)
14. Ghadekar, P.P., Chopade, N.B.: Modelling nonlinear dynamic textures using hybrid DWT-DCT and kernel PCA with GPU. J. Inst. Eng. Ser.-B (Springer Journal) **97**(4), 549–555 (2016)
15. Ghadekar, P.P., Chopade, N.B.: Content-based dynamic texture analysis and synthesis based on SPIHT with GPU. J. Inf. Process. Syst. (JIPS) **12**(1), 46–56 (2016)

Exploration of Apache Hadoop Techniques: Mapreduce and Hive for Big Data

Poonam Rana[1], Vineet Sharma[1], and P. K. Gupta[2(✉)]

[1] Department of CSE, KIET Group of Institutions, Ghaziabad, India
{poonam.rana,vineet.sharma}@kiet.edu
[2] Department of CSE, Jaypee University of Information Technology,
Solan, HP, India
pkgupta@ieee.org

Abstract. With the rapid growth of technology, huge amount of data is being proliferated from various sources like sensor networks, IoT, online transactions, social media, etc. Big data is a collection of huge voluminous and complex data sets that include the large amount of data, social media analytics, real time data and data management capabilities. In some cases, the volume of this data has reached upto ZettaBytes. To analyze such a huge amount of data, traditional technologies are found inefficient. So, the new technologies of Apache Hadoop Distributed File System (HDFS) came into existence. In this paper, we have presented tools and technologies used in big data along with detailed description of MapReduce and Hive programming framework of Hadoop. Apache Hadoop consist of techniques and technologies that require new forms of combination to reveal large unknown values from large data sets that are diverse, complex and of massive scale.

Keywords: BigData · HADOOP · HDFS · MapReduce · Hive · Pig

1 Introduction

Role of Big Data Analytics is getting wider day by day and now it is getting used to process the complex datasets [1,2]. BigData retrieves and analyzes the useful information from the stored data and also finds the hidden patterns and other related useful information that can be required for further processing and analysis [3].

1.1 The Importance of Big Data

Investigative computing platform is required by organizations to know the full value of Big Data. This platform can be used by various users to use, analyze and structure Big Data to access relevant information related to that

© Springer Nature Singapore Pte Ltd. 2018
M. Singh et al. (Eds.): ICACDS 2018, CCIS 905, pp. 543–552, 2018.
https://doi.org/10.1007/978-981-13-1810-8_54

business. The important points related to use of Big Data can be summarized as follows [4]:

- Big data is gaining more interest and popularity from both point of view IT industry and business users.
- From an analytics view, it is still representing analytic workloads and data management solutions that cannot be previously supported because of cost considerations and/or technology limitations.
- Analytics on multi-structured data enable smarter decisions. Using traditional analytical processing technologies, the processing is difficult to be applied on these types of data.
- Big Data supports rapid analysis and decision making over high volume of detailed data.
- Data that is outside of the enterprise data warehouse can be easily processed and analyzed by the organizations. MapReduce programming model is used by programmers to retrieve important information from such Big Data. Different types of large data sets can cause handling problems [5].

1.2 How Big Is Big Data and Evolution?

The data is being proliferated across the world from last good many years and volume of this proliferation is keep on rising day by day. Some facts about the proliferated data are that there are 2 million/minute Google search queries, 277,000 tweets/minute, new videos are getting uploaded on Youtube in bulk, also a huge amount of data is getting processed by Facebook and Emails, and more than 550 websites are being created every minute [6].

1.3 The 10 V's of Big Data

Currently, Big data comprises of 10 V's as shown in Fig. 1 includes: $Volume$ - amount od data, $Variety$ - refers to the different types, $Velocity$ - corresponds to speed of data transfer, $Value$ - process of discovering huge hidden values, $Variability$ - inconsistencies in the data and in consistent speed, $Veracity$ - refers to the provenance or reliability, $Validity$ - refers to accuracy and correctness of data, $Vulnerability$ - refers to security concerns, $Volatility$ - ensures about the oldness of collected data, $Visualization$ - refers to visualizing the BigData [7,8].

1.4 Hadoop Architecture

Hadoop is a combination of two services: store and process and what it consumes is Big Data. Hadoop is a giant system and categorized into two parts $Hadoop = Store + Process$. The following case study describes about the concept of Store and process:

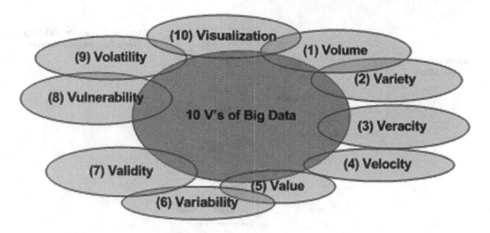

Fig. 1. The 10 V's of big data.

A company called CAVA Consultancy Services and it is present in 159 countries and people admire them. Just day before yesterday, its page got 1 billion likes. Now CEO is excited and wants a huge dashboard where we can see whole globe and an hover of each country. We see how many likes we got from each country. He calls Rajat who is Project Manager and asks him to get his dashboard made in 4 days duration.

- *Rajat contacts two persons- Mr. Admin and Mr. Developer.*
- *Admin purchases 5 machines, where one will be master and four slaves.*

Admin tell Rajat setup is done, proceed and write programs. Now Facebook.Json file that consist of 640 MB data is divided into 5 chunks or blocks, each block is of size 128 MB as shown in Fig. 2. Hadoop default replication factor is 3 and each block is copied three times on storage slave/ processing slaves. When we install core Hadoop, by default we have only HDFS (Hadoop Distributed File System), MapReduce and YARN. Other components like Hive, Sqoop, Impala, Spark, Flume, Hue, Pig, Oozie, Senteryare needed to configured separately.

- **Sqoop:** It is like RDBMS to Hadoop or Hadoop to RDBMS.
- **Flume:** Real time logs to Hadoop.
- **Oozie:** Workflows for Hadoop
- **Hive:** SQL on Hadoop
- **Impala:** SQL on Hadoop (faster than Hive but does not have failover capability)
- **Spark:** A new framework that is much faster than MapReduce
- **Hue:** Hadoop on browser
- **Sentery:** ACL (Access Controll List) for Hive tables that is grant, insert, select kind of layer on Hive table

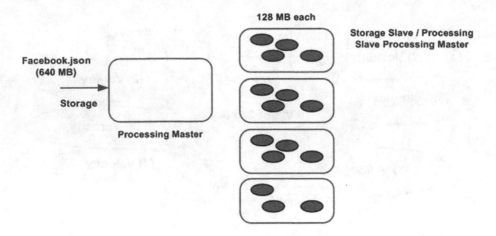

Fig. 2. Hadoop storage and processing

Typical components of HDFS are:

- Namenode → Master for Storage
- Datanode → Slave for Storage
- Secondary → backup of Namenode
- ResourceManager → Master for YARN
- NodeManager → Slave for YARN
- JobHistoryServer → Status archival for MR Job

2 Reference Architecture of Big Data and Hadoop

Extracting the knowledge from Big Data is getting one of the most challenging and difficult task [9]. Scalability in BigData can be discussed in two ways. First, we give reference to a very large databases and Secondly for processing and analysis parallel programming models must be used. Regarding the first issue, distributed databases for intensive updating workloads is the standard solutions in this field [10], and parallel database systems for analytical workloads [11].

2.1 Techniques to Handle Big Data

(a) **NoSQL:** It stores the information as 'Key-Value' pairs. NoSQL provides flexible data models and can be easily used with large amount of data. NoSQL donot support updates and deletes whereas traditional databases do

(b) **Data Mining:** Here, mining related algorithms plays the important role and loads the data into the main memory.

(c) **Dynamo system** [12]: is also a milestone for NoSQL DBMSs. It was originally built to support internal Amazon's applications, and to manage the state of services that have very high reliability requirements.

(d) **HBase** [13]: follows the scheme of the BigTable and supports compression, in-memory operations, and Bloom filters.

(e) **Cassandra** [14]: It has a hierarchical architecture in which the database is based on columns (name, value and timestamp).

(f) **HyperTable** [15]: It is a low-level API provided by the HyperTable systems and the HyperTable Query Language, which allows the user to create, modify, and query the underlying tables.

(g) **MongoDB** [16]: It is written in C++ with MapReduce support for a flexible data aggregation and processing [17].

(h) **CouchDB** [18] A CouchDB document is an object that contains name fields, such as strings, dates, numbers, or even ordered lists and associative maps and allows use of queries and indexes using Java Script following a MapReduce style, i.e., using JSON to store the data.

(i) **HDFS** [2]: is a block-structured distributed file system which collects huge amount of Big Data. It is client-server architecture consisting of NameNode and many DataNodes.

- Metadata is stored in the NameNode.
- The file system operations is the responsibility of NameNode [2].
- If failure occurs in Name Node, the Hadoop doesn't support automatic recovery.

2.2   Hadoop's Components [3]

(a) **HBase:** Written in Java, a non-relational, open source, distributed database system and utilizes HDFS.

(b) **Pig:** It is high-level platform that creates MapReduce programs which is used with Hadoop.

(c) **Sqoop:** A command-line interface platform used to exchange the data between relational databases and Hadoop.

(d) **Avro:** It is basically used in Apache Hadoop as a data serialization system and data exchange service.

(e) **Oozie:** Helps in managing the Hadoop jobs.

(f) **Chukwa:** It is designed over HDFS and MapReduce framework for processing of large amount of data logs.

(g) **Flume:** It is a high level architecture which focus on streaming of data.

(h) **Zookeeper:** It acts as a centralized service and supports distributed synchronization.

We have summarized some of the important characteristics of Big Data in Table 1.

3   Description on Hadoop's MapReduce and Hive

3.1   MapReduce

MapReduce is divide and conquer technique that process large amounts of data. It is a framework that process on map and reduce task [19, 20]. It gives the sorted

Table 1. Characteristics of several Big Data Techniques

Name	Cassandra	Hbase	Hive	MongoDB
Typing	YES	NO	YES	YES
Secondary indexes	RESTRICTED	NO	YES	YES
SQL	NO	NO	NO	NO
APIs and other access methods	Proprietary Protocol	Java API, Restful HTTP API, Thrift	JDBC, ODBC, Thrift	Proprietary Protocol Using JSON
Partitioning methods	Sharding	Sharding	Sharding	Sharding
Durability	YES	YES	YES	YES
Server-side scripts	NO	YES	YES	Javascript
Triggers	YES	YES	NO	NO
Replication methods	Selectable replication factor	Selectable replication factor	Selectable replication factor	Master-slave replication
MapReduce	YES	YES	YES	YES

output of the map task which further becomes the input for the reducer task. Two tasks are associated with MapReduce. First is the Map job which takes a set of data where single elements are broken down into tuples - key/value pair. The input file is passed to the Mapper function line by line. It process the data and creates several blocks of data. The Reduce job takes the output from the mapper as input and combines those data key/value pairs into a smaller set of tuples. The working of mapreduce is shown in Fig. 3 [21]. The programming queries is similar to SQL as in the relational databases where the data is totally structured. MapReduce deals with all types of data, i.e., unstructured, semistructured and structured. The sample of query in MapReduce query is presented in Fig. 4.

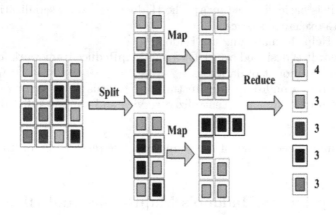

Fig. 3. Working of MapReduce.

```
Query:
SELECT Country, Count(*) from Students Group By
Country
Explaination:
Scans each and every record        //  Map Phase
If the group is created then        //Reduce Phase
Insert in the group else            // .................
Create the group and insert it      // ..................
```

Fig. 4. Query in MapRedue.

3.2   Parallelization Techniques and MapReduce

With the exponential growth in raw data, a number of extraction methods and models are being used to process the hidden valuable information from the collected raw data. Unfortunately, only few models and methods can meet with the growing size of data and processing of valuable information. To perform computations at large scale and to extract information various algorithms related to parallel and concurrent algorithms are being used. These different parallelization techniques but some traditional computing problems utilize multiple CPUs to perform some sort of numerical calculation concurrently. For such style of working, they use libraries like MPI, OpenMP, CUDA, or pthreads. Problems that can be aptly solved by using these traditional methods typically share two common features:

- **Almost CPU bounded:** Much of the time is consumed in doing calculations that involve floating point or integer arithmetic.
- **Less amount of data(GB-Scale):** the required data for the calculation is typically less than a hundred gigabytes, and mostly found in few hundred megabytes.

While performing parallel computations MPI model respond better but it is difficult to implement in routine activities and this is the main reason behind the popularity of MapReduce model. it provides sufficient flexibilty and processing environment over the growing size of data.

3.3   Hive

It provides the SQL interface and relational model in a Data warehousing application, executes on the top of Hadoop and also help in providing summarization, query and analysis.

- Hive uses MapReduce and HDFS for processing and storage/ retrieval of data.
- Advantages:
  - Used as an ETL
  - Provides capability for querying and analysis
  - Can handle large datasets

Figure 5 represents the working of Hive with all its components, as:

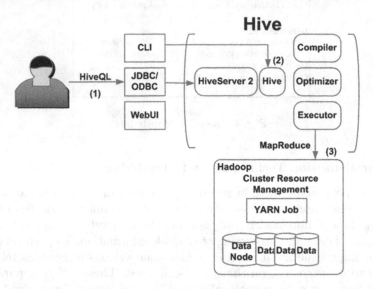

Fig. 5. Working of Hive.

3.4 Pig

Pig and Hive were invented almost at the same time to solve the same problem. Pig is also used to analyse the datasets using Mapreduce Programming Framework. Hive and pig and provided the simplified framework of programming otherwise Data Science and Data Analysts had to do core programming on Java and Python. With the evolution of Hive and Pig Latin one should have basic knowledge of SQL queries as similar to Relational Database Management System (RDBMS).

Pig is a scripting language which is designed to explore large datasets. Components of Pig are as follows:

– *Pig Latin:* a language used to express dataflows.
– *Pig Engine:* a Engine on top of Hadoop.

Pig Latin is a flow language. It provide support data types-long float, char array, schemas and functions. It is extensible and supports user defined functions. In this metadata not required but used when available. It operates on file in HDFS and supports various functions like JOIN, FILTER, GROUP, SORT.

3.5 MapReduce vs Hive

All Hive queries as shown in Fig. 6, will be converted to Map Reduce job for execution, but understanding the internals of Hadoop framework is must to write Map Reduce job. Anyone having SQL knowledge can quickly write Hive scripts and get the results.

```
Syntax:   To create a table
hive> Create Table<table-name>
(<column name> <data type>,
(<column name> <data type>;
Example:
hive> Create Table Student (name string, age int) ROW
FORMAT DELIMITED FIELDSTERMINATED BY ',';
```

Fig. 6. Query in hive.

4   Conclusion and Future Work

As we know that data is being generated at a very high rate approximately in ZettaBytes. The various sources of Big Data are data being generated from sensor devices, IoT, social networking sites, E-commerce website product reviews, scientific calculations etc. Now the problem arises that how to deal with this data which is unstructured, structured and semi structured. In this paper, we have presented various tools and technologies to deal with Big Data and also present the comparative analysis of them. Map Reduce and Hive has been explored in detail. We will include their working scenarios and applications in future work.

References

1. Shilpa, M.K.: BIG data and methodology-A review. Int. J. Adv. Res. Comput. Sci. Softw. Eng. **3**(10), 991–995 (2013)
2. Garlasu, D., Sandulescu, V., Halcu, I., Neculoiu, G.: A big data implementation based on grid computing. In: Grid Computing (2018)
3. Sagiroglu, S., Sinanc, D.: Big data: a review. In: Proceedings of International Conference on Collaboration Technologies and Systems (CTS), pp. 42–47. IEEE (2013)
4. Maitrey, S., Jha, C.K.: MapReduce: simplified data analysis of big data. Procedia Comput. Sci. **57**, 563–571 (2015)
5. Big Data: A New World of Opportunities. NESSI White Paper, pp. 1–25 (2012)
6. Micro Focus Blog. https://blog.microfocus.com/how-much-data-is-created-on-the-internet-each-day. Accessed 15 Mar 2018
7. The 10 V's of Big Data. https://tdwi.org/articles/2017/02/08/10-vs-of-big-data.aspx. Accessed 15 Mar 2018
8. Laney, D.: 3D data management: controlling data volume, velocity and variety. META Group Res. Note **6**(70), 1–4 (2001)
9. Chen, C.P., Zhang, C.Y.: Data-intensive applications, challenges, techniques and technologies: a survey on Big Data. Inf. Sci. **275**, 314–347 (2014)
10. Rothnie Jr., J.B., et al.: Introduction to a system for distributed databases (SDD-1). ACM Trans. Database Syst. (TODS) **5**(1), 1–17 (1980)
11. DeWitt, D.J., Ghandeharizadeh, S., Schneider, D.A., Bricker, A., Hsiao, H.I., Rasmussen, R.: The Gamma database machine project. IEEE Trans. Knowl. Data Eng. **2**(1), 44–62 (1990)

12. DeCandia, G., et al.: Dynamo: Amazon's highly available key-value store. In: Proceedings of ACM SIGOPS Operating Systems Review, vol. 41, no. 6, pp. 205–220 (2007)
13. Dimiduk, N., Khurana, A., Ryan, M.H.: HBase in Action, 1st edn. Manning, Shelter Island (2010)
14. Lakshman, A., Malik, P.: CASSANDRA: a decentralized structured storage system. ACM SIGOPS Oper. Syst. Rev. **44**(2), 35–40 (2010)
15. Khetrapal, A., Ganesh, V.: HBase and Hypertable for large scale distributed storage systems, Department of Computer Science, Purdue University, pp. 22–28 (2006)
16. Chodorow, K.: MongoDB: The Definitive Guide: Powerful and Scalable Data Storage. O'Reilly Media Inc. (2013)
17. Severance, C.: Discovering javascript object notation. Computer **45**(4), 6–8 (2012)
18. Anderson, J.C., Lehnardt, J., Slater, N.: CouchDB: The Definitive Guide: Time to Relax. O'Reilly Media Inc., Sebastopol (2010)
19. Dean, J., Ghemawat, S.: MapReduce: simplified data processing on large clusters. Commun. ACM **51**(1), 107–113 (2008)
20. Landset, S., Khoshgoftaar, T.M., Richter, A.N., Hasanin, T.: A survey of open source tools for machine learning with big data in the Hadoop ecosystem. J. Big Data **2**(1), 24 (2015)
21. Maitrey, S., Jha, C.K.: An integrated approach for CURE clustering using mapreduce technique. In: Proceedings of Elsevier, pp. 563–571 (2013). ISBN 978-81-910691

Author Index

Printed in the United States
By Bookmasters

Printed in the United States
By Bookmasters